CEYLON
AND ITS CAPABILITIES

CEYLON
AND ITS CAPABILITIES

AN ACCOUNT OF ITS

NATURAL RESOURCES, INDIGENOUS PRODUCTIONS,
AND COMMERCIAL FACILITIES

TO WHICH ARE ADDED

DETAILS OF ITS STATISTICS, PILOTAGE AND SAILING DIRECTIONS

AND
AN APPENDIX,
CONTAINING THE ROYAL CHARTER OF JUSTICE, THE KANDYAN CONVENTION OF 1815, ORDINANCES OF THE COLONIAL GOVERNMENT ON VARIOUS MATTERS CONNECTED WITH THE COMMERCE OF THAT ISLAND, ETC. ETC.

WITH PLAIN AND COLOURED ILLUSTRATIONS

J. W. BENNETT

GYAN

Published by

Gyan Publishing House
5, Ansari Road
Daryaganj, New Delhi-110002
Phone: 011-47034999, 9811692060
E-mail: books@gyanbooks.com

Distribution Network
gyanbooks.com
India, USA, Canada, UK, Australia, France

ISBN : 978-81-212-3209-8 (PB)
First Published, London, 1843

2nd Impression 2020

Printed at: Gyan Press, Delhi.

Ceylon and its Capabilities
Author: J. W. Bennett

CEYLON

AND ITS CAPABILITIES;

AN ACCOUNT

OF ITS

NATURAL RESOURCES, INDIGENOUS PRODUCTIONS, AND COMMERCIAL FACILITIES;

TO WHICH ARE ADDED

DETAILS OF ITS STATISTICS, PILOTAGE AND SAILING DIRECTIONS,

AND

AN APPENDIX,

CONTAINING THE ROYAL CHARTER OF JUSTICE, THE KANDYAN CONVENTION OF 1815, ORDINANCES OF THE COLONIAL GOVERNMENT ON VARIOUS MATTERS CONNECTED WITH THE COMMERCE OF THAT ISLAND, ETC. ETC.

WITH PLAIN AND COLORED ILLUSTRATIONS.

BY

J. W. BENNETT, ESQ., F. L. S.,

LATE CEYLON CIVIL ESTABLISHMENT.

LONDON:

WM. H. ALLEN AND CO., 7, LEADENHALL-STREET.

1843.

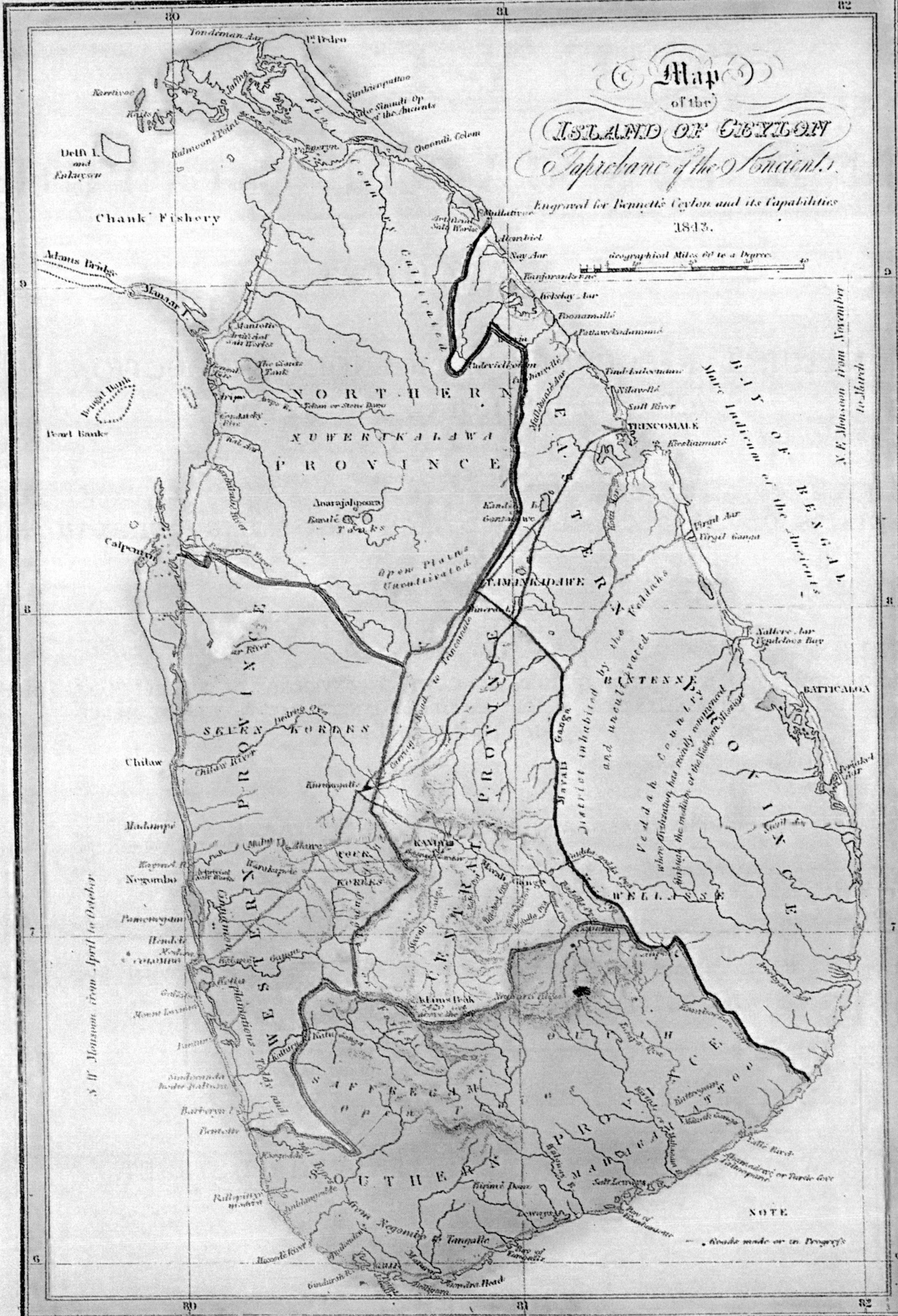
Map
of the
ISLAND OF CEYLON
Taprobane of the Ancients
Engraved for Bennett's Ceylon and its Capabilities
1843.
Geographical Miles 60 to a Degree
Chank' Fishery
Adams Bridge
Pearl Banks
NORTHERN
NUWERAKALAWA
PROVINCE
TRINCOMALE
BAY OF BENGAL
BATTICALOA
SEVEN KORLES
Chilaw
Madampé
Negombo
Colombo
KANDY
CENTRAL PROVINCE
WESTERN PROVINCE
SOUTHERN
EASTERN PROVINCE
Adams Peak
NOTE
Roads made or in Progress

TO

THE RIGHT HONORABLE

THE EARL OF RIPON,

D.C.L., F.R.S., H.S., R.G.S.,

PRESIDENT OF HER MAJESTY'S BOARD OF CONTROL FOR THE AFFAIRS OF INDIA,

PRESIDENT OF THE ROYAL SOCIETY OF LITERATURE,

&c. &c. &c.

UNDER WHOSE BENIGN ADMINISTRATION OF THE COLONIES, BETWEEN THE YEARS 1830 & 1833, INCLUSIVELY.

THE MONOPOLIES WHICH THE PORTUGUESE AND DUTCH HAD ORIGINALLY ESTABLISHED,

AND THE BRITISH GOVERNMENT HAD CONTINUED,

IN THE ISLAND OF CEYLON,

FROM THE PERIOD OF ITS CESSION IN THE YEAR 1796, TO THE YEAR 1832,

WERE ABOLISHED;

A MOST INTOLERABLE INCUBUS UPON NATIVE INDUSTRY REMOVED;

THE LABOURING CLASSES RELIEVED FROM THE OPPRESSIVE SYSTEM OF FEUDAL SERVICE;

EXTENSIVE REDUCTIONS EFFECTED IN THE PUBLIC CIVIL DEPARTMENTS:

AGRICULTURE EXTENDED; COMMERCE PROTECTED; THE REVENUE INCREASED;

AND THE MOST IMPORTANT INTERESTS OF THAT INVALUABLE COLONY, EITHER PROMOTED OR SECURED

THIS VOLUME,

UPON

"CEYLON AND ITS CAPABILITIES,"

IS HUMBLY DEDICATED,

BY

HIS LORDSHIP'S VERY FAITHFUL AND MOST OBEDIENT SERVANT,

THE AUTHOR.

LONDON, JUNE 20th, 1843.

PREFACE.

WHATEVER original materials, whether derived from my own observations or the communications of others, during a long residence at Ceylon, may have been employed in the compilation of the following pages, it would have been difficult to have satisfied myself, or to answer the anticipated purpose of my undertaking, if I had not also drawn largely from the best ancient and modern historians, who have (partly) preceded me in the same route; although without having the same object in view;—that of drawing the attention of British capitalists to the most important and valuable of all the insular possessions of the Imperial crown.

Ceylon, though comparatively but little known, is pre-eminent in natural resources, and abounds in all the necessaries and most of the luxuries that minister to the gratification of human nature. Its vast importance in every sense, political, fiscal, agricultural, and commercial, has hitherto been too much overlooked by capitalists; a neglect, which, I would fain hope, has arisen from the want of detailed information, or the pressure of other objects, apparently more interesting, only because better understood.

The object of my humble description is, to submit to public view the great capabilities of this magnificent island;—its fertile soil, indigenous vegetable productions, including dyes, medicinal plants, gums, and naturalized exotics; its minerals; wild and domestic animals; varieties of timber for construction and ornament; fisheries; immense uncultivated tracts of arable and other lands; employed and unemployed population; and its exports, already large, and easily to be increased.

To these, I have added my humble suggestions for establishing farms for the improvement of the native breed of cattle and other domestic animals, and for supplying the Royal Navy and Commercial Marine with stock of every description; factories for curing the varieties of useful fishes which abound on the coasts, and for the manufacture of important articles of commerce, easily obtainable, but now altogether neglected,—all offering ample employment and prompt returns for British capital and enterprise: and I have not omitted to point out how a gratuitous supply of Teak timber may be provided for the future exigencies of the Royal Navy.

PREFACE.

And further, in the hope of affording all useful and practical information, for merchants, visitors, naval and military officers, emigrants, manufacturers, and colonists, I have detailed the statistics, &c., of the island, including climate, provinces, judicial circuits, revenue, ecclesiastical, judicial, civil, and military establishments, missions, schools, public societies, and charities, native festivals, and the features of the country and roads; together with pilotage and sailing directions along the coast and into the harbours and roads of the island, which I have extracted, at large, from the last edition of "Captain James Horsburgh's Directory, improved from the correct surveys of Captain David Ross, marine surveyor to the Honorable the East India Company," and published in the year 1836; and I am not aware, that any thing strictly connected with the object in view, has been omitted.

I have also added the latitude and longitude of various given points in the island, derived from the surveys of James Twynam, Esq., master attendant at Gàlle, and of the late Richard Brook, Esq., master attendant at Trincomalè.

I have preferred citing the best authorities now extant upon the mineralogy of the island, to giving my own plainer and humbler remarks, because the latter must altogether have excluded scientific information upon this important branch of natural history.

In conclusion, I thankfully acknowledge that I have derived much of my information from the priest and the chief, the merchant and the agriculturist, the astrologer and the culler of simples, or doctor, the mechanic and the husbandman, the sea fisherman and the humbler angler for the finny tribes of the fresh-water streams and tanks; and, in acknowledging my obligations to my several authorities, both ancient and modern, dead and living, I hope I have done them all the justice in my power, by this candid avowal.

THE AUTHOR.

TABLE OF CONTENTS.

CHAP. V.

CHAP. VI.

CHAP. VII.

CHAP. VIII.

CHAP. IX.

CHAP. X.

CHAP. XI.

CHAP. XII.

CHAP. XIII.

CHAP. XIV.

CHAP. XV.

CHAP. XVI.

CHAP. XVII.

CHAP. XVIII.

CHAP. XIX.

CHAP. XX.

CHAP. XXI.

CHAP. XXII.

CHAP. XXIII.

CHAP. XXVIII.

CHAP. XXIX.

CHAP. XXX.

CHAP. XXXI.

CHAP. XXXII.

CHAP. XXXIII.

CHAP. XXXIV.

CHAP. XXXV.

CHAP. XXXVI.

CHAP. XXXVII.

CHAP. XXXVIII.

CHAP. XXXIX.

CHAP. XL.

CHAP. XLI.

***

CHAP. XLII.

CHAP. XLIII.

CHAP. XLIV.

CHAP. XLV.

CHAP. XLVI.

CHAP. LI.

CHAP. LII.

APPENDIX.

CEYLON AND ITS CAPABILITIES.

CHAP. I.

Geographical position—Dependencies—Ceylon occasionally confounded with Sierra Leone—Gulf and Strait of Manaar—Island partially known to the ancient Romans—Various Names of the Island—Its position upon the Geographical Lotos of the Hindoos—Popular tradition of its separation from the Peninsula of Hindostan—Adam's Bridge—Hindoo history respecting it—Sir W. Jones's remarks—Indian Satyrs—Hypothesis respecting the Garden of Eden—M. Tournefort's opinion—Variety of Climate—Pedrotalagalla the highest land in Ceylon—Verdant appearance of the Island—Sea-breezes—Monsoons and their causes—General Salubrity of the Interior dependant upon the progress of Agriculture—Area of the Island and Population to the square mile—Official Census of 1835.

THE most magnificent of the British insular possessions, styled, "Ceylon and its Dependencies," lie between the parallels of 5° 50′ and 10° of north latitude, and between 79° 42′ and 82° of east longitude, at the west entrance of the Bay of Bengal, and distant about ten leagues from the peninsula of Hindostan,* extending from S. S. E. to N. E. between Capes Comorin and Negapatam; in circumference about nine hundred miles; in length, from Dondra Head in the southern to Point Pedro in the northern province, under three hundred miles; and in extreme breadth from one hundred and forty to one hundred and fifty miles.

The "Dependencies" are the islands of Kalpentyn—Karetivoe—Manaar—Trentivoe, or Two Brothers—Kakeritivoe—Paletivoe—Nedoentivoe, or Delft†—Mandetivoe—Poengertivoe—Kayts, or Leyden island—Nayntivoe—Anelativoe—Northern Karetivoe, or Amsterdam island—Jaffna, formerly the kingdom of Jaffnapatam, upon which the town and fort of that name are situate—and the largest, containing the Districts of Wadenerratchie, Temmoratchie, and Patchilapelle.

Ceylon, too often confounded in common parlance with our West African settlement of Sierra Leoné, from neglecting to accentuate the last syllable of the latter, is separated from the southern extremity of Hindostan by the Gulf and Strait of Manaar,‡ which is not frequented except by small coasting vessels; the water being usually shoal

* From *Hindû*, black, and *St'han*, place.

† Called also by Captain Horsburgh *Polandiva, Cat-Island,* and *Enkhuysen.*

‡ From the Malabar word *Man*, sand, and *Aar*, river.

all over it, six or seven fathoms in some places, to four, three, and two fathoms towards the main, renders the navigation unsafe for vessels above a certain tonnage. It is bounded by Adam's Bridge to the southward, and by Calymere Point and the coast of Tanjore to the northward. The Dutch describe *three* channels formed between Calymere Point and the north end of Ceylon, which lead into Palk's Bay; but the southern channel, called Palk's Strait, contiguous to the north coast of Ceylon, is probably the only one that may be considered safe for large ships.

Adam's or Rama's Bridge, a narrow ridge of sand and rocks, mostly dry, for on its whole extent there is said not to be more than three and four feet of water in any part at high tides, extends nearly E. S. E. and W. N. W. six or seven leagues, and joins the island of Manaar on the east, and the island of Ramisseram, which lies close to a peninsula of the continent, the extremity of which is called Point Ramen, on the west. Between the main island and Manaar there is a narrow gut, only navigable by coasting vessels, which is commanded by Fort Tannacudia on the eastern extremity of Manaar.

That Ceylon was partially known to the ancient Romans may very reasonably be inferred from the names they gave to some of its principal places; and probably that knowledge of the island originated by means of their coasting vessels along the western side of India, or of their fleet from the *Sinus Arabicus*, or Red Sea. But the island lay so directly in the course of vessels venturing beyond Cape Comorin, viz. according to the ancient mode of "hugging the shore" as closely as possible, that one can scarcely suppose its position to have been left to doubt; but, on the contrary, that it had been precisely determined. Nevertheless, there is hardly any point in ancient geography less certain and more undecided.

The Amasian stoic, Strabo, who composed his great work upon geography in the time of Augustus Cæsar, describes Taprobane as equal in size to Britain, and "by reports" varying from seven to twenty days' sail from Cape Comorin, the southernmost point of the peninsula of Hindostan, the *Comaria Promontorium* of the Romans. But he erroneously describes the island as extending to the westward of its true position five hundred stadia, or rather more than twenty leagues. By this same author we are informed that the most valuable productions of Taprobane were carried to the various emporia of India.

Pomponius Mela, in his "De sitû orbis," could not decide whether Taprobane, which name was not known in Europe antecedently to the æra of Alexander the Great, was the commencement of a new world, or an island, because no one had ever sailed round it at the time he wrote, but he himself inclined to the former opinion; and the Roman augur, C. Plinius Secundus, instead of elucidating doubts, in his more copious description of Taprobane, which he also alludes to as *Terra Anticthonum,* or the Antipodes, involves it in deeper obscurity, and gives a most ridiculous account of an embassy to Claudius Cæsar from a sovereign of the island. The ambassadors must have entertained a very humble opinion of Roman science, when they ventured to affirm, that "in their country the moon was invisible for eight days after the change, and then only visible for the same period of time."*

Ptolemy, the famous Alexandrian geographer in the time of Marcus Aurelius, who wrote after Pliny, describes Taprobane as an island nearly opposite to Cape Comorin, and at no great distance from that part of the peninsula of Hindostan, but extending two degrees to the southward of the equator. Ptolemy appears to have been ignorant of Pliny's account of Taprobane, and informs us that the native name was *Salice,* which is preserved in that of *Selendive,* from the proper name *Selen,* and *divé,* an island.† Both, however, of these writers concur in describing the island as intersected by the equator, a circumstance that has led many to maintain that Sumatra is the island which during the middle ages was almost uniformly called Taprobane; and in the fifteenth century Nicolo di Conti, the Venetian traveller, on his return from India, described Ceylon as *Zeilam,* and after noticing its cinnamon and other productions, states that he sailed from thence to the great island of Sumatra, "which the ancients called Taprobane," and describes the durian *(Durio zibethinus)* as a fruit indigenous there, but which is not known to this day at Ceylon. But notwithstanding the obscure and contradictory descriptions both of the ancient Greek and Roman as well as of the Indian writers, upon this particular point, scarcely a doubt now exists that their celebrated Taprobane is the present Ceylon.

The Nubian philosopher, El Edrisi, in his work dedicated to Roger, king of Sicily, in the twelfth century, calls the island by the name of *Serandib;* and the Venetian traveller, Marco Polo, who visited it in the thirteenth century, by that of *Seilam* or *Zeilam.*

Cosmas, an Egyptian merchant, subsequently sirnamed *Indicopleustes,* who made several voyages to and from India during the reign of the emperor Justinian, mentions the island as *Sielediba,*‡ and as an emporium of commerce into which was imported the silk of the Sinæ, and all the precious productions of the Eastern Countries, with which all parts of India, Persia, and the Arabian Gulf were supplied.§

The island has also been known from the remotest periods of Singhalese history by the Elu name of *Lakka* and Sanscrit *Lanka,* the world, to which latter has been prefixed the Sanscrit adjectives *Tevé* and *Devé,* signifying famous and holy: and in the Geo-

* C. P. Hist. Nat., lib. vi. cap. xxii.

† According to Ptolemy its *ancient* name was *Symondi.*

‡ Cosm. lib. xxi. 336.

§ Ib. lib. xi. 337.

graphical Lotos of the Hindoos, which is supposed to be floating upon the vast expanse of ocean, Ceylon, described as *Sinhala,** lies between the southernmost upper petal and the *Maha Lanka* or Malacca petal, upon the *under* south-eastern petal.

But whether the popular tradition that Ceylon originally formed the south-eastern extremity of the peninsula of Hindostan, and was detached from it by some extraordinary convulsion of nature, aided by the rushing in of the sea through the division of the lands, be deserving of credit; or that it was an island de principio, at a greater distance from the Malabar and Coromandel coasts, and stretching so much further to the southward and westward as to be the Lanka or equinoctial point of the ancient Hindoos, but gradually approximating the continent by the accumulation of sand and madrepore, and the consequent shoaling of the Strait of Manaar,—is matter for the attention of the geologist.

Hindoo history evidently alludes to Adam's Bridge, in recounting the wars of Lanka, and attributes to Rama,† an incarnate deity of the first rank in the Hindoo mythology, the conquest of the island with an army of *Indian satyrs,* and states that Rama's general, the prince of satyrs, named HANUMAT‡ from his high cheek bones, soon raised with workmen of such agility a bridge of rocks over the sea; part of which, say the Hindoos, yet remains. This Rama is described as a conqueror of the highest renown, and the deliverer of his consort Sita from the giant Ravanen, king of Lanka. Sir William Jones, in alluding to the above,§ inquires "if this army of satyrs might not have been only a race of mountaineers, whom Rama, if such a monarch ever existed, had civilized?" and concludes with this remark,—"However that may be, the large breed of Indian apes is at this moment (1794) held in high veneration by the Hindoos, and fed with devotion by the Brahmins, who seem, in two or three places on the banks of the Ganges, to have a regular endowment for the support of them: they live in tribes of three or four hundred, are wonderfully gentle, and appear to have some kind of order and subordination in their little sylvan polity."

It may much more reasonably be conjectured, that the Bridge of Islets, bearing the name of the common father of mankind, from the Mahomedan fable that angels formed it for Adam to pass over to Hindostan, after having dropped upon the mountain Hamalell, when expelled from the celestial Paradise, was the route by which the persecuted followers of the god *Bod,*|| or Buddha, when driven from the continent by the Brahmins, sought a secure resting-place for themselves, and for the unmolested exercise of their religion, in Ceylon.

* Asiatic Researches, vol. viii., 8vo edition, p. 376.

† The son of *Cush.*

‡ The son of *Pavon*, the Indian god of storms and winds, and one of the eight Genii.

§ Asiatic Researches, vol. i., 4to edition, p. 257.

|| *Bod,* a contraction of *Buddha,* which signifies wisdom.

Ceylon abounds with traditions, and amongst others, that it was the site of the terrestrial Paradise; and inquiry has scarcely done more than cause a wide diversity of opinions upon that point. Tartary, China, Persia, Mesopotamia, Chaldæa, Arabia, Syria, Ethiopia, and Ceylon, have all, in turns, been objects of research upon this great point; and whilst some have concluded that the scriptural description of Paradise was either allegorical, or that if such a perfect place really existed, the subsequent terrible concussions of the earth at the time of the deluge have so altered the face of nature as to render it now impossible to discover where the true garden of *Eden* or *Aden* lay, (synonymous in the Arabic, and signifying pleasure,)—others have been led astray as much as the Jews themselves, who were totally ignorant of the geography of the Old Testament. Josephus supposed the Ganges and the Nile to be two of the four rivers that went out of Eden.

There exists to this day such a variety of *Edens* and *Adens*, one near Tripoli in Syria, another near Telassar in Chaldæa, a third an island in the Tigris, a fourth near Tarsus in Cilicia, and a fifth upon the coast of Arabia Felix, that authors have given it in favour of either of the *two former*, as being, I presume, the same with that of Moses.*

There can scarcely be a doubt that Eden was not an imaginary but a real Paradise, bounded by the countries and rivers described in the Mosaical topography, but no one author seems to have decided the point so satisfactorily *to himself* as Mons. Tournefort. "The commentators upon Genesis, even those who keep most closely to the letter, do not think it necessary, in order to assign the place of Paradise, to find a river which divides itself into four branches, because of the great alteration the Deluge may have occasioned; but think it sufficient to show the heads of the rivers mentioned by Moses, namely, the Euphrates, Tigris, Pison, and Gihon. It cannot, therefore, be doubted but that Paradise must have been in the way between Erzerum and Teflis, if it be allowed to take the Phasis for Pison, and the Araxes for Gihon.—And then, not to remove Paradise too far from the sources of these rivers, it must of necessity be placed in the beautiful vallies of Georgia, which furnish Erzerum with all kinds of fruits. If we may suppose it to have been a place of considerable extent, and to have retained some of its beauties, notwithstanding the alterations made in the earth at the flood, and since that time, I do not know a finer spot to which I can assign it than the country of the Three Churches, a town about twenty French leagues distant from the heads of the Euphrates and Araxes, and almost as many from the Phasis. The extent of Paradise must at least reach to the heads of these rivers; and so it will comprehend the ancient Media and part of Armenia and Iberia. Or, if this be thought too large a

* 2 Kings xix. 12. Isaiah xxxvii. 12.

compass, it may be confined only to part of Armenia and Iberia; that is, from Erzerum to Teflis. Our learned men may think as they please, but as I have never seen a more beautiful country than the neighbourhood of the Three Churches, I am strongly persuaded it is the place where Adam and Eve were created!"

Ceylon presents a variety of climate, which may be classed as the hot, the intermediate, and the temperate: the first, that of the maritime provinces; the second, between the maritime provinces and the mountainous region; and the last, that of the convalescent station of *Neuwara Eliya*, literally, city of light, adjoining the highest land, called Pedrotalagalla, which is 8280 feet above the level of the sea, and 860 feet higher than the far-famed *Samenella*, or Adam's Peak, erroneously cited by many authors as the highest land in Ceylon. At Neuwara Eliya the mean daily variation of the temperature is stated to be as high as 10°, and from that to 11° of Fahrenheit, which is more than three times the mean daily variation at Galle and Colombo; and the annual range of the thermometer from 36° to 81°. The mean annual temperature of the maritime provinces is between 78° and 80°, according to the only data I possess, but as they are from uncertain sources, I think Dr. John Davy's the best authority upon all these points, and he, from practical observation during his residence in the island as Physician to the Forces, states the mean annual temperature of *the coast* at between 79° and 81°; the extreme range of the thermometer between 68° and 90°, and the medium range between 75° and 85°.

A stranger approaching Ceylon after a long voyage and the monotonous prospect of boundless ocean, during which the imagination, connecting the island with its proximity to the equator,* may have pictured to itself nothing but barren sand-hills, parched trees, and sun-burnt fields, is agreeably surprised at the first view of a verdant island, whose northern and north-eastern coasts are belted with intermingled palmyra and coco-nut palms, and its southern and western shores covered with myriads of the latter to the very verge of the sea.

This interesting country is highly favoured with continual sea-breezes, which render its hottest parts much more temperate than the climate of Hindostan. The coolest season is during the prevalence of the south-west monsoon, or periodical wind, which sets in about the latter part of April, and continues till the end of October, when the sun is to the northward of the equator. The change of the monsoon is generally ushered in by abundant and refreshing rains, which continue at intervals, more or less, for ten or twelve weeks. The north-east monsoon is of shorter duration; it begins in November, and prevails till March, when the sun is to the southward of the equator.

* The difference between day and night is about fifteen minutes.

It is also attended by heavy rains in the northern parts of the island: and both monsoons bring their share of the most tremendous thunder and vivid lightning that the eye of man has ever witnessed, or his mind conceived. Nevertheless the occurrence of fatal accidents during a thunder-storm, when contrasted with the violence with which it rages, and the population of the island, bears no proportion to that of the casualties from lightning in more northern countries.

Rowning, in his natural philosophy, thus explains the occasion of these periodical winds or monsoons within the tropics. "When the sun approaches the northern tropic, there are several countries, as Arabia, Persia, India, &c. which become hotter, and reflect more heat than the seas beyond the equator which the sun has left; the winds, therefore, instead of blowing from thence to the parts under the equator, blow the contrary way; and when the sun leaves those countries and draws near the other tropic, the winds turn about and blow on the opposite side of the compass. At the time of the shifting of those winds, the *Indian* seas are very subject to be tempestuous, and the navigation becomes unsafe."

So much depends upon the progress of agriculture, that the climate of 1838 may be altogether changed for the better in 1841, in one and the same place. As this important point can only be partially ascertained until cultivation, which scarcely exceeds one fourth of its superficies, shall have been extended over the whole island, it is but fair to form a criterion for anticipations of the ultimate result, by that which has already attended it in places where it has superseded densely-wooded and impervious forests, and where the decomposition of vegetable matter had continued through countless ages, and every natural impediment was opposed to evaporation; for there has not been an instance of the continuance of malaria where the underwood has been thoroughly cleared; and even places that are only partially cleared, and where sickness was a few years back prevalent and periodical, are become comparatively salubrious. Thus if a judgment may be formed of the climate of the future whole, by that of the one fourth part of the area of the island now under cultivation, it will be impossible for a healthier to be found in any part of the habitable globe than that to which Ceylon may then justly lay claim.

Taking the superficies of the island at 24,448 square miles, and estimating its present population at a million and a half, the product would give about sixty in round numbers to the square mile; and of this population, the number employed may be set down at the maximum as follows:—

In agriculture	400,000
In manufactures	55,000
In commerce	45,000

CENSUS OF THE POPULATION OF THE ISLAND OF CEYLON AND ITS DEPENDENCIES,

Taken by order of His Excellency the Right Honourable Sir Robert Wilmot Horton, Bart. G. C. H. Governor, Commander in Chief, and Vice Admiral, In the Year 1835.

Provinces.	Area in Square Miles.	Whites.		Free Blacks.		Slaves.		Total.		Aliens and Resident Strangers.	Population to the Square Mile.	Persons employed in			Births.	Marriages.	Deaths.
		Males.	Females.	Males.	Females.	Males.	Females.	Males.	Females.			Agriculture.	Manufactures.	Commerce.			
Western Province	4,452	1,275	1,273	257,144	235,461	373	332	258,792	237,066	1,829	111.78	†111,601	13,391	†11,456	10,377	4,960	6,887
Southern do.	6,032	559	599	142,810	121,780	431	342	143,800	122,721	573	44.27	71,694	11,366	9,040	11,292	1,787	5,087
Eastern do.	4,895	*415	*395	*25,844	*23,536	*12	*11	*26,271	*23,942	*3,143	10.90	*8,930	*3,017	*1,427	*1,546	*465	*1,165
Northern do.	6,053	478	518	112,223	112,928	12,605	11,910	125,306	125,356	‡1,446	41.65	‡67,662	‡18,992	‡12,454	‡4,323	‡1,174	‡2,491
Central do.	3,016	185	144	84,821	71,541	687	694	85,693	72,379	3,834	53.68	84,727	3,931	8,531	2,431	1,816	1,570
Total, Exclusive of the Military ..		2,912	2,929	622,842	565,246	14,108	13,289	639,862	581,464	10,825	50.39	344,614	50,697	42,908	29,969	10,202	17,200
Military & Civil Ordnance Officers with their Families —																	
Western Province		1,145	292	1,482	1,183	,,	,,	2,627	1,475	,,	.92	,,	,,	,,	88	36	121
Southern do.		209	79	522	496	,,	,,	731	575	,,	.21	,,	,,	,,	28	9	36
Eastern do.		521	124	352	253	,,	,,	873	377	,,	.25	,,	,,	,,	25	6	89
Northern do.		14	21	266	210	,,	,,	280	231	,,	.08	,,	,,	,,	13	6	12
Central do.		715	160	1,001	629	,,	,,	1,716	789	,,	.83	,,	,,	,,	77	25	28
Total Military		2,604	676	3,623	2,771	,,	,,	6,227	3,447	,,	.39	,,	,,	,,	231	82	286
Grand Total	24,448	5,516	3,605	626,465	568,017	14,108	13,289	646,089	584,911	10,825	50.79	344,614	50,697	42,908	30,200	10,284	17,486

POPULATION OF CEYLON......1,241,825.

† Excepting the Seven Korles Division, where no Return has been kept.

* Excepting the Bintennè Division, where no Return has been kept.

‡ Excepting the Nuwerakalawiyé Division, where no Return has been kept.

CHAP. II.

Existing Slavery—The Honorable Sir Alexander Johnston, Chief Justice, originates the preparatory measure towards the abolition of slavery, in which he is zealously supported by His Excellency the Governor—Address of the proprietors of domestic slaves to His Royal Highness the Prince Regent, tendering the manumission of all children born of their slaves on and after His Royal Highness's birth-day of 1816*—No part of the Parliamentary grant of* £20,000,000 *appropriated to the Ceylon slave proprietors—Paternal care of the slaves by the Ceylon government—James Sutherland, Esq.—James Nicholas Mooyaart, Esq.—Foreign employés in the civil establishment—Extraordinary results of their peculations and perjuries—Degradation of the service and loss to the public—Consequences of individual comments upon the measures of the colonial department, in re-employing or pensioning convicted peculators—Number of female children of slaves enfranchised by the government—Substance of the provisions of the government ordinance for the more efficient registration and protection of slaves.*

THAT Asiatic Slavery should still exist in Ceylon, whilst the African Negro is altogether free to work or be idle, as may suit his purpose or his inclination, will appear incredible to those who may have given the appropriation of the twenty millions sterling, granted by Parliament for the abolition of Slavery in the British Colonies, one moment's consideration;—nevertheless, the foregoing Census of the population of the island, taken in the year 1835, exposes the real state of the case; the number of slaves being 27,397, including 14,108 males, and 13,289 females.

To the eternal honor of the humane Dutch and native proprietors of domestic slaves in the Singhalese districts of the maritime provinces, Ceylon was the first and only colony under the British flag to make a voluntary concession of prospective slave property to the principle upon which the Imperial legislature subsequently acted.—The Honorable the Chief Justice (the present Right Honorable Sir Alexander Johnston) had only to suggest a plan to the slave proprietors, to have it adopted. It was not merely from the respect in which the community held Sir Alexander, for his able, just, and patient exercise of the power attached to his high and important office, that such ready deference was shown to his philanthropic recommendations, every way congenial with the general feeling of the British nation and the best interests of humanity, and presenting a moral basis for the ultimate abolition of slavery throughout the island, but because they loved him with more than common affection, for his general humanity and charity, and zeal for the welfare of them all.

The cause which the Chief Justice had so warmly espoused, found a strenuous supporter in His Excellency the Governor, the late General Sir Robert Brownrigg, Bart., G. C. B.; and the principal proprietors of domestic slaves amongst the Dutch inhabitants, burghers, and native castes of Colombo, acting upon the conviction that the Government and Parliament of the United Kingdom took a warm interest in the cause of those branded with the name of slaves, and of the moral and religious obligation of commiserating the situation of that unfortunate class of their fellow creatures, unanimously resolved to address a petition to His Royal Highness, the then Prince Regent, (in which they were subsequently joined by the proprietors of domestic slaves throughout the Singhalese districts of the maritime provinces,) declaratory of their determination to emancipate all children born of their slaves on, and after, His Royal Highness's birth-day, the 12th of August, 1816.

Of this document, so every way worthy of being recorded upon a more imperishable tablet than paper, I feel both pride and pleasure in submitting a copy to my readers; for by this act of justice to the petitioners, I also confer a lasting honor upon my own pages.

TO

HIS ROYAL HIGHNESS THE PRINCE OF WALES,

REGENT OF THE UNITED KINGDOM OF GREAT BRITAIN AND IRELAND,

&c. &c. &c.

"We His Majesty's loyal subjects, the Dutch inhabitants, burghers, and native castes of the maritime settlements in the island of Ceylon, animated with sentiments of sincere and fervent loyalty towards the person and government of His Majesty, and your Royal Highness, and emulating the humane and disinterested spirit with which our fellow subjects in the United Kingdom have moved the Legislature in favour of that unfortunate class of beings, placed in the degraded condition of slavery, beg leave to approach your Royal Highness with an humble tender of such tribute, on our parts, in furtherance of the same benevolent object, as our circumstances enable us to afford.

"In families long settled in this island, of whatever class, the household establishment is usually so much dependent on the service of slaves, that a general discharge of those persons would subject the inhabitants to privations, losses, and expense, such as ordinary prudence forbids us to encounter; at the same time we have reason to know, that to great numbers of the persons now in our houses in the character of slaves, bred up under our roofs, supported for a course of years with kind and considerate treatment and comfortable subsistence, many of them far advanced in life, and the greater part established in habits of attachment, a general emancipation would withdraw the source of their support, without advancing their happiness, or improving their condition.

"We therefore humbly incline, both in consideration to them and to ourselves, to adopt the principle sanctioned by the wisdom of British Legislation, of a gradual abolition; that which we beg leave to offer, being indeed gradual in its progress, but in its issue certain and complete.

"We respectfully and dutifully propose, that the era of future freedom to the slaves of this colony shall take its commencement on the auspicious occasion of your Royal Highness's birth-day, the 12th of August in the present year 1816. And we declare all children born of our slaves, from that date inclusive, to be free persons.

"Some incidental provisions will be perceived to be necessary with regard to the support and tutelage of these liberated children during their tender years. The leading articles of enactment, which appear expedient for this purpose, have already been indicated in Resolutions conveyed by the Honorable the Chief Justice for the information of His Excellency the Governor; and we doubt not that these and such other regulations as may be found calculated to place the intended measure on a footing of mutual comfort to the emancipated slaves and their masters, will be distinctly and favourably represented by His Excellency, and receive in substance the gracious acceptance and confirmation of your Royal Highness."

(Signed by the petitioners.)

His Royal Highness's reception of this petition was as gracious as the most sanguine philanthropist could have anticipated from the enlightened prince, who, "Patriam, pro patre, regens," swayed the Imperial sceptre of these kingdoms: and its provisions, having been confirmed by His Royal Highness, took effect agreeably to the intentions of the petitioners.

At that period, the domestic slaves were generally much happier than hired servants, or free labourers, whose daily wages never exceeded sixpence for twelve hours' labour; but, upon what moral principle, the claims of the proprietors of African slaves should have been considered so very paramount to those of the owners of Malabar slaves in Ceylon, that not one shilling of the £20,000,000 could find its way nearer to that island than the Mauritius, no one has hitherto attempted to explain.

Humanity will admit, that if the example set by the proprietors of domestic slaves in Ceylon did not give them a priority of claim, in point of justice, over those of African slaves, their voluntary relinquishment of their rights of ownership over the issue of their slaves from the 12th of August, 1816, had at least entitled them to an equitable compensation out of the twenty millions of the public money voted by Parliament for the enfranchisement of colonial slaves :—but these philanthropic individuals, instead of sharing in the public grant, are now doubly burthened through their own humanity; for by slavery continuing until death shall have carried off the present number of domestic slaves, they are bound to support the old and feeble, and consequently useless individuals, without receiving any allowance whatever for their maintenance; little chance of obtaining relief by selling their rights as owners, because few will purchase under the circumstances; and no succession of service to anticipate from the offspring of the slaves whom they are bound to maintain.

Ceylon had no agent in Parliament to advocate either the claims of its slave proprietors, or of the slaves themselves; or, surely, the noble conduct of the Dutch inhabitants, burghers, and native castes of Ceylon, who had set such an example of humanity, and indeed of deference to the call of the nation, would not only *not* have been overlooked, but have been deemed entitled to a fair and adequate compensation; and the Asiatic slaves of Ceylon to an equal right to emancipation with their African contemporaries of the West Indies and Mauritius.—For the sake of justice to the one, and of humanity to the other, I hope it is not even yet too late for their relative claims to be considered and admitted by the British Legislature.

But whether the extinction of slavery in Ceylon is to be effected, or the evil to continue for an indefinite period, every benevolent heart will rejoice at the paternal care manifested towards those degraded beings by the local government, although it may have overlooked certain rights of the owners in dispensing its own will and pleasure in regard to *their* slaves.

The first enactment of a Regulation for the Registration of slaves in the Malabar districts of the island, took place in the year 1806, during the administration of His Excellency the late Right Honorable Sir Thomas Maitland, G. C. B.; and so important has this measure been considered by His Excellency's successors in the government, that a strict attention to its provisions has been continued, and is still enforced.

During the administration of His Excellency the late General Sir Robert Brownrigg, the registration of slaves was attended to with a still greater surveillance on the part of the government than at any former period, from the circumstance of its being entered into with all the ardour of personal interest, by the late James Sutherland, Esq., the then talented superintendent, as deputy secretary to government, of the home and judicial department of the Chief Secretary's office.

In the furtherance of this important measure, Mr. Sutherland found an active and able coadjutor in James Nicholas Mooyaart, Esq., the humane and enlightened fiscal of Jaffna at that period; who, although a natural-born subject of Holland, has since been appointed to the civil service; in which, much to the satisfaction of all who know him, he now holds a high and lucrative office.

I may, perhaps, be allowed to digress, for a moment, from the direct line of route I had sketched for myself, to remark, that it would have been a wise precaution, if the government had been equally as select in all its other appointments of forcigners, including the Frenchman, the Greek, the Italian, and the German: for, in that case, the records of the civil establishment of Ceylon would not have exhibited the numerous pollutions, which, through favoritism, the personal convenience of former Governors, and the impunity with which private interest induced the then noble secretary for the colonies to allow the official convicts to escape, it now does.

The enormous peculations, and subsequent innumerable perjuries, committed by these foreign employés, (from which British subjects were not, I regret to say, altogether exempt,) with a view to conceal their repeated breaches of official trust, with the public monies under their charge, were either allowed to be committed with impunity, or, if such total destitution of public duty and private principle did temporarily subject them, after discovery and conviction, to the displeasure of the Right Honorable Lord, who then held the seals of the colonial department, it was either followed, through private influence, by restoration to the service, to secure a pension, or employment, with an increase of salary, (to £2000 a year in two instances,) in defiance of the recorded judgment of the Governor in council; but if an unfortunate critic of such measures of encouragement to official villainy, gave vent to his opinions, even while dispensing hospitality at his own table, it was sure of repetition, at "Head Quarters," by some "China carrier" or other; and Homer's truism, "He who has the power will have the revenge," exemplified, as a matter of course!

To return to the subject of slavery:—The government has enfranchised about three thousand five hundred female children of slaves within the last twenty one years, and the number of adult slaves who have purchased their own manumission, may be estimated in round numbers at a thousand, including male children: but the Malabar slaves do not now show so much anxiety, as formerly, to become free. This may arise from their increased value, since their owners manifested such great objections to the government system of compelling them to accept whatever sums the arbitrators might fix for the manumission of adult slaves at their own cost; and the consequent amelioration of the condition of these unfortunate beings may have reconciled them to a quiescent submission to their fate.

In the year 1837, the government extended the Registration of slaves, (which by the former Regulations, and prior to the acquisition of the Kandyan kingdom, had been limited to the maritime provinces,) throughout the island, by an Ordinance of the Governor, with the advice and consent of the Legislative Council, of which the following is the substance.

" 1. The registration by proprietors or persons in charge of slaves in parts of the island of Ceylon to which former Regulations did not extend, of the name, age, sex, and description of their several slaves in the register of the District Court, before the first day of July, 1838.

" 2. The notification of the death of a registered slave, or of the birth of a child of a slave, within eight days after the event, to the Secretary of the District Court; and if the mother of the child whose birth is so reported, have not previously been registered in that District, the proprietor or person in charge to produce a certificate of the last registry of such mother.

" 3. Upon the acquisition of any registered slave, whether by purchase, gift, legacy, inheritance or otherwise, the person acquiring the same, or his or her agent, to give notice to the Secretary of the Court of the District in which such proprietor or agent resides, within eight days; and if the slave had not previously been registered in that District, to produce a certificate of the last registry.

" 4. The Secretary of the District Court, within forty eight hours (exclusive of Sundays and Holidays) after the receipt of notice of the birth, death, or acquisition of a slave, and on production of the certificate required in the two preceding clauses, to register the same; and if the slave whose death, or the mother of the slave whose birth is reported, or the slave reported to have been acquired, had not previously been registered in that District, to transmit, within forty eight hours of such notice, a full report of particulars, to the Secretary of the District Court in which the slave had been registered.

" 5. Certificates of registry to be issued by the Secretary of the District Court to persons making such registry (unless in cases of reasonable cause for delay) within twenty four hours (exclusive of Sundays and Holidays) after the application; and in the absence of the Secretary, the District Judge to order the certificates to be prepared and issued by some other Officer of his Court.

" 6. The certificates to be written upon a stamp of one shilling, if applied for within three months after registration, and of five shillings at any subsequent period, at the expense of the slave owner or holder; and from and after the said first day of July, 1838, no Court to consider any person a slave unless a certificate of the last registry be produced.

"7. A registered slave to be furnished by the Secretary of the District Court with a copy of the registry within twenty four hours (exclusive of Sundays and Holidays) after application, free of all charge.

"8. A proprietor or person in charge of a slave failing to comply with the provisions of the said Ordinance, is liable to the following penalties, viz.—For failing to enregister any slave as required by the first clause, or acquisition of any slave, or birth of any child of a slave, within the periods prescribed, the forfeiture of all right in any slave or child not registered, and all the children of such slave if a female, who are declared enfranchised; and for omitting to notify the death of any slave, a fine not exceeding five pounds, one half thereof to the informer; and in all cases the Defendant to prove his compliance with the provisions of the said Ordinance: and the penalties it imposes to be over and above all such punishment as may by law be inflicted, or civil damages for detaining free persons in slavery or selling them as slaves.

"9. The Secretary of a District Court neglecting or refusing to comply with the provisions of the said Ordinance, is liable to a fine not exceeding ten pounds.

"10. Any person claiming to register any slave under the first clause of the said Ordinance, to bring such slave openly before the District Court on the day of registration; and the Judge to put such questions to the person claiming to enregister, or the person to be registered, as he may think necessary to satisfy himself that the said person is actually the person intended to be registered, and cause it to be explained to the said person that he is alleged to be a slave; and further compare the slave with the description given for the purpose of registration, and sign his name in the original register opposite to the slave's name and in the proper column, in token that the said person agrees with the description; and a copy of each register of a slave, and of any alteration thereof, to be translated into the native language of the District and placed in a conspicuous place at the Court House for three months after such registration.

"11. The forms of registers and certificates to be according to the Schedules annexed to the said Ordinance, and a correct transcript of each registry to be transmitted by the District Judge of the District to the Colonial Secretary's Office immediately after the said first day of July, 1838, and of all new entries or alterations in the registers for every three months subsequent thereto to be also sent to the Colonial Secretary's Office within one month after the termination of each quarter.

" 12. Any person making a false report to the Secretary of a District Court, or bringing any person not being the person intended to be registered, with a view to make a false or fraudulent registry, or any person wilfully making any false entry in the original registry or in the transcripts thereof for the Colonial Secretary's Office, or fraudulently erasing or altering such entry, or, being an Officer duly authorised to issue extracts from the same, issuing any false or fraudulent paper purporting to be an extract therefrom, to be deemed to be guilty of a misdemeanour.

" 13. Every proprietor or person in charge of a slave to be held liable to support every sick or infirm slave registered as his property or in his charge, and the District Court, on application by or on behalf of any such sick or infirm slave, to ascertain the truth of such complaint, and to make such order as it shall deem fit for the due support of such slave, or medical assistance to such slave, at the cost of the owner or person in charge, to be recovered from him by distress on his property.

" 14. Within three months after the termination of three years from the closing of the register directed by the said Ordinance to be opened in each District, or within three months after the termination of three years from the registry of the birth or acquisition of a slave, according to the circumstances of the case, and thereafter in like manner trienially, every proprietor or person in charge of a slave to take out from the District Court a renewed certificate of the registry of such slave, upon a stamp of one shilling, at the cost of the proprietor or person in charge of such slave; and prior to the issue thereof, each slave for whom such renewed certificate is claimed to be taken out to be brought before the District Court, when the registry is to be examined, and such questions put as the Court shall deem necessary to satisfy itself that the person before the Court is the person registered; and the District Judge to enter in the register, the date of such slave appearing before the Court, and such alteration of the description of such slave as he shall find necessary, and affix his initials thereto; and where the proprietor or person in charge of a slave shall omit to take out a renewed certificate of registry, such slave to be declared absolutely free; provided, that such neglect shall not exonerate the owner or holder from the obligation to maintain any sick or infirm slave to which he is liable by the said Ordinance; and such renewed certificates of registry shall be issued in like manner as certificates of original registry."

CHAP. III.

Facilities of irrigation—Culture of Rice very inadequate to the consumption—Classification of Rivers—Mavali-Ganga, Kalané-Ganga, Kalu-Ganga, Wallewé-Ganga—Analysis of their waters—Second-rate Rivers, Maha-Oya, Parapa-Oya, Dedroo-Oya. Navil-Aar—Inferior Streams—Mountains—Lakes or Tanks of Padeviel-Kolom, Kandellé, and Mineré—Suggestions for the introduction of Hindoo Agriculturists from the Peninsula of India—Ralph Backhouse, Esq.—His description of the Kandellé Lake—Singhalese King Maha-Sen, A. D. 275*—Dedication of Lands to Temples—Oppressive system of Rajah-Karia, or royal service, abolished by Lord Viscount Goderich, His Majesty's principal secretary of state for the colonies, in* 1832*—Suggestions for the restoration of the ancient tanks—Duties upon paddee fields and coco-nut topes—Amount paid for rice to French colonies in* 1840*—Suggestions to Her Majesty's secretary of state for the colonies, for a general survey of temple and other lands adapted to the culture of rice—Caution as to the reports made by natives—Suggestions for the non-removal of provincial agents.*

The means of irrigation are boundless; for the island being intersected in almost every direction by perennial mountain streams, every facility is afforded by nature for the formation of canals, where they do not yet exist; and where these may not be practicable, for the formation of tanks and reservoirs, and the restoration of many ancient ones, that are capable of being repaired.

These cover an immense area, sufficient for the inundation of hundreds of thousands of acres for the cultivation of rice, by which the island, instead of being, as it is now, partly dependent upon extraneous supplies of that staff of life to the native inhabitants, may again become one of the principal granaries of India, and, as in the year 1639,* supply the whole coast of Coromandel from the surplus of its produce.

A chief river is locally styled *Ganga,* but this term is indiscriminately applied to streams of minor importance; a second-rate river, *Oya.*

Of the former, the principal is the Mavali-Ganga,† which river has its source in the mountainous region of Neuwara-Eliya, flows through part of the Kotmalé district, where it is called the Kotmalé-Ganga, and washing the capital of the interior, Kandy, the *Muragramum* of the ancient Romans, rapidly descends through the plains of the district of Bintenné, and part of the savage country called Vedahratté, about thirty five

* Mandelsloh's Travels into the Indies, book ii. page 115.

† According to Chambers's account of the Tamul language, the Tamulians (or Malabars) having no *h* in their alphabet, are under a necessity of shortening the Sanscrit word *Maha,* great, and write it *Ma.* They are obliged also for a similar reason to substitute a *v* for a *b* in Sanscrit words or other foreign originals that begin with that letter. Hence the *Mavali-Ganga,* which waters the eastern side of Ceylon, where the Tamulic prevails, has probably taken its name from *Bali,* the famour hero of Hindoo romance, and *Ganga,* one of the Indian goddesses of the waters, who is painted as a beautiful woman walking upon a river, and bearing in each hand a flower of the *Nymphæa Lotos.*—Ganga is described as having sprung, like the armed Pallas of the Romans, from the head of *Indra,* the Indian Jupiter.

miles from Kandy, where its fall is calculated at from 900 to 1000 feet, and receiving in its way various tributary streams, meanders through a dry and almost level country, whence it diverges into several branches; and finally forming a delta of the district of Kottiaar, the northern branch, which is there called the Kotti-Aar, debouches at the bay of that name, and the southern branch between the ports of Trincomalé and Batticaloa, on the east side of the island, where it is called the Virgel-Ganga.

That the Mavali-Ganga may be made navigable, and of boundless utility to the interior, by means of locks, there can scarcely exist a doubt; and as cultivation extends, and additional means are required for transporting the increased quantity of produce to a port of export, it will become a matter of general importance to the country. But so long a period must elapse before there would be a return for capital employed, that it would be nothing less than madness for private speculation to attempt it. Whether made navigable or not, there is nothing to prevent the agriculturist from turning the waste waters of this splendid river to the advantageous irrigation of the valuable lands through which it meanders.

In the rainy season the Mavali-Ganga has been known to rise sixty feet above its usual level at Paradenia, near Kandy, in the course of a few hours, overflowing the road to Colombo, which could only be traversed in boats.

The second river in magnitude, but chief in point of importance, is the Kalané-Ganga, which derives its name from a very ancient city, called Kalané, whose sovereign, Kalanetissa, is said to have flourished about 250 or 260 B. C.,* but the date of his reign is not definitively ascertained. Kalané, now a mere village, has a celebrated temple, and its banks are washed by this stream, which rises in the mountains of Saffragam, near Hamalell or Adam's Peak, in the southern province; but it only takes that name at the confluence of the Maskelli-Ganga and Kehelgamua-Ganga, whose united waters form the Kalané-Ganga, at Weraloo-Ella, and debouches at Modera, about four miles north of the fort of Colombo, where it is called the Mutwaal river; but a bar of sand at the entrance occasionally acts as effectually as a dam, and greatly increases the width of the river, which is crossed at Pasbetal, on the northern road, by a bridge of boats.

The third is the Kaltura river, called by the Singhalese Kalu-Ganga,† and Setagongola-Oya at its source, about 4000 feet above the level of the sea, in the mountain called

* Turnour's Epitome of Singhalese History.

† From *Kalu*, black, and *Ganga*, river, owing to the deep shade over its waters, which,—

"Darkened by their native scenes,
Create wild images, and phantoms dire,
Strange as their hills, and gloomy as their storms."

Adam's Peak, and flowing past Battugeddera and Ratnapora, (where, in the rainy season, it has been known to rise twenty five feet above its usual level, in the course of a few hours;) and receiving several tributary streams, rapidly descends to Kaltura, and joins the sea through a narrow channel formed by two sand banks.

The Wallewé-Ganga is the fourth; but of much less importance than either of the former, and a bar of sand forms a dam at its extremity, except during the rainy season. when it rises full twenty feet above its usual level. At other times it is almost everywhere fordable, from about half a mile above the ferry at the village of Wanderopé, (which is about two miles from the sea,) to its source in the mountains of Ouva, in the southern province.

These mountain springs form the grand drains of the high lands of the interior. and are remarkable for their purity, differing only from rain water in containing slight traces of muriate of soda, or common salt, or of vegetable matter, and occasionally of carbonat of lime and suspened clay.* But nevertheless the natives residing upon the banks of the Wallewé-Ganga, will not even bathe in that river during the rainy season, on account of the quantity of decomposing vegetable matter carried down by the stream, rendering not only the water but the air unwholesome, and producing jungle fever if drunk or bathed in. Perhaps this very circumstance may be one cause of the great salubrity of the interior, by washing the dead and putrifying vegetable matter from the surface, and preventing its accumulation.

Of the second-rate rivers, by which the country between the mountains and the low lands, as well as the latter, are drained, the Kaymel river, as it is called at its mouth in the western province, and Maha-Oya at its source and intermediate meanderings, is the most important. The next are the Parapa-Oya, which has its source to the east ward of the mountains of Ouva, and flowing past the Hindoo temple of Kattregam. enters the sea, under the name of the Yallé river, in the southern province; the Chilaw river, called also Dedroo-Oya in the interior, which debouches at Chilaw in the western province; and the Navil-Aar, which rises in the mountains of Bintenné, and debouches between Karetivoe and Singharetopoe in the eastern province.

The other streams which have their sources and flow into the sea on the east side of the island are the Waroewekalé-Aar, Nay-Aar, Kokelé-Aar, Malekanté-Aar, Irikanté-Aar, Virgel-Aar and Virgel-Ganga, the latter being the largest stream, and both rivers merely branches of the Mavali-Ganga; Pannitchicanie-Ganga, also a branch of the Mavali-Ganga; Bampore or Nallore-Aar, Batticaloa river, Viriadi-Aar, Periekel-Aar, Mootoe-Aar. (a branch of the Navil-Aar,) Aroekgam-Aar, and Konokan-Aar.

* By Dr. John Davy's analysis.

The rivers which disembogue on the western side of the island are the Mandekal-Aar, Pali-Aar, Perie-Aar, Kambotokké-Aar, Awarie-Aar, Kal-Aar, Marchikatté-Aar, Pomparipo-Aar, Wellikar-Aar, Pantura-Oya, and Bentotte-Oya (a branch of the Mapelgam-Ganga), which rises in the Saffragam mountains.

Several streams which also branch from the Mapelgam-Ganga, debouche at Ballepitié-Modera, Amblamgoddé, Hiccodé, Dodandewé, and Gindurah, as well as the Matura, Tangalle, Ranné, Yallé (a branch of the Parapa-Oya), and Kirindé rivers in the southern province.

The mountains, from whence these perennial streams derive their sources, are not situate in the middle of the island, as many imagine, from the circumstance of that part of it being called Kandy, or Highlands, from the Singhalese word *Kandi*, high, but between the parallels of 6° 40′ and 7° 40′ of north latitude, about the middle of the southern half of it.

Lieut. Colonel Fraser, the Deputy Quarter Master General to the Forces in Ceylon, ascertained the height of the principal highlands by geometrical operations; the following is the ascending scale of elevation of the several mountains in English feet, as given by that highly respected and gallant officer.

The highest point in the road leading through the *Kadooganawa* pass, 1731 feet; this was ascertained by levelling; the hill above *Mattan Pattanna*, 3192 feet; *Alloogallé* near *Amoonapoorré*, 3440; *Amboolluawa* near *Gampalla*, 3540; *Oorragallé* the rocky ridge of *Hantanné* to the southward of the town, 4380; *Hoonasagiria* peak, 4990; *Diatatawé*, near *Hangorankketté*, 5030; the *Knuckles*, a part of the same chain of mountains as the *Homasagiria* peak, 6180; plain of *Neuwara-Eliya*, 6210; *Kammoonakoolé* near *Badula*, 6740; plain of *Wilmanie*, 6990; *Adam's Peak*, 7420; *Totapella*, 7720; *Kirigalpatta*, 7810; and *Pedrotallagala* close to the Rest House of *Neuwara-Eliya*, the highest land in Ceylon, 8280 feet above the level of the sea. This proves that the far-famed Adam's Peak, heretofore described as the highest of the Ceylon mountains, holds only the fourth rank in point of altitude.

According to the author already cited, and whose analysis may be relied on, the difference between the water of the smaller rivers and that of the mountain springs consists in their containing, with the exception of the suspened clay, larger proportions of common salt, carbonat of lime, and of vegetable matter.

But these are not the only means of irrigation that the island possesses; for its artificial lakes or tanks, in repair or capable of being repaired, may be called innumerable.

Of the most ancient and extensive, those of Padeviel-Kolom in the northern, and of Kandellé and Mineré in the eastern province, are deservedly the chief objects of the traveller's attention; and it is to be hoped, that at no very distant period the government of the country, if individual speculators will not, will set a proper estimate upon their value and importance; and by restoring them to their pristine efficiency, induce Hindoo agriculturists from the peninsula of India to settle in this part of Ceylon. The agriculture of the country will soon recover its former wholesome state of vigorous usefulness, and the island once more become independent of other countries for rice, and an exporter of the surplus of its produce of that prime necessary of native consumption.

According to the late Mr. Ralph Backhouse's description to me of the lakes of Kandellé and Mineré, both of which he visited, as well as the ancient capital of Anaradahpoora, between the years 1820 and 1822, at which period he was collector (synonymous with government agent) of the district of Manaar, the extent of the former was fifteen miles in circumference; but as upon this point authors differ greatly, one making it three or four miles, and another twenty miles, perhaps Mr. Backhouse was governed by his own ideas of extent and distance in judging of its superficies.—Mr. Backhouse however measured the height and length of the embankment, which rested upon solid rock at one extremity, and upon an artificial mound of earth at the other, and found the former 22 feet, the latter 11 furlongs, and the base 180 feet.

However greatly inferior in size the Kandellé tank to that of Mineré, its construction affords proofs, by the hewn blocks of rock composing its solid wall, of the superior skill in the art of masonry which the ancient inhabitants of the country possessed, and almost everywhere displayed in their public works. The lake is environed with extensive and verdant plains, capable of affording pasturage to many thousands of cattle, or for an unlimited cultivation of paddee,* and the neighbourhood has almost inexhaustible resources in timber trees of great bulk, adapted for every useful and domestic purpose of construction and ornament.—Kandellé is situate in the Tamblegam district, in the eastern province, and about thirty miles S. W. of Trincomalé.

The lake of Mineré is about the same distance and bearings from that of Kandellé, and in the district of Tambankadewe, also in the eastern province. The country between them is diversified with woods and plains, which latter are in some parts inundated during the rainy season. The tank of Mineré is twenty miles in circumference, surrounded with marshy lands, capable of a very extensive cultivation of rice, and having abundant forests of the most valuable timber trees in their vicinity.

These lakes were formerly connected by an aquaduct; and there is a connexion between that of Kandellé and the Mavali-Ganga by what may be called the western branch of the Virgel-Ganga, and with that of Mineré by the western branch of the

* Rice in the husk, or state of culture.

same river, there called the Kotti-Aar. There are but very few inhabitants occupying the village of Mineré.

These lakes, together with that of Padeviel-Kolom in the northern province, are the chief of that denomination in the island; but Singhalese history affirms that there were at one time above 200,000 artificial tanks in Ceylon; and that the immense work called the lake or tank of Mineré, or Mennairia, was formed in the reign of the Singhalese king, Maha-Sen, whose capital was Anaradahpoora, (now a mere village,) in the year of Christ 275, and of Buddha 818; and that, by means of dams, the stream of the Kara-Ganga was turned into it.*

To this king, the same orthodox authority attributes the formation of sixteen other tanks, and of the Tallawattuella canal, by which 20,000 paddee fields were formed and dedicated to the temple of *Danawetta,* whereby the fields got the name of *Dantalawé,* (synonymous with *Gantalawé,* which signifies a voluntary gift to temples,) and are now called Kandellé.

Though the sovereign was considered to have been originally the sole landlord, extensive lands belonged to lay individuals and to the priesthood. Temple lands were chiefly royal donatives; and we may infer that the same were originally granted by the king for signal services to the state. It is true that they might become retainers to the crown or to the temples; but, as the latter service was less oppressive, and held out spiritual consolation, they generally dedicated their lands to the vihare in preference to the rajah.

When lands had thus been consecrated to the temple, the donor received protection, and pledged himself to perform certain personal services. In cases where lands were dedicated to temples by rajahs, the services to be rendered by cultivators of the soil, were minutely detailed in inscriptions upon stone, still extant, and even upon solid rocks, near the temples to which such lands were appropriated by the rajah or king.

Temple lands are free frem *Rajah-Karia,* or royal service; and that duty, which in the king's villages was paid to the king, was then paid to the temple. This ancient system may be traced to have obtained antecedently to the Christian era.

Forced labour however no longer exists, either under the name of *Rajah-Karia,* or any other definition; but it is almost incredible that Englishmen, naturally jealous of their own rights, could have really desired the continuance of the feudal oppressions. which Lord Viscount Goderich took the best means of removing, root and branch, from the Singhalese nation, by an order in council, which abolished personal service, or forced and unpaid labour, and placed them upon equal privileges with ourselves,

* Turnour's Epitome of Singhalese History.

their fellow men and fellow subjects; and yet this glorious act of the most consummate and benevolent policy was condemned by many in the colony!

The restoration of the ancient tanks would certainly be a work of time; and as cultivation only could be the result of that elementary measure, the settler would naturally look to the Government for assistance in carrying the latter into effect, for he would hesitate to make any considerable outlay where the prospective advantages were so very distant. By holding out adequate encouragement by a guarantee of certain immunities and privileges for a fixed period, the principal of which should be the grant of lands free of taxes for a certain number of years, (but *charging a water rate upon lands deriving benefit from the repaired tanks,*) and further that the extension of such term should be made proportionate to the increase of agriculture, the Government will insure the cultivation of the entire country by Hindoo settlers.

The Hindoos are a very superior race, in as far as regards industrious habits, to the Singhalese, who are naturally inclined to indolence, for they are more sanguine in their speculations, provided they have corresponding encouragement: and the more liberal the conditions of settlement in Ceylon, the more beneficial will be the result to the government and colony at large. In the list of advantages may be classed the increase of trade coastwise, which would be more than an equivalent for the interest of capital advanced by the local government for the restoration of the tanks to their original state of agricultural utility.

But notwithstanding all the existing facilities for the cultivation of rice, the staple of chief importance to the natives, what is the state of Singhalese agriculture connected therewith?

The duties upon paddee fields scarcely yield a moiety of the collections upon coconut and toddy topes; and in the year ending the 5th of January 1841, the quantity of rice produced in Ceylon was so very inadequate to the consumption, that the value of the paddee and rice imported, amounted to £114,866, 1*s.* 4*d.*, of which sum £20,489 16*s.* was paid to French colonies!!

Such then is the state of the production of the staff of life for the population of nearly a million and a half of British subjects; and should this book be honored with even a cursory perusal by Her Majesty's principal Secretary of State for the Colonial department, I do humbly but earnestly implore his Lordship to give this one point his deliberate consideration.

I would begin by causing a survey of all crown lands to be made by district surveyors, under the immediate inspection of the agents of government and their assistants, in their respective provinces and districts, distinguishing such lands as are capable of producing mountain rice, from those that have the means of irrigation; for we all know, who have resided in India, that certain qualities of excellent rice are adapted solely to the former, but the greater variety to the latter mode of culture. Every tank capable of repair should be also surveyed and reported, as to its extent, and embankments, the sources that supply it with water, and the means of carrying off its superabundance, during the rainy season, so as to prevent those lands which it supplies when the rice plant requires water, from being inundated at other times when it equally requires the evaporation of moisture to attain maturity.

The report should also separately express the position and extent of the temple lands, and those of private individuals, adapted to the growth of rice, and the quantity of that staple that had been produced in each during the preceding seven years. It may then be easily ascertained, upon a fair comparison of the superficies of the province with the number of its population, how far rice has been adequately cultivated in that province.

But prior to any such survey being made, or report called for by the government, there are a few important points deserving attention. First, the colonial government should demand and seal up all former reports from the different cutcheries, so as to prevent a reference thereto by the present government agents. I speak from my own knowledge during my residence in the island, that in very many instances the annual reports of the districts were merely transcribed by collectors, with here and there a few alterations for the sake of consistency, from the reports of their predecessors. By this means, the work was easily got rid of by the temporary occupier of office, and the government not much enlightened by any report subsequently to the *original* one. The qualification of a provincial agent for the office he holds might be ascertained by his report of the capabilities of the province under his superintendence; and it would be a wise determination of the government to allow of no removal of its provincial agents, except for misconduct and incapacity, during their period of service in the colony; and that would ensure a perfect acquaintance with the resources and population of their provinces. Their rank might be defined by long standing, and their services be rewarded by a gradual increase of salary. Secondly, no dependence should be placed upon *native returns*, but sufficient encouragement be held out to young and well-qualified civil surveyors to serve in Ceylon, in addition to the present limited local establishment of civil engineers.

CHAP. IV.

Fiscal division of the Island into Provinces—Variety of Soil—Unsuccessful Sugar speculation at Kultura—Successful experiments with the Sugar cane at Koondesalé—Local Revenue—Exports—Imports—Suggestions for extending the hours of business at the Colombo custom-house—Vexations to the Mercantile community and suggestions to H. M. Secretary of State for the Colonies for their removal—Imports at Colombo for the years 1840 *and* 1841*—Increase of Exports from that port—Imperial Standard weights and measures—Dutch Standard measures—Singhalese specification of the nature and tenure of Lands.*

THE island is divided into five fiscal provinces, styled eastern, western, northern, southern, and central, which are subdivided into districts. Each province is superintended by an agent of government, with a limited number of assistant agents, to whom the charge and collection of the land revenue and sea customs are entrusted, with the exception of the customs of the port of Colombo in the western province; where, of late years, the new and distinct situation of comptroller of customs for the island, with a salary of £600 a year, and an establishment of three clerks, has superseded the former method of conducting this duty, which was executed conjointly with that of commissioner of stamps.

The eastern province comprises the former districts of Trincomalé, Batticaloa, and the interior provinces of Tamankadewé and Bintenne, except Wegampaha, Kooloogampaha, and Miganagolla-Palata. The agent of government at Trincomalé superintends the custom-house duties there, and the assistant agent, at Batticaloa. The superficies of this province is 4895 square miles.

The western province comprises the former districts of Colombo, Chilaw, and Putlam, upon the sea; the Dessavonies* of the Seven Korles, Four Korles, Three Korles, and province of Lower Bulatgammé. The agent of government resides at Colombo, and his assistants (including the superintendent of the salt department) at Chilaw, Calpentyn, and Negombo. The customs' department is distinct and superintended by a collector, who has five assistants, by whom the duties of the minor custom-houses of Pantura, Caltura, Negombo, Chilaw, and Calpentyn are executed. The superficies of this province is 4452 square miles.

* A native term, synonymous with that of a provincial collectorship of revenue.

The northern province comprises the former districts of Jaffna, Manaar, Wanné, the Dessavony of Neuwarakelawiyé, and the island of Delft. The agent of government at Jaffna acts also as collector of customs, and his assistants superintend the minor custom-houses of Cayts, Point Pedro, and Manaar. The superficies of this province is 6053 square miles.

The southern province comprises the former districts of Galle, Tangalle, Matura, and Hambantotte, upon the coast, the Dessavony of Saffragam, and province of Lower Ouva and Wellassé in the former Kandyan territory. The customs' duties are executed by the agent of government, who resides at Point de Galle, and by his assistants at the minor custom-houses of Dodandoowé-Moderé, Ballepitté-Moderé, and Bellegam. The superficies of this province is 6032 square miles.

The central province comprises the whole of the former districts of Kandy, Yatti-neuwara, Udu-neuwara, Harasia-Pattoo, Tumpané, Doombera, Hewahetté, Kotmalé, Weyaloowa, Upper Bulatgammé, Wegampaha, Kooloogampaha, Miganagolla-Palata, and the Dessavonies of Uwa, Matellé, Udapalata, and Wallapané. The superficies of this province is 3016 square miles.

Every province presents such a varied soil, that whether alluvial, kabook,* sandy, or vegetable mould be requisite for different objects of culture, settlers will find no difficulty in fixing upon suitable localities. Opinion was at one time pretty general, although I never concurred in it, that sugar could not be grown in the island, so as to insure a sufficient return for capital laid out. This, I believe, originated in the failure of experiments at Kaltura, upon the estates of Charles Edward Layard and James Anthony Mooyaart, Esqrs., who were alike indefatigable in every undertaking of public or private utility. These gentlemen introduced the culture of the sugar cane, but upon too extensive a scale for a first experiment; and, owing to the quantity of iron with which the soil there is almost everywhere impregnated, were unsuccessful.

That sugar is now grown, equal to any produced in Siam or China, recent extensive experiments at Koondesalé, in the central province, have fully established. In a few years the island will become independent of other countries for this article of domestic consumption, whilst its greater cheapness, by rendering it accessible to the lower classes, will increase the demand for it to an extent that must ensure its general cultivation wherever the soil may be found adapted to it. And it is therefore to

* Ferruginous clay-soil, derived from the decomposition of clay-iron stone, of a reddish brown, of which a well-dried specimen was found to consist, according to Dr. John Davy's analysis, of 83.5 of ferruginous clay, and 16.5 of water, with traces of vegetable matter.

be anticipated, from the justice and good policy of Parliament, that long before this island produces a surplus for exportation, the import duties upon East and West India sugars will have been equalized in the home tariff. If a judgment may be formed from the few samples that have been brought by private individuals to this country, the quality of the Kandyan sugar is not surpassed by that of Mauritius or Bengal, either in the quantity of its saccharine matter, or in point of crystalization. It would, however, be more satisfactory if those proofs could be established, by larger samples of Ceylon sugar being analyzed with equal quantities of the produce of Mauritius and Bengal, by disinterested parties, and for the result of such analysis to be made generally known in the British market.

The local revenue is derived from the duties on cinnamon, salt, tobacco, fish farms, pearl and chank (*Voluta gravis*) fisheries, marriage and spirit licences, judicial and commercial stamps, fines, land commutation tax, auction duties, post-office receipts, charges for boat hire and pilotage, anchorage dues, sales of gunpowder, horses from the government stud at Delft island, Ceylon Gazette, and Calendar, house and land rents, premiums upon sales of bills upon the Treasury, timber, Vedah tribute, and customs' duties upon exports and imports.

Ceylon exports arrack (distilled from the toddy of *the Cocos-nucifera*), arrow root (*Maranta arundinacea*), Areka nuts (*Areka Catechu*), bark for tanning, bees' wax, betel leaves and flower (*Piper Betel*), bicho de mar or sea slug (*Holothurion Tripan*), castor oil and seed (*Ricinius palma Christi*), cassia fistula, greater and lesser cardamoms, cummim seed, cinnamon, cinnamon oil, clove oil, coffee, coco-nuts, coco-nut oil, copperah or sun-dried pulp of the coco-nut for making oil, coir cordage, and loose coir for rope making, stuffing mattresses, &c. chunam or shell lime, cotton, chank shells (*Voluta gravis*), chaya root (*Oldenlandia umbellata*), country manufactured cotton cloth, dornatil or wood oil, elephants' tusks, fruits, gingely seed (*Sessamum orientale*) and oil, dried ghorkas (fruit of the *Gambogia gutta*), ginger, ghee or clarified buffalo's butter, fine hemp called hané (*Crotolaria juncea*), honey, hides, Aralu nuts (*Terminalia Chebulla*, L.), Illepei seed and oil (*Bassia longifôlia*), Margosa seed and oil (*Melia Azaditrachta*, L.), mats, marmelle water (extracted from the flower and fruits of the *Cratæva Marmelos*), Odil or Palmyra roots (*Borassus flabelliformis*), coco-nut oil-cake or *Poonac*, pearls, precious stones, resin, sappan wood (*Cæsalpinia Sappan*), shells, sharks' fins for the China market, taggary seed (*Cassia Tora*), tamarinds, twine, tobacco, turmeric, timber, vinegar, and country winnows.

The imports consist of ale, almonds, anchovies, aniseed, ambergris, antimony, white, red, and yellow arsenic, assafœtida, astronomical instruments, salted beef from Bengal and Europe, beer of all kinds (including spruce), biscuits, blacking, books, boots and shoes from Europe and Bengal, bottles, brandy, bullion, salt butter, black hellebore root, camphor, chocolate and cocoa (*Theobroma Cacao*), chamomile (*Anthemis Pyrethum*), cloves, broad cloths, wax and spermaceti candles, hemp and cotton canvas from Europe and Bengal, capers, cards, canary seed, cattle, cordage, chalk, cheese, China root (*Smilax aspera*), cables, cordials, bottled cider, cinnabar or vermillion, European, Indian, and Chinese cottons, nankins, and chintzes, colors, confectionary, copper, crapes, currants, cutlery, earthenware from Europe and China, dholl or guinea pea (*Cytisus Cajan*, L.), fireworks from Europe and China, flannel, garden seeds, gauze, gin, gloves, glue, gram, gum Benjamin (*Ficus Benjamina*), guns, gunpowder, copper caps, shot, hams from Europe and China, hardware, hats from Europe and China, smoked and salted herrings, horses, iron hoops for casks, indigo, jewellery, looking glasses, glass, rock salt, incense, iron, thread, cotton, gold, and silver lace ; lacksay or Chinese vermicelli, pig and sheet lead, liqueurs, mace, manna, marble, maps, mats from China and the Maldive islands, medicines, millinery, music and musical instruments, needles, nutmegs, linseed, salad, and turpentine oils ; onions, opium, paints, pearl barley, pease, black pepper (*Piper nigrum*), cotton root (*Gossypium herbaceum*), perry, porter, philosophical instruments, pickles, salt pork, quicksilver, rice, rosin, rattans (*Calamus Rotang*) from Acheen, Batavia, Malacca, and Pulo Pinang or Prince of Wales Island ; sal-ammoniac, salt petre, saffron, preserves, pickled salmon, salted tongues, humps, and briskets from Bengal ; sandal wood, sarsaparilla, sashes, smoked sausages, saddlery, raw and manufactured silk, sitaratta or the lesser galangal root, raw and tanned goat skins, snuff, soap, stationery, staves for casks, spirits, sugar from Bengal, Batavia, China, and Siam ; sulphur, tar, tea, gold and silver tinsels, foils of all colours, tobacco pipes, toys, tutenague from China, varnish, verdigris, vinegar, wines of all descriptions and qualities, wheat and other grains from Bengal and the coasts of Coromandel and Malabar.

The very short time (between four and five hours a day, Sundays excepted,) for the exporter to transact business at the Colombo custom-house, is too limited, without the further impediments which embarrass the commerce of that port. In addition to other difficulties, the merchant incurs serious risk of injury to colonial produce, particularly coffee, during bad weather, by any delay in its transmission from the jetty to the shipping in Colombo roads. The accommodations at the custom-house are very inadequate to the wants of the exporters ; and during the rainy season considerable damage may be done to coffee intended for exportation, by exposure, and even by absorption, during that damp period, in the custom-house godowns or export warehouses. It is therefore to be hoped, that Her Majesty's Secretary of State for the Colonies will be pleased to remove these and all restrictions upon the commerce of the island; and, by commanding an extension of the hours of business at the Ceylon custom-house, afford every requisite facility to merchants.

Amongst other vexations, the Ceylon merchant is obliged to submit to the weighing of his consignments of coffee before shipment; just as if the local government was ignorant that by the exporter neglecting to take the exact weight of all coffee exported the loss would be his own. The merchant's interest is to make his returns to the custom-house as correct as possible, for he himself places the valuation thereon, and pays 2½ per cent. duty on that valuation; and he has then to get the custom-house certificate that the coffee so returned is the produce of the island, without which it would not be admitted for home consumption at the *low* duty: and surely that of itself is a sufficient guarantee for the full weight being given; for otherwise, the coffee so imported into this country would be liable to an extra duty of 28*s*. per cwt. for the surplus accruing from a false return to the Ceylon custom-house on the part of the exporter.

The imports into the port of Colombo for the year ending 5th Jan. 1841, were :—

		£	s.	d.
From Europe	Cotton goods	£49,892	13	9
	Haberdashery and millinery	5,626	4	1
	Cutlery and hardware	1,078	19	2
	Machinery and tools	4,997	7	3
	Malt liquor	7,934	16	6
	Bullion and sundries	56,514	8	1
		126,044	7	10
	Ditto, 1840, £153,063 14 9			
From Asia	Cotton goods	8,109	4	11
	Paddee	7,188	8	1
	Rice	87,178	17	3
	Bullion and sundries	258,236	18	5
		360,713	8	8
	Ditto, 1840, £419,135 17 3			
From French Colonies	Rice	20,498	16	0
	Sundries	5,358	11	5
		25,857	7	5
	Ditto, 1840, £27,190 14 1			
From sundry places		28,892	17	7
Grand total of imports for 1841		£541,508	1	6

The duty levied upon the above imports amounted to 36,082*l.* 15*s.* 6*d.*, or about 6½ per cent. The decrease on goods from Europe, as compared with the imports of 1840, was chiefly to be attributed to the falling off in the demand for cotton goods, haberdashery, millinery, cutlery, hardware, machinery, and tools; whilst the import of malt liquor had been increased by 1,197*l.* 18*s.* 3*d.* The decrease on the imports from Asia was owing to the lesser demand for cotton goods; and from the French colonies, to the smaller supply of rice.

The exports for the same period were:—

		£	s.	d.
To Great Britain	Coffee	£197,387	10	4
	Cinnamon	28,866	5	6
	Coco-nut oil	29,284	6	1
	Precious stones	6,112	17	6
	Sundries	15,937	7	5
		277,588	6	10
	Ditto, 1840, £215,101 4 6			
To Asia	Arrack	3,283	3	2
	Areka nuts	12,701	0	0
	Bullion	1,489	0	0
	Cotton goods	1,092	12	2
	Sundries	7,773	3	3
		26,338	18	7
	Ditto, 1840, £46,536 8 4			
To France	Cinnamon	73	15	0
To sundry places		6,359	9	11

The increase in the exports to Great Britain consisted principally of coffee, coco-nut oil, and precious stones; and the decrease to Asia was occasioned by the falling off in the demand for arrack, betel nuts, and bullion. The duty paid on goods exported amounted to 49,677*l.* 1*s.* 7*d.*, or equal to about 16 per cent. The great difference between the rate of duty levied on imports and exports (*nearly* 250 *per cent. against the productions of the island!!*) cannot fail to excite attention.

		£	s.	d.
The total value of imports, in	1840-1841	£541,508	1	6
Ditto	1839-1840	483,627	16	5
	Increase	57,880	5	1
The total value of exports, in	1840-1841	310,360	10	4
Ditto	1839-1840	275,592	10	1
	Increase	34,768	0	3

Vessels entered inwards, for the year ending 7th Jan. 1840	740
Ditto .... ditto .... 5th Jan. 1841	667
Decrease	73

Vessels cleared outwards in 1840	538
Ditto 1841	585
Increase	47

These tables show the growing importance of Ceylon, and the little fear that can exist of too much land being brought under cultivation, when one-fifth of the value of the imports had been paid to other countries, including French colonies, for food only.

Notwithstanding the adoption of the imperial standard for colonial weights and measures, by the ordinance of the governor and councils (No. 2 of 1836), the speculative capitalist disposed to purchase lands from the natives, will find it convenient to understand both their original tenure under the former Dutch government, and the native standard of dry measure connected therewith.

The former dry measure was the Dutch *parah,* a cylinder of $11\frac{57}{100}$ inches in depth and breadth, which was divided into twenty-four seers, and the seer, a cylinder of depth equal to its diameter, subdivided into half and quarter seers. Standard gauges were deposited for reference in every cutcherry,* as a protection against fraud through defective measures; an indispensable precaution where the natives are such adepts at cheating, that they first place the wooden measures in boiling water, then dry them in the sun, and complete their roguery by coating the interior surface with a thick layer of transparent dammer.†

Dry Measure.

4 (cut) chundoos make	1 (cut) measure or seer,
4; seers	1 coorney,
$2\frac{1}{2}$ coornies	1 markal,
2 markals	1 parah,
8 parahs	1 ammonam,
$9\frac{3}{8}$ ammonams	1 laste.

* Revenue office and residence of the agent of government.

A kind of resin extracted from a species of *Pinus,* (*Dammara alba,*) a native of Malacca and Sumatra.

Two hundred seers of paddee, when cleared of the husk, will yield about one hundred and seventy six seers of rice.

There is a great difference in the paddee of various districts, and particularly between that of the highlands and lowlands: the former is smaller, and of the latter there are several varieties; but the most nutritious and the most palatable rice, although considered common, and known by a reddish film, is the sort called *Patcherie* by the Singhalese.

Singhalese Specification of the Nature and Tenure of Lands.

Owitté Lands . .	Meadows on the borders of rivers and canals.
Wattoewaré . . .	Muddy grounds overgrown with thick jungle or underwood.
Moellawé	Where the jungle has been burnt and the ground cultivated for the first time.
Dewie	At the base of hills or mountains.
Chena	Cleared of jungle or underwood every ten or twelve years, and then sown with small grains, such as tala (*Sessamum orientale*) and korakan (*Cynosurus Coracanus*).
Bandaré	Crown property.
Devill	Exempted from all taxes on condition of personal service upon public occasions when required by the provincial agent of government.
Malapalla . . .	Originally leased, but reverted (upon the lessees' death) to the landlord.
Ratmaheré . . .	Originally the property of the crown, but granted to individuals in consideration of the payment of ten per cent. upon the produce.
Moetettoo	Assigned and cultivated gratuitously by the villagers for the support of the dignity of their headmen.
Andé	Of which the crown receives one half the produce.
Ottoe and *Parvené* .	Nearly synonymous, both being liable to the tax of ten per cent. upon their produce. *Parvené* literally means private lands.

CHAP. V.

Improved state of the colonial revenue under the Right Honorable Sir George Murray's administration—Lord Viscount Goderich renders it permanent—Governor Sir Robert Wilmot Horton succeeds Lieut. General Sir Edward Barnes—Reduction of the civil expenditure—Reform of the chief secretary's office—His Majesty's representative hanged in effigy—China carriers—Suggestions for the restoration of the civil and widows' pension funds—Lord Goderich's liberality insufficiently appreciated—Civil and military pay, and enormous and unmerited pensions to widows of civilians, contrasted with the pittances allowed to naval and military officers' widows—Revenue and expenditure—Heavy imposts—Excess of revenue—Apathy of colonists as to the culture of cotton—Suggestions for the formation of government cotton plantations, and for training thousands of idle females and children to habits of industry and profitable employment—Trade of Ceylon quadrupled since the acquisition of Kandy in 1815—Extraordinary contrast between the current prices of certain articles of British manufacture and of colonial produce—Partiality of the Singhalese for British productions—Exceptions in favor of Dutch manufactures—Singhalese require British example, and reductions in taxation and customs' duties, to stimulate them to industry and agricultural improvement—Anticipated result to the home manufacturer and local revenue.

ALTHOUGH it was under the administration of the colonies by the Right Honorable Sir George Murray, G. C. B., that, for the first time for many years, the public revenue of Ceylon yielded an excess over the expenditure, it was during his successor, the Right Honorable Viscount Goderich's (now Earl of Ripon) second tenure of the colonial seals, from 1830 to 1833 inclusively, that it assumed the appearance of permanency which it has since maintained.

In the year 1831, the Right Honorable Sir Robert Wilmot Horton was appointed to succeed His Excellency Lieut. General Sir Edward Barnes, as governor and commander-in-chief of Ceylon and its dependencies, upon the appointment of the latter to the command-in-chief of the Bengal army; and, as if example were in some degree expedient to reconcile the heads of the civil departments to the reductions that awaited them, His Excellency accepted the governorship at the reduced salary of £7,000 a year.

His Excellency Sir Wilmot Horton was instructed to effect reductions in the civil expenditure to the amount of £38,000 a year;* and Lord Goderich deserved the gratitude of the colony for having delegated this peculiarly unpleasant task to the management of a gentleman, pre-eminently qualified for carrying it into effect with the utmost delicacy towards those who were about to suffer by the long-required reforms, which had, at length, been determined upon by his Lordship, as His Majesty's secretary of state for the colonies.

* Communicated to the Author by letter from the late governor, Sir Robert Wilmot Horton, Bart., G. C. H

A single instance may suffice to show the excessive amount that was expended for the support of one department only; and the manner in which the same duties have been since executed at the reduced rate, affords a clear proof that it has sustained no loss, in point of efficiency, by the alteration.

In 1816, the chief secretary's office at Colombo was superintended by two deputy secretaries, (the chief secretaryship being a mere sinecure of £3000 a year,*) of whom the senior held also the office of secretary for the Kandyan provinces, at salaries of £2000 and £1500; a first assistant at £640, a second assistant at £512, and an indefinite number of extra assistants at £300 a year each; but, allowing two extra assistants, as an average, the seven salaries amounted to £8252!—and, in the year 1838, the same department was equally as efficient under the management of a "Colonial Secretary" at a salary of £2000 a year, (which is more by £500 a year than the pay of Her Majesty's under secretaries of state for the still more laborious duties of the colonial department,) and one assistant at £620 a year.

Thus, in one civil department, and without the slightest detriment to the public service, Lord Goderich effected a saving of £5632 per annum, which, if it had been carried into effect, as in common justice to the state of the revenue it ought to have been, at least thirty two years earlier, (or rather, such a burden upon the public ought never to have been tolerated,) would have made a difference of £180,224 in favor of the colony and at a time when its public expenditure considerably exceeded its income.

Notwithstanding the governor's anxiety to act with the utmost delicacy towards those civil servants, whose offices were to be abolished or salaries reduced, His Excellency did not fare better than others similarly employed upon an ungracious mission; but the governor had surely no reason to expect, that by conscientiously fulfilling the grand objects of his mission, as commanded by his noble superior, he would subject himself to personal insult: and it will scarcely be believed, that there were individuals rancorous enough to cause the representative of their Gracious Sovereign to be hanged in effigy, ('tis true it was a splendidly-dressed and decorated effigy, and "pity 'tis, 'tis true,")

* Although the chief secretary had enjoyed a salary of £2000—£3000 a year for nearly twenty years, he was not in the "Civil Service" until the year 1821; but, upon its being resolved that the benefit of the projected "Widows' Pension Fund" should be limited to the widows of subscribers to the "Civil Fund," he was allowed to subscribe to the latter, although contrary to the established rules of the service, because he had for so many years previously refused to do so; and consequently the fund was a considerable loser by his not subscribing *de principio*.—This was an act of great injustice to others similarly circumstanced, (including the judges of the Honorable the Supreme Court,) who were precluded from securing a similar pension of £300 a year for their widows, upon the grounds that they were not subscribers to the Civil Fund; which, nevertheless, included the superintendent of Delft Island, and the chief gardener!

but it actually took place; and in addition thereto His Excellency was as much cut up and hashed behind his back (very probably by those most *obsequious*, and the greatest "China carriers,"* to his face) as if he had originated the objectionable reductions.

Nothing would make Her Majesty's present secretary of state for the colonies more deservedly popular at Ceylon, than by restoring the civil fund to its original state; making, however, sixteen or twenty years, instead of twelve, the period of actual service in the island, as the title to a pension upon retirement; and admitting all civilians, whether on half-pay or otherwise, who might choose to subscribe to it, from its institution, or upon their first appointment, but not afterwards, to that privilege.

This would have the effect of annulling all grounds for that prevailing heartburn between those who do, and those who do not, subscribe to the civil fund; and be more just than the measure adopted some years ago by the colonial department, of taking out of the hands of the *civil fund committee*, into its own, the treasure of that and the widows' pension fund, and charging itself with the pensions due, or falling due, upon the old system; but precluding all further subscriptions, in order to abolish that excellent institution, and avail itself of the large surplus of the accumulated funds.

But Lord Goderich's liberality in allowing so extensive a civil establishment as the island even now supports, to continue, ought to have been done more justice to by the civilians in general, when the cheapness of living, and the large fortunes that have been accumulated in the colonial service by those who went out with *nothing*, or *were involved in debt* at home, be fully and fairly considered, and candidly contrasted with the pay of the naval and ordnance civil establishments, and the very inadequately paid (upon the same comparison) military staff of the colony. The military secretary draws but 9*s*. 6*d*. a day, in addition to his pay as a captain in the army, and island allowance of 13*l*. 16*s*. per mensem; the deputy adjutant general, who has held that situation twenty-three years, but 19*s*. a day, in addition to colonel's half pay; and the deputy quarter-master general, a lieutenant colonel (half pay unattached), the same very small pay, when compared with that of the junior civil servants of the year 1830, after having held that very arduous situation longer than the colonial secretary has been in the public service.

* "*China carriers*,"—a local name, meaning the despicable sycophants, tale-bearers, and toad-eaters who have been too much encouraged by more than one governor; and who, instead of meeting their just deserts, a kicking down the grand staircase, have been appointed to colonial situations. In some instances it mattered little whether their qualification for it reached so *high* as to know a Bible from Johnson's Dictionary, or to write a common letter upon any common subject!—So much for *China carrying!* nevertheless it has long proved a very *lucrative* business in Ceylon!

These are but a few instances to what might be adduced, but they will, I hope, be sufficient to merit attention from Her Majesty's principal secretary of state for the colonies, and, without doing injustice to any, induce justice to every branch of the Ceylon service.

So reckless was the colonial government at one period about granting pensions, and the colonial department at home in confirming them, without requiring any proof of merit, that the following instances, of which I select but two in confirmation of my statement, will, at this day perhaps, appear incredible, but do not these very abuses still exist?

A foreigner and his wife (also a foreigner), without any claim upon the government or connexion in the colony, went to Ceylon from the Cape of Good Hope, where, report stated, he had served as a soldier in a French regiment. He soon wormed himself into a situation of £800 a year as a provincial judge!! and in that capacity he appropriated to his private purposes all the deposits belonging to the poor suitors in his court, to the amount of 32,000 rix dollars; and when called upon to account for the deficiency, he poisoned himself. An annuity of £300 was conferred by the governor upon the widow, and her five sons were subsequently provided for by commissions in the army, or civil situations, by which they receive nearly £3000 a year between them, and yet allow their mother to continue a pensioner upon the colony!!!

The next case is not so bad; because although the widow is a French creole lady, her husband had been a lieutenant in the army. This gentleman failed in trade,* whilst belonging to the civil service, and died in less than three years after his appointment, when a pension of £300 a year was settled upon his widow, which she still enjoys; but although her sons have been provided for in the army and civil service, and one of them (a bachelor) enjoys a salary of £2000 a year, the mother still continues a burthen upon the colony.

That I have limited myself to only *two* instances, does not arise from having exhausted my data, as Her Majesty's secretary of state may easily ascertain, by referring to the Ceylon pension list, and inquiring upon *what grounds* such pensions were originally granted, or subsequently confirmed at home.

With these incontestible facts on the one hand, it may not be considered anomalous to cite a few naval and military officers' widows' pensions by way of contrast on the other; widows, whose husbands, after having passed their lives in one unsullied career of glory, have died, perhaps fallen on the field of battle, in the service of their king and country!!

* Neither his bankruptcy, nor the peculation or insolvency of other civil servants, have hitherto affected their official positions.

E. G. Seven widows of full colonels, or of post captains of three years standing, at £80 per annum	560
One lieutenant's widow (army)	40
	£600 !!

Or twelve captains' widows (army), or twelve lieutenants' widows (navy), at £50 a year; or fifteen lieutenants' widows in the army at £40 a year.

I must stop here! for if I were to detail *the official iniquities that fell under my own view, whilst I served in the island, I should have no room left for other matters.*

"Revenons à nos moutons,"—the revenue of Ceylon. The last data, or rather the most recent that I possess, is "a statement of the revenue and expenditure of Ceylon for the year 1836." The amount in that year of the *fixed revenue* from sea customs, export duty on cinnamon, cinnamon oil, land rents, land customs, licenses, pearl fishery, fish farms, salt farms, assessment tax on houses, commutation tax, tithes redeemed, tobacco tithes, auction duty, collection of postage, sale of stamps, &c., was as follows,—

	£	s.	d.
Total fixed revenue	£354,491	0	11¼
Incidental receipts	41,629	0	4
Receipts in aid of revenue	6,254	11	4¾
Arrears of revenue of former years	4,413	0	11½
Grand total	406,787	13	5½

Expenditure for the year 1836.

	£	s.	d.	£	s.	d.
Arrears of former years	£ 23,328	7	3			
Ordinary civil, judicial, revenue, and ecclesiastical charges	106,819	3	8			
Extraordinary ditto	117,177	7	5			
Miscellaneous charges, including colonial agents, loss in exchange of bills and remittances, surcharges refunded, old unsettled advances written off, sundry incidental receipts repaid	5,950	5	6¾			
Ordinary military expenditure	37,742	9	9½			
Extraordinary ditto	8,111	2	5½			
Ordinary commissariat expenditure	2,307	5	0			
Extraordinary ditto	29,769	4	3¾			
Expenditure of the agent for Ceylon in London.						
Agent's salary and establishment	500	0	0			
Civil and widows of civil servants' pensions	14,268	8	1			
Pensions to judges, &c.	5,513	5	0			
Stores, supplies, and miscellaneous charges	1,499	19	8			
	352,986	18	2½	352,986	18	2½
Balance of revenue over the expenditure				£ 53,800	15	6

This proves that in spite of the heavy imposts to which the natives of Ceylon are subject, by their taxation, first upon every article of European manufacture, and secondly upon the export of their principal staple, cinnamon; and the subsequent levy of duties upon every other article of Ceylon produce when imported into this country, and notwithstanding that scarcely a fifth of its immense area is under cultivation, the island of Ceylon, after paying for the support of an enormous civil establishment, and "an adequate military defensive force," *as it is called,* but what may be called scarcely large enough for "these piping times of peace" for the regular garrison duties of the colony, yielded an excess of revenue over the public expenditure, for the year 1836, of 53,800*l.* 15*s.* 6*d.*

In 1829 Sir George Murray was colonial secretary, and the excess of the revenue of Ceylon over its expenditure, the first time that it had occurred for some years, amounted to	£44,777	0	0
In 1830 Lord Goderich succeeded Sir G. Murray, and the excess was	56,446	0	0
1831	73,605	0	0
1832	31,337	0	0
1833 the excess was larger than at any former period	105,791	0	0
1834	43,117	0	0
1835	48,718	0	0
1836	53,800	15	6
	£457,591	15	6

Showing an excess of income over expenditure, in eight years, spite of all mismanagement, and oppression of the native agriculturist, of £457,591 15 6!!!

If the government, acting upon the justifiable grounds for its interference, the *apathy* of individuals as to the cultivation of *cotton,* (principally arising from the belief that less ground planted with coffee affords a greater profit,) were to cause a third of the crown lands to be at once cleared and planted with the best varieties of cotton, (giving a fair trial to the Maltese, Sicilian, Egyptian, American, and Bourbon cotton shrubs,) it would cause such a revolution in the opinions of the present speculators in colonial produce, as to insure a ready sale of all such crown lands, as soon as the first proof, of the immense returns to the government that will undoubtedly result to it, shall have excited their cupidity.

Ceylon will never be benefited in a right proportion to its claims, *unless the government sets the example.* There would be no occasion to appoint one additional agent or assistant agent, unless from the military officers quartered in the districts where the culture of cotton might take place, for, and on account of the government, by way of preliminary experiment in different districts, upon a moderate scale, under the superintendence of the several assistant government agents, who have sufficient native headmen to keep the labourers to their duty.

But, for the purpose of a more extensive establishment, the appointment of a well-informed individual, possessed of adequate local knowledge, as "Superintendent of Cotton Plantations," with a moderate salary, accompanied by the stipulation that its continuance and increase will be made to depend upon the successful result of his exertions, for the first five years, is indispensable.—This would afford ample time to establish the fact, that my anticipations of its eventually eliciting propositions to the government to transfer its interest in such establishment to an incorporated company of British capitalists, or for the subdivision and sale of the cotton grounds, as in the case of the late government cinnamon plantations, at a remunerating price to the crown, are by no means Eutopian; for there are many individual capitalists, who only now require a more intimate acquaintance with Ceylon and its capabilities, to put the latter to the test of practical experience.

The successful result of such a measure, under the immediate auspices of the government, will not be considered hypothetical, by those, who are capable of forming an opinion of it, from local experience and observation; and if it be the moral duty of the government to avail itself of the ample means at its own disposal in Ceylon, for lessening the dependence of the mother country upon foreign nations for the supply of one of the principal staples of British manufacture, the gradual cultivation of 4000 square miles of now waste lands (less than one fourth of the present uncultivated portion of the island) with cotton, would materially assist towards its accomplishment.

Women and children might be employed to clear and pick the cotton for exportation, with their little cross sticks, without injury to the staple; and thousands of now idle people be thereby brought into habits of industry and profitable employment, at a less expense than the cost of machinery; and all that would be requisite in the latter shape, would be cotton screws to prepare it for shipment.

Whether the government, or a company of British capitalists, adopt my humble suggestions, which are grounded upon a thorough conviction of their feasibleness, there would be no deficiency of labourers; for although many thousands of Malabar slaves are now supine under their somewhat improved position, from having enfranchisement at their command, if they possess the means and inclination to pay for it, (as I have already explained in the preceding pages,) they would eagerly embrace an arrangement for the purchase of their freedom by others, and for their services as apprentices, for a given term, at a proportionately low rate of wages, in return for their emancipation.

With fair encouragement to native agriculture, and proper management of the natural resources of Ceylon, the island might be made to yield an incalculable excess of colonial produce over its consumption, and consequently of revenue over its expenditure; but the value of this splendid colony will scarcely ever be fully known and appreciated, if the time for ascertaining it by experiments be further indefinitely deferred, as it has been, with but limited exceptions on the part of individuals of small and inadequate capital, for the last forty six years.

Although the trade of Ceylon has quadrupled since the amalgamation of the Kandyan kingdom with our former dominions in the island, in the year 1815, it may with propriety be said to be only now in its infancy; and therefore improved measures are indispensable to insure relief to the native agriculturists, and stimulate them to abandon their present habits of comparative indolence and inaction for those of industry, by a more certain prospect of remunerating prices for their produce.

During the short period that I acted as Collector of Customs at Colombo, in the year 1816, a very inteligent Dutch gentleman drew my attention to the fact, that the quarter's pay of a clerk, after having served the government long and faithfully in the civil departments, would barely supply him with an English broad cloth coat, and a beaver hat; the cost of the former being 42 rix dollars, or 3*l.* 13*s.*, and of the latter 32 rix dollars, or 2*l.* 16*s.*; and at the same time 250 lbs (avoirdupois) of black pepper, or 360 lbs of coffee, or 200 lbs of tobacco, or 80 gallons of arrack, of colonial produce, could be purchased at a less price.

The Singhalese are partial to Manchester, Leeds, Sheffield, and Birmingham manufactures, except certain agricultural implements, manufactured in the latter place, which, they consider inferior to those of Holland. The higher ranks indulge in the best wines, particularly Madeira and Champagne, which are liberally dispensed at their parties to European guests; and no people in the world set a higher value upon British medicines, stationery, and perfumery; or relish with a keener zest, English hams, cheeses, butter, porter, pale ale, cider, perry, herrings, salmon, anchovies, pickles, and confectionary; all which, they prefer to similar imports from France and America, except in regard to price.

But to bring these articles into more general demand, the Singhalese must first be taught to appreciate the value of industry, which can only result from British example: this, and a considerable reduction in the taxes and customs' duties, will conjointly operate to increase the demand for British productions, and consequently the revenue of the crown.

CHAP. VI.

Judicial division of the Island—Circuits of the Honorable the Supreme Court of Judicature—District Courts and extent of their jurisdiction—Charter of justice—Suggestions for the appointment of barristers at law as judges of the superior district courts—Supreme court of judicature—Rank of judges—Proctors for paupers and prisoners—Queen's advocate—Laws of bankruptcy and cessio bonorum—No jury in civil causes—In criminal causes jury decides by the majority—Judges—Introduction of trial by jury—Native attachment to that system—Improper mode of administering oaths to Buddhists in courts of justice—Hallan—Extraordinary consent to a nonsuit by a Singhalese plaintiff—Buddhist priests, how sworn in courts of justice—Original Dutch method of swearing Buddhist witnesses, the best to elicit truth—Extraordinary coincidence respecting the Aspen, or Populus tremula, and Boguha, or Ficus religiosa.

The Judicial division of the island comprises three Circuits, styled the Eastern, Northern, and Southern Circuits of the Honorable the Supreme Court of Judicature: but this is exclusively of what might very appropriately have been styled the Home or Western Circuit, now designated the Colombo District Courts.

The district of Colombo, as regards the exercise of the jurisdiction of the supreme court, consists of that space of country heretofore forming the collectorship of Colombo, together with that of the Three Korles and Lower Bulatgammé, and the dessavony of Saffragam. This district is bounded on the north by the Kaymel river, on the south by the Bentotte river, and on the west by the sea. The district of Colombo is subdivided, according to its present limits and jurisdiction, into six districts, known and designated respectively as—District No. 1 north of Colombo, district No. 1 south of Colombo, and districts No. 2, 3, 4, and 6 of Colombo.

The Colombo district No. 1 north, consists of so much of the town and the space contained in the four gravets of Colombo as is bounded on the south by St. John's river, Dam street, Hulfsdorp street, Silversmith street, and the high road to Kandy as far as the bridge of boats—so much of the Allootkoor Korle as is situated to the southward of the Dandogam river, and of the Addicaré-pattoo and Medde-pattoo of the Sina Korle (excluding the two Vidhan villages of Benmoelle and Galgomoowe)—and of so much of the Gangebadde-pattoo in the said Korle as is situated west of the road from Hangwelle to Attenegalle. The district court is held at Colombo.

The Colombo district No. 1 south (court held at Colombo) consists of so much of the town and the space contained within the four gravets of Colombo as is bounded on the north by St. John's river, Dam street, Hulfsdorp street, Silversmith street, and the high road to Kandy as far as the bridge of boats—of the Meddepattoo, the Pallepattoo, and the Addicaépattoo of the Hewagam Korle—the Salpitty Korle, and the villages of the Vidhan of Pantura north of the Pantura river.

The Colombo district No. 2 (court held at Negombo) consists of the town of Negombo, and so much of the Alootkoor Korle as is situated north of the Dandogam river; the Hapitigam Korle; and so much of the Sina Korle as is comprized within the divisions known as the Vidhan villages of Galgomoowe and Benmoelle in the Meddepattoo.

The Colombo district No. 3 (court held at Ruanwelle) consists of the space forming the Three Korles, and Lower Bulatgamme, together with the Oodoogaha Pattoo of the Sina Korle; so much of the Gangabadde Pattoo of the Sina Korle as is situated east of the road from Hangwelle to Attenegalle; and the Oodoogaha Pattoo of the Hewagam Korle.

The Colombo district No 4 (court held at Caltura) consists of the Pasdoon Korle, and so much of Walalawitty Korle as is attached to it; Welapora Caltura and all the villages between the Bentotte river and the Caltura river, or Kalu-Ganga, which are situated between the Pasdoon Korle and the sea—the town of Pantura and adjoining villages south of the Pantura river; and the Raygam Korle.

The Colombo district No. 6 (court held at Ratnapoora) consists of the dessavony or province of Saffragam.

The Eastern Circuit is divided into eight districts, viz. the districts of the Seven Korles, Four Korles, Kandy, Madawalatenné, Matelé, Neuwara-Eliya, Badula, and Alipoot. The district court of the first is held at Kornegalle; of the second, at Ootuankandy; of the third, at Kandy; of the fourth, at Madawalatenné; of the fifth, at Fort Mac Dowall; of the sixth, at Neuwara-Eliya, of the seventh, at Badula; and of the eighth, at Alipoot.

The district of Seven Korles consists of the dessavony of that name.

The district of Four Korles consists of the dessavony of that name.

The district of Kandy consists of the provinces of Udunuwara, Yattinuwara, Dumbera, Hewahette, Megoddatihé, the Hangurankettē and Gannawé Korles of Hewahetté Eggodatihé, Udapalata, Udabulatgama, and Dolosbagé.

The district of Madawalatenné consists of the provinces of Harasiapattoo & Tumpané.

The district of Matelé is the dessavony of that name.

The district of Neuwara-Eliya includes the province of Kotmalé and the Maturatta and Kohoké Korles; of Hewahetté, Eggodatihé, and the portion of the province of Uwa contiguous to Neuwara-Eliya and to the northward and westward of the Hakgalla range of mountains.

The district of Badula consists of the provinces of Wallapana, Weyaloowa, Oudakindé, Meddakindé, and Yattekindé of Uwa; Wegampaha, Kooloogampaha, and Miganagollapalata of Bintenné; and Pattipola and Polwatté of Welassé.

The district of Alipoot consists of the province of Welassé, and Kandukara, extending from the Wallawé river to Welassé.

The Northern Circuit comprises eleven districts, viz. the districts of Chilaw and Putlam, Manaar, Neuwarakalawiyé, Jaffna, Walligammo, Waddimoratchie, Tenmoratchie and Patchelapelle, the Islands, the Wanné, Trincomalé, and Batticaloa. The district court of the first is held at Putlam and Chilaw; of the second, at Manaar and Silawatorré; of the third, at Anarajapoora; of the fourth, at Jaffna; of the fifth, at Mallagam; of the sixth, at Point Pedro; of the seventh, at Chavagacherry; of the eighth, at Kayts and Delft; of the ninth, at Moolitivoe; of the tenth, at Trincomalé; and of the eleventh, at Batticaloa.

The district of Chilaw and Putlam consists of the several divisions of Chilaw, Putlam, Calpentyn, and the Demellepattoo.

The district of Manaar consists of the province of that name, together with the parish of Illepecadadewe, and the following provinces, which formerly formed part of the collectorship of the Wanné,—Kelekomolé north, Kelekomolé south, Odeaoor, Nadoe Chetty Kolom, Sinne Chetty Kolom, Meerkomolé, Pannengammo, and Toonukay.

The district of Neuwarakalawiyé consists of the province or dessavony of that name.

The district of Jaffna consists of the parishes of Nalloor, Wanarponné, Chundicooly, Kopay, Poottoor, Oodooville, Manipaay, Poonoryn, Polwerayencadoo, and Trentivoe or Two Brothers' Island.

The district of Walligammo consists of the parishes of Atchowely, Mylitty, Mallagam, Tellipallé, Pandeterrippo, Changané, and Batticotté.

The district of Waddimoratchie consists of the parishes of Oodopitty, Cattewelé, and Point Pedro.

The district of Tenmoratchie and Patchelapellé consists of the parishes of Nawakooly, Chavagacherry, Warrené, Elludumutual, Catché, Mogomalé, Tambogammo, Plopallé, Mullipattoo, and Caretché.

The district of the Islands consists of the parishes of Kạyts, Welené, and Alleputté; and of the islands of Pungertivoe, Anneletivoe, Nyhativoe, Karativoe, and Delft.

The district of the Wanné consists of the following provinces, which formerly formed a part of the district or collectorship of the Wanné, — Karrikattemollé North, Karrikattemollé South, Mulliawellé, Melpattoo North, Melpattoo South, Melpattoo East, Karnawelpattoo North, Karnawelpattoo South, and Poodookoodieruppoo.

The district of Trincomalé consists of the district of that name and the province of Tamankadewé.

The district of Batticaloa consists of the district of that name, and the province of Bintenné, excepting Wegampaha, Kooloogampaha, and Miganagollapalata.

The Southern Circuit is divided into five districts, viz. the districts of Amblangodde, Galle, Matura, Hambantotté, and Tangalle. The district court of the first is held at Ballepitté-Moderah; of the second, at Galle; of the third, at Matura; of the fourth, at Hambantotte; and of the fifth, at Tangalle.

The district of Amblangoddé consists of the upper division of the Welleboddépattoo, being that situated to the northward of Hickodé river, and the Wallallawitté Korle, excepting so much as is included in the Colombo district No. 4.

The district of Galle, consists of the town and four gravets of Galle, the Gangebodde Pattoo (of Galle), the Talpepattoo, and the lower division of the Walleboddé Pattoo, being that situated to the southward of the Hickodé river.

The district of Matura consists of the whole of the Bellegam Korle and Totemoone, four gravets of Matura and the Angooroogams, Makawitte, the Gangeboddepattoo of Matura, and the four Baygams, the Kandeboddepattoo, the Welleboddepattoo of Matura, and the Muruwé Korle.

The district of Hambantotte consists of the Mahagampattoo.

The district of Tangalle consists of the Girewah-Pattoo, Kiremé, Cattoné, Oedoebokké, and Julampityé.

Many and greatly beneficial changes were effected by the charter of justice granted by his late Majesty king William IV., on the 18th of February, 1833, in the third year of his Majesty's reign; but a few judicious alterations might be made for facilitating justice to the people, and conjoining greater weight and dignity with the judicial office.

A new, or amended, charter of justice * became a matter of expediency, consequent upon the annexation of the Kandyan kingdom to the British territories, in the year 1815, during the late gallant General Sir Robert Brownrigg's administration of the island.

The principal alteration to be now desired, is the appointment of junior barristers at law from the English, Scotch, and Irish bars, as *senior* district judges: instead of allowing colonial civil servants, who have not received a legal education to qualify them for such duties, to preside over the superior district courts.

But in order to induce the acceptance of such situations by barristers, it should be established as a rule by Her Majesty's secretary of state, that these learned gentlemen, after having served a certain period as senior district judges, shall be eligible for the appointments of Queen's advocate and Queen's deputy advocate; and ultimately for the bench, as vacancies occur by the death or retirement of the chief and puisne justices of the Honorable the Supreme Court.

A succession of legal functionaries for the higher offices would thus be ensured to the colony, and the executive be relieved of the necessity of appointing persons who are not duly qualified for permanently holding such judicial situations; or, as upon former occasions, of applying to the Madras bar, for acting chief, or puisne justices, much to the prejudice of the learned gentlemen, for after having sacrificed a lucrative practice in India in the justifiable anticipation of succeeding to the Ceylon bench, they have been cruelly disappointed, and superseded in their temporary judicial appointments by barristers from the English courts, without compensation or pension.

At the present moment, the salaries of the chief and puisne judges are scarcely adequate to the proper support of their high colonial rank; the former having only £2500 a year, and the latter £1500 a year, instead of the £7000 and £4000 enjoyed by their predecessors, which, by stipulations upon that point in the former charter of justice, were considerably increased by payment in gold, instead of in currency.

The Supreme Court possesses all the powers vested in the High Court of Chancery and Court of Queen's Bench; and the officers of the Vice-admiralty Court are selected from those of the Supreme Court. The chief justice is, ex-officio, the deputy and surrogate of the vice-admiral, who is His Excellency the Governor for the time being.

The chief justice takes rank in the colony immediately after the governor or lieut.-governor, and the several puisne justices according to their patents, and next after the commander of Her Majesty's forces in the island.

* Vide Appendix.

Two proctors of the Honorable the Supreme Court are appointed to officiate for paupers and prisoners, with the small salaries of £180 and £150 a year!

By the authority of the charter, appeals are made from the different district courts to the supreme court; and in criminal cases offences are prosecuted by information, in the name of the Queen's advocate, without previous inquest by a grand jury.

All questions of law are decided by the judge of the circuit, who may reserve them for the opinions and decision of the whole court; but no sentence of death can be executed until it has been approved by the governor.

The laws in regard to bankruptcy and cessio bonorum are similar to the Scotch. There is no jury in civil actions, and, in criminal cases, it consists of thirteen members: but the unanimity of the jury, how much soever to be desired, is not indispensable; for the majority, as in Scotland, decides the guilt or innocence of the prisoner.

Of the Ceylon judges the country may well be proud; for whilst justice, humanity, and patience have been their characteristics on the bench, so urbanity, charity, and benevolence have distinguished them in private life. There may have been a solitary exception perhaps, but even the sun has spots upon its disk.

Since the benefit of trial by jury was established in the island, through the active energy and devotion to the welfare of Ceylon which characterized the whole career of its then chief justice, the Honorable Sir Alexander Johnston, that inestimable privilege has gained an extraordinary influence over the affections of the native people.

Very soon after the introduction of trial by jury into the maritime provinces, and long before its advantages were sufficiently known to be fairly appreciated, it became a favourite with the natives; and now, after thirty years' experience of its blessings, which the wisdom of the supreme court of judicature had adapted even to their prejudices, the attachment of the natives to the system, from conviction of its inestimable value, as the palladium of their civil liberties, is boundless; and well may every class and caste of the native population be proud of the supreme court's administration of justice, under a government administered upon truly British principles; and which, so long as it continues to be conducted with firmness and integrity, will retain a paramount interest in their affections, which neither the Portuguese nor Dutch, during their long possession of the maritime provinces of the island, were ever able to establish.

It can truly be said, in the language of a former chief justice, "Armies may waste away by disease or climate, navies be dispersed by storms and shipwreck, seasons and circumstances may baffle the utmost exercise of human foresight, but firmly-rooted in the attachment of the people of Ceylon to our British jurisprudence, the security of our national interests and dominion in that island may be deemed impregnable."

The Singhalese, taken collectively as a nation, may be justly described as most litigious; and their general disregard for truth is only equalled by their readiness, whenever it suits their purpose, to commit wilful perjury. It would be extraordinary indeed if there were not numerous exceptions, but these are limited to the highest classes, and to educated persons of other grades; and yet throughout the nation there prevails a leaning towards the degrading vice, politely designated "courtier-like evasion."

In the several courts of justice, oaths are administered to Hindoos upon the water of the Ganges, and *Tolse* leaves; to Arabs and other Mahommedans upon the Koran, by a priest; and to the Singhalese, whether Buddhists or devil-worshippers, upon the *Hallan*, which consists of a couple of large cylindrical copper rings, containing small iron balls. These rings are of an oblong form, about twelve inches in circumference, and represent the Bangles of the Hindoo goddess *Pattiné*, which, at devil-ceremonies for the sick, the Kapuralé places between the first and second toes of each foot, and keeps in a revolving motion at certain intervals throughout the night, to the mis-called music of conch-shells and tam-a-tams. But when produced in court for the purpose of administering an oath to witnesses, these bangles, which are wrapped in a red handkerchief or cloth, and kept in a round box, ornamented with annular stripes of red, yellow, and black paint, are held by the Kapuralé towards the witness, who, extending his hands in an attitude of prayer, and bending his head at the same time, repeats the usual oath according to the custom of courts of justice at home.

But it is lamentable to observe the readiness with which the Singhalese perjure themselves. This may partly be ascribed to the indifference which the local government has too long manifested to the mode of administering oaths to Singhalese witnesses; and for this among other reasons none but persons descended from the Portuguese and Dutch families. and styled Europeans, should be selected for police Vidahns.

The facility of suborning evidence is as well known as the impossibility of eliciting the truth from Buddhist witnesses, unless by an appeal to their superstitious fears; and therefore the sooner the *Hallan* is excluded from courts of justice, except for those who are professed devil worshippers, the better; and a reference to my official representations upon this subject to the government, and advocate fiscal of Ceylon, between the years 1823 and 1827 inclusively, will show that this is not the first attempt to bring the subject under the most serious consideration.

I derive my authority for stating that the *Hallan* is any thing but sacred in the eyes of true Buddhists, from Buddhist priests in the Galle district, in answer to very pertinent questions upon that point, during the time I was magistrate there, from 1823 to 1826 inclusively. A defendant in a civil action proposed that judgment should be given in favor of the plaintiff, instead of the trial proceeding, if he would make oath that the debt claimed was just;—the plaintiff readily advanced with the palms of his hands pressed together, to be sworn upon the *Hallan;* but to *that* form of oath the defendant objected, for the reason that the plaintiff was a known Buddhist, and, according to his ideas of right, ought to be sworn upon the sacred books, within a temple, or under a *Bogaha.** The priests of the temple could alone decide the point raised by the objection; for no other mode of swearing Buddhists except upon the *Hallan* was provided for by the government, and the code of regulations laid a veto against resort being had to "any unusual way of administering oaths to Singhalese witnesses," but when the plaintiff heard the interpreter repeat the court's directions to send for the priests from the temple, he, fearing that the oath was about to be put to him in the form that had obtained during the occupation of the maritime provinces by the Dutch government, namely, under a *Bogaha,* or in a Buddha temple, voluntarily submitted to a nonsuit! This mode, if re-adopted, would render the course of justice smoother and much less troublesome to its dispensers.

Buddhist priests are sworn upon the sacred books of the temple. The *Bogaha* is of rapid growth, and easily propagated, so that a court of justice should not be without one near or within its precincts. By this simple method, the truth may be expected from Buddhist witnesses, even if it suited their purpose to commit perjury.

* *Bogaha.—Bo,* abbreviation of *Bod* or *Buddha,* and *gaha,* tree,—the *Ficus religiosa,* L. There is a remarkable coincidence between the stories told in Syria of the aspen tree, *Populus tremula,* L., class Dioecia, order Octandria, and the Singhalese stories of the *Bogaha,* or *Ficus religiosa,* class Polygamia, order Triæcia. The Syrians aver that the wood of the cross of our Saviour was made of aspen, and that the leaves of the aspen have trembled ever since, in commemoration of that event. The Buddhists attribute the similar property in the foliage of the *Bogaha,* or Buddha's tree, to Buddha's preferring, when on earth, a seat under its shade to that of every other tree; since which period its leaves have always an apparent motion, whether there be any wind stirring or not.

CHAP. VII.

Ecclesiastical establishment—Unjust distinctions among the clergy—Suggestions for Ceylon being made a bishopric—Consistory of the Reformed Church of Holland—Portuguese mission of the Oratorio of San Felippe de Neri—Papal mission from Rome—Suggestions for its removal—Baptist mission—Wesleyan mission—American mission—Church of England mission—Caste of Sorcerers—Conversion to Mahommedanism—Military establishment—Civil branch of the Ordnance—Pay and Island allowances—Batta to Naval officers—Staff allowances.

THE ecclesiastical establishment, in official language, includes only the clergy of the Established Church of England and Ireland, and the consistory of the Reformed Church of Holland.

The seniors of the colonial clergy enjoy the privileges of the pension fund, in common with those civil servants who subscribed to it prior to the year 1822, agreeably to the regulations established by the late Earl Bathurst, at that time His Majesty's secretary of state for the colonies; but those who have since been appointed, have no such advantages; this causes serious heart-burnings, which, however concealed, are deeply felt as a most undeserved and unjust difference.

Considering the population of the island, the establishment of a separate bishopric in Ceylon would afford general satisfaction to all sincere Protestants, for the diocese of Madras, of which it at present forms an archdeaconry, is so extensive, that a very small proportion of the Lord Bishop's attention can be devoted to Ceylon, if justice be done to the rest of his diocese.

The consistory of the Reformed Church of Holland comprises four elders and six deacons; but it cannot boast much of the liberality of the British government; for the president has but £350 a year, which is less by £50 than the stipend of the native Singhalese colonial chaplain; and the consistory's exemplary proponent at Galle has but £54 per annum, after having preached in Dutch and Portuguese in that church for upwards of thirty years.

Of Christian missions, the Roman Catholic mission of the Oratorio of San Felippe de Neri of Goa is the most ancient. The Portuguese take credit to themselves for having been the first to introduce Christianity into Ceylon; but history informs us that they were preceded by Persian missionaries of the Nestorian churches, who planted churches there, subsequently to the subversion of the Parthian empire by the Persians, and the restoration of the ancient line of the Persian monarchy; and that the functions of religion were performed by priests ordained by the archbishop of Seleucia, at that time the capital of the Persian kingdom.—But there are no known records of the Nestorian churches now extant in the island; and the next power, to whom credit is due for its christian zeal in favour of the heathen, is Portugal.

The chief residence of this mission is at Santa Lucia, near Colombo. Three missionaries reside at Colombo; three at Negombo; one in the southern province, who officiates at Galle and Matura; one at Kaltura, who also has the church at Morotto under his cure; one in Kandy, and for Alootkoor; one at Chilaw, and for Calpentyn; one at Arippo, and for Bangallé; one at Manaar, and for the Wanné district; one at Kaits, one at Jaffnapatam, one at Walligammoe, one at Point Pedro, and one at Trincomalé, who also officiates at Batticaloa; but the immense tract of country from Tangalle to Batticaloa, where devil worship now reigns paramount, is destitute of the means of acquiring the light of the gospel.

This mission estimates its converts at 150,000, for which number, seventeen missionaries may well be considered a very scanty establishment. Perhaps the poverty of the Roman Catholic churches in Ceylon, and the limited number of padres,* may arise from the apathy of native converts; but such is the present very degenerated state of the Roman religion in the island, that those who have been accustomed to the splendid cathedrals of Malta, Spain, and Italy, can scarcely imagine it possible, when they enter a Santa Gri, or holy church, in Ceylon, that the same faith is professed by both.

The reverend fathers of this mission are subjects of Her Most Faithful Majesty: they superintend 118 schools, and are humane, pious, charitable to the poor, and hospitable to the stranger.

Upon the anniversary of St. Cecilia's day, (Nov. 22,) a splendid dinner is given in the refectory of Santa Lucia, where religion presents no bar to the equal enjoyment of the genuine hospitality of the reverend fathers by their Protestant as well as Roman Catholic guests.

About two years ago, His Holiness Gregory XVI. despatched a vicar apostolic and several priests from ROME to Ceylon. For this there was no occasion, and it is hard upon the numerous and well-educated English and Irish Roman Catholic clergymen,

* The general name, among the natives, for the clergy and missionaries throughout the island.

that the government should allow the ministry of that church to be exercised by foreign priests in a British colony, for which our own and sister country could have better and more consistently provided. These reverend intruders would very soon take their departure, if Her Majesty's secretary of state for the colonies were to stipulate with His Holiness the Pope, for the establishment of a Protestant church and mission at Rome, as the condition of their continuance in the island.

The first British mission to Ceylon was that of the Baptists, in the year 1812, but it only now occupies four stations; namely, at Colombo, Byanville, Matellé, Hanwellé, and the adjoining villages. This mission superintends eleven schools, and two Sunday schools, consisting of between 400 and 500 children.

There are but two missionaries, with five native teachers to assist them; these gentlemen are themselves so very exemplary in every moral and religious duty, that they are universally respected; and for their genuine zeal in promoting the objects of their mission, they will ever stand high upon the records of the colony, for it has effected great good, in spite of the disadvantages of limited funds and paucity of labourers.

The next, but *nulli secundus* in good works, is the Wesleyan mission, established in the year 1814.

I must leave it to an abler pen to do justice to the reverend gentlemen of this mission; their works speak for themselves; these are not limited to matters of religion, and are productive of great and universal good throughout the island. Every month is ushered in with the publication of "The Friend," and "The Protestant Vindicator," the former a miscellany for the promotion of the moral and social, as well as religious interests of the colony, the latter that which its title implies.

The natives of Ceylon might be much benefitted, if, amongst other means adopted for extending the blessings of useful knowledge amongst them, a translation of the Penny and Saturday Magazines were published in the island;—the engraved wood-blocks belonging to these works, after having answered all the purposes of the "Society for the Diffusion of Useful Knowledge," might be well devoted to this object, and it would be a boon of such incalculable benefit to the rising native population, that it would be unjust to doubt the readiness of the Wesleyan mission to translate, and publish them in the native languages. The demand for these works would gradually become extensive, for they would find their way throughout India.

The Wesleyan missionaries minister in the Hindoo-Portuguese, Singhalese, and English languages; and their chapels are conspicuous for the plain, but convenient and well-ordered regularity of Protestant places of worship. The affairs of this mission are regulated at annual meetings, held at Colombo in January, the decisions of which are subject to the control of the general committee of the home mission. From the funds of this last, that of Ceylon is supported; but much more might be realized by the friends of missions in this country, if they would but do their *utmost* to increase them; for Ceylon, although presenting a most ample field for the labours of at least ten times its numbers of Wesleyan ministers, is now limited to eight missionariés and fourteen assistants, who have the management of the education of nearly *six thousand scholars*, in eighty one schools.

Never did the ministers of the Established Church, of which at that time the Honorable Thomas James Twistleton, afterwards archdeacon of Colombo, was the senior colonial chaplain, do themselves greater honor than by the manner in which they collectively and individually extended the right hand of christian fellowship aud hospitality to the Wesleyan missionaries, upon the first establishment of their mission in the island in the year 1815. This laid the foundation for that long continued and existing cordiality, which the then government appeared most desirous of encouraging; for when the Wesleyan chapel was first opened at Colombo for divine service, His Excellency the governor (Sir Robert Brownrigg, G. C. B.) with his family, the clergymen of the Established Church, and the majority of the civil and military officers, whose duties would admit of it, were present at that most interesting ceremonial to the Almighty's honor, and for the propagation of "peace on earth, and of good-will towards men!"

The American mission was first establised in the northern districts of Ceylon, in the year 1816, and many still living will recollect the official jealousy with which the settlement at Jaffna, of the very exemplary individuals who originally composed it, was regarded. Experience has proved that it was unjust and unworthy of the generous character of a British government; and it would be difficult to find an individual in the colony, who has had an opportunity of witnessing the conduct of the respectable and respected persons of the American mission, at all disposed to believe, that even if the government of the United States would so far compromise its own dignity, as to endeavour to induce its missionary citizens in Ceylon to exercise the degrading office of spy, there would be found one amongst them so lost to his own character, as to prostitute it for any national or worldly advantage.

This mission occupies seven stations in the northern province, to which its attention is exclusively limited: namely, Tillipallé, Batticotta, Oodoovillé, Pondeteripo, Manepé, Chavagacheré, and Varané; and they employ native catechists at Oodopitté, Achoowelé, Changané, Caradivé, Valané, and Pungertivé.

At Batticotta there is a seminary, superintended by a principal, a professor, a native tutor in mathematics and natural philosophy, and a native teacher of arithmetic and astronomy, according to the Hindoo system; the number of pupils is 101; of girls in the central school, 90; native free schools 42; boys 1200, girls 300. The seminary is entirely supported by the American Board of Commissioners for Foreign Missions.

The printing and book-binding establishment belonging to the mission employs three presses, and fifty workmen.

Although last in the field, having been established in 1818, the Church Mission has distinguished itself for its christian zeal, and in promoting native education: occupying four stations, and having but nine missionaries in holy orders, their labours, in which they are assisted by about 110 native catechists, school-masters, and school-mistresses, may be estimated by the number of congregations and schools belonging to the mission.

The number of communicants bears no proportion to the attendants at public worship, the former amounting, in 1838, to 133, and the latter to 2418. Of scholars, male and female, there are, in the sixty-two schools, thirty adults, 2048 boys, and 426 girls.

A lay agent transacts the temporal concerns of this mission, and the number of tracts already distributed amounts to 420,000.

The whole of the Scriptures and Book of Common Prayer have been translated into familiar Singhalese, besides numerous elementary school books, and religious tracts: all these have been printed at the Kotta Mission press, and extensively circulated amongst the natives, by whom they are sought with avidity, and readily purchased by those who can afford it; whilst those who cannot, accept them with apparent thankfulness.

The prospects of this mission are evidently great and very encouraging; and as the only rock upon which they can possibly be wrecked, is the want of competent funds, it is earnestly to be hoped that the pure doctrine they preach will not be allowed to fail of producing the desired effect, by adequate pecuniary support being niggardly withheld at home. The scholars make constant and creditable progress in the acquirement of religious information and general knowledge.

It is, however, a subject of general regret to the missions, that although in the immediate neighbourhood of a nominally christian population, scarcely one native family out of a hundred, unless immediately connected with them, abstains, on religious principles, from the ceremonies and practice of devil worship. When their wizards, astrologers, and conjurers are converted, they will quit the devil practices by which the native minds are so extraordinarily worked upon as to render them pliant and subservient victims to the grossest impositions that ever fettered the spirit of man. This may be calculated on as a certain effect of the light of christianity upon the minds of the *soi-disant* magi, who now hold bodies and souls in perpetual thraldom. But until this grand evil be removed, and by the assistance of the magistracy wherever it may be needful, in severely punishing all such impostors, the fears of the ignorant natives will not be overcome by merely professing themselves converts to christianity. The conversion of one greatly dreaded astrologer and devil worshipper will do much to reconcile the natives to the power of christianity over the wiles of the evil one, and tend to reduce their fears of the *maha yaka,* or great demon, more than can be hoped for by other means.

The caste of Seppidiwigie Karayo, or sorcerers, is one of the greatest stumbling blocks to christianity that now presents itself, and on its gradual conversion very much depends; for the superstitious natives will never altogether abandon devil worship, so long as its priests have such power over their minds, as to inspire these deluded creatures with the dreadful conviction that both their own bodies and the lives of their cattle, are at their (the sorcerers') command. May the Almighty's blessing enable the ministers of Christ to effect this grand object, and may it light upon the efforts of all employed in so great and glorious a cause, whatever the denomination of the christian church, mission, sect, or creed, they profess to belong to!

Too much cannot be said of the amiable and exemplary divines to whom the affairs of this mission are so happily entrusted; for, like those who have preceded them in the office, they are altogether unexceptionable, whether in a religious or moral point of view.

Our missionaries may make proselytes of Singhalese, and Malabars, but they appear to have little or no chance with any of the many thousands of the followers of Ali and Mahommed, of whom I have not yet heard that they have converted even a solitary individual; but Ceylon has witnessed the conversion of an apostate Englishman to Mahommedanism. The first and most ready Singhalese converts have been those who anticipated employment in the missionary establishments.

The Peace establishment of the army in Ceylon consists of two companies of the royal artillery, commanded by a lieutenant-colonel; two of the royal engineers; four regiments of the line; the Ceylon rifle regiment, consisting of sixteen companies, and a troop of mounted orderlies.

The present governor, Lieut. General Sir Colin Campbell, K. C. B., is also commander of the forces.

The general staff consists of a military secretary, two aids-de-camp, a deputy adjutant general, deputy assistant adjutant general, deputy quarter-master general, deputy assistant quarter-master general, and a deputy commissary general.

The medical staff includes one deputy inspector of hospitals, one staff surgeon, and nine assistant staff surgeons.

The civil branch of the ordnance consists of two store keepers, one (who is also the paymaster) at Colombo, and one at Trincomalé; four established clerks, two assistant clerks, and one extra assistant clerk.

The amount of officers' pay and island allowances, and of the latter to naval officers, when employed as agents of transports, during their detention by, or employment under, the orders of Her Majesty's colonial government, is given in the following tables.

Military and Army Medical Establishment at Ceylon.

		£	s.	d.
Military Secretary's Office.				
Military secretary	per diem	0	9	0
Five clerks, senior at	per annum	135	0	0
and junior at	—	27	0	0
Adjutant General's Office.				
Deputy adjutent general	per diem	0	19	0
Deputy assistant general	—	0	10	0
Three clerks, senior at	per annum	103	10	0
and junior at	—	49	10	0
Quarter-Master General's Office.				
Deputy quarter-master general	per diem	0	19	0
Deputy assistant ditto	—	0	10	0
Two clerks, the first at	per annum	103	10	0
and the second at	—	72	0	0
Two draftsmen, the first at	—	54	0	0
and the second at	—	36	0	0
Staff Officer's Office.				
Staff officer	per diem	0	10	0
Clerk, at	per annum	40	10	0
Royal Engineers' Office.				
Three clerks, the first at	per annum	96	0	0
the second at	—	60	0	0
and the third at	—	36	0	0
One draftsman, at	—	69	6	0
Principal Medical Officer's Office.				
Two clerks, the senior at	per diem	0	7	0
and the junior at	per annum	54	0	0
Kandy.				
Staff Officer's Office.				
Staff officer	per diem	0	10	0
One clerk, at	per annum	27	0	0
Royal Engineers' Office.				
One clerk of the works, at	per annum	72	0	0
One assistant ditto	—	36	0	0
Trincomalé.				
Staff Officer's Office.				
Staff officer	per diem	0	10	0
One clerk	per annum	27	0	0

Island allowances to officers, in addition to their Queen's pay, in lieu of lodging-money, fuel, candles, &c.

		£	s.	d.
Colonel	per mensem	45	9	0
Lieutenant-colonel	—	32	2	0
Major	—	23	19	0
Captain	—	13	16	0

		£	s.	d.
Lieutenant	—	8	5	0
Second lieutenant or ensign	—	6	6	0
Paymaster	—	13	16	0
Surgeon	—	17	10	0
Assistant surgeon	—	12	10	0
Adjutant	—	10	4	0
Quarter-master	—	10	4	0

When officers, having been relieved, have ceased to do duty in the island, they are allowed the following rate of island allowances, to the day of their embarkation inclusively.

		£	s.	d.
Colonel	per mensem	22	14	6
Inspector-general of hospitals	—	22	14	6
Lieutenant-colonel	—	16	1	0
Deputy inspector-general of hospitals		16	1	0
Assistant inspector of ditto	—	13	15	0
Major	—	11	19	6
Staff surgeon	—	11	19	6
Surgeon	—	11	13	4
Captain or paymaster	—	9	4	0
Apothecary or assistant surgeon	—	8	16	8
Adjutant	—	8	16	0
Lieutenant or quarter-master	—	5	10	0
Second lieutenant or ensign	—	4	4	0

Lieutenants or masters in the Royal Navy, acting as agents of transports, are entitled to 13*l.* 16*s.* per mensem, being island allowances to captains of infantry, during their detention or employment by Her Majesty's colonial government.

Additional allowances to officers in command of corps.

		£	s.	d.
Colonel	per mensem	5	4	0
Lieutenant-colonel	—	5	4	0
Major	—	8	3	0
Captain	—	10	4	0
Lieutenant	—	5	11	0

Additional allowances to officers in command of garrisons, with the exception of Colombo, Trincomalé, Kandy, and Galle.

		£	s.	d.
Colonel	per mensem	29	11	0
Lieutenant-colonel	—	8	18	0
Major	—	6	14	0
Captain	—	3	19	6
Lieutenant	—	2	14	0
Second lieutenant or ensign	—	2	0	6

The allowance of the commandant of Colombo is fixed at ...... per mensem 29 11 0

		£	s.	d.
Ditto of Trincomalé	—	30	0	0
Ditto of Kandy	—	25	0	0
Ditto of Galle	per diem	0	10	0

N. B. The allowance to the commandant of Colombo is not drawn, except when the offices of governor and commander of the forces are held by the same officer.

General and Medical Staff.

		£	s.	d.
Major-general	per mensem	275	13	4½
Deputy quarter-master general, being a lieutenant-colonel.....................		16	1	0
Deputy assistant ditto, being a lieut. ...		4	2	6
Deputy adjutant-general, being a lieutenant-colonel		16	1	0
Deputy assistant ditto, being a lieut. ...		4	2	6
Assistant military secretary		6	18	0

But if this office be held by an aid-de-camp, then it is not drawn, there being no island allowance for more than one staff situation to the same officer.

	£	s.	d.
Aid-de-camp to the governor and general officer, whether captains or subalterns	6	18	0

Besides the regimental allowance thus regulated, and where the ranks of staff officers do not correspond with this table, the addition equals one half the regimental rate of island allowances.

Aids-de-camp, if subalterns, have the staff and island allowances of captains.

		£	s.	d.
Brevet inspectors of hospitals,	per mensem	68	3	6
Staff surgeon	—	23	19	0
Assistant ditto	—	12	10	0
Apothecary to the forces ...	—	13	5	0

In 1827 the inspector of hospitals enjoyed the lucrative posts of inspector of vaccination, at 45*l.* per mensem, and deputy inspector, at 84*l.* 10*s.* per mensem, together with a commission of half a pice per pound upon all cinnamon assorted !!

CHAP. VIII.

Cinnamon first introduced into Europe from Ceylon by the Portuguese—Tribute of the Singhalese Rajah D' Harma Praakramabahoo IX., to Emmanuel, king of Portugal—Cinnamon uncultivated until Governor Falck's administration of the government—Cinnamon plantations and roads a general benefit—Casual remarks in the plantations—Dutch and British monopolies—Lord Viscount Goderich abolishes the cinnamon monopoly and all its penalties and oppressions—Nature of the former oppressive system—Ceylon jackdaw and cinnamon pigeon—Classification and varieties of the cinnamon laurel—Nepenthes distillatoria, Gloriosa superba, Ixora coccinea, and Vinca rosea—Soil of the cinnamon plantations near Colombo—Chalias or cinnamon peelers—mode of ascertaining the maturity of the bark—process of barking, assorting, and tasting—Cinnamon tasters—Prices of cinnamon lands at the sale in 1840—Prices of the spice—Revenue from cinnamon—Cinnamon oil, water, and candles—Clove oil made from the leaf of the cinnamon laurel—Cinnamon known to the ancient Greeks and Romans—Best quality known by the bark—Black pepper indispensable to the preservation of cinnamon—Cinnamon breezes bubbles of the imagination—Pandanus odoratissimus—Arum fœtidum—Hoax upon Griffins practised on board an East Indiaman.

It is scarcely possible to present much novelty to the reader upon a subject which has been extensively handled by the many abler writers who have preceded me; but as no account of this interesting island can be even moderately perfect without some notice of the cinnamon laurel, I avail myself of the correctest information that I could obtain upon the spot where it is principally cultivated, and from the best authors who have described its characters and properties.

When the cinnamon of Ceylon first attracted the attention of the Lusitanian discoverer of the island* in the year 1506, it was only known in its wild state; nevertheless this spice was at that period so highly esteemed, that the Portuguese admiral at once determined to turn it to the advantage of his country; and he consequently entered into a treaty with D' Harma Praakramabahoo IX., the rajah of Ceylon, whose capital was Kotta, for an annual tribute of 2500 quintals or 250,000 pounds avoirdupois of cinnamon; for which he guaranteed the then powerful protection of his sovereign, Dom Emmanuel, king of Portugal, to the Singhalese rajah and his dominions.†

* Admiral Lourenço D' Almeyda, son of the Count D' Abrantes, at that time vice-roy and governor general of the Indies.

† Papal permission was deemed necessary to authorize a commercial intercourse with the heathen; and as a license had previously been granted by His Holiness, Nicholas V., by *bull*, in favour of prince Henry of Portugal,

Cinnamon had never been cultivated in Ceylon until about the year 1770, when the Dutch governor, Iman Willem Falck, determined to try the effect of culture upon that laurel, malgré the opinions of the headmen that the result would be an useless expenditure of time, labour, and money, and the quality of the spice be deteriorated by the projected undertaking.

To this excellent governor is to be attributed the twofold benefit which resulted to the public, from the adoption of a line of policy, calculated, in his opinion, to increase the value of the principal staple of the colony in the European markets, and the general salubrity of Colombo, by clearing the impervious underwood in its immediate vicinity, and forming roads through the cinnamon plantations. These roads were subsequently improved by the British, and perfected during the late Sir Edward Barnes's administration of the government.

Very many Europeans traverse the cinnamon gardens, as the plantations are locally designated, at full gallop, without allowing a single remark to escape them upon this elegant and aromatic laurel, except in the language of disappointment at the absence of all odour of the spice from its innumerable blossoms: some may pluck a cluster of the small white monopetalous flowers, and express surprise that they exhale a slight perfume of the tuberose (*Polyanthes tuberosa*) instead of that of cinnamon; others may admire only the bright scarlet foliage of the extreme branches, or the purple acorn-shaped drupe, which contains the seed, merely because it bears a miniature resemblance to that of the oak tree; or perhaps pluck a leaf, as they ride or drive, and, upon crushing it in the hand, wonder that it exhales the odour of the clove only.

We readily accuse the Dutch of monopolizing the principal staples of colonial commerce, and we call that policy illiberal which restricted the culture of cinnamon to Ceylon, of the clove to the Moluccas, and of the nutmeg to the Banda islands; but what did *not* the British government in Ceylon monopolize, over which it had power? and even during the continuance of its own monopolies of cinnamon and salt, cum multis aliis, which had obtained from the cession of the island by the Dutch in 1796, the Kandyan kingdom had scarcely been *eighteen* months in our possession when the government declared the late king of Kandy's "monopoly in areka nuts, cardamoms, bee's wax, coffee, and pepper, to be highly prejudicial to the growth of those valuable articles of inland produce, and injurious to the commercial interests

to trade with the Mahomedans, and which referred to similar concessions from his papal predecessors, Martin V. and Eugenius, to the kings of Portugal, so it was continued in favour of Dom Emmanuel.—*Osorio*, vol. i. p. 253.

of the colony!!" and it was thereupon abandoned by proclamation dated 15th June, 1816, in the Kandyan territories: but it was not until the Right Honorable the Lord Viscount Goderich, His Majesty's principal secretary of state for the colonies, from 1830—1833 inclusively, abolished the iniquitous and arbitrary system altogether, that the monopoly in cinnamon ceased in the maritime provinces.

For nearly three centuries before Lord Goderich's fiat went forth, every regulation of the Portuguese, Dutch, and British governments, in regard to cinnamon, teemed with tyranny and oppression. The proprietor of the soil, whether European or native, dared not destroy a plant, which a passing jackdaw* (*Corvus Monedula* of Pennant) or pompadour pigeon† (*Vinago aromatica* of Shaw) by dropping its ordure, containing the indigested seed, might have been the vehicle of generating in his grounds; and a penalty was attached to the party omitting to report to the superintendent of cinnamon plantations the presence of such an unwelcome intruder upon his property.

But this was not all that was expected from the occupier of the soil. He neither dared to cut a cinnamon stick for his own use, nor a particle of the bark for his domestic purposes, nor to distil camphor from its roots, or clove oil from its foliage,

* This, the most impudent and numerous of the Ceylon birds, is described by all authors who have preceded me, except by the celebrated ornithologist, Dr. Stanley, the present Lord Bishop of Norwich, as the *Corvus Corax*, or crow; and some very tolerable anecdotes have been related, with, I doubt not, a very scrupulous adherence to truth, but which are nevertheless calculated to raise doubts in the minds of the majority of those whose fate has limited them to the perusal of the statements of what others have seen.—This bird is much smaller than the European crow, and I prefer adopting the opinion of the Right Reverend Prelate, that it is the *Corvus Monedula*, P., and not the *Corvus Corax*, L., that inhabits Ceylon. It is thus described in the work alluded to. "In the island of Ceylon, these birds are extremely impudent and troublesome, and it is found very difficult to exclude them from the houses, which, on account of the heat, are built open, and much exposed to intruders. In the town of Colombo, where they are in the habit of picking up bones and other things from the streets and yards, and carrying them to the tops of the houses, a battle usually takes place for the plunder, to the great annoyance of the people below, on whose heads they shower down the loosened tiles, leaving the roofs exposed to the weather. They frequently snatch bread and meat from the dining table, even when it is surrounded with guests, always seeming to prefer the company of man, as they are continually seen hopping about near houses, and rarely to be met with in woods and retired places. They are, however, important benefactors to the Indians, making ample compensation for their intrusion and knavery, for they are all voracious devourers of carrion, and consume all sorts of dirt, offal, and dead vermin: they in fact carry off those substances which, if allowed to remain, would in that hot climate produce the most noxious smells, and probably give rise to putrid disorders. On this account they are much esteemed by the natives; their mischievous tricks and impudence are put up with, and they are never suffered to be shot or otherwise molested.

† *Columba pompadoura*, Gmel. Syst. Nat. 1. 775. 9.

because a heavy penalty stared him in the face, for all cinnamon plants and bushes were public property: and whenever the superintendent chose, he despatched *chalias* to decorticate them and carry the bark to the government godowns or stores, without the slightest remuneration to the landlord. Not only the proprietors, but every body and thing, including *bullocks* and even *carts*,* were made liable to *prosecution* and *imprisonment*.†

The following is the classification of the *Laurus Cinnamomum*, according to the Linnæan system.

Class IX. Enneandria—Order I. Monogynia. Flower white, having a brownish shade in the middle; monopetalous; stellated, having six points; fruit a drupe, about the size of a small hedge strawberry, containing one seed, and of the shape of an acorn; leaf trinervous, egg-oblong, nerves vanishing towards the tip, and reticulated.

The principal, and the only cultivated species, is distinguished above all others by the Singhalese name of *Penné* or *Rassé Kuroondu*, which signifies honey or sweet cinnamon; the second variety is called *Naya Kuroondu*, or snake cinnamon; the third, *Kapooru Kuroondu*, or camphor cinnamon; the fourth, *Kabatté Kuroondu*, or astringent cinnamon; the fifth, *Sevel Kuroondu*, or mucilaginous cinnamon; the sixth, *Dawool Kuroondu*, or flat or drum cinnamon; the seventh, *Nika Kuroondu*, or wild cinnamon, whose leaf resembles that of the nicasol, or *Vitex Negundo;* the eighth, *Mal Kuroondu*, or bloom or flower cinnamon; and the ninth, *Tompat Kuroondu*, or trefoil cinnamon.‡ But it is only the first four that are strictly varieties of the *Laurus Cinnamomum*.

When in full bloom, the cinnamon bushes have a very beautiful appearance; the small white petals affording a most agreeable contrast with the flame-coloured extremities of the upper, and the dark green of the inferior foliage, intermingled with the climbing monkey or pitcher plant (*Nepenthes distillatoria*), which, conjointly with

* Bandies.

† GOVERNMENT ADVERTISEMENT.—"Notice is hereby given, that no Bullock Bandies, *loaded* or *unloaded*, are allowed to pass through the Cinnamon Gardens, on the roads or otherwise, on any pretence whatever; and all *Bullock Bandies* found so trespassing, with the *Cattle* belonging to the same, will be seized *by* and prosecuted *before* the Sitting Magistrate.

Signed, JOHN RODNEY,
Chief Secretary to Government.

Chief Secretary's Office,
COLOMBO, 14th Feb. 1812."

‡ *Burmanni Thesaurus Zeylanicus.*

the flame-coloured *Gloriosa superba,* entwines its tendrils around this umbrageous and spicy laurel, and the scarlet-flowered *Ixora coccinea,* and pink-petaled *Vinca rosea,* enjoying the shade beneath it.

The best cinnamon is obtained from the shoots which spring almost perpendicularly from the roots, after the parent bush or tree has been cut down;—these afford the hazel-like walking sticks so much esteemed by persons visiting the island, and which, although very great difficulty formerly existed in procuring them, owing to the oppressive nature of the cinnamon regulations, may now be very easily obtained from proprietors of grounds producing that spice.

The external appearance of the cinnamon suckers, prior to their decortication, resembles that of the hazel. The best soil for cinnamon is a pure quartz sand; which, from the surface to the depth of a few inches, is as fine in its nature and as white in its appearance as the best table salt; but below that depth, and near the roots of the bushes, the sand is greyish.*

There are two regular seasons for barking cinnamon, namely from April to August, and from November to January, but considerable quantities are collected at other times, as the spice attains maturity.

In order to ascertain the maturity of the *liber,* or inner bark, which is the cinnamon of commerce, the peeler gives the stick a diagonal cut with a heavy knife, and if the bark readily separate itself from the wood of the shoot that he has selected, he cuts it down, and having scraped off the outer brown and green pellicles with a blunt knife, he removes the bark by passing a sharp-pointed knife longitudinally from one extremity to the other. He then places the smaller portions of the bark within the larger, and dries it in the air and shade, where it curls and contracts, as it is imported into Europe.

The peelers form the cinnamon into bundles, from three to four feet in length, and 85 pounds avoirdupois in weight, but reckoned only as 80 pounds, the surplus being allowed for waste; and they have so delicate a sense of taste, that they can distinguish either of the four best sorts of cinnamon in the dark. The government cinnamon tasters are necessitated to eat bread and butter at intervals during that pungent duty, in order to preserve the skin of their tongues.

* According to Dr. John Davy's analysis, the greyish sand, thoroughly dried, consists of 98.5 silicious sand,
1.0 vegetable matter,
0.5 water.
100.0

At the time of the abolition of the monopoly, a sort of *cinnamo-mania* prevailed for purchasing the partitioned plantations from the crown; but in 1840 cinnamon lands sold for about 4*l.* to 4*l.* 10*s.* per acre.

This spice is sold at 6*d.*, 9*d.*, and 1*s.* per pound avoirdupois; the duty upon exportation of the first and second sorts is 2*s.* 6*d.* per pound, and upon the third sort 2*s.*, provided it be assorted by the government assorters; and 3*s.* 6*d.* per pound upon its importation into this country. The oil of cinnamon, which is made from the refuse of the stores, is subject to a duty of 1*s.* per ounce. The Dutch limited the quantity of cinnamon for exportation, in order to maintain high prices for it in the home markets.

The Ceylon government derives an average revenue of £120,000 a year from cinnamon, cinnamon oil, and clove oil. In the year 1836 it amounted to 127,164*l.* 18*s.* 3½*d.* which included the export duty of 74,631*l.* 0*s.* 10*d.*

It may naturally be inferred, that the increased production of cinnamon will eventually cause a glut, which nothing less than a reduction of duty will obviate, or the accumulated stock must sell much below remunerating prices.

The most pungent and delicious cinnamon water, which, after having undergone adulteration in the proportion of four to one, would still excel the best that is sold as such at home, does not exceed 2*s.* 6*d.* per gallon in the island.

Amongst the Kandyan spoils were some cinnamon candles belonging to the rajah, of which Lieut. Lyttelton, of the 73rd regiment, gave me a few specimens; but they exhaled no very grateful odour, nor was there any peculiar brilliancy in their light.

Nature in some degree thwarted Dutch policy, in as far as regards one staple of Ceylon production; namely, that called *clove oil*, which is there manufactured solely from the cinnamon *leaf*, and equal, in point of aromatic pungency, to the oil made from the clove itself at the Molucca islands.

Cinnamon was well known to the ancient Greeks by the name of Κιννάμωμον, and to the Romans by that of *Cinnamomum*. It was chiefly used in perfumes and unguents, but its price was so exorbitant that none but affluent people could purchase it. Genuine cinnamon oil is made in this country, and is considered equal to the best that was formerly imported from Holland; and the essential oil, distilled from cinnamon grown in Jamaica, cannot be distinguished from that imported from Ceylon.

The best cinnamon is not thicker than stout writing paper, of a light yellowish red color, and of a sweetly pungent taste. The inferior sort is thicker and darker in color, hot and pungent to the taste, which subsequently becomes most unpleasant. Many impositions are practised in this country by selling the bark, as genuine cinnamon, after its essential oil has been distilled from it.

Owing to the limited quantity of black pepper that is produced in Ceylon, in proportion to the demand for it, and the means of growing it, the island is dependent for supplies of that spice upon the coast of Malabar. Ships, chartered for the purpose of conveying cinnamon to England, have been detained for several weeks through the want of pepper to fill the interstices between the bales of cinnamon in the ships' holds; without which, the latter spice would lose one half its value upon being imported into this country; but, by being stowed together, each spice is preserved in the utmost perfection during the homeward-bound voyage. The apathy shown to the culture of the pepper vine is altogether as unaccountable as the neglect of the other very many valuable productions that are noticed in these pages.

But as to those bubbles of imagination, the *cinnamon breezes* of Ceylon, many leagues at sea, they explode before the experience of the resident in the country.— If all the cinnamon trees growing in the island were being barked at one and the same time, it is impossible to say whether or not, or how far at sea, with the wind off shore, the perfume of the spice might extend; though as there is nothing peculiar in its diffusiveness, it is fair to infer that its influence would not extend *very* far. As the operations are now effected, in particular spots as the cinnamon becomes mature for the purpose, and over an extensive surface, at uncertain periods and in *limited* quantities, in comparison with its produce, it is physically impossible that *cinnamon breezes* can be perceived at sea.

Whatever fragrance may accompany Ceylon breezes, near and from the island, is more likely to arise from the immense variety of the odoriferous blossoms and flowers, of the wild orange, lime, and shaddock, and varieties of the white and yellow jessamine, and above all, in its diffusive properties, the *Pandanus odoratissimus*, a species of *Mellori*, or Nicobar Islands' bread fruit, most objectionable as the latter name is, when contrasted with the produce of the true bread-fruit tree (*Artocarpus incisa*, L.), for none but the lowest and poorest natives will eat it, and then only after having been prepared in a manner peculiar to themselves.

It's common name among Europeans is the wild pine apple, from the great resemblance it bears to the *Bromelia Ananas*;* but it is of a very different nature, class, and order.† The fruit of the Pandanus is composed of wedge-shaped drupes, angular, and

* *Bromelia Ananas*, L. Class IV. Hexandria, Order I. Monogynia.

† *Pandanus odoratissimus*, L. Class XXII. Diœcia, Order I. Monandria.

one-seeded; the leaf is much longer than that of the pine apple, but is also serrated and spinous; and its flower, which is indispensable at all the native devil-ceremonials, exhales so powerful an odour, that when dried it becomes the best preservative of clothes, and of specimens in natural history, from the ravages of the *Termes*, or white ant. The flower is an erect spike, thick and silky, of a lightish brown color, and rises from a spathe, which is double, strong, and similar in substance to that of the Indian corn (*Zea Mäis*).

The Singhalese call it *Wetta-gaha*, and they aver, that unless the male and female plant be near each other, the fruit never becomes edible. The seed is oval and glossy.

But odours "not of Araby" sometimes prevail within the island: such are those which are wafted by the sea-breezes from the southward, and assail the traveller upon the coast of the southern province, particularly between Rogallé and Mirsé, arising from a large species of the *Arum fœtidum*, which taints the air, to a considerable distance, with a smell scarcely inferior to the noxious effluvia which some hundreds of decomposing carcases would diffuse.

If proof were wanting *of the effect of imagination* in regard to *cinnamon breezes* off Ceylon, I might adduce an incident that occurred on board an outward bound East Indiaman, whilst standing along the island, but not in sight of it, and with the wind *dead upon the land*. The surgeon having rubbed a little oil of cinnamon upon the weather hammock nettings, the *Griffins*,* who formed a majority of the passengers, and who generally assembled on the poop just before the dinner hour, were so convinced of the *reality* of the *cinnamon breeze*, that one of them actually published an account of it, "from his own experience of its fragrance many leagues at sea."

* *Griffin*, an East Indian term, synonymous with the West Indian, *Johnny Newcome*.

CHAP. IX.

The culture and manufacture of indigenous Indigo entirely neglected—Apathy displayed by the government and individuals almost incredible—Every thing favourable to the culture of Indigo—None of the vicissitudes of climate, as in Bengal, to be dreaded—Varieties of indigenous Indigo—None exported since 1794—District of Tangalle in the southern province abounds with Indigo—Facilities for establishing an Indigo factory—Mr. Fawkener, an eminent Indigo planter, proposes to the government to establish an Indigo farm and manufactory—This proposition refused—Extraordinary hypothesis—Indigo largely exported by the Dutch government of Ceylon—Governor's protracted stay in Kandy—John Tranchell, Esq.—Projected Indigo company of Tangalle—Stipulations in favour of the proposed superintendent—The company to be a body corporate—Anticipation of profit—The governor readily supports and becomes the patron of the company—Protracted correspondence—Questions of the committee—Mr. Tranchell's death—The governor's promotion and removal—Abandonment of the scheme—Fæcula of the Indigo leaf a valuable manure—Madung Appo—Specimens of Indigo made from other indigenous plants—Best mode of selecting Indigo seeds—Linnæan classification—Different methods of manufacturing Indigo—Cost of establishing an Indigo factory—Indigo maistry and labourers—Indigo sown every second year—Singhalese anxious for Indigo plantations in the Tangalle district—Cultivation of coffee—Land not in the same insecure state in Ceylon as in India—Hints to intending emigrants—Suggestions to Her Majesty's secretary of state for the colonies for encouraging the cultivation of Indigo—Settlement in Ceylon and in Australia contrasted.

Perhaps I cannot do better than continue, consecutively, the subject, connected with the capabilities of the island, and with the grand staples of commerce, for which Providence has pre-eminently qualified it.

The local agriculture does not yet include the culture of indigo; nor, during the forty-four years that Ceylon has been under the British flag, has a pound of indigo been manufactured for exportation, from the indigenous material, which is both excellent and abundant; but, on the contrary, manufactured indigo is still imported from the Indian continent.

The apathy of the government to an object of such incalculable importance to the colony, is almost incredible; but the neglect of this valuable dye by individuals, can only have arisen from a lamentable state of ignorance respecting it, or from the want of capital.

Here every thing is favourable to the speculation, if it may be called one, where the prospect for early and abundant returns for capital laid out is not clouded with the remotest probability of a contrary result; for there are none of the vicissitudes of climate to be dreaded, that in the course of a night have devastated the most extensive plantations in Bengal, which, on the preceding day, had appeared in all the luxuriance of approaching maturity, and, with their destruction, annihilated the hopes and calculations of the planter.

It is almost incredible, but nevertheless an absolute fact, that although the plant itself, (*Indigofera tinctoria*, L.), in both the varieties, *sativa* and *agrestis*, grows in the most prolific abundance, the last export of that dye took place, under the Dutch government of the island, in the year 1794 !!

The district of Tangalle, in the southern province, is the best adapted to the culture and manufacture of indigo, for various reasons ; namely, abundance of the indigenous material—similarity of climate to that of the coast of Coromandel, where the best indigo is produced—facility of transport by water to either of the ports of export, Galle or Colombo, during the north-east monsoon, or to Trincomalé by the south-west—and every necessary material for building a first-rate indigo factory, including drying yards, leaf godowns, steeping vats, and presses, (except roof and floor tiles, which may be obtained in any quantity from Colombo, during the south-west monsoon, at a moderate rate, compared with their cost at home,) is at hand ; for wood is abundant, and may be obtained in any quantity, upon a license from government to fell it, for which a trifling duty is charged ; and shells or coral for lime, for the mere expense of collecting and burning, upon the spot ; and any number of carpenters, bricklayers, masons, and labourers may be had at moderate wages, the latter for sixpence a day.

In the year 1817, a gentleman named Fawkener, an extensive indigo planter in Bengal, came to Ceylon for change of air. He soon became delighted with the climate, and having accidently seen the true and bastard indigo growing spontaneously in my compound at Colpetty, he forthwith submitted a proposition to His Excellency General Sir Robert Brownrigg, Bart., G. C. B., the then governor, to establish an extensive indigo farm and manufactory in the island, provided the government would assign to him certain waste lands, the property of the crown, free of the usual taxes upon *Parveny* or private lands, for thirty years ; and at the expiration of that period, to be subject to the usual duty of ten per cent. upon the produce. Mr. Fawkener offered full security for continuing the cultivation of indigo, and that in failure thereof, the lands were to revert to the crown.

This proposition was replete with *certain* advantage to the revenue, because there was no stipulation made that government should allow indigo to be exported *duty free ;* and one successful speculation would have induced others. The benefit to the colony, and the increase of agricultural labour, would have been certain and progressive, and the profits to Mr. Fawkener, incalculable.

It may be presumed that the multiplicity of business which then pressed upon Governor Sir Robert Brownrigg, who was occupied in suppressing the Kandyan rebellion that had broken out, precluded the deliberate attention to Mr. Fawkener's proposition which it might otherwise have received, for sound policy would surely have dictated its acceptance, both as a certain means of increasing the revenue, and of extensively benefitting the agriculture of the colony, by introducing at one and the same time an improved method of cultivation, and bringing into general notice as a grand staple of colonial produce, a most valuable and indigenous, but altogether neglected dye.

It was stated, but how far correctly I cannot vouch, that doubts were expressed by the executive, whether indigo could be successfully cultivated in the colony! But surely, that point was for the speculator's consideration, and Mr. Fawkener had no doubts whatever upon the subject; for he had found it growing spontaneously, and subsequently ascertained that in certain localities it was most abundant, and required nothing but culture to improve it, when the manufacture would follow as a matter of course; and secondly, such a doubt on the part of the executive would have betrayed gross ignorance of the history of the colony, for it had long been a recorded fact, that during the Dutch administration of the government, vast quantities of indigo had been manufactured for the European market, and exported from Trincomalé: besides which, a preliminary trial of its growth and manufacture upon a limited scale, would have soon solved the hypothesis.

The governor's protracted stay in Kandy, and the very uncertain state of affairs in that country, together with Mr. Fawkener's desire to avail himself of the south-west monsoon, to return to Bengal, determined him to abandon his original intention, which may be justly considered a very severe loss to the island, for no similarly advantageous propositions were subsequently made.

The next in the field was Mr. John Tranchell, a Swedish gentleman of great ability, skill, and enterprise; but unfortunately without capital. Mr. Tranchell had long previously ascertained that an abundance of indigo grew spontaneously in the Tangalle district, and at length, failing in private channels, he proposed to the then governor, His Excellency, Lieut. General Sir Edward Barnes, G. C. B., to patronize the formation of an indigo factory, by a joint-stock company, in fifty shares of 500 rix dollars, or *37l. 10s.* each share. The governor approved of the plan, and most cheerfully consented to become the patron.

It was then proposed, that as original mover of the scheme, Mr. Tranchell should be appointed the company's resident superintendent of such factory, and have a vested right to ten shares for his own benefit, such ten shares to be paid for by the subscribers, in proportion to the number of shares purchased for themselves—that the land should be granted by the government as the bonâ fide property of Mr. Tranchell, subject to the cultivation of indigo, so long as it should be found to make an ample return to the company, or that the company continued to exist—that the said company should be a body corporate, under the title of The Indigo Factory Company of Tangalle, with the privilege of being allowed to sue and defend, in all causes of action before the supreme court of judicature, and minor courts, as a body corporate.

"That two thousand acres of crown lands, in the province of Tangalle, to be chosen by Mr. Tranchell, should be granted, free of all tax to government, for thirty years; and after that period, to be chargeable, as the property of Mr. Tranchell, with the usual duty upon private lands, namely, one tenth of their produce per annum; and that the proprietors, or a majority of them, at public meetings, should nominate a committee of inspection, from time to time, of the progress of the establishment."

It was calculated, after a liberal estimate of the expenses, that the proprietors would only have to make a sacrifice of the *interest* of their capital for the first *eighteen months*, and that in the *third* year a *considerable dividend* might be anticipated; and it was at the same time suggested, that as an encouragement to the superintendent to give up all his time to the concerns of the factory, he should have the right of preemption of such shares as might at any time be offered for sale, and also the power of disposing of all his own shares above five, which number he was to be obliged to retain: but that if, at any subsequent period, the superintendent should desire to relinquish that situation, it could only be done with the consent of three-fourths of the proprietors.

His Excellency the governor readily entered into the spirit of the propositions, but with certain modifications. The formation of the company was then proposed to the literary and agricultural society of Ceylon, and that measure eventually decided its fate; for protracted correspondence ensued, innumerable questions were asked, and answers required for the "select committee's" information; which led to an extensive correspondence between Mr. Tranchell and some eminent indigo factors in India, with a view to give every satisfactory information to the select committee, as to the cost of erecting the necessary buildings, from such plan as might be received from Madras.

The committee next wished to ascertain if a less sum than £2000 would not be sufficient, taking it for granted that the government would give the land required—secondly, whether the previous appropriation of a number of shares to Mr. Tranchell in the outset, might not be impolitic; and in lieu thereof, to remunerate his services according to the profits of the concern—thirdly, whether the company might not proceed upon a less scale at first, and have the conveyance of the land to trustees for the subscribers generally; and finally, suggested, in order to secure Mr. Tranchell against caprice on the part of the proprietors, that he should not be liable to removal from the office of superintendent, except by the vote of four-fifths of the company.

To all these suggestions Mr. Tranchell readily assented; for he felt satisfied that the speculation would succeed, and surpass all possible expectation or calculation. But alas! L' homme propose, mais Dieu dispose! Mr. Tranchell died; the principal subscribers, upon whom the formation of the indigo company of Tangalle depended, did not complete its establishment; most probably from the difficulty of finding a competent superintendent; and the subsequent promotion of the governor to the chief command of the Bengal army, put a finishing stroke to the abandonment of a scheme, by which numerous families might at this moment have been in the full enjoyment of independent incomes, obtained with but little comparative trouble, and altogether without risk of capital; because such speculation must have been a lucrative one where the climate is every way congenial to the plant itself, and altogether exempt from the vicissitudes affecting either its growth or manufacture.

It would not be difficult to select 500,000 acres, the property of the crown, which, at a comparatively small expenditure, might be brought into a proper state of cultivation for the reception of indigo seed; for very little would be required to be done beyond clearing the ground of weeds, and burning the grass, and then lightly ploughing and levelling the ground; and whenever manure might be requisite, the fœcula of the leaf affords one of the richest that could be employed: nothing indeed is wanting to ensure success but a moderate capital and perseverance. I brought with me to England full powers for establishing an indigo company in this country, in the year 1827, but Mr. Tranchell's death in 1828, cancelled the power of attorney that I held to act in his behalf.

Ceylon produces two other plants that I am well acquainted with; from which a very valuable blue dye may be obtained by a similar process to that of making indigo. An intelligent Singhalese doctor at Gallepiaddé, near Galle, in the southern province, named Madung Appo, brought me samples of the dye, which were extensively shown to Anglo-Indian merchants connected with the indigo trade in this country, by the late Lieut. J. W. Philips, royal navy, (who at that time commanded the ship Elizabeth,) by whom it was declared to be a very *superior violet-colored indigo.* Here then is a new and extensive field for further speculation and energy in developing the natural capabilities of this incomparable island.

Mr. Fawkener pointed out to me the best mode of selecting seeds of the true indigo (*Indigofera tinctoria var sativa,* L.) from the bastard variety (*Indigofera tinctoria var agrestis,* L.) by the leaf. The first, when held between the thumb and forefinger of each hand, divides upon the least distension transversely; the latter, tried in the same way, breaks with a swallow-tail.

The Egyptian name for indigo is *Nil,* which is also the Singhalese name for it, and one of many proofs of the great affinity between the Egyptian and Pali languages.

Linnæus classifies indigo as of the XVII. class Diadelphia, and order III. Decandria. Of this genus there are twenty five known varieties, but only two are natives of Ceylon.

The best plan for ascertaining the maturity of the indigo plant is by gently shaking it, and if the leaf begins to fall, it is fit for the steeping vat. The plant, which is then about two feet high, is cut with a sickle; the smaller branches are stripped off, and infused in water for about thirty six hours; after which, the water is turned off into a sort of churn, which is worked until the water is covered with a scum-like foam—olive oil is then added in the proportion of one pound to sufficient water to produce seventy five pounds of indigo—the oil causes the scum to separate, and appear like curdled milk; it is then allowed to settle for some time, when the water is drawn off, and the sediment removed into straining bags, and allowed to drain for some time. It is then made into lumps or cakes, and, when dried, forms the indigo of commerce.

There is another method of making indigo, by infusion of the smaller branches in boiling water, after the manner of tea, and employing quick lime as a precipitate; but if it were not for the additional expense of labour, a superior indigo would be obtained by *using the leaf only.*

The expenses of erecting a substantial indigo factory upon a large scale, including leaf godowns, drying yards, and every necessary apparatus for the manufacture, would not exceed £1500 sterling; and, admitting that 2000 acres of land were to be purchased from the government, at *5s.* per acre, the whole outlay would not exceed £2000 sterling.

An indigo maistry may be obtained from Madras for about four pagodas, or thirty two shillings sterling a month; and any number of labourers may be procured at sixpence a day in the maritime provinces. It is only in the interior that labour is higher, because labourers are not to be procured there in sufficient numbers for the plantations now under cultivation; and Hindoo labourers are consequently hired from the continent, for the natives of the maritime provinces have great objection to service in Kandy, or (adopting their own words) "that other country."

Upon the coast of Coromandel, the Ryots, who grow indigo, sow the crop but every third year, permitting the ground to lie fallow during the intermediate period, and feeding sheep on it; or else they cultivate it with dry grains, oil plants, &c. Good and well-manured ground may be sown with indigo every second year; the fœcula of the indigo leaf is a very powerful manure, and requires caution in its employment.

The Singhalese headmen of the Tangalle district in the southern province have long been anxious for the establishment of an indigo plantation and factory there, and would readily take shares in a company established for that purpose; but the government must set the example, if it wish to extend and improve the agriculture of Ceylon, as regards a more extensive culture of rice by the natives, and of cotton, indigo, cocoa, cochineal, pepper, annatto, silk, hemp, and opium by Europeans.

I repeat that it must not be left to the private energy of the present colonists, or cultivation, as far as regards these articles of commerce, will be just in the same state of abeyance twenty years hence, as, with all the great natural capabilities of the island, it is at this moment.

The cultivation of coffee will run away with all the capital that the Europeans in the colony can command, because the foundations for it had been laid long before the present proprietors ventured upon the speculation; and because they imagine that more profit is likely to accrue from the culture of a less quantity of land with coffee; and therefore, other equally important articles of commerce (except sugar, which begins to attract attention) are to be left to chance, or to be altogether neglected, except in such small proportions as may suffice for private instead of national wants.

Land is not in the same insecure and unsettled state in Ceylon, that it is in India, notwithstanding the proximity of the two countries; and, moreover, Ceylon offers that which India does not, a fair field for the adventure of capital, accompanied by permanent settlement; and particularly in the interior, without risking any disastrous effects of climate upon European constitutions.

If Ceylon were better or sufficiently known to the generality of persons, intent upon emigration to new and almost unknown lands, for its great and indigenous resources to be fully and fairly appreciated, speculation would not long remain idle; but the encouragement of hope or of even the slightest prospect of success to any other than *possessors of moderate capital,* would be both criminal and delusive. To officers disposed to become settlers, the government has a variety of means at its command to augment the "advantages" held out by the colonial minister's memorandum of August 15, 1834, and now extended to Ceylon; amongst the rest, by advances of money *out of the annual excess of the local revenue over the expenditure,* upon the security of the produce, to enable them to form plantations of the valuable productions mentioned above.

If Her Majesty's secretary of state for the colonies would, in his wisdom, follow the precedent for encouraging the cultivation of indigo set by the Honorable the East India Company in 1799, or adopt the plans now acted upon for the promotion of the culture of cotton in India by the same Honorable body, many enterprising and intelligent officers and private individuals would eagerly grasp at the opportunity of further developing the resources of Ceylon, and of encreasing its revenue; and, at the same time, their own means of providing for their families and dependents.

But without *moderate capital,* it would mislead an officer to recommend him to avail himself of what are termed "advantages" of emigrating to Ceylon, upon the same terms provided for settling in the Australian colonies, south Australia excepted.

It is evident from the perusal of those documents to which I have given a place in the appendix for general information, that the government has allowed one grand point to escape its observation. An officer accustomed to society and the comforts, and I may add, elegancies of life, resigns them the moment he becomes a settler in a country like Australia. There, all settlers are bent upon the same objects;—a location, fencing, planting, &c., and however happy they may be to greet each other over the *same prog*, they have no one better off than themselves, that may place them within the pale of invidious comparison in the same neighbourhood, or country. But it is different, widely different, in Ceylon; and wretched will be the settler, who may have inconsiderately proceeded to that island upon any such most discouraging terms. The best inducement to officers to become settlers in Ceylon, would be to grant them as much land, at a nominal quit rent of a peppercorn, as they may undertake to bring into cultivation, and advance them money upon the terms I have already suggested.

CHAP. X.

Conflicting descriptions of the Palms of Ceylon—Extraordinary accounts of the process of Sura or toddy drawing—Classification and description of the coco-nut tree—Process of toddy drawing, from personal observation—Sinnet for sailors' hats—Toddy, or palm wine—Varieties and domestic uses of the Cocos nucifera—Arrack—Oil—Vinegar—Jaggery—Native method of planting it, and their superstition about salt—Uses of the fronds—Coco-nut timber—Adhesive properties of the water of the green coco-nut—The Hiromané—Average produce of a coco-nut tree—Uses of the shells—Medicinal oil from the bark—Medicinal properties of the root, leaves, and flowers—Extraordinary notions about the superabundance of the coco-nut palm, and facility of planting it—Coco-nut oil used in the manufacture of soap and candles—Suggestions for extending the culture of the coco-nut palm in the British West Indian and West African colonies.

So many conflicting and erroneous accounts have been given of the palms of Ceylon, in travels, and extracts from the travels of various writers, that if I were not satisfied to the contrary, I might be disposed to think the authors endeavoured to mislead, instead of inform, their readers; and if the former will be governed by *native* statements only, instead of witnessing the processes which they pretend to describe, one cannot expect that the latter, how much soever they may be amused, will be enlightened by accounts at variance with facts.

The subjoined notes* from the works of authors who have obtained general credence for the correctness of their representations, are (as all who have really witnessed the

* "Toddy is the juice running from an incision made in the stem of the leaves; and constitutes a very pleasant beverage when first gathered in."—*Statham's Indian Recollections,* page 29.

"A pot sufficient to hold two quarts is fixed to a shoot where an incision is made in the evening, and is brought down full at sunrise in the morning."—*Cordiner's Ceylon,* vol. i. page 352.

"A small incision being made, there oozes in gentle drops a cool pleasant liquor, called *tarce* or *toddy,* the palm wine of the poets."—*Forbes's Oriental Memoirs,* page 24.

"Toddy is procured by incision. It is only necessary to make a slit in the top of the tree, where the leaves shoot up, with a knife over night, and suspend a chatty, or earthen pot, from the branches so as to receive the juice, which immediately begins to distil, and continues to do so till next morning, when the pot is removed."—*Percival's Ceylon.*

"Between the cabbage-like shoot and the leaves, there spring several buds, from which, on making an incision, there distils a juice differing little from water in color or consistence. This liquor is sold in the bazaars by the natives under the name of toddy."—*Tennant's Indian Recreations,* vol. ii. page 283.

See also Kerr's Voyages, vol. vii. page 476; and Pennant's Hindoostan, vol. i. page 139.

tedious process of preparing the coco-nut tree for the production of toddy will admit) absolute illusions.

Let it be supposed, for instance, that a planter in the West Indies, (where toddy drawing was, some few years ago, and probably continues to be, entirely unknown,) being desirous of testing these plans, adopted either one or all of them; and let his disappointment be imagined, when, anxiously anticipating the assured morning's draught of the "Palm wine of the poets," he found it altogether Eutopian! and if either of these incisive measures had been resorted to, and the pot hung up at the times these accounts were written, the authors would have waited a long time for their toddy; for it would not, even yet, after an interval of so many years, have begun to distil.

I will, therefore, briefly describe the various natural properties and domestic usefulness of this splendid palm, from my own personal observations.

The Coco-nut palm (*Cocos nucifera*, L., and *Polgaha* of the Singhalese, Class XXI. *Monœcia*, Order VI. *Hexandria*, Natural Order *Palmæ*), delights in a sandy soil, and the nearer to the margin of the sea, the quicker its growth, and the more abundant its produce. It requires little or no care, beyond being well fenced from the inroads of cattle, for, fanned by the winds of the Indian ocean, it gains fecundity by exposure: and although its general height is from sixty to eighty feet, it is not uncommon for it to exceed a hundred. Its diameter, at the base, is from two to three feet; and the root, which is composed of strong flexible fibres, about the thickness of a small rattan cane (*Calamus Rotang*, L.), spreads in a circle; and of these, some run to a great depth, and others creep along the surface of the soil.

One may imagine a beautiful and verdant circle, formed of feathery fronds, from fourteen to sixteen feet in length, radiating from a common centre at the top of a tapering stem eighty feet in height, and that will afford some idea of the magnificence of the coco-nut palm.

The fronds are supported at the base by diagonal and horizontal layers of strong elastic fibres, capable of sustaining great weight, and so closely united as to form, when gently stretched, an excellent substitute for a hair sieve for straining liquids. This fibrous support lies in *laminæ* between the branches, which it envelopes, as well as the incipient ones, even to their rudiments, or what is commonly called the *cabbage*, and seems providentially adapted for the security of the passing traveller from the constant danger that would otherwise attend him, whilst traversing the coco-nut topes, from the sudden falling of decayed branches, which its very firm adhesion to the trunk prevents; but it is not made into gunny bags, (*Gungesaaken* of the Dutch,) as some authors have stated, and is merely used for straining toddy and other liquids, and for kindling fires.

During the many years that I resided in Ceylon, I never heard of but one fatal accident from the falling of a coco-nut; a remarkable circumstance, when one considers the many thousands of people constantly passing and repassing through the topes.*

Trees, intended for toddy drawing, are prevented from producing fruit by the following process. The toddy drawer first ties the spathe in three places, with strips of the tough white *pinnæ*† of the young fronds; which latter shoot perpendicularly at first, and are then of a beautiful white, but soon change to a straw color; these are concave towards the heart of the crest, and when they are successively forced from their position by new fronds, they gradually expand their pinnated leaves, and ultimately become horizontal. The old fronds have a strong mid-rib, with the footstalks nearest the tree proportionally thick; these embrace the stem, and as they gradually fall off, after hanging for weeks together by their fibrous support, or are pulled down for fuel, torches,‡ and fences, they leave successive and very visible scars.

The purpose of tying the spathe is to prevent its expansion; it is then cut transversely, to the extent of about two inches from the point, and beaten with an ebony or iron-wood batoon, by the toddy drawer, for five or six mornings and evenings successively. The next operation is to remove a portion of the footstalk of the spathe, so as to admit of its depression, for the juice to flow freely, and it is kept in that position by attaching it to an inferior branch; in the course of five or six days, the toddy drawer suspends a calabash, or earthen pot, called a *chatty*, from the decapitated spathe, so as to receive the juice as it exudes from the flower, and this he repeats every morning and evening, taking off a slice of the flower as occasion requires. whilst any part of it remains.

This delicious liquid, combining a pleasant but slight degree of sweetness with a still less degree of acidity, when fresh, and of peculiar flavor, is called by us toddy;

* An Indian name for groves. In Bengal, Mango plantations are called *topes*, as well as those of the coco-nut tree; but where groves of palms are reserved for toddy drawing, they are called *toddy topes*.

† These are in general request by sailors in India, for making hats. Jack first reduces the pinnæ into very narrow strips, then plats them into what he calls *sinnet*, and, with a needle and thread, soon forms a good but heavy substitute for a chip hat; for it wears remarkably well, and, being cooler than one of glazed leather, is better for inter-tropical service. Of the mid-rib (*costa*) the natives make neat whisks and bird cages.

‡ *Chulos*, and, (Anglicé,) *Chules*. These the natives make, by laying down the pinnæ horizontally from the footstalk towards the point; but they leave one or two, at certain distances, in their natural position, for the purpose of tying the others round the mid-rib, or rather, the longitudinal section of it, for each frond makes two chules.

Ra, by the Singhalese; and *Suri* or *Sura,** (which means palm wine,) by the Hindoos and Hindo-Portuguese; and, being esteemed a gentle aperient, it is very often resorted to at the earliest peep of dawn, by the *bon-vivant,* by way of removing the unpleasant effects of more potent libations over night.

There are five varieties of this palm at Ceylon, and the grounds adjoining the Buddha temples generally contain the best specimens of the indigenous species. The priests readily afford strangers every information, but only upon inquiry, for their diffidence, which arises from the dread of being considered obtrusive, does not proceed from disinclination to gratify the curiosity of the European visitor; and without *asking* for information when required, one may remain all one's life-time in Ceylon and know no more of the varieties of the coco-nut palm than casual observation might suggest, from the mere circumstance of the difference in point of color of the nuts, from the *Koroomba,* or water coco-nut, to that which approaches, or has attained maturity.

The peculiar shape and bright orange color of the *King coco-nut* cannot fail to attract observation, but it is scarcely ever to be seen in the bazaars. It is occasionally presented, by the priests, or headmen, by way of compliment, to Europeans.

The next in beauty is of an orange color, but not of the beautiful pear shape of the king coco-nut. The third is of a pale yellow, rather cordiform, and the fleshy substance of its husk, which is between the epidermis and the nut, is edible in its green state. The fourth is the common coco-nut, which is abundantly imported into this country from the West Indies; and the fifth is a sort of Maldive,† or dwarf coco-nut, about the size of a duck's egg; this is esteemed as a rariety.

I have remarked the coco-nut palm, in its various stages, in many countries; namely, the Azores, West Indies, Mauritius, Coast of Coromandel, Bengal, Pinang, Malacca, Moluccas, Banda Islands, Celebes, and Timor; but I never saw it attain the height that it does in Ceylon.

The finest arrack in the world is distilled by the Singhalese from the fermenting toddy, (which, owing to the rapidity of that process, becomes an intoxicating beverage in the course of a few hours,) and not from sweet toddy, as some travellers have erroneously

* "The word *Sura* in Sanscrit signifies both wine and true wealth; hence in the first *C'hand* of the *Rámáyan* of *Válmic,* it is expressly said that the *Devatás* having received the *Surá,* acquired the title of *Suras,* and the *Daityas* that of *Asura,* from not having received it. The *Véda* is represented as that wine and true wealth; and the *Devatás* as enjoying it, in a superior degree, being termed *Suras,* the prince, or supreme leader of the *Suras,* became, in the Grecian deity Bacchus, (by a confined translation of the word,) the god of wine and drunkards."—*Asiatic Researches,* vol. viii. page 50.

† So called, because the Maldivian boats which visit the island bring a few extremely small nuts as curiosities.

asserted. One hundred gallons produce, by the simple chymical process of the Singhalese, twenty five of arrack,* (*Polwakéré,*) which, when very new, is injurious to the constitution, but gradually acquires wholesomeness by age. Toddy is also used by bread bakers for the purposes of yeast.

Pine apples, steeped in arrack, impart a delicious flavor, and reduce its strength to that of a liqueur, unrivalled for making nectarial punch, or *Puntjee* of the Hindoos, meaning five :—thus our compound of sugar, limejuice, spirit, water, and lemon-peel, derives its English name from a Hindoo numeral.

Lamp oil is made from the kernel of the ripe coco-nut, after it has been exposed to the sun on mats until it has become rancid and discolored, (in which state the natives call it *Kopperah,*) by means of a simple press turned by bullocks; and oil for culinary purposes, by boiling the fresh pulp, and skimming it as it rises. The former is now made into candles and soap, and the oil-cake, or *Poonac,* is used for feeding cattle and poultry.

Vinegar is made by putting toddy, drawn in dry weather, into jars, and keeping them closely covered, but exposed to the sun, for a month; the toddy is then strained, and replaced in the same jars, with a little bird pepper (*Capsicum frutescens,* L.), a small piece of the red Ghorkah (*Cambogia gutta*), and of Moringa pod (*Hyperanthera moringa*), the jars are then laid in the earth for a month or five weeks, and thus a very excellent vinegar is produced.

Jaggery, a sort of sugar, is made by suspending a clean and dry calabash, or chatty, instead of one in common use for toddy drawing, and containing some chips of the bark of the *Shorea robusta,* (*Halghas* of the Singhalese,) which will cause the toddy to become sweet. Eight gallons of it boiled over a slow fire, yield two gallons of syrup, called in Singhalese *Penni;* which, being again boiled, produces a coarse brown sugar, called *Jaggery;* this is formed into cakes in bottoms of coco-nut shells, by way of moulds; which, having been enveloped in pieces of dried plantain leaf, are hardened, and preserved from humidity by being suspended where smoke has free access to them.

A coco-nut tree, planted near the sea, generally blossoms in the fourth or fifth year; but in elevated situations of the interior, six or seven years may be considered the average period; and from that time to upwards of sixty years, this most prolific palm will continue to produce fruit in abundance, unless the tree be devoted entirely to the toddy-drawer, in which case it produces no fruit.

The maturity of coco-nuts, reserved for planting, is indicated by the brown color of the husk; they are then plucked, and, having been laid aside for a few days, are

* Batavian arrack is distilled from rice.

ranged in rows, and partly covered with earth; or, as in many parts of the country, suspended from the branches of trees until vegetation has commenced. In about three months, more or less, the plant will have appeared, and in less than five months from that time, will have attained the height of sixteen or eighteen inches, and have thrown out three or four foliacious fronds. The best time for transplanting is during the rainy season, when the plants receive that abundant nourishment which their nature requires.

The Singhalese are so extremely superstitious, that they invariably throw a little salt into the holes, before they place the coco-nut plants in them; and they observe great regularity in forming their topes, by making holes for the plants in parallel lines, from twenty to twenty four feet apart, about three feet deep, of the same diameter at the top, and in the shape of inverted cones, for the purpose of collecting the necessary moisture. If the salt were omitted, they would not expect the plant to flourish.

The green fronds split, and their pinnated leaves interwoven, make covers for plants, baskets, and thatch;* and, when burnt, produce a superior alkali. The young *pinnæ*, which are white and tough, make beautiful mats, baskets, and boxes for ladies' work.

The stem is at first of a very spongy nature, and full of tough perpendicular and ligneous fibres; and, until it is about twenty years old, is applicable only to the purposes of gutters, water pipes, and fences; but when it becomes old, it is fit for rafters, shingles, ornamental cabinet work, rice pounders, walking sticks, and for building country vessels, called *Dhonies.*†

The water of the green coco-nut is a delicious drink, if it be plucked before sunrise; it is also used by house-plasterers, for its adhesive quality, in mixing their white and colored washes, and, conjointly with Jaggery and shell-lime, for stucco.

The pulp of the young coco-nut is an admirable vegetable *blancmange;* and the kernel of the seed coco-nut, after vegetation has commenced, is among the delicacies of a Singhalese dessert. It is spongy, but pleasant to the taste, and greatly esteemed by the natives. The expressed juice of the pulp of the ripe nut is properly the milk, and is obtained by first rasping it with an instrument called *Hiromané*,‡ then soaking it in

* Called by the natives, *Cajan*.

† From 80 to 200 tons burthen.

‡ The *Hiromané* is the best kind of grater that can be employed to reduce the kernel for culinary purposes, because it obviates the necessity of breaking the nut-shell in pieces, or the previous removal of the kernel from it, which, in its ripe state, is no very easy matter. It consists of a circle of notched iron fastened to the end of a stout piece of wood, cut in a peculiar shape, which immemorial custom has induced the Singhalese to consider the most convenient for this domestic purpose; and considered by Europeans to resemble a *boot-jack*, but why, I have yet to learn.

water and pressing it through a cloth, when it forms an ingredient in all good curries. The cabbage is delicious, whether fricaseed, or pickled, or in its raw state, when it is as sweet and crisp as the Catappa almond (*Terminalia Catappa*, L.).

A bunch of coco-nuts seldom exceeds fifteen or twenty good ones; and from trees growing in sandy situations, the fruit is gathered four or five times a year. The external husk, after having been soaked in water for a certain period, is beaten out into a fibre called *Koir* or *Koya*, of which, yarn, ropes, cables, brooms, plasterers' brushes, bed and sofa mattresses, and bags, are manufactured. Coco-nut shells* are made into cups, basons, lamps, sportsmen's liquor flasks, ladles, skimmers, spoons, lampblack, and charcoal; which latter, when pulverized, forms an excellent dentifrice.

A powerful oil is extracted from the bark of the coco-nut tree, which is employed as a liniment in cutaneous diseases, and considered by the Singhalese doctors eminently efficacious, provided that, in such cases, a free use of the green coco-nut, as the principal article of diet, be strictly adhered to; and an ointment is prepared from the kernel, which is a certain cure for the ring-worm in children.

The root is considered by the native doctors so efficacious in intermittent and remittent fevers, that it is almost invariably employed by them. Small pieces of it are boiled with dried ginger and jaggery, and the decocture is given to the patient at regular intervals. The same decocture, when used as a gargle, is mixed with the oil of the nut, freshly made, and generally affords considerable relief to the patient, in cases where pustules have formed in the mouth or glands of the throat.

In hemorrhoids, the expressed juice of the leaves, mixed with fresh oil of the nut, and taken internally, is considered a sovereign remedy; and in ophthalmic complaints, the external application of the expressed juice of the nut, mixed with new milk from the cow or goat, mitigates, if it do not entirely remove, inflammation.

The juice of the flower is of so astringent a nature, that it has the same effect as a solution of alum upon the inside of the mouth; this, mixed with new milk, and taken in small quantities, not exceeding a wine-glass full, but at regular periods, affords almost immediate temporary relief, and, if persevered in, effectual cure, in that most debilitating disease in tropical climates, *Lues Gonorrhœa*.

The shade of the coco-nut tree is wholesome; for wherever there are coco-nut topes, very little underwood is found.

An odd notion has long prevailed, that if all the coco-nut trees in Ceylon were cut down, the natives would be obliged to cultivate rice more extensively, and that it

* See page 103, for the Singhalese musical instrument, the *Vinah*.

would operate as a general blessing!! To me it appears a subject of regret, that the many virtues of this invaluable palm, apparently bestowed by the hands of a beneficent Providence, for the use and happiness of the natives of tropical climes, are not more universally known and encouraged throughout the British West India Islands. Those whose duties may have called them, as in my own case, to both countries, cannot have failed to remark the apparently degenerated state of the coco-nut tree of the West Indies, in comparison with that of the East.*

The facility of planting the coco-nut palm,—the small portion of care requisite for its growth and preservation,—the multiplied benefits which, in its maturity, it bestows on man,—all tend to render it an object of peculiar regard to those who are the guardians, deputed by the Giver of all good, of the labourer of the tropics.

The Singhalese are very remarkable for their luxuriant and beautiful hair, and attribute it to the use of coco-nut oil, which, in a perfumed state, is also employed by Europeans; but it is only by habitual use that its virtues can be sufficiently ascertained to insure its general adoption as a promoter and preserver of the hair, unless its natural properties are destroyed by adulteration; and as steam and other English oil-mills are now used, and the demand for coco-nut oil has greatly increased, since its employment in the manufacture of candles and soap, it may be anticipated, that from the recent improvement of the quality of the coco-nut oil for table use, by its being rendered free from smoke, its importation will continue in an increasing ratio; and consequently, too much attention and encouragement cannot be given to a more extensive cultivation of this invaluable palm, not only at Ceylon, but throughout our West Indian and West African colonies.

Independently of the general consumption of the produce of the coco-nut palm by the native inhabitants, and its extensive employment in the domestic economy of Europeans, it finds a ready market for exportation; and the manufacture of koir yarn, ropes and cables, oil, vinegar, arrack, jaggery, and cajans for thatching bungalows and native houses, affords employment to a considerable portion of the Singhalese and Malabar population.

* If the reader have not previously read "A Treatise upon the Coco-nut Palm, by a Fellow of the Linnæan and Horticultural Societies," published in the year 1830, and a second edition of it, in my own name, in 1836, it will afford him some amusement to compare the former with the second volume of "Wanderings in New South Wales, Batavia, Pedir Coast, Singapore, and China, by George Bennett, Esq., F. L. S., and fellow of the Royal College of Surgeons," (published by Mr. Bentley in 1834,) pages 297 to 335 inclusively. AUTHOR.

CHAP. XI.

The Areka Palm and its Linnæan classification—Flower and fruit used for ornamenting temporary buildings for festivals—Areka nut anti-scorbutic—Spathe, and its uses—Terra Japonica—Properties of the areka nut as a dye—Suggestions for condensing the dye—Heat generated by the nuts—Barter through the agency of Buddhist priests—Wood excellent for bows—Palmyra (Borassus flabelliformis, L.) common in the Northern and Eastern Provinces—Buddhist priests and their fans—Native books—Palm oil—Kellingo—Palmyra toddy and Jaggery—Timber and its principal uses—Sugar palm (Caryota urens, L.)—Kettule fishing rods—Sago—Elephant bows, and snares or nooses—Kettule toddy and Jaggery—Hookahs—Calabashes—Sugar palm chiefly cultivated in the Southern Province—Talipat tree (Corypha umbraculifera, L., and Licuala spinosa of Thunberg)—Its classification—Talipat leaf—Its uses—Conflicting accounts of the report caused by the bursting of the spathe of the talipat tree—Mabolé—Talipat sago—Talipat palm at Colombo—Privileges of the priests of Buddha—M. de la Loubère's notice of the use of the talipat fan by the priests of Siam—Talipat plants sent to England by the author—Tavelam tents—Palms from Mauritius introduced into Ceylon—Phœnix sylvestris, L.—Dwarf palm.

In a commercial point of view, the Areka palm (*Areca Catechu*, L., Class *Monœcia*, Order *Monadelphia*, and Natural Order *Palmæ; Puak-gaha* of the Singhalese, *Faufel* of Bauhine, and *Pinanga* of Rumphius) is next in value to the coco-nut tree.

The flower, which, like that of the coco-nut palm, is white, is used, conjointly with its beautiful drupes, and the flower and fruit of the coco-nut tree, and the wild flowers and moss (*Lycopodium Zeylanicum*) with which the cinnamon gardens abound, in ornamenting temporary buildings for balls and other festivities.

This palm so greatly resembles the cabbage palm (*Areca oleracea*, L.) of the West Indies, that, upon a cursory view, it is scarcely to be distinguished from the latter, except by its drupes. The heart of the crest of the *Areca Catechu* is also edible, but it is both inferior to that of the cabbage and coco-nut palms.

The drupes are about the size of a hen's egg,* with a smooth epidermis of a bright gold or orange color, occasionally speckled with brown; these grow in clusters, like coco-nuts in miniature, but at the very base of the verdant crest, instead of between the fronds, as in the coco-nut palm. The average annual produce is from 280 to 300 nuts.

The nut forms a principal ingredient in the betel masticatory, so general throughout India and the Eastern Archipelago, where it is called *Paän* or *Pawn*, and is the first thing offered by way of compliment by natives of all classes. It is considered an anti-scorbutic for the teeth and gums, and to give the breath an aromatic odour; but its

* Described in the *Hortus Botanicus Americanus* as of the size of a *coco-nut!!*

habitual use imparts an appearance of bleeding at the mouth, which is particularly disgusting in women. The pulverized charcoal of the nut forms an excellent dentifrice.

The fronds are more bushy in foliage than those of the coco-nut tree, and about half their length; they have also a strong mid-rib, but the leaflets are *folded back*, and being more irregular in shape, and thicker than those of the coco-nut palm, cannot be interwoven into *Cajans*.

The base of the crest, to the height of three feet, is enveloped in a sort of spathe, which the Singhalese call *Puak-pata;* this being extremely tough and elastic, is of great utility to the natives for domestic purposes, particularly for carrying milk and oil, and their curry and rice, when travelling; but where the sugar palm (*Caryota urens*, L.) abounds, it is principally in request for the purpose of holding the *Kettule Penni*, or sweet syrup, and will retain its original elasticity for many years.

I have heard it asserted, that the extract of the areka nut is the *Terra Japonica* of commerce, and if a few of the nuts are boiled in water with a little chunam, the decoction has both the taste and odour of that drug; but if this be the case, its present name is greatly misapplied.

The properties of the areka nut, as a dye, are well known in Scotland; it is of a peculiar red, and cannot be mistaken by any one accustomed to the color. I should conceive it practicable to condense the dye, so as to save a great deal in freight, instead of importing the nuts; and strong objections to their exportation to any great distance arises from the excessive heat which is generated by their stowage in bulk; this is perceptible even whilst lying in heaps for a few days before they are shipped.

The Ceylon areka tree is famous for the superior quality of its nut, which was always a great article of barter between the Kandyan inhabitants of Saffregam, and Barberyn, viâ Kaltura, long before our occupation of the interior. This traffic was chiefly carried on through the agency and connivance of the Buddhist priests, who allowed depôts of nuts to be formed at the various *Panselas** on each side of the Kalu-Ganga, from whence they were conveyed away, in *Pardie*† boats, to the sea coast.

The tree itself is beautiful, and delights in a sandy soil. The stem slender, and, with occasional exceptions, straight as an arrow to the height of seventy or eighty feet. Its circumference varies little throughout its length, seldom exceeding two feet at the base, from which to the crest, the annular marks of the fallen petioles are distinct. When very old, the wood is as tough as whalebone, and the best in the world for bows and pingos.—There is a wild species of this palm (*Areca sylvestris*), which the Singhalese call *Lenatesi gaha*.

* Temporary residences for priests; derived from the Pali words *Pan*, leaf, and *sala*, shed.

† Flat-bottomed boats, iron fastened, and with sliding roofs, thatched with *Cajans*.

The third palm, in point of value for its domestic properties, is the fan palm, or palmyra (*Borassus flabelliformis*, L.), class XXII. Diœcia, and order VI. Hexandria. The Singhalese call it *Talgaha*. Linnæus describes the male tree by the Malabar name of *Ampana*, and the female tree by that of *Carim-pana*.

Male flower, *calyx;* universal *spathe*, compound; *spadix* amentaceous, imbricated; *corol* three-parted; *petals* egg'd, concave; *stamens*, filaments six, thickish, anthers thicker, striated.—Female flower, *calyx; spathe* and *spadix* as in the male; *corol* three-parted; *petals* roundish, small, permanent; *pistil*, germ roundish, styles three, small, stigmas simple; *pericarp*, drupe roundish, obtuse, rigid, one-cell'd; *seeds* three, rather egg'd, compressed, distinct, filamentous.

Like all the other palms, the fronds of the palmyra grow on the top of the tree only; but as these are cut down, or fall off, they leave their *vestigia* much more distinct than either of the other palms, and the bark is consequently so much rougher, that the tree may be ascended with less difficulty, by inexpert climbers, than either the coco-nut, areka, or sugar palms.

The spathe resembles that of the *Areca Catechu* in toughness and elasticity, and is used by the natives for similar purposes.

This tree is more common in the northern and eastern provinces, than in any other part of the island; and those that I have seen, seldom exceeded thirty or forty feet in height. The fronds are fan-leaved, armed with spines, radiating from a common centre, and the *stipes* sawed at the edges. The fan-part is about four feet in diameter; the spines are cut off, and the middle is formed into fans, or *Punkahs;* these are lackered for sale, or used plain, as may suit the taste of the purchaser; but one never sees a Buddhist priest without one of the smaller sort, or a fan of some kind or other; of which, some are heart-shaped, others circular, with handles of carved ivory.

I have heard many arguments as to the fan being an emblem of authority;* and some pretend that the degrees of the Buddhist priesthood may be distinguished by their fans; but I do not state this as an ascertained fact, although I have myself oberved, that the handsomest *Punkahs* are carried by the higher orders of the priesthood.†

Palmyra leaves are subdivided longitudinally into strips for native books and letters, and bear the general name of *Olas*. These are written upon with an iron style, and

* St. Matthew particularly alludes to the fan (or winnow) in his 3rd chapter, verse 12.

† *Maha Nayeka Oonansé* signifies a high priest, and *Oonansé* a priest.—*Gooroonansé* a teacher, and *Tirinansé* a reader.

lampblack is then rubbed over the writing, which makes the characters more legible; this, from the smoothness of the surface, is easily wiped off, leaving the part that is not impressed by the style perfectly clean.

The fruit, which is a large three-seeded drupe, grows in bunches, and is much esteemed. Palm oil is made of the pulp, after having been exposed to the sun and become rancid. The spring leaf, or *Kellingo,* is a most excellent vegetable, when boiled or fricasseed; this the natives manufacture into a nutritious meal, or flour, of delicious flavour, by cutting it off close, after the seed nuts have been sown a few months, then drying it in the sun, and afterwards pounding it in a rice mortar. The Dutch formerly considered palmyra flour so very valuable as a convalescent diet, as well as for presents to their friends, that they often exported it to the Cape of Good Hope and Holland:—in both places it was much esteemed, and used for thickening, and imparting its peculiar flavor, to soups and made dishes.

Palmyra toddy is drawn from the flower, and good *Jaggery* is made from it, by a similar process to that described in the preceding pages.

On the outside and at the base of the fronds, just where they rise from the stem, there is a soft cotton-like substance, of a light brown color, which is collected and employed by the native doctors for staunching blood, or hemorrhage.

The timber, being dark and beautifully striated, is very much esteemed for cabinet work; and by builders, for rafters, &c. It is extremely durable, becoming harder and tougher with age.

The next of the indigenous palms, in point of domestic utility, is the sugar palm (*Caryota urens,* L.), or *Kettule-Gaha* of the Singhalese, of class XXI. Monœcia, and order VIII. Polyandria.

Male flower *calyx;* universal *spathe,* compound; *spadix* branchy; *corol* three-parted; *petals* lanced, concave; *stamens,* filaments many, rather longer than the corol; *anthers* linear.—Female flower upon the same *spadix* with the male ones; *calyx* common with the males; *corol* three-parted; *petals* pointed, very small; *pistil,* germ roundish, *style* pointed, *stigma* simple; *pericarp,* a berry, roundish, one-cell'd; *seeds* two, large, oblong, roundish on one side, flat on the other.

The berries are about two and a half or three inches in circumference, and are thickly studded upon dependent stems, from four to five feet in length, and about three feet in circumference, like a mass of closely knotted ropes, diverging from a common centre; these, when ripe, are of a brilliant red color, from which the *trivial* name of this palm is derived.

The tree is very straight in growth, and without fronds except at the top, where they form a dark green crest, but are different to those of the other indigenous palms, being *twice-feather-leaved;* and the leaflets are of triangular shape. The transverse divisions of the fronds are much esteemed by the native fishers, for angling rods.

The *Kettule* seldom exceeds forty feet in height. The petioles leave their annular *vestigia* upon the bark, like those of the coco-nut and areka palms. The pith produces a nutritious sago; but, according to my humble judgement, it is very inferior to the brown sago of the Moluccas, or the white sort of China. The wood, when very old, is tough and heavy, and is made into rice pounders, bows,* and pingos for carrying burthens. The outer cuticle is so very strong and elastic that the natives make it into nooses and ropes for securing elephants.

The toddy, which is also drawn from the flower, is so very luscious, that it is only drunk when that from the coco-nut tree cannot be readily procured. Eight gallons of this liquid, boiled over a slow fire, will produce four gallons of a very thick syrup, called *Kettule Penni;* to this is also added small pieces of the bark of the *Halgas* (*Shorea robusta*), and, being again boiled, double the quantity of *Jaggery,* and of a superior quality to that from the coco-nut palm, is the product.

The Kandyan *Jaggery* is made entirely from this syrup, and will keep good for several years. Although the common sort is of the color of the coarsest Muscovado sugar, a finer sort, of very superior quality, and the best substitute that can be obtained for Chinese sugar-candy, which it greatly resembles, is made for headmen. *Jaggery* is a principal ingredient in the *Chillum* used throughout India by *Hookah, Gur-Gurrée,* and *Habble-bubble* smokers.

Clean chatties, or calabashes, are indispensable for collecting *sweet* toddy, which would otherwise be affected by the acidity inseparable from using the same vessel twice, without being well washed and dried. The Ceylon calabash is a gourd (*Cucurbita Lagenaria,* L.); that of the West Indies is the fruit of the calabash tree (*Crescentia Cujete,* L.), which is not produced in Ceylon.

The *Jaggery,* or sugar makers, are called *Hakooroos,* and toddy drawers, *Chandoos;* but both are included in the subdivisions of the same caste, (*Shudra Wansé,*) the second in rank of the principal Singhalese castes.

Each cake of *Jaggery* is separately enveloped in a piece of the dried leaf of the plantain (*Musa sapientum,* L.), or banana (*Musa Paradisiaca,* L.), and then suspended where smoke has free access to it, until required for the market or other purposes.

* The elephant ows used by the natives of the Mahagampattoo, in the southern province, are made of this wood, and tempered in the smoke of wetted rice straw, thrown upon a fire made of jungle leaves.

The shape and size of a cake of common *Jaggery* is that of the bun of our English pastry cooks. The *Kettule* tree is more extensively cultivated in Saffragam, in the southern province, than in any other.

The next in value, but the most magnificent of Ceylon palms in appearance, is the talipat, or umbrella-bearing palm (*Corypha umbraculifera*, L.); the *Licuala spinosa* of Thunberg, and *Talagaha* of the Singhalese. Its classification has for many years been in a most undecided state.

Thunberg describes the flower as follows,—*Calyx; perianth* one-leaved, three-parted, hairy within; *corol* three-parted almost to the base, the divisions egg'd, acute, concave; *nectary* garland form, twice as short as the corol; *stamen*, filaments six, inserted into the nectaries, erect, very short; *anthers* oblong, twin; *pistil*, germ above, convex, furrowed, three-parted, smooth; *style* one, simple; *stigmas* two.

The talipat leaf is the largest known; it is circular, feather handled, folded, and intercepted with a thread. The natives subdivide it into eight parts, and these are sewed at the side with the natural thread, and ornamented with talc and various colors for the use of headmen. Its circumference is from thirty to forty feet; and it is so thoroughly impervious to the sun and impenetrable by the heaviest rains, that its value to the native traveller may be easily imagined. The most valuable of the Singhalese books are formed of strips of the leaf; these are engraved with an iron style, and some now extant, although written many centuries back, have all their original freshness of appearance. Tents, of all forms and sizes, are also made of the leaf, supported by bamboo poles, than which, nothing can be lighter for carriage, or better for the purpose of temporary shelter.

One of the specimens of the talipat leaf that I brought with me from Ceylon, which measures thirty six feet in circumference, may be seen in the museum of King's College, with my name attached to it; but *how* it got there, I have yet to learn. It is, however, most satisfactory to know that it is so well disposed of. The fate of the other is still a mystery; for although they were borrowed to be shown at certain scientific institutions, neither of them have found their way back to the proper owner for the last fourteen years.

There have been many conflicting statements published of this palm; and although I never was within view of a talipat tree at the moment of its spadix bursting the spathe, it has been stated in one of the "Annuals" that I had witnessed it several times. This perhaps was not the first, nor has been the last, of the same author's *mistakes;* but I am not at all disposed, because I was not present, to dispute the native accounts of the loud report, with which the bursting of the talipat's compound spathe, is accompanied, until it be refuted by some individual of unimpeachable veracity, who may have been *near the tree* at the time of its taking place; feeling satisfied, notwithstanding the opinions as to its gradual expansion, that, in calm weather, it may be heard at a considerable distance; for I was positively assured by several respectable Dutch inhabitants at Grand Pass, as well as by two intelligent Malays, who had resided for a considerable time at Matelé, now part of the Central Province, where the *Talagaha* abounds, that the bursting of the spathe is attended with a loud report.

The natives entertain a similar belief to that commonly entertained of the American aloe, that the talipat lives a century before it blossoms; but it is too well known, that the growth of all the palm family is extremely rapid, and moreover that the heart of the talipat stem consists of a spongy fibre, for this part of its description to be credited.

In 1822, a talipat palm blossomed at Mabolé, about six miles to the northward of Colombo; and for nearly three months, viz. from the time of the spadix bursting its spathe to the flower attaining its full height, (nearly thirty feet,) and for a further space of four months before it seeded, the road was occasionally thronged with the curious, and among them the "evening beauties" of the Pettah, on their way to view this wonder of the vegetable world, ere its floral magnificence departed.

Sago is prepared from the granulated pith of the talipat palm, which some consider equal to the true sago of the Moluccas; but if I may judge from the specimen that I brought with me to this country, it is even inferior to that of the *Caryota urens*, or *Cycas circinalis.*

There are very few objects in the vegetable kingdom more beautiful or remarkable than this palm, or more useful to the countries where it is indigenous. There is a beautiful specimen of it in the compound of the Cutchery at Colombo, where the casual visitor, who may not have time or opportunity for seeing it in the interior, may gratify a very commendable curiosity.

The Buddhist priests had the same privilege as Royalty, in the reign of the late King, as to the talipat fan being borne over them with the broad end foremost; and M. de la Loubère, in his account of Siam, in alluding to the priests of Buddha, particularly mentions the talipat fan, "Pour se garantir du soleil, ils ont le talapat qui est leur parasol en forme d' ecran."

In 1822 and 1825, I sent several talipat plants to the late Earl of Tankerville, Lord Bagot, and the Horticultural Society of London, from Ceylon; and, in 1839, I presented the only perfect talipat seed that I had left, to Mr. James Carter, the eminent seedsman of High Holborn.

Be the quantity of rain what it may, not a particle of moisture is imbibed by the talipat leaf; and, exclusively of the uses made of it by all classes of the natives, as a defence from sun and rain, the Tavelam* people employ it for tents to cover their bags of salt on their journies from the coast to the interior. A Tavelam *bivouac* is by no means an uninteresting sight to an European. The bags of salt are piled together, and the pointed ends of the segments of the talipat leaf are laid on the uppermost bag, so as to radiate from the centre, by means of a heavy weight, which keeps them in that position; and, by means of *koir* or jungle lines and pegs, the whole are kept in a circular shape, like a bell tent, and afford a sufficient covered space around the salt bags, by way of verandah, for the traders and drovers to cook their victuals and take repose.

During my stay at Reduit, the Governor's country house at Mauritius, in 1821, I availed myself of His Excellency's (the late lamented Sir Robert Townshend Farquhar, Bart., K. S. L.) kind permission to select whatever plants I pleased, from the Government garden; and, amongst very many others, I took two of the date palm (*Phœnix dactylifera*, L.), and two of the *Cycas circinalis*, L., to Ceylon; both the former died, but one of the latter, which I planted at Bagatelle, near Colombo, was a very fine tree when I left the island, and the other was transferred, by the late Honorable the Chief Justice, Sir Hardinge Giffard, to whom I had given it, to the Royal Botanic Garden at Paradenia, near Kandy, where it flourished as well as in its natural soil.

Although Ceylon does not produce the date palm, there is no reason why it should not, for two wild varieties of that palm (*Phœnix sylvestris*), called by the Singhalese *Indi* and *Mahindi*, are plentiful enough, and well adapted for fences, owing to their extremely strong and sharp spines. The drupe, which is rather more oblong, but not larger than a common Bullace plum (*Prunus insititia*, L.), and of a purplish black, is insipidly sweet.

There is also an indigenous species of dwarf palm, or palmetto (*Chamerops*, L.), Class *Polygamia*, Order *Diœcia*, Natural Order *Palmæ*, of which, small baskets (*Hembili*) are made, the only purpose to which its leaf is applied.

* See page 295.

W. C. Edwards foulp

A Singhalese Gentleman in his Triacle.
From a Native Drawing.

CHAP. XII.

Digression—The Singhalese—Extraordinary effeminacy of the men in habits and dress—Singhalese women—Betel or Pawn—Kissing—Female dress—Inferiority of Singhalese to Malabar women—Dress of headmen—Mr. John Brexius de Zielfa—Extraordinary decision respecting his assumption of shoes and stockings—Predictions fulfilled—King William IV.—Lord Viscount Goderich—Sir R. W. Horton—Petty tyranny—Singhalese theatricals—Amphitheatre—Tragedy—Mode of illuminating the amphitheatre—Coco-nut lamps—Native music—Actors' dresses—Native musical instruments of percussion—Wind instruments—Vinah the only stringed instrument.

By way of change to the reader, I beg leave to digress a little from the vegetable productions of Ceylon, instead of postponing an account of the inhabitants, as I had originally intended, upon the principle that the last of the Almighty's creation was man.

The higher castes of the Singhalese are, generally speaking, a fine handsome race; but the men are as notorious for the effeminacy of their appearance and habits, as the women for their docility, industry, and devotion to their domestic duties. The men allow their hair to grow to its full length, and support it with tortoise-shell combs of an extravagantly large size; this, together with their very prominent breasts and effeminate costume, but more particularly when returning from bathing, at which time they wear their hair loose upon a handkerchief, spread over the shoulders and back, and tied upon the forehead, gives them such a feminine appearance, that even at a moderate distance, strangers very often mistake them for women; and their light white jackets, and cloths (*Sarongs*) wrapped round the waist and descending to the ankles like a petticoat, heighten the deception. The painted cloth worn by modeliars and others of rank among the Singhalese, is called *Soman.*

The women are generally of an olive complexion, well formed, and pretty until about twenty years of age, when they begin to fall off as much as females in England do at fifty, without having any of the various resources of art that enable the latter to affect youth, and keep off the dreaded wrinkles of age as long as they can.

From the vile habit of masticating *Pawn,* Singhalese ladies (for it is common to both sexes) always appear as if their mouths and lips were bloody; this, however, is no loss to the Singhalese lover, for saluting the lips is unknown; he merely applies his nose to the cheek of his intended, and gives a sniff or two, which species of gallantry is the native substitute for the more ardent kiss of the British islanders.

This national masticatory is general throughout India and the Eastern Archipelago, and consists of a leaf of the betel vine (*Piper betel*), a small piece of the nut of the areka palm (*Areka catechu*, L.), but erroneously called betel nut; a little betel chunam (shell lime prepared for the purpose), and occasionally tobacco or cardamoms, or a small portion of the leaf of the *Alpinia nutans*, which is very aromatic.

The female dress consists of a deep folded cloth or *Cambay* worn like a petticoat, a neatly plaited chemise, and a white jacket trimmed with country lace, tight at the arms, and thickly studded with small gold buttons from the wrist nearly to the elbow. In full dress, the Singhalese ladies confine their hair by small arrows of gold or silver filigree-work, and diamond ornaments, to the exclusion of combs. But in point of figure and carriage they are generally very inferior to their more sable neighbours of the Malabar coast; who, from twelve to twenty years of age, display the natural graces and proportion of the Medicean Venus in all the elegance of living originals.

The Portuguese government established, and the Dutch subsequently improved, a descriptive dress for the various ranks of Singhalese headmen. As this dress is still in use, but with the gentlemanly addition of shoes and stockings, I have detailed it for the amusement of my readers.

Descriptive Dress of the Native Headmen.

WELLALE CASTE.

Maha Modeliars—Velvet, silk, or cloth coat, with gold or silver lace, loops, and buttons: sword hilt and scabbard of pure massive or wrought gold, or silver inlaid with gold, and shoulder belt of gold or silver lace, or silk embroidered or spangled with gold or silver.

Modeliars of the gate or guard—Silk or cloth coat, with gold or silver lace, loops, and buttons; sword hilt and scabbard of silver inlaid with gold, and belt of gold or silver lace, or silk embroidered or spangled with gold or silver.

Modeliars of the Attepattoo, Modeliars of the Korles, Mohotiars of the guard and Attepattoo, and Mohandirams of the guard—Silk or cloth coat, with gold or silver lace, loops, and buttons; sword hilt and scabbard of silver, hilt inlaid with gold, and belt of gold or silver lace, or silk embroidered or spangled with gold or silver.

Mohandirams of the Attepattoo and the Basnaiké and Padicarré Mohandirams employed as interpreters in the courts of the several provincial judges—Silk or cloth coat, with gold or silver lace, loops, and buttons; sword hilt and scabbard of silver, and the eyes and tongue of the lion's head of gold; the belt of gold or silver lace, but not spangled.

The Corals, Mohandirams, and Mohandirams employed as interpreters in the courts of the sitting magistrates—Silk or cloth coat, with gold or silver lace and buttons: sword hilt and scabbard of silver, and in the middle of the scabbard a plain silver plate; the belt of gold or silver lace, but not spangled.

Arrachies—Cloth or linen coat, with silver buttons and loops; sword hilt and scabbard of silver, with two plain plates of tortoise-shell on the scabbard; the belt of colored ribbon, embroidered with flowers of silver or silver thread.

Canganies—Cloth or linen coat, with silver buttons and loops; sword hilt of horn inlaid with silver, the scabbard of horn or wood with eight silver bands, and belt of colored ribbon without embroidery.

FISHER AND CHANDOO CASTE.

Modeliars and Mahavidahn Modeliars—Silk or cloth coat, with silver buttons and loops; sword hilt and scabbard of silver, and the eyes and tongue of the lion's head of gold; the belt of gold or silver lace, but not spangled.

Mahavidahns, Mahavidahn Mohandirams, Patengatyn Mohandirams, and all other Mohandirams of the same caste—Cloth or linen coat, with silver buttons and loops: sword hilt and scabbard of silver, and in the middle of the scabbard a plain plate of tortoise-shell; the belt of gold or silver lace.

Arrachies—Cloth or linen coat, with silver buttons and silk loops; sword hilt of horn, embellished with silver, with three tortoise-shell plates; the belt of colored ribbon, embroidered with silk.

Canganies—Linen coat, with silver buttons and silk loops; sword hilt of horn, embellished with silver, the scabbard of horn or wood, with two silver plates, and the belt of plain colored ribbon.

BLACKSMITH AND WASHER CASTE.

Mahavidahns and Mahavidahn Mohandirams—Cloth or linen coat, with silver buttons and loops; sword hilt and scabbard of silver, with one plate of tortoise-shell on the scabbard, and two plates of tortoise-shell on the scabbard worn by the washermen; the belt of ribbon, embroidered with flowers of gold or silver thread.

Arrachies—Linen coat, with silver buttons and silk loops; sword hilt of horn, embellished with silver, the scabbard of horn or wood, with silver bands, and the belt of plain colored ribbon.

Canganies—Linen coat, with horn or covered linen buttons; sword hilt of horn, the scabbard of horn or wood, with three copper bands, and the belt of plain ribbon.

BARBER CASTE.

Vidahn Mohandiram—Cloth or linen coat, with silk buttons and loops; sword hilt and scabbard of silver, but on the scabbard there must be two plates of tortoise-shell; the belt of colored ribbon, embroidered with flowers of silver thread.

N. B. Titular headmen of each rank dress in every respect as the headmen of the rank and caste to which they belong, but the word "Titular" is engraven on their sword hilts.

It may scarcely be supposed credible, but it is an absolute fact, that Englishmen in the nineteenth century have wished for the continuance of native oppression, and for the headmen to be compelled to leave their sandals at the cutcherry doors.

Mr. John Brexius de Zielfa, the present assessor to the district-court of Galle, who formerly held the office of Mohandiram interpreter of the magistrate's court of that district when I presided there, and who wore shoes and stockings in court with my unqualified approbation, was refused admission to the cutcherry with such European appendages. That gentleman felt that, as a British subject, he had as great a right to wear shoes and stockings as those who were of European birth; but as the collector chose to make a reference to the governor, which was followed by the most extraordinary decision, that "His Excellency would not sanction the adoption of the most comfortable portions of the European and native costumes, and that the interpreter must choose one or the other," Mr. de Zielfa relinquished his visits to the cutcherry, rather than the comforts of his adopted dress.

This was a most inconsiderate decision, because every step towards the adoption of the English costume, was an advance in civilization; and it ought to have been recollected, that as natives do not suddenly relinquish either their dress or habits, individuals were entitled to credit for setting an example fraught with advantages to the manufactures and commerce of the mother country.

My predictions at that time (1825) as to the future admission of natives to the rights and privileges of British subjects, have been since fulfilled by Lord Viscount

Goderich's abolition of all that militated against the equal enjoyment of those blessings, in 1832. If this had been the only one out of very many acts of sound and humane policy, which characterized his Lordship's *second* administration of the colonies, (for the *first* was so short as to afford his Lordship no time for acquiring much acquaintance with their state and wants,) it was sufficient to immortalize his Lordship's memory: and whilst Ceylon and the Singhalese exist, the reign of King William IV. will be held in veneration, the name of Goderich be considered synonymous with true liberty, and that of Horton with humanity and justice.

I trust the time is now for ever passed, when a British magistrate, whilst driving his buggy through a town, may presume to lay his whip violently over a black merchant's umbrella, because he was not quite so quick in doffing it as "his worship" considered due to his own consequence.—This I myself witnessed at Colombo, in the streets of the Pettah; but although my blood overboiled at the time, I knew that he "*was in favor at court*," and that a representation of it would have had no better effect than an exposition of the various abuses and impositions upon the public and the secretary of state for the colonies, would have had, through a *private channel*, at home.

Singhalese theatrical performances invariably take place in the open air; generally in some spacious compound, or garden, where abundance of jack, bread-fruit, and other trees can be made available to the purposes of illumination; and where also, from the quality of the ground, a natural amphitheatre is easily fitted for the purpose. The erection of booths, covered with white cloths and ornamented in a very tasteful style, for which the natives are celebrated, with mosses, wild flowers, of the *Nelumbium speciosum*, *Coffea triflora*, *Ixora coccinea*, and *Vinca rosea*, white and yellow jessamine, fruits of all sorts in clusters, interspersed with the white flowers and *olas* or leaflets of the coco-nut palm, and bunches of areka nuts in the bright yellow and orange of maturity; all these add to the beauty of the scenery, and give an air of richness and luxuriance to the whole.

Tragedy alone is worthy of native attention; the everlasting subject of it being kingly depravity or virtue; the latter of which is still more rare in Asiatic than in European record. After multiplied scenes of bloodshed, the usurper's destruction and the lawful sovereign's restoration, form the chief characteristics of the native drama, in which all is pantomime. Several splendid thrones in elevated positions, and extravagantly large but superb crowns, displaying a magnificence and taste for which one would not give the Singhalese credit, are distinguishing features in their theatricals.

A tragedy occupies several consecutive nights in the performance. All the avenues, trees, and booths are illuminated with coco-nut oil, in lamps made with the shells of green or water coco-nuts stuck upon stakes, the green husk of the fruit being kept on for the purpose of receiving their points; and thus the shells are properly fixed previous to being filled with oil and trimmed as lamps.

The plays are very well attended; and the order, so necessary to the immense assemblage of persons of all ranks and classes, is invariably maintained without the intervention of police or constables. The music is extremely barbarous, and monotonous to an European ear. The instruments are *Berrigoddeas, Doolahs, Tam-a-tams, Oodikeas, Taleahs* (a sort of brass cymbal beaten with a stick), and the country hautboy, called *Horanawa;* these together, make noise enough even for the halls of Pandemonium.

The dresses of the actors are very gaudy, being set off with every possible variety of foil and tinsel. There are no actresses. The admissions are gratuitous, the costs being defrayed by collections from the native audience.

The Singhalese have but seven or eight musical instruments; of which five are instruments of percussion.

The first is the *Oodikea;* this in shape somewhat resembles an hour glass; but instead of the three wooden supporters of the circular extremities, it has four braces, which are compressed towards the middle by an elastic ring; the body is of jackwood (timber of the *Artocarpus integrifolia*, L.) and cylindrical, the middle just large enough to be grasped in the hand; the ends are covered with a coarse parchment, made of deer skin, which is laid on wet, then tied with thongs, and dried in the sun.

The next, a sort of long drum with eight braces, is called *Doolah.* It has one end larger than the other, which end is beaten with a drumstick, slightly convex on one side and concave on the other; the body, usually made of thin jackwood, is cylindrical; the ends are covered in the same manner as the *Oodikea's.*

The third, which is also a cylinder of thin jackwood, is the *Berrigoddea.* This instrument has nine braces, and is beaten with the hands; it is very convex in the middle, where it's circumference is double the size of the extremities, towards which it gradually slopes; these are covered with deer-skin parchment, in the same manner as the instruments already described.

Tam-a-tam, vulgarly, *Tom-tom,* is the fourth: in shape it resembles kettle-drums. This instrument is also covered with deer-skin parchment, and is beaten with two sticks, having an elastic circle, of about an inch in diameter, at one end.

The fifth and last of the native instruments of percussion is a sort of brass plate, of the size of a small cymbal, and called *Taleah.* It is suspended by a loop, which is just large enough to admit the left thumb, and is beaten with a stick. This most noisy instrument is used by auctioneers, to assemble people, and is a great annoyance to the inhabitants of the neighbourhood where auctions are held.

The only stringed instrument that I have seen among the Singhalese is the *Vinah*, but it is altogether different from the Hindoo instrument of that name. The Singhalese *Vinah* is formed of a neatly carved or polished coco-nut shell (of which about a third part is cut off) and covered with guana skin (*Lacerta Iguana*, L.); to this is fixed a solid handle of about an inch in diameter, which is generally lackered with various colors, and, on the opposite side of the shell, a sort of peg is fixed, to which two strings, one of horse-hair, and the other of fine bow-string hemp (*Sensivierra Zeylanica*), are attached; these strings are passed over a wooden bridge, upon the centre of the covering, one horizontally, and the other upon an inclined plane, the slope commencing from within three inches of the extremity of the handle, where it is perforated large enough to receive a strong peg of nearly half its circumference, and of about a fourth part of its length, having at the point a notch for the reception of the strings, which, by turning the peg, are kept in a state of tension, like the strings of a violin.—This instrument is played upon with a bow, convexing largely from about two-thirds of its length from the point, near which a couple of small brass bells, something similar to horse bells, are attached.

The only itinerant *Vinah* player that I recollect, usually took his post at the bridge leading to the Bazaar at Point de Galle, where the poor lepers, who usually congregated there for charity, appeared the most delighted of his auditors.

Except the trumpet shell; (*Fusus Zeylanicus*,) to which is affixed a brass or ivory mouth-piece, the only wind instrument of the Singhalese is the *Horanawa*. This native pipe is cylindrical, and trumpet-shaped; the middle is of wood, and the rest of brass; the mouth-piece is made of two pieces of a talipat or palmyra leaf, one of which is of some length, and attached to a peg near the third hole from the opposite end; by which, when necessary, the orifice between the parts composing the mouth-piece is extended. One side of the instrument is pierced with seven holes, and in tone it resembles the Irish bag-pipe.

Ancient Portuguese names are so mixed with the *Rice* names and patronymics of the Singhalese, that nothing is more common amongst the higher classes of the maritime provinces, than for the Lusitanian names of *Dons* Christian de Abrew, Salamon de Zouza, Theodoris Mendis, Migel Fernando, Johan de Zilva, Carolis de Lewera, Paulus Pereira, Adrian de Alvis, Louis de Saram, Louis Pieris, Salomon Dias, Cornelis de Fonseka, Louis de Sampayo, and Simon de Melho, to be prefixed to the Singhalese surnames of Wajesondra, Rajepaksé, Wijesinké, Wijesiriwardené, Wijenaiké, Jayetilleké, Illangakoon, &c.; and it is not uncommon for a *low* caste Singhalese to be ambitious of the name of European; and as the Hindoo-

Portuguese, who have all the privileges of Europeans in courts of justice, are as dark in color as the Singhalese, and often much darker than the higher castes of the latter; the ambitious aspirant thinks it no greater difficulty to get upon the first bar of the European ladder, than to prove that he possesses some portion of Lusitanian blood; and therefore the moment he can raise sufficient cash for a second-hand coat or jacket, or if these are not to be obtained at his own price, a white cotton jacket, waistcoat, trousers, shirt, a hat (*Chapé*), and shoes (*Zapatas*), the candidate for *European honors* is complete in point of dress; he next wants a Portuguese name, and of course a *title*. German Barons are scarcely less plentiful than Ceylon Doms and Dons, and the latter appendage is just as easily assumed as the former title.

For the first six weeks, the poor "European's" shoes inflict as severe a pedal penance as was endured by Peter Pindar's pilgrim, "who forgot to boil the peas"; the *Chapé* is scarcely less troublesome; but having, with his new dignity, acquired the Portuguese complimentary style of doffing it, our *European* salutes every one who wears a hat, from the governor to the nearest counterpart of the pseudo-European himself, a tame ourang-outang. He is now Don Abram, Don Louis, Dom Christoffel, or Dom Adrian, "*et le jeu est fait.*"

Among other oppressions of the natives, the following may be classed as an abuse of power that was very commonly practised by former collectors of districts.—When native cattle feeders have objected to sell their young calves to Europeans, the collector of the district, upon being applied to, has compelled them to do so, upon being paid for them; to this stretch of power the poor unprotected creatures have acceded, but with a very bad grace, upon the ordering of the modeliar of the cutcherry.

These tyrannical times have also passed away, never to be recalled whilst Ceylon belongs to the British crown; for the government will no longer recognize such tyranny and oppression as an official privilege of its provincial agents or collectors.

CHAP. XIII.

Specimens of Singhalese proverbs—Dutch language but little known among the natives—C. A. Prins, Esq.—Prevalence of the Hindo-Portuguese language—Singhalese generally acquainted with the properties of their indigenous plants—Madung Appo, a native botanist and doctor—Instance of extraordinary cure of blindness—Native doctor's objections to name the composition of the salts employed—Obligations to him—Major General Thomas Hardwicke, Bengal artillery—Pariar dog nuisance—Government precautions against hydrophobia—John Tranchell, Esq.—Sudden entry of a rabid pariar dog during dinner—The host's coolness, and assurance of curing his guests if bitten—Death of the dog from the effect of rain—Singhalese cattle—Swine—Improvements suggested—Rabbits—Poultry—Seir fish—Shell fish—Turtle—Establishment of farms and agricultural prizes suggested—Singhalese a litigious nation—Pointed knives illegal—Caste—A beautiful girl nearly murdered for covering her bosom with a kerchief—Nothing to be dreaded in Ceylon by protecting all as British subjects should be protected.

THE Singhalese have several books of proverbs; and an acquaintance with these "wise sayings" is considered to display great knowledge. A few are here given, as specimens of the native phrases, and their meaning.

"Do not wear a *Wallah** in your native place, nor carry a large stick in another."—That is, Be not too proud at home, nor display more power than belongs to you elsewhere.

"Although a man with large teeth dies, no one will believe it."—No one will believe a man, who is known to be rich, when he talks of his poverty.

"Scraps of chunan are found in every one's betel box."—The best of men have faults.

"Buying a house for five hundred dollars, and selling it at half-price."—A person reduced from riches to comparative poverty.

"Although the *Ambalama*† be unroofed, will it shorten the journey?"—A good reputation survives poverty.

Another proverb of synonymous interpretation is, "Although an elephant may become lean, he cannot wash in a barrel."

"The horn, which came last, has more power than the ear which preceded it."—The lowest in his own village has become head in another.

* *Wallah,*—A cloth worn by the Singhalese, of which one end hangs lower than the other—a mark of ostentation.

† *Ambalama,*—A rest-house for natives upon high roads.

"Even in *Gilimala** there are people with white teeth."—Amongst the best people, some are bad.

"Even in the salt *Leeways*† people live without salt."—There are affluent persons who derive no enjoyment from their fortunes.

"A foreigner and a parasite plant are synonymous."—One is as ruinous to the place he inhabits, as the other to the tree it embraces.

"Tanks do not fill with the night dew, but with rain."—Men become rich by honesty, and not by roguery.

"Where is the honor of being born at *Totaganawa*, if you cannot read and understand *Bana?*"—Totaganawa is famous for literature and learned men, and Bana‡ signifies the history of the god Buddha.

"First look at the lime,§ and then open the mouth."—Bribe the judge well, and success is certain, whether the cause be right or wrong.

It is a subject of general remark, that but few of the Singhalese, and those of the higher castes only, understand the Dutch language. A very intelligent Dutch gentleman, the late Carolus Arnoldus Prins, Esq., informed me, that his countrymen would not employ any domestics that were acquainted with that language, that they might not know the subjects of conversation at their masters' tables. The very different policy of their predecessors, whilst in the possession of the maritime provinces, may be inferred, from the prevalence of the Hindo-Portuguese language, and the extension of the Roman Catholic religion throughout the whole track of their original conquests; than which, no greater proof need be adduced of the original power of the Lusitanians of the sixteenth century, or of the spirit of adventure by which they distinguished themselves.

The generality of Singhalese have a considerable knowledge of their indigenous plants, and some of their doctors are very clever in medical botany. As oculists, they may be said to excel; and this is the more extraordinary, because they know nothing of the anatomical structure of the eye or head.

Madung Appo, a native doctor of Galpiaddé, near Galle, from whose skill in botany I derived much useful information, gave it as his opinion, that "*Ceylon produces such*

* *Gilimala*, a place famous for the cultivation of the betel plant, or *Bulack*, which blackens the teeth.

† *Leeway* or *Leawawa*, natural salt pans. ‡ The place where Bana is read, is called Bana Madewa.

§ It was the custom formerly for bribes to be inclosed in limes, (the small variety of the *Citrus medicus* or lemon,) which generally consisted of as many gold star pagodas, value about eight shillings each, as it could be made to contain. To this day, limes are offered, upon all occasions of ceremony, by the Singhalese.

an infinite variety of medicinal plants, that if a botanist were to devote a long life to their investigation, he would still leave an ample field for the labours of very many equally zealous successors."

This culler of simples was extremely well acquainted with the nature and properties of all plants included in the native Materia Medica. As an oculist, he was justly celebrated; and one of his cures was regarded with admiration by many who had heard four English medical gentlemen, including two physicians, previously declare the case *altogether incurable and hopeless.* In the case alluded to, his proposition to cure a little Portuguese girl, about seven years of age, after she had been declared incurable by four of the European faculty, appeared so preposterous, and indeed ridiculous, that it was only upon his positive and repeated assurances that "he could and would cure her, if permitted to try his own remedies, even were a hundred European doctors of the same opinion as those who had already declared the case hopeless;" and this too after the child had been for several weeks under the care of an English surgeon, that the mother consented to allow him a trial of his skill.

The proposition, on Madung Appo's part, was, that if the girl recovered her sight, he was to be paid thirty rix dollars, or 2*l.* 5*s.* sterling; but if otherwise, that he was to have nothing for his attendance and medicines. This preliminary having been assented to, he began by ordering the child a milk diet; and during the six weeks that she was his patient, he employed no other medicine than a fine white powder, having all the appearance of quinine; this he gave in doses at stated periods, and occasionally blew a similar powder, by means of a quill having a piece of clear muslin at the end, into the child's eye. At the expiration of six weeks, to the surprise of every one, and to the delight of many, who were interested for this amiable little creature, her vision was perfectly restored. A continuation of the same diet was prescribed for some time, and then gradually changed; and the only particular care this native doctor recommended, was, that light should be excluded as much as possible from the room until the child's sight could bear it without inconvenience.

I could not obtain from him the name of either medicine; but to my questions, why he would not inform me, and whether the same was employed externally and internally, his answer to the first, was, "I dare not give you the name, (as if he was under some superstitious fear or obligation,) but I will say thus far, it is a *salt* obtained from the bark of various trees;" and, as to the second, "The medicines were altogether different, but both were *vegetable salts.*"

I acknowledge great obligations to Madung Appo, for the native names of a variety of plants, and for a copious description of their medicinal properties, notwithstanding his great and insuperable objection to make his eye remedy known. By his aid I obtained a great variety of medicinal plants, which I dried and sent to my respected friend, the late Major General Thomas Hardwicke, of the Bengal artillery.

The *Pettahs*, or, vulgarly speaking, black towns and native villages, swarm with pariar dogs; and it is only in such places as are occupied by Mahomedans, who detest the whole canine genus, that these mangy curs are not to be met with; for the Singhalese will not destroy any of the progeny of these mongrels, and the government is necessitated to adopt measures for the general safety, during the hottest season of the year; viz. the months of January, February, and March, when a body of Malays is employed, under the superintendence of police *Peons*,* to destroy all dogs found in the streets that have not collars by way of passport.

When the immense and daily increasing numbers of these animals are considered, one may well wonder at the comparative paucity of cases of hydrophobia that occur. Many native doctors pretend to have certain cures in indigenous roots and vegetables; but if ever there was a known remedy in the possession of an European, it may be believed, from the following extraordinary occurrence, to have belonged to the late Mr. John Tranchell of Belligam.

On the 12th of June, 1827, whilst we were at dinner with Mr. Tranchell and his family, a rabid pariar dog, which had been chased from a neighbouring village, through the sacred grounds of the Moorish mosque adjoining Mr. Tranchell's estate, ran into the room. My first impulse was to seize a loaded gun that stood in a corner, and present it at the animal; but my host intreated me not to fire, "*because* (said he very coolly, and without rising from his chair or altering a muscle of his countenance) *if the poor devil bites you, I can cure you.*"

But no one present wished to be made the subject of such an experiment; and I drove the dog from under the sofa, where he had taken refuge, into the compound, when a sudden shower of rain saved me from the expenditure of powder and shot; for the moment the animal felt its deadly influence, it was seized with convulsions, and expired upon the spot.

The stoical indifference of Mr. Tranchell was not assumed, and arose from a thorough confidence in his means of cure; but whether he relied upon the same nostrum in hydrophobia, with which I had seen him perform most extraordinary cures of snake bites, (as I have related elsewhere in these pages,) or not, it is to be hoped that the papers he left behind him will explain. For the latter, he employed, in addition

* Literally, running footmen or messengers.

to Eau de Luce, given internally, a mixture of nitric and muriatic acid, which was labelled upon a bottle always at hand in his dressing room; but I am ignorant of their relative proportions.

The breed of Singhalese cattle is very inferior; the small black bullock of the country being rather more than a third, and occasionally about half the size of an English bullock; the native Jaffna sheep are long legged, and may well be called goat-sheep, the best name I have for the breed; the swine are also long legged, and allowed to feed where food of any kind can be picked up, it matters not what, nor where, to the native owners. Notwithstanding that the Singhalese are as much attached to hogs' flesh as ever Otaheitans were in the time of the celebrated Captain Cook, (for they never have a feast or festival without a hog being served at it,) yet I never saw swine penned for feeding at any native cottage or farm.

The doubtful reputation of Bazaar pork and ducks is the same at Ceylon as it is throughout India; and whenever the one or the other appears on the dinner table, it is absolutely necessary for the host to vouch for its "education," for otherwise, notwithstanding that silver dishes contained the suspicious food, neither would be tasted.

The Ceylon buffalo (*Bos bubulus* of Shaw) is a large and valuable animal for agricultural purposes, and the flesh is by no means despisable, although rarely, if ever, seen at the tables of Europeans. The milk of the cow buffalo is much richer than that of the common island cow, (a species of *Zebu*,) and the butter made from it, and clarified, is known by the general name of *Ghee* throughout India.

Ceylon bullocks may be purchased for about thirty or forty shillings a head; cows for less; Jaffna sheep at three, four, and five shillings; a sow and litter of pigs from twelve to fifteen shillings, and occasionally for less; but Bengal sheep (which, after being well fed, afford delicious mutton) and kids vary in price, according to the demand for them—the latter, depends upon the caprice of the Moormen and Hindoos, who are the principal feeders. That these animals are in the greatest abundance, one may be fully convinced, by merely riding through the quarters of the towns and villages occupied by these people, for their verandahs teem with goats and their kids: these, when about to be fattened for sale, are previously castrated.

Cape sheep (*Ovis Steatopyga* of Shaw) thrive remarkably well; but Bengal sheep require a great deal more care, when first landed in the island, owing to their sudden transition from dry to green fodder; the reason there is occasionally such great mortality among Ceylon sheep on board ship, arises from their being shipped without previous preparation for the dry food usually provided for sea stock; for their general fodder is green jack leaves (*Artocarpus integrifolia*, L.), grass, and other vegetables; and they are often fattened for the table entirely upon the former, which possess very mucilaginous and nutritious properties. Bengal sheep are usually fed on dholl (*Cytisus Cajan*, L.) and paddee, and are consequently better for sea stock.

An importation of domestic animals of each kind from England and the Cape of Good Hope would soon improve the native breed. The camel is never to be seen at Ceylon, and but very few mules and asses.

The wild rabbit is not indigenous, and tame rabbits are scarce.

Every sort of poultry is extremely cheap, except turkies; for even at Matura, in the southern province, which is a noted place for breeding them, these birds are seldom purchased for less than 72*s*. to 80*s*. per dozen; and a sovereign is not an uncommon price for a fat cock turkey at Colombo.

There is occasionally a very great mortality amongst turkies during the rains, which makes that species of poultry so much dearer than any other. The owner considers himself fortunate, if fifty out of a hundred arrive at maturity for sale. But all this loss is to be obviated by care; for turkies require an elevated and dry roosting place to retire from wet, and black pepper is indispensable with their food.

Geese are smaller than those of Europe, and remarkable for their brownish color and black bills, having the upper part surmounted with a black bony protuberance or knob; their usual prices are from 2*s*. to 3*s*.

Ducks are considered dear at 6*d*. or 8*d*. each.

Chickens may be purchased in some places for 1*s*., at others for 1*s*. 6*d*. and 2*s*. per dozen; and 100 eggs at the same price.

Reddish brown widgeon, erroneously called teal, are abundant, and easily domesticated. The guinea fowl, pea fowl, Malay fowl (*Gallus giganteus*), common fowl, European, Persian, and Indian pigeons, and Brahminy and Muscovy ducks, complete the list of domestic poultry.

Ceylon poultry, when fed by natives, invariably tastes of *Poonac*, or coco-nut oil cake, which imparts an oily flavor to whatever is fed on it; this, they give, as being cheaper than paddee, which is a favorite food of poultry, and of most domestic animals. But even the *Poonac* would be very different, if pressed whilst the nut is fresh, which should be the case when intended for feeding cattle or poultry.

Too much cannot be said in favor of the fishes of Ceylon, particularly of the *Seir* fish, called by the Singhalese *Tora-malu*, for the female has the same flavor as the salmon (*Salmo Salar*) of Europe; many varieties are elsewhere noticed in these pages; and the *Crustacea* include a small but delicious crab, prawns from six to eight inches in length, cray-fish, oysters, and shrimps; all which are excellent of their kinds.

As to the Ceylon Turtle, great caution is requisite, because it is not generally known that the *Testudo Imbricata*, called by the Singhalese *Lili-kas-bewa*, which produces the transparent shell, is not only unwholesome, but, at certain seasons, absolutely poisonous. Several natives died from eating its flesh at Ahamadewé, or Turtle Cove, in the Mahagampatto district, in 1826. Their illness exhibited every symptom of Asiatic cholera.

The edible turtle is the *Testudo Mydas*, the *Gal-kas-bewa* of the Singhalese; and the small fresh water turtle is also wholesome and nutritious. The Singhalese call it *Kiri-ba*, from *Kiri*, milk; because, when boiled, the flesh is milk white. This last is given by the native doctors to cure the abdominal obesity to which children are subject from the effects of rice diet.

Notwithstanding the island has been in our possession for a period of forty five years, no general and but very little partial improvement has taken place in the breed of the more useful animals, horses alone excepted!!

To obviate all the apparent difficulties to the improvement of the breed of the domestic animals, no plan appears to me more feasible, or more likely to insure a productive result, than the establishment of five large farms; viz. one in the best situation for grazing lands in the central province; and a farm at each of the towns of Colombo, Galle, Jaffna, and Trincomalé; or in the best locality near them that can be fixed upon for the purpose.

The object being the general benefit of the island, and of great importance in whichever light it may be viewed, will no doubt receive the support of the government, in so far as the grant of lands belonging to the crown may be required for the purpose, at a low rate, to such joint-stock company or individual capitalists as may be most forward in this national as well as private object of improvement and profit.

Prizes for the best specimens of the several animals might be held out by the government, as well as by an agricultural society,—of medals for Europeans, but in cash to the natives, as the surest *ad captandum modus* that can be held out to the Singhalese, and the only one that never fails.

The Singhalese are naturally a litigious nation; and it is not uncommon for a plaintiff and defendant, each accompanied by a number of suborned witnesses, to walk together from their village to the district court, perhaps a distance of fifteen or twenty miles, the former to prosecute a claim, and very probably an unjust one, to the eighth share of a jack or coco-nut tree. Then is the time for hard swearing! but the witnesses are generally so perfect in their lessons, as to baffle the cleverest of the native proctors in their cross examinations.

Some cases of murder have displayed a ferocity that one would scarcely have supposed such an effeminate race to be capable of; and their proneness, upon sudden quarrels, to resort to the knife, rendered it necessary for the government to pass an ordinance, in the year 1816, by which it was made unlawful to carry any pointed knife, except that called *Ulkatoo-peheyé*, or knife fixed to the same handle as the iron-pointed style with which the natives write upon strips of the leaves of the talipat and palmyra.

As regards the observance of caste, the abolition of all degrading distinctions as to dress, during Lord Viscount Goderich's last administration of the colonies, in conjunction with the extension of Christianity, will hasten its abandonment. A woman of low caste may now cover her shoulders with a cloth or kerchief, or wear a waistcloth below the knees, which she dared not have done some twenty years ago.

I was once passing through the Bazaar at Barberyn, in the western province, when an unusual mob had collected in the street; and I learned that a woman of the *Padua* caste* had been nearly killed by some indignant *Wellales* and *Chandoos*, for "*having presumed so far to forget her degraded lot in life as to throw a kerchief over her neck and shoulders !!*" She was a girl of about sixteen years of age, and the prettiest native that I ever beheld; her beauty, however, seemed to excite, instead of allay, the brutality of these sticklers for the strict observance of the *rights* (?) of caste.

The European eye cannot well be accused of fastidiousness in such matters; custom soon reconciles even our modest countrywomen to the all but naked coolies, whose "fine sleek backs," were particularly noticed in the travels of a fair authoress.†

It is said that nothing can be more conducive to British interests, than to consult the feelings and humour the prejudices of our unenlightened sable fellow subjects, until education (to which, if an estimate may be formed by the rapid strides it is now making in the island, under the auspices of the government and the zealous missionaries of the various establishments, every one, in the course of a few years, will have free access) shall have paved the way for a voluntary relinquishment of them.—This may be all very fine, and near the truth; but there is nothing to be dreaded, in Ceylon, from protecting *all*, by the strong arm of the law, and preventing individuals from taking the law into *their own hands*, whether they be called *Europeans*, or *high caste* natives.

* One of the subdivisions of the *Shudra Wansé* caste.

† Maria Graham.

CHAP. XIV.

Exaggerated stories about Snakes—Singhalese catalogue of venomous and harmless Snakes—Reported extraordinary transformation of the Coluber Naja, L.—Corroborated by a Singhalese in this country—Dia Naya—Ahedoella—Pimbera or Python—Buddhists will not kill the sacred snake, but have no objection to send it to sea, without a chance of escape—Cobra di Capello easily kept alive—Charles Peter Layard, Esq.—Snake deprived of its eyes by mice—Caution to be observed in purchasing snakes—Samp Wallahs—Snake exhibition—Providential escape—Successful application of Eau de Luce, and of nitric and muriatic acid in the cure of snake bites—John Tranchell, Esq.—A coroner's reason for not holding an inquest—Supposed cause of the paucity of snakes in the Mahagampattoo—Viverra Ichneumon attacks the Cobra di Capello—Various plants named as antidotes—More caution requisite against leeches than against snakes—Cobra di Capello in houses—Superstitious notions respecting snake charming.

If a tenth part of the stories related about the superabundance of snakes in the island were true, one might expect to find them in every house, in every compound, or on every lawn, as well as upon the branches of every tree. Where jungle is being cleared, numerous snakes are found, as they are in similar places in almost every intertropical, and even temperate clime. Now and then, they are met with upon the ramparts and esplanades of forts, and occasionally in houses built upon ground that may have been recently cleared or near to uncultivated land; but where one snake, so found, is venomous, ten are harmless; and sportsmen often meet them in jungles, but that is never an obstacle to "following up the game."

To assist the ophiologist to procure snakes, I subjoin the native names of a few of the principal ones, with which the most intelligent in the natural history of their country are acquainted; of these, there are several *varieties* that are not enumerated, and it will be for him to class them agreeably to the authorities to which he may have the means of referring.

* 1	Naya	* 6	Dia Naya
* 2	Berawah Naya	* 7	Polonga
* 3	Koboe Naya	* 8	Lee-Polonga
* 4	Soeloe Naya	* 9	Nidi-Polonga
* 5	Deput Naya	*10	Pala-Polonga

* 11	Tic-Polonga	* 21	Doenoo Karewella
12	Pimbera and Anaconda	22	Mal Karewella
* 13	Ahedoella	* 23	Tib-Karewella
* 14	Mapilla	24	Kan-Köenda
* 15	Karewella	25	Galgoloowah
16	Pala Panoowa	26	Hotambeyah
17	Dia Berya	27	Etetullah
18	Garrendiya	28	Mal-Karabeta
19	Aharé Kocka	29	Mal-Polon
20	Wal-Garwendiya	30	Matribilla

31 Duberriya is a harmless water snake.

Of the above list, the Singhalese aver that all are venomous that I have marked with an asterisk; but the position of the teeth will soon convince the naturalist how far their statement may be depended on.

The Singhalese positively assume that the *Koboe Naya* is the Naya (*Cobra di Capello-Coluber Naja,* L.) in its last stage; that every time it has expended its poison, the reptile loses a joint of its tail; and so on every year, until its appearance and nature become totally changed, by the addition of wings, similar to the pectoral fins of the flying fish (*Exocœtus volitans,* L.), at which time the head and mouth resemble the toad's! But nature is altogether so extraordinary in her various transformations, and so many productions, formerly considered as the mere fictions of the traveller, are now known to exist, that, at the present day, one might be premature in doubting even this extraordinary Singhalese report on the subject of the natural history of their country.

In October, 1839, I made particular inquiries of an intelligent Singhalese respecting the *Koboe Naya,* when he not only confirmed the foregoing statement, but assured me that a very fine specimen of that snake, in its last transformation, and preserved in spirits, is in the possession of Mr. W. H. Kellaart, assistant apothecary to the forces at Colombo.

The *Dia Naya,* according to the Singhalese, is amphibious in a peculiar sense, independently of the Linnæan classification, living six months in water, during which period it is venomous, and for a similar length of time on land, when it is altogether innocuous.

The *Ahedoella,* from its rapid movement and power of springing, is called a "flying snake;" and mortiferous sleep is said to follow the bite of the *Nidi Polonga.*

The *Pimbera,* or rock snake, (Genus *Python,* C.), is said to be the *Anaconda* or *Anacondia* of ancient writers.

It is by no means uncommon, in crossing or in excursions upon Ceylon rivers, to fall in with bags (made of matting and tied at the mouth) floating with the stream; and great caution is necessary in opening them, for they generally contain one or more snakes of the sacred kind, (*Naya,*) that some devout Buddhist had dispatched upon a cruize, with a stock of provisions, consisting of boiled rice, an egg or two, and perhaps a "Bellerophon's letter" upon a talipat or palmyra leaf. From these facts it may be collected, that if Buddhists object *to kill* the Naya, from religious motives or superstitious veneration, they nevertheless think it no sin to send it upon an *aquatic excursion,* without a possibility of escape from its place of confinement, and with the certainty, if met by Europeans, that the reptiles will change their temporary immersion in water for a more permanent one in spirits.

The Cobra di Capello may be kept alive for years upon eggs and frogs. A remarkable instance of instinct in mice, as connected with this snake, fell under my own observation on the voyage homewards from Ceylon. One of the passengers (Charles Peter Layard, Esq.) had a very fine living specimen in a case adapted for the purpose, of which a portion was glazed. At the usual time for giving it food, which was about once a week, two small mice were put into the case; and upon looking at the snake the next day, we found both the mice alive and uninjured, but the reptile deprived of both its eyes, and in a few days it died. Instinct therefore must have pointed out that the only means of preserving their own lives from the destroyer, was by depriving it of sight, which no doubt the little animals effected by eating its eyes.

Europeans cannot be too cautious in purchasing Cobras di Capello from itinerant snake charmers, for no reliance can be put upon their assurances that the reptiles are harmless. I can vouch from experience, that nothing but the fullest proof, upon inspection, that the fangs and poison ducts have been *extracted,* ought to satisfy the intending purchaser; and, for want of such precaution on my part, in buying a Cobra di Capello, it might, but for a most providential circumstance, have been attended with fatal consequences.

A Dutch gentleman who very obligingly assisted me in collecting natural specimens, sent a Bengal samp wallah or snake charmer to me. This man brought with him several Cobras for sale, and proceeded to exhibit them. A cooley, who accompanied him carried two circular baskets at the ends of a pingo, which he placed upon the ground, and commenced playing the *Horanawa,* or country pipe, whilst the charmer beat with his right hand upon a small *Oodikea* that he held in his left. In about a minute or two the covers of the baskets were gradually raised, and as the snakes left the baskets, the music (if such a most anti-melodious din may be called) increased in quickness; the snakes moved about the circular space allotted to them with part of their bodies erect, and the rest of their lengths coiled, but their hoods, upon which the "painted spectacles" showed to great advantage, were expanded, and their forked tongues in the continual motion of projecting and retracting.

The snakes were irritated to strike at the charmer's arms and knees, and blood flowed; after which he took the reptiles by the neck and held their mouths close to his forehead, which however was mere display, because in that position they were perfectly harmless; he then declared them to be perfectly innocuous, or what he called *kutcha*.

Under this impression, I bought one of the snakes, and in the full belief that it had been deprived of all power to do mischief, I occasionally placed it upon the table, and as the animal moved about, displaying its hood, my wife would pass and repass her hand under its mouth, without the slightest dread or idea of danger.

Some months had elapsed, after the purchase of the snake, when some French officers paid me a visit, and upon their evincing great dread of the animal, I, in order to convince them it was groundless, grasped the animal by the back of the head, as it lay upon the table, without any other precaution than that of covering my hand with a handkerchief; and having employed a pair of nail scissors to open the mouth, I discovered to my horror, which may be imagined, but cannot be described, the *fangs perfect*, and the animal in full possession of its deadly power. The snake had coiled itself so tightly round my left arm and neck, that, feeling a numbness coming on, and being certain that I could not much longer retain my hold, I, upon the spur of the moment, again forced open the animal's mouth, and extracted the fangs and poison ducts from its jaw, which having done, I flung the snake into the air with all my force, and afterwards replaced it in the basket where it had been kept: there it lived for several months, and appeared to suffer no ill effects from the forcible removal of its fangs. Feeling certain that the charmer had shown one snake and sold another, I caused every search to be made for the impostor, but he had long previously left the island.

Eau de Luce has been successfully employed in the cure of the bite of the Cobra di Capello, in various stages of the patients' sufferings, which place the efficacy of that remedy beyond all doubt, when properly administered at an early period after the bite.*—The late Mr. John Tranchell of Belligam cured two Singhalese, natives of that

* Asiatic Researches, vol. iv.

Hamlet, after having been some time in strong convulsions, (one of them a woman, whose speech had entirely left her, and who foamed at the mouth in a dreadful manner,) by dropping and rubbing into the punctures made by the snakes' fangs a mixture of nitric and muriatic acid, and giving them each fifty drops of Eau de Luce in a little water. They recovered in a few hours; but as the snakes were not caught or killed, and were only seen by the parties, who declared the animals to be *Nayas*, Mr. Tranchell did not feel that he could so positively vouch for the truth of their report, as to make the circumstances the subject of a communication to the Literary Society of Colombo, as he had at first intended; but that he did not do so, arose from no doubt in his own mind, or that the preparation he had employed, conjointly with Eau de Luce, would ever be an inefficacious remedy.

Upon another occasion I accompanied Mr. Tranchell to a village about two miles from Belligam, upon receiving a report that a woman had been bitten by a *Polonga*. That gentleman, arming himself with his nostrum, lost no time in going the nearest way to the poor woman's residence; but we arrived too late, for she had died in less than half an hour from the time she was bitten, and her corpse was then lying upon a couch under a lactera tree in the compound, and the snake, which her husband had killed, lying by its side. The face was so very much disfigured as to have lost the appearance of any thing human; the mouth was covered with saliva, and the right hand and arm, which had been bitten, were swollen to a monstrous size.

The answer of Mr. Porlier, the Belligam magistrate, and coroner *ex-officio*, to a question put to him on the following day, as to the verdict of the coroner's jury, shows the apathy with which such a death was regarded. "It was unnecessary, (said he,) to hold an inquest, because it was evident enough the snake had killed the woman!!"

I attribute the paucity of snakes in the Mahagampattoo, for I had more difficulty in procuring them in that district than in any other part of Ceylon, to the immense number of peafowl with which the plains and trees abound, whose partiality to snakes as food renders them the chief destroyers of these noxious reptiles.

The *Viverra Ichneumon* is the deadly foe of all venomous snakes. To this little animal, called by us *Mongoose*, and by the Singhalese *Goodoowa*, is attributed the power of distinguishing venomous from harmless snakes by the pupil of the eye. It resembles the common ferret in shape and size, and when young its fur is of a pencil grey, which changes by age to an iron grey, tinged at the extremities with brown. By way of experiment I placed a tame Mongoose, which was accustomed to run about the house, in a room where I kept a very fine specimen of the Cobra di Capello. Having closed the doors, I removed the cover from the basket in which the snake was kept, which, upon seeing the Mongoose, expanded its hood, and rapidly darting forth and as rapidly retracting its forked tongue, displayed the greatest excitement; but the Mongoose, so far from showing a disposition to attack the snake, exhibited a great sense of fear, for it ran about the room, poking its nose under the doors, as if eager to escape.

Having closed the basket, I removed the snake to the compound, where many visitors and lookers-on were soon assembled; and having formed a circle at a reasonable distance, so as to prevent the escape of the snake, (for which purpose some had cloths to drop over it, and others *kettule** fishing rods with snares at the ends,) the Mongoose was introduced, but escaped through the circle and retreated to the hedge that divided the compound from the cinnamon gardens, which was covered with wild plants. As every one expected, from an acquaintance with its habits, it returned in about five minutes and re-entered the arena. It showed no fear then, but made several detours, each time reducing the circle and nearing the snake, which also was upon the qui vive, watching every motion of the enemy. The Mongoose suddenly crouched with its nose close to the ground, and having waited its opportunity, sprung forward within the twinkling of an eye, and fastened its teeth in the back of the Cobra's neck. The snake twisted itself in every direction, vainly endeavouring to envelope the Mongoose in its folds, and lashing its tail against the ground, but all to no purpose; the little animal maintained its hold until the snake became completely exhausted, when giving it a farewell shake, it relinquished the Cobra, but only as life departed. This occupied nearly an hour; the Mongoose was neither bitten nor in any way injured; but, upon quitting the snake, it again repaired to the hedge, whither it was followed by the most inquisitive of the party, who were anxious to discover the plant that it resorted to, but it is even now difficult to name the correct one. Some aver that it is the *Mendi* of the Singhalese, (*Ophiorhiza Mungos*, L.), because almost every part of the tree is employed by the native doctors in curing snake bites; others that it is a variety of *Mimosa sensitiva;* others, that the plant is the *Ophioxylon serpentinum*, L., which is everywhere abundant. Both these plants, which are of the same Linnæan classification, namely, Class V. Pentandria, Order I. Monogynia, are of the *Eka-wariya* family of the Singhalese botanists, but the stem of the former is herbaceous, and of the latter ligneous. One of the most positive upon this point, Madung Appo, a native doctor at Galpiaddé, assured me that he had watched the Mongoose

* Smaller branches of the *Caryota urens*, L.

after having been bitten by a Cobra di Capello, and that the animal ran immediately into a hedge, where there was no other plant but the ayapana, (*Eupatorium Ayapana*), of which it ate both root and leaf; and moreover that he had cured a native, when bitten by a Cobra di Capello, by giving him tea made of the aromatic leaves, then suspending the wounded leg over a pan of boiling hot water, in which a quantity of ayapana leaves was infused, and keeping it in the steam until every bad symptom had disappeared, when he perfected the cure by giving his patient half a coco-nut-shell full of old Madeira wine. The leaves are lanceolate, of a very dark green in the centre, gradually becoming lighter towards the edges, and have a very conspicuous gloss upon the upper surface.

The snake charmers or *Samp Wallahs* are Hindoos; and it is well known that they irritate the Cobra to bite at red rags, by which means it expends it's venom; but the reptile can only be temporarily innocuous, for so long as thc cylindrical fangs and poison ducts remain perfect, its power to inflict mischief will be restored by a re-accumulation of the venom.

The botanist, or the collector of natural specimens, not only in the interior, but in every uncultivated place where there is long grass, has more occasion to guard against the small but most troublesome leech of Ceylon (*Hirudo Zeylanica*) than against snakes; and if he can bring his mind to think no more about the latter there than he would at home, he would probably meet with as few snakes, *except it be in the jungles of the island*, as in the country in England in the hot months of summer.

During many years' residence in Ceylon, and in all the variety of my rambles both in the interior and maritime provinces, although I have repeatedly seen Cobras di Capello in hedges, I never but once fell in with any venomous snake directly in my pathway, so as to endanger myself; but I have upon two occasions fallen in with Cobras di Capello in houses; the first of which was on the night I landed at Trincomalé, in my bed-room at Mr. James's (the hotel keeper) Bungalow, which had been for some time previously unoccupied; and the last, at the rest-house at Mahagam, which is seated in the midst of jungle; where, finding the mosquitos extremely troublesome, my palankin was brought into the room for the purpose of sleeping in it, but upon opening the door, in order to put in my pillows, I found I had been anticipated by a very fine *high-caste Naya*, which was coiled upon the mat, and showed no disposition to relinquish his berth; but with the ramrod of my gun, and a packthread noose at the end of it, I was soon enabled to secure the animal without injuring it, and to present it to a friend who considered it an acquisition to his ophiological collection.

It is no less extraordinary than true, that many, whom, one would suppose, from their education and position in society, to be free from superstitious notions, will positively support the vulgar opinion of snake charming, and cite scripture and the ancients as their authority; but why this power should have survived the age of miracles, or why, because Virgil wrote, "Frigidus in pratis cantando rumpitur anguis," and Ovid, "Vipereas rumpo verbis et carmine fauces," it should be believed in the nineteenth century, I have yet to learn. It is probable that the samp wallahs, as a precaution, saturate their hands and faces with a vegetable juice to which the snakes have a known repugnance, (for even the rattle-snake dreads the wild pennyroyal, and dies from its application) perhaps of the very plant resorted to by the Mongoose.

CHAP. XV.

Indigenous vegetable productions—Valuable in themselves, but their culture altogether neglected, although capable of great improvement, and of increasing the public revenue—The French manage these things better in their colonies—Forest timber trees—Singhalese list of ninety varieties—Bombyx pentandrum—Asclepias gigantea—Annatto—Plants producing substitutes for flax—Mons. Plassiard—Specimens of cord from the Musa sylvestris—His Grace the Duke of Portland—Crotularia juncea—Bowstring hemp—Naval contractors prefer Laccadive to Ceylon Koir—Suggestions for its improvement—White, and Digitated mulberry trees—Their cultivation—Silk worm—Cassada or Manioc—Canna glanca—Arrow root—Turmeric—Ginger—Sun-flower, its valuable properties—Elastic gum trees—True gum Arabic tree indigenous—Euphorbium antiquorum—Gum Euphorbium unnoticed in the Ceylon tariff of exports.

Having taken leave of the snakes of Ceylon, but with some regret on my part that I had not the good fortune to fall in with any of the *flying* ones that others have seen, and that those I fell in with, lay under the original curse,* I will beg leave to continue my account of some of the more useful and beautiful of the indigenous productions; namely, those of the vegetable kingdom, in succession to the palms, already described.

These, I lament to say, however valuable in themselves, and, as articles of commerce, capable of increasing the revenue, either of the colony, by duties levied upon their exportation, or, if exported duty free, that of the mother country, by duties upon their importation here, and of rendering us independent of foreign colonies, or countries, have been too long neglected, by those who are, one would reasonably suppose, the most interested in becoming acquainted with the indigenous resources of the island, and expect to be foremost in developing and turning to the advantage of their country.

That "the French manage these matters much better," is a truism as indisputable as it is discreditable to English colonists.

The island abounds with teak, nadoon, satin-wood, black and variegated ebony timber, commonly called calamander,† red-wood, satin-wood, and innumerable other trees, for which I have no other than a Singhalese list of Kandyan *Wal-Gahas;*‡ amongst which number will be found a variety of all sizes and qualities, adapted to every

* Genesis. chap. iii. ver. 13.

† *Kalu-mindrie,* from *Kalu,* black, and *mindrie,* flaming.

‡ *Wal-Gahas,*—Forest trees.

purpose to which the ship and house builder, the cabinet and musical instrument maker, the wheelwright, and the gunmaker, could possibly apply them.

There is abundance of a sort of zebra-wood, called *Kombook;* but I never heard of rose-wood or mahogany growing in Ceylon, although I inquired particularly about both trees, for the information of one of the principal importers of foreign timber in the city of London, who had been informed to the contrary.

Some specimens of jack and bread-fruit-tree wood, when very old, equal the finest Honduras mahogany, but these are of a very different class and order to the latter; the former being of the class Monœcia and order Monandria, and the latter of the class Decandria and order Monogynia.

Native List of Kandyan Forest Trees, or Wal-Gahas.

1. Kotala gaha
2. Wal-kiri gaha
3. Wal-duru gaha
4. Ketiya gaha
5. Gokara gaha
6. Bol-pana gaha
7. Maralhan gaha
8. Rilla gaha
9. Heen-weli-damba gaha
10. Goda-ran-mala gaha
11. Diya-kolla gaha
12. Ran dawoola gaha
13. Diya-mee gaha
14. Ran damba gaha
15. Rikilla gaha
16. Kikivi-messa gaha
17. Diya-mee-gaha
18. Sulu-galu-kalu gaha
19. Maha-mora gaha
20. Rat kihiriya gaha
21. Kalu kihiriya gaha
22. Ela-kihiriya gaha
23. Tela-kihiriya gaha
24. Tel-kekuné gaha
25. Diyė-rat-mal gaha
26. Kayapu gaha
27. Maha gaha
28. Lunu-bee gaha
29. Mas-bedde gaha
30. Onital gaha
31. Runu-mella gaha
32. Bo-me gaha
33. Riri-rong gaha
34. Ralu-rela gaha
35. Maha-dia-dal gaha
36. Wal gaha
37. Okuru gaha
38. Kara gaha
39. Gona-pana gaha
40. Bu-terana gaha
41. Wal-leeta gaha
42. Rattan-beriya gaha
43. Katu-reené gaha
44. Wan gaha
45. Damunu-andara gaha
46. Wal-kaju gaha
47. Yon-tumbé gaha
48. At-pila gaha
49. Gorandia gaha
50. Ratane gaha
51. Mas-badda gaha
52. Ek mee gaha
53. Kurutiaya gaha
54. Pat-beriya gaha
55. Bara gaha
56. Geta-kula gaha
57. Gojaru-ruritiya gaha
58. Pada rurutiya gaha
59. Wal-kiri-kon gaha
60. Kalu-mella gaha
61. Malu gaha
62. Wal-wareka gaha
63. Reliya gaha
64. Bol-wila gaha
65. Ura tana gaha
66. Liniya gaha
67. Goda kirilla gaha
68. Dada kirila gaha
69. Meti bembrya gaha

70. Geta wilamba gaha
71. Weli-ana gaha
72. Gal-kune gaha
73. Uruta gaha
74. Geta-rulu gaha
75. Armatilla gaha
76. Hela gaha
77. Ros-ata-pala gaha
78. Sulu kiri messa gaha
79. Tun-hiriya-messa gaha
80. Dambu gaha
81. Ma-tambala gaha
82. Rat-timbiri gaha
83. Hœ-kolon gaha
84. Kalu timbiliya gaha
85. Un-sulu gaha
86. Geta-pota gaha
87. Rok-kandi gaha
88. Ralu ronda gaha
89. Wane sapoo gaha
90. Rarelu gaha

It is by no means improbable, from what is generally known of the foreign timber imported into Great Britain, that scarcely one of the ninety Kandyan forest trees, here enumerated, has ever been seen in the London market; and as it is but natural to suppose, that these various woods partake of the colors that many of their local names imply, such as red, black, yellow, stone, and white; and also of the intermediate shades, for the Singhalese have no definition except of the primitive colors, the variety is very great.

After the forest timber trees, it may be as well to describe those, whose produce, if properly applied, would prove a new source of revenue, and show that the vegetable capabilities of this incomparable island are deserving of the earnest attention of the capitalist, the merchant, and the manufacturer, instead of that extraordinary neglect to which the rage for coffee and sugar planting has hitherto consigned them.

Some authors have described trees as producing fit materials for manufacturing purposes; which, upon fair trial, have been pronounced the reverse: but still they have their uses.

The silky cotton tree (*Bombyx pentandrum*, L.) is quite common throughout the maritime provinces, and in the lower parts of the central province; but its produce, which is something similar to that of the gigantic swallow-wort (*Asclepias gigantea*, L.), is only fit for the stuffing of pillows and mattresses, notwithstanding the very different notions that have obtained with many individuals, who have superficially observed the silky cotton as it appears upon the tree, that it might be turned to good account by our manufacturers; but if they had given the slightest consideration to the neglected state of culture of the true cotton in Ceylon, they would have thought otherwise of the value of an article, whose shortness of staple, and want of elasticity of fibre, render it unfit to be employed even as a substitute for beaver. For this purpose it was tried by the Dutch; who also sent a quantity of the raw material to China, in the very reasonable expectation that if "the most ingenious nation in the world could not convert it into cloth of some kind or other, it was not to be effected;" but it proved a fruitless speculation. The best use that can be made of the timber, is for insect boxes; the tenacity of the wood preventing the pins from dropping out, and thereby preserving insects from injury through loco-motion.

The much neglected annatto (*Bixa orellana*, L.), class Polyandria, order Monogynia, is another valuable dye, which is unknown in the tariff of Ceylon exports, notwithstanding the great facility with which its cultivation there would supersede the necessity of our dependence upon South America for an article that could be produced in any quantity, and of the best color and quality, in our own colony. This valuable shrub thrives best in a sandy soil, and stands the sea-breeze well; and it has often surprized me, that this luxuriant and ornamental production should be so generally neglected as it is; for it is of rapid growth, requires but little care, and, from the density of its cordiform foliage, which must not be judged by the specimens of the plant in our hot-houses and conservatories, is impervious to the rays of a vertical sun.

The seeds contain the coloring matter, and are enclosed in a capillary almond-shaped capsule, which, in an unripe state, is pink, but changes to brown as it ripens: and, at maturity, divides and exposes to view its bright vermillion seeds.

The present duty on foreign annatto is sufficient *encouragement to cultivate* an indigenous production, whose various uses, in medicine, varnishes, for dying silks and wools, and coloring cheese, entitles it to more attention, on the part of our colonists, than it has hitherto had. The elastic bark of the *Bixa orellana* is used by the natives for making strong ropes and elephant nooses.

As a substitute for flax, and for all the purposes of grass-cloth manufacture, in which the Chinese almost equal the cambric of the best French looms, the fibre of the wild pine or silk grass (*Bromelia Karatas*, L.), of every variety of *Musa*, including the seed-bearing or wild plantain (*M. sylvestris*), and of the leaves of the aloe (*Aloë perfoliata*, L.), and Mellori (*Pandanus odoratissimus*, L.), is well adapted.

My attention was first drawn to the *Musa* genus, for the manufacture of cordage and cloth, by seeing some excellent specimens of both in the possession of Vice Admiral Stirling, the commander-in-chief, whilst I was upon the Jamaica station, in the year 1813; and, in 1822, I sent a specimen of plantain fibre to France, by Mons. Plassiard, the commander of the French ship Le Henri; together with about half a pound weight of the dried fibre of the *Bromelia Karatas*, and *Pandanus odoratissimus*, in order to see if French ingenuity could not effect something equal to Chinese manufacture; and with the hope of surprising those of my countrymen and contemporaries, who treated with levity any novel suggestion for adding to the common catalogue of colonial produce. The result remains with Mons. Plassiard, who did not return to Ceylon, as he

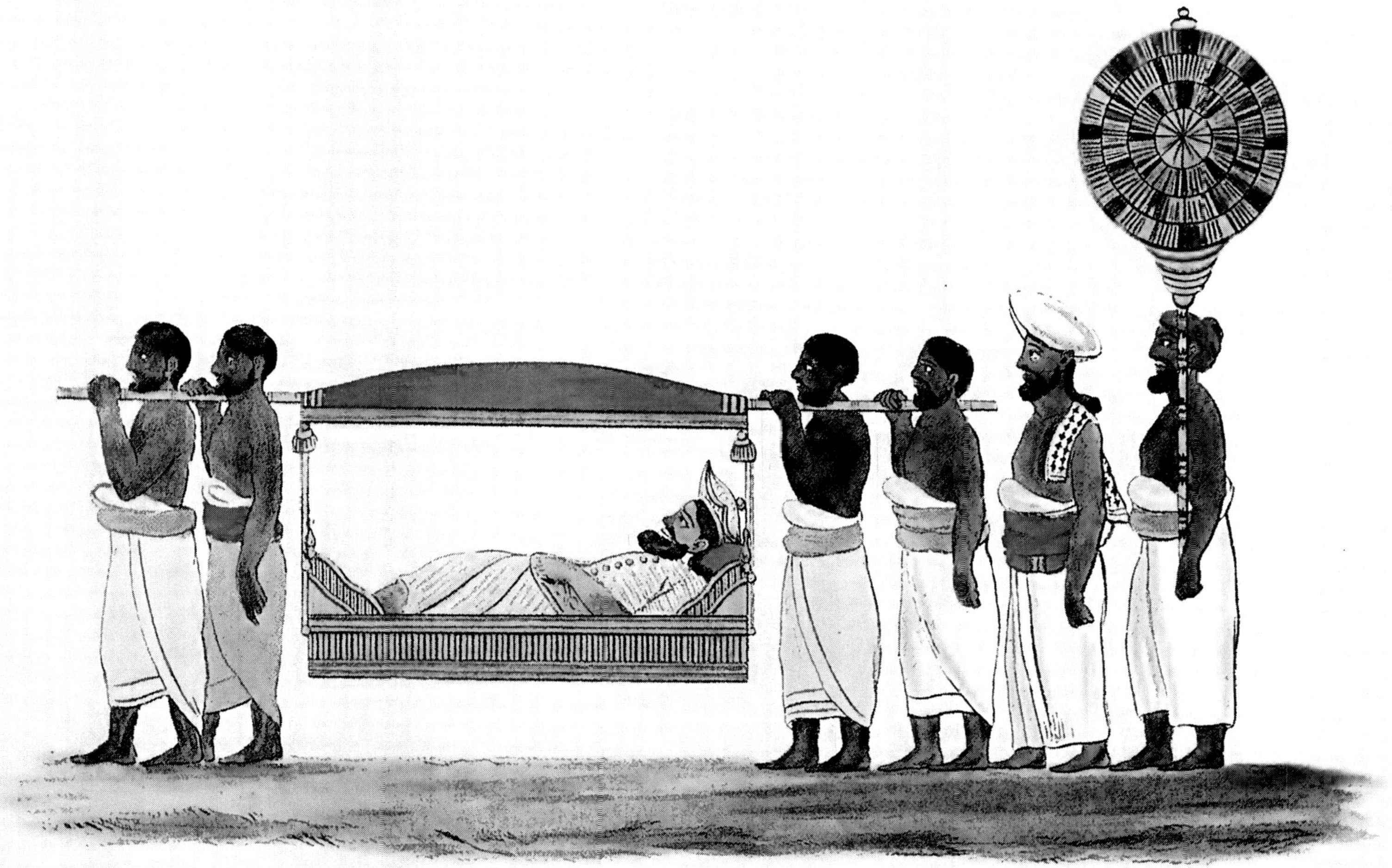

A Kandyan Defsave in his Muncheel,
from a Singhalese drawing.

Engraved by W. C. Edwards.

had intended, and of whose address I am, at this moment, ignorant. I have since submitted to His Grace the Duke of Portland, some specimens of the fibre of the *Musa sylvestris*, and also of white and strong cord manufactured from it.

The Singhalese fishermen make their *finest* nets of the *Hané* plant (*Crotalaria juncea*, L.), which grows upwards of five feet in height, and is more cultivated in the western province than in any other. They also make nets of *Koir* cord, and of the *Sensiviera Zeylanica* of Thunberg.

If it be considered, that in one year, during the last war, Great Britain imported 37,000 tons of hemp, it will occasion much surprise, that the apathy of the government, and the supineness of individuals, in regard to its cultivation in Ceylon, or of the valuable substitutes for it which everywhere present themselves, should keep pace with each other; for surely where so many thousands of square miles of rich land, belonging to the crown, are now lying waste, the profit of an extensive cultivation of hemp and flax would not only abundantly repay the expense of fencing and clearing the land, but leave a considerable surplus profit, and justify the government in monopolizing their culture, if private individuals will not undertake it.

Rope making is here a most profitable business; and there is ample field for many additional manufacturers of that article, from the largest cable to sail-makers' twine; for which latter the *Hané* plant is a very superior material.

At one time, the culture of hemp was thought of so much importance, that it was introduced into Delft Island, and Lieut. Edward Nolan, of the 3rd Ceylon regiment, appointed to superintend it, with a salary of £500 a year, and the privilege of subscribing to the Civil Fund, for an annuity of £400 for life, after twelve years' service in that situation; but, although in addition thereto that gentleman had the troublesome office of superintending the government breeding stud, he was most illiberally restricted from civil promotion or increase of salary.

In all naval contracts, rope made from Laccadive *Koir* was always preferred to that of Ceylon; but that the latter might be improved there can scarcely exist a doubt; or that the process of Kyan, in the prevention of dry-rot, might not be beneficially applied to the rope itself.

In introducing the white and digitated mulberry plants into Ceylon, where the original plantations of the black mulberry (*Morus nigra*, L.) had dwindled into a few stunted trees, here and there, of which the fruit was smaller than the common hedge strawberry, I had fully anticipated that I was laying the foundation of a permanent good to the island. My first distribution of cuttings was, to the late Honorable Sir Hardinge Giffard, D. C. L., the then chief justice, (in 1821,) through whom it was introduced into the botanic gardens at Colombo and Kandy; to Henry Augustus Marshall, Esq., auditor and accountant general; Captain Schneider, surveyor general; Lieut. Colonel Alexander Watson, of the royal artillery; George Turnour, Esq., collector of Kaltura; Captain Crisp, master attendant; the Wesleyan mission gardens at Colombo and Calpetty; and subsequently to Charles Edward Layard, Esq., provincial judge of Galle and Matura, and James Agnew Farrell, Esq., collector of revenue at Chilaw.

The culture of the mulberry plant was an indispensable preliminary to my projected introduction of the several varieties of the silk worm, from Malta, Bengal, China, St. Helena, and the south of France. Had this plan been carried into effect, it would soon have determined *which species* of silk worm would best agree with the humid atmosphere of Ceylon; and as both species of the mulberry tree succeeded beyond my most sanguine hopes, the speculation might have been proceeded with, safely and successfully; and silk have become, long ere this, one of the most valuable exports of the island.

This is one of its capabilities that deserves the attention of capitalists; for there can be very little, if any, difficulty in inducing experienced persons to proceed to Ceylon. A preference might be given to those who had been some time employed in the service of the British, Irish, and Colonial Silk Company; and they would soon be qualified to decide as to the species of silk worm best adapted to the climate, and to select localities for silk factories.

The growth of the mulberry is so extremely rapid, that in less than six months the plantations would be in full bearing; and it might easily be propagated to any extent, by cuttings from the produce of my original introductions from the Mauritius.

The Chinese, who are the greatest silk growers in the world, consider the mulberry tree that bears the least fruit, the best; and adopt a curious method to increase the quantity of foliage, and decrease that of the fruit; namely, by feeding hens upon the ripe fruit of the mulberry tree, after it had been partly dried in the sun; the ordure of the fowls is subsequently collected and steeped in water, and the undigested seeds, having been again soaked in water, are sown, and produce trees of the desired preponderance of foliage. These ingenious people select rising grounds, near rivulets, for the habitations of their silk worms; for the eggs require frequent washings, and the purest running water is considered the best. The place must be kept free from fetid or bad smells, and noise; for when the silk worms are fully hatched, even the barking of a dog, or the crowing of a cock, throws them into confusion.

If I were to plant the mulberry extensively, I would sow indigo by way of undercrop; and, in order to secure shade for the mulberry plants, which would not injure indigo, plant plantain trees at fifteen feet distant from each other, in rows, until the mulberry trees had attained a sufficient height to withstand the sun; and, as the plantain affords a succession of suckers, the ground can always be kept clear enough by their early removal; and the parent trees, after having borne their respective bunch of fruit, (for that is all the plantain or banana tree produces,) can be cut down, for the sake of their fibre, and for their leaves to be employed for fodder; or be allowed to die away gradually, as the necessity for shade or otherwise may obtain.

I also introduced the cassada or manioc (*Jatropha Manihot*) from Mauritius in 1821, but notwithstanding the great and gratuitous distribution of cuttings from the produce of the original stock, this invaluable plant has been so lightly valued, (from, it is to be presumed, ignorance of its inestimable qualities,) that, with the exception of some Malays in the Mahagampattoo, only one individual, Charles Edward Layard, Esq., has paid any sort of attention to its culture. There is no root which is so well adapted, from its nature, to become a substitute for rice; and one or two failures in the rice crop would not only point out the value of the *Jatropha Manihot,* but its cultivation would be considered an object of paramount necessity, as the only certain and easily obtained substitute for that chief article of native consumption. But I have seen so much of the apathy of my countrymen in regard to this invaluable esculent, that until they shall have been convinced by necessity that "prevention is better than cure," I can scarcely hope that its importance will be sufficiently estimated and acted upon.

Another extremely common plant, the *Canna Indica*, or Indian shot, of which there are both the *glauca* and *coccinea*, is equally neglected. The roots of the *Canna glauca* yield a more nutritious farina than the arrow root (*Maranta Arundinacea*, L.), and the process of manufacturing it is equally simple, viz. the roots having been well washed, are rasped upon a large tin or copper grater, and if not quite fine enough, are pounded in a wooden mortar; the pulp is then put into a large tub, and a quantity of water having been poured over it, is stirred well; every particle of fibre is then removed, and the residue allowed to settle for the night; in the morning the water is strained off, and the sediment spread upon clean cloths (under which mats have been previously spread) and dried in the sun.

The light soils of Ceylon are admirably adapted to the cultivation of ginger, cardamoms, *Canna glauca*, *Maranta arundinacea*, and turmeric (*Curcuma longa*, L.), the *Saffran des Indies* of the French. The latter is not so extensively cultivated as might be expected; for although, as a dye, it is in occasional demand, its use is general and indispensable in the native diet. Like the *Amomum Zingiber*, or ginger, its roots spread to a considerable distance under ground, and it resembles that root in shape.

The plant attains the height of from twelve to fourteen inches; the external color of the root is ashy, but internally a bright yellow; the robes of the Buddhist priesthood are dyed with it, yellow being the sacred color.

The common sun-flower's (*Helianthus annuus*) seed is a most valuable article of food for cattle and poultry; and as it attains the greatest perfection in Ceylon, one is almost lost in astonishment at the entire neglect of its cultivation, except as an ornament to the parterre or flower garden. Every part of it is useful. The most delicious oil is expressed from the seed; the oil-cake is a fattening diet for cattle and poultry, and does not impart the rancid flavor to either that the *Poonac* or coco-nut oil-cake does; the stalks produce a great deal of alkali; the dried leaves afford an excellent substitute for straw for cattle; and subsequently form a rich manure for sandy soils.

Various indigenous trees yield elastic gum, nearly equal to the South American caoutchouc; but it has not hitherto been thought worthy of speculative competition. Amongst these may be named the *Ignatia elastica*, L.; *Ficus religiosa*, L.; *Ficus Indica*, L.; *Cecropia peltata; Carica papya*, L.; *Jatropha elastica*, L.; *Artocarpus incisa*, L.; and *Artocarpus integrifolia*, L.

Ceylon produces the true gum arabic (*Mimosa Nilotica*, L.), class Polygamia, order Monœcia, in abundance; nevertheless not a pound of it has been collected for exportation since our first occupation of the island in 1796. Madung Appo, observing that I employed the white of an egg to give a gloss to my drawings of the fishes of Ceylon, (published under the auspices of the Ceylon government in 1830,) brought me a very fine gum, equal to the best gum arabic, which he had obtained from a tree called in Singhalese *Kattoon-daru Gaha;* and he subsequently brought me a branch of the tree with flowers and seeds; the siliquose of the latter emitted a fine aromatic odour. Of the flowers and gum I brought specimens to England, by which it was proved that Ceylon produces the true gum arabic tree.

During my superintendence of the Mahagampattoo district, in 1826 and 1827, I made a few successful experiments with a common augur, in tapping the *Euphorbium antiquorum*, in the presence of several natives, from the orifices of which a thick caustic milky juice abundantly exuded, that soon acquired the consistency of bird-lime, and afterwards hardened to a gum. I recommended it to their notice, as an article of commerce that would amply reward their exertions, as well as afford constant employment in collecting the gum that had formed upon the trees in considerable quantities, through the casual wounds inflicted by animals or insects. They shook their heads, as in distrust of any benefit likely to be derived from it; and as I was then upon the eve of leaving the district, I could do no more than reiterate my advice; but the gum *Euphorbium* is not yet included in the tariff of Ceylon exports.

CHAP. XVI.

Continuation of the vegetable productions of Ceylon—Cachew gum, a substitute for gum Senegal, and for many of the purposes to which gum Arabic is adapted—Sir Joseph Banks's endeavours to find a substitute for foreign gums, during the last war with France—Ceylon could have supplied the British market, but no one knew of it—Gum lac tree, not the Lacsha of Bengal—Singhalese lackerers—Lac insect not indigenous—Kauffman's description of the varieties of gum lac—Suggestions for making the vegetable lac of Ceylon equally profitable with the Coccus lacca—Gum Tarahama—Sap of the bread-fruit tree a substitute for pitch, and also for caoutchouc—Gumboge—Introduction of the coffee tree from Java—Governor Zwaardenkroom—Louis XIV.—Value of coffee exported from Colombo in one year—High duties on cinnamon injurious to that trade, for it encourages the sale of Java cinnamon, under the name of Cassia lignea, which bears a less import duty—Java cinnamon the produce of the Laurus cinnamomum—Clandestinely introduced into that island from Ceylon—Suggestions for assorting the cinnamon imported as Cassia lignea, and protecting the revenue—Cotton neglected in Ceylon, notwithstanding the example set by the East India Company to extend its culture in India—Culture of opium introduced—Its use increased by teetotalism.

THE next valuable gum, but altogether neglected, is that of the cachew tree (*Anacardium occidentale*, L.* and *Acajou* of Tournefort), which is only to be seen in a wild state. It yields a beautifully transparent gum in large masses, from its trunk and branches; and its thick and astringent bark contains a great proportion of tannin, equal, if not superior, in quality to that of the oak (*Quercus Robur*, L.)

In the year 1826, I sent about fifty pounds weight of cachew gum to Messrs. Muskett and Young, merchants at Colombo, for the purpose of being submitted to manufacturers in England for trial; and the report made of it, was to the effect, "that

* Linnæus first placed the *Anacardium* in class IX., and then transferred it to class X. M. Rottröell, Fellow of the Medical College of Copenhagen, after a full examination of several specimens of the inflorescence, fixed the character of the genus in the following manner, which placed it in class XXIII. Polygamia, order I. Monœcia.

The Hermaphrodite Flower. CALYX—*Perianth* five-leaved; *Leaflets* egged, concave, erect, colored, subvillous. COROL—*Petals* five-lanced, acute, &c., as in the character of Linnæus. STAMENS—*Filaments* eight to ten, connected at the base; one of them thicker than the rest and one third part longer, answering to the greater lobe of the germ, which has an *Anther* three-sided, large, fertile, *deciduous*; the rest have *Anthers* less, fruitless, permanent, the figure of the former. PISTIL—*Germ* oblong, kidney-form, with one lobe layer placed higher; *Style* single from the bottom of the germ, awled, equal to the corol; *Stigma* small, roundish, depressed, concave; receptacle and fruit as in Linnæus.

The Male Flower on a different plant. CALYX, COROL, STAMENS—as in the Hermaphrodite flower. PISTIL—*Germ* 0 or abortive.

a superabundance of *Gum Senegal* was then in the market; but that in time of war, cachew gum might be employed to great advantage as a substitute for the former, in dying silk; and also for almost all the purposes to which gum arabic is adapted."

At an early period of the last war with France, the late Sir Joseph Banks, G. C. B., held out great encouragement for the discovery of a substitute for gum in our manufactures; for an opinion at that time obtained, that the supply of foreign gum would soon prove inadequate to the demand. This simple fact is sufficient to show how little was then known of the indigenous productions of our own possessions in Ceylon, which might, at that very time, have supplied all the demands of the British market.

The cachew tree grows to the height of eighteen or twenty feet, and spreads much at the top; but its timber is of little value: the leaves are glossy and thickly set. The gum exudes in such large drops, that insects are occasionally caught in its progress, and are soon covered with a transparent mass, which, upon becoming hard, may be polished. Very beautiful specimens of gum necklaces and bracelets are too often imposed upon purchasers in this country for amber ornaments of Chinese manufacture.

A resinous gum is produced in Ceylon, with which the natives form a lacker of the consistency of sealing-wax, and color it; but I do not recollect seeing it of a greater variety of colors than red, yellow, black, and a sort of bluish or *Vishnu* green. It is not the production of an insect, like that of the *Lacsha* of Bengal (*Coccus lacca*, L.), but exudes from the trunk and branches of the *Croton lacciferum*, L., the *Kapitya gaha* of the Singhalese, wherever punctured by insects, or from incisions made for the purpose of collecting the gum. When quite fresh, it is of a transparent straw color; but, with age, it becomes of a muddy brown hue.

This substance might be turned to good account in this country, as an auxiliary to the fine arts. The Singhalese, and particularly those of the interior, lacker their ceremonial bows and arrows, walking sticks, wooden bowls, and all sorts of boxes, which they make, by a very simple turning lathe, in great perfection, and finish in beautiful style, with the *Kapitya* lac, leaving the surface as smooth and brilliant as the best French polish could effect, but of a more durable nature.

Animals have so great a dread of the tree itself, that they cautiously avoid coming in contact with it; this may be owing to the very nauseous odour that it emits, which is almost as bad as that of the green or winged bug.

I have particularly sought after the lac insect in Ceylon, but without success, and yet the tree that it makes its usual habitat in Bengal, the *Mimosa cinerea*, L., is indigenous and abundant.

According to Kauffman, the substance called *gum lac* in the British market, is the cell of the *Coccus lacca,* colored red by the dead body of the insect contained in it; *stick lac,* the white membraneous substance found in the empty cells, which, when separated from the adhering sticks, and grossly powdered, is called *seed lac;* which last, being freed from impurities by melting over a gentle fire, is called *lump lac;* and lastly, that called *shell lac,* is the cells liquefied.

Now as the Bengal *Coccus lacca,* and the Ceylon *vegetable lac,* are known to possess the same resinous properties; and as the former is made the basis of many varnishes, and of the finest kinds of sealing wax, and is also used in painting, it seems to me to require little more than the spirit of speculation, and the funds of a very moderate capitalist, to render the latter equally valuable as an article of commerce. At present it belongs to the catalogue of the already too long neglected *capabilities* of this incomparable island.

Gum *Tacamaha* may be procured in any quantity from the roots of the *Domba* tree (*Calophyllum Inophyllum,* L.), the *Domba gaha* of the Singhalese, which is indigenous and most abundant. This resinous gum is called by the Malabars *Tacamaha.* Its smell is fragrant, approaching to that of ambergris: but the *Tacamahaca* of commerce exudes from the bark of the balsam tree (*Populus balsamifera,* L.) The native doctors employ the gum externally, in cataplasms, &c.

Although other indigenous trees yield resinous gums, their number is too limited, in comparison with the abundance of those already described, to render their produce worth the trouble of collecting.

The sap of the bread-fruit tree (*Artocarpus incisa,* L.), when hardened in the sun, and subsequently boiled, forms a tolerable substitute for pitch; but, even if that tree were not otherwise so useful as it is, the sap would be more profitably employed in a raw state, by being converted into India-rubber.

Gumboge may be obtained in any quantity from the *Cambogia gutta,* L. (*Ghorkah* of the Singhalese); *Stalagmites Cambogioides,* and *Xanthochymus ovatifolius.* It is sold in the Bazaars, but has not hitherto been an export from the colony. The home market is chiefly supplied from the Indian continent.

Coffee (*Coffea Arabica,* L.) was first introduced into Ceylon from the island of Java, where it was originally planted by the governor general of Batavia, Zwaardenkroom, who procured the seeds and plants from Mocha, in the Arabian Gulf, in the year 1723. This public benefactor did not limit his views to the mere benefit of the islands under his control, but sent the coffee plant from Batavia to Amsterdam; for with him nothing was thought of too little importance for grave consideration, when the national advantage lay even in the most distant prospective; and so ought all to think who have the management of colonies, and love for their country.

The coffee plants sent from Batavia to Amsterdam, soon attracted public attention; and, amongst others, the French consul seemed to take a particular interest in the novelty that had been introduced; and he subsequently succeeded in obtaining one of the plants, which he sent to his sovereign, the then Grande Monarque, Louis XIV.

This plant having been placed in a hothouse, throve admirably well and seeded; and the French government attached so much importance to its naturalization in the West Indies, that three plants of the first produce were transmitted to the island of Martinique; and never were crown diamonds or regalia guarded with more care: but, notwithstanding every precaution and attention, only one plant survived the voyage. That plant was the original parent of all the present coffee plantations in the British, French, and Spanish West Indies; and I much question if all the glories of Louis the fourteenth's reign together, entitle him to more honor than his introduction of the coffee plant into culture at Martinique. It rendered his country and humanity a benefit that will survive a million of victories:—laid the foundation for an extension of commerce; from which various nations derive immense revenues, merchants increase of riches, and mankind one of the most exhilarating and wholesome beverages, of which, nature has, hitherto, produced the means.

In the year ending the 5th of January, 1841, the value of coffee exported to Great Britain, from the port of Colombo alone, amounted to 197,387*l.* 10*s.* 4*d.*; but there was not a single bale of cotton or silk, or a pound of cocoa, indigo, gum, opium, annatto, or cochineal, of the produce of the island, exported; and not even pepper enough of Ceylon growth to pack the cinnamon; and yet all these articles are either indigenous, or may be easily naturalized.

The present mania for coffee planting daily increases; and will continue to do so until the government either reduces the cinnamon duty, upon the export of cinnamon from Ceylon, and upon its importation here, or places the cinnamon grower upon a more equal footing with the cultivators of coffee and other produce. It is the great difference in the duty which causes the present high price of coffee grounds, and the low price of cinnamon plantations, and consequently increases the value of the former article, whilst it depreciates that of the latter.

The injury done to the Ceylon cinnamon grower, by the importation of the same spice, the produce of Java, under the *pseudo* denomination of *Cassia lignea*, at an inferior duty of, I believe, one shilling per pound avoirdupois, may easily be imagined; for although there may be, and, no doubt, is, a large proportion of *Cassia lignea,* probably of the produce of Malabar and China, mixed with the true spice, for sinister purposes, as regards the import duty; a similar process to that of assorting cinnamon in Ceylon, would, if adopted in our import warehouses, soon establish the fact, that of the quantity imported as *Cassia lignea,* the proportion of *true* cinnamon will be found to predominate.

In corroboration of my statement, I may venture to state one or two facts, of equal importance, at the present moment, to the Ceylon cinnamon grower and exporter, and to the revenue derived from its importation here.

When Lord Glenelg avowed to certain merchants, by letter dated 6th March, 1838, that "he is unable to say whether coffee is grown in West Africa," the most satirical reflections were cast upon the colonial department by the commercial community; and that same body, so far as it includes those who are profiting at the expense of the Ceylon cinnamon grower, would also, there can be little doubt, be better pleased than otherwise, if the noble president of the board of trade and foreign plantations were to avow himself equally unable to decide the point to which his Lordship's attention has been recently drawn, by merchants connected with the Ceylon trade, in regard to the cinnamon of that island.

It is not, however, unknown to his Lordship, that the island of Java, whilst Ceylon formed one of its dependencies, was not considered by the Dutch government to produce cinnamon or *Cassia lignea,* although the latter *might* have been wild in certain districts of the interior of that immense island; the former, the *Laurus Cinnamomum,* L., the latter, the *Laurus Cassia,* L.; for the Dutch, pursuing the same policy by which they destroyed every nutmeg and clove tree in Ceylon, and restricted the culture of the former to the Banda islands, and of the latter to the Moluccas, prohibited the growth of cinnamon, except in Ceylon, throughout their Eastern colonies.

Consequently all the spice *denominated Cassia lignea,* or base cinnamon, now imported from Java, must be the produce of trees planted subsequently to the cession of Ceylon to our flag, on the 14th of February, 1796; for it is well known, that many of the Dutch families, who quitted Ceylon for Java with the former Dutch garrisons of the forts that had been ceded, did not go empty-handed, either in regard to cinnamon plants or seeds.

But it is not from that original introduction only, of the cinnamon plant into Java, that all the spice now imported as *Cassia lignea,* to the prejudice of the Ceylon cinnamon trade, is obtained; for, in the year 1825, upwards of three thousand cinnamon plants, were, through the connivance of interested persons, smuggled off the island by a brig bound to Batavia.

The brig, when she first arrived at Galle, was commanded by an Englishman; but the Dutch owner, fully aware that the commander was too honourable a man to listen to a proposition of so illicit a nature as the contemplated removal of cinnamon plants, managed to quarrel with him first, and then to discharge him; and subsequently engaged a ready coadjutor in his nefarious scheme among his own countrymen.

The best protection that can be afforded to the Ceylon cinnamon trade, would be, to subject all *Cassia lignea*, imported from Java, or other Dutch settlements, or elsewhere, to the same process of assortment as is adopted in Ceylon; and by charging an increased rate of duty upon all cinnamon found mixed with, and imported as, *Cassia lignea*, and continuing the duty on the rest, as at present; viz. 2*s*. 6*d*. per pound.

The external appearance of these two varieties of the aromatic laurel, cannot be distinguished while growing, except by the leaf; and that only by those who are accustomed to both trees.

As to cotton, the great exertions made by the Honorable the East India Company to extend and improve its culture in India, by engaging planters from America, is a convincing proof of the importance attached to it by that preeminent body in the commercial affairs of this great country, "whose merchants are princes;" and a sufficient excitement, one would think, for the employment of capital for the same purpose in Her Majesty's island of Ceylon.

Hitherto the chief objects of *European* culture in the interior, exclusively of esculent vegetables and fruits, have been the coffee tree and sugar cane; both of which flourish in the greatest perfection; and Ceylon coffee, by the rapid improvements in its cultivation, may soon be expected to equal the produce of Mocha.

The Kandyans select the best coffee by its bluish color, and by its weight; but they are perfectly *au fait* at giving it an artificial weight, by the soaking process, in order to profit by the difference. Coffee sells at Colombo at about 6*d*. per pound, or 1*s*. per measure, which will contain about two pounds avoirdupois weight, more or less. The lighter and whiter coffee is called second quality. Raw sugar is considered dear at 4*d*. per pound.

Opium, the inspissated juice of the white poppy (*Papaver somniferum*, L.), was first cultivated in the Mahagampattoo, in the year 1826. I obtained the original seeds from Malwah, where the finest opium is produced, through the kind offices of Captain John Morris, who was at that time editor of the Bombay Gazette. Having ascertained, by trial, that the soil and climate of the banks of the Wallewé river were well adapted to the culture of the opium poppy, I sent for a further supply of seed; the produce of my own plantation, which, after the first successful experiments, had been reserved for that purpose, having been swept away, by the sudden rise of the Wallewé river, in October of that year, just as the capsules had attained maturity. The second importation of opium poppy seed, which was sufficient for general distribution, I placed at the disposal of the governor, in February, 1827; His Excellency having previously taken an opportunity of acknowledging me, as the first introducer of the culture of opium into the island, at a general meeting of the Literary and Agricultural Society of Colombo, in December, 1826.

I had subsequently the great satisfaction of seeing that my public objects in the introduction of the culture of the white and digitated mulberry, and of the opium poppy, were likely to be realized, under the fostering care of the local government; for, on the 21st of September, 1829, a regulation of government was passed by the governor in council, "*for promoting the growth of certain articles of agricultural produce, in the island of Ceylon, and for the encouragement of agricultural speculation,*" in which the articles silk and opium were included, for the first time, in a regulation of the Ceylon government.*

But the great difficulty to be overcome, in all matters connected with native industry, was very obvious to Sir Edward Barnes; who, in a letter to me, dated the 14th of February, 1827, thus pointedly alludes to it,—"I have to return you my thanks for the packet of Malwah poppy-seed which you forwarded, and likewise for the paper of instructions relative to the cultivation of the plant, and preparation of opium from its capsules; and I have no doubt that it, in common with many other articles of commerce, might be brought to perfection in the island, *could the natives be convinced of the importance of attention to agricultural industry.*"—"Hic labor, hoc opus!!"

The poppy plants appeared above ground in six days after the seed was sown, and in less than six weeks were in full bloom: abundance of capsules soon formed; from the juice of which, about a pound of opium, of good quality, was procured by my Malay gardener, (who withheld it from my knowledge till I was upon the eve of quitting the district,) and sufficient seed was reserved for twelve large beds, exclusively of the quantity distributed to some Malays in the district. The second crop was totally destroyed, as I have before stated.

The juice of the opium poppy is of a very thick nature, and of a milky white; the incision is made in the green capsule in the shape of a T, and the juice that flows during the night, congeals before morning, when it is scraped off with a blunt knife;

* Vide Appendix.

this is subsequently formed into small cakes, and is the opium of commerce. East Indian opium is now rendered, by a peculiar process, as pure as that of Turkey. An acre will produce about forty pounds; but the growth of the opium poppy soon exhausts the best soil, and renders the application of a powerful manure, of which the fœcula of the indigo leaf is one of the best, indispensable.

The natives of India are quite *au fait* at the adulteration of opium with resinous gums and an extract from the leaves and flower stalks of the poppy.

Many objections have been started to the culture of the opium poppy; and China is cited for an example of its injurious effects upon the population; but notwithstanding that it has been prohibited from immemorial time, by a succession of *Vermilion* edicts, the vicious appetite of the people has been found much too strong for legal restraint.

In this country, as teetotalism extends, so will the use of opium increase; and already has its use taken deep root amongst that class of the people which has determined to abstain from the use of wines, spirits, cider, and the less wholesome *melange* of hops, malt, and narcoctics. As well may the use of spirits be prohibited in England, as that of opium in China; or let the duty upon either be what it may, those who are slaves to either habit, will indulge it at all costs and risks, when and where they can.

CHAP. XVII.

Extreme opinions as regards the Fruits of the island—Natives have no method of engrafting or improving fruit trees—Naturalized exotic fruits—Native Materia Medica and medical books—Classification of fruits—Mangosteen—Ramboutan—Nam-nam—Rose Apple—Sour-sop—Brazil Cherry—Grape—Lo-quat—Star Apple—Canary Almond—Lemon—Bladder Cherry—Fig—Lovi-lovi—Stripe-leaved Pine Apple—Mandarin Orange—Wampi—Pomegranate—Melon—Strawberry—Mulberry——Indigenous fruits: Pine Apple—Orange—Shaddock—Guava—Papaw—Mango—Custard Apple—Cœur de Bœuf—Bilimbing—Cherimelle—Carambole—Jack Fruit—Bread Fruit—St. Helena Almond—Caffrarian Lime—Jambo—Trefoil Limonia—Plantain and Banana—Cachew Apple.

As regards the fruits of Ceylon, the superficial observer may be led into extreme opinions, by esteeming them too much, or too little. It should be recollected, that the natives know nothing of engrafting, and are equally ignorant of any other method for improving fruits or vegetables; everything is therefore left to nature, except where Europeans have adopted the horticultural systems of their own country, for improving the several indigenous varieties, and perfecting the exotics, that, from time to time, have been introduced from various parts of the world.

Of the number of edible fruits, the best are from naturalized exotics, originally introduced by the Dutch, from Guiana, and the islands of Java and Amboyna; but these are only to be found in the gardens of the principal European and native inhabitants; and as the native *Materia Medica* is chiefly, if not altogether, composed, of simples, which include the roots, leaves, and bark, as well as the gums, of fruit-bearing and other trees, I have included a description of the medicinal uses to which they are applied by the Singhalese.

The native doctors possess many ancient medical books; of these, the best are said to be in Sanscrit and Pali; between which languages, the learned in Eastern literature trace a near affinity; but, as to the productions of Singhalese writers, they are stated to consist chiefly of incantations, and magical jargon about the influence of the moon and the stars upon the several plants, and the proper, or *most fortunate* time, for the simpler to collect them.

The fruits may be described in three classes; the first, to consist of such as are only to be found in private gardens; the second, of those that are procurable in almost every bazaar; and the third, of the wild fruits that are eaten by the lowest class of the natives.

The Mangosteen (*Garcinia Mangostana*, L.), was originally introduced by the Dutch, from the island of Great Banda, whilst Ceylon was a dependency of the government of Batavia. This fruit has a smooth epidermis, is round, and of a purple color, and rather larger than a St. Michael's orange; it rests in a permanent green calyx, and the top is surmounted by an eight-rayed corona. It is usual to cut it transversely in the middle, but not deeper than the rind, which is about a third of an inch thick; the top part is then taken off, and exposes the pulp; this is of a pure white, and divided into eight lobes, each containing a seed, convex on one side and angular on the other. The Mangosteen is considered the *ne plus ultra* of all tropical fruits. The astringent juice of the rind stains linen of an iron-rust color; and, when combined with oxide of iron, makes a beautiful purple ink, which, when dry, has a brilliant gloss.

The Ramboutan (*Euphoria nephelium*, the *Nephelium lappaceum*, L.), originally introduced from Java, is much smaller in size, and more oblong, than the European horse-chesnut, which it resembles externally; but its bristles, instead of being green, as in the latter, are beautifully tinged with crimson and yellow. The fruit grows in large clusters; and the edible part of it is a pure white mucilaginous pulp, very cooling and wholesome, and of a peculiarly pleasant sub-acid flavor.

The Nam-nam (*Cynometra cauliflora*, L.), originally introduced from Malacca, grows from the trunk and branches of the tree. It is flat and kidney-shaped, has the color of a ripe russet apple and the flavor of a green one.

The Rose Apple (*Eugenia fragrans*, L.), originally introduced from Java, partakes both of the smell and flavor of the moss-rose, and has the color of an apricot. It is sweeter, but as insipid to the taste, as the petals of the flower from which it derives its English name.

The Sour-sop (*Annona muricata*, L.), originally introduced from the Dutch settlement of Surinam, in Guiana, is extremely scarce. The pome grows to a large size, and has a green murexed rind, which, at maturity, bursts and exposes its woolly pulp, in appearance like wetted cotton. This has a pleasant sub-acid taste. The creoles of the West Indies make a very choice liqueur from it, called, from the French name of the tree, *Corossol*.

The Brazil Cherry (*Eugenia uniflora*, L.) was introduced into Ceylon by myself, from the governor's garden at Reduit, Mauritius, in 1821. The French call it *Roussail*. When ripe, it is about the size of a small green-gage plum, of a bright orange color, ribbed like a melon, and has a peculiar but pleasant flavor.

The Grape (*Vitis vinifera*, L.) was originally introduced from Goa, on the coast of Malabar, by the Portuguese; whose envoys, amongst other presents, carried grape vines to the Rajah of Ceylon, which throve very well in Kandy. Knox mentions both black and white grapes, in his account of Ceylon, published in 1681. The vine flourishes better at Jaffnapatam, than in any other part of the maritime provinces.

The Lo-quat (*Eriobotrya Japonica*), originally introduced by the Dutch, from China or Japan, is a small oblong fruit, of an apricot color. It grows in bunches, and has a very agreeable sub-acid flavor. The flower has the exquisite perfume of the hawthorn (*Cratægus odoratissima*, L.) blossom.

The Star Apple (*Chrysophyllum Cainito*, L.) is an extremely scarce fruit, of a purple color; and when divided transversely, the pulp, which is very luscious, displays the figure of a star. The juice is white, and of the consistence of cream. It was originally introduced by the Dutch from Surinam. I never saw but two or three specimens of this fruit, and these were sent me by the Count Van Ranzow, in 1820.

The Canary Almond (*Canarium communis*, L.), originally introduced from Batavia by the Dutch, is a very sweet nut, of superior flavor to the filbert, and yields a valuable oil.

The Lemon (*Citrus Limonum*) was originally introduced by the Portuguese; but the people take no trouble to cultivate it; the more juicy lime (*Citrus limetta vulgaris*) being both indigenous and abundant.

The Bladder Cherry (*Physalis Alkahengi*, L.) was introduced from the Cape of Good Hope. When the flower drops, the calyx swells to the size of a small walnut, and forms a pentagonal covering, blown out like a bladder, for the fruit, which is about the size of a large white currant, and generally used for tarts. There is a wild plant in Ceylon that greatly resembles this *Physalis* in appearance, but is most nauseous to the taste.

The Fig (*Ficus Carica*, L.), introduced by the Portuguese, grows freely, but requires artificial caprification to ripen it. This is easily effected by the French (Provence) plan of dipping an orange spine into olive oil, and gently puncturing the fruit. The admission of atmospheric air soon causes the flower, which is within the receptacle, to expand, and the fruit to ripen.

The Lovi-lovi, (as the Malays call it,) introduced from Amboyna by the Dutch, is like the large red cherry in appearance. This fruit is very acid; its pulp makes an excellent jelly, quite equal in flavor to red currant jelly; and the tree altogether resembles the cherry tree of Europe.

The Stripe-leaved Pine Apple (*Bromelia Ananas, variegata*, L.) was originally introduced by myself, from Mauritius, in 1821; the leaf is striped longitudinally with light yellow or straw color, but the fruit is not better than that of the indigenous species.

The Mandarin Orange (*Citrus nobilis*, L.) was originally introduced from Java. Of this delicious fruit there are three varieties; one, about the size of a common orange, having so very fine and loose a rind, that, if taken by the crown, the pulp is easily shaken out of it; the second sort is smaller, with a thicker rind; and the third is about the size of a golden pippin, and very luscious.

The Wampi (*Cookia punctata*, L.) was originally introduced from China, *viâ* Java, and is rare. In shape, it resembles the *Li-tchi* of China (*Dimocarpus Litchi*), but differs in taste, the pulp of the former having a sub-acid, the latter a sweet flavor.

The Pomegranate (*Punica granatum*, L.) was introduced by the Portuguese, from Goa, and is abundant. The rind of the fruit is much employed by the native doctors, and is in great esteem for its astringent properties.

The best Melons are produced from English and Persian seeds; of the latter, the sorts called *Dampsha* or *Zamsksy*, and the *Geree* or ostrich-egg, are the best. The plants require no transplanting, but much shade.

The Strawberry (*Fragaria vesca*, L.); and the Mulberry, of the white (*Morus alba*, L.), black (*M. Indica*, L.), and digitated (*M. digitata*, L.) species, complete the list of naturalized exotic fruits.

The Pine Apple (*Bromelia Ananas*, L.), *Anasi* of the Singhalese, in greater abundance than variety. The White, and the Black (or Stone) Pines, are the best; but the most common is the Red or Orange Pine.

The Orange (*Citrus Aurantium*, L.) is either of a deep green or of a russet color, when perfectly ripe. This most cooling and delicious fruit is not excelled in flavor by the best Barbary orange; and, together with the lime (*Citrus limetta vulgaris*), and citron (*Citrus medica*), is in the greatest abundance.

The Shadock or Pumplenose (*Citrus decumana*, L.), both of the white and red varieties, and of a very large size; and there is a smaller species, which is very juicy, but scarce.

The Guava (*Psidium pyriferum*, L.) is found wild, walk where one may, near a village; but it is seldom cultivated. The fruit is cooling, and has the flavor of a strawberry; but, owing to the superabundance of its seeds, is best when stewed, or made into a jelly. Its size and flavor are both easily improved by grafting.

The Papaw (*Carica Papya*, L.) is a valuable fruit. There is a male, female, and hermaphrodite Papaw tree. The female produces such a quantity of fruit, in clusters round the stalk, for the depth of two or three feet between and beneath the fronds, that nature forces off a great many, to afford room for the rest to ripen. The fruit of the hermaphrodite tree is smaller, and more melon-shaped than that of the female tree, and grows at the extremities of the dependent flower stalks. The white flowers hang in long clusters, are very fragrant, and have a beautiful appearance. The Papaw is somewhat pear-shaped, and ribbed longitudinally; the rind is of a bluish-green color, from which, upon the least puncture, drops of a milk-white liquid exude; the inside is of a bright orange color. The seeds lie closely united by a sort of gluten in the cavity of the fruit, and are enveloped in a brownish-green pellicle; these have all the pungency of seeding cress (*Lepidium*, L. and T.), and are a specific remedy for the ill effects of too great indulgence in the fruit itself. The pulp is of a similar nature to the flesh of a very ripe melon, and possesses the peculiar flavor of the Tonquin bean. In a green state, the Papaw makes an excellent pickle, and sweetmeat; and, when boiled and mashed, is a substitute for the turnip, in places where the latter is not to be procured; this answers the purpose so very well, that it is in general use at the tables of Europeans; where, a leg of veal, doing duty for a leg of mutton, is not very uncommon. The acrid juice of the green fruit is medicinally applied to remove worts, and specks on the eyes; and it is also considered efficacious in destroying the ringworm. The odoriferous blossoms are so very wholesome, that no dread need be entertained of having any number of these herbaceous trees near one's residence. Their growth is so rapid, that seedlings produce fruit in about six months. The red-flowered, or dwarf variety (*C. Posoposa*), common to the West Indies, is not known in Ceylon.

The Mango (*Mangifera Indica*, L.) comprises several varieties; but the large Jaffna cordiform mango, the almond-shaped Matura mango, which is not more than one inch and a half in length, and the kidney mango, about six or seven inches in length, are the best; the last grows in large pendent clusters. The common mango is stringy, and has more of the turpentine flavor, peculiar to the genus, than the other sorts: when green, it makes an excellent pickle; the only purpose for which it is adapted. There is also a species of the mango tree that produces no fruit; this is called *Colu-ambo*, or mango leaf, from which the town of Colombo is said to have derived its name: and not, as some have averred, in honor of the celebrated Columbus.

The Custard Apple (*Annona squamosa*, L.) has a white pulp, so like custard, that were it not for its black seeds, and a drop or two of noyeau were mixed with it, one might be deceived to eat the natural for an artificial custard.

The Bullock's Heart (*Annona reticulata*, L.) is more luscious than the custard apple, but not so delicate. From its resemblance to a heart, it was originally called *Cœur de Bœuf*, by the French. A branch of the leaves, laid where there are bugs, will attract them all, as I have proved by experience;—this should be generally known, for these disgusting insects infest the chairs and sofas of many rest-houses, much to the annoyance of the traveller.

The Bilimbing (*Averrhoa Bilimbi*, L.), the Cherimelle (*A. acida*, L.), and the Carambole (*A. Carambola*, L.), are three species of a very acid genus; but they are excellent tart fruits, and are also used in the native curries.

The Jack Fruit (*Artocarpus integrifolia*, L.) is the largest the island produces. The fruit grows from the body of the tree, and is sack-shaped, large, and heavy, occasionally exceeding thirty pounds avoirdupois in weight. Its juice is an elastic substance, of a milky white, and so tenacious, that it is used for the purposes of bird-lime. The pulp is eaten in curries; the luscious bright yellow and fleshy coverings of the seeds are generally served at table in salt and water; and the roasted seeds are used as substitutes for chesnuts. The odour of this fruit is very fetid and diffusive.

The Bread Fruit (*Artocarpus incisa*, L.) might more properly be classed among the esculent vegetables; for it can only be eaten after having undergone a culinary process. It is by no means so palatable in the usual native way of currying every thing, as when parboiled and baked, or boiled and served as a substitute for the artichoke, or fried in thin slices: in this last way, it certainly resembles crisp pie-crust; but, according to my experience of its use for several years, and, I believe, in almost every way known to the native cooks, I never could carry my imagination so far, as to agree in opinion with those who describe the bread fruit as very like new bread, or (when baked whole) hot rolls; "sed, de gustibus, nil disputandum!"

The St. Helena Almond (*Terminalia Catappa*, L.), the *Kattamba* of the Singhalese, is served at desserts; it is extremely sweet and pleasant to the taste.

The Caffrarian Lime* (*Citrus tuberöides*) is occasionally preserved as a sweetmeat; but the principal use made of it by the Singhalese, is for cleaning their long black hair. The entire fruit having been first boiled, is then mashed to the consistency of a thick paste, which they rub well into the hair; this, they aver, makes it hard, and the head clean; and, for the purpose of cleansing the hair of the pulp, the white and yolk of eggs, beaten together, is employed as a succedaneum. Europeans call the fruit Caffrarian Lime, and the Singhalese, *Koodalodeyé*. The natives praise it for its various medicinal properties; but the most useful purpose to which I have seen it applied, is for curing the bite of the diminutive but most troublesome Ceylon leech (*Hirudo Zeylanica*).

The Jambo* (*Eugenia Malaccensis*, L.) is a beautiful and very juicy fruit; of this there are two varieties. The epidermis of the largest sort looks like white wax,

* For a full account of these fruits, vide Bennett's "Fruits of Ceylon," 4to. Wood, 1842.

delicately tinged with red; the other is nearly of the color of a half-ripe Orleans Plum, with an occasional tinge of deep red, where the fruit has been most exposed to the sun. The pome is juicy, cooling, and of an agreeable vinous flavor and smell; the latter partaking, but in a very slight degree, of the perfume of the *Eugenia fragrans*, L., or rose apple. It forms part of the usual dessert at European tables; and is also stewed or baked, after the manner of pears in Europe, and occasionally preserved as a sweetmeat. In order to give it a pink or deeper red color, to resemble baked pears, the native cooks employ the petals of the shoe-flower* (*Hybiscus rosa Sinensis*, var. duplex). The large bats, called flying foxes (*Vespertilio Vampyrus*, L.), are extremely partial to this fruit; and, if the natives did not, in some measure, provide against their night attacks, by stretching lines, attached to a bell, from branch to branch, these destructive animals would devour the produce of a large tree in a few hours.

The Trefoil Limonia (*Triphosia Aurantiola*), the *Macunjé* of the Singhalese, is a little aromatic fruit, having the flavor of citron. When ripe, it is of a crimson color, and is chiefly used for sweetmeats. There are two other indigenous species, *T. monopylla* and *T. acidissima*.

The Plantain (*Musa sapientum*, L.) and Banana (*M. Paradisiaca*, L.). Of the former there are sixteen varieties; but the gigantic red (*Tanjore*), the green sugar (*Madras*), and the speckled (*Tellicherry*) plantains are the best. The Hindo-Portuguese call the plantain tree, the fig-tree (*Figuera*) of Paradise; and very properly so, for one leaf of it, wrapped round the loins, is sufficient for all the purposes of the strictest modesty; and if the plantain leaf split, it still hangs pendent in a double row from its mid-rib; and, when dry, is much tougher than in a green state. There is also a peculiarity and virtue in the plantain leaf but little known; and when we connect it with the scriptural records, that our original parents "sewed fig leaves together, and made themselves aprons;" and observe the brittle substance of the *common fig leaf*, and then examine the great size and substance of the plantain leaf, we shall be disposed to think that instead of "sewed fig leaves together," the text should have been, "they *formed* aprons of fig leaves." There is also a most wonderful provision of nature in the leaf of the *Musa;* the upper surface is of a glossy green, the under surface covered with a sort of bloom; the former is generally employed for healing blisters, the latter for exciting them. The Divine intention might have been, for the upper or healing surface to have been worn next the skin, and the under surface externally; for if water be thrown upon that surface, it runs off like globules of quicksilver.

* So called because its bruised petals are occasionally used as a substitute for *blacking*.

In its green state, and roasted, the plantain is eaten in lieu of bread, and forms a better substitute for it than the bread-fruit itself. It is also a general ingredient in native curries; and if it be dried in the sun and pulverized, and kept in closely-corked bottles, it will retain its flavor for many years. This flour might also be made a valuable article of domestic economy and of commerce. I first learnt to prepare it in the West Indies, where it is called *Congontay*. The root of the plantain tree is also edible; but it is only the very poorest class of natives that makes use of it. The juice of the herbaceous stalk, combined with oxide of iron, makes a fine *blue-black* dye.

The Cachew Apple* (*Anacardium occidentale*, L.), the *Cajhu* of the Singhalese, is juicy and of rather a spongy nature; but has an unpleasant smell, which some people assimilate to garlic. The apples that are most exposed to the sun, are largest and best, and are of a bright yellow, variegated with red; their juice is of a restringent acid flavor, but custom soon reconciles one to its use, notwithstanding the temporary contraction of the skin of the mouth, consequent upon eating the fruit. Dutch families occasionally manufacture a superior spirit from the cachew apple, which some prefer, as a liqueur, (but not for diluting with water,) to the best brandy. The cachew apple, stuck with cloves and roasted, gives a peculiarly delicious flavor to arrack punch; and its juice may be used for marking linen; for by the application of lime water upon the writing, after it is dry, the color becomes black. The kernel of the nut, which grows from the crown of the apple, is eaten both in a green and dry state; but the natives roast the ripe nut, in order to get rid of the hard acrid pellicle that envelopes it. The nut-shell contains a powerful oil, which might be usefully employed for a variety of purposes, and particularly as a varnish to wood, for the white ant (*Termes*) will never attack any thing besmeared with it. In some instances, I have seen the leaf of this tree so much like that of the jack tree, that I could scarcely tell the one from the other; and in two specimens, brought to me at the same time, by a native doctor, the fruits were unusually large and alike in shape and color, but the distinction of the leaf was so remarkable that I made drawings of both. I have heard, that as much gas may be obtained from an ounce of the nut-shells, as from three pounds of the best coal; but as no known authority was given for the assertion, it must be considered altogether hypothetical for the present.

* The gum of this tree has been already described in page 129.

CHAP. XVIII.

Indigenous fruits continued: Ghorka—Champaka—Kirila—Marsan Apple—Jar Plum—Wood Apple—Khon—Tamarind—Pharaoh's Fig—Rattan Fruit—Ceylon Olive—Melon—Slime Apple—Myrobolams—Red and yellow fleshed Water Melons——Esculent vegetables: Horseradish tree—Kallaloo—Purslane—Spinach—Jerusalem Artichoke—White Radish—Asparagus—Indian Corn—Gourds—Sorrel—Bamboo sprouts—Beans—Carpintchee leaf—Brinjals—Suggestions to the English market-gardener—Cress—Lettuce—Celery—Endive—Beet—Carrots—Cucumbers—Cabbage—Bandika—Parsley—Mint—Borage—Roots—Sweet Potato—Yam—Iris—Moon-flower—White and red Water Lilies—Eschelot—Garlic—Capsicum—Tomato—Snake Gourd—Sour Gourd—Mushroom—Nol-col—Red Sorrel—Green Pea—Arrow Root; Difference between that of Ceylon and Bombay—Sweet Fennel—Ginger—Illepei—Bird's-nest Cucumber—Tala—Carraway Seed—Fenugreek—Sweet Sorrel—Cardamoms—Mustard—Guinea or Pigeon Pea, supplied to the royal navy in the Indian seas, under the name of Dhol, as a substitute for pease—Rice, and other grain; Native Agriculturists deficient in the selection of the best species.

THE Ghorka (*Cambogia gutta*, L.). This fruit is round and ribbed like a rock melon, and of the size of the Mangosteen; but, although *somewhat* resembling it in flavor, the Ghorka has a great degree of acidity, which the former has not. There are two sorts of this fruit, the red and the yellow; but the latter is the most pleasant to the taste; and, when cut transversely, the pulp resembles in shape, and is divided into lobes, like that of the Mangosteen; but instead of being white, as in the latter, it partakes of the color of its own epidermis. That the Ghorka is not sufficiently esteemed by Europeans, may arise from its cooling and wholesome properties not being so generally known as they deserve to be. The natives dry the rind in the sun, and employ it in their curries; and their doctors prescribe the yellow concrete juice of the tree, which is the gumboge of our dispensaries, in dropsical, cutaneous, and leprous cases.

The Champaka (*Michelia Champaca*, L.). This elegant fruit grows in clusters, like grapes. The saffron-colored flowers are much esteemed by the Buddhists, it being their sacred color, and the robes of their priesthood are of that hue. Devotees make offerings of these flowers to Buddha.

The *Kirila* of the Singhalese (*Sonneratia acida*, L.) is, as its Linnæan name implies, a very acid fruit, but is eaten by the natives. Linnæus describes it as "sitting on the expanded permanent calyx, globular, smooth, succulent, and many-celled." The most useful parts of the tree are the straight and conical roots: these strike upwards in the water, the *habitat* of the tree being marshy places. At one time, during the war, the Dutch being driven to great straits for corks, brought the elastic roots into general use as a substitute; and I have occasionally employed them for the same purpose.

The Marsan Apple (*Zisyphus spinosus*, L.), *Wal-Hambilla* of the Singhalese, resembles the Siberian crab in shape, but is larger, and yellow instead of red. The tree grows rapidly, and its branches and leaves are so beset with spines, that a more admirable production for fences cannot well be imagined.

The Jar Plum (*Calyptranthes Jambolana*, L.), *Maden* of the Singhalese, is of an oblong shape, about the size of a half-grown damson, and of a purple color, but reddish within. It yields a milky juice, of insipid sweetness.

The Wood Apple (*Cratæva Marmelos*, L.), *Beli gaha* of the Singhalese. The pulp is yellow, and covered with a hard rind, which has the smell of a ripe apricot. It is not liked at first, but one soon becomes partial to it. The Dutch and Portuguese distil an exquisite cosmetic from the rind and blossom, called *Marmelle* water, and the Singhalese doctors employ the leaves for curing inflammations and pains in the head and ears.

The Khon or Koang (a species of *Dimocarpus*) grows in clusters. It is like the Wampi (*Cookia punctata*, L.) in shape, and has a slightly acid pulp. The tree, at a short distance, resembles the oak.

The Tamarind (*Tamarindus Indica*, L.) is common and abundant. The method of preserving this acid fruit is very simple; the pods having been shelled, the pulp (inclosing the seeds) is laid in jars, over which boiling sugar is poured, and the jars are then closely covered. The native doctors prescribe tamarind water in fevers, and a decoction of the leaves, as a vermifuge.

Pharaoh's Fig (*Ficus Sycamorus*, L.). This is smaller than the common fig (*Ficus Carica*, L.), and grows in masses from the branches and body of the tree, but is only fit for preserving. The wood is of the most durable nature, and is supposed to have been that which was employed by the ancient Egyptians for the coffins of their mummies.

The Rattan fruit (*Calamus rotang*, L.) grows in clusters, and has a very pretty appearance. It is covered with small gold-colored scales; the pulp is gelatinous, and of a pleasant acid flavor; but the cane itself is of very inferior quality to the rattan of Batavia.

The Ceylon Olive (*Eleocarpus serratus* of Loureiro), *Wierelu* of the Singhalese, resembles the Spanish olive in size, shape, and color. It is edible, but has a mealy and acid pulp.

The native Melon (*Kekirya* of the Singhalese) is a tasteless fruit; probably degenerated by an alliance with the cucumber, which it resembles in shape.

The Slime Apple (*Embryoptoris glutinifera*), *Maha Timbiri* of the Singhalese, is one of the wild fruits that are eaten by the natives. The tree yields a medicinal gum, which is esteemed by their doctors. Carpenters use it as a substitute for glue.

Myrobolams (*Myrobolanus Zeylanicus*), *Kaekuna* of the Singhalese, who are almost as partial to it as the monkies; but these animals generally contrive to get the best share. A soft, resinous, concrete juice, of a whitish yellow, inclining to a greenish hue, and somewhat transparent, exudes from the tree; this has a strong but not unpleasant odour, and is the gum *Elemi* of commerce.

The Water Melon (*Cucurbita Citrullus*, L.), both of the red-fleshed and yellow-fleshed sorts, is not so abundant as might be expected, which arises from an indifference to its culture by the natives. It grows very rapidly in sandy soil, and might be cultivated to advantage for feeding cattle; for it attains an enormous size. I have seen water melons thirty two inches in length, and twenty eight in girth; these are naturally insipid, but very cooling in their nature. The Persians and Arabians cut the fruit, transversely, at one end; and then bruize the pulp, with a long piece of bamboo cane, shaped like a paper knife: they then add to the juice, lemon acid and sugar, and thus prepare a very grateful and wholesome sherbet.

Of the esculent vegetables there is an abundance, exclusively of the number already noticed in the preceding pages; and, among the best, may be classed the following.

The green capsule of the Horseradish tree (*Guilandina Moringa*, L.), *Merikulumulu* of the Singhalese, (a long triangular siliquose, containing, in its cavities, several angular, alated seeds,) is so delicate and wholesome, that parents who object to their children partaking of other vegetables, allow a free use of it, because it is entirely devoid of flatulent properties. The leaves and flowers, which are also edible, are much esteemed by the natives; and the root, as a substitute for horseradish, by Europeans; for, with a sweeter taste, it has equal pungency, and the same flavor. A very powerful oil, considered efficacious in rheumatism, and in the *Barbeers*, or, as it is locally called "a stroke of the land wind," is extracted from the seeds; and the native doctors prescribe decoctions of the root in fevers and paralysis. The gum is of a reddish hue, and is used as a substitute for gum *Tragacanth*.

The country Kale, or Kallaloo (*Amaranthus sanguineus*, and *A. viridis*, L.). The young stalks are dressed and served as asparagus, and the leaves have much of the flavor of the English spinach (*Spinacia oleracea*, L.). This esculent might be improved in England by the hot-bed; and if once introduced into use, it would doubtless become a favourite table vegetable, instead of merely occupying a place in the flower garden, as it now does.

The Purslane (*Portulaca oleracea,* L.) in the greatest abundance and variety.

Two varieties of a mucilaginous vegetable, called *Brettalé* by the Portuguese, and Spinach by the English. One is a dwarf, the other of rapid growth, and propagated so easily by cuttings, that within four months it will cover a cottage.

The Jerusalem Artichoke (*Helianthus tuberosus,* L.). This thrives well in sandy soil, and produces roots equal in size and flavor to the best specimens of European horticulture.

The White Radish (*Raphanus sativus,* L.) attains a large size, without getting coarse or fibrous; and is served, *à la Hollandaise,* as a substitute for asparagus (*Asparagus officinalis,* L.), which latter is much neglected, although it attains maturity in about six months.

The Indian Corn (*Zea Mays,* L.) grows everywhere, and is increased in size by topping the plant, soon after the beard appears, at the joint immediately above the glume. In its green state, it is parboiled whole, and then fried or devilled for the table; and, when ripe, it is ground into farina for various domestic purposes.

Of the Gourd genus there is a great variety, but the indigenous sorts are smaller than the European. The most common are—the pumpkin (*Cucurbita pepo,* L.), calabash (*C. lagenaria*), egg-gourd (*C. ovifera*), and squash (*C. Melopepo*).

A species of Sorrel, called *Surée* by the Singhalese, with no perceptible difference in taste from the English sorrel (*Rumex acetosa,* L.); but the classes and orders differ, the former being of class Hexandria, and order Monogynia; the latter of class Hexandria, and order Trigynia.

The young sprouts of the Bamboo (*Arundo Bambos,* L.) are excellent, either as a table vegetable, or pickled in the Singhalese manner.

Beans are in great variety, including the Sabre Bean (*Dolichos ensiformis,* L.), Three-lobed Bean (*D. trilobus,* L.), called *Binné* by the Singhalese; Lablab Bean (*D. Lablab,* L.), China Bean (*D. Sinensis,* L.), Four-lobed Bean (*D. tetragonolobus,* L.), Awned Bean (*D. aristatus,* L.), Kidney Bean (*Phaseolus vulgaris,* L.); and also of the genus *Phaseolus* they have the following varieties, according to the native list of them,—*Adsaryapala, Actokola, Avorapolu, Bumum, Bunkäe, Hindamini, Joywya, Kiripuswal, Maemung, Maha-wampala, Meekaree, Mam, Meang, Mundumala, Wal-undoo, Wal-undoowal, Wal-unae, Wandoroomé.*

The leaf of the *Carpintchee* of the Singhalese (*Cookia Anisetta,* L.) is greatly esteemed for the peculiar flavor it imparts to the native curries; and, when properly dried, retains its aromatic properties.

The Brinjal (*Solanum Melongena,* L.) includes the Egg-shaped, Green, and Purple varieties, and is so generally esteemed, throughout India, among the very best of table esculents, that no description of mine can add to its praise. Where is the "East Indian" to whom a prawn and brinjal curry would not be a truly welcome dish in any part of the world; or the brinjal itself, whether sliced transversely and fried plain, or divided longitudinally and cooked *à l' écrivisse?* Nevertheless, this nutritious esculent, although everywhere plentiful in Spain and Portugal, is never to be procured, except of the egg variety, in Covent Garden or other English markets, and then only in flower-pots;—this is the more strange, because the numerous families from the East and West Indies, would ensure a profitable sale of it, by the speculative gardener. The best sorts of it are the Green and Purple Brinjal, called by the Spaniards *Beringena* (pronounced *Berinkena*). The wild Prickly-stem Brinjal is edible, but so full of seeds, that it is used only by the poorest natives.

The Water and Garden Cress, Lettuce, Celery, Endive, (which latter grows remarkably large, and is usually bleached by covering it with pan-tiles), Beet, Carrots, and Cucumbers from English seed, are only procurable from private gardens. The country Cucumber has a smooth epidermis, is very common, and attains maturity within six weeks from sowing the seed. The natives never transplant cucumber or melon plants.

The Cabbage (*Brassica*) genus does not attain perfection in the maritime provinces, but in the interior it equals the best specimens of English horticulture.

The *Bandika* of the Singhalese (*Hybiscus esculentus*, L.) is mucilaginous and wholesome; and, if dried in the sun and pulverized, it may be taken to any part of the world, and made a valuable article of commerce. If once admitted into our English cookery, it would soon establish a character for itself. I never saw the flour prepared in Ceylon, except by myself, and I first learnt its valuable properties in the West Indies.

The Parsley (*Apium Petroselium*, L.) is common enough, and procurable in the principal bazaars, as well as Mint (*Mentha sativa*, L.), and Borage (*Borago Zelanica*, L.).

The Singhalese cultivate a variety of esculent roots, chiefly of the genus *Arum*; but, with the exception of the Purple-stalked Dragon (*Dracontium polyphullum*, L.), *Kana Kidahran* of the Singhalese, and the *Habarellé* of the Singhalese (*Arum Macrorhizum*, *A. esculentum*, and *A. Peregrinum*, L.), I have only been able to obtain a few of the *native* names for them, namely, *Kandellé*, *Kocconallé*, *Kaccotoorallé*, *Dekehallé*, *Gahallé*, *Enguralé*, *Jambowallé*, *Javakallé*, *Junallé*, *Kidakaran*, *Ratullé*, and *Welhallé*: all these are planted in May, and become ripe in June.

The leaf of the *Arum esculentum* is a wholesome vegetable, when dressed as spinach.

The Sweet Potato (*Convolvulus Batatas*, L.) is much cultivated. The leaf affords a fattening fodder for domestic animals, and deer are also partial to it.

The Purple Yam (*Dioscorea bulbifera*, L.) is very farinaceous, and generally grows from eight to twelve pounds in weight; the stalks, when entwined round some neighbouring tree, have a pretty appearance, and produce small yams of the size of a moderate potato; these are white, but not so farinaceous as the root. Owing to the great length of time it takes to ripen, this root is but little cultivated.

The edible Iris (*Iris edulis*, L.). The first plant I ever saw in Ceylon, was from a root that had been accidently sent me with some almonds from the Cape of Good Hope; and from its offsets I raised sufficient for use. It is a very wholesome esculent, delights in a sandy soil, and is well worthy of extensive culture.

The green capsules of the Moon-flower (*Ipomea bona nox*, L.) make excellent pickles and curries.

The root and corol of the White and Red Water Lilies (*Nymphæa alba* and *N. Nelumbo*, L.) are both edible; the latter has a strong almond flavor. Both are wholesome; particularly the large white sort, or Egyptian bean. The petals, root, and pulpy pericarp, are equally esteemed, and very nutritious.

The Eschelot (*Allium ascalonicum*, L.), and Garlic (*Allium Sativum*, L.), are extensively cultivated, being indispensable ingredients in the native cookery.

Of Capsicums, there is a great variety, including the *Capsicum frutescens*, of which Cayenne pepper is made; and the *C. annuum*, *C. grossum*, *C. baccatum*, *C. purpureum*, *C. minimum*, and *C. Caffrariensis*, L.

The Common and Cape Tomato (*Solanum Lycopersicum*, L.) are cultivated pretty generally in the gardens of Europeans.

The Snake Gourd (*Cucumis anguinus*, L.). The native cooks take out the pulp, and stuff the gourd with minced meat.

The Sour Gourd, *Angelica* of the Singhalese, is common, and is said to be a variety of the Monkey-bread (*Adansonia digitata*, L.). The tree attains a very large size; but it appeared to me more like a variety of the *Artocarpus incisa*, L. The fruit is oblong and cucumber-shaped, with a woolly epidermis. It has an acid taste, and produces a quantity of small round seeds.

The Mushroom (*Agaricus*, L.) is in variety and plentiful, on plains where buffalos graze; these fungi are generally of the esculent species, and of a large size. The best are the *Agaricus deliciosus*, *A. campestris*, and *A. Georgii*. The natives prefer the latter, with its white foldlets, to the red sort, or *Campestris*. I have seen the last species, upon the plains between Wanderopé and Hambantotte, in the southern province, fourteen inches in diameter; but it is only during, or soon after, the rainy season, that they are to be procured.

The Turnip Cabbage, or Nol-col (*Khol-rabi*) is an excellent vegetable, and grows well throughout the island, from Cape seeds.

The calyx of the Indian Red Sorrel (*Hibiscus sabdariffa*, L.) is made into a jelly, which is scarcely to be distinguished, either in color or flavor, from that made from the red currant of Europe.

The Green Pea (*Pisum sativum*, L.) grows freely, with proper attention to its culture, but it requires to be transplanted; and the plant, when about four feet high, should be topped.

The Arrow Root (*Maranta arundinacea*, L.) is extensively cultivated at the Church Missionary station at Baddegammé, in the southern province, and prepared in a similar manner to potato starch in this country. Ceylon was formerly supplied with it from Bombay, where it is made of the *Koray Kalung* of Malabar (*Curcuma angustifolia*, L.), which is very inferior to the true Arrow Root (*Maranta arundinacea*, L.); this has been so extensively cultivated for the last twenty years, that the island now produces abundance for home consumption, and for exportation.

The Sweet Fennel (*Nigella sativa*), *Kaluduru* of the Singhalese, abounds.

The Common Ginger (*Amomum Zingiber*), *Ingoroo* of the Singhalese. Green ginger is a general ingredient in curries, and distinguished from dry ginger by the name of *Ammu-ingoroo*. The native doctors prescribe an embrocation made of the juice of the former, conjointly with new coco-nut oil, for rheumatism, and it is a most efficacious remedy.

The Illepei (*Bassia longifolia*, L.). Every part of the *Illepei* tree is useful: the flowers are edible, after having been first dried, and then roasted; the ripe fruit is eaten by the poorer classes; a decoction of the bark, and also of the leaves, is used medicinally; a valuable oil is made from the ripe and unripe fruit; from the former, when required as a substitute for clarified (buffalo's) butter, or *Ghee*; and from the latter, for medicinal purposes. After it becomes rancid, it is thicker than coco-nut oil, and emits a most disagreeable smell, when used in lamps; but it is chiefly employed in the manufacture of country soap.

The Bird's-nest Cucumber (*Momordica cylindrica*, L.), *Vetta Koloo* of the Singhalese, grows like the cucumber, and is deserving of particular notice. In a green state, it is used in curries; and when dry, if cut transversely, its inside, which has the smell of honey, consists of longitudinal and transverse fibres, beautifully interwoven, and forming three cells the whole length of the fruit. These are full of round black seeds; and the native doctors form a decoction of the fibre, which they use as an emetic.

The Tala plant (*Sesamum orientale*, L.), a species of *Digitalis*. The seeds yield a wholesome and aromatic oil, called *Gingili* oil by the Singhalese, who use it both for culinary and medicinal purposes.

The Indian Carraway Seed (*Anethum graveolens*), *Sattacupa* of the Singhalese.

The Fenugreek (*Trigonella fœnum Grecum*), *Oloowa* of the Singhalese, is generally used in their condiments.

The Sweet Sorrel (*Anethum fœniculum*), *Dewaduru* of the Singhalese, abounds.

The Greater Cardamom (*Amomum grana Paradisi*, L.), and the Lesser Cardamom (*Eletaria cardamomum*, L.), *Ensal* of the Singhalese, are used in the native condiments, and by the ladies, for sweetening the breath, after meals; a very necessary succedaneum to the free use of garlic.

The Mustard (*Sinapis orientalis*, L.), *Raumanissa* of the Singhalese, is extensively cultivated. It is very insipid, being destitute of the pungency of the European white mustard (*Sinapis alba*, L.), which is largely imported. The most luxuriant crops are produced on the banks of rivers.

The Guinea Pea (*Citysus Cajan*, L.), *Tovaray* of the Malabars, thrives best in a sandy soil. It is a triennial; rapid in growth, prolific in produce, and a succession of plants is easily obtained; for, from the force with which, upon the bursting of the legume, the seeds (little oblong yellow peas) are scattered, they rapidly vegetate, under the shade of the parent shrub. Cattle, poultry, and pigeons, are extremely partial to it; and, in some countries, it is called the Pigeon Pea. It is an excellent substitute for pease on shipboard, and is supplied to the navy in the East Indies under the name of *Dhol*.

The native agriculturists are deficient in the selection of the best species of Rice (*Oryza Sativa*, L.) and other grain. As the culture of these has been extended, numerous varieties have formed; indeed, the several seasons of cultivation, and difference of soil, have multiplied them into an almost endless variety.

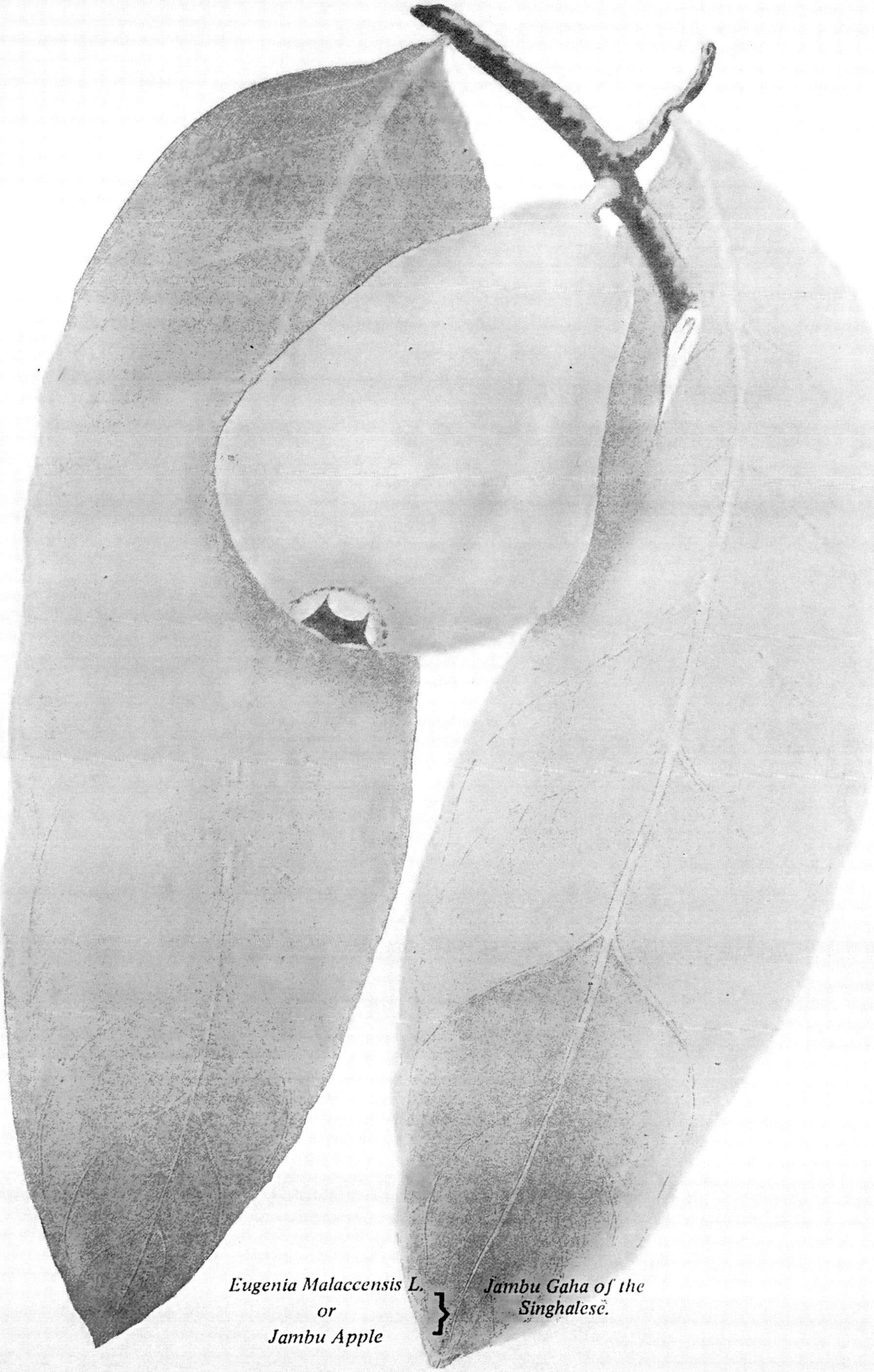

Eugenia Malaccensis L. } *Jambu Gaha of the*
or } *Singhalese.*
Jambu Apple

J. W. Bennett del.

Citrus tuberoides or *Caffrarian Lime* } *Koodalodeye of the Singhalese*

CHAP. XIX.

Western Province—Maritime capital—Master attendant's directions for the guidance of ships to the anchorage in Colombo roads—Sand bank—Drunken sailor rock—Adam's Peak—Pilotage—Fort of Colombo—Queen's house—Library—Officers of the garrison without quarters—Parsees—Pettah—Schools—Hindo-Portuguese and Dutch families—Black-eyed belles—Government clerks—Garrison of Colombo—Face of the country—Soil—Slave Island—Lake of Colombo—The Tamarind tree—Panorama of Colombo—Bazaars well supplied—Newspapers—Etiquette upon arrival—A British merchant—Horticultural society—Mail coach establishment—Widows' and orphans' fund—Savings bank—Charitable institutions—General wish for a Ceylon bank.

THE Western Province is bounded on the north by the Pomparipo river and Northern Province, on the south by the river Gindurah and part of the Southern Province, on the east by the Central Province, extending to within a short distance of Kandy, and on the west by the sea. Its principal towns and villages are,—Colombo, Negombo, Chilaw, Putlam, Calpentyn, Galkisse, Pantura, Kaltura, and Barberyn, on the sea, and Kornegalle and Ruanwellé in the interior.

Colombo, the maritime capital and seat of government, is situate in latitude 6° 57′ north, and longitude 79° 56′ east, distant about six leagues S. S. W. from Negombo. The bottom between these places is chiefly mud, with regular soundings; but the coast should not be approached close, on account of some rocks stretching out about two miles from the north point of the Kalané river, here called the Mutwal; and in passing along shore, a ship should keep in ten or twelve fathoms, and may anchor in Colombo road in six-and-a-half or seven fathoms, with the flag-staff or light-house in the fort bearing from S. to S. by E., off the town one-and-a-half or two miles.

Mr. Steuart, master attendant of Colombo, gives the following useful information for the guidance of ships to the anchorage.

"A brilliant light now exhibited from a light-house in the fort every night, which is ninety seven feet above the level of the sea, will direct ships approaching the road. Ships requiring pilots, should make the usual signal, to be conducted to the anchorage, which is free from foul ground, and *now* frequented at all seasons of the year, as a severe gale of wind is seldom experienced here.

"The best berth during the S. W. monsoon, from April to October, is in from seven to eight fathoms, with the light-house bearing S. by E. half E., and the Dutch church E. by S. In the N. E. monsoon, from November to April, it is more convenient to anchor in six-and-a-half fathoms, with the light-house bearing S. or S. half E., and the Dutch church E. S. E. In the night, when proceeding into the road, bring the light of the fort light-house to bear S. by E. or S. half E., and anchor in eight or nine fathoms, about half a mile off shore.

"The bar is a bank of sand, with seven feet of water on its shoalest part, the northern extremity being about four hundred yards N. W. of the custom-house point. Small vessels, drawing less than ten feet of water, ride within the bar, protected from the sea and S. W. wind. The sea breaks heavy on the bar in bad weather, rendering the crossing it, from the shipping in the outer road, dangerous for small boats. The native boats usually pass out and in to the southward of the bar, close to the breakers on the rocky point of the custom-house; which, being a narrow pass, should not be attempted by strangers, when the sea breaks on the bar. It is best to proceed round to the northward of the bar, which is easily distinguished by the breakers. Some rocks, projecting from the custom-house point, ought to be avoided in passing.

"The *Drunken Sailor Rock*, bearing by compass about S. W. by W. half W. from the light-house, distant one thousand yards, is very dangerous, being situated in the track of ships coming from the southward, when bound into Colombo road in the N. E. monsoon, for the sea *does not break upon it* in fine weather; and even in the S. W. monsoon it is not always visible, for at times only a small white roller can be perceived to rise over it once in six or eight minutes. According to the statement of Lieut. Colonel Wright, of the royal engineers, who examined this rock, it is of an oval shape, twenty or thirty feet in circumference, having only three-and-a-half feet of water on its summit at low tide, and about six at high water, with nine fathoms very near it, and eight or nine fathoms between it and the shore. This must refer to the shoalest patch only at its southern part, because Mr. Steuart found not less than seven feet on it at low water, and he estimated the ledge to be one hundred yards in length, and 20 yards in breadth. Several ships have passed very close to the *Drunken Sailor*, ignorant of its existence; and others have even passed between it and the shore, without knowledge of the danger, which is avoided in coming from the southward, by keeping in eleven or twelve fathoms water, until the flag-staff bears E. or E. by S."

Ships, late in the season, ought to anchor *well out*, to be enabled to proceed to sea in case of necessity. The barque Ceylon, Captain Francis Davison, did not arrive at Colombo till the beginning of June, 1827, and continued taking in cargo until the 26th, when she sailed for England. During the month there had been much rain, thunder, and lightning, the weather latterly threatening, with a heavy swell from the south-westward, which was followed by a gale of wind soon after the Ceylon had left the anchorage.

The land about Colombo is low near the sea, with some hills to the south-eastward, a little way in the country. The high mountain, having on it a sharp cone, called Adam's Peak, is nearest to this part of the coast, being about two-thirds of the distance that it is from the east side of the island. Captain Ross, the Honorable East India Company's marine surveyor, in January, 1824, made Adam's Peak eighteen-and-a-quarter miles east of Point de Galle flag-staff, by angles taken with the theodolite. Adam's Peak is in latitude 6° 52½' north, and bears E. seven degrees S. from Colombo, distant twelve-and-a-half leagues. When the atmosphere is very clear, it may be seen about thirty leagues; but this seldom happens, excepting in the N. E. monsoon, dense vapours generally prevailing over the island during the S. W. monsoon.

A steep bank of coral, about half a mile broad, having fifteen fathoms water on it, lies seven miles west of Colombo, stretching a few miles to the southward, and in a northerly direction towards Negombo, where its surface is sand. The water deepens at once to twenty three fathoms outside the bank, and to twenty eight fathoms greenish sand at two miles distance, which is not far from the edge of soundings. Within the bank are twenty five fathoms, gradually shoaling towards the shore.

Pilotage is *not* now charged at Colombo, as it formerly was, *unless a pilot be employed;* and in that case the charge, according to the most recent regulation of the governor and councils, is 15*s*.

The fort of Colombo is an irregular octagon, built upon a rocky peninsula, which projects considerably into the sea, and may be easily insulated. As it is not commanded in any direction, and is strong by nature and art, this fortress, adequately provisioned and garrisoned, may be considered tenable for a long time against a large force by sea and land. The main or King's street is wide and well planted with umbrageous tulip (*Hibiscus Zeilanicus*, L.) and bread-fruit trees, and several of the best houses have gardens for shrubs and flowers in their front, and coach-houses and stables in their rear. The streets are well watered during the day, and the fallen foliage is regularly removed every morning and evening. One may walk from either extremity of the fort to the other, in the heat of the day, without being incommoded by the sun's rays.

The governor's residence is styled the Queen's house; nearly opposite to which is the Colombo library and reading room, well supplied with books upon every scientific and amusing subject; periodical publications from Europe and the Indian continent, army and navy lists, and newspapers. The situation of the library, which is considerably elevated above the street, and with its spacious verandah delightfully shaded by umbrageous trees, and exposed to the sea breeze, presents an agreeable lounge during the heat of the day.

It is certainly an anomaly for officers of regiments forming the garrison of a fortress in India, to be necessitated to hire houses, (for there are no lodgings,) where by right, if not by custom, they are entitled to free quarters; but, notwithstanding the great reductions that have taken place, in the course of the last twenty years, in their colonial, or, as it is locally called, "island allowance," its present very limited amount is expected to cover all the expenses of lodging, fuel, and candlelight. The prospect of *free* quarters at Colombo is extremely distant: but if ever the day arrive for the town to be in a state of siege, officers will be sure of having choice of all the best houses in the fort, for those chiefly in request at the present time, would then be the most exposed to all the varieties of shot, shell, and rockets.

Several respectable Parsee tradesmen are settled in the fort and pettah of Colombo; they are all connected with the Bombay trade, from which island they receive supplies during the south-west monsoon, and make their returns, chiefly in produce, during the north-east monsoon; and, as their custom is elsewhere, they occupy houses as near as possible to each other.

Notwithstanding the hopelessness of discovering who the so called *Parsees* are, or from what nation descended, it must be admitted that they are a most inoffensive and industrious race, and strict in the observance of their religious rites, as prescribed by Zoroaster or Zerdhusht, the founder of the religion of the Magi, which admitted the existence of two principles—the cause of all good, and the cause of all evil. These Parsees worship one Supreme Being, under the most glorious symbol, the sun; and venerate fire, as the type of that grand source of light and heat.

The *Pettah*, or black town, as it is called in Indian parlance, lies on the north side of the fort of Colombo, upon the margin of the sea, and consists of two principal streets, intersected at right angles by cross streets, in all which the houses are substantially built with *Kabooc* or iron-stone. Several of these streets have a row of trees on each side, chiefly of the *Guilandina Moringa, Hibiscus Zeilanicus* (*Soorya gaha* of the Singhalese), *Hibiscus albemoschus* (*Kapu Kinaisa gaha*), or *Melia sempervirens* (*Kassambu gaha*). The town has a large and airy hospital, leper hospital, public library, and several boys' and girls' schools; namely, the Colombo academy, St. Paul's schools, Dutch consistorial school, Hulfsdorp school, and St. Thomas's schools; all which are under the patronage of the government, and contain about one thousand scholars, of both sexes.

The Hindo-Portuguese and Dutch families, the descendants of European connexions with native ladies, are an intelligent and respectable community; but altogether distinct from British society, except upon certain public or *pell-mell* occasions. The ladies, when young, are generally pretty, and marriageable at an early age; but it is only in the evening, at which time the streets are watered, the air cool after the burning heat of the day, and scarcely a bullock bandy, out of the hundreds that pass and repass between sunrise and sunset, to be seen, that these black-eyed *belles* display their pretty little figures in the verandahs or *stoups* of their paternal residences. Habited in the newest London or Paris fashions, but in the chaste and becoming native style as regards the hair, these *brunettes* display the latter ornament, with which nature has blessed them with a profusion, to the greatest advantage, aided by the natural beauty of the fragrant flowers of the yellow and white Ceylon jessamine, Arabian jessamine, *Moogrie* (*Nerium coronarium*), tuberose (*Polyanthes tuberosa*), *Champaka* (*Michelia Champaka*), and occasionally the starry corols of the *Mimusops Elengi*, L., which they intersperse with, and by way of contrast to, their jet black ringlets.

These families are all styled, and have the privilege of, " Europeans," in the supreme and minor courts of justice. English officers have occasionally intermarried with the offspring of such Dutch and Portuguese connexions, but it is a rare occurrence.

The government clerks are selected from these families, and manage all the clerical duties of the public offices in an admirable manner; and fortunate it is that their economical habits of life enable them to support their families upon their scanty and altogether inadequate pay. Their great claims upon the consideration of Her Majesty's secretary of state for the colonies are just and strong, for there is not a public department in the United Kingdom in which the details of office and punctuality in attendance are more regularly performed than in Ceylon; and whatever may be the difference expected from gentlemen doing duty as clerks in the former, in point of dress, appearance, and society, even then the difference is in the greatest degree invidious, and the balance too great against the latter. The pay of Ceylon clerks bear no fair proportion to that of English civil servants; for there is no such an existing anomaly in this country, where, in the treasury for instance, the secretaries may have 2000*l.* a year, for the junior clerk to have only 22*l.* 10*s.* a year; but in Ceylon, where the vice-treasurer has 1750*l.* a year, the chief clerk has but 250*l.* a year, the first clerk 63*l.*, and the junior 22*l.* 10*s.*—In the colonial department, where an under secretary of state has but 1500*l.* a year, which is 500*l.* a year less than that of the colonial secretary at Ceylon, what would the junior clerk think of 30*l.* a year, which is the salary of his contemporary in the colonial secretary's office at Ceylon: and in the auditor and accountant-general's office, where the head of the department has 1750*l.* a year, the junior clerk receives but 31*l.* 10*s.*—By these data, a fair judgment may be formed of the inadequacy of the salary of the clerks, and their relative disproportion to the emoluments of the heads of departments.

The general and disgusting habit of masticating betel, obtains among the elder ladies, and the young folks will clandestinely enjoy it. At their parties, the former range themselves in chairs against the walls of the rooms, in a straight line, as if drilled into it to the command of "eyes right" or "eyes left," and by the side of each chair stands a well-polished brass spittoon, for the reception of the blood-colored saliva which the *Pawn* produces; whilst the middle is occupied by the latter, for quadrilling and contre-dancing.

The garrison of Colombo consists of two regiments of the line, the head quarters of the Ceylon rifle corps, a company of artillery, with a proportion of engineers, and the requisite medical and military staff, together with a small troop of mounted orderlies, and a body of gun Lascars.

The country about Colombo is flat, except a small part to the northward; soil alluvial and sandy in some parts, and iron-stone clay and gravel in others—extremely fertile, the shores covered to the verge of the sea with coco-nut palms; and, inland, beautifully diversified with umbrageous fruit and other trees, cinnamon plantations, gardens, and pasture lands, intersected by canals, and a fresh-water lake; and, to the northward, by the Mutwal river or Kalané-Ganga, and the grand canal.

Soon after day-break, when the lofty mountain of the *Sri Pada,** or Adam's Peak, is seen in the distance from the south esplanade or Galle face, the view of Slave island rising out of the placid bosom of the water, called the lake of Colombo, with its pretty houses, bungalows, and other buildings, interspersed amongst stately areka trees, bread-fruit trees, and coco-nut palms, the bugles of the Ceylon rifle corps alone breaking the tranquility of the scene, affords indescribable pleasure to the recently-arrived European. It is at this hour, that, upon review days, the troops are seen marching to their ground upon the race course; and that the early risers of Colombo are setting out upon their morning drives, rides, or walks, very many of whom look forward with unalloyed pleasure, except when the rainy season prevents it, to the general rendezvous of the European civil and military officers and merchants—the well-known *Tamarimd Tree,* (near the three-miles' stone on the Galle road,) to quaff the wholesome and renovating nectar fresh from the toddy palm, before fermentation, which is very rapid, commences. It is then that the natural sieve which nature presents, in the envelope of the petioles of the coco-nut fronds, is employed in one of its most useful offices; namely, for straining the liquid, and clearing it from the various insects that may have fallen victims to their love of sweets during the night, and are generally of the genus *Scarabæus,* of which, the blue and green are the largest and most beautiful.

The whole way from the esplanade to the tamarind tree is a wide carriage road, shaded with tulip, coco-nut, teak, bamboo, banyan, silky cotton, areka, Adam's apple (*Cerbera Manghas,* L.), and various other useful and ornamental trees: but the road

* Venerated foot.

generally preferred for returning to the fort, leads along the margin of the sea, through a dense coco-nut tope, to the verge of the esplanade.

Emerging from the line of native huts, upon the sea-side of the high road, the splendid fortifications of Colombo, which form a prominent part of the grand panorama that presents itself, are viewed with admiration.

The various Bazaars are situated in the *Pettah* of Colombo, and are well and regularly supplied; every day, except Sunday, being alike in point of supplies; but no traffic is now allowed, as formerly obtained, during stated hours, on the Lord's-day. Grain, beef, mutton, veal, kid, pork, poultry, fish, fruit, and vegetables, including potatos, for which, some few years ago, the island was altogether dependant upon Bombay and Madras, but are now abundant and cheap, are exposed for sale soon after daylight, and fish is also supplied every evening in great variety.

There are three weekly newspapers, namely, the Colombo Herald, the Observer, and the Government Gazette; these, it is to be hoped, are too liberally conducted to descend to personal attacks upon individuals; and that the editors, in availing themselves of their now indisputable right to question the official conduct of *public servants*, will be satisfied with having that power; for it is within my recollection, that to have so done, would have ensured their deportation, if not the seizure of their presses.

Europeans arriving at Colombo, are expected to report themselves without delay at the colonial secretary's office; and at the other ports of the island, to the agents of government. Gentlemen for the civil establishment will, of course, feel it their duty, after having paid their respects to His Excellency the Governor, and commander-in-chief, to whom they will be introduced by the private secretary, to wait upon the heads of departments; and they cannot do wrong by paying similar respect to the commandant.

Naval and military officers require no information upon the observance of local etiquette, for it is everywhere the same to them; but Griffins may derive great assistance from Mr. Dionysius de Neys, librarian of the Colombo library, in procuring a residence, servants, &c., if, through want of introductory letters, they find themselves "alone in their loneliness."

The surviving partner of the oldest commercial firm in the island, (that of Messrs. W. C. Gibson & Co.) Joseph Read, Esq., who resides at Colombo, than whom, few if any, are better acquainted with the internal and external commerce of the colony, is an admirable specimen of the *old British merchant*; combining with every quality that can fix confidence, and ensure esteem, the most genuine Caledonian hospitality; for which, distinguished as his countrymen are everywhere, (and where they are not it is next to an impossibility to discover,) Mr. Read may perhaps be equalled, but cannot be excelled.

The Horticultural Society of Colombo is under the patronage of the governor, and it is to be hoped that it will prove more stable in its nature than its predecessor, the Literary and Agricultural Society.

The Mail Coach Establishment, commenced in 1832 by a joint stock company, conveys passengers from Colombo to Kandy (which formerly took several days to accomplish by palankin travelling) in less than twelve hours. The coach starts from Colombo every Monday, Wednesday, and Friday morning, at gun-fire, and reaches Kandy, a distance of seventy eight miles, between five and six o'clock of the same day; and leaves Kandy every Tuesday, Thursday, and Saturday morning, at gun-fire, and reaches Colombo about five P. M.; the former journey having more up-hill work than the latter. The fare to and from Kandy is 2*l.* 10*s.*

The Ceylon Widows' and Orphans' Fund is under official management and security; and cannot fail to prove a blessing to those widows and orphans whose provident husbands and fathers may, by their contributions, have preserved them from destitution.

The Colombo Savings' Bank is another excellent establishment, and worthy of general support. It has branch committees at Trincomale, Galle, Kandy, and Jaffna, by which loans are advanced upon good security, and deposits received and business transacted, between twelve and three o'clock on the first and third Monday in every month; and, in case of extraordinary business, on the second and fourth Monday, from one to three o'clock.

Of charitable institutions, there are—the Leper Hospital; Pettah Hospital; District Committee of the Society for Promoting Christian Knowledge; Bible Association for the Dutch and Portuguese inhabitants; Colombo Friend-in-need Society, (for the purpose of relieving the really necessitous, and for suppressing mendicity,) under the able management of a highly respectable and numerous committee; over which, the senior colonial chaplain is president, and the governor, for the time being, the patron;—A Commission for the General Superintendence of Education in the Colony, of which the members are selected from the ecclesiastical, judicial, and civil establishments;—and the Colombo Ladies' Branch Society, to the immortal honor of those amiable, accomplished, and benevolent ladies, who compose the committee.

Both Europeans and natives appear equally anxious for the establishment of a Colonial Bank. The mercantile interests, as well as those of individuals, must be sensibly alive to the disadvantages of being altogether dependant upon the limited sale of government and missionary bills, for remittances to England; and it is to be anticipated that public-spirited individuals will yet be found in this country, to carry the general wish of the colonial community into effect, by the establishment of a Ceylon Bank, which cannot fail to conduce to the welfare of that important island.

CHAP. XX.

Ceylon fishing boats—Their extraordinary shape and swiftness—The fishery one of the most important of the capabilities of the island—Regulation of government for encouraging the salting of fish within the island—Insufficient protection—Fish rents—Restrictions upon fishermen—Suggestions to His Majesty's secretary for the colonies, in 1832, for increasing the sale of salt, decreasing the expense of gathering it, reducing the price to the consumer, and encouraging settlers in the Mahagampattoo for curing fish—Abolition of the monopoly recommended—Leways or natural salt pans—Salt stealing—Military guards—Sentinels' pay liable to stoppage for stolen salt—Two salt stealers killed—Bullocks confiscated—Double wages to labourers in the Mahagampattoo—Impressed salt gatherers—Adulteration of salt—Expense of gathering salt and transmitting it to Colombo—Salt naturally formed at the distant Leways placed under military guard until dissolved by the rain—Price of salt—Importation of salt fish—Coup de grace to salt-water invoices—Native process of salting fish objectionable—Its results—Suggestions for improving the mode of salting fish—Proposed plan for curing fish by smoke—Country salt fish very little in request among Europeans—Salt fish from Europe and America—Fish common to the coasts of Ceylon.

THE innumerable sailing canoes that are daily engaged in fishing, in the offing of Colombo, during the S. W. monsoon, attract the attention of every new-comer. These extraordinary boats are formed of a single tree, which is either hollowed by means of fire, or scooped out by the simplest tools, and generally from fifteen to eighteen feet in length. The body has a considerable bilge, and gunwales are raised upon it, consisting of two planks of light wood, from 20 to 24 inches in breadth; these run the whole length of the boat, and are united at the head and stern by a transverse plank of the same breadth as the longitudinal ones, by means of regularly drilled holes, through which strong *Koir* cord is passed, and neatly interlaced crosswise: this is afterwards *payed* over with a coat of dammer as a preservative.

The breadth of beam of the Ceylon canoes is from 20 to 24 inches; and their great height and extreme lightness would render it impossible to keep them upright, without being balanced by an outrigger from one side. This is formed of a *solid* log, shaped like a canoe, but with pointed ends, and is extended for about six or seven feet from the side, by two arched stretchers, convexing towards the false canoe, to which they are lashed by strong *Koir* cord, passed through neatly drilled holes, in order to prevent friction as much as possible. These canoes have one mast, upon which a very large square sail, of country cotton canvas, is hoisted; and the head and stern being alike, the sail is carried either way, and the course altered in a moment to the opposite direction, without shifting or neutralizing the outrigger. The velocity with which these boats skim over the surface of the water, (for so light is their draught, they can scarcely be said to sail through it,) surprises every beholder.

The Colombo Fishery might be made one of the most important of the capabilities of this island, whose coasts may literally be said to teem with fish of the best kinds, for all the purposes of home consumption, as well as for exportation; and a more ample field for lucrative speculation cannot possibly present itself.

The natives, whether Singhalese or Malabars, are so accustomed to a light diet; and, with the exception of swine, to which the former have all the partiality of the Otaheiteans, eat so very little animal food, that a method of curing fish, upon an improved system to the primitive one, that has obtained in the island from immemorial time, would both ensure very ample profits to those concerned in it, and prove a blessing to the colony.

I do not find, among my various data, and notes collected in the island, that the notice of any one British governor had been applied to this most important, but, I am sorry to say, still neglected subject, until the late Lieutenant General Sir Edward Barnes, G. C. B., at the time he was lieutenant governor of Ceylon, deemed it worthy of attention, amongst the other objects of his patriotic zeal for the general welfare; and the Regulation of government, No. 6, of the year 1821, "for encouraging the preparation of salt fish within the island," was accordingly promulgated.*

That ordinance expressly provided for its protection, by imposing a duty of fifteen per cent. upon the invoice value, or prime cost of salt fish of every description, imported from, and after the first of April of that year; and, for the further encouragement of the fishery, all salt fish cured within the island was permitted to be exported duty free. But it escaped His Excellency's attention, that the most likely mode of promoting the object in view, was to excite the cupidity of the Singhalese, by granting a liberal *drawback* to the exporter, even to the extent of the amount of the import duty.

The average annual value of the fish rents to government, may be estimated at from £7000 to £8000 sterling. These rents, or tenths of all fish caught upon the sea-coasts of Ceylon, are annually sold by public auction, and the duty is collected by the farmer of the revenue of each district. This is a most vexatious duty, both upon the native fisherman, and the consumer desirous of having fish as fresh as possible from the sea:—for instance, a person living between Galkisse and Colombo, which places are seven miles distant from each other, sees abundance of the best fish carried past his house every morning and evening, and yet he cannot buy any, because it must first be taken to the Bazaar, for the fish-renter to have his share; so that a servant has to travel several miles to, and from the Bazaar, to get fish in a wholesome

* Vide Appendix.

state, merely because the fishermen dare not sell, what may have been caught, perhaps within a mile or two of his (the servant's) master's residence.

Until the government removes such restrictions upon the fisherman, and reduces the price of salt, little or nothing can be expected from any plans for establishing factories for the curing of fish.

In the year 1832, I solicited the attention of Viscount Goderich, at that time His Majesty's principal secretary of state for the colonies, to my suggestions for the improvement of the revenue derived from salt, by diminishing the expenses of its realization, and for extending its sale, by reducing the price to the consumer; and for the better encouragement of settlers in the Mahagampattoo, for the purpose of curing fish, by reducing the price of salt used for that purpose to one half of the market rate of it elsewhere in the island. Nevertheless, this oppressive monopoly still exists, and the natives cannot obtain salt at a less price than 2*s.* 4*d.* per bushel, of four pecks.

Surely the government might adopt some better system for the gathering and sale of salt, (the expense of the present establishments may be estimated at from £6000 to £7000 per annum,) or be satisfied with a less amount of nett profit than £20,000 or £21,000 per annum, which is about the average value of this monopoly.

Some *less objectionable* tax might be substituted, so as to relieve the population of so oppressive an impost upon this grand necessary of life, and put a stop to the long-prevailing smuggling system to which the natives are tempted, by the high price of salt, and the heavy restrictions upon that article.

Abolish the monopoly, I would say, and levy a customs and excise duty, from 4*d.* to 6*d.* a bushel, upon all salt conveyed by *land* carriage, or *coastwise,* by *Dhonies,* &c.; and if that be insufficient, make it up by a *charge upon licenses* to the renters of *natural Leways,* and salt manufacturers at other places: and thus remove the hardships that are now too justly complained of.

The natural salt pans, or *Leways,* are situate in the Mahagampattoo, a district of the southern province, which, although formerly flourishing and well-inhabited, is now, in proportion to its extent, almost destitute of population. Its numerous ruined tanks, and other agricultural vestiges, are proofs of its pristine importance; but its chief place, Hambantotte, contains no more than fifteen hundred inhabitants, including the garrison. Nevertheless, by a better system of management of the salt department, and adequate encouragement for the establishment of a factory for curing fish, this place may again become a prolific source of public prosperity and of private wealth, and one of the most populous of the maritime districts of Ceylon.

The stealing of salt from the temporary depôts at the *Leways,* has for many years prevailed to an almost incredible extent; and neither the penal enactments of the governor in council, nor the risk of life itself, which has often proved fatal, have had the effect of deterring the natives from availing themselves of every opportunity to obtain it. This determination to possess themselves of an absolute necessary of life, by plundering the salt heaps at the *Leways*, arises from the exorbitant price set upon a natural production, which poverty precludes them from obtaining honestly: this is so general, as to hold out no expectation of its being overcome, whilst the present system incites them both to steal for themselves and to supply the smuggler.

The revenue is exposed to much loss, owing to the great distance of the storehouses from the *Leways*, or natural salt pans; where the salt, instead of being lodged under cover, is collected into large heaps, which are clayed over; for as the salt does not always form in one place in a *Leway*, the positions of the collected heaps vary according to circumstances; and therefore such divisions as are not contiguous, require a separate military guard, and temporary guard-house, for their protection; which renders it expedient to keep a garrison of one hundred and fifty invalids of the Ceylon rifle corps, for the duties of the salt department.

The expense of so large a military force, is not the only objection to its employment. At one time, the question "Quis custodes custodiet ipsos?" was justly applicable to the military guardians of the government salt heaps; for without their connivance, or with common vigilance on their parts, no great excess of plunder could possibly have been effected: therefore a security, that should be made available to the public, was indispensable; and the pay of the sentinels having consequently been made liable for the value of the salt, stolen during their respective tours of *Leway* duty, their self-interest became inseparable from the preservation of the government property.

A different system was thenceforth adopted; and subsequent attempts to steal salt from the heaps, were regarded by the soldiers as personal injuries; and whenever, owing to the number of natives, who, at one and the same time assailed the salt heaps, the guards could not seize individuals, they employed their firearms. In 1826, two Singhalese were shot dead by the Malays, whilst in the act of stealing salt at the Koholoncalé *Leway;* and between three and four hundred bullocks, belonging to salt smugglers, were confiscated during my superintendence of that district.

The distance of the *Leways* from the storehouses, renders an establishment of one hundred carts, some hundreds of bullocks, with a number of headmen, drivers, smiths, and carpenters, indispensable; and as no native will serve there under double pay, so great is their dread of the climate of the Mahagampattoo, the expense of it, independently of contingent expenses, of which, the loss of bullocks, killed by wild beasts, is not the least, in the course of a year, is worth saving to the public.

One fourth of mud or sand may be considered the average quantity collected out of every parah * of *Leway* salt; and it often happens, that no more than half the quantity of good salt is produced by evaporation: but this entirely arises from the *impressment* of natives to gather the salt, who, notwithstanding that they are paid the very fair wages of four fanams (6*d*. sterling) a day, hurry through the business, they care not how.

The headmen are so few, in proportion to the hundreds of salt gatherers, who are scattered over an extensive *Leway*, that the latter cannot be individually overlooked by those who superintend the general business of the salt department.

It is only during the salt harvests, that these wretched inhabitants of the villages near the *Leways* are able to obtain subsistence, except upon wild roots, (the majority of which possess acrid properties,) and the bitter leaves of the wild tea tree: these they boil and eat with sour curd, and use an infusion of the leaves for drink; and yet so great is their natural idleness, that they are compelled to be *pressed* as salt gatherers, where their only alternative is starvation, or the vile diet already described!!

Singhalese coolies from other parts of the island go to the Mauritius for employment, notwithstanding that every thing is dearer there than at Ceylon. What then must be the state of agriculture, where, with a population of only 1,500,000, at the maximum, to an area of 24,448 square miles, agricultural labourers emigrate to other colonies?

The high price of government salt encourages every species of roguery. The ports of Colombo, Galle, and Trincomalé, are chiefly supplied from Hambantotte, by large native vessels, called *Dhonies;* and scarcely a season passes without complaints against the quality of the salt conveyed by them; this the natives so ingeniously contrive to adulterate, that, in appearance, their cargoes, on arrival at the ports of destination, agree with the samples, which, sealed in bamboo canes, accompany them. The adulteration is effected at certain creeks on the coast, where, by pre-concerted arrangements, smugglers are in waiting, with sacks, and bullocks, to carry away the stolen salt, which they replace with an equal proportion of grey sand. This might certainly be prevented, by sending a trustworthy person with each cargo; but where so many vessels are employed, an establishment of such officers would be required.

The deteriorated quality of the salt, as it is now gathered, occasions an expense of at least a fourth more freight than would be required under the plan I submitted to the colonial department. The expense to the government of gathering salt, and transporting it to Colombo, may be estimated at sixpence the parah; and the *nett* revenue from this monopoly, at £20,000 per annum, which includes the produce of all the natural and artificial salt works in the island, which are about forty eight in number.

* A parah is about two-thirds of a Winchester bushel.

It often happens, that when salt has formed at the more distant *Leways*, instead of being gathered, guards are posted there, perhaps for months together, until the rains shall have set in, and *dissolved* it. The guards may then connive at the clandestine removal of the salt with impunity, because their pay is only held liable for the loss of salt, where it can be *ascertained by admeasurement;* and serious loss to the revenue is thus occasioned, which the erection of a storehouse on the margin of each *Leway*, for the reception of the salt as soon as gathered, would effectually obviate.

The price of salt is fixed at two shillings the parah measure; and I have seen a parah of the grey mixture called government salt, submitted to what is called the boiling process, just after it had been received from the salt stores at Galle, which produced only twelve-and-a-half pounds of pure salt; but this occasionally varies in the same place, a similar quantity sometimes yielding thirteen or fourteen, at others, sixteen pounds.

Thus the high price of salt operates so much to the prejudice of the Ceylon fisheries, that the island is dependent for supplies of salt fish, *which is an article of general consumption, and in constant demand, throughout the interior*, on its importations from the Maldive Islands, and places within the East India Company's territories, (where, notwithstanding the monopoly, salt is cheaper); and a ready sale is found for it, *malgre* the *protecting duty* of ten per cent.

If the government was not originally aware of the salt water invoice system, the ordinance No. 5 of 1837 gave the *coup de grace* to that disgraceful practice, by reducing the import duty to ten per cent., but upon the *value* of the article in the *Ceylon market*, instead of the original cost or invoice price: nevertheless this was little or no relief to the public, for in very many instances it operated equally against the consumer and the importer; and consequently the government was the only party benefitted: for, whilst the fish-rent system prevails, very many years must elapse, before the island can be independent of foreign supplies of salt fish for home consumption; and a much longer time will be required, even if a considerable drawback were allowed, for the local fisheries to have a surplus for exportation.

The native process of salting fish is altogether most objectionable. In the first place, no care is taken to obviate the rapid progress of putrefaction; for, instead of salting the fish, as soon as it is taken out of the water, which is indispensable within the tropics, it is carelessly done after having been some time landed, (and then, of such part only of the cargo as could not be sold in its fresh state,) and exposed upon a sandy beach to a vertical sun. The consequence may be easily imagined; fish so exposed, is soon impregnated with almost as much sand as salt; and, if affected by casual moisture, or absorption, it becomes rotten before it can be conveyed to the interior, where it is chiefly in demand.

As the Ceylon fishing boats are built exclusively for sailing; they have no room to stow more than a few fish, and consequently have no stowage for salt, for the purpose of curing the fish in the only way that can be effectual in so hot a climate.

This might be obviated, by a certain number of fishing boats being attended by a *Dhoney,* as a rendezvous, and for the purpose of carrying salt; and for the crew of the latter to salt the fish as soon as caught and conveyed to them. This, however, would require more capital than the *native* fishers can command, or would be disposed to risk, if they could. But an additional and great advantage would attend the plan; for the crews of the fishing boats could keep much longer at sea, and cook their victuals and sleep on board the *Dhoney,* until it was fully freighted.

Those who are accustomed to salt and cure fish in cold climates, would require considerable experience to become equally perfect within the tropics, where the fish requires air and shade, as well as occasional exposure to the sun.

Upon casually looking over the notes that I made during the time I was on garrison duty at Fort Belgica, in the island of Banda Neira, in 1811, it occurred to me, and I mention it with all deference to superior judgment, that the mode adopted by the nutmeg curers there, would answer very well for fish; namely, by open platforms of split bamboo canes raised in tiers at regular distances, with proportionate, and of course larger spaces between each bamboo slip than would be required to support the nutmegs, and according to the size of the fish.

By this means, the objectionable mode of letting the fish come in contact with the sand, would be obviated; and any quantity might be entirely cured by smoke, by lighted wet rice straw being laid under the lower tier, which would ascend through all the intermediate spaces to the roof, and a more convenient or cheaper contrivance could not, in my humble opinion, be adopted.

Country salt fish, owing to the improper manner in which it is cured, is very seldom in request for the tables of Europeans, compared with what it would be under an improved system; for, even if the sand can be got rid of, there still remains an incipient degree of putrefaction, which renders it necessary for charcoal to be boiled with it; and even then, when served at table, the effect is too potent for either mustard and egg-sauce, or acids, to overcome.

Independently of salt fish being an article of great and general consumption in the interior, the fact that there are upwards of 150,000 Roman Catholics, who are rigid in the observance of their religious fasts, will be considered a sufficient guarantee for the success of a fish factory upon a very extensive scale.

It is well known, that salt fish from Europe and America is rotten, unless very particular care be taken in packing it, before it reaches India; and I have known the late Egbert Bletterman, Esq., of Ceylon, pay thirty rix dollars, (at that time 1*s.* 9*d.* sterling each,) for a jar containing about four dozens of half putrid red herrings. I therefore earnestly endeavour to impress upon the attention of individual capitalists, that there is no speculation more certain of success, amongst the many other very encouraging ones that present themselves at Ceylon, than that of establishing factories for the curing of fish at such places upon the coasts as have the best fishing, and little or no demand for fresh fish.

The principal of the more useful fishes are—the Albicore or Thunny (*Scomber Thynnus*, L.), Bonetta (*Scomber Pelamis*, L.), Scad (*Scomber Trachurus*), Coal fish (*Gadus carbonarius*, L.), Pomfret, Bull's eye (*Holocentrus ruber* of Bennett's fishes of Ceylon), Snook or Cape Salmon, Parawah (*Scomber Heberi* of Bennett's fishes of Ceylon), Sea Perch (*Perca marina*, L.), Bearded Ophidium (*Ophidium barbatum*, L.), Pampus (*Stromaticus Paru*, L.), Sword fish (*Xiphias Gladius*, L.), Gemmenas Dragonet (*Callionymus Lyra*, L.), Kurtus (*Kurtus Indicus*, L.), Dorado (*Coryphæna Equiselis*, L.), Doree (*Zeus Faber*, L.), Sole (*Pleuronoctes Solea*, L.), Red or Sur Mullet (*Mullus barbatus*, L.). Striped Sur Mullet (*Mullus Surmuletus*, L.), Great Gar fish (*Esox osseus*, L.); a species of *Clupea*, very like the Sprat, which, at certain seasons, is poisonous; several species of Rock Cod, of large size and excellent quality; the Seir fish (*Tora-malu* of the Singhalese), already described in page 110; Skate (*Raia Batis*, L.), and a variety of Rays of enormous size; all which are detested by the natives, and returned to the sea as soon as caught. The Singhalese have a great dread of the Sting Ray (*Raia pastinaca*, L.)

The most valuable of all fishes for the China markets, are Sharks. Of these viviparous monsters, the largest, and most esteemed, for their fins, are the White Shark (*Squalus Carcharias*, L.), Saw fish (*S. Pristis*, L.), some of which are from twelve to eighteen feet in length; Balance Shark, or Hammer Head (*S. Zygæna*, L.), the Tope (*S. Galeus*, L.), Blue Shark (*S. glaucus*, L.), and the Shagreen, or Basking Shark (*S. Maximus*, L.); the skin of this last is much in request by the Chinese, for the purpose of making it into shagreen, of which a great quantity is annually sold to the Russians, upon the frontiers; so that shark catching might be made a separate and most profitable speculation; for the simple mode of drying the skins and fins in the sun, without a particle of salt, is greatly in favor of the undertaking; and the saving to be effected by that mode of curing them for the China market, would be, under all the circumstances of the price of salt, a paramount consideration.

CHAP. XXI.

Fresh-water fishes—Original establishment of the Portuguese at Colombo—Portuguese surrender it to the Dutch—Dutch capitulate to the British—Insulting conduct of the Dutch troops to their forbearing victors—Absurd claim of Portugal—Clandestine attempt to inspect, or possess, the records of the colony by a Portuguese officer—Mr. Deputy Secretary Sutherland's inquiry, at the request of Governor Sir Robert Brownrigg—Route from Colombo to Kandy—Roads of Ceylon—Governor Sir Edward Barnes—Just tribute to his memory—Great sacrifice of human life in forming the roads—Families consequently destitute—Suggestions for relieving them—Preliminary hints to travellers—Best mode of travelling—Suggestions for canteens—Pistols and swords, except for officers, incumbrances—Chatty bath—Batta to coolies—The three grand maxims for the tourist's observance—Umbrella indispensable—Important addition to its usefulness—Mosquito—Northern route—Jayellé—Road to Negombo—Sailing directions from Captain Horsburgh's Directory.

HAVING described, to the best of my power, the several sorts of sea fish that are most common and abundant upon this coast, for the purposes of home consumption and exportation, I regret that I have but little to say in favor of the fresh water varieties. Of these, the best that the lake, fort ditch, and canals produce, are the Cat-fish, *Angoloowa* of the Singhalese, the Eel, the Burbot (*Gadus Lota,* L.), by many mistaken, from the cirri on the jaws, for a variety of the Barbel (*Cyprinus Barbus,* L.), and the Grey Mullet (*Mugil Cephalus,* L.).

The Portuguese first established a factory at Colombo in the year 1515, and then erected a small fort for its protection, which, from time to time, they enlarged; and, notwithstanding the hostilities in which they were subsequently involved with the natives, and, ultimately, with the combined Dutch and Kandyan forces, they maintained their footing, and extended their conquests, for a period of one hundred and twenty two years. The Portuguese governor and captain-general, Antonio de Zouza Continho, surrendered Colombo to the Dutch in 1656, when the administration of the Batavian governor, Van der Meyden, commenced.

The Dutch having, in turn, enjoyed their tyrannical sway for nearly one hundred and forty years, were dispossessed of Colombo, by capitulation to the British force, under the command of Major General Stewart, on the 16th of February, 1796; at which time, the ordinary counsellor of Dutch India, Johan Gerard Van Angelbeck, was governor.

The British force consisted of His Majesty's 52nd, 73rd, and 77th regiments, three battalions of the Honorable East India Company's Madras Sepoys, and a detachment of Bengal artillery. This small army had landed at Negombo without opposition, on the 2nd of that month, and immediately proceeded to the attack of Colombo; which it could not have taken, if the Dutch had availed themselves of the natural obstacles of the intermediate country to oppose its progress. But the Dutch troops, although superior in numbers, were bordering upon a state of mutiny, and their officers, however brave and disposed to defend the fort, had no control over them; for even after the British flag had been hoisted, upon the capitulation of Colombo, the Dutch soldiers, as they filed past to lay down their arms, spat their saliva at their brave and indignant but forbearing victors.

The first British administration was formed "in the name of the Honorable the Governor of Fort St. George (Madras) in Council;" and in the forty six years that have since passed, we have not had less than thirteen governors and lieutenant-governors of Ceylon. The following is a list of these functionaries, with the dates of their accession to the government; and of the lieutenant-governors, acting as governors, in the intervals of succession of the latter.

The Honorable Frederick North assumed the government, October 12, 1798.—Lieut. General Honorable Thomas Maitland, July 19, 1805.—Major General John Wilson, lieutenant-governor, March 19, 1811.—Lieut. General Sir Robert Brownrigg, G. C. B., March 11, 1812.—Major General Sir Edward Barnes, K. C. B., lieutenant-governor, February 1, 1820.—Lieut. General the Right Honorable Sir Edward Paget, G. C. B., February 2, 1822.—Major General Sir James Campbell, K. C. B., lieutenant-governor, November 6, 1822.—Lieut. General Sir Edward Barnes, K. C. B., January 18, 1824.—Major General Sir John Wilson, K. C. B., lieutenant-governor, October 13, 1831.—The Right Honorable Sir Robert Wilmot Horton, Bart., G. C. H., October 23, 1831.—The Right Honorable James Alexander Stewart Mackenzie, November 7, 1837.—The Honorable Major General Sir Robert Arbuthnot, K. C. B., until the arrival of the present governor, Lieut. General Sir Colin Campbell, G. C. B.

Notwithstanding the long interval of nearly a century and a half that the Dutch retained possession of the former Portuguese settlements in Ceylon, Portugal has even now a hankering after the original seat of its power in the island; and public attention has been recently drawn to the claim, preferred by the latter, to the fort and town of Colombo.

How far this claim may be well founded, or otherwise, the following may tend to elucidate.

In the year 1816, a colonel in the Portuguese army, who wore the decoration of the order of Christ, arrived at Colombo, by one of the annual China ships, from Macao, bound to Goa. He soon became acquainted with one or two of the principal Portuguese families, and clandestinely endeavoured to obtain a sight of the old records of the Portuguese and Dutch governments. Mr. Sutherland, at that time deputy secretary to the government, and secretary for the Kandyan provinces, having been informed of the latter circumstance, took an opportunity of questioning the colonel upon his object; and, at the same time, intimated the impropriety of applying to those who could not assist him, except at the risk of their own official situations.

The colonel was very ready with an apology; and having entered upon the subject of our being in possession of the *whole* island of Ceylon, Mr. Sutherland jokingly observed, that "we had not yet turned out the wild Veddahs from the forests of Bintenné."

Mr. Sutherland subsequently asked the governor, (Lieut. General Sir Robert Brownrigg,) if he had ever heard of the treaty by which Colombo was to revert to the Portuguese, in the event of the entire island becoming, as it was at that time, (1816,) subject to the British crown; and he also remarked to His Excellency, that from the sinister manner, in which the colonel had endeavoured to obtain a sight of the records, or, probably, to possess them, there could be no doubt of the real object of his visit to Colombo; although that officer was very desirous that it should be attributed to mere accident, and as the casual one of a passenger, *en route*, from China to Goa.

His Excellency acknowledged that he had heard, or read, reports very similar to the Portuguese colonel's statement: and requested Mr. Sutherland to search the records, and make such extracts as he might consider expedient.

By these, it appeared, that in 1661, a treaty had been entered into between Great Britain and Portugal; by which, if Portugal recovered Ceylon from the Dutch, the port and fortress of point de Galle were to be ceded to the former; but that if Great Britain should wrest the island from the Dutch, Colombo was to revert to the Portuguese flag. It further appeared, that by two *subsequent treaties*, one in the year 1661, (the very year in which the preceding treaty had been entered into,) and the other in 1669, between the Dutch and Portuguese, the former were to retain *all* their conquests in Ceylon, without any stipulation or reservation whatever; and that in 1692, Portugal had definitively recognized the right of the Dutch to all the territories they had acquired there; by which treaty, whatever claims upon Colombo Portugal might originally have had, were for ever set at rest, whether preferred against the British, or any other power that might subsequently be in possession of Ceylon.

The whole island presents a scene of much interest to the emigrant and the naturalist; and it is not to be presumed that either will have a disposition to make a flying journey through it. There are many, however, who prefer starting for the interior, almost immediately after arriving at Colombo. Whether one travels by mail coach or not, the following is the route from the maritime capital to that of the interior.

From Colombo to the bridge of boats across the Mutwal river, which is one of the numerous improvements introduced into the colony by the late Lieut. General Sir Edward Barnes, G. C. B., soon after his succession to the government, as lieutenant-governor, in 1820; in order to obviate the delay, to which, travellers, and particularly troops, were subjected, when there was merely a ferry boat to convey them, the distance is $3\frac{1}{4}$ miles. To Mahara, where there is a rest-house on the right, 5 miles. To the mail coach station of Kosrupé, $6\frac{1}{2}$ miles. From thence to the rest-house of Henneratgodde, where there is also a barrack, 2 miles. To Kellegeddehainé, (mail coach station,) about 5 miles. To Viangoddé rest-house, 3 miles. To Walweldenia, (mail coach station,) about $4\frac{3}{4}$ miles. To Ambapasse rest-house, $6\frac{1}{2}$ miles. To the mail coach station of Ambapittia, through Maha-Hainé, $9\frac{1}{4}$ miles. To Ootooankandé rest-house and mail coach station, $8\frac{1}{2}$ miles. To Kadooganava rest-house, about 7 miles. To Paradenia, $6\frac{1}{4}$ miles; and from thence to Kandy, 4 miles. In all, about 72 miles from Colombo.

The formation of these military roads, which had been the first grand consideration of the executive, after the conquest and annexation of the Kandyan kingdom to the British empire, in 1815, as the surest means of retaining possession, but which the rebellion of 1817 and 1818 had, in a great degree, suspended, was resumed, with the return of tranquillity, in the year 1820, and upon an extended scale. Assistant engineers, selected from officers of different regiments, were appointed, with additional pay; every necessary arrangement for the work was put in train. Additional stimulus was given to the energies of those employed in these important undertakings, by the opportune arrival of Major General Sir Edward Barnes, K. C. B., from England, early in the year 1819, as second in command of the forces in Ceylon.

The formation of a carriage road from the port of Colombo on the west, to Trincomalé on the east side of the island, was of paramount importance to the commerce of the colony, in order to establish the means of transport between those places, when interrupted by sea, during the periods that the north-east and south-west monsoons respectively prevailed. These, however, although still incomplete, afford comparative facility to commerce.

Besides rest-houses on the roads for Europeans, and *Ambelamas* for native travellers, at regular distances, useful trees were planted on each side of the road, from the knotty bamboo to the umbrageous Sea-Pomegranate tree (*Barringtonia speciosa*, L.).

As regards the splendid roads already formed, there is scarcely a spot throughout the line, whether bridge, or tunnel, or rest-house, that does not justify the application to the memory of the late Lieut. General Sir Edward Barnes, G. C. B., of the tribute paid to that of Sir Christopher Wren, *for everywhere a monument presents itself*: and if His Excellency had not long previously distinguished himself as a gallant follower of his unrivalled chief, the Duke of Wellington, (whom may God long preserve to his country and sovereign!) the great and incalculable benefits, which, whilst governor of Ceylon, his unwearied zeal for, and devotion to, the best interests of the commerce and agriculture of the colony, have conferred upon it, are sufficient to immortalize his memory:—the public acknowledgments of its population best mark the general sense of them; nor will the name of any governor of that part of our Indian empire stand higher upon its records than that of Sir Edward Barnes.

There are, however, some classes of persons, the relatives of the brave and zealous European and native officers and soldiers, who fell victims to the malaria of the jungles of the interior, in cutting roads through the almost impenetrable fastnesses of the Kandyan kingdom, who cannot feel these public benefits. They can derive no consolation for the loss of husbands, fathers, and brothers, upon whom, perhaps, was their sole dependence, from the reflection that they had died in the performance of such a duty: for although it has secured possession of the interior, ensured the safety of the maritime provinces from a foe in their rear, promoted the commercial interests of the colony, and augmented its resources and revenue, very many of these families remain destitute.

These roads were made by the compulsory labour of the natives, (conjointly with military working parties,) who from their several tenures were liable to it themselves, or served as substitutes for others; and although the government legally possessed the power to avail itself of the monstrous system of oppression, which it had inherited from its Portuguese and Dutch predecessors, the great number of families left destitute by the loss of fathers, sons, and brothers, may still be deemed worthy of the humane consideration of the government, by which, compulsory labour was subsequently abolished: and even now, at this distant period, it is not too late to afford them some compensation, in proportion to the great public benefits, thereby achieved; for it cannot be a very difficult matter for the headmen of villages to report the names of parties, who died, whilst employed upon the roads, and of their existing families;

and surely some proportion of the annual surplus of revenue over expenditure, and which, by judicious management, every succeeding year will increase, cannot be more benevolently or honestly applied, than in performing an act of strict, though of tardy justice, to the native population of Ceylon, from a protecting and magnanimous government.

The following preliminary suggestions may be useful to the tourist in Ceylon, both in regard to his personal comfort and to economy. The emigrant, desirous of forming an opinion for himself, respecting an incomparable and magnificent country, and to seek for a location where he may expend a part of his capital to the best advantage, would not think flying through the island in a mail coach, the best way to attain his object; and, by buggy, it is hazardous and inconvenient, even with relays of horses, and fodder and medicines for them, at command. To be perfectly at one's ease, to stop when one pleases, to view the country, or to collect specimens in natural history, there is nothing like the old-fashioned way, by palankin; for any number of bearers may be engaged, casualties by sickness or desertion be provided against by due precaution, and the traveller is always sure of a bed.

From Colombo to Kandy by the mail coach, there is no occasion for more luggage than may be carried in a carpet bag; but by the route round the island, by the northern road from Colombo, occasionally diverging from the sea coast, as the roads toward the central province may present opportunities for investigating soil, climate, productions, and sites for intended agricultural or other speculations, and returning to that capital by the eastern and southern road, the traveller must be independent of accident for supplies.

I would earnestly recommend the traveller in Ceylon to have nothing to do with those pretty looking *canteens*, shining with patent leather and brass nails, at every outfitter's warehouse in town; for there are places, where, unless the greatest care be taken, the white ants will soon devour the leather, and perhaps the wood; and as to the ornamental brass nails, they are sure to exchange their brilliancy, in the humid atmosphere of the island, for the green hue of old copper.

I have always found japanned tin boxes the securest and best; and the traveller may have as many as his habits require; but he has one thing to bear in mind, viz., that the government regulations do not allow coolies to be compelled to carry more than forty pounds (avoirdupois) to a greater distance than two miles from any town; and as they travel best with their burthens slung at each end of a *pingo*, a canteen, when full, should not exceed twenty pounds. Therefore, a sufficient breakfast equipage, with supplies of tea, sugar, coffee, powder, shot, caps, a small lamp fitted to a low candlestick, with a couple of glass shades, wax candles, &c. &c., may be easily fitted into compartments in a tin box, twenty inches long, by fifteen in depth and width, and sufficient space to be left for a tray, of light cedar, over all; and the dinner canteen should be similarly fitted.

The Parsee and other shopkeepers have always hampers, containing an exact cooley load of wine, &c., at hand; and the gridiron and kettle may be slung upon the pole-irons of the palankin. A couple of good guns are indispensable, but pistols and swords, except for military men, are positive incumbrances.

The traveller's cook should always precede his master by some hours, to the rest-house, where he may intend to halt during the heat of the day; and be directed to have a sufficient number of chatties of water (which, if exposed to the night air, becomes the more cooling and wholesome) in readiness by his master's arrival.

Chatties, of the common size, hold about a gallon of water; these, emptied consecutively over the head, impart a delightful coolness to the frame, that disposes the tourist for one of those excellent breakfasts, *à la fourchette*, which the native cooks are second to none in preparing.

During this gastronomic enjoyment, and whilst coolness of temper conjoins with the temperature of early morning, let the traveller treasure the following in mind, as the best advice that he can act upon. First, Never to strike a native, how much soever his temper may be put to the test. Secondly, that for every day's halting, Sundays included, his coolies are entitled to *Batta*,* at the rate of threepence each, in addition to their regular hire. Thirdly, that they must not be compelled to travel more than two stages, or twenty five miles, in twenty four hours; or to proceed in cases of actual illness; under penalty, to their employer, of fine or imprisonment, at the discretion of the nearest district court.

An umbrella should be carried, whenever practicable, during the heat of the day: and I have found a circular curtain of green mosquito net, about twelve feet in depth, with a centre ferrule fitted to the curtain, so as to admit the point of an umbrella, a most excellent defence against that inveterate enemy of the new-comer, and constant annoyance to European travellers, the mosquito; for when the umbrella is expanded, and the handle tied to the head of a common rest-house bed, or couch, one may anticipate a night of comparative comfort, without having recourse to a *mosquito dose* as a soporific.

To make a circuit of the island, by the coast, tourists should proceed by what is called

* Extra allowance.

the northern route. This, after having crossed the Mutwal river by the bridge of boats, lies through the village of Jayellé, a distance of $9\frac{1}{4}$ miles, through a fertile and populous country; and from thence to Negombo the road lies chiefly through cinnamon plantations. Everywhere the sight and the smell derive gratification; for, on each side, may be seen the beautiful crimson *Clerodendrum infortunatum*, L., the *Pinna-mal-geddi* of the Singhalese, *Coffea triflora*, *Ixora coccinea*, *Nepenthes distillatoria* of the climbing and dwarf varieties (*scandens* and *nana*); the former, clinging to the cinnamon bushes for support, and displaying its "pitchers," some with the lid closed, others with it open, and in an erect position, half full of water, like so many fly traps, as if the liquid they contained was too valuable to be lost; the latter, shrinking from exposure, under the shade of the overhanging trees and grass: whilst the wild orange, lime, and shaddock trees, ever in fruit and blossom at the same time, impart the most delicious fragrance to the surrounding atmosphere.

For a considerable distance through the cinnamon plantations, the road is sandy: and, in many places, it leads through large tracks of the pure white quartz sand, already described in page 69, to which the cinnamon tree is partial.

Negombo is twenty four miles distant from Colombo,* and two leagues to the S. S. W. of Caymel. It lies in latitude 7° 15 north, and is a place of some trade, but frequented solely by coasting vessels. The coast between Negombo and Caymel forms a *bight*; and the former is known from the offing, by the point projecting a great way out, covered with coco-nut trees, and defended by a long reef beyond it. The *bight*, as sailors call it, should not be approached by large vessels nearer than two leagues off shore, nor in less than eight fathoms water, until the fort flag-staff bears S. E. by S., by which, the rocky ledge projecting from this part of the coast, and a rock with ten feet water on it, and six fathoms close by, bearing from the flag-staff, or north point of the fort, N. N. W., will be avoided.

For vessels bound to Negombo from the southward, the fort should be brought to bear S. E.; a ship ought then to steer direct for it, without borrowing any more to the northward, and may anchor in five or six fathoms, abreast of the fort.

The present fort was built by the Dutch, more for a protection to the cinnamon peelers, and storehouses of that spice, than as a sea defence. The only garrison, in time of peace, consists of a few rank and file of the Ceylon regiment, under the command of a non-commissioned officer.

* The roads, throughout the island, are measured from the Queen s house, Colombo.

CHAP. XXII.

Negombo admirably situated for grazing farms—Suggestions for supplying Colombo, and the shipping, with butcher's meat, and stock, and the navy with salted provisions—Naval dependance upon Bengal for supplies—Ceylon capable of supplying boatswains, carpenters, and other stores—Dutch families—Native women—Rest-house—Wesleyan mission-house and chapel—Superintendant of revenue and customs—Medicinal plants—Road from Negombo to Kandy—Native pastimes—Northern route by the coast from Negombo—Recreations for the naturalist and sportsman—Nattandé—Madampe—Pepper plantations—Game—Harvests in the Chilaw district—Chilaw—Sailing directions—Manufacture of coarse paper and cotton cloths—Mr. Wallbeoff's escape from a leopard—The plant called Rajah Wanya, or Jungle King—Artificial Leways.

NEGOMBO is an admirable place for establishing a grazing farm; and for improving the method of rearing and fattening cattle, sheep, swine, and poultry, for the Colombo market; for every variety of green and dry fodder is produced here with very little trouble; and the inland communication by water would enable the farmer to have the animals slaughtered over night at Negombo, and in the Colombo market soon after day-break in the morning.

Ships touching at Colombo, might thus be supplied with live stock, and fodder, at a few hours' notice, equal to any that the very best farms in Bengal can produce; but this certain lucrative speculation, like many others, has been hitherto neglected or unthought of, although a variety of projects, and many of them Eutopian ones, are constantly in agitation or progress.

The establishment of farms for the improvement of the breed of domestic cattle, and for salting and curing meat, could not fail to prove a successful speculation; and, in the cooler regions of Neuwara Eliya, all the advantages possessed for the *latter* grand object, are equal to those of the most temperate clime. It really astonishes the considerate mind, that a country so highly favoured by nature, and the head quarters of the British navy in India, should never yet have supplied that navy with a cask of salted beef or pork from its own resources!

Whatever the distress of our fleet might be, the naval dependence for salt provision, in India, is upon Bengal; and yet there is not a single article that could be required for the use of the navy, in point of boatswains' and carpenters' stores, and provisions, which Ceylon, if her natural resources were properly applied to that grand object of national importance, could not abundantly supply; from sail-maker's twine, to the main-mast; from the biscuit, to the cask of beef and pork; rum, arrack, lime-juice, vinegar, sugar, raisins, potatos, rice, pease, coffee, cocoa, pepper, oil, salt fish, live stock, grain, dry fodder, spices, fruits, vegetables, tapioca, arrow root, and a variety of the most useful drugs for the sick, at a cheaper rate than any other place in the British dominions.

Negombo is famous for its fish; and, at certain seasons, the Sea Woodcock, or Red Sur Mullet (*Mullus surmuletus*, L.) is caught in the greatest abundance and perfection. Pliny, Seneca, Horace, and Martial, bear testimony to the great estimation in which this delicious fish was held by the Romans, who purchased it at the very high rate of its weight in silver. Apicius too, considered nothing more delightful than to view the change of its beautiful colors, when expiring; and nothing more exquisite than to feast on it, when dressed with the "*Rien que manque*," or Carthaginian sauce of his age of gluttony. Here, they are exposed in heaps, just after being taken from their native element, at a few challies for half a dozen.

Kid, poultry, eggs, bread, fruit, and vegetables, may be obtained here in great plenty, at moderate prices; and the sportsman will find excellent snipe, curlew, and widgeon shooting. The water is extremely brackish, unless it be obtained from Kottidewé, or Children's Island; where persons are employed for the purpose of sinking pitchers in the sand over night, which, in the morning, are found full of pure and sweet water, that had filtered in the interim. Very fine mushrooms are found here, during, and for some time after, the rainy season; and, from the facility with which the country is irrigated, a great deal of paddee is produced: indeed, fertility and cultivation are everywhere conspicuous, the pastures being of a rich and delightful green, interspersed with magnificent teak (*Tectona Grandis*, L.) and fruit trees, and toddy topes.

Several respectable Dutch families formerly resided here, whose gardens were famous for their exotic fruits, (originally introduced from Java and the Malay peninsula,) but very few Dutch or Portuguese families, possessing wealth, remain in any part of the island, in comparison with their former numbers.

The native women of Negombo have the credit of being prettier than at most other places in Ceylon, and are generally modest and domestic in their habits.

The rest-house is a large and substantial stone building, with a spacious avenue of very fine teak trees in its front.

The Wesleyan mission-house is large and commodious, and the chapel a particularly neat building, having all the characteristics of a Protestant house of prayer.

The revenue and customs are superintended by an assistant government agent, who is also a judge of the Colombo District Court, No. 2 south.

The neighbourhood of Negombo abounds with medicinal plants: of those used by the native doctors, the following are the most generally known.*

The Indian Lilac (*Melia sempervirens*, L.), *Kassambu* of the Singhalese, is much esteemed for the medicinal properties of its bark and root. It yields a gum, that smells like garlic; and a valuable oil (*Margosa*) is extracted from its fruit, which is of the size and shape of a French olive, with a part of its top cut off transversely, of a yellow color, and grows in thick bunches.

The ripe fruit of the *Domba gaha* (*Calophyllum Inophyllum*, L.) yields an oil which is efficacious in rheumatism and rheumatic gout.

The Castor Oil plant (*Ricinus Palma Christi*, L.) is so abundant, that it may be regarded as a mere weed; for when once it gets into a garden, it is as troublesome to a gardener as the tobacco plant. The oil is generally esteemed for its medicinal properties, and the leaves make a cooling dressing for blisters.

The Thorn Apple (*Datura Stramonium*, L.). Of this common but invaluable plant there are the white (called in Singhalese *Attana*) and purple (*Kalu-Attana*†) varieties; these bear prickly pericarps, full of seeds, of narcotic qualities. The native doctors make an ointment of the flower, for burns and contractions of the nerves; and of the leaves for curing the gout: but the leaf is not used, as with us, in asthmatic affections, for the native doctors consider it injurious; and prescribe the root only, after it has been thoroughly dried, and chipped very fine, to their patients, who are then allowed to smoke it *ad libitum*. The seeds of the white species are efficacious in dental complaints; but these are seldom known where the use of *Betel* prevails.

The Wild Liquorice (*Abrus precatorius*, L.), *Olinda* of the Singhalese. The leaf has the taste of liquorice, and the native doctors make a decoction of it, with sugar and lime juice, for coughs.

The Vanilla (*Vanilla aromatica*, L.), *Hinninwela gaha* of the Singhalese, abounds; and yet not an ounce is prepared for exportation!

The Galangale Root (*Kœmpferia galanga*, L.) is equally neglected. The flower is white, with a violet spot in the centre: root bulbous, palmate; leaves egg-shaped.

* Where there are no English names, the Singhalese precede the Linnæan ones.

† The Singhalese have no definition of purple, and apply the word *Kalu*, or black, in lieu of it.

Its medicinal virtues are aromatic and diaphoretic. The broad-leaved galangale (*K. latifolia*), round-leaved (*K. rotunda*), and narrow-leaved (*K. angustifolia*), are also indigenous.

The *Jacberi* of the Singhalese (*Crotalaria laburnifolia* and *retusa*, L.). Both have yellow flowers, and the former is said to be the *Radix Colombo*, but, I believe, erroneously.

The *Tebu-gas* of the Singhalese (*Costus speciosus*), an excellent substitute for ginger.

The *Wal-pupulu* of the Singhalese (*Eupatorium Ayapana*), used to cure snake bites

The *Sacsanda* of the Singhalese (*Aristolochia Indica*, L.). The root, steeped in brandy or old arrack, is an invaluable tonic.

The *Nil Kataroodoo* of the Singhalese (*Clitoria Ternatea*, L.), a very common creeper, and extremely ornamental, from its blue flowers and bright green leaves. The root is used as an emetic.

The Angular-leaved Physic Nut (*Jatropha curcas*, L.), *Jarrack* of the Singhalese, of which two or three seeds, cleansed from the skin, are a sufficient purge. Oil made of the nuts is used in the cure of the itch, and the pounded leaf for ulcers; and, when mixed with tobacco, as an enema.

The *Cocculus Indicus*, L., mixed with moistened rice, is employed to intoxicate birds and fishes.

The Coral Shrub (*Jatropha multifida*, L.).

The *Mendi* of the Singhalese (*Ophiorhiza mungos*), used in the cure of snake bites.

The *Godogandu* of the Singhalese (*Ophioxylon serpentinum*, L.), also used for snake bites, and as a tonic.

The *Ratnethul* of the Singhalese (*Plumbago rosea*, L.).

The *Rat Binungé* of the Singhalese (*Periploca Indica*, L.), with red flowers; and the *Ellé Binungé* of the Singhalese (*Periploca sylvestris*, L.), with white flowers. Both possess similar properties to the Ipecacuanha (*Euphorbia Ipecacuanhæ*, L.), and delight in a sandy soil.

The *Arooloo* of the Singhalese (*Terminalia chebulla*), *Booloo* of the Singhalese (*T. bellerica*), and *Nelli* of the Singhalese (*T. emblica*).

The *Jayapala* and *Nepalam gaha* of the Singhalese (*Croton tiglium*, L.), wild and abundant. A very powerful oil is extracted, called *Croton* oil, and used in cases of spasmodic cholera.

Lemon Grass (*Andropogon Schœnanthus*, L.), used in decoction as a cooling drink in fever, and by the Dutch and Portuguese, for giving a lemon flavor to tea.

The Prickly Poppy (*Argemone Mexicana*, L.).

J. W. Bennett del.

Citrus tuberoides or *Caffrarian Lime* } *Koodalodeye of the Singhalese*

The *Cassia Fistula*, L., abundant in jungles, and much used as an aperient medicine.
The *Dewool gaha* of the Singhalese (*Feronia elephantum*), produces a medicinal gum.
The Jalap plant (*Convolvolus turpethum*, L.), *Tristawalla* of the Singhalese.
The *Wanassa* of the Singhalese (*Ballota disticha*, L.), a species of horehound.
The *Lineya gaha* of the Singhalese (*Helicteres Isora*, L.).

From Negombo there is a road through Miniwangoddé and Veangoddé to Kandy, distant 66½ miles; but I enjoyed the more unfrequented road, which, although in many places it was with difficulty passed on horseback, I recommend to the naturalist; namely, by the left bank of the Kaymel river, through Halpé, Kotadenia, Girulé, (at which place there is a ferry, and the name of the river is there changed to Maha-Oya,) and Negahagidera, to the wretched cowshed, miscalled rest-house, at Nagahattoo, and from thence to Kurunagallé, or, as we call it, Kornegalle.

The whole country, except where there are occasional patches of jungle, is everywhere cultivated and well irrigated, producing large crops of paddee, and small grains; and abounding in pasture lands, some of which have all the appearance of an extensive English park: these teem with buffalos and bullocks, and the jungles with game.

Birds and insects, in great variety, and of the most brilliant colors, meet the eye in every direction.

The villagers throughout the line of the bridle road, chiefly spend their afternoons in cockfighting; and, at night, are often successful in spearing elephants. At Kotadenia, I mounted on a dead elephant, to make a sketch of a group of six which lay dead within twenty yards of my position: but not one of them had tusks. The villagers informed me, that the animals were surrounded by so great a number of people, with *Chulos* and *Tom-toms*, that they appeared paralyzed, and were speared without making an attempt to defend themselves. I should not suppose the largest of these elephants exceeded eight feet in height, and two of them were very small. I never saw one in Ceylon, that, to the best of my judgment, exceeded ten or eleven feet in height.

Five miles beyond Negombo, the Kaymel river (as the Maha-Oya is called at its mouth) is crossed at Topoo Ferry; from thence to Kirimetteané the distance is six miles, and to the bridge of Ging-Oya about 4¼ miles; the road flat and sandy, and the land but partially cultivated. The next rest-house is that of Nattandé, about a mile from the bridge over the Ging-Oya.

The naturalist and the sportsman may find the most delightful recreation and exercise in this neighbourhood; the former in collecting specimens of the various aquatic plants, ferns, mosses, land shells, insects, and birds; and the latter may select any game he pleases; for he has not to go far inland to find elephants, leopards, deer, elk, hares, and almost every variety of animal and bird the country produces.

But if the tourist be neither botanist, naturalist, nor sportsman, and desire to have game procured for him, he has only to hint his wish to the keeper of the rest-house where he may halt, and a number of native sportsmen will soon be collected about him, with their uncouth guns, ready to bring him whatever game he may require, upon receiving a charge or two of powder and shot, and a promise of a similar quantity, as their subsequent reward; for as they never fire until *too close* upon their object to run the least risk of missing it, they invariably earn the promised gratuity.

From Nattandé rest-house to the bridge over the Kuddoopitté-Oya the distance is $5\frac{3}{4}$ miles; and half a mile further is Madampé, formerly a place of importance, and the residence of native sovereigns; and subsequently a swampy unhealthy locality, tenanted by mosquitos, jackalls, monkies, and alligators; until the late Mr. Peter Engelbert Vanderstraaten obtained a grant of land from the government, and formed pepper gardens there, in the hope of eventually rendering the island independent of the Malabar coast for that most important spice, without which, the cinnamon would lose its aromatic properties, and consequently its value, during the homeward voyage.

If Mr. Vanderstraaten had been supported by the government to the extent he had been encouraged to anticipate, Madampé would have proved pre-eminently productive, particularly in pepper, which is now produced there, but in a very limited quantity to its capabilities. The clustering pepper bines unite the most stately trees, all valuable for their timber, as if in one family compact; these form cool and delightful avenues; and in every direction near his spacious bungalow, Mr. Vanderstraaten planted the best and rarest varieties of the plantain tree, (*Musa Sapientium*, L.) that the island, and the neighbouring continent of India produced.

Madampe abounds with widgeon, snipe, curlews, sand pipers, the large and small white and brown paddee birds, flamingos (*Phœnicopterus ruber*, L.), and other aquatic birds. The flesh of the flamingo is, at certain seasons, white and delicious, and entirely free from the peculiarly fishy flavor of its genus that it possesses at others. Elk,* deer,† wild hogs, the stock or original of the common domestic hog, and not the Babyroussa (*Sus Babyrussa*, L.), as some have stated it to be, for that animal is not known in the island; Indian musk of Pennant (*Moschus Meminna*, L.), pea fowl, jungle fowl (*Gallus Indicus* of Leach), small red-legged partridges (*Perdix Janninus*

* Elk, the roe-buck (*Cervus Capreolus*, L.).

† Deer (*Cervus Axis* of Shaw, *Cervus Dama*, L.), amongst which there is a variety perfectly white, with red eyes.

of Shaw), Coromandel quails (*Coturnix textilis* of Shaw), and hares, abound throughout the province.

The canal contains abundance of small mud fish, of the genus *Perca*, L., and eels.

The beautiful *Nymphæa alba* and *N. Nelumbo* cover the water tanks with their odoriferous red and white (esculent) corols.

The Ceylon hare resembles the common European hare in every respect, except that the fur on the nape of the neck is black. The flesh of the wild hog is a wholesome food, but altogether unlike pork; and next to it, in point of flavor, but more delicate, is the flesh of the porcupine, an animal easily domesticated; for, though "fretful" by nature, it will feed, and keep upon excellent terms with pigs in a stye.

The *Maha* or great harvest in the Chilaw district, of paddee sown between the 1st of September and 31st October, takes place in February; and the *Yalla* harvest, or second crop of paddee, sown between the 1st of April and 31st of May, takes place in August. Twelve sorts of this grain are cultivated here; and as many sorts of "fine grains," of which, those sown between the 1st of September and 15th of October, are reaped at the *Maha* harvest in January; and those sown between the 1st of April and 31st of May, are reaped at the *Yalla* harvest in July and August.

The directions for sailing along this coast are thus given by Horsburgh: "Seven miles north of Madampé is Chilaw, which village lies in about latitude 7° 48′ north, and may be known from the offing by a sand hill, having on it some bushes, and near it a round hummock. In coming to this place from the northward, a vessel should keep two miles outside the reef of rocks projecting from Calpentyn, until clear of its southern extremity, then haul in towards the Ceylon shore. Coming from the southward, a vessel may, if bound to Chilaw, steer along shore to the anchorage abreast of the river.

"From the north point of Calpentyn to Chilaw, the distance is about nine leagues; and when a vessel has got an offing, the course is about S. S. W. along the west side of the island. A reef of rocks stretches along that side, nearly from the middle part beyond the southern point, where it projects nearly three miles from the shore, requiring great attention to the lead in passing. The bottom between Calpentyn and Chilaw is mostly sand, with a little coral at times: the nearer the former is approached, the worse it becomes for anchoring."

The fort of Chilaw has a small garrison, and is a dependency of that of Putlam. The rest-house is roomy and airy. At the time I first visited it, in 1816, the best pack of dogs (I cannot say hounds) in the island was kept there, by the then collector of the district, Mr. Wallbeoff, who was a great sportsman. Chilaw, which is now superintended by an assistant government agent, has manufactories of coarse paper, and also of common cottons, table cloths, and towels: these are preferable to linen articles for wear and tear, because the latter cannot withstand the Ceylon washerman's principal soap (beating against a stone) as the former does, to the tune of " Europe, Europe, Europe," until the article, subjected to his manual operations, is more *holy* than sound.

The tiger is unknown in Ceylon, although that name is applied to the chetah or leopard (*Felis Leopardus*), which is as great an authropophagist as the former, whenever opportunity admits of it.

Mr. Wallbeoff, whilst in search of a leopard, which had severely lacerated a native, observed the animal crouched behind a fallen coco-nut tree. He fired both the barrels of his gun at the animal; one ball perforated the near hind leg, and the other, passing through the lower jaw, lodged in the off shoulder. Turning round for his rifle to the native to whom he had entrusted it, and who had *faithfully promised to keep close to him*, he found himself deserted; for his followers had all decamped, upon seeing the danger he was in. At this moment, Mr. Wallbeoff received a violent blow on the back of his shoulder, from the animal's paw, which felled him to the ground, when the enraged beast fastened its teeth in the back part of his head, and its hind claws into his back; but, owing to the wounds it had received, and its struggle with a strong muscular man, the animal relinquished its hold, and retired into a bush.

As soon as Mr. Wallbeoff had so far recovered himself as to reload his gun, he pursued the leopard and shot it through the heart. The animal, when measured, was found to be seven feet ten inches from the nose to the tip of the tail; and, after all, Mr. Wallbeoff's injuries were not very material.

From Chilaw, the northern route lies to the Dedro-Oya, distant two miles; from thence to the rest-house of Battooloo-Oya, 10¼ miles; to Moondel, 4 miles; to Marrundamkoollé, 7½ miles.

The botanist will be delighted with the beautiful little plant, called *Rajah Wanya*, or *Jungle King*, which delights in marshy places, and abounds in this neighbourhood. The plant bears a delicate white flower, upon a pink capillary stalk; leaves cordiform; upper surface, resembling black velvet, striped with gold-like color, and veined after the manner of a butterfly's wing; under surface, a light lake, inclining to ash color. The natives, ignorant of the attractive influence of water upon trees, ascribe the bending of their branches over the water and marshy places, inhabited by the *Rajah Wanya*, to their natural homage to the *Jungle King* plant!!

The artificial *Leways*, or salt pans, are situate at Oedepencarré, Alempitty, Pulletchacalom, Mundel, Anea Kadda, Pallandowé, Perrea Natchicalé, Karativoe Island, Calpentyn, Chinné Natchicalé, and Rattandé.

CHAP. XXIII.

Putlam—Its garrison—Artificial salt pans—Face of the country—Crocodiles—Native devoured by a crocodile—Living crocodile presented to the Author—Difference between the Ceylon and Ganges crocodile—Mosque—Burial ground—Remarkable tree—Moorish dancers with a double-edged sword in each hand—Milk purveyors—Tyre—Native Vermicelli—Road to Kandy through Kornegalle—Water conveyance to the islands of Calpentyn and Karetivoe—Sailing directions along the coast—Farm of the Chank fishery—Its extent—The Chank manufactured into bangles and spoons—Estimated value of a Chank with its valve opening to the right instead of the left—Hint to the naturalist—The sea weed Fucus aurylaceus, commonly called Jaffna moss—Custom-house establishment at Calpentyn—Inadequate salaries, and contrast—The late Earl of St. Vincent's illiberal maxim for naval officers not likely to ensure honesty in civil departments—Anecdote of a provincial judge of Calpentyn—Northern route continued—Pomparripo—Face of the country—Wild animals—The great crane—Right Honorable Sir Alexander Johnston—Ancient tank of Bawalé—Singhalese records—Capabilities of the soil—Extent and population of the western province.

Putlam is the next stage from Marrundamkoollé. It is a populous village, principally inhabited by Moormen and Hindoos, and has a small fort and garrison, commanded by a lieutenant, with a medical staff of one assistant surgeon, and one native medical assistant.

The commandant is also superintendant of salt under the civil assistant government agent of Chilaw. This great staple of human economy is manufactured here in large quantities; the coast being very flat and sandy, and evaporation extremely rapid, the artificial pans, soon after the salt has formed, appear, at a distance, as if covered with snow.

The face of the country is flat, and abounds in tanks and patches of water, all which are infested with crocodiles. The Ceylon species is the *Lacerta Crocodilus*, a very sluggish animal. The natives catch them in nets, and also in traps, and with baited hooks. In the former way, they have more sport; for they spear and shoot them, ad libitum, after having dragged them upon terra firma.

The crocodile possesses great strength, and is equally dreaded by men and animals. It has been occasionally caught in the jungles. The only instance of its destroying human life, that fell within my own knowledge, was at Hiccode, in the Galle district, in 1824; when a native, in the act of bathing, was seized by a crocodile, and swallowed, with the exception of the head and one hand, which were found on the margin of the river; from which it was inferred that the poor victim had seen the animal approach, and had endeavoured to save himself, but was overtaken just as he had grasped at an overhanging branch of a tree in the last fruitless effort to escape.

Immediately upon the report reaching the collector of the district, James Agnew Farrel, Esq., he ordered a general search for the amphibious monster; which, on the second day, proved successful; for just as our pic-nic party was about to sit down to dinner, two carts lashed together, and containing the body of the animal, which was $17\frac{1}{2}$ feet in length, were driven to the door. We had it removed instantly to the sea-side and opened; when the body of the native, already a mass of putrefaction, was taken out, and a coroner's inquest held upon the spot.

The Ceylon crocodile differs greatly from the *Lacerta Gangetica*, which has a snout thrice the length of the head, and the eyes very prominent, and so constructed that the animal can see above the water when its body is below the surface. In the Ceylon species the head is long, and flat towards the extremity of the jaws; the eyes very small, and so placed within their orbits that the outer part, when shut, is not above an inch and a half in length, and parallel with the opening of the jaws; the nose is directly in the middle of the upper jaw, and about an inch and a quarter from the extremity of it; the neck is carinated, and both the head and back are covered with a hard coat; the tail rough, with two lateral crests; but the belly is not proof against a musket ball.

In 1827, the bullock drivers belonging to the salt establishment at Hambantotte, brought me a living crocodile, which they had caught in a jungle near Magam. It measured sixteen feet four inches from the extremity of the head to that of the tail.

This animal is called Kayman by the Dutch and Portuguese of the island, and *Kimbolah* by the Singhalese; and whatever is once seized by it can never escape; for there are alternate cavities between the teeth in both jaws. The living specimen had twenty five sharp-pointed teeth in the upper, and fifteen in the lower jaw, of different sizes; but it evidently had had more in the former, by the remains of stumps that had the appearance of broken teeth.

The crocodile lays from eighty to a hundred eggs, which are white, and of the size of a goose's egg, but more oblong, and convex at the extremities.

The Moormen have a mosque at Putlam; and, in the burial ground, there is a fine specimen of a species of tamarind, which is distinguished by the Malabars from the common tamarind (*Tamarindus Indica*, L.), which they call *Bolam-Pulli* and *Maderam-Pulli*, by the name of *Papara-Pulli*; as large as the one, under which Baldæus is said to have first preached the gospel in Ceylon, and which lies in the direct route to

Jaffna, near the village of Illipekadewé. In 1816, this tree was thirty four feet in girth, and nearly eighty feet in height.

Some of the young villagers display great agility in dancing with a double-edged sword in each hand; and in attack and defence, whilst rapidly moving to the sound of native music.

The Moormen are the principal huxters, jewellers, and butter and milk purveyors, in the island. At "out-stations," the last two articles may be obtained free from adulteration; but at Colombo, where the demand is greater, the adulteration of the former, with flour, and the latter, from "the standing cow in the yard," is proportionally great.

At this place, and other country villages, the best *Tyre* is to be procured morning and evening. This cool, wholesome, and very nutritious curd, is prepared by boiling new milk until one third of the quantity has evaporated; it is then removed from the fire; and when cool, the addition of a table spoonful of butter-milk converts it, in a very few hours, into a solid curd; in which state it is eaten with sugar, nutmeg, and boiled rice. Nothing can be more wholesome for children; and it is a great favorite, at breakfast, with all ranks and classes, both European and native. The Singhalese call it *Midi Kiri*, or hard milk; the Hindo-Portuguese, *Tyro*; and the Malabars, *Tyree*. This curd is also eaten with a species of Vermicelli, which is formed of rice flour and the expressed juice of the pulp of the ripe or curry coco-nut, forced through the bottom of a chatty, which is perforated with small holes for the purpose, into a common rice winnow, and held in the steam of boiling water until it acquires the consistency of boiled Maccaroni.

From Putlam there is a tolerable road to Kandy, through the romantic station of Kornegalle; which, for the traveller's guidance, may as well be set down in Ceylon road order; because, if in search of a location, he would scarcely confine himself to the line of road, and might prefer extending his tour, by diverging to the right and entering the central province, so as to obtain information as to the nature of the soil, its productions, and capabilities for being made available to any speculation that he may have in prospective; and, after having so done, return to the place from whence he diverged, for the purpose of continuing his route round the island.

From Putlam to Katjemadowé, 12 miles; to Dohanneamma, 11 miles; to Bogallegamma, 10 miles; to Padennie, 10 miles; to Kalloomooné, 8½ miles; to Kornegalle, 7½ miles; to Kospotté-Oya, 8½ miles; to Madawalletenné, 6¼ miles; to Mavali-Ganga, 8¾ miles; to the entrance of the tunnel (500 feet in length), 1½ mile; to Kandy, 1½ mile;—total from Putlam to Kandy, 84 miles.

There is also conveyance by water from Putlam to Calpentyn; and as the islands of Calpentyn and Karetivoe lie parallel with this coast, and between Putlam and Point Koedeemalé (which forms a small bight between it and the south bank of the Marritchicatty river); and the island of Manaar, forming, with the north end of Karetivoe,* a considerable bay, the directions for sailing along them may be of sufficient utility to justify a temporary digression from the route by land.

According to Captain Horsburgh's sailing directions, "There are many dangerous banks interspersed from the east end of the island of Manaar to Calpentyn island, rendering the navigation unsafe for large vessels near the shore; but small ones, drawing seven or eight feet water only, and acquainted with the coast, pass inside or between some of them. The east end of Manaar is in about latitude 8° 57′ north, having coco-nut and palmyra trees upon it; also a fort, and several houses; and in the gut which separates it from the opposite point in Ceylon, Mantotte, there is said to be ten or twelve feet water in some places."

"Calpentyn island, situated to the southward of Cardiva island, near to, and parallel with, Ceylon, appears as part of the principal island, when viewed from the offing. It is low, abounds with coco-nut trees, and extends from latitude 7° 56′ to 8° 18′ north."

"The fort and village of Calpentyn stand on the north end of the island, between which and the south end of Cardiva island, there is a group of islets, with a larger one, called Long Island,† adjoining the north point of Calpentyn, of which it seems part. Close to this, vessels may anchor in four or five fathoms; or farther to the N. E. near Cardiva; but the bottom being mostly rocky and foul, they will be liable to lose their anchors. The best track in, is thought to be near the N. W. side of the island, on account of dangerous overfalls on the rocky banks a little to the northward. The bank of soundings is said to stretch from this island about six or seven leagues to the westward."

In the rainy season, the *peninsula* of Calpentyn becomes an *island*, and the mud renders crossing impossible.

"The rocky banks or reefs off this place are very dangerous; one lies to the W. and S. W. five or six miles off shore, with four fathoms water close to it, and the outermost are said to be five leagues distant from the land. Ships bound to Manaar from the southward, when 3 or 3½ leagues to the westward of Cardiva island, may steer about north, till the breakers on the reef are discerned; then haul to the west-

* Called also Cardiva and Nallandine Island.

† Distant from Chilaw by sea eight or nine leagues.

ward about a league in rounding it. From this place, Manaar island will be seen to the N. E., for which they should steer, *keeping a good look-out, and the lead going*, the soundings being irregular over a rocky bottom, until seven or eight fathoms near the island; under these depths they decrease gradually towards it to five fathoms sandy ground. In this track there are sometimes overfalls from twenty to twenty five fathoms, to two or three fathoms less at a cast. If a vessel shoal to eight fathoms hard ground, in passing near the reef or outermost banks, she ought instantly to haul to the westward."

"From this part of Ceylon to the Tinevelly coast, soundings extend across the gulf to the southward of Adam's Bridge; but the outer limit of the bank is not exactly known to Europeans, as seldom any other than small coasting vessels navigate in the gulf to the northward of Colombo."

The farm of the exclusive right of fishing for the shell fish called Chank (*Voluta Gravis*), which extends from the northern extremity of Calpentyn island, round by Jaffna, to Moelletivoe on the east side of the island, is usually sold to the highest bidder for a term of two years.

This univalve is an article of considerable commerce throughout India; for it is manufactured into bangles for women and children, by whom these ornaments are worn, round their arms and legs, in indefinite numbers, as their circumstances may admit of the display. Spoons are also made of it, which are occasionally purchased by the curious European.

A chank shell with its valve opening to the right instead of the left, is considered of very great value. I once heard a native estimate it at 10,000 rupees, or about £1000 sterling.

The palankin boys and baggage coolies will be much relieved by boating it from Putlam to Calpentyn; and by keeping close along the shore of Navakarré, the naturalist may obtain shells, specimens of mollusca, madrepore, pearl-oyster spawn, coral, sea weed (*Fucus aurylaceus*), commonly called in the island Jaffna moss, which is in general demand and estimation throughout India; and, as it is superior in quality to the Iceland moss, it might be made a profitable speculation, as an export to this country.

The custom-house at Calpentyn is the only civil establishment on the island, and is superintended by an assistant custom master, whose salary is 67*l.* 10*s.* per annum, with a supervisor at £30, a conicoply or cash-keeper and cloth-taxer (*unus et idem*) at £20, and a searcher at £10 per annum!! Is this enough to support them and their families, and at the same time keep them honest in the midst of temptation?

I have seen £2000, £1600, £1200, and £800 a year, insufficient to keep certain Europeans, called Ceylon civil servants, faithful and honest in their public duties; but perhaps the indigenous breed are expected to be composed of more tsustworthy materials, although, by comparison, expected to live on chameleon diet. The late Earl of St. Vincent's illiberal maxim in regard to naval officers, "Keep them poor, and they will serve you well!" will not do to ensure honesty in *post office, revenue*, and *custom-house* departments.

The very name of Calpentyn is so connected with colonial anecdote, that I cannot refrain from relieving the monotony of the route, by relating one, as I received it: but without vouching for its authenticity.

Formerly, Calpentyn was the residence of a provincial judge; and a vacancy having occurred, a civil servant was appointed to that judicial office, who was as notorious for his *orthographical independence*, as for his habitual boast "that although he was eight years fagging at Latin and French, he knew no more of either than when he left school; and, that at that time, he was just as wise as on the day he entered it!"

This new provincial judge proceeded to the King's house, as the Governor's residence was then called, with the twofold object of returning thanks for the appointment, and of getting the Governor's consent to the usual advance of six months' salary, in order to fit out for his new station. After having been, according to court parlance, "most graciously received," his request was granted; and just as the Governor was about to give him his *congé*, the Stentorian voice of a neighbouring Dutch auctioneer's clerk, whose name was Terry, and who was about to sell a lot of cast cavalry horses, was heard in the street facing the King's house: "Going,—going,—can't dwell, gentlemen,—going,—gone!" attracted his attention. He was a good judge of *horse-flesh*, if not of Greek and Latin, and therefore anxious to depart from "the presence," in order to attend the sale.

Upon rising to take leave, the Governor good-humouredly said to him, "I presume, Mr. ——— that you are very intimately acquainted with the *Lex terræ*,"—and, if the judge had not suddenly interrupted him, His Excellency would have added, "according to the Dutch code, as administered in this island." The judge changed color, as if gazing upon a ghost; for his dignity was much hurt at the serious charge, as he considered it; and so anxious was he to acquit himself, that he very gravely assured the Governor, that "if His Excellency did not joke, he must have been grossly misinformed; for that upon his honor, as a gentleman, except that he knew the fellow's surname was Terry, and that he was the auctioneer's clerk, he knew not whether his christian name was *Lex*, or if he had ever been christened at all!!"

Reader! imagine, if thou canst, the surprise, or rather mute astonishment, of His Majesty's sole manufacturer of provincial judges, His Excellency the Governor of Ceylon!

To resume our route by land, the next stage from Putlam is to Pomparripo rest-house, beyond the river of that name, (through the village of Nelliobar, distand 5 miles, and Wannativillé, 6½ miles from the former village,) distant 18½ miles; and to the village of Pomparripo a further distance of four miles.

The face of the country is flat; but although none of the scenery of the more elevated parts of the island diversifies the prospect, magnificent forest trees, and verdant plains, interspersed with neat native cottages and paddee fields, form as interesting a landscape as any champain country can present. The sea is skirted by low sands, with here and there an occasional *Cactus opuntia,* or *Pandanus odoratissimus.*

The neighbouring jungle abounds with elk, deer, wild hogs, elephants, chetahs, bears, sloths, monkies, and various other animals; besides birds and insects in great variety, and most interesting to the collecting naturalist. Of the stork or *Grus* genus, which is numerous throughout the island, and particularly in the northern and eastern provinces, the *Maha Kokah** is a splendid specimen, and its elegant white feathers over the shoulders and back are much esteemed by the fair sex. My attention was first drawn to its delicate plumage by the Right Honorable Sir Alexander Johnston, with whom I had the honor to travel, some years since, when Sir Alexander was chief justice of Ceylon, from Jaffna to Colombo; during which period, I shot a superb specimen of the *Maha Kokah;* but not having any preparation at hand for preserving the skin, putrefaction followed death most rapidly, and I contented myself with sketching the bird, and presenting the valuable portion of its feathers to Sir Alexander.

The northern part of this province is chiefly inhabited by Moormen and Hindoos; and there are so many vestiges of its original agricultural importance, that one is lost in surprize at the apparent apathy of former European governments.

The naturalist or the botanist may not be disposed to lose an inch of ground; but the antiquarian will find little for research, unless he diverges very much to his right, through jungle and cattle tracks, until he reaches the remains of the Bawalé tank; for which place he can procure a guide at Pomparripo.

* *Maha Kokah* signifies the Great Crane,—*Maha,* a Sanscrit word, in general use by the Singhalese, for Great, and *Kokah,* Crāne.

This ancient tank is one of the very many vestiges of the former agricultural prosperity of the northern districts; for although the cultivation of rice had subsequently become so neglected, that in the year 1785 Ceylon was supplied from Java, it is a recorded fact, that in the year 1693 the whole Coromandel coast was supplied with that grain from this part of Ceylon! It is estimated, that if the Bawale tank was restored to its original state of usefulness, the lands which would thereby be rendered capable of irrigation, would afford employment to at least fifteen hundred or two thousand labourers.

Although it is mortifying to the inquiring mind, that the period of authentic history is so extremely limited; and that, as it is generally understood, we cannot trace it antecedently to Herodotus, unless we include the sacred writings of the great lawgiver of the Jews, about eleven hundred years more remote, the Singhalese priests do not hesitate to aver, *that they have correct national records for upwards of two thousand years.*

The soil of this district is admirably adapted for the cultivation of cotton (*Gossipium herbaceum*, L.), both of the white and Nan-Kin varieties; Dhol (*Citysus Cajan*, L.), sun-flower (*Helianthus annuus*, L.), Cassada (*Jatropha Manihot*, L.), ginger (*Amomum Zingiber*, L.), pepper (*Piper nigrum*, L.), annatto (*Bixa orellana*, L.), turmeric (*Curcuma longa*, L.), and the greater and lesser cardamom (*Amomum grana Paradisi*, and *Eletaria cardamomum*, L.).

The superficies of the western province of Ceylon is 4452 square miles. White population, including military and their families, 3982. Free blacks, 492,605. Slaves, 606. Aliens and resident strangers, 1829. Thus giving a population of 111.78 to the square mile.

CHAP. XXIV.

Northern Province—Pomparripo river—Pomparripo—Native inhabitants—Capabilities of the province for supplying the whole island with rice—Anticipated result of a liberal encouragement of Hindoo immigration—Indispensable elementary improvements—Increase of revenue from sea customs one certain result of Hindoo colonization—Depression of native agriculture—Singhalese landlords—Cultivators pay fifty per cent. upon advances of seed corn—Consequence of non-payment after the harvest—Native proctors—The law of primogeniture would be a blessing to the Singhalese—Minute division of landed property—Northern route continued—Marritchicatty rest-house—Padoua caste—Covia and Nallua slaves—Headmen support caste from interest and prejudice—Assumption of the rank of headmen in the Malabar provinces—Penalty attached—Kallaar pagoda—Ashes exchanged for money—Malabar improvisatori—Scenery from Pomparripo to Kallaar—Apician luxuries—Common oyster abundant, but neglected, although it might be made a profitable speculation—A Singhalese mile—Jaffna moss—Description of the Hirundo esculenta—Its edible nest—Dutch partial to it as a delicacy—Its virtues—The prepared birds' nest humbly presented to His Majesty King George the Fourth, who commands it to be cooked for his Royal use—Sir Henry Halford's communication to the Author.

THE Pomparripo river separates the Western from the Northern Province, and takes its rise in the mountains of the interior, near Nallandé, in the former Kandyan Dessavony of Matellé, now part of the central province. The village of Pomparripo, about four miles north of the ford, is chiefly inhabited by industrious Moormen and Hindoos. These people are of very contented habits; and the province possesses great natural and artificial capabilities of irrigation. If therefore the government would but encourage Hindoo immigration, by grants of the crown lands, tax-free, for a certain number of years, there would be no want of native capitalists to advance money and seeds, upon the security of the crops; and sufficient rice, cotton wool, and tobacco, might be grown in this province to supply the whole island, and leave a large surplus for exportation.

But, as an indispensable preliminary to the great and important measure of extending the culture of these staples, the government will have to effect extensive elementary improvements; such as the restoration of the ancient tanks, and the formation of canals and bridges, in order to increase the means of transit; the want of which, are the chief physical obstructions to commerce: for it is by such works that the capital of a country is formed, and they ought to be promoted, if it be the object of the government to attract, and render profitable, the capital of individuals.

For this grand object, it would be sound policy to encourage an extensive colonization of the northern parts of the western, and the northern provinces, by Hindoos; and it is morally impossible to estimate the extent of the local benefits, to which, such a measure may lead.

Whether the Hindoos were the primitive inhabitants of the country or not, they form one of the most ancient nations in the world, and were distinguished by letters and arts, at a time when the major part of their Asiatic neighbours were scarcely advanced beyond the first stage of civilization. Let it be recollected, that this race is humane, gentle, and brave, (for there are nowhere better native soldiers than the Hindoos, under proper discipline and European officers,) their manners obliging, and their habits frugal, hospitable, and temperate.

If the latter be, as we are told, one of the effects upon society of Hindoo superstition, whose positive injunction to rigid temperance preserves its votaries from many of the gross irregularities, which, in our own country, sap the foundations of all social happiness, let us hope, that the extension of christianity will not introduce its antithesis to this now contented race of people.

It may be anticipated, that Hindoo immigrants would bring with them, exclusively of those practiced in agriculture, cattle breeding, fishing, hunting, and mining, manufacturers of cotton and silk cloths, shawls and mats, and tanners of leather, equal to those of Cordova. As they are also inimitable dyers, there is not a fairer field for their operations than Ceylon, where every kind of vegetable dye may be said to be indigenous.

Although the restoration of the ancient tanks would be a work of time, yet cultivation would be gradually extending itself, as the means of irrigation progressed; and one grand result of the occupation of the soil by industrious Hindoos, would be a gradual, but important increase of the local revenue, through the additional stimulus that would thereby be given to the trade between Ceylon and the opposite coasts.

The next important object, and not the least to a naval power, to which I would beg leave most earnestly to draw the attention of Her Majesty's government, is the culture of the indigenous hemp (*Cannabis Sativa*, L.), and the formation of teak (*Tectona grandis*) plantations, upon the crown lands of the maritime provinces. That the Ceylon teak is not inferior to any that India produces, is, I believe, undeniable: and, however great the supply that may now be obtained from the Malabar and Burmese coasts, a time may come when Great Britain may have to depend upon its own resources for shipbuilding materials; and all will admit, that it is the duty of the present to anticipate the naval wants of succeeding generations. The teak flourishes best upon the sea coast; and the neighbourhoods of Galle, Colombo, Negombo, and Trincomalé, offer every facility for forming plantations of this invaluable tree, for the future purposes of the British navy.

Many objectionable circumstances still tend to depress native agriculture in Ceylon, notwithstanding the abolition of forced personal service, or *Rajah Karia*, in the year 1832; a measure by which the Earl of Ripon, when Viscount Goderich, immortalized his Lordship's second administration of the colonies.

We must not look at the improved system introduced by a few speculative English capitalists, or their agents, (for those gentlemen do not *condescend* to cultivate rice, or the smaller grains,) in the few thousands of acres devoted to coffee, sugar, &c., but to the general agricultural system of the colony; for "the greatest happiness of the greatest number" ought to be the grand object of every good government.

The Singhalese landlords care not one straw for the interests of the cultivators. The latter must contrive to pay them a clear profit of fifty per cent. for their advances of seed corn, whether the harvest be good or bad;* and they are naturally such a litigious race, that if this exorbitant premium be not duly paid, upon the grain being trodden out, (for they have no other than the primitive mode of detaching it from the straw,) the omission is sure to be followed by a proctor's summons; whereupon, the debtor, in his anxiety to save further costs, grants a bond for the value of the corn, which he was to have paid *in kind*, at the rate of fifty per cent., upon the market price, and bearing the usual legal rate of interest, in the colony, viz. twelve per cent per annum. If, again, that bond be unpaid when due, wo betide the unfortunate cultivator!—the law is resorted to—followed up *gradatim*—and unmercifully, as far as it depends either upon the Singhalese plaintiff or his proctor; execution follows, and all the poor defendant's little property is seized and sold!

This curse upon agriculture, though great, is not the greatest. The law of primogeniture, which is elsewhere considered a very unjust hardship upon the younger branches of a family, would, if established in Ceylon, be the greatest blessing that a wise government could possibly confer upon the country. It would decrease the number of those *pests*, the Singhalese proctors, who infest every minor court of justice; and a corresponding benefit to the agricultural classes would be one of the first results of its enactment.

If a person, possessing landed property, die, its value is estimated, as the system now obtains, by the produce of so many Jack or Coco-nut trees; or, of so many

* When advances of seed corn are made by the government, twenty five per cent. is the usual charge

acres (I suppose one must adopt the English term, according to the new system introduced into the country, and which has puzzled the natives to understand our superficial measure,) of paddee; and if he leave a dozen children, the trees are shared between the *heirs*, either conjointly with, or without, the land. And, if the owner of one twelfth share dies, leaving twelve children, away goes that twelfth among *his heirs;* and so on, *ad infinitum*, until, perhaps, each share might cover but a penny piece in size.

The least trespass, the taking of a Coco-nut, or Jack, beyond the share, would inevitably be followed by a "law-suit:" and in this manner the time and patience of district judges are occupied and put to the test. The price of judicial stamps might be so increased as to operate as a *damper* upon such eternal litigation; but nothing can effectually remove it, except by establishing the law of primogeniture; or by allowing the richest heir to buy the whole, and for the proceeds to be divided between the rest; giving always the preference to the eldest son, or to his eldest son, if the former have died and left an heir.

If the crop be on the ground at the time a "land suit" is commenced, the proctor moves the court "for sequestration," until final adjudication; thus much time is lost, and money expended, that would have been sufficient to buy up all the original shares; and who is the party ultimately benefitted? the proctor! no one else; for after the land, or produce, or both, is sold, if the share, or shares, for which the action may have been brought, be insufficient to pay *his costs*, he forthwith brings actions against the parties who have employed him, for *the balance!*

Can any country under heaven, let the Almighty's bounty to it, be what it may, prosper, where such glaring mismanagement, injustice, and litigation prevail? The picture is not overdrawn.

The next stage from Pomparripo is through the village of Marrandé, distant 8¾ miles, to the rest-house of Marritchicatty, 16½ miles from Pomparripo. The rest-house is on the north bank of the river; the road is very sandy, and, except in certain places, and close to the villages, where there are paddee fields, skirted on the east by dense jungle, which abounds with wild animals. There is but one inducement to halt at this place, and that is to see a dance of the *Padoua* caste,—a class of people, considered so very low and degraded, that they are restricted from playing on any musical instrument whatever; and therefore they adapt themselves to a necessity which cannot be overcome; and display no small share of ingenuity in drawing sounds, by blowing into earthen chatties; to which they keep admirable time. The males of this caste dare not wear cloths below their knees, nor dare the females cover their breasts. A few measures of rice will be well bestowed amongst these poor people.

There is every reason to believe, from the system of slavery that still obtains in this province, that many of the inferior castes were originally slaves; who, in the frequent revolutions of the country, were left to serve the superior castes for their means of support. In this province, slavery still exists; and the registry of slaves, which commenced in the year 1806, distinguishes them under the heads of "*Covia* and *Nallua* castes."

In the year 1817, the government, in its wisdom and humanity, passed a regulation, which, without infringing much upon the right of ownership, abolished joint property in slaves; and, by the same regulation, slaves were allowed to purchase their emancipation, when they could obtain the means of so doing. In 1821, by another regulation, the government, in order to hasten, as far as lay in its power, the abolition of slavery, pleged itself to pay the owners of slaves from 3*s.* 6*d.* to 5*s.* 3*d.*, according to the caste of its mother, for the freedom of each female infant, at its birth; but this small sum was greatly objected to by the Malabar proprietors; and with some reason, when it is contrasted with the manner in which the value of adult slaves was fixed; namely, by arbitration.

Here, again, I cannot refrain from referring to the circumstance of Negro manumission; the benefit of which was extended to the Mauritius, but not to the wretched *Covia* and *Nallua* slaves of Ceylon; the purchase of whose freedom would have made but a small indent upon the £20,000,000 granted by parliament for that benevolent object.

The headmen support the distinctions of caste from motives of interest, as well as from prejudice; and, for these reasons, all attempts, on the part of the inferior castes, to improve their lot in life, are resisted and counteracted. This system must be expected, until the headmen become more enlightened, by education and christianity: but ages may pass away, ere that grand object be attained; for it is extremely remote in the prospective; notwithstanding the rapid strides, which, by all our missionary reports, the light of truth is making in the island.

The unauthorized assumption of the rank of headmen, in the Malabar provinces, had become so notorious, that, in the year 1820, the government passed a regulation, by which it involved a penalty of 500 rix dollars,* or imprisonment (not exceeding six months) in default of payment; but it is difficult to conceive upon what grounds of justice the same regulation abrogated all former effective, as well as titular acts,† granted by the authority of the government, antecedently to the fourth of June, 1809.

* £43 15*s.*

† Local name for the warrants, by which Headmen hold their titles.

From Marritchicatty to Kallaar pagoda, which is a Hindoo temple, the distance is 7½ miles. At this place, the poor coolies exchange money for ashes; and consequently ashes are never at a discount. This precious humbug is held in such veneration by these untutored pagans, that they believe the effect of rubbing the ashes over their foreheads and arms, will be, to protect them from all danger on the road, and to preserve them and their families in health!!

These "palankin boys," as the bearers are generally called, are principally Malabars. They are naturally *improvisatori*, for sing they must, and have responses: and it matters not what the burthen of the song be, but the more ridiculous the better. The Right Honorable Sir Alexander Johnston, when chief justice, was so well acquainted with the Tamul language, that he required very little aid from his interpreter. Upon one occasion, a friend, travelling with Sir Alexander, being amused by the chaunt of his palankin bearers, requested an interpretation of it; this Sir Alexander did not readily give; but, upon being pressed to do so, his friend was informed that the burthen of the song was, "*Tamby, tamby,* (or brother, brother,) shake him well, shake the great fat English pig!"

The scenery from Pomparripo to Kallaar, and its immediate neighbourhood, only requires a mountain or two in the distance, to stamp it as magnificent. The trees to the right of the road are of the most splendid description, in point of girth, spread, and height; and the foliage is of every hue that the most perfect landscape painter can imagine.

As to gastronomic luxuries, the Apician might justly include the snipe and ortolan (*Emberiza Hortulana*, L.), as well as the sur-mullet and oyster of this coast, in his catalogue of "ways and means to provoke appetite."

The common oyster (*Ostrea communis*) abounds; but is altogether neglected, although the native inhabitants of the coast, between Putlam and Kallaar, might make a very profitable speculation of gathering and pickling oysters for the Colombo and Kandyan markets; but, satisfied with a few paddee and fine grain fields, and cotton, arum, or yam, and plantain grounds, they seem to have no care beyond the common necessaries of Indian life; this may arise from want of capital, or of example, to stimulate them to speculative exertion.

The naturalist would find much to gratify and amuse him in this province: for the jungles, tanks, and paddee fields teem with a great variety of birds, reptiles, and insects; of which, very many are still undescribed.

After a few hours' travelling by palankin, one is often induced to inquire of his attendant *Appo*, how much further it is to the rest-house, where his *avant courier*, the cook, may have a good dinner or breakfast under preparation for "master," (which will be the case, if *Cookée* be worth the salt he eats:) and it may so happen that the answer is, "only one mile, Sir!" whereupon, "master" continues tolerably tranquil until the lapse of a quarter of an hour or twenty minutes, every now and then anxiously peeping through the front venetians of his palankin, for the desired rest-house; another quarter of an hour passes, and still nothing before him but a sandy shore on the one hand, and occasional paddee fields and jungle on the other. Appo is again applied to: "now only two trees (thirds, of one mile, Sir!" "Long mile, Appo! what, in half an hour, only travelled a third of a mile?" "I think bearers tired, very much, Sir, walk plenty too much slow." Patienza per forza! Another quarter of an hour, and another half hour succeeds; when, at length, something *white* appears in the prospective, which proves to be the long wished for rest-house, (where it was formerly the custom for the tables and chairs to be covered with white cloths;) and in a very short time "master" and his legs will have occupied three chairs in the virandah. "Master" at length discovers that a Singhalese *mile* is two English *leagues!* "Verbum sap."

The sea weed (*Fucus aurylaceus*) locally called Jaffna moss, is peculiar to this province; but, although the same production is common to Java and other islands belonging to the Dutch, where it is said to form the exclusive food of the swallow (*Hirundo esculenta*), whose nest forms a chief luxury of the Chinese gourmand, the bird itself does not belong to the ornithology of Ceylon.

There is no peculiar beauty in the *Hirundo esculenta*; it appeared to me almost all feathers; for half a dozen of these birds, presented to me by the first lieutenant of the Piedmontaise frigate, (the late Captain Sir Thomas Carew,) did not weigh more than two Spanish dollars. The color of the back was of a dark grey, tinged with green, which showed more plainly when held in the sun; the belly light grey, inclining to fawn color; tail forked, but not so much as that of the common swallow, and marked with a round white spot; middle toe remarkable for its great length, compared with the others.

The edible swallow's nest resembles a small circular, or rather oblong, piece of Dutch cheese, hollowed and scooped thin, with a feather here and there upon the concave side, more than any thing else; but when prepared for sale to the mandarins and other great men, it has a totally different appearance; for by the process, it is drawn out into long strips, about a third of an inch in width, having something of the appearance of hartshorn shavings: these are tied in bunches, of about four inches in circumference, and fourteen in length, with the fine flax prepared from the stalks of the wild plantain (*Musa sylvestris*), and dissolve in water as easily as isinglass.

I have occasionally eaten "birds' nest soup," at the resident's, and at Captain Chinaman's tables, both at Amboyna and Banda; but it was highly spiced, and withal so very gelatinous, that I could not distinguish any very peculiar delicacy in its flavor.

The Dutch relish the soup best when it is prepared by the Chinese; and they ascribe to it the inestimable property of restoring the tone and powers of the stomach, after they have become altogether debilitated, by excess in the use of opium, or ardent spirits; and they are at no loss to adduce instances of its great and renovating effects, where medicine had altogether failed.

Having brought with me to England, in 1827, some of the "*very first chop*"* prepared birds' nest, which had been presented to me by the late Mr. Blettermann, of the Ceylon civil service, who had received it from his brother, a Dutch factor at Canton; it occurred to me, at the time of the last illness of His Most Gracious Majesty King George the Fourth, that it might produce a beneficial effect; if not, that so novel an article of diet might prove a grateful change to His Majesty, and could not do harm; and I accordingly transmitted it to Sir Henry Halford, one of His Majesty's physicians. Sir Henry acknowledged its receipt, by letter dated Windsor Castle, 18th May, 1830, in the handsomest terms that language could convey, and thus concluded it,—"I did not fail to present it to the King in your name, when His Majesty was pleased to desire that I would thank you for it, and to give orders for preparing it to-day."

* Chinese definition of the *superior* sort of the edible swallow's nest. This article of Eastern commerce was considered the most valuable part of the cargoes of Dutch vessels, or Malay *Proas* under Dutch colors, that our cruizers made prizes of in the Eastern seas during the late war.

CHAP. XXV.

The Kallaar river—Route to Kandy—Thomas Ralph Backhouse, Esq.—Brief description of the ruins of the ancient capital of Ceylon—Pilgrimage from the coasts of Coromandel and Malabar to Anarajahpoora—Kondatchie, the rendezvous of adventurers, jugglers, and thieves, during the pearl fishery—Various accounts of the pearl fishery—Committee's report of the pearl banks, prior to a fishery—Rocky bank—The island of Cardiva, a protection to the pearl banks from the south-west monsoon—Superstition—Shark charmers—Roman Catholic priests distribute amulets to the divers—Sharks—Boats—Mode of diving—Objections to the use of the diving bell—Pearl oyster spawn, and opinion of the divers in regard to it—Average daily produce of each boat—Putrefaction of the pearl oyster—Field for naturalists—Kola or leaf oyster—Betel oyster—Position of pearls in oysters—Pinna Marina—Difficulty of transferring the habitat of the pearl oyster considered insuperable—Various methods of clearing the pearls from the oyster—Pearl oyster of Ceylon (Mytilus margaritifera) a variety of the mother o' pearl oyster—Pearls most valued at Ceylon for their golden hue—Suggestions for disposing of the pearl fishery by lottery—Impolicy of abandoning the monopoly—Suggestions in regard to reduction of the rent—Suggested panorama—Arippo rest-house—Roman Catholic chapel—Kondatchie destitute of water

THE Kallaar river takes its rise near Anarajahpoora, the ancient capital of Ceylon, through which place there is a road from Kallaar pagoda to Kandy, by thè following route :—From Kallaar to Kiritenna Venditté rest-house, 6½ miles ; to Paymaddoo, 8½ miles ; to Oyamaddoo rest-house, 8¼ miles ; to Alleaparte, 1¾ miles ; to Anarajahpoora, 6¾ miles ; to Tirapankadawetta, 12½ miles ; to Manawevva, 9½ miles ; to Nickinnawé, 8½ miles ; to Damboola Vihare rest-house, 16 miles ; to Leenadora post station, 7 miles ; to Natandé post station, 7 miles ; to Palapawella Ella rest house, 4 miles : to Fort Macdowall, the station of the assistant government agent and district judge, 11 miles ; to the top of Ballacadua Pass, 6¼ miles ; to Mavali-Ganga Ferry, 7 miles : to Kandy, 2¾ miles ;—total from Kallaar to Kandy, 129 miles.

The ancient city of Anarajahpoora was the capital of Ceylon for eleven or twelve centuries ; and I avail myself of the information respecting it, with which I was favored by my esteemed friend, the late Thomas Ralph Backhouse, Esq., of the civil service, after his ramble, (as well as the jungle would admit of it,) in the year 1823, over the extensive site of its pristine splendour : but although even now scarcely worthy of the name of village, Anarajahpoora has been raised from the almost total oblivion, in the *official* scale, to which it had been consigned for more than three centuries, by being made the station of one of the assistant government agents of the province who also holds the office of a district judge of the northern circuit of the supreme court

" I fell in with a very intelligent Budhoo priest at Mantotte," says Mr. Backhouse, " who, at my request, accompanied me to Anarajahpoora; but his account of this deserted city borders so much upon the marvellous, that I shall limit *my* relation of it to its probabilities. His story is, that the first Budhoo's tree, or *Bogaha*, was miraculously conveyed to Anarajahpoora from Siam, where it is held sacred to Sommocodom, (another name for Buddha,) which took root instanter, (without, I suppose, waiting for the common course of nature,) and was there cherished by the royal hand of Petissa Rajah, who flourished, according to his account, more than two thousand years ago, and was the origin of the subsequent annual pilgrimages to that ancient city.

" The Archdeacon has a fine copy of Ptolemy, with a map, to which you may as well refer for Anarajahpoora; the position is correctly given, under the name of *Anurogrammum*.

" This ' city of the ninety sovereigns,' according to the Singhalese derivation;* but, by the late Mr. William Tolfrey's, which is the most probable, from the planet *Anoorada*, is stated to have been surrounded by a wall, from nine to ten Singhalese miles, or from fifty to sixty English miles, in extent, and in a most fertile and well-cultivated country: this is now a mere desert; but amongst the jungle that surrounds it, there exist innumerable vestiges of the former magnificence of Anarajahpoora;—granite pillars, shafts, bases, and capitals, of an order unknown to the modern architect: remains of stone bridges over the Malwatté river, and of several spacious tanks, still capable of being restored, to contain water for the irrigation of many lacs† of acres.

" Notwithstanding the great difficulties interposed by the jungle, I examined the bases of two temples, and found them geometrically correct as to the positions of the angles at the cardinal points; there are also vestiges of magnificent palaces, and of an extensively paved road; and the more I see of the antiquities of this (the northern) province, the more I am convinced that it was originally peopled by a nation pre-eminent in architecture and civilization, whose language is said to have been obliterated from the earth, leaving only gigantic records of its characters in granitic rock, that seem to set time and nature at defiance.

" This ancient seat of long-departed royal magnificence and superstition, (the Kandyan *Anurodgeburro*,) is frequented by numerous pilgrims from the Malabar and Coromandel coasts; these are encouraged by their Brahmins, particularly by those of Ramisseram, to believe that their future state of existence, in the metempsychosis assured by their religion, materially depends upon their undertaking this pilgrimage

* *Anoo*, ninety; *Rajah*, king; *Poora*, city.

† *Lac*. 100.000

and, as the devotees cross from the peninsula to Ramisseram, where they make offerings to the temple, for a safe journey to, and from thence, *via* Adam's Bridge and Manaar, and from thence to Ceylon; returning by the same route, and renewing their offerings for their safety on their way home, the motives of the priesthood require no explanation.

"Whether Anarajáhpoora was destroyed by some awful visitation of Providence, or deserted upon the invasion of a barbarian conqueror, are at best but hypothetical, for there is no record that may be relied on."

From Kalaar pagoda, the next stage is Kondatchie; which, at the time of the Pearl Fishery, becomes the general rendezvous of all boats to be employed, and of adventurous traders, jugglers, and thieves; for as the government Gazettes of the several presidencies previously give six months' notice of it throughout their extensive circulation, there is scarcely a nation or caste of the immense continent of India, exclusively of Parsee and Arabian traders, of which there are not many individuals, whom the thirst of gain allures to this grand field of speculation.

Since the time of Pliny the elder, there has not appeared a work, professing to treat of Ceylon, in which the pearl fishery has not been noticed; and yet, as connected with the capabilities of the island, no novel method has hitherto been suggested for increasing the revenue derived from this source.

It is not my intention to tread in the direct footsteps of some of my predecessors, who have written elaborately upon the subject; nor to adopt the brief reasoning of others, "that the pearl fishery is too well known to render further information necessary;" for although very many of my readers may have their own libraries at hand, and not consider it much trouble to refer, either to the ancient or modern authorities upon this point, the majority may find it attended with inconvenience, if not with expense.

Since the British government superseded that of the Dutch in Ceylon, the appointment of supervisor of the pearl fishery has been held conjointly with that of private secretary to the Governor. But as that office is materially connected with the revenue, it ought, in strict justice, to form a part of the duties of the agent of revenue for the northern province, by which means the salary would be saved to the public: for a supervisor may be from three to seven years in the receipt of £500 a year, and not be called on more than once, or twice at furthest, to attend a pearl fishery; and then only for about fifteen or thirty days. If the salary of the private secretary, at the present rate of £500 a year, be inadequate, some less anomalous means might be adopted for increasing it.

In the preceding November, the government institutes an official inspection of the pearl banks, by a committee of the civil servants, including the supervisor. This is indispensable; and, upon its report, the banks selected for the purpose, which of course will depend upon the maturity of the oysters, and value of the pearls obtained from the samples examined, are advertised to be fished. The report of the committee, according to the following formula, is then published in the Ceylon and other Indian newspapers.

Statement of the Inspection of the Pearl Banks of Arippo, in Nov. ——.

Number of Parcels.	Number of Oysters.	Description of the Bank.	Quality and quantity of the Pearls extracted.				Value of the Pearls.		Size.	Rate of Valuation
				Chow.	Kalingi.	Manjade.	P. N. Pagodas.	Fanams of Madura 20 pr. Pag.		

It has happened, upon more than one occasion, that an over anxiety on the part of a colonial governor to make a very favourable report of the revenue derived from the pearl fishery, has placed the future produce of the pearl banks in jeopardy, by over-fishing them. In April, 1820, the Madragam Paar was found to be the only bank where the oysters had attained sufficient maturity. It was then fished on account of government, and the oysters were sold, in lots, upon the beach. The government seldom fishes in *Aumanie*, (viz. upon its own account,) if an average price be offered for it by individual speculators, who can give the requisite security, or make an adequate deposit.

In the year 1814, the boats employed in the *Aumanie* fishery (after the rented fishery had ceased) landed 76,000,000 of oysters during the first twenty days' fishing.

About the middle of January, the boats begin to assemble; between which period and the commencement of the fishery, the medley of adventurers will have constructed their various dwellings, with areka or bamboo poles, and the fronds of the talipat, palmyra, and coco-nut palms, paddee straw, and colored cotton cloths, in endless variety, and in tolerable order, upon the arid sands of Arippo; at which place stands the beautiful Doric mansion, built by Governor North. This is occupied by the supervisor (who is vested with full magisterial powers) and his friends. All persons frequenting the pearl fishery, are privileged from arrest upon any *civil* process; but the powers of the supreme court, in criminal matters, are not affected: and justice is summarily administered in disputes, arising from matters connected with the fishery.

During the stay of the supervisor and his department, a strong military guard, with a proportion of artillery, is stationed at Arippo. This place is rather less than five miles north of Kondatchie, and is a small trading village, with a fort and barracks, and, from the offing, bears four leagues south of the east end of the island of Manaar.

Arippo is situate at the mouth of the Aweria-Aar, which takes its rise beyond the ancient capital of Anarajahpoora, in the central province; and, about two leagues off the land, a rocky bank, or reef, lies to the west and south-west. The island of Cardiva, or Nalladive, which is very low, narrow, and crooked, covered in some places with sandy patches, and in others with jungle, and about seven leagues south of Arippo, affords ample protection to the pearl banks from any injurious effects of the south-west monsoon; and they are protected from the effects of the north-east monsoon by the main land of Ceylon.

Prior to the divers commencing operations, those most useful humbugs, the shark charmers, or *Kadel-Kutties*, are in general requisition; for their services are indispensable, to give confidence to the superstitious divers; who, upon their assurances that they may fearlessly follow their submarine occupation, for that "the mouths of the sharks had been closed at their command," divest themselves of all fear.

Although all the divers are not pagans, superstition so predominates in almost every thing connected with the native character, that, however incredible, it is an indisputable fact, that even the Roman Catholic priests impose a similar farce upon the divers of their faith; for not one of them will descend without a charm, composed of brief extracts from scripture, fastened round the arm, which he is told will protect him from danger.

This shark charming trade is a very lucrative one, because as it is not the mere government stipend that satisfies them, they insist upon the additional *daily* tithe of ten or a dozen oysters from each boat, which is readily paid.

Of the varieties of the shark (*Squalus*) genus, upon the coasts of Ceylon, the most dangerous is the saw-fish (*Squalus Pristis*, L.), the *Depta Mora* of the Singhalese, from its long projecting and dreadful beak; but fortunately it is less numerous than the *Squalus Carcharias*, and *S. malleus*.

The boats employed at the pearl fishery are built upon the old Portuguese model, without keel; and head and stern nearly alike. These are from twelve to fifteen tons burthen, and carry a crew of twelve or fourteen hands, and from eight to ten divers.

The inspector of the pearl banks makes a signal from the government vessel, for the commencement of, and for leaving off, diving.

A stone, of a conical shape, and weighing from forty to fifty pounds avoirdupois, is slung to a double rope, which is passed over a boom projecting from the boat's side. The *charmed* diver then places the great toe of his right foot into the space between the double rope; and, with his left, he keeps a net, in shape like an angler's landing net, and capable of holding some dozens of oysters, close to the stone. The rope having been adjusted for lowering, the diver, pressing his nostrils with his left hand, and holding on by his right, descends as rapidly as the weight will admit of. Upon reaching the bottom, he suddenly jerks the rope; upon which, the stone is hauled up; and, upon a similar signal, he intimates that he has filled his net, (which may occupy about a minute, or a minute and a half,) and then, holding on by the net or rope, he is drawn up within a fathom or two of the surface, when he relinquishes his hold; and having reached the boat, and taken breath, he is very soon ready to descend again.

Such is the process of diving upon the old system. The diving bell was first introduced for use upon the pearl banks, by the late indefatigable Governor, Sir Edward Barnes; but time alone must decide, whether the predictions of one of the most intelligent Master Attendants in the Ceylon service, the late Captain James Chrisp, formerly of the Honorable the East India Company's marine, be verified, or not.

"The diving bell," said he, "may answer very well at first; but it will ultimately be the means of destroying the oysters: for it must *crush a great many*, which will putrify; and so extremely delicate is the nature of the oyster, that it will spread like a plague, gradually extending its vortex, and destroying all within it."

The oysters lie in layers, from four to five feet deep: and when about five or six years old, they abandon the madrepore, to which they had attached themselves, from their first sinking, after the formation of the shell, (for the spawn floats about until that process has taken place,) and ramble about the sandy regions of the bottom.

The divers entertain the belief, that the oyster spawn descends in showers during the rainy season.

Each diver sends up about 3000 oysters, upon an average, daily: and from 20,000 to 25,000 have been taken by one boat in a day. In the year 1836, the revenue derived £25,816 from the pearl fishery.

It is not uncommon for fifty or sixty, or even eighty pearls, of various sizes, to be found in one oyster. The natives consider it a disease, or rather, the effect of a disease, to which the animal is liable. If a pearl be cut transversely, and observed through a microscope, it will be found to consist of minute layers, resembling the rings which denote the age of certain trees, when cut in a similar manner.

After the second or third day's fishing, the stench of the dead oysters becomes intolerable to all, except those whose thirst for gain absorbs every other sense. But, as use reconciles one to most things in this life, custom soon neutralizes the olfactory effect of the nuisance; for the stench is considered less diffusive, as the process progresses.

It is here that the naturalist may devote a considerable portion of the day to collecting and classifying the great variety of the class *Mollusca*, which, according to Cuvier, is furnished with a heart and circulating system; and almost every batch of oysters is accompanied by specimens of zoophytes, which have neither the one nor the other: and every day affords additional treasures, particularly in polypes, fuci, and madrepore, for his information and amusement.

The *Kola*, or leaf oyster, represents an inverted hollow cone, and is one of the most curious; and the small red-tinged, or *Betel* oyster, which produces a superior pearl, is well worthy of being included in the collection of the naturalist.

The largest pearls are found in the thickest part of the flesh of the oyster; but it does not follow that the largest oysters produce the finest pearls.

The oysters cluster together by a fine silky filament, of a similar nature to that of the *Pinna Marina* of the Madaleine islands, (dependencies of Sardinia,) but it is destitute of the valuable qualities to the manufacturer, that distinguish the latter.

As no means of successfully transferring the pearl oyster (*Mytilus margaritifera*), for the purposes of increasing its *habitat*, has yet been discovered, it may be more advantageous to leave the natives to their old customs and mode of fishing, than to adopt any new-fangled European methods, which may tend to the ultimate destruction of the oyster beds.

There are so many different methods of clearing the pearls from the fleshy part of the oyster, that one can scarcely determine which is the best plan; but certainly, that in which putrefaction is resorted to, though it may be the most lucrative, is the most likely to induce disease amongst the human myriads that attend the fisheries; amongst whom, there is no deficiency of dexterous thieves, who set detection at defiance, by very extraordinary means; de quo nil amplius dicendum!!

The pearl oyster of Ceylon (*Mytilus margaritifera*) has a similar hinge to the mother o' pearl oyster; but the former, which is scarcely one half the size of the latter, is more oblong, and seldom exceeds the Concale bay, or Jersey oyster, in size. Its interior surface is equally, if not more, resplendent than that of the larger species.

The pearl oyster's spawn may be seen floating in apparently coagulated masses upon the western coast of Ceylon during the north-east monsoon; and the uncouth anchors of the native *Dhonies*, or coasting vessels, which are composed of a thick wooden shank, with large stones lashed between transverse beams of wood, in lieu of flukes, are often found, upon being weighed, enveloped in spawn.

For the first year, the oyster seldom exceeds the size of a shilling, and is not at maturity for seven years. When it has attained the age of three or four years, or is half grown, seed pearls only are found in its flesh; but after that period, they gradually increase in size, until the maturity of the oyster; when the disease, which produces them, destroys its bivalve victim. The pearl is not valued for its silvery whiteness, at Ceylon, but for its golden hue.

The government has never yet tried the plan of a lottery for realizing the revenue upon the pearl fishery. I never heard it suggested by any one; but it occurs to me, that as the pearl fishery, under all and every circumstance, involves extensive gaming transactions and risk, the government may as well make the best of the prevailing mania; and by that means obviate the applications to which it is now constantly liable, for a reduction of the sum, originally agreed upon with the farmer of the pearl fishery, in the event of an unsuccessful fishery. By this means, the proceeds of lottery tickets would realize treble the average amount of a successful year; and, by being made transferable, the tickets would find their way, as those of the continental lotteries do, throughout India, and perhaps Egypt, Persia, and Arabia; and the government would incur no further expense than that of the superintendence of the fishery, and the conservation of the public peace.

It could not benefit the colony, and would be the acme of bad policy in the government, to abandon the pearl fishery monopoly; a lottery might be preferable to farming it (whenever the committee report the beds, or any proportion of them, in a fit state for a fishery to take place) to the highest bidder: but it is very bad policy to hold out an expectation, that, in the event of failure, the speculator may claim a reduction of his rent; for these gentry take very good care, in the event of the profits *exceeding* their calculations, to keep the overplus to themselves. The sale should be peremptory; and the speculators forewarned, that, in the event of failure, the government will not, under any circumstances whatever, entertain their claims to a reduction of the rent.

The medley of colors, nations, castes, and trades, (amongst which pearl-drilling is a very lucrative one,) upon the Arippo sands, would form a panorama, which, if taken from the flat roof of the *Doric*, would be well worthy of Barker's pencil.

There is an excellent rest-house at Arippo, and plenty of good water, which is there a treasure of great value, owing to the difficulty of obtaining it elsewhere for very many miles. There is also a Roman Catholic chapel in the village, but it is not much attended, except during a pearl fishery, when it proves a good thing for the priests; their Malabar communicants being a very numerous class, many of them wealthy, and all very superstitious. The whole of the beach that borders the bay of Kondatchie is a sandy waste, without a coco-nut tree or palmyra (except a few stunted ones of the former in the distance) to relieve the eye of the monotony of the desert; but to the right, or eastward, of the sands, dense jungle, teeming with every variety of game and beasts of prey the island produces, courts the sportsman's attention.

The moment the fishery is over, Kondatchie's glory ceases; and it then becomes the same miserable, waterless, (for it has no water except from Arippo,) and arid spot, that it has been for ages past.

CHAP. XXVI.

Route from Arippo to Bangallė—Island of Manaar—Soil—Fish abundant—Suggestions for a factory for curing it—Cheapness of the principal necessaries of life—Manaar sheep and cows—Agricultural encouragement suggested—Harvests—Headmen—Sailing directions—Coasting trade—Mantotte church or rest-house—Missionaries' journey—Giant's tank—Gentoo city—Antiquity of the Hindoos—Singhalese records and traditions—Sir William Jones—Racshasas or giants—Invention of the game of chess—Magnitude of architectural works no proof of extraordinary stature of the workmen—Suggestions to the traveller to proceed by sea to Jaffna—Native cottages—Useful properties of cow dung—Route from Mantotte to Poonerym—Scenery—Poonerym to Jaffna—Jaffna formerly a kingdom—Principal villages of the northern province—Inhabitants—Cession of Jaffna by the Portuguese to the Dutch—Fruits—Coasting trade—Chitties—Tamul year—Hegira—Goldsmiths—Their mode of selling gold and silver plate—Exports for the China markets—Culture of cotton too limited—Its extension suggested—Jaffna tobacco—Its value exemplified—Rajah of Travancore—His monopoly in tobacco—Contracts with the Ceylon government—Maintains a body of troops by the profits—Countervailing monopoly—Its injury to the native tobacco grower—Abolition of the monopoly, and substitution of a duty of 200 per cent.—Decline of the Ceylon tobacco trade in the Eastern markets—Reduction of the duty to 2½ per cent.—The trade recovers and flourishes.

FROM Arippo to Bangallė, the distance is eight miles; and from thence the traveller may as well vary his course, by proceeding to the island of Manaar: this he can do, with more convenience to himself, from Bangallė than from Mantotte.

The fort of Manaar is a dependency of the garrison of Jaffna, and was at one time commanded by a field officer, but is now without even a subaltern's guard. There are several villages in the island, with churches for native (Malabar) christians, and a Dutch church. The soil is sandy, as its name implies,* but not barren, for it abounds with coco-nut and palmyra trees; and fish is so abundant, that if a factory were established, for curing it in a proper manner, (upon a limited scale at first, by way of experiment,) a very profitable result may be justly anticipated; because a better article of food would be sold at a less price than that now paid for an inferior one; thereby ensuring an increase of the consumption, whilst its improved quality for exportation would cause an extension of the coasting trade, to the benefit of the revenue, and the profit of those concerned in the speculation.

Butcher's meat, poultry, game, fruit, rice, and vegetables, may be obtained at Manaar at very low prices; and sheep appear to thrive better there than in any other part of Ceylon, except in the extensive sheep walks between Jaffna and Point Pedro.

* From the Tamul words *Man*, sand, and *Aar*, river

Manaar cows give double the quantity of milk (viz. three pints a day) yielded by the Colombo cows. Here is an irrefragable reason for the establishment of an energetic agricultural society, for the improvement of the native breed of domestic animals, and a proof of their present degeneracy.

Paddee is sown in the Manaar district in September and October, and reaped in March. Korakan (*Cynosurus Coracanus*, L.) is sown in September, and reaped in December. Gingillie seed (*Sessamum orientale*, L.) is sown in March, and reaped in May.

Twenty four native headmen of rank are attached to the revenue department of the Manaar district, which is superintended by an assistant to the government agent at Jaffna, who is also a district judge of the northern circuit of the supreme court.

According to Captain Horsburgh, "the east end of Manaar is in latitude 8° 57 north, and may be known from the offing by the fort and houses on it, as well as numerous coco-nut trees. The gut between Manaar and Mantotte has in some places ten and twelve feet water; but the only anchorage is on the south side of the island, in four or five fathoms, and four or five miles to the westward of the gut."

A considerable coasting trade is carried on, by the gulf of Manaar, between Ceylon and the Coromandel coast, by Chitties and Malabars, who are principally christians: but if the channel were deepened, by a few of Colonel Pasley's operations, so as to admit of the passage of *large* vessels, it would be of more benefit, and of less expense, to the island, than even if the Eutopian scheme of building a bridge across to Ramisseram, and another between that island and the main land of Hindostan, were to be realized.

The distance from the island of Manaar to Mantotte, across the gut, is not more than three miles at high water; and at ebb tide, the channel appears more like a small meandering stream than an arm of the sea. The rest-house at Mantotte, which is distant 4½ miles from Bangallé, was formerly a Dutch church, and was built, according to the date upon its northern gable, in the year 1607. An amusing account of a journey from Calpentyn to Mantotte, by two Wesleyan missionaries, was sent me by my late highly esteemed friend, the Rev. William Buckley Fox, which will give the reader a good idea of travelling in this part of Ceylon in 1822. It also shows the spirit which animated the amiable and indefatigable individual by whom it was written, and displays the character and zeal of the christian missionary.

"After thirteen days of sailing, wading, and walking, here I am, without a cooly. You have a tolerably correct, though rough, view of my habitation. I have got coolies from Manaar for Mr. Newstead, but I must wait till I get the means of proceeding myself, and patiently.

" A harder journey I never had. This day week we reached Calpentyn, after many Quixotic adventures, and then found that we could not go to Jaffna by sea, the wind being dead against us. Our commission mentioned nothing about turning back; so we sought for coolies, but could get but few, amongst whom were six Malays, (better men I have never travelled with in Ceylon,) but these will not touch a palankin. We procured as many as we could, and set off in a *Pardie* boat, across the Calpentyn gulf. The sea was high, and our flat-bottomed conveyance was famously tossed: but, being both large and new, we crossed the gulf, (about four miles,) with very hard rowing, and then hauling *our house* about two miles along shore, we came near Karetivoe. There we anchored for the night, and sent for the postholder and headman, one as *commissariat*, the other as *tower-hill* overseer. Our coolies were barely sufficient to carry our empty palankins, and the little baggage we had reserved.

" The following morning one of the coolies ran away; and, after an hour's labour, I got a malefactor in his room. Our first stage was through a jungle, or what they call the *Tappal* road. It was hard walking. I waded the Pomparripo river seven times. It is this way We stopped at Pomparripo all night, and were there told, for our consolation, that a palankin could not go: that the *Tappal Peons* waded up to the neck on the plains of Pomparripo. Not wishing to give up the business that called us northward, so quietly, I engaged a *Tappal Peon* as a guide, and, where the water was very deep, to cut us a way through the jungle. From the description he gave us of the country, I imagined we should not have to wade above a quarter of a mile. Off we went; and, in about three miles, came to the water, and waded to near the waist, about half a mile; when our guide informed us we were "just upon a very deep place," and he took us through a swampy jungle for a full quarter of a mile. we then waded half a mile further, and through several pieces of water, before we came to Mardodé. Having refreshed, we took to the water again; and before we had reached Marchicatty, we had not waded less than four miles. A very large leopard had crossed our road just before us. We should not have got through our journey, had we not fallen in with eight Bengal palankin bearers, on their way to Madras, who rendered us great service. The rest of the journey has been hard walking, on bad roads, with no water of importance to impede us.

" Except being sadly pricked with thorns and bitten by leeches, and the loss of the skin of my face, from exposure to the sun, I am not much the worse for the journey I have walked fifty seven miles, and have been carried two miles and a half; and, as I am not a prophet, I shall say nothing of the part of the journey before us till another time."

——"These zealous christians steadily proclaim
To listening worlds the glory of HIS name!
Greatness with goodness infinite combined;
Wisdom and might and mercy unconfined!
HIS eye the sun; HIS heart the living breeze;
The clouds HIS chariot; and HIS path the seas!
Pervading all things—boundless in HIS sway!
Such is the God, to whom the Christians pray.
Such is the God, who from his throne above,
Sends to this isle the messengers of love!"—POLYNESIA.

At Mantotte, the antiquarian will find an ample field for research, in the still extant remains of remote antiquity; amongst which, are the vestiges of an immense tank, (Giant's Tank,) but inferior in size to many in the island; and the ruins of a former Gentoo city, built of brick.

The antiquity of the Hindoos, by whom, I humbly presume, the island was originally peopled, and their civilization, at the remotest period of history, are accorded by all the ancient Eastern philosophers; and, of our modern literati, very few will be disposed to dispute the late Sir William Jones's title to be considered pre-eminent in Asiatic literature, and thorough acquaintance with Eastern customs and history.

Notwithstanding the antiquity of the Singhalese records, (some of which, that are extant, are said to have been written many centuries before the birth of Christ,) tradition goes great lengths in Ceylon. Giants, forty feet in stature, are named as the architects of the wonderful buildings, canals, and viaducts; and the immense blocks of granitic rock, prepared in a masterly way, are cited as proofs. Sir William Jones, in his eighth anniversary discourse before the Bengal Society for inquiring into the arts, sciences, and literature of Asia, remarks,—"For Silán itself, we know, from the languages, letters, religion, and old monuments of the various inhabitants, was peopled beyond time of memory, by the Hindû race; and formerly, perhaps, extended much farther to the west and the south, so as to include Lanka, or the equinoctial point."

But, notwithstanding Singhalese traditions, and Sir William Jones's allusion, in his discourse upon the Indian game of chess, to the *Racshasas*, or giants, the people of Lanka,*

* This name (Lanka) was originally given to very extensive territory, the bounds of which do not appear to have been defined in any history to which I have had access. It is almost as vague as the mythology of Buddha; into which, if the curious be disposed to dip, a volume might easily be compiled from the Asiatic Researches. For this, in addition to the comments on the *Vedas*, or social history of the Hindoos, (in vol. viii appendix, page 529,) I would beg leave to refer the reader to the introductory remarks which were intended to have accompanied Captain Mahony's "Papers on Ceylon and the doctrines of Buddha, *which are given at length in the seventh volume of the Asiatic Researches*. The peninsula of Malacca is called, in the Sanscrit, "*Ma or Maha Lanka*," the Great Lanka.

or Ceylon, where the game was invented by the wife of Ravan, king of Lanka, in order to amuse him with an image of war, while his metropolis was closely besieged by Rama, in the second age of the world, there is nothing to justify the belief, or supposition, that the ancient inhabitants of Ceylon were forty feet in stature; for, until we are better acquainted with the state of the arts and sciences in those days, (and it may reasonably be inferred, from the splendid remains of cities, and temples, still extant, that the island was extensively populated, by a highly civilized race, ages before the Christian era,) the enormous masses of granitic rock which are found indented together, and forming part of the ruins of canals, bridges, and temples, are no proof of their having exceeded the present race of mankind in strength or stature.

Much trouble and inconvenience will be obviated, by coasting it (by boat) from Mantotte to Jaffna, a distance of nearly sixty eight miles; but it cannot be expected that a botanist will adopt this plan, because he may lose the opportunity of collecting a number of plants, which, though common to this province, are rare in others.

The whole route is sandy, in many places inundated, and bordered by jungle; and, although cultivation is well attended to in the immediate vicinity of villages, and cattle are abundant throughout the country, there is a great extent of uncultivated and desert land, which is solely occupied by the wild beasts of the forest. No stranger, however, can fail to remark the general neatness which characterises the native cottages; where, whilst some of the industrious housewives, at sunrise and at sunset, sweep up and burn every decayed leaf within their respective compounds, others are busy in plastering their cottage floors with diluted cow dung, which they level; and, when dry, coolness and comfort follow; for the mosquitos retire from the smell of the sacred animal's ordure, although it is far from disagreeable to the native inhabitants.

Every Budhist temple, and Hindoo pagoda, has its flooring covered with this cooling composition, which is regarded as anti-contagious, and wholesome to the human frame.

From Mantotte to Woodettidivo, the distance is 9 miles; to Illipekadewé rest-house, 6 miles; to Paliaar, 6¼ miles; to Pulleverayenkottoe rest-house, 8¾ miles; to Vauwattoregé, 6¾ miles; to Sembencoondu, 5 miles; to Pooneryn, 5¼ miles;—total from Mantotte to Pooneryn, 47½ miles.

The fort and rest-house of Pooneryn are beautifully situated; and the scenery, notwithstanding that the whole coast is both flat and sandy, delightful; for the country is remarkable for its being well cultivated and verdant, interspersed with abundant coco-nut and palmyra palms, and forest trees of the most magnificent and picturesque variety that the arboriculturist can well picture to his imagination. Here, indeed, not the romantic, but the simple charms of nature, are most bountifully displayed, untainted by the *improvements* of art.

From Pooneryn fort to Kalmooné (often written *Calimony*) the route lies across a long neck of land, very often inundated by the sea, and the distance is 14 miles; but it may be accomplished in less time by sea, during the south-west monsoon. From Kalmooné to Colombo Torré (by water) 3¼ miles; from thence to Jaffna (by land) 3 miles;—total from Pooneryn to Jaffna, 20¼ miles.

Jaffna, or Jaffnapatam, once a kingdom of Ceylon, and now the chief town of the northern province, is situate in latitude 9° 43′ north, five leagues to the eastward of *Hamsheel* (or *Hamenhiel*) fort; so called by the Dutch, who assimilated the shape of the island to that of a ham.

The channel is within the islands; but, having scarcely four feet water in some places, it is only frequented by country boats; by which, a very considerable coasting trade is carried on. The course from Jaffnapatam to Calimooné point is E. S. E.

Jaffna is extremely populous, and so indeed is the whole of the northern parts of the province. There are no other places entitled to the name of towns; but the principal villages are, Arippo, Tillipally, Batticotta, Oodoovillé, Pandateripo, Manepy, Cayts, Manaar, Chavagachery, Vareny, Point Pedro, Moelletivoe, Nuwerakalawiyé, Tamankadewé, and Anarajahpoora.

The Moormen (of Malabar) and Hindoos form the majority of the population of Jaffna; but many respectable Dutch and Portuguese families reside there.

Jaffna was the last fortress held by the Portuguese in Ceylon: of this, they were dispossessed, by the Dutch, in 1658. The fort is regularly built, and contains several excellent houses, barracks, a church, and court house. The *Pettah* is extensive, and contains a great many large and well-built houses, with delightful gardens, in which, many delicious exotic and indigenous fruits are cultivated. The necessaries of life are cheaper and more abundant here, than elsewhere in the island; and the best materials for building are to be obtained at an unusually cheap rate, when contrasted with their prices at Colombo and Point de Galle.

The grape-vine flourishes luxuriantly; and Jaffna grapes, both of the white and purple sorts, are not inferior in flavor to the produce of our hot-houses: but, although excellent wine has been made in small quantities, by private individuals, the cultivation of the grape-vine has never yet been exclusively devoted to that object; and, as the demand for the fruit is general, the profit is much greater to the grower than would accrue from manufacturing it into wine and brandy.

Next to its grapes, Jaffna is famed for its large and delicious Mangos, which are often sent as presents to different parts of the island. In its green state, the mango makes a very fine marmalade and pickle;—these, with ghirkins and preserved fruit, are so much in request, that their preparation is a source of employment and profit to several respectable Dutch and Portuguese families, whose incomes have been reduced by misfortune.

The principal part of the coasting trade is in cotton manufactures, and is carried on by Chitties, who are also the bill discounters and money changers throughout the island. These merchants import calicos, muslins, handkerchiefs, palempores, mosquito-net, &c., from the Coromandel coast, and realize enormous profits. The christian Chitties are pretty numerous, both here and at Colombo. They are Protestants, and extremely regular in their attendance at church, where the service is performed in the Tamul language, by the Rev. Christian David, (a pupil of the venerated Swartz,) the Malabar colonial chaplain at Jaffna, who was ordained priest in the year 1817, by the Right Rev. Dr. Fanshawe Middleton, the then Lord Bishop of Calcutta.

The Tamul year, *Sreemoega*, is the same as that of the Hegira, in reference to time; thus their year 1256, corresponds with our year 1842.

The Portuguese are the principal manufacturers of the much-admired Jaffna rose chains, and also of silver plate, which is usually massive and handsome; but their dinner and tea services do not show the exquisite polish of British workmanship: owing, perhaps, to the metal being nearly pure in the one case, and possessing a certain quantity of alloy in the other, by which the hardness is increased, and the metal better adapted for receiving a high polish. The usual way of selling gold plate, or jewellery, is, by putting it into one scale, and gold (star) pagodas into the other; at the market price of the day, for the quality of the gold employed, with an additional charge for the workmanship; which amounts to a mere trifle, when compared with the high price demanded for *fashion* at home. Silver plate is sold by the Sicca rupee weight.

Dried sharks' fins, and sea slugs, are exported from this province, and fetch a ready sale, and high prices, in the Chinese markets; where they are so highly valued, that the Chinese esteem them next to the highly prized delicacy, the edible swallow's nest, already described.

Although more cotton is grown in this province than in any other, there is very little cultivated in proportion to its extent and capabilities; and it is to be regretted, that whilst the East India Company is sparing no expense to extend the cultivation of that valuable staple upon the Indian continent, and sending out experienced persons from America to superintend it, and improve the native methods of planting, cleaning, and sorting it, nothing is being done in Ceylon towards rendering the mother country independent of Egypt and America for cotton wool.

Tobacco, known by the general name of "Jaffna tobacco," is largely cultivated in this province, and is of a very superior quality and flavor, and of a peculiarly dark color. The ground is previously manured, by sheep being penned upon it.

I knew a Dutch gentleman, a connoisseur in tobacco, to whom several boxes of the best Havannah cigars had been presented, offer them to an officer of the medical staff for one basket of Jaffna cheroots, the price of which in the market would have been about three shillings, or less; "for (said he) in all the world there is no tobacco like that of Jaffna:" and it is so much esteemed above the produce of Malabar, that the Rajah of Travancore, who had a monopoly in this article throughout his dominions, contracted with the government of Ceylon for all tobacco grown in the province for the purposes of exportation. This, was locally called the "Travancore investment:" and the Rajah was enabled, by the high price he charged for tobacco, to pay a subsidy to the government of Madras, for the maintenance of a body of native troops, under the command of an officer of the army of that presidency, in Travancore.

By this contract, the government of Ceylon averaged an annual profit of at least £10,000; but as the arrangement was followed by serious loss and detriment to the Jaffna tobacco grower, by increasing the consumption of the inferior production of Malabar, the government established a countervailing monopoly in 1812; but as it failed of the anticipated effect, recourse was had, in 1824, to an export duty of nearly 200 per cent., in lieu of it. This, displayed very little fiscal knowledge on the part of the governor and council, by whom it was enacted: and, as might have been foreseen, the result was, that, notwithstanding the drawback allowed upon exportation, the trade rapidly declined in the Eastern markets, where Jaffna tobacco had long been in great request by the Malays.

In 1837, the government of Ceylon determined upon a reduction of the enormous duty of 200 per cent., *ad valorem*, on tobacco; in lieu of which, a duty of 2½ per cent. was substituted: the consequence was, that in less than three years, the trade in Ceylon tobacco had doubled itself. A similar result may be anticipated as regards cinnamon, by a similar reduction of the present enormous rate of duty upon exportation.

CHAP. XXVII.

Climate of the northern province adapted to the growth of silk—Hindoo culture of the mulberry plant—Introduction of the silk-worm suggested—Cooley labour cheapened—Suggestions for reducing the colonial import duties upon the raw productions and manufactures of British India, as an inducement to the Indian presidencies to abolish their export duties upon cotton and silk to Ceylon, when intended for exportation from thence to the home markets—Choya root indigenous—The culture of the Cacao, or chocolate-nut tree, altogether neglected, instead of being made a profitable speculation—Provisions abundant—Game—Native cattle—Pasturage—Provincial breed of sheep—Cape of Good Hope cows—Culture of grass, and hay-making, entirely neglected—Suggestions for providing pressed hay for ships' stock—Timber trade of Jaffna—Hindoo festival of the idol Jagan-Nath—The Pranava or mystical tri-literal character—The author accompanies the chief and puisne justices to view the triumphal car of the idol—Decorated booth—Reception by the chief Brahmin—Sacred honors conferred upon the judges—Consecrated limes—Description of the car—The bride of Jagan-Nath—Temple mysteries—Brahaminical humbug—The Devadasi of the Deura—Native musicians—The Hindoos—Their diet—Domestic life—Amusements—Power of the Brahmins—American missionaries—Their usefulness—Pringle's account of missionary privations inapplicable to Ceylon missionaries—The moral of an old adage equally neglected by the American and British nations—First Tamul translation of the Liturgy at Ceylon at the sole expense of the governor, who subsequently presented an offering to a Budhoo temple—The national religion sometimes incompatible with sound national policy.

THE climate of this province being much less humid than that of the other maritime provinces, the silk-worm might be advantageously introduced, the mulberry plant extensively cultivated, and silk become a principal staple of commerce, instead of being, as at the present time, one of the entirely neglected capabilities of the island.

The Hindoo mode of culture may be the best for the native agriculturist, because it is perfectly simple; and cooley labour may be cheapened, by the employment of children to prepare and lay down the sets, as soon as the nurseries of the mulberry plant are sufficiently stocked to admit of the operations of the planter.

In Bengal, the land, having been cleared of weeds, and, where necessary, manured, is lightly ploughed; and pits, large enough for the reception of eight or ten sets, having been prepared, in parallel lines, with a space of two feet between each pit, the planter has nothing more to do, than employ children to cut the mulberry plants into sets of about fourteen inches in length, whilst others distribute them, by laying down the requisite number at the side of each pit, ready for being planted; these having been inserted, the planter presses the mould with his hands around each set, and loose earth having been scattered over the whole, leaving only the tops to appear, the primary object is effected. If this be done just before the rains set in, the fields will exhibit, in the course of a week or ten days, a most verdant appearance; for, in that short space of time, the little clumps will be covered with foliage; and thus, any required quantity of mulberry leaves may be ensured for the ulterior purposes of the silk grower.

It may be worthy of the consideration of the local government, whether the admission into Ceylon of the raw productions and manufactures of the East India Company's territories upon the continent of India, at the same rate of duty as is there levied upon our home produce and manufactures, and reducing the import duties upon paddee and rice, until the island produces sufficient for the consumption of its population, might not induce the governments of the several presidencies of British India to allow cotton and silk to be exported to Ceylon duty free, (if intended to be shipped from thence to Great Britain,) and materially diminish the price of labour in the colony.

It is to be expected, that such a change of system, in regard to the importation of the raw materials and manufactures of British India, would materially affect the importation of British cottons, because the native green or unbleached cloths would then compete with those of the mother country; but the result of such an arrangement would benefit the native consumer in an equal ratio, which should be a primary object of colonial legislation.

Choya root (*Oldenlandia umbellata*, L.), which yields a valuable red dye for manufacturing purposes, is both indigenous and abundant in this province; nevertheless, its culture, which would naturally tend to the improvement of the dye, has been hitherto entirely neglected. This useful staple was formerly a government monopoly, and at one time yielded a revenue of £2000 a year; but it subsequently declined to about a tenth part of that sum. The trade in it being now open, its culture offers a new source of profitable speculation.

The soil is also admirably adapted to the growth of the hitherto much neglected chocolate-nut tree (*Theobroma Cacao*, L.), which, in the course of a few years, might rank as a staple of the island. I have had very fine specimens of the fruit in my own garden, from trees planted by the late Jacobus Burnand, Esq., a Dutch gentleman, whose name is deservedly remembered at Ceylon with respect and regard; for he was distinguished, both by his zeal for the welfare of the island, through the introduction of the culture of valuable exotics from the Malay peninsula, and the Dutch islands of Java, Banda, and Amboyna, and by his botanical acquirements. The nuts were equal to the finest I had seen at Penang and Malacca, or in the West Indies, and in no degree inferior, either in size or nutritious properties, to the best productions of South America.

This tree requires shade; and, for that purpose, plantations of banana and plantain trees, which are of rapid growth, might be formed in parallel lines, leaving spaces of ten or twelve feet between each, for the reception of the chocolate plants.

I am well aware of the objections likely to be opposed to my suggestions upon this subject, arising upon a *primâ facie* view of it, from the comparatively slow return for the outlay, owing to the great difference of time between the produce of the chocolate tree and that of the coffee bush attaining maturity: but it should be taken into consideration, that here "the steed does *not* starve, whilst the grass grows:" for, independently of the annual value of the fruit* of the banana and plantain trees, which is in general request by the natives of all classes, the medicinal usefulness of the leaves, which also afford excellent fodder for cattle, and the several mechanical purposes to which the fibrous stalks may be applied, as already described † indigo, ginger, turmeric, cardamoms, cassada, arrow-root, maize, Guinea grass, and the principal grains, after rice, to which the native farmer turns his attention, particularly those called—Gingillie *Sessamum orientale*, L.), Mun and Mung, a species of *Phaseolus*, Meneri (*Milium Zeylanicum, minus*), Korakan (*Cynosurus Coracanus*, L.), Badhaamu, a species of *Dolichos* and a few others, known by the native names of Mutches, Cadecourie, Cambanpullo, Warego, Swamy, Tinnéswamy, Panneswamy, and, although the last, not the least in value, for its domestic purposes, Dholl and Horse Gram, might be planted and sown, by way of under crop, without injury to the chocolate plants. To these might be added, an extensive cultivation of the black pepper vine; for, notwithstanding the soil is well adapted to its growth, the island is still dependent upon Malabar for supplies of this spice, which is indispensable for the preservation of cinnamon bark during the homeward-bound voyage.

Surely, this is a speculation worthy of the attention of British capitalists; indeed, but a moderate capital would be required, to bring very large tracts of ground into a profitable state of cultivation; and if a few zealous individuals would but determine to adopt this system of agriculture, and give it a fair trial, it would establish the truth of my assertions, that the returns from the under crops would be as rapid as the most sanguine could have anticipated, and be ultimately increased by an abundant harvest of the chocolate nut.

The whole coast of the province abounds with excellent fish, and the interior part of it with fresh-water fish. Cattle and sheep are extremely cheap; the former, varying from twenty to thirty shillings a head: and the latter, from two shillings to half-a-crown

* Mandrakes of Scripture, *Dodaim* of the Hebrews. Gen xxx 14

† Page 125

Poultry and eggs are abundant, and proportionally cheap; but swine are less plentiful than in the Singhalese provinces, the Hindoos and Musselmans holding the "unclean animal" in almost equal abhorrence. Game abounds in every jungle, and a variety of wild fowl, including wild duck, widgeon, teal, and snipe, in every swamp and water tank.

There is great room for improvement in the native breed of cattle, here and throughout the island, by crossing it with that of England, or of the Cape of Good Hope; and if more regard be not paid to their feeding in this province than elsewhere, it certainly does not arise from a deficiency of excellent pasturage, either here, or in the several small islands to the westward. The native list of grasses contains 36 varieties.

As to the provincial breed of sheep, it is somewhat difficult to determine, by the appearance of these animals upon the extensive sheep walks between this place and Point Pedro, to which of Shaw's genera, *Capra* or *Ovis*, they bear the nearest affinity. Nevertheless, Jaffna sheep, after having been fed, for a few weeks, upon jack leaves, paddee, or dholl, yield a tolerable substitute for Bengal or Cape of Good Hope mutton.

Cows, imported from the Cape, have been found to answer very well; but, owing to the immediate neighbourhood of lakes, rivers, and canals, being the most favourable site for paddee fields, the appropriation of meadows, for the cultivation of grass, is as much neglected as the making of hay, which the sun would fully effect in a few hours; and although the latter is altogether unnecessary for local purposes, where winter is unknown, it might be prepared for the supply of shipping, if mechanical means of pressing it for that purpose were introduced from England.

A very considerable timber trade in Palmyra rafters and laths, (locally called *Paralies* and *Reepas*,) which are in great request, both for public and private buildings, is carried on coastwise between Jaffna and the other ports of the island.

About the beginning of August, the Hindoos celebrate the annual festival of their idol, *Jagan-Nath*, or *Parameswara*, the Lord of the Universe; but it is unaccompanied by the tragic scenes of self-immolation which are occasionally displayed at the grand *Deura* (temple) at Jagan-Nath, upon the coast of Coromandel, where pilgrims throw themselves under the wheels of the stupendous car of the idol, and are crushed to death. To this act, their religion incites them, as one so acceptable to *Jagan-Nath*, that a new birth, in felicity and honor, in the present world, is thereby assured to these voluntary victims of superstition and error.

Patterson, speaking of the origin of the Hindoo religion, describes the temple at Jagan-Nath as a famous resort for pilgrims of all sects; "for it is generally revered by them, as a converging point, where all contending parties unite in harmony with each other:" and, in describing the *Pranava*, or mystical character, which represents the *name* of the deity, from which cypher they have made three distinct idols, viz. *Bal-Ram*, *Sabhadra*, and *Jagan-Nath*, he calls it "a stroke of refined policy in the first founders of the temple, to present as an object of worship, the personification of the tri-literal word, which is held in reverence alike by all sectaries, and to give it a title, which each sect might apply to the object of its particular adoration;" and considers "that the intention of the foundation was evidently to render the temple a place of pilgrimage open to all sects, and to draw an immense revenue from the multifarious resort of devotees."

Having been invited to accompany the chief and puisne justices of the supreme court, (the Honorable Sir Alexander Johnston and Sir William Coke,) at that time on their northern circuit, to see the pagan ceremonies observed at the festival of *Jagan-Nath*, I gladly availed myself of so favorable an opportunity for viewing the triumphal car and procession of the idol.

A spacious booth, brilliantly illuminated, and decorated with white cloth, and natural fruits and flowers, among which the white, pink, and blue varieties of the *Lotos* were conspicuous, had been erected in front of the triumphal car, expressly for the reception of the judges, who were received, upon their arrival, by the chief and other Brahmins; after which, the head Brahmin placed over the shoulders of the chief justice three chaplets of fragrant flowers; of which, one was composed of the beautiful rose-colored corols of the double oleander (*Nerium odoratum*, L., *var duplex*), and the others of the moogrie, or Arabian jessamine (*Nerium coronarium*, L.); and the puisne justice was decorated with two white chaplets of moogrie flowers;—consecrated limes were, at the same time, presented to the judges, and the chief Brahmin paid me a similar compliment.

The car of the idol, formed of wood, about twenty or twenty five feet in length, and of proportional width, above its huge wheels, was highly gilded, and painted with emblematical figures, (among which the *Lingam* was prominent,) surrounding the carved figure of the idol.

According to the best account that I could collect from the Malabar interpreter of the custom house, the festival continues for several successive nights, as the time most adapted to the rites of pagan superstition; and he positively asserted as a matter of fact, "that it commences by the presentation of a beautiful virgin to the Brahmins, for the bride of *Jagan-Nath*, in whose temple (*Deura*) they leave her all night, after persuading her to believe, that the deity will himself visit her during that period. *Jagan-Nath* is then personated by one of the chief Brahmins; to whose lust, the poor victim is first sacrificed, and then instructed in the part she is to perform at the ensuing ceremonial; especially in the various stories which she is publicly to declare, from her seat by the idol's side, upon his car of triumph, as the commands received from *Jagan-Nath* himself, during the preceding night. "Tantum religio potuit suadere malorum."

The *Devadasi*, or dancing girls of the *Deura*, having been introduced by the head Brahmin, commenced their lascivious gestures, mis-called dancing. The prima donna was a Malabar girl of great beauty, and, in point of figure, a personification of the Medicean Venus; the others were also pretty, and of good figure; but the profuse use of turmeric, with which their faces, arms, necks, and breasts were covered, however charming to the native eye, neutralized the interest, with which, their otherwise attractive appearance might have inspired the more fastidious European.

The dress of the *Devadasi* consisted of a robe of spangled muslin, which partially covered the left breast, but exposed the right; this was confined round the waist by a massive zone of pure gold, of about three inches in width, and resplendent with pearls and precious stones; chiefly diamonds, emeralds, rubies, and sapphires. Splendid jewels of similar materials ornamented their ears, nostrils, (descending over the mouth and chin,) fingers, arms, ankles, and toes.

The *Devadasi* performed their parts to admiration; their various positions and movements were, perhaps, unequalled in point of lasciviousness, which gradually increased with their excitement, until it apparently bordered upon Bacchanalian madness, to the sound of the most barbarous *music*, if that word be not altogether misapplied, that ever deafened ear.

But, as if the horrid din of perforated shells, native drums, cymbals, and pipes, were considered insufficient to delight the European visitors, recourse was had to vocal music, by way of auxiliary. The Hindoo *artistes* were chiefly old men with snow-white beards; but these anti-harmonists, instead of clearing their mouths of the *Pawn* which they had previously been masticating, crammed into them additional rolls of it, and then commenced their monotonous *tic-tic-ticky-taw-tic-taw-ticky-taw*.

The dancing having terminated, the procession commenced its usual circuit:—the *Devadasi*, preceded by the singers and musicians, placed themselves in front of the car, which, upon a given signal, and amidst innumerable Chinese fire-works, myriads of torches, and the firing of small arms, was slowly dragged along by about a hundred devotees, who seemed to vie with each other for the honor of buckling themselves to the consecrated ropes of *Jagan-Nath's* car. The order of this heathen ceremonial recalled to mind the more sacred one described by the royal Psalmist, "The singers went before; the players on instruments followed after: amongst them were the damsels playing with timbrels."

All castes of Hindoos acknowledge the Brahmins* for their priests, and derive from them their belief of the metempsychosis, or transmigration of souls. Although many of the higher castes are extremely particular as to diet, and object to the use of animal food, the greater number are less scrupulous, and eat, sparingly, but not indifferently, of fish, flesh, and fowl. Their chief diet, however, consists of vegetable curries, in which butter, made of buffalo's milk, and clarified, is very generally employed; and they esteem milk as the purest of food, because the cow is regarded as a divinity.

The best native condiments used by the higher classes, are compounded of coriander seed, turmeric, black pepper, white mustard, green ginger, allspice, lesser cardamoms, cummim seed, fenugreek, and cayenne; but the lower classes are contented with the simpler ones of turmeric, green ginger, cayenne, and a leaf of the carpintchee tree (*Cookia anisetta*).

The chief amusement of the Hindoos consists in assisting at the religious ceremonials prescribed by their Brahmins, who appear to have established among themselves a regular hierarchy, and gradation of ranks, thereby securing subordination in their own order, weight to their authority, and dominion over the minds of the people. To enter into a detail of the complicated system of Hindoo superstition, is as far beyond my power, as it is foreign to my present object. The village people appear contented; and, as if their happiness consisted in domestic life, being taught by their religion that marriage is the indispensable duty of all, except those who separate themselves from the world for the sake of religion, polygamy is allowed; but they are generally contented with one wife, who is distinguished for fidelity to her vows, and solicitude for her family.

Native philanthropy displays itself, equally in the Malabar and Singhalese districts. At certain distances on the public roads, the way-worn traveller is sure to find the means of assuaging thirst, from a large earthen chatty, filled with water, to which a coco-nut-shell ladle is attached; this is placed upon a rest, about two feet from the ground, by the road side; and the neighbouring villagers never fail to replenish the "travellers' cistern," morning and evening.

As already stated in the preceding pages, the Americans have a large missionary establishment in this province. The first missionaries were acquainted with various

* According to Dr. Hyde's history of the religion of the ancient Persians, they believed their religion to have been that of the patriarch Abraham; and it appears to have been his own opinion, that the ancient Brachmans and modern Brahmins, derived their names from Abráhám, or rather Brâhâm, which is the common way of pronouncing that word amongst the Persians.—The Brahmin caste is distinguished by threads worn over one shoulder, and called *Zennaar*.

mechanical trades, and were not above imparting their knowledge of them to the natives; and they have done much good throughout their respective localities. They have a Hindoo professorship of astronomy, which is taught upon the native system; and if their number of converts to christianity be bounded, the social good they have effected is boundless.

"He left his Christian friends and native strand,
By pity for benighted men constrained;
His heart was fraught with charity unfeigned;
His life was strict, his manners meek and bland.
Long dwelt he lonely in a heathen land,
In want and weariness,—yet ne'er complained;
But laboured that the lost sheep might be gained,
Not seeking recompense from human hand.
The credit of the arduous works he wrought
Was reaped by other men who came behind:
The world gave him no honour—none he sought,
But cherished Christ's example in his mind.
To one great aim his heart and hopes were given,—
To serve his God, and gather souls to heaven."—PRINGLE.

Pringle's account of missionary privations, however applicable to those he might have had in view when he wrote, are certainly inapplicable to Ceylon missionaries of any denomination. In all other points, those who know those gentlemen will very probably agree with the author as to the applicableness of the above lines; but, in Ceylon, missionaries are, as I would wish they should be in every quarter of the globe, subject to no want or privation except such as are common to other gentlemen, in the public service and commercial community, arising from climate and distance from their native country.

But, like the good and well-intentioned of this country, the Americans have equally forgotten an old but true adage; for they too are more intent upon disseminating christianity amongst the pagans of India, than amongst the immense numbers of their worse than heathen brethren at home; who, according to that adage, have the nearest and greatest claim.

The first Tamul translation of the Liturgy was made by the Rev. Christian David, now Malabar colonial chaplain in this province, and was printed at the Serampore mission press, at the sole expense of the then governor, the late General Sir Robert Brownrigg, Bart., G. C. B.; but it is probable that even this will not be considered, "sanctis et inter sanctos" of this country, to be a sufficient expiation for the *deadly sin* of having made, as I shall show in the following pages, an offering to a Budhoo temple!!!—I much fear, that every attempt to reconcile the conflicting duties of religion with sound national policy will ever be an insuperable task to even the most zealous of our colonial governors.

CHAP. XXVIII.

Garrison of Jaffna—Provincial head quarters—Extensive culture of the Betel pepper—Esteemed for its astringent properties by native doctors—Flower and leaf of the wild and cultivated Betel—Mode of culture—Water conveyance to Point Pedro—Point Pedro Shoal—Route by land—Bitter Aloes—Villages of Kopaay and Atchoéwelle—Veteran magistrate who served under Frederick the Great—The ruling passion—Route from Jaffna to Trincomale—Katchay—Elephant Pass—Choondi Colom—Mullativoe—Face of the country—Postholders supply provisions to travellers—Jungles—Game—Mullativoe house—Dangerous coral shoal—Sailing directions—Alembiel—Superficies and population of the Northern Province—Numbers employed in agriculture, manufactures, and commerce Eastern Province—Nay-Aar—Kokelay—Sand-flies—Kokelay river—Fish—Dead shells for lime abundant—Scenery—Inhabitants—Terria—Banyan fig tree—Wild hogs—Hint to sportsmen—Cutchiavellé—Nilavelle—Salt River—View of Trincomale—Trincomale the chief town of the Eastern Province—Fortifications—Harbour—Society—Garrison—Suggestions for establishing farms for supplying shipping with salted and fresh provisions—Anticipated favorable result to Trincomale.

In time of peace, the military command of the province is held by a captain of the army; and the garrison of Jaffna, the "head quarters," consists of a few Europeans and a detachment of the Ceylon rifle corps: with a medical staff, consisting of an assistant surgeon, and a native medical sub-assistant: besides whom, there are a native medical sub-assistant, and a medical pupil, for the express purpose of vaccination. The civil departments are filled, as described in page 34, under the head "Fiscal division into provinces."

The culture of the Betel pepper (*Piper Betel*, L.) is more extensive in this, than in any other province; because its proximity to the Indian peninsula, enables the grower to export the leaf and flower, in a fresh state, to a market, where these articles, being scarcer, and indispensable necessaries of general consumption, are sure of a prompt sale at remunerating prices.

The Malabars call it *Betélé* or *Betré*, and the Singhalese *Booläāk* or *Booläāt-waela* and their doctors esteem it one of their best astringents. The Dutch formerly exported the dried flower, both of the cultivated and wild species, to the Cape of Good Hope:—the former is about an inch and a half in length, of a bright yellow; and the latter about five inches, and of an ash color. The leaf of both species is septinervous; but the upper surface of that of the cultivated has a peculiar glossiness, of which, the wild is destitute.

The Betel is propagated by layers;—these are cut into sets of about two feet in length, and the middle having been covered with earth, the extremities are left exposed; in the course of a few days, roots strike forth, and when the plant requires support, poles are employed, as in the hop-grounds of this country.

From Jaffna to Point Pedro there is conveyance by the river, which is only navigable by boats, and debouches near that port, where there is a small fort, but it has no garrison in time of peace. Point Pedro is the northernmost land of Ceylon; and from thence, during the north-east monsoon, Trincomalé may be reached by a country boat or *Dhoney* in a few hours.

According to Captain Horsburgh, "Point Pedro Shoal encompasses the N. E. extremity of the island; and, from thence, stretches nearly parallel to the coast, about six leagues to the S. S. Eastward, having only 3 and 3½ fathoms on it, in many places, and 2½ fathoms on two patches; one of these bears nearly E. ¾ S. from Point Palmyra, the N. E. extremity of Ceylon, distant about five miles; the other N. E. from the same Point, distant four miles.

"Between this extensive narrow shoal and the coast, there is a safe channel, about three miles wide; with regular soundings, soft mud, 7 fathoms close to the shore, 7, 8, or 9 fathoms in mid-channel, and five or 6 fathoms close to the inner edge of the shoal. To the Eastward of it, the bank of soundings is also flat, with regular depths; decreasing to 5 and 6 fathoms close to the S. E. and Eastern parts of the shoal, and to 4 fathoms, coarse brown sand, close to its N. Eastern verge.—The whole of this coast is low, and abounds in palmyra trees."

If the tourist intend to travel by land to Point Pedro, his route lies through Kopaay, passing to the left of Poetoer, through a low country, where there are extensive sheep-walks, to Atchoéwellé. The soil is sandy, but produces certain plants which are not indigenous elsewhere in the island, and are consequently attractive to the botanist; amongst others, the Aloe (*Alöe spicata*, L.), *Komarita* of the Singhalese, which yields the *Bitter Aloes* of commerce.

The inhabitants of the villages of Kopaay and Atchoéwellé, are an obliging, well-disposed, and contented race of people; and at Point Pedro, where there is a small establishment for collecting the customs, one is sure to meet with every kindness and hospitality from the resident civilian, who is an assistant government agent of the district.

Formerly the sitting magistrate at Point Pedro, was a Prussian gentleman of the name of Theile, who had served under Frederick the Great. He was a fine specimen of the Prussian grenadier of the old school, being not less than six feet three inches in height. Mr. Theile entertained the late Sir William Coke (puisne justice of the Honorable the Supreme Court) and myself, upon our landing at Point Pedro from Trincomalé, with the greatest hospitality; and, after dinner, a few extra glasses of Sir William's Champagne took a pleasant effect upon the old gentleman, who was eighty years of age; for instead of shouldering a crutch, "to show how fields were won," he desired his daughter, a very pretty girl, to play a favorite Prussian march; and "advancing arms" with my gun, marched about the room as erect as if he had been sixty years younger than he really was.

The direct route by land from Jaffna to Trincomalé, after having crossed the ferry, at Nawakooli, lies through Katchay, distant $17\frac{1}{2}$ miles; and from thence to Elephant or Bischuter Pass, 16 miles. The line of road is tolerably good, for a low champaign country, where sand is the predominating soil; and continues so to Choondi Colom, a distance of 15 miles; and from thence, to Moolladivo or Mullativoe, a further distance of $10\frac{3}{4}$ miles.

The face of the country is nearly the same throughout; in some places well cultivated, and studded with palmyra trees, with patches of jungle interspersed, and, here and there, a few straggling coco-nut trees. So few Europeans travel in this part of the island, that there are no regular established rest-houses between Jaffna and Mullativoe; but, at the several stages, the postholders provide eggs, milk, poultry, fish, and fruit, at the rates, established by the agent of government for the province, including a certain per centage upon the bazaar prices, for their own trouble and attention.

At almost every step, novelties present themselves to the attention of the naturalist and the sportsman. The jungles abound with game, of which, the most sought after are the Indian Samver (*Cervus Aristotelis*), commonly, but erroneously called Elk, and the Axis deer (*Cervus Axis*); but, amid the variety of wild animals, none is more curious, or perhaps novel to the newly-arrived European, than the toothless ant eater (*Manis tetradactyla*, L.), the *Kaballe* of the Singhalese. This singular creature forms itself into a ball, when suddenly obtruded upon, or at the approach of an enemy, after the manner of the hedgehog (*Erinaceus Europæus*, L.); the whole body is covered with imbricated scales, whose resisting power, arising in a great measure from the convexity as well as substance of its scales, (between every two of which a solitary bristle protrudes,) renders it impenetrable either by a spear or musket ball. The animal is of a greenish ash color, and obtains its food by laying its tongue, which is protrusile to the length of 16 or 18 inches, upon the ground, and as soon as it is covered with ants, it suddenly doubles it back into the mouth, and rubs them off against the palate.

The Wattoewékal-Aar is crossed at the ford, about a mile and a half or two miles from Mullativoe, which has a small fort, and a good rest-house, and is situate in latitude 9° 13' north, and longitude 81° 1 east, close to the sea, and bears about N. W. by N. from Pigeon Island, distant thirteen leagues; but, in time of peace, it has no garrison or European resident.

Captain Horsburgh, in the last edition of his Directory, (1836,) calls Mullativoe, *Molawal* or *Molatuwa*, and if one take the trouble to look at six or seven maps of Ceylon, scarcely two will be found to agree in point of orthography.

"From 'Mullativoe House, a dangerous coral shoal, having only two fathoms water on it, called Molawal shoal, extends to the eastward and north-eastward near four miles from the shore, which ought not to be approached nearer than thirteen fathoms. As there are twenty and twenty-one fathoms water about four miles from the shore, and four or five miles to the south-eastward of the shoal, a ship should edge out a little when near it; but when abreast of its eastern extremity, she may with the land wind borrow towards it to thirteen or fourteen fathoms. The north side of this shoal is not so steep, but composed of detached knowls, the depths decreasing regularly to nine or ten fathoms, close to its northern verge, and to six and seven fathoms along the N. W. part, close to the shore. From this, the coast is low to the N. E. point of Ceylon, with seven fathoms near to the sandy beach, but care is requisite to avoid the Point Pedro shoal."

The same orthodox authority in regard to Eastern navigation, describes the coast between Mullativoe House and Pigeon Island as "low and safe to approach, to eighteen or twenty fathoms in the night, if the lead be kept going, or to twelve fathoms occasionally when working in daylight. About 3½ leagues from Pigeon Island there is a small river, and four leagues further to the N. W. the river Kokelay is situated."

From Mullativoe the next village is Alembiel, distant 8¾ miles; and from thence to the Nay-Aar, which river separates this part of the Northern from the Eastern Province, 7½ miles.

The superficies of the northern province is 6,053 square miles; and the population, (excepting that of the Nuwerakalawiyé division, where no returns had been kept,) agreeably to the last Census, taken in 1835, is 252,619, making the average number to the square mile, 41.73; viz.

	MALES.	FEMALES.	TOTAL
Whites, including Military and their families	492	539	1,031
Free Blacks, ditto ditto	112,489	113,138	225,627
Slaves	12,605	11,910	24,515
Aliens and Resident Strangers	.	.. ...	1,446
			252,619

The number employed in agriculture, 67,662; in manufactures, 18,992; and in commerce, 12,454. The marriages, in the year 1835, were 1,180; births, 4,336; and deaths, 2,503; leaving a surplus in favor of the population of the province, of 1,833.

From the Nay-Aar, the distance to Kokelay, which is situate about mid-way between Alembiel and Kanjarankenné, is rather more than 10 miles, During the heat of the day, the glare and the sand-flies are so embarassing, that no one travels between 9 A. M. and 4 P. M. if it can well be avoided; but during the N. E. monsoon, the road is rendered comparatively pleasant, by the refreshing breezes from the sea, to what it is when the S. W. prevails.

The Kokelay river, and indeed the whole line of coast, abounds with fish, including the Sole and Sur-mullet, and several varieties of the Ray (*Raïidæ*, C.) and Mackarel (*Scomberoidæ*, C.) families; and there is such an accumulation of dead shells, that sufficient lime might be burnt upon the spot to supply the whole province.

At early dawn, flamingos, widgeon, curlews, herons, and snipes, congregate in the watery patches near the plains; and these, covered with verdure and bordered by magnificent forest trees, upon whose topmost branches innumerable peafowl await the first rays of the rising sun, to exhale the night dew from their splendid plumage,

> " ——— While o'er the forest glade
> The wild deer trip, and, often turning, gaze
> At early passengers!"

delight the eye in every direction: but so little is produced by human exertions, to what the country is capable of, that one naturally arraigns the neglect of man, whilst he acknowledges, and is lost in admiration of, the bounty of the Creator.

The Hindoo villagers are an industrious race of people, and seem contented and happy. Their usually plain diet includes the *Kellingo*, or meal made from the spring leaf of the palmyra; and their chief employment is in salting fish for the Kandyan market, or attending to their humble husbandry. Every cottage has its garden, in which, capsicums, tobacco, cotton, Indian spinach, water melons, ginger, pumpkins, betel, cucumbers, turmeric, pepper, yams, beans, sweet potatos, and plantains, are the principal objects of culture. The people of the village are generally well-grown and handsome; the women are pretty, and extremely diffident in their appearance and demeanour; but all their children appear, as elsewhere in the island, subject to obesity; which, if one ask them the reason, is attributed to the rice, and they seem to have the same remedy for it everywhere, in the flesh of the river tortoise or *Kiri-Ba*. The villagers use the Caffrarian lime (*Citrus tuberoïdes*) as commonly here as in the southern and western provinces, for cleansing their long and redundant black hair.

The next stage to the southward is Terria, distant $11\frac{3}{4}$ miles; the natives pronounce it *Pehria.* The neighbourhood exhibits immense rocks of singular appearance; and the surrounding scenery is altogether worthy of a master pencil. The native cottages, which are built of sticks (*Warretchie*) and clay, and whitewashed with chunam, are extremely neat.

The banyan tree (*Ficus Indica*) is common here; and, during the time its red figs are ripe, the sportsman has no further trouble than to station himself in a good position, under cover, and within gun-shot of the trees, soon after dusk, when he may kill wild hogs *ad libitum* for these animals are so eager for their favorite food, that they return, after a short time, to the spot, (where they may have left many of their original number "dead upon the field,") and continue to run from, and return to, the same place, several times during the night, until the sportsman is actually tired of slaughter; but not being one myself, I am indebted for my information upon this point, to some of the most experienced of my contemporaries, both English and Dutch.

From Terria to Cutchiavelle rest-house, the distance is rather more than $8\frac{1}{4}$ miles road still sandy, with jungles abounding with wild hogs, deer, and buffalos. The place contains but few inhabitants, and their appearance is not so pleasing and contented as that of the people of the villages of Kokelay and Terria; but they are equally civil and obliging.

The next stage, to Nilavellé rest-house, is rather more than 13 miles; from thence to the Salt river, $4\frac{3}{4}$ miles; and to Trincomalé, $3\frac{1}{2}$ miles further; road sandy, with thick jungle, and occasionally undulating and hilly; affording magnificent views of the bay of Trincomale, and of the numerous fortifications by which that most important place, the Head Quarters of His Excellency the Commander-in-chief of Her Majesty's ships and vessels in the Indian seas, may be rendered, when adequately garrisoned, impregnable.

Along this coast, there is little for remark, beyond a bold shore, immense tracks of wood inland, and the abundance of the palmyra palm; but the country is better inhabited and cultivated than appears to the superficial observer.

Trincomalé, the chief town in the province, (Batticaloa being the next, but scarcely deserving the name,) stands in a N. E. direction along the bay, in a woody and hilly country, interspersed with coco-nut and palmyra trees; but the appearance of it is extremely wild, owing to the general neglect of agriculture; and, like most seaport towns, whose dependence is upon the navy, it experiences the inconvenience of peace; for it is so little frequented by free traders, that it has nothing to compensate it, for the loss of its grand support.

From its position, Trincomalé is naturally strong, and art has since made it impregnable, by fortifications; but although it occupies a larger area than the maritime capital, it has scarcely half the number of houses; and these are very inferior, with the exception of the late naval commissioner's spacious mansion, built upon the Madras plan, with flat roof, and verandah, whose pillars rival in appearance Parian marble, and a few other public and private buildings.

The fort commands the bays, and particularly the entrance to the inner bay, which being nearly as much land-locked as Portsmouth harbour, ships of every rate and class may ride secure there throughout the year; but this very circumstance, as opposing great natural obstacles to a free circulation of the sea breezes, is considered by many medical men as a principal cause of the proverbial unhealthiness of the place; to this may be added, the swampy grounds on the land side, as another reason.

The strong brick-built fortification, called Fort Ostenburg, which also commands the harbour, projects so far to seaward, that before an enemy can attack it, possession must first have been obtained of the fort of Trincomalé, as well as of the grand harbour itself; but, notwithstanding the importance attached to this naval station by its former possessors, the French and Dutch, as well as by ourselves, for its proximity to our possessions on the coast of Coromandel and bay of Bengal, it has never possessed any trade of importance, in a national point of view; and this not only deserves the greatest consideration, but an adequate remedy.

The European society of Trincomalé is limited to the families of those employed in the public service; and their general hospitality is such as Ceylon has been famed for from the earliest period of our possession of it.

The garrison consists of a regiment of the line, with a company of royal artillery and a detachment of the Ceylon rifle corps.

The medical department comprises a staff surgeon, one assistant staff surgeon, and a native medical sub-assistant. The former duties of fort major and fort adjutant, are now performed by the "Staff Officer," with an extra allowance of 10*s*. per diem.

The agent of government, district judge, colonial chaplain, and master attendant, are, ex-officio, members of the Sub-committee of the commission for the general superintendence of education throughout the colony.

During the war, Trincomalé was, comparatively speaking, a flourishing place, when contrasted with its present state; but since the breaking up of the dockyard establishment, which caused the circulation of a great deal of money, and made it profitable to the inhabitants, it may be said, "Stat nominis umbrâ:"—but it might soon be made a place of great resort by ships of all classes in the India trade, if a few speculative capitalists were to establish an extensive farm in the immediate neighbourhood, for the purpose of rearing and improving stock of every description for ships' use, and for growing fodder and grain for its support on shipboard; as well as for supplying good beef and wholesome esculents to the royal navy in the harbour, as suggested in page 111.

The patronage of the naval commander-in-chief, as well as of the army commissariat, might be calculated upon, as one certain consequence of the speculation; because it would display a degree of public spirit that would unite all in a zealous desire to support it; and, for my own part, I would desire no better fortune than a *tenth* share of the profit, for as many years, which might be realized by its efficient management.

The establishment of a "model farm" in this part of the island would prove of more real importance to the country than a hundred upon the fatal banks of the Niger; not only as regards the comparatively small cost, but the almost incalculable saving of human life. The culture of grains, including the millet (*Panicum Italicum*, L.), which was originally introduced by the Portuguese, and called by them *O milho painço*, instead of paddee, now in general use, would throw a much larger supply of rice into the market, and supersede the too general employment of coco-nut oil-cake.

This, in conjunction with a central farm in the highlands of Kandy,* would prove a very lucrative speculation, for their temperature is every way favorable to the curing of provisions for supplying the royal and commercial navies, for which they are now dependent upon Bengal and Bombay; and would soon render Trincomalé as much frequented by trading vessels as it is now neglected.

It cannot reasonably be doubted, but that such an extensive farm, capable of supplying shipping with stock, equally good and perhaps cheaper than either Madras or Calcutta, and which might also include a depôt for supplying steamers with coals, would scarcely have had time to perfect itself, ere ten ships would put into Trincomale, where one does now; for everything would then be against Madras for supplying ships, upon an equality, in point of goodness or cheapness, with Trincomalé, independently of the difficulty of access at all times, owing to its surf, and the danger, if not impracticableness, of lying in that roadstead, between the period of striking the flag-staff of Fort St. George, in October, and re-hoisting it, at the change of the monsoon; and consequently Trincomalé would naturally be resorted to for stock, instead of the river Hooghly, if it could be obtained there equally as good and cheap at all seasons of the year.

* Vide page 177

CHAP. XXIX.

Malacology of the island—Cabinets of shells got up for sale—Best method of procuring perfect specimens—Caution to strangers in buying jewellery from natives—Their importunate method of obtruding it upon notice—Adepts at transforming broken glass into varieties of precious stones—Laws to restrain imposition effectual, when appealed to, in time—Jewellery expressly made for "Chip Gentlemans"—Ear-cutting—Ineffectual punishment for it—Suggestions for suppressing it—Rains—Lord Valentia—Crocodiles—Hot wells of Cannea—Little white ants (Termes) great public peculators—Sailing directions into the harbour of Trincomalé—Reasons for not building ships at Trincomale, inapplicable to the neglect of growing Teak for the future exigencies of the royal navy—Suggestions for rendering grants, or sales of crown lands, more beneficial to the public, in proportion to the advantages derived by grantees or purchasers.

TRINCOMALE has been proverbial for its marine shells, for centuries past; and it is no less capable of affording perfect specimens of the Malacology of the island at the present day, than when it was considered, by our Dutch predecessors, in the zenith of its fame, for this interesting and extensive branch of natural history, which appears to be in more general request than any other; arising, perhaps, from the lesser degree of care required to preserve shells for an indefinite period, and with but little loss of substance or color.

The principal varieties to be obtained here, belong to the following genera of the Linnæan or Lamarchian systems, viz. *Anomia, Arca, Buccinum, Bulla, Cardium, Chama, Chione, Carocolla, Carinaria, Ceritheum, Columbella, Conus, Cypræa, Dentalium, Donax, Glycimeris, Harpa, Haliotis, Helix, Mya, Mactra, Murex, Mytilus, Nautilus, Nerita. Ostrea, Pholas, Pinna, Pleurastoma. Pteroceros, Sufula, Solen, Strombus, Sponsylus. Tellina, Teredo, Turbo, Trochus, Venus,* and *Voluta.*

Shells are sold, *en masse,* in very pretty cabinets of indigenous satin wood and ebony. which are occasionally ornamented with mother-o'-pearl; but these, although at first sight attractive to the new comer, are generally found, upon individual examination, to be scarcely worth the trouble of carriage; the most valuable part of the purchase being the drawers which contain the trash, as such shells are justly considered by the Conchologist. The best way to obtain perfect specimens, is to get a recommendation from the government agent to the renter of the shell fishery; and, as the latter will expect to be paid in proportion to the value of the shells he procures, the purchaser may rely on his strenuous efforts to get the best for him.

Strangers landing at Trincomalé, as casual visitors, are apt to be misled by the showy appearances of the jewellery offered by itinerant venders, who crowd together at the landing place, upon the first signal of a ship standing into the harbour, to take advantage of "*Griffin Gentleman.*"

These fellows, who are chiefly Moormen and Malabars, vie with each other in vociferously obtruding their "*Tort-shell boxes.*" "*Not jeweller's gold,*"—"*All first touch star pagoda gold shaines*"—"*He all, he stone rings,*" (representing those of the island; some of the commonest of which may be genuine,)—"*He mooney-stone rings,*"—"*He Chinnamon stone*"—"*He safeer,*" (sapphire)—"*He rubal,*" (ruby)—"*He imral,*" (emerald)—"*He topaze,*"—"*He water safeer,*"—"*He ambetyst,*" (amethyst)—"*He tourmaline,*"—"*He opal,*"—"*He agga marina,*" (aqua marina)—and lots of other "*He*"-prefixed humbugs upon "*Chip Gentlemans;*" for they know well enough how to transform broken blue, green, purple, and yellow finger glasses into sapphires, emeralds, amethysts, and topazes; veneered tortoise shell, into solid "*Tort-shell snuff-boxes,*" and Birmingham gilt chains, into "*Real Ceylon gold shaines, Masta,*"—et cæteris paribus!

As the local laws impose heavy penalties upon persons convicted of selling counterfeit, or inferior, gold to the quality bargained for, these Jews of the East, relying upon impunity in their nefarious transactions ashore, or with officers and passengers on ship-board, keep their several false and real *Bijoux* in separate boxes; and it is by no means uncommon, when they are displaying their best jewellery to residents, and are asked to show what their "other boxes" contain, to be told, "*that* not do for *Masta* or *Lady*; that for *Chip Gentlemans!*"

Strangers being desirous of purchasing jewellery, and of knowing what they do purchase before they pay for it, will find it best to apply to the secretary of the district court, who will introduce them to the Assayer (generally a headman of the goldsmiths) employed by the court; and he will test the quality of the gold, and fix its value, so that the purchaser will not be imposed on in the weight or quality of the gold; and the working goldsmiths' charges for "fashion" are extremely moderate.

The lower classes of Malabars about this place are a very bad set, and notorious for "*ear-cutting;*" a crime which is peculiar to the northern and eastern provinces and, as it does not enter into the catalogue of European felonies, may require some explanation.

The rich Malabars, Hindoos, and Chitties, ornament their ears with enormous gold rings, about three inches in diameter, reaching from the lobes of the ears to the shoulders; these rings are generally of the purest gold, and set with resplendent jewels, chiefly emeralds, rubies, sapphires, and cats'-eyes, and, occasionally, pearls of a large size; sometimes the former, although merely polished, are considered of greater intrinsic value than cut stones. This display causes frequent robberies; and the thieves, having waylaid their victims, instead of unfastening the ornaments, hastily clip the lobes of the ears, and make off with their valuable plunder.

Although the supreme court has never allowed an opportunity to escape of punishing this crime to the utmost extent of the law, it has hitherto failed to suppress it; but as the natives dread deportation more than any other penalty, (death excepted,) which does not extend to ear-cutting, one would imagine that a Legislative enactment for the transportation of persons convicted of it, to New Zealand, where they might be usefully employed in the construction of roads and public buildings, would tend to suppress this Malabar *penchant* for plundering their neighbours' ears.

"The rains" set in with the north-east monsoon, in October and November, during which time the mean temperature is about 77°, by the late Mr. Richard Brook's observations; but Trincomalé is visited with heavy, although partial, showers in July, during the south-west monsoon, when the mean temperature is about 82°; at which time, this side of the island is as little affected by it, owing to the intervening range of mountains, from 1000 to 8280 feet above the level of the sea, as the western and southern provinces are during the prevalence of the north-east.

Lord Valentia (the late Lord Mountnorris) has been unjustly accused of recommending "the cutting down of coco-nut trees, as the means of improving the salubrity of the place near which they abound;" for, in his Lordship's "Travels," the noble author, in allusion to the coco-nut tree, gave his opinion, that "when close-planted, it seems to prevent the growth of underwood," but that "if all shelter were removed, even in the lowlands, the ground crops might be injured by too much opening them to the sun and wind, and the effects, even on the fruit trees, might be unfavorable. But tall trees would protect, without stopping the circulation of air. Clumps of them, and hedge-rows, ought to be planted, when the jungle and underwood are cleared."*

As regards the felling of coco-nut or other trees, by which a fort or fortress is immediately overlooked or commanded, Lord Valentia displayed more sound judgment than otherwise, in a military point of view; and probably the recommendation "to cut down the coco-nut topes at Trincomalé," was but a natural consequence of that view of their position.

* Lord Valentia's Travels, vol. i. page 313.

Lord Valentia has, however, exposed himself, with more justice, to strictures, by the severe remarks his account of Ceylon contains upon Professor Thunberg. Whatever local privileges the professor may have enjoyed under the Dutch administration, there are no just grounds for doubting an iota of that gentleman's account of them; and if Lord Valentia, as the "lion of the day" there, could not get his coolies to keep together, notwithstanding his peerage, and the Governor's avowed anxiety to afford every possible accommodation, his Lordship might have supposed that times were altered for the worse, instead of doubting the facilities for travelling which the Dutch government appears to have readily afforded to Dr. Thunberg: or, there might have been reasons in the back ground for the obstacles that the noble Lord complains of; because violence, or irritability of temper, on the part of Europeans, have operated as effectually as the withholding the pay or *Batta* from their coolies, in causing desertion at the first opportunity; whilst a contrary system has been equally successful in securing the retention of their services throughout the journey.

The crocodile abounds here: and the jungles teem with game and other wild beasts. At Cannea, about eight miles from Trincomalé, there are hot wells, but their waters do not possess any mineral properties: they are walled in, and the enclosure forms a parallelogram of about forty feet by twenty; it is just a pleasant distance for a breakfast party; starting at daylight, and returning before noon.

According to Dutch tradition, one of their Collectors of Revenue for this district, being unable to account for the disappearance of a few thousands of rix dollars, reported to the government, that "the white ants had eaten them;" and as these insects are believed to possess most extraordinary powers of digestion, from their forming their "covered ways" through walls and beams of wood, it was not altogether incredible; but one of our own Head Civil Servants, similarly circumstanced, and for very little less than 100,000 rix dollars, (when he had only the *small* salary of £2000 a year and *pickings*,) upon being ordered to make up his accounts, instead of endeavouring to impose a similar story upon the government, (for the missing treasure included gold star pagodas, as well as rupees, and it was the second time that he had been so *unfortunate*,) merely accused the *white ants* of having eaten the "*vouchers*" for the expenditure of that sum!! This way of "*doing*" the public was a very thriving trade in the colony for a number of years, because it seldom failed to insure impunity, and was generally followed by promotion or a pension; but let us hope that these "*sweating*" times are past.

"Ridentem dicere verum quid vetat?"

As the best ascertained sailing directions into the bay and harbour of Trincomalé, are those given in Captain Horsburgh's Directory, I have adopted his authority; but I have used the name of "Ostenburg," which is the *proper* one, instead of "Osnaburg," employed by Captain Horsburgh.

"Foul Point, the S. E. point of Trincomalé Bay, named from a dangerous reef projecting from its extremity upward of a mile to the N. N. Eastward, is low and woody, and the breadth of the entrance of the Bay, between it and Flag-staff Point, is about five miles, this point bearing from the former about N. W. ¾ W.

"Flag-staff Point, in latitude 8° 33½′ north, and longitude 8° 19′ east of Madras, by Captain Horsburgh's chronometers, and 8° 26′ east from Bombay castle, by Captain F. Heywood's observations, is high, steep to seaward, covered with trees, and has on it several forts.*

"This point is the northern extremity of a narrow and crooked peninsula, that bounds the E. and S. E. sides of Trincomalé Harbour, and separates Back Bay from it and from the great Bay to the southward; this peninsula being steep, bluff land, fronting the sea, is easily known, as the coast is low near the sea, both to the northward and southward.

"The S. E. point of the peninsula, called Chapel Point, has some islets near it on the south side, called Chapel Island, and to the eastward a reef of rocks, distant a large half mile, nearly on the edge of soundings, having 20 and 30 fathoms very close on the east and south sides: on the inner part of the reef, one of the rocks is seen above water. Flag-staff Point is bold to, and safe to approach, but between it and Chapel Point, rocks stretch out from two small projections, which ought not to be approached under 14 fathoms.

"The S. W. point of the peninsula, called Elephant Fort Point, has an island called Elephant Island, near it on the S. E. side, from which a reef, having 5 feet water on its shoalest part, projects to the westward. Ostenburg Point, the westernmost point of the peninsula, is a little farther to the N. W., between which and Elephant Fort Point there is a cove or safe harbour, with soundings in it from 8 to 14 fathoms.

"The entrance of the Inner Harbour is not a quarter of a mile wide, formed by Ostenburg Point to the eastward, and Great and Little Islands to the westward, Little Island being the easternmost, and close to the other.

"About half a mile south from Great Island, and one mile to the west of Elephant

* Captain Basil Hall, R. N., in 1814, made it in longitude 81° 21′ east, by stars east and west of the moon; and he made the variation of the compass, 1° 9′ west.

Island, Clappenburg Island is situated, close to a Point of the same name, and about a mile further to the southward is a point, where the land is elevated a little, called Marble Point, with rocks projecting around.

"Marble Point forms the western entrance of the Great Bay, separating it from the entrance of the Harbour, and affords a mark for going in. To the westward of Marble Point, there is an island, called Birds' Island, near the entrance of a lagoon, and shoal water. To the S. E. lies Pigeon Island, distant a large half mile, having 10 and 12 fathoms water close to; and Round Island, nearly the same distance from the Point, to E. N. E., having 30 fathoms water near it on the outside, then suddenly no ground. On the south side of this island there is a rock above water, and between it and Clappenburg Island, but nearest the latter, called Government Rock. The entrance leading to the Harbour, is formed by these Islands and Rocks to the S. W., and Elephant Island and Point to the N. E.

"Four rivers, navigable by small boats, fall into the south part of the Bay, nearly at equal distances from each other, of which, the principal is the Mavali-Ganga.

"The bank of soundings lining the shores of the Bay, extends very little outside the islets or rocks, except at the S. E. part, between the rivers Cotiaar and Sambar, where ships may anchor in 10 or 12 fathoms, regular soundings, soft mud, sheltered from easterly and southerly winds.

"The east side of the Bay is bounded by Norway Point to the northward, which is about two miles to the W. S. W. of Foul Point. Norway Island lies on the west side of the Point, having a rocky reef encompassing it, and the islets near it and the Point. From this Point and the Island a sandbank stretches about a mile to the south, with soundings on it 3 and 3½ fathoms, and 20 or 25 fathoms close to. To the west of it a quarter of a mile distant there is no ground; but to the south, between it and the river Sambar, there is good anchorage near the shore.

"Norway Point and Foul Point must be avoided, on account of reefs projecting from them about three-quarters of a mile; nor ought the shore between them to be approached, the soundings being irregular, and about half-way there is a very dangerous rock, about a mile distant from the shore, called Northesk Rock, from a ship of that name, lost there in 1748. Close to it, on the outside, there are 12 and 14 fathoms, and 8 or 9 fathoms inside. When on it, Flag-staff Point bears N. 35 W., Norway Island S. 33 W., and a hill in the country, touching Marble Point, W. 10 S., and Foul Point E. 10 N., it making a transit line with these Points.

"*To sail into the Bay, and to the Harbour*, with a fair or leading wind, a ship may enter the Bay, keeping nearly equal distance from each side; when Round Island and

Marble Point are discerned, the Point ought to be kept about W. by S. ½ S. open to the northward of that Island, until the Harbour's mouth is open. No soundings will be obtained in the middle of the Bay. When Round Island or Elephant Island is approached, she ought to steer in about mid-way between them, and will then have soundings: after hauling to the N. W. for the Harbour, care must be taken to give berth to a reef stretching from Elephant Island, by not coming under 10 or 12 fathoms toward it. When a ship, going into the Harbour, first opens the channel between Elephant Island and the main land, she is nearly abreast of that reef; when wide open, she is past it. On the hill of Ostenburg Point, there is a battery built with brick, on the eastern part of the fortification, higher than any battery there, and easily distinguished. The flank of this battery kept on with Elephant Fort Point, would carry a ship close to the shoalest part of the reef, where there is only 5 or 6 feet water; but the battery kept open with the Point, (which is the best mark,) will carry her clear of it, in not less than 10 fathoms. There are 24 and 30 fathoms between the Points that form the entrance of the Harbour, and after passing the reef contiguous to Elephant Island, a ship should steer direct for it; although narrow, either of the Points may be approached within a ship's length, and when through this narrow part, a spacious harbour appears, where a *great navy* may anchor in good ground, sheltered from all winds, exclusive of several coves convenient for careening ships.

"When within the entrance, it is prudent to steer to the N. N. W. to avoid the shoal within Ostenburg Point, and York Shoal further to the northward. The former has only 11 feet water on it; with York Island and Flag-staff Point in one, and Pigeon Island and the low part of Ostenburg Point in one, a ship will be in 5 or 6 fathoms water on it, and close to the shoalest part. It is small with deep water all round, between it and the shore near Ostenburg Point there are 7 and 8 fathoms.

"York Shoal has only 5 feet water on its shoalest part; to avoid it, a ship in steering up the Harbour must keep Round Island a little open with Ostenburg Point; but there seems no good land-mark to point out when a ship is to the northward of it, that she may haul to the eastward, for the anchorage abreast the town. When the Intrepid's boat was at anchor on its outer edge, in 3¼ fathoms, within a ship's length of its shoalest part, Round Island bore S. ¾ E., seen over the low part of Ostenburg Point; the centre of York Island E. N. E. ¾ N., and the N. W. point of Great Island nearly W. S. W. ½ W.; with this bearing of Round Island, the shoal is not more than half a cable's length from north to south, and is steep all round.

"Ships may moor abreast the town, to the N. Westward of York Island; also to the northward of Great Island, or in any other part of the Harbour, clear of the shoals."

No saving whatever is made, by not making a signal for a pilot, to enter the Inner Harbour of Trincomalé; for pilotage is charged under either circumstance.*

The late intelligent Captain James Chrisp informed me, that the grand obstacle to ship-building here, for naval purposes, was the limited rise of the tides, which seldom exceeded thirty eight inches. But although *this* is a good reason for not *building* ships, it is none for not growing the best timber for the purpose of the future exigencies of the British navy, upon all the waste lands of the Crown, near this, and the ports of Colombo and Galle.

Ceylon teak (*Tectona Grandis*, L.) is considered of an excellent quality; and if the government were to make it a condition, in all its grants or sales of Crown lands, that the grantee, or purchaser, should plant and protect a proportionate number of teak trees, posterity would derive incalculable advantages from this timely provision for its naval wants. Lands might be marked out by rows of teak trees; and these, being the property of the Crown, and the landlords or tenants compelled by their title deeds, or leases, to protect them, and to replace all casualties with young trees, there could be none of the disputes among neighbours, as to the right to the trees, which now too often lead to endless litigation; and the Crown may, with full justice to all, insist upon some more proportionate benefit to itself, for the advantages which its grants, or sales of lands, confer upon individuals.

Crown lands are sold by auction, at an upset price of 5*s.* per acre; and, in the year 1841, the government of Ceylon disposed of nearly 80,000 acres, chiefly at the upset price; but some, as high as 17*s.* to 17*s.* 6*d.* per acre:—and therefore, if only six teak trees to an acre were planted, the Crown would possess 480,000 saplings, gratuitously planted, for the future purposes of the British navy, as some additional acknowledgment for the lands so cheaply sold.—The government might realize from £1 to £2 an acre, by affording purchasers the facility and certainty in the acquisition of land. which, in the Australian colonies, may be expected from the provisions of the recent Land Act.

Trincomalé, once considered very unhealthy, is now greatly improved in that respect; and as draining the marshy lands and clearing the jungles of underwood proceed, so will its salubrity increase, until it equals that of the most favored parts of the island.

* Vide Appendix, for the Laws relating to the Ports and Customs.

CHAP. XXX.

Anticipated extension of the culture of the Cassada—Its valuable properties—Local names in various countries—Crops safe from the vicissitudes of weather—Method of preparing the stalks for transit from Mauritius to Ceylon—Sweet variety edible, without previous preparation—Primitive method of preparing the Bitter Cassada—Casleep—Tapioca—Substitute for mushroom spawn—Ant-hill clay—Native goldsmiths—Their simple implements—Route from Trincomale to Kandy—Kandellé—Tamblegam—Hindoo temple—Kottiaar—Anedivoo—Tapootorre—Patcherie rice—Native varieties—Mode of culture—Scarcity seldom attributable to natural causes—Java formerly supplied Ceylon from its surplus produce—Pumpkin Governors—General Sir Hudson Lowe, G. C. B.—Anticipated justice to that gallant officer, who was expected to have succeeded Sir Edward Barnes as Governor—No one more capable of developing the capabilities of Ceylon—Virgel-Oya—Kaddiravallé—Pannitchancanne—Kommollandam Moone—Air plant—Nalloor—Erraoor—Region of mosquitos, Batticaloa—Lacerta Iguana, L.

As the establishment of farms, for the purposes suggested in the preceding chapters, would naturally lead to an extensive culture of useful roots, whose applicableness, as food for man, or fodder for domestic animals, might render them worthy of the attention of the agriculturist, my long entertained hope, that the much-neglected Manioc, or Cassada, will cease to be dreaded as poisonous, and be brought into general use, may ultimately be realized.

Its valuable properties only require to be more generally known, to establish a claim to universal regard, as an object of primary importance to the colony. I have partially alluded to this exotic, as a farinaceous esculent, in page 127; but some further notice of its usefulness to the agriculturist, may not be uninteresting to the reader; who, if he be an intending settler at Ceylon, will do well to treasure it in memory.

This species of Jatropha, (*Jatropha manihot*, L.), known by the several names of *Manioc*, *Cassada*, *Cassavi*, and *Cassava*, in various countries, is either changed by culture, or preparation, to an article of the greatest utility, both as food for man, in a variety of wholesome forms, and for fattening every description of domestic animal; particularly swine and poultry.

Being safe from the vicissitudes of weather, the manioc root is rendered a certain succedaneum for rice, in the event of failure in the crops from drought or blight, which makes its value inestimable: and moreover, the facility of propagating it, and the rapidity of its growth, ensuring a regular succession of crops, week after week, and month after month, throughout the year, render it worthy of general and particular attention.

I adopted a very simple plan for conveying the manioc to Ceylon. Having selected from the grounds of my excellent friend Madame Luzardin, (widow of the late Doctor Luzardin, Ancien Chirurgeon-Major du Regiment de Bourbon,) at Mauritius, as many manioc sticks as I required, from four to five feet in length, and dissolved a sufficient quantity of rosin and mutton suet over a slow fire, the ends of the cuttings were dipped into it to the depth of an inch; and, when dry, the whole were formed into a fagot, and covered with coarse *gunny* cloth.*

When required for planting, the sticks are cut into sets of about fourteen inches long; these, having been laid down horizontally in trenches, either singly, at about two feet apart, or doubly in parallel lines, leaving a space of twelve or fourteen inches between the sets, are lightly covered with earth and watered. The plants appear above ground in about a week; and, as the growth is very rapid, the planter's chief care is to keep the ground free from weeds. One great advantage is, that the manioc will grow any where in a tropical climate, and thrives well in a sandy soil.

Notwithstanding the lapse of twenty one years since I first introduced the *Cammanioc,*† or sweet cassada, into Ceylon from the Mauritius, at which time my recommendation of the root as an esculent for the table, (for it requires no caution in its preparation, as the *bitter* variety does, and may be boiled or baked as a yam or potato,) was regarded with suspicion and dread, even by those whom I considered some of the most enlightened of my contemporaries, its culture is still almost entirely neglected:—and when we recall to mind, how long Ceylon has been, and still is, dependent upon other countries for rice; and the repeated failures it has experienced of the paddee crops, subjecting the poorer classes to all the horrors of famine, the apathy shown, in regard to the manioc, is almost incredible, and must arise either from absurd notions of danger, or ignorance of its domestic value.

By encouraging the natives to cultivate the manioc, as a resource against failure in the rice crops, prejudice will soon cease; and, by way of more speedily overcoming it, I submit the following extracts from my notes, made during my stay in the West Indies, and at the Mauritius, to the notice of the sceptical, in the hope that they may be induced to test their correctness, if only by way of experiment, upon a limited scale.

* Made from the hemp of the *Crotalaria juncea,* L.

† Linnæus makes no distinction, which may be merely accidental, as in the case of sweet and bitter almonds.

If this were done, the result would probably lead to its general culture throughout the island, and be followed by the beneficial effects that I originally anticipated, when I gave up the personal comforts of a cabin, during the voyage from Teneriffe to Mauritius, and from thence to Ceylon, to ensure the safety of the several exotics, which I had shipped at these places, in the sanguine hope that their introduction would prove lasting benefits to the island; and that the invaluable properties of the manioc would recommend it to public notice, as one of the chief blessings, next to vaccination, that had ever been conferred upon the colony by the hand of man.

The sweet cassada (*Jatropha manihot*, L., *var dulcis*) never flowers; and its bark is of a reddish brown, instead of the ashy color of the common or poisonous sort:—but the *bitter*, or common cassada, may be rendered equally wholesome; for, by expressing its juice, that very liquid, which, if mixed with wheaten flour and made into pellets, will destroy rats, and is used by the Indians, of some countries, for poisoning arrows, may be manufactured into a delicious sauce for a variety of domestic purposes.

The roots, which grow as large as parsnips, but not so tapering at the extremity, having been peeled, are reduced to a pulp by a large tin or copper grater; (the latter is generally employed at the Mauritius,) and as this mode is more primitive, it is consequently better, at present, for Ceylon, (where manual labour is so very cheap,) than the horse-hair bags, or machinery, employed for it in the West Indies:—the pulp is then enveloped in coarse cloth, and laid in an oblong trough, perforated with holes, and standing within a receiver of sufficient depth to contain the juice; and a board, fitted to the inside of the trough, having been laid upon the pulp, as much weight as may be required is placed upon it, until the juice is thoroughly extracted, when the farina is removed from the press, and prepared for use in the following equally simple manner.

A smooth circular plate of iron, of about eighteen inches diameter, and two-thirds of an inch thick, supported by stones over a wood fire, is first made nearly red hot; the person employed to make the cakes, then spreads half a coco-nut shell of the farina over the iron plate, of an equal thickness (about the fourth of an inch) throughout, with a small whisk of split bamboo; and, when required, a flat piece of iron or wood (shaped like a paper knife, but wider and longer) is introduced between the plate and the cake, and the latter is turned as dexterously as any expert cook would a pancake. By this simple process, the cassada bread—the negro's staff of life—is prepared for use. These cakes are rather thicker than the "Passover" biscuit of the Jews, and of similar size.

The juice of the *bitter* cassada, having been drawn from the sediment, and boiled over a slow fire till it has attained the consistence of treacle, (by which process the deleterious but very volatile principle is quite dissipated,) is seasoned with pepper and salt, and bottled for use. This sauce, which will keep good for many years, bears the name of *Casleep*, and is a principal ingredient of the far-famed West Indian *olla* called "Pepper Pot."

The sediment having been laid on mats and dried in the sun, (when it resembles arrow root, and may be used in a similar manner for invalids and children,) is formed into a thick starch; which, having been sprinkled with cold water, and laid on a cloth over a pan of boiling water, is closely covered, and soon becomes condensed by the steam into a viscid irregular mass: and this, having been dried in the sun until it is quite hard, is broken into small grains for use, and forms the Tapioca of commerce.

The rind of the cassada is employed, in a rotten state, at the Mauritius, as a substitute for mushroom spawn, for which it answers remarkably well.

Such then are the domestic uses to which a naturally deadly poison is applied: a proof, amidst the millions the creation affords, that there is nothing in that creation without its utility to mankind.

It may with truth be said, that even the very ant-hills, which abound here, may be turned to useful purposes. The trading goldsmiths, who are very ingenious, or they could never manufacture such beautiful ornaments as they do, particularly rose and snake chains, with their simple and uncouth materials, form their finest crucibles of the red earth or clay of the ant-hills. These, with an earthen chatty, full of saw-dust, or fine sand, and containing a small charcoal fire, under which is laid a short cylinder, of the size and shape of the spout of a small coffee pot: an anvil, a pair of tongs, (just like those that are used by cooks to turn a steak,) a piece of bamboo cane for a blow pipe, a few hammers, files, and some straight pieces of metal, compose the whole of their working implements.

The direct road from Trincomalé to Kandy, lies through the following villages: to Pallampoota rest-house, $10\frac{1}{2}$ miles: from thence to Wenyron Colom, $12\frac{1}{2}$ miles; to Gantelawa rest-house, $2\frac{1}{4}$ miles; to the Kandyan Limits, $4\frac{1}{4}$ miles; to Talgaha Ella, $2\frac{1}{2}$ miles; to Alootveva-Oya, excellent water, and post station,) 6 miles; to Nayapane Pass, $1\frac{3}{4}$ mile; to Gal-Oya right bank, (excellent rest-house, and post station,) $4\frac{3}{4}$ miles to Talbaddegalla, or Three-wells, $6\frac{3}{4}$ miles; to Haboorenné village, (large tank, and post station,) 3 miles; to Oulandangawa village and tank, $2\frac{1}{2}$ miles; to Innamallowe post station, $6\frac{3}{4}$ miles; to the Junction Kandy Road, $3\frac{3}{4}$ miles; to Damboola rest-house, $\frac{3}{4}$ mile; to Leenadera post station, 7 miles; to Nalandé post station, 7 miles.

to Palapatwella Ella rest-house, 4 miles; to Fort Macdowall, (the station of the assistant government agent and district judge,) 11 miles; to the top of Ballacadua Pass, 6¼ miles; to the Ferry of the Mavali-Ganga, 7¼ miles; and to Kandy, 2¾ miles. Total, from Trincomalé to Kandy, 113¼ miles.

Leaving Trincomalé, the next stage to the southward is Tamblegam, distant 15¼ miles. The road is sandy, and bordered with jungle; but, upon nearing the village, the country appears fertile and well cultivated, and the view of the bay is magnificent.

Kandellē lake supplies water for irrigating the paddee fields:—these either wear the verdant appearance of fields of young wheat, or the golden richness of that grain at maturity, as the season may be commencing, or advanced; and nothing can be more grateful to the eye, in this climate, than a field of young paddee, sugar-cane, or maize.

Tamblegam has a good rest-house, but is without a postholder, the road being seldom frequented by Europeans. May speculation and capital yet give it a different appearance; every road throughout the island be bordered with cultivated grounds and verdant pastures, and covered with the busy transporters of produce to ports of export!!—There is a Hindoo temple here, but it is scarcely worth a visit.

From Tamblegam to Kottiaar the distance is about 12½ miles, partly along the bed of a stream that issues from the lake, or tank, of Kandellé, and occasionally through fertile vallies, interspersed with dense jungle. Kottiaar is situated between the two branches of the Mavali-Ganga, both which are fordable.

From Kottiaar, the route southward is through Tapootorré, distant 9⅛ miles from Kottiaar, and 13½ from Anedivoo; chiefly through well-cultivated paddee fields, interspersed with palmyra, coco-nut, tamarind, and wild tea trees;—the country is rather populous, and the plains are covered with cattle, particularly buffalos.

A peculiar kind of rice is grown here, called by the natives *Patcherie*. Its grain, when boiled, is nearly twice the size of the Patna rice, and more oblong and egg-shaped, having thin strips of reddish skin attached to it, which is not altogether got rid of by the operation of pounding. This rice, not being so white as the Patna, or other varieties, is never set before Europeans, except when none other may be at hand; but it is of a more mucilaginous nature, and has a fine and peculiar flavor which makes it worthy of notice.

Ceylon, however, has such varieties of rice, that it is a hard task to make one's self acquainted with them. Linnæus limits his information upon the subject to the generic and trivial name of one species only; namely, *Oryza sativa*, class Hexandria, order Digynia: but the natives have several distinguishing names; such as, Elenkalyen, Gotiaran, Handiran, Podé-wee, Coloocombelé, Henetté, Ratte-wee, Mornaga-wee,

Pollé-ellé-wee, Karté-Elenkaylen, Panengeallyn, Mootomanica, Radecatten, Eki-chamba, Hadellé, Pondichambé, Noorocengau Chienetté, Moroega, Pallechederie, Mahama-wee, Gedeme-wee, Balema-wee, Seeniették, Manelworie, Perocriellé, Moe-raingew, Patjedroema, Kottéhandiram, Nandoohandiram, Ellé-wee, Kallukarayel, Ratkarayel, Sooderkarayel, Kahattenhamba, Kahaniman, Galpé-wee, Mukelu-wee, Ratkondé, Tawalvé, Sooderkuru-wee, Polevel or Hatiel, Kotukuru-wee, Roombolé, and Danchala.

These include both the Malabar and Singhalese names of paddee grown in the several districts. The natives grow both upland and lowland paddee; the former is not transplanted, and does not require so much irrigation as the latter, which is grown in swamp and water till nearly ripe.

When lowland paddee has shot up a few inches above the ground, it is transplanted by half a dozen plants at a time, in rows, subsequently inundated; by opening the dams of the reservoirs, and kept under water until the stalks become quite strong; the land is then drained, by opening the dams of each paddee field, and the sun soon dries it. The natives both reap with a sickle, as with us; and they also cut off the stalks about a foot below the ear separately, and bind them into small sheaves.

Paddee grows in loose spikes, like our common oat; and is divested of its husk (when it is called rice) by beating it with a heavy rice pounder, (*Mol-Kotta,*) made either of iron-wood or of very old *Kettule* wood, in a huge wooden mortar.

It is almost incredible to the observant traveller through the provinces of Ceylon, that this natural granary should ever have been dependent upon any other country for the grand staff of human life in India. That it has been most discreditable to the British government to attribute scarcity in this colony to natural causes, where, let the heat of the weather be what it may, irrigation is ever at command, by the application of industry, no one will deny: and that it was still more so to the Dutch government, to depend upon Java for supplying grain to Ceylon, until the presence of British cruizers upon the coasts, made it necessary to depend upon its own local resources for grain for its consumption, will be apparent to all whose inquiry may have enabled them to form an opinion upon this most important point of local polity.

In the year 1767, Java supplied 14,000 tons of rice to Ceylon and Banda, from the surplus of its produce, after all the wants of its own population had been provided for!!

At Tapootorré there is a very extensive tank; but want of capital unfortunately prevails, or this country would produce a thousand-fold where it now does one. Much depends upon the appointment of Governors; and such as are most active and energetic, and general officers, instead of civilians, are the best everywhere. The natives cannot reconcile what they call "arrack and onion," or "pumpkin Governors," with the dignity of the British nation.

These people are very observant;—they do not like to have a Governor who stoops to the degradation, in their opinion, of cutting his own vegetables, and filling every space of the public grounds, upon which his residence may stand, with pumpkins, &c., instead of encouraging horticulture amongst the natives, and depending upon the *markets* for supplying his own table.

Neither Sir Edward Barnes, nor (his, at one time much hoped for, and, as it was believed, intended successor in the government of Ceylon,) the much calumniated Lieut. General Sir Hudson Lowe, G. C. B., were ever stationary; but here, there, and everywhere; investigating the resources of the island, and running their chances of jungle fever and malaria, as well as other people; for they knew that nothing but cultivation could rid the island of those most unwelcome colonists.

Sir Hudson Lowe no sooner became thoroughly known at Ceylon, than he was praised as much as he was elsewhere calumniated; although but a very short time prior to his arrival at Colombo, as second in command, the prejudice against him appeared as insuperable there as it did in France; but it was as transient as a passing cloud, and those who were the most prejudiced, and the highest in the colony, were the first to express their opinion, that "Sir Hudson had been sacrificed to his soldier-like obedience of orders," and that "he could only be done justice to, in England and France, by Lord Bathurst's despatches, from *first* to *last*, including the "*most secret*" and "*most confidential*" *ones*, (addressed to Sir Hudson, as Governor of St. Helena,) being laid upon the table of the House of Commons!" What an exposé this would produce!

If fortunately this be read by some independent member of that Honorable House, who, in addition to moving for these papers, will act upon the motto, "Fiat justitia; ruat cœlum!" now is the time, befitting the occasion, for doing justice to as brave, generous, and intelligent an officer as ever yet drew sword in the service of his sovereign and his country. Under the auspices of such a Governor, Ceylon might yet display all its "capabilities."

The tourist having crossed the Virgel-Oya at Molcade, about 2⅜ miles from Anedivoo, (where boats are always at hand, and a palankin is soon ferried across for a few fanams,) will find a well-cultivated and delightful, but low country before him. The pagoda upon the left or north bank is of great antiquity, and worth examining.

From the Virgel-Oya to the village of Kaddiravallé, the distance is 4 miles; and from thence to Pannitchancanné, where the ferry is crossed over the river of that name, or Pannitchan-Oya, (which is most probably another branch of the Mavali-Ganga,) 9 miles. Wild orange, lime, and cinnamon trees abound here, and attract myriads of monkies.

From Pannitchancanné, the next stage is Kommollandam Mooné, distant 15¾ miles, a small and thinly populated village, with but little cultivation, and surrounded, except upon the east, by dense jungle: the road good throughout. The next village is Nalloor, distant 4½ miles, abounding in wild cinnamon, and a very beautiful species of air-plant, the petals of which are of a bright yellow, partially marked with dark purple specks.

At one time I collected several specimens of the indigenous *Orchideæ*, of the Mahagampattoo, some of which were tied to the pillars of the verandah, and others to the backs of chairs, where they both flowered and seeded, in as great perfection as in their native jungle.

Nalloor, called also by the natives *Bapoor*, is in a populous neighbourhood, and the country between it and Erraoor, 10 miles further south, extensively cultivated with paddee fields, and plantations of yams and plantains; but the road for the latter part is over very deep sand. Cotton is grown here, but in a limited quantity, instead of whitening thousands of acres with its produce.

Ferry-boats are always at hand, for crossing the Nalloor and Erraoor rivers; and a further distance of nine miles from the latter, which is salt, and a part of the Batticaloa river, ushers the tourist into that meridian of mosquitos,—Batticaloa.

Throughout the whole of this route, from Trincomalé to Batticaloa, game will be found in abundance, as well as the Guana, (*Lacerta Iguana* of Shaw), whose flesh equals, if it does not excel, that of the rabbit, in delicacy and flavor. There exists a great antipathy to its use at English tables but the native Dutch and Portuguese esteem it as much as the West Indians do, and make exquisite soups, curries, and ragouts with it. This animal burrows, the same as the rabbit, but is oviparous, and lays from fifty to seventy eggs, which are considered delicate food, after the first prejudice against them is overcome.

CHAP. XXXI.

Sailing directions along the easternmost coast of Ceylon—Batticaloa—Its small commercial importance—Civil and judicial departments—Island—Fort—Garrison and medical establishment—European Society, famed for its unanimity and hospitality—No Protestant church or chapel, clergyman or missionary—Roman Catholic chapels—Bazaar—Suggested establishment of a factory for curing fish—Anticipated increase of the coasting trade—Green beetle (Buprestis chrysis)—Employment of its irridescent elytra for ladies' dresses and other ornaments—Appearance of Batticaloa from the sea—Sandstone rocks—Veddah country—Mr. Lambias, secretary of the magistrate's court at Hambantotté, wanders into the Veddah country—Kindness of the Veddahs—Their language—Method of preserving flesh—Manner of shooting elephants—Veddahs visit Hambantotté—Primitive method of kindling fire—Veddah gratitude—Caste—Extensive area of forest lands occupied by the Veddahs—Their mode of disposing of their dead—Inhuman custom of the inhabitants of the Mahagampattoo—Author's endeavours to suppress it—Report to the Governor.

The following sailing directions along the easternmost coast of Ceylon, according to Captain Horsburgh's Directory, may assist the navigator, in the case of his being unsupplied with that valuable work.

"Agaus or Aganis, in about latitude 6° 50′ to 7° north, a space of land with some hillocks near the sea, is the easternmost part of the island, and situated about six miles east of the meridian of the Little Basses; being 1° 41 east from Point de Galle flag-staff, by chronometers, and in longitude 81° 58½ east, by mean of many lunar observations taken by Captain James Horsburgh, F. R. S., at various times.

"Between the hillocky land of Aganis and the hills to the N. Westward of the Little Basses, there is a considerable space of low land, excepting an isolated mount on it, which has a regular peaked appearance when viewed from the eastward; but resembles a saddle, having a gap in it, when seen from the southward.

"From the Little Basses to the land of Aganis, the course is N. N. E. ½ E., and N. N. E., distance ten leagues: between them the coast may be approached with safety to 17 or 18 fathoms, about 1½ league off shore, the depths on the bank being pretty regular, generally sandy bottom; and the edge of it, where there are 45 and 50 fathoms, is distant 4½ or 5 leagues from the shore.

"At a considerable distance inland from Aganis, in about latitude 7° north, there is a table mount, called Westminster Abbey, with a large square nob or turret on its north end; and there is another peaked hill near the sea, generally called Aganis Peak: these are in one with each other, bearing W. by S.

"The whole of the S. E. coast of Ceylon forms a convex curve, rounding gradually, without any conspicuous head-lands projecting into the sea. Between latitude 6° 30' and 7° north, is an advisable place to make the land, for ships running toward the eastern part of the island in the N. E. monsoon: taking care in the night to fall in with it to the northward of the Little Basses.

"Batticaloa River's entrance, in latitude 7° 44 north, and longitude 81° 50' east, by chronometers, bears from the land of Aganis, in latitude 7° north, about N. by W., distant 14½ or 15 leagues, the coast between them having a little convexity, and generally very low near the sea, interspersed with coco-nut topes and houses or small villages. In this space a ship may generally borrow to 19 or 20 fathoms, these depths being from 2½ to 3 or 4 miles off shore, and the bank of soundings extends out from it to the distance of 2½ or 3 leagues, where the depths are from 45 to 70 fathoms, but not always regular; for in a few places within 4 miles of the shore there are 35 and 38 fathoms. In working during the day, a ship may in some parts venture into 15 or 16 fathoms, and tack within two miles of the shore: but 20 or 22 fathoms is as near as it should be approached in the night: for in these depths, if the moon shine bright, the surf will be seen breaking on the sandy beach, or the noise of it may sometimes be heard with the land wind. From some of the small projecting points, foul ground is said to extend about 1 or 1½ mile, rendering it prudent not to come under 20 or 22 fathoms near them, particularly in the night.

"The coast contiguous to Batticaloa is low, but several circumjacent mountains or hills, situated inland, are conspicuous in sailing along this part of the island; the most remarkable and highest of these is the Friar's Hood, in latitude 7° 29½ north, and longitude 81° 36' east, about 4½ or 5 leagues from the sea, and leans over to the left, resembling a friar's hood, when bearing to the S. Westward, but has the form of a pyramid, when it bears to the N. Westward. To the southward of it there is another mountain, somewhat similar in appearance, called the False Hood, which is not so high as the former. Far inland, about 7 leagues to the westward of the Friar's Hood, there is a round conical hill, called the Kettle Bottom, visible in clear weather; and on the middle of the great level plain, in latitude 7° 49 north, is situated, about 6 leagues W. by N. from the entrance of Batticaloa river, the Sugar Loaf, a sharp isolated cone. Nearly abreast the Friar's Hood, but rather to the southward, is the entrance of a river which extends a great way inland, having to the southward a pagoda, among a grove of coco-nut trees, at a place called Tricoil.

"Batticaloa river is narrow at the entrance, not discernible except from the northward, the opening being in that direction; but it may be known by a house and flag-staff, where the colors are usually shown to passing ships. There is 6 feet water on the bar, (at low water,) and the tide rises about 2 or 3 feet perpendicularly; high water at four hours on full and change of moon, but not always regular.

"The Fort is four or five miles up the river, on an island where water may be procured, by landing casks at the wharf and rolling them to and from the well. Plenty of wood may be cut near the bar on the river's banks.

"The anchorage in the road is not always safe in the N. E. monsoon, when a gale from that quarter may be liable to happen from September to February; but in the S. W. monsoon it is safe. Ships generally anchor to the N. W. or westward of the reef, with the entrance of the river about south, the Friar's Hood S. S. W., distant about two miles from the river's entrance, abreast of a cluster of rocks projecting from the shore to the northward of the river."

Batticaloa is, unfortunately, of small commercial importance, owing to its having but little connexion with the southern and western provinces, and no very great coasting trade with the northern province, or coast of Coromandel.

The revenue and customs' duties of the district are superintended by an assistant government agent, who is also the district judge.

The island of Batticaloa is about four miles in extent, and defended by a small square fort of four bastions, capable of mounting from twenty to thirty guns, and containing a barrack, magazine, and a spacious house for the commandant.

The garrison consists of a company of the Ceylon rifle corps, and a native medical sub-assistant for the hospital duties.

At one period, when the necessity of watchfulness against Kandyan irruptions was a matter of primary consequence, this fortification was of the utmost utility, for the Kandyans always took care to keep out of the reach of shot; and, within that range, every native subject of the British flag felt secure, both in person and property: but it has no longer an internal enemy to threaten it; and, in the event of a naval war, the fort would afford sufficient protection to such small craft as might shelter in the river.

The limited society of Batticaloa has long been famed for hospitality and friendship, notwithstanding the variety of changes to which it has been, like all our small colonial settlements, continually subject. At a distance from the other stations, and depending upon unanimity for the chief comforts of life, the European military and civil servants seem to have successfully studied, and, spite of the fable, adopted, "il modo di piacere a tutti;" for I have never once met an individual of either service, who was not sorry, *malgré* the mosquitos, to quit that station: and several instances are recorded of the expression of the kindliest feelings, by farewell parties, and occasionally by presentations of plate, at parting.

It is remarkable, that although Batticaloa has neither Protestant church nor chapel, and is without either a clergyman or missionary to perform divine service, it has two very neat Roman Catholic chapels, which are built of stone, with tiled roofs, and are the best ornamented in the island. The *Fishers* are Roman Catholics, and occupy one chapel exclusively to their own use; the other, is open to all comers.

The Bazaar, as it is called, is a straggling village of huts throughout the island, occupied by venders of fruit, vegetables, fish, poultry, eggs, rice, and other articles of native consumption; all which, are abundant and cheap.

As the coast abounds with fish, a factory for curing it for the Kandyan markets, and for exportation, might be established here; for any quantity of salt may be obtained from Hambantotté during the S. W. monsoon. This could not fail to prove a profitable speculation, a ready sale being at all times certain, as well as quick returns for the outlay of capital; and the consequent increase of the coasting trade would prove an additional source of revenue to the crown.

Batticaloa has a very pretty appearance from the sea; and the adjacent country is both fertile and romantic. The shore is bold, and those immense sandstone rocks, known as the "Friar's Hood," "Elephant Rock," and "Pagoda Rock," afford excellent land-marks to the navigator.

The beautiful green beetle (*Buprestis chrysis*), so much esteemed at home and upon the continent of India, is very common here. The most splendid ladies' dresses are ornamented with the elytra of this insect; which are also mounted in gold, and formed into necklaces, tiaras, and armlets: for the colors they display, arising from an unrivalled richness of tints, brilliance of metallic lustre, and the irridescence of their ever-varying hues, according to the change of light in which they are viewed, may be considered the most splendid in nature.

Batticaloa is bounded on the west by the country of the wild Veddahs (*Veddah Ratté*); of which most extraordinary people, there exists a great difference of opinion: for whilst some aver that they are the aborigines of Ceylon, others are as positive of their descent from a race of Malabar fugitives.

The best information in my power to obtain, when I was almost, it may be said, upon the spot, (for the Mahagampattoo district extends very nearly to the confines of the Veddah country,) I derived from Mr. William Lambias, the secretary of the revenue and sitting magistrate's court at Hambantotté, during the time that I presided there, in the years 1826, 1827.

السلطان محمد معین الدین [illegible]

[illegible]

Mr. Lambias, who was an excellent shot and had in his time bagg'd many a "tusker," having, upon one occasion, rambled rather too far from Mattawillé, in the Nadekadoe district, at present part of this (the eastern) province, fell in with a party of straggling Veddahs, armed with bows and arrows, who had several dogs with them, by whose barking, he was first made aware of his danger.

Expecting nothing less than death, Mr. Lambias determined to sell his life at as dear a rate, as any one man with a couple of guns, could possibly do against so many; but he was in no danger, for one of the Veddahs directed another "to bring the Portuguese some flesh and honey," and thereupon laying down his arrows, he respectfully approached Mr. Lambias with repeated *salaams*;—this inspired confidence, and Mr. Lambias, addressing them in low Singhalese, inquired if they had many elephants in their country. They understood him, and one of them ran and brought some arrows to him, which, he said, had been headed by a smith at China-Kanda; to whom they had taken some honey and bees' wax, together with a Moöua (*Cervus Aristotelis*), in return for the arrow heads, some of which were about three inches long, and of the exact shape of the leaf of the Naghas (*Mesua ferrea*, L.) or iron-wood tree; and the rest about fourteen inches long, and an inch and a half broad, for killing wild buffalos and elephants.

These savages were extremely civil; and so far from offering Mr. Lambias the slightest annoyance, they asked him to their village, which greatly surprised him, because he had always understood that they lived in trees. In full confidence in his safety, (for he acknowledged to me, that "he had abandoned all idea of danger from the moment he heard their original conversation respecting himself," and he was perfect master of both high and low Singhalese, as well as of Tamul,) he visited their village, as they called it, upon their promising to conduct him to Mattawillé afterwards.

Although these people resembled the Singhalese, and spoke to him in that tongue, their general language amongst each other, seemed, to his ear, to be a mixture of Malabar and Singhalese. Mr. Lambias did not see any huts in trees, and their village consisted of straggling sheds, constructed like the habitations of the lower classes of Singhalese, with sticks and mud, (the smoke issuing from every aperture,) and surrounded by thorn bushes, scattered about without regard to order.

When he asked them if any of them lived in trees, they shook their heads; and, pointing towards the Kandyan mountains, said, "those in the high and very far country did." All the Veddah party had scraps of cotton round the waist, and chewed betel. which must have been obtained at some bazaar. They talked much of Kattregam Dewalé, where two of them had been, as well as of Hambantotté.

The Veddahs preserve the flesh of deer and buffalos in honey, and stow it away in hollow trees, as described by Knox, for use when fresh game is scarce; and they also cut it into long slices and dry it in the sun; but I never yet knew any one disposed to partake of it, for the best Ceylon venison is rather *lean* food; and, as to dried deer flesh, it is merely fit for the grater.

The Veddah mode of killing the larger animals, such as the elephant, wild buffalo, and samver, is by lying on their backs, holding the bow with their toes, (which they use with the same facility that we do our fingers,) and drawing the arrow to the head with all the force of both hands, let fly: and so near do they contrive to place themselves to the elephant, unseen, that they seldom fail to hit the animal in its most vulnerable part, viz. behind the ear. They wing their arrows with the deep red feathers of the peacock.

The Veddahs showed Mr. Lambias various roots, (their chief subsistence except game and wild honey, of which they have abundance,) and a wild species of Brinjal (*Solanum insanum*, L.), called *Wal-Bambuttoo* by the Singhalese.

During my residence at Hambantotté, two village Veddahs were brought to me, who were any thing but fine specimens of the *Homo Sapiens*. Their jargon was with difficulty understood by my Malay interpreter, although they comprehended his Singhalese easily enough; and Mr. Lambias being absent on leave, I had not the benefit that I otherwise should have derived from his acquaintance with their dialect.

These Veddahs were not more than five feet two inches in height; their hands small, but feet long and flat; hair matted, and tied in a bunch at the back of the head; large bushy beard, almost covering the face; eyes small, piercing, and constantly in motion to the right and left, and their ears seemed almost as restless as their eyes. They showed no surprise at a looking-glass, nor any of the curiosity of the monkey to see what was at the back. I gave each a Malay knife, some nails, a common bazaar handkerchief, a betel knife, some tobacco, several sorts of seeds, and cuttings of the cassada; at which latter they at first sneered, but upon my showing them how to plant it, and giving them some specimens of the roots that would be the produce of their labour, they seemed more pleased than otherwise.

Upon being told, by the Mohandriam, to show how they kindled a fire, they proved their independence of flint and steel for that purpose; for in less than three minutes, with two dry sticks, of which, one was hollowed a little in the middle, and the other pointed at one end, the elder Veddah, steadying the former on the ground, by placing a foot upon each extremity, inserted the latter in the hole, and then whisked it about rapidly between his hands, after the manner of making chocolate; whilst his companion, holding a handful of dry leaves to the orifice, caught the sparks elicited by the friction, which he soon blew into a flame.

Some claret was given them, which they received in their joined hands, so as to form a substitute for a cup; but it had scarcely entered their mouths ere it was spouted over the floor, whilst their countenances exhibited all the effect that the most nauseous medicine could have had upon the palate.

These people defraud the Singhalese who venture to barter with them, by concealing a lump of clay in the centre of each cake of bees' wax. It is so artfully effected, that it cannot be discovered, unless by means of an intense light, or by breaking the cakes; and therefore the Singhalese think it safer to put up with the roguery, than, by exposing it, to run the risk of Veddah revenge.

Nevertheless, they have virtues; and, from what I saw of these two Veddahs, I would no more fear going through their country, (unarmed,) than, except for the comparative comforts one must abandon in the one, for the privations of the other, to travel in any other part of the island; for I am convinced that it only requires tact and kindness to bring the wildest of them within the pale of civilized life.

Upon being informed, in the usual way, that "they might go," the Veddahs *salaamed* very low, touching their foreheads with the palms of their hands. One of them having dropped a small nail, instead of taking it up with his fingers, did it equally well with his toes, which he seemed to have just as much at command.

About two months after this interview, (at the conclusion of which I had directed every kindness to be shown them throughout the district,) a couple of elephant's tusks, nearly six feet in length, found their way into my front virandah at night; but the Veddahs, who must have conveyed them, never gave me any subsequent opportunity of rewarding them. What lesson in gratitude and delicacy even a Veddah may teach!

It appears to me quite irreconcileable with various accounts of these people, that, notwithstanding their seclusion from the rest of the community by their savage life and roving habits, they belong to the highest in the classification of Singhalese castes; viz. the *Goewansé* of the highlands, and *Vellalé* of the maritime provinces, (cultivators of the soil); by whom, all temple and state honors have been monopolized from immemorial time; although, according to the specification of the employments peculiar to each caste, agriculture is the exclusive privilege of the *Goewansé*.

The Veddahs occupy an immense area of forest lands, (which may be estimated at a rough calculation, at 1500 square miles,) distinguished as Veddah Ratté, and Maha-Veddah Ratté; the former, in the district of Bintenné, and the latter, in Wallassé and a part of Ouva, to the east and south-eastward of the Kandyan mountains, and to the westward of the district of Batticaloa in the eastern, and of a part of the Mahagampattoo in the southern, province.

Divided into two distinct communities, one of which Europeans denominate "the wild," and the other "the village" Veddahs, these savages seldom meet but to commit hostilities; for the former, who build their huts in trees, and display no trace of even incipient civilization, are held in great dread by the latter, who congregate in villages, live in huts, as already described in Mr. Lambias's account of them, and cultivate, if raking the earth, scattering seeds, and sticking roots into the ground, may be so defined, small patches of Korakan (*Cynosurus Coracanus*, L.), maize (*Zea Mais*, L.), and a species of the *Arum esculentum*, called by the Singhalese *Wal-Kidahran*.

The Veddahs observe no rites of marriage or of sepulture, neither do they give their children "rice names," after the custom of the Singhalese; but they believe that they propitiate the great demon with offerings; and resort to the abominable custom of consigning their dead to the wild beasts of the jungle, instead of burning, or burying, the bodies. If, however, they do not anticipate the death of their relatives, but wait for that event, ere they throw their bodies into the jungle, they are more humane and civilized than their neighbours of the Mahagampattoo; where, so recently as the year 1826, many cases occurred of parents, brothers, sisters, and children, having been consigned, during

"That awful pause, dividing life from death,"

with a portion of rice and a chattie of water placed by the side of each dying individual, to the "*tender mercies*" of bears, leopards, crocodiles, and jackalls.

But, notwithstanding my great anxiety and strenuous endeavours to suppress such inhuman and detestable practices in the district, my avowed determination, which was proclaimed by beat of *Tam-a-tam* in every village and bazaar, to commit all who might be guilty of, or accessory to, this species of murder, for trial by the supreme court of judicature, and my successful intervention in several instances, through the zealous co-operation of the native headmen, I much fear that I failed in altogether preventing their clandestine continuance.—In the hope that it may not be considered supererogatory by the reader, I insert an extract from my official report to His Excellency the Governor of Ceylon, in the year 1827, upon this subject.

"4thly. I have put a stop, as far as my preventive means could enforce it, to the unnatural exposition of parents, when considered in a dying state, to the wild beasts of the jungle, by their own children; and, in several instances, I have succeeded in impressing upon the minds of the natives, a conviction of the iniquity and ingratitude of thus disposing of the authors of their being, at that awful period."

CHAP. XXXII.

Route southward continued—Naypattri-Moonné—Wambimodoo—Asclepias gigantea—Its medicinal properties—Tourist recommended to travel only by day—Wild beasts abundant—The jungle bear will attack man, notwithstanding its frugivorous and insectivorous habits—Field for the sportsman and naturalist—Caution necessary in entering a jungle—William Gisborne, Esq., an excellent elephant shot—Death of Major Haddock—Natives killed by elephants—Elephant catchers—Pliny s account of Ceylon elephants—Distinction between the Indian and African elephant, according to Cuvier—Ceylon ivory—Anecdote respecting elephants' petit-toes being sent to the late Earl Bathurst—Lord Charles Henry Somerset's enigma—The sloth—Squirrels—Maucauco—Ternate bat—Racoon—White baboon—Black baboon—Brown monkey—Anecdote of a Wanderoo—Summary of migratory and indigenous birds—Native summary of indigenous birds.

Leaving Batticaloa, the next stage is to Naypattri-Moonné, distant 17¼ miles, where there is a tolerable rest-house, but the neighbourhood presents little in the shape of cultivation to attract attention; from thence to Wambimodoo, where there is also a temporary rest-house, the distance is 7¾ miles.

The line of road abounds with the gigantic swallow-wort (*Asclepias gigantea*, L., *Calotropis mudarii*, R. Brown), *Manughawael* of the Singhalese, a beautiful plant when in flower; its corolla being of a lilac color, powdered, and the leaf a bright sea-green. The native doctors dry the root, which they consider a powerful sudorific; this has the extraordinary property of gelatinizing with heat, and becoming liquid as it cools. It is considered efficacious in rheumatism and cutaneous diseases, and is exhibited in syrups and decoctions. This plant has been already noticed in page 123, but without reference to its medicinal properties. There is another indigenous species, which the Singhalese call *Walanghuna*.

This is the wildest part of Ceylon, except the Veddah country, and the tourist is recommended to travel only during the day, for elephants, bears, and leopards abound throughout the district; and, in the rainy season, the former, being driven by mosquitos from the jungles, infest the roads and plains almost as much by day as by night.

The jungle bear (*Ursus labiatus*) is quite black, and a very awkward acquaintance, unless one is well armed. It is much dreaded by the natives, for it will attack man, notwithstanding that some historians aver to the contrary, because its general food consists of fruit, honey, and insects. Would they have put their theory to the test of experience, by trusting themselves near a hungry Ceylon bear?

This animal obtains fruit and honey without difficulty, being an excellent climber, and devours insects, particularly white ants, with great facility, through the elongation of the cartilaginous part of the nose, and of the extremity of the under jaw, which act as prehensile instruments, as effectually for the purpose as the tongue of the *Manis tetradactylus*, already described.

If the tourist be both a sportsman and a collector of specimens in natural history, he has only to diverge to the right, throughout this route, to have as much elephant, bear, deer, samver, wild hog, chetah, jackall, monkey, squirrel, and guana shooting as he pleases, amid the extensive forests with which this part of the country abounds; for it is so seldom traversed by Europeans, that the *feræ naturæ* have it all their own way:—but the greatest caution is necessary, whenever, led by the eagerness of pursuing his object, the naturalist enters a Ceylon jungle, and one barrel of his gun should always be kept loaded with ball, as a reserve, (I strongly recommend the American plan, of cutting a small portion of the surface of two balls flat, and screwing them together,) for as the jungles are interspersed with small patches of herbage, he may suddenly find himself in most unwelcome company, unless actually in quest of elephants, upon turning the corner of a jungle clump, by being close upon a herd of these animals. If to windward of an elephant, he will not have been allowed to approach very near without receiving timely notice, by the animal's trumpeting; but if to leeward, he may approach very close without much danger, its sense of sight being very inferior to that of smell.

The late William Gisborne, Esq., of the civil service, (who has immortalized his name in Ceylon by forming the Kirimé canal, which was completed under his personal superintendence, whilst collector of Tangalle,) would approach an elephant, to leeward, so closely as to touch it; he would then clap his hands and shout, and, upon the animal looking round, plant a two ounce ball in the centre of the *os frontis*, (where the bone plates are extremely thin,) or immediately *behind the ear;* when, within the twinkling of an eye, the stately animal would "lick the dust."

It is surprising, when the great risk is considered, and the quantum of nerve required to face an elephant within a few yards, that so few accidents occur to English sportsmen. Major Haddock, of the 97th regiment, was the only one killed by an elephant for many years, during my residence in the island; but several others had narrow escapes from the leviathan of the jungle.

In the years 1826-7, several native labourers were killed by elephants, in the Mahagampattoo district, whilst harmlessly going to their daily work. This generally happened upon suddenly turning the corner of the jungle; and two Singhalese were killed on the same morning, just after having left their own cottages; so that I am not at all disposed to concur in opinion with those who attribute "generosity and magnanimity to the elephant, in its wild state," for I have had very many proofs of its being a naturally vicious and destructive animal.

It is by no means uncommon for elephants to enter villages at night, remove the thatch from houses containing a store of paddee, deliberately help themselves, and walk off leisurely before daybreak. The damage done to paddee and other fields in the course of a night is so great, that whenever these destructive animals are known to be near, watchmen are stationed under a shed upon a platform fixed upon four lofty poles, (having a rustic ladder at one side,) or against trees, commanding a view of the whole field, to give an alarm upon their approach.

The apparently unwieldy bulk of the elephant is no bar to its activity, for its common walk will keep a man upon the run, or native jog-trot; and, when put to its mettle in pursuit, very few horses will beat it in swiftness.

When elephants emerge from the jungle, they are of a dusky red color, from the quantity of sand and red earth with which they cover their hides, as a preventive against the jungle tick, and their much-dreaded foe, the tiny mosquito.

Gangs of elephant catchers from Bengal, under the command of a captain in the army, are occasionally employed to procure elephants for the East India Company's service. The Ceylon "Elephant Establishment" is attached to the civil engineer and surveyor general's department.

The island has been famous for its elephants from time immemorial. Pliny has thus recorded their superiority to the elephants of India, "Elephantas ii multo majores erant quam quos fert India;" and the immortal Cuvier has more recently defined the existing difference between the African, and Ceylon (or Indian) elephant: "Elephas Capensis, fronte convexâ, lamellis molarium rhomboidalibus."—"Elephas Indicus, fronte plano-concavâ, lamellis molarium arcuatis undatis."

The tusks* of the male elephant (but scarcely one in a hundred has tusks exceeding the size of the grubbers common to all) are from six to seven feet long, and those of the female about half that length. The *modus copulandi*, long doubted, has ceased to be a mystery, and is the same as that of the horse.

Ceylon ivory is considered the most valuable for all the purposes of the manufacturer, being whiter, of finer grain, and retaining its whiteness much longer, than any

* Amongst the prize property captured in Kandy, in 1815, there were 289 elephants' tusks, weighing altogether 5951½ lbs avoirdupois.

other. There is no probability of any visible decrease in the immense herds of wild elephants, notwithstanding the daily slaughter that takes place in the interior, (where it is not uncommon for a single sportsman to kill several before breakfast, and some have been known to "bag" from forty to fifty, sometimes more, in a week,) as well as in some districts of the maritime provinces, until cultivation shall have made greater inroads upon their jungle *rights* and *royalties;* for thousands of square miles of land, equal, in point of fertility, to any in the known world, are now occupied solely by wild beasts; of which, elephants are the most destructive.

An anecdote was at one time very current at Ceylon, of "Elephants' *petit-toes*" having been anonymously sent to the late Earl Bathurst, at that time His Majesty's secretary of state for the colonies, at the suggestion of the late Samuel Daniels, Esq., the ranger of the woods and forests; which, from the known eccentricity of that facetious gentleman, is far from improbable. The present was rather an extraordinary one to a secretary of state for the colonies, not celebrated for a propensity to Apician gormandizing. If the facts were as stated, the preparatory pickling of the "*petit-toes*" in strong toddy vinegar and cayenne pepper had failed of their usual effects in obviating putrefaction, and that when the case was opened in his Lordship's presence, if all the sewers in London had been at once let loose, into what the late Lord Charles Henry Somerset characterized as "*the grand sewer, requiring a second Hercules to cleanse it,*" the stench could not have been more intolerable or diffusive than that emitted from the elephants' *petit-toes,* and their pickle.—His Lordship's meaning as regards the "grand sewer," although quite an enigma to *me,* may not be difficult of solution by those who were in his Lordship's confidence, at the period of his return from the Cape of Good Hope.

Elephants' tusks are occasionally found buried in the jungle, but whether it be done by the animals themselves, or, for concealment, by the natives, is hitherto hypothetical. Even in districts apparently the most barren, the bones of innumerable animals (those of the elephant in particular) meet the eye in almost every direction, rotting where they lie, and altogether neglected, although they might be converted into valuable manure; and the jungles and plains are in many places strewed with the cast antlers of deer, of which, I have had a cart-load picked up in the course of a few hours: but as the natives now begin to find a market for deer horns, they will soon reap the benefit of collecting and selling them for exportation to Europe.

Of the lesser animals the most worthy of powder and shot, exclusively of those already named, are, the Sloth (*Bradypus dactylus,* L.) with two toes, as its trivial name implies, on its fore feet; this animal has no tail, and is much smaller than the South

American Sloth (*B. tridactylus*, L.);—a variety of Squirrels (including the *Sciurus volans*, L.), called by the general name of *Dandooleyna* by the Singhalese; of which, one large species is very beautiful, having a pink nose, a deep glossy black and bright yellow body, the fur of which is long and silky, and may be easily tamed;—the Maucauco (*Lemur tardigradus*, L.), whose trivial name is a sad misnomer, for the little animal is remarkably active; it is of a pretty light brown color, inclining to that of burnt T. Senna, has no tail, hind toes short and pointed, and the others round;—the Ternate Bat (*Vespertilio Vampyrus*, L.), commonly called the flying fox, about the size of our common squirrel (*Sciurus vulgaris*, L.), whose large black leathern wings, which, when extended, are from four to five feet between the extremities, give it a terrific appearance; and, notwithstanding that its habits are well known to be frugivorous, it would be presumptuous to doubt a positive affirmation of the celebrated Linnæus, that it sucks the blood of a human being, sleeping in the open air, whilst fanning the air with its wings;—the Racoon (*Ursus Lotor*, L.);—the White Baboon, called by the Singhalese *Tannia* or *Wannia*, which I have never seen, and it may be an Albino; but the natives relate strange stories of its lying in ambush and attacking women and children;—the Black Baboon, with white beard, (*Simia Silenus*, L., and *Macacus Silenus*, C.), *Wanderoo* of the Singhalese;—and the Brown Monkey, *Rilawah* or *Rollawai* of the Singhalese.

On the homeward voyage, in the ship Princess Charlotte, in 1819, I had a *Wanderoo* on board, which showed a great degree of cunning, as well as of partiality for English cookery. His residence was under the tarpauling cover of the launch, from whence he would keep a look-out upon the cook, whenever meat was being roasted at the caboose fire. Jackoo usually remained very quiet, taking an occasional peep at the spit, until the joint before the fire was nearly dressed; and when the cook temporarily left the caboose, the animal would jump from cover, rub his paws over the surface of the meat, and lick them, repeating it until retreat was necessary to his own safety, and leaving it for the cook to discover the plunderer of the fine brown surface of the cuddy dinner, who never failed to accuse the soldiers' children of it. But justice determined that Jackoo should be detected; and having been caught in the act, the animal showed such dread of the consequences, both by his face and manner, and by scratching his side, and then extending his open paws, as if pleading, in extenuation, that they were free from grease, that the cook was more mercifully disposed than one would have expected. "You would (said he to the culprit) speak if you could; but although your hands may be clean, you smack your lips, and some of the *brown* is upon your whiskers, which is enough, if I had not caught you, to prove you guilty:

however, as you are a black fellow, and don't know better, I'll let you off this time." In justice to Jackoo, it must not be omitted, that he was never known to repeat his attempt upon the cuddy dinner. He weathered the cold off the Cape of Good Hope very well, (from which circumstance, the crew named him "Corporal Hardy," and dressed him *en militaire*, with a corporal's chevron on the arm,) but died from eating too much fruit, soon after being landed at Cape Town.

In this, and the adjoining district of the Mahagampattoo, the patches of water, bordering upon jungle, are very well tenanted by the Black-backed Goose (*Anas Melanotos**), Spotted-billed Duck (*A. Poecilorynсha*), Wigeon (*A. Penelope*), Pelican (*Pelicanus Onocratolus*, Lin.), white, with a bag at its throat, for carrying its finny prey; Common Kingfisher (*Alcedo Ispida*), Violet Kingfisher (*A. Coromanda*), Pied Kingfisher (*A. rudis*), Smyrna Kingfisher (*A. Smyrnensis*), Spoonbill (*Platalea Leucorodia*, Lin.), Grey Sandpiper (*Tringa Squatarola*, Lin.), White-headed Ibis (*Tantalus Leucrocephalus*), Black-headed Ibis (*T. melanocephalus*), Curlew (*Scolopax arquata*, Lin.), Snipe (*S. Gallinago*, Lin.), and Jack Snipe (*S. Gallinula*, Lin.), both of which latter are very numerous, and equal, if not superior, to their kinds in England.

I have heard of the Woodcock (*Scolopax Rusticola*, Lin.) having been killed in the interior, but I never saw it in any part of the country where I have travelled; nevertheless, its presence is by no means improbable on that account, for a great variety of migratory birds periodically visit the island; of which, the most numerous is the Flamingo (*Phœnicopterus ruber*, Lin.). These birds come in large flocks, and plant centinels to give notice of an enemy's approach; hence the Dutch sportsman's maxim, "the longer the gun, the better the chance of killing flamingos." But the kingfishers, on the contrary, appear as if they were disposed to be domesticated; for they take post upon the stumps of trees, close to houses, and wherever there is water, and allow one to approach very near before they take the trouble to move off, and then to a short distance only.

The jungles bordering upon this line of road contain many a novel and undescribed species of the indigenous genera, worthy of the attention of the Ornothologist; for the birds that are named in the following catalogue, exclusively of those elsewhere noticed in these pages, as being commonly known to have their *habitat* in Ceylon, form but a small proportion of the whole: viz.—

The Malabar Hornbill (*Buceros Malabaricus*), Yellow-throated Toucan (*Ramphastos*

* The birds are named agreeably to Smellie's translation of Buffon's Natural History, and Latham's Indian Ornithology, unless specified to the contrary.

dicolorus), Preacher Toucan (*R. precatus*), Indian Parrot (*Psittacus Orientalis*), Ceylon Parakeet (*P. Zeylanicus*), Pygmy Parakeet (*P. pygmæus*), Boulboul Shrike (*Lanius Boulboul*), Indian Roller (*Coracias Indica*), Grey-tailed Roller (*C. vagabunda*), Fairy Roller (*C. Puella*), Faciated Curucui (*Trogon fasciatus*), Spotted Curucui (*T. maculatus*), Indian Vulture (*Vultur Indicus*), Cheela Falcon (*Falco Cheela*), Rhomboidal Falcon (*F. Rhombeus*), Black-and-white Falcon (*F. melanoleucos*), Brown Hawk (*F. Badius*), Ceylonese Eared Owl (*Strix Ceylonensis*), Coromandel Eared Owl (*S. Coromanda*), Indian Eared Owl (*S. Bakkamuna*), Tufted Fly-catcher (*Muscicapa Comata*), Red-vented Fly-catcher (*M. Hæmorrhousa*), Yellow-breasted Fly-catcher (*M. Melanictera*), Cinnamon Fly-catcher (*M. Cinnamomea*), Malabar Lark (*Alauda Malabarica*), Cinnamon Creeper (*Certhia Cinnamomea*), Indigo Creeper (*C. parietum*), Yellow-billed Creeper (*C. Lepida*), Tufted Creeper (*C. Erythrorynchos*), Red-crowned Barbet (*Bucco rubricapillus*), Yellow-cheeked Barbet (*B. Zeylanicus*), Blue Barbet (*B. Gerini*), Green Barbet (*B. viridis*), Red-headed Cuckoo (*Cuculus Pyrrhocephalus*), Bombay Goat-sucker (*Caprimulgus Asiaticus*), Green Wagtail (*Motacilla viridis*), Pink Warbler (*Sylvia Caryophyllacea*), Green and Yellow Fig-eater (*S. Zeylonica*), Black-necked Warbler (*S. nigricollis*), Tailor Warbler (*S. sutoria*), Gaur Bunting (*Emberiza Asiatica*), Olive Bunting (*E. olivacea*), Red-winged Woodpecker (*Picus miniatus*), Malacca Woodpecker (*P. Malaccensis*), Ceylon Finch (*Fringilla Zeylanica*), Green-rumped Finch (*F. butyracea*), Yellow-crowned Thrush (*Turdus Ochrocephalus*), Long-tailed Thrush (*T. macrourus*), Yellow Grosbeak (*Loxia flavicaus*), Yellow-rumped Grosbeak (*L. Hordacea*), Eastern Grosbeak (*L. undulata*), Brown Grosbeak (*L. fusca*), Ash-headed Grosbeak (*L. Indica*), Malabar Grosbeak (*L. Malabarica*), Dwarf Grosbeak (*L. minima*), Black Tanagre (*Tanagra atrata*), Indian Plover (*Charadrius Indicus*), Ceylon Rail (*Rallus Zeylanicus*), Indian Jacana (*Parra Indica*), Crested Gallinule (*Gallinula cristata*), Common Hoepoe (*Upupa Epops*), Purple-shouldered Pigeon (*Columba Phœnicoptera*), Spotted Green Pigeon (*C. maculata*), Ring Dove (*C. palumbus*, Lin.), Turtle Dove (*C. Turtur*, Lin.).

Of the genus *Columba* there is a great variety, from the Cinnamon Pigeon to the smallest of the innumerable doves of the jungle. Some of the latter are of the most brilliant hues, particularly the Great, and the Lesser Green or Bamboo Dove. The wild Blue Pigeon is very common throughout the island, and particularly upon the coasts of the southern and eastern provinces.

Of widow birds, (as they are called, but they probably belong to the genus *Upupa*, the two Ceylon varieties are, the rufous brown with black crest, and the white and black with raven black crest. The Singhalese call the former *Rattoo Pili Hora*, and the latter, *Sudu Pili Hora*. These birds are more plentiful upon the Kalu-Ganga, than in any other part of the island; but there is no known instance of their having survived twenty four hours' confinement in a cage.

Orlotans (*Emberiza Hortulana*) are abundant, particularly in the southern province; and the common house sparrow is as plentiful as in any part of Europe.

I wish I could offer the naturalist a more detailed list of the Ceylon Birds; but this will materially assist him with his native guides in collecting specimens, which can be classed, at leisure, agreeably to the System he may prefer.

1 Monara
2 Rana Koka
3 Rajah Ali
4 Walé-Kukoola
5 Dia Kawa
6 Karawal Koka
7 Indoora Koka
8 Maha Koka
9 Koka
10 Kaportoo Koka
11 Seraa
12 Mäe Seraa
13 Söemba Seraa
14 Getta Seraa
15 Rena Kewa
16 Dia Toedewa
17 Beli Kawa
18 Maana
19 Wattoevandewa
20 Kebbe Lita
21 Baké-moena
22 Basa
23 Metti Koroewaka
24 Korowaka
25 Kirilla
26 Koleya
27 Rena Wattoewa
28 Kobeya
29 Kas-wattoewa
30 Pili Hodoowa
31 Hella Leniya
32 Kaha Koroola
33 Battoe Goya
34 Alloo Kobeya
35 Nil Kobeya
36 Rattoo Pili-Hora
37 Sudu-Kalu Pili-Hora
38 Poto-Koroola
39 Goon Kawediya
40 Tootiya
41 Wie Koroola
42 Key Koroola
43 Kolowêwa
44 Mäe Rotorewa
45 Malletjé
46 Girrawa
47 Laboo Girrawa
48 Rena Girrawa
49 Battoo Girrawa
50 Kandoo Panikia
51 Pooroo Kandata
52 Kandata
53 Mäe Kandata
54 Awetja
55 Parendella
56 Oekosoewa
57 Demeditiya
58 Weserima
59 Politija
60 Haban-Koola
61 Olema
62 Kurundu Kobeya
63 Maha-nilla-Guya
64 Iri-Kahawa
65 Getté Poli-Hoedoowa
66 Kottoreya
67 Moodoo Kirilla
68 Gaulama
69 Weggi-Lena
70 Koerool-Goya
71 Kalu Koerool-Goya
72 Mal-Koha

J. W. Bennett del.

W. C. Edwards foulp

A species of Indigenous Thea L.
presented by Assistant Staff Surgeon Crawford – Batticaloa.

CHAP. XXXIII.

Pensile nests of the Yellow Grosbeak—Its partiality for the fire fly—Tailor warbler—Mode of forming its nest—Its familiarity—Employment of a botanist skilled in practical chymistry suggested—Official employés incapable of affording much time to philosophical researches—Route southward continued—Tricoil or Tricowillé—Komarie—Face of the country—Hints to the traveller—Pattivilla—Oohundemallé—Village of Kombookanaar—Black paddee—Time of sowing and reaping—Devil worshippers—Offerings at the conclusion of harvest—Kombookan-Aar—Kombook trees—Area and population of the Eastern Province——Southern Province—Potané—Yallé—Suggestions to the tourist, if intending to proceed to Kattregam Dewalé—Total absence of splendour there—Human victims to chetahs—National religion of the Singhalese a medley of Hindoo and Buddhist worship—The god of Kattregam—Dewalés and Vihares—Approach to Kattregam Dewalé—Head Brahmin—Confers with the Basnaike Rale—Supposed subject of their conference—Timely suggestions—Water of the Parapa-Oya—Priestly ablutions—Chief Brahmin's Residence—Image and slippers of a god—State chair of sacred clay, the founder's stepping block from earth to heaven—Present from the priests—Temple lands—Buddhist and devil priests—An easy going set of fellows—Malay officer commanding at Kattregam—Medley of superstitions—Contrasts between the worship of Buddha and that of Brahma.

THE very curious and pensile nests of the Yellow Grosbeak (*Loxia flavicans*), which is of a yellowish brown, and in some respects resembles our yellow hammer (*Emberiza Citrinella*), cannot fail to attract attention. I have counted forty three of these nests upon one tree, all of which were suspended from the extremities of the spinous branches of the *Mimosa pennata*, L., that overhung a patch of water. These exhibited an extraordinary and beautiful appearance, when illuminated with fire flies at night, and waved by a gentle breeze.

The Hindoos, who call it *Baya*, and are adepts at taming it, describe it as being partial to the fire fly (*Buprestis vittata*); and so careful is this bird of the insects which it selects for the purpose of feeding its young, that it does not kill them in transitû to its nest, as if it intended that they should first illuminate it, and afterwards serve for a living prey to its young. This Grosbeak has no note beyond a chirp: it deposits several eggs, which are as white, and almost as glossy, as pearls, and of the size of our common sparrow's eggs. The nest, which in shape resembles an inverted Bengal water goglet, is about twenty six inches in length.

The next, in point of ingenuity, is the beautiful little Tailor Warbler (*Sylvia sutoria*), which forms its nest by attaching a dead leaf of the *Domba* tree (*Calophyllum inophyllum*, L.) to a living one;—these it sews together, by making holes in the leaves with its pointed bill, through which it passes a fibre of the plantain tree, as fine as thread, and then lines the cavity with silky cotton and feathers, for the reception of its tiny white eggs.

A pair of these pretty little creatures having formed their nest in a *Domba* tree, within twelve or fourteen feet of my verandah, I would not allow them to be disturbed; and there they reared their young, until their little wings had acquired sufficient strength to enable them to shift for themselves. They latterly became almost as familiar as a robin red-breast in winter, seldom attempting to fly away when I approached them, as they had done during our first acquaintance: and, by way of protecting them by day from the attacks of the ever-vigilant and voracious jackdaws (*Corvus monedula*), I kept a gun and pellet bow in the verandah, as near the tree as possible; both these weapons being so well known to these audacious birds, that every deference is paid to their presence, except by some very old ones, who are daring enough to approach them, as if they knew that neither a gun nor a pellet bow could do mischief of itself.

It is here that a botanist, combining the qualifications of a practical chymist, would prove a most important acquisition to the government, and the public; for he would not only satisfy himself as to the abundance of the trees that produce medicinal, elastic, and other gums, (which might have been made, for the last forty six years, available to British commerce,) but that many a valuable production, by which the trade of the country may hereafter be extended, and the revenue increased, now lies hidden in the heart of the jungle, for want of energetic examination and developement. It cannot be denied, however discreditable it be to the nation, that hitherto, "most of our varieties have been found out by casual emergency, and have been the works of time and chance, rather than of philosophy."*

It cannot be expected that official employés have sufficient leisure for acquiring any very great knowledge of the natural productions of the island, from their own researches, even if the climate were as favorable to study and exertion as it is congenial with indolence and relaxation; and therefore qualified professors, who devote their time exclusively to the pursuits of botany, or natural history in general, would be invaluable members of society in this extensive, but little known, colony.

Much self-command and great patience is necessary in prosecuting any particular study in a climate where one hand is constantly employed in endeavouring to keep off the mosquitos, or to kill them as they alight upon one's face, which often sustains a hard slap, without the satisfaction of having "bagged" the winged annoyance.

* Glanville.

To resume our route southward;—the next stage from Wambimodoo is to Tricoil, or Tricowillé, distant 16½ miles, a small straggling village, but well populated for its position in a part of the country but little cultivated, and that only in scanty patches, which is also the case for a part of the way to Komarie, a further distance of 11 miles, where the country begins to wear a more general appearance of cultivation; chiefly of black paddee (*Karpoo nillo*), yams, maize, *Payro*, a grain sown with maize, *Natcherie*, or *Korakan*, and other small grains.

At every *bazaar* along this coast, which may here be considered synonymous with village, plenty of fish, poultry, eggs, rice, milk, common fruits, and vegetables, may be obtained at moderate prices. The traveller will find it very useful to have with him some of the smallest copper coin of the country; and, having his bed with him, and, it is to be presumed, a supply of good brandy, as a necessary qualifier of some of the water that he will have to drink, if he drink it at all, when he can get green coco-nuts, any shed (where there is neither a rest-house nor Buddha temple to receive him) that will shelter his palankin from the sun, will also afford his bearers a resting-place, and his cook a kitchen:—but this he will have found out before he reaches Komarie.

From Komarie to Pattivilla, the distance is 9 miles; from thence, through the small village of Arookgam, (distant 2¾ miles,) to Panoah, near which village the Arookgam-Aar is crossed twice, 12 miles; the face of the country continuing the same, with very little variation, to Oohundemallé, a further distance of 8½ miles, where there is a tolerable rest-house; and to the village of Kombookanaar, the last stage in the Eastern Province, 12½ miles. This is just the place for an Icthyophagist, for the finest sorts of fish, green turtle (*Testudo Mydas*, L., *Chelonia Mydas*, C.), oysters, cray-fish, prawns, and small but delicious crabs, are abundant and ridiculously cheap.

Black paddee is sown towards the end of October, and reaped about the middle of April; but the few other species of paddee cultivated here vary in the time of attaining maturity,—that called *Samba* requires five months; *Chinetté* or *Hinetté* eleven or twelve weeks; and *Perianelloo* is sown from the middle of January to the beginning of May, and reaped in four months.

The inhabitants of this province are chiefly "Devil-worshippers," and undertake neither sowing nor reaping, without propitiating Pattiné with their offerings. At the conclusion of harvest, they form a circular road, by removing the paddee stubble from a space about ten feet in diameter, and then making a large hole in the centre, they fix several stakes around the opening, and decorate them with coco-nuts, areka nuts, white olas, sheaves of paddee, and the flower spikes of the *Pandanus odoratissimus*, which last are indispensable, it being supposed that their diffusive odour is a most acceptable perfume to the *Maha Yaka;* to whom, they hold it as sacred as the Syracusans of old did the Cypress, Maiden-hair, and Narcissus to Pluto; but more merciful than the Syracusans, they shed no black bull's, or other blood upon the ground, by way of sacrifice.

After certain ceremonies, they deposit bunches of areka nuts, several small pieces of wood, a hen's egg, enveloped in an ola of the talipat or of the palmyra tree, and inscribed with certain invocations by a *Kappuralé,* or priest of the goddess Pattiné, in the hole; and, over all, they place a stone with great ceremony.

The women, who have borne, as the poor creatures do throughout the island, the burthen and heat of the day, then approach, bearing on their heads sheaves of paddee; and after having thrice walked round the stone, in solemn silence, they deposit the sheaves upon it, as a "first-fruit offering" of the harvest to the dreaded *Maha Yaka.*

This ceremony concluded, the natural loquacity of the women resumes its reign, and amidst a confusion of tongues, which a stranger to the language can compare to nothing less than that recorded of Babel, they collect and bring in the reaped paddee; and, upon that work being completed, they vociferously lay claim to a portion of the grain, by way of "largess," sufficient to cover, to a certain thickness, the stone upon which the devil offerings rest!!

The Kombookan-Aar takes its name from the innumerable Kombook trees that border its banks. The timber is a sort of zebra wood, which, but for its distance from ports of export, might be turned to a good account as an article of commerce. It is a species of *Terminalia,* L.; and, from its affording a resinous juice, which makes a superior varnish, is, probably, the *Terminalia vernix,* L.

The superficies of the eastern province is 4895 square miles; and the population, (exclusive of the Bintenné division, where no returns had been kept, nor are likely to be for many years to come,) agreeably to the Census taken in 1835, was 54,606, making the average number to the square mile, 11.15; viz.

	MALES.	FEMALES.	TOTAL.
Whites, including Military and their families	936	519	1,455
Free Blacks, ditto ditto	26,196	23,789	49,985
Slaves	12	11	23
Aliens and resident strangers	......	......	3,143
			54,606

Of whom, there were employed in agriculture, 8930; in manufactures, 3017; and in commerce, 1427. The marriages, in the year 1835, were 471; births, 1571; and deaths, 1254; leaving a surplus in favor of the population of the province, of 317.

Having crossed the ferry, the traveller enters the Southern Province, which comprises the former districts of Hambantotté, Tangalle, Matura, the dessavony of Saffragam, and province of Lower Ouva and Wallassé; and the Southern Circuit of the Supreme Court of Judicature includes the district courts of Hambantotté, Tangalle, Matura, Galle, and Ballepittyé Modera.

The first stage from Kombookanaar is to Potane, distant 7¾ miles; and the next, through low jungle, filled with every description of game known to the island, to Yallé rest-house, upon the left bank of the Manick-Ganga, (also called Parapa-Oya and Yallé river, which takes its rise in the Ouva mountains, and flows past Kattregam Dewalé, to its *emboucheure* at Yallé,) 11¼ miles.

If the tourist be disposed to visit Kattregam Dewalé, instead of crossing the Manick-Ganga, native guides, and a *Tamātāmé*, or *Tam-a-tam* beater, to scare the chetahs and bears to a respectful distance, should be procured at Yallé to accompany him through the jungle, to that meridian of paganism, which is situate upon the left bank of the river.

One must not expect splendour, neither "Barbaric gold nor pearl," at Kattregam, notwithstanding the innumerable pilgrims who visit it from all parts of India; very many of whom annually leave their bones there to whiten in the sun, after having been well picked by chetahs and jackalls; for in the hot months of June, July, and August, (during which period not a drop of rain falls to refresh exhausted nature, and the periodical fever, which carries off great numbers, prevails,) the pilgrims are most numerous, it being the time of the great festival; as if, the more deaths that resulted from attending it, made the *Holocaust* * the more acceptable to the much dreaded and sanguinary deity. It is an almost daily occurrence for pilgrims, whilst resting themselves upon the arid sands of the desert, in which stands this curse of humanity, to be carried off to the jungle, by chetahs, and devoured.

The national religion of the Singhalese, although said to be the exclusive worship of Buddha, is a medley of Buddhist and Hindoo worship. The temples of the former are called *Vihares*,† and of the latter *Dewalés*; of which, the most dreaded is Kattregam Dewalé, or temple of *Kartikeya*, son of the mountain-born goddess, or *Pārvāti* of the

* This word is here used metaphorically, in allusion to the great heat of the sands of Kattregam, where a body is more likely to be *burnt* than *frozen*, and where so many *devils* are worshipped.

† In Siam, the temples of Sommona-Codom, another name for Buddha, are called *Pihân*; those of Buddha in Ceylon are called *Vihâr*, which is Sanscrit, and written by the Bengalese *Bihâr*. According to Ferishtah's History of Bengal, "the name was given to the province of Behâr, because it was formerly so full of Brahmins as to be, as it were, one great seminary of learning; as the word imports."—Both in Siam and Ceylon, there are two orders of Buddhist priests; both of which are distinguished by the yellow, or saffron colored robe.

Brahmins, who is represented riding on a peacock, and having six crowned heads, and twelve arms; two of which hold swords, two grasp spears, and one holds a small punkah or fan. So that it will not be thought extraordinary that a Dewalé and a Vihare should stand contiguous, or, as it occasionally happens, under the same roof, as if by way of compromise between Buddhists and their original Brahminical persecutors.

There are several Dewalés here, besides that of the Kattregam *Dewiyo;* but, when I visited the place, in 1826, most of these buildings were in a state of decay and dilapidation, and the grand Dewalé, as well as the much-neglected Vihare of Buddha in the large square, (where the only object really worthy of admiration is a magnificent *Bogaha,* or sacred fig tree,) were also much out of repair.

The former temple, which is approached by a long and spacious front and back avenue, the one terminated by a large Dagobah, much dilapidated, and wearing all the appearance of great antiquity, and the other by a small Hindoo temple, or Dewalé, consists of an outer and inner apartment only. The walls of the former are bedaubed with representations of the Hindoo mythology; amongst which, are those of *Sheva, Vata, Vishnu,* and *Pattiné,* and a Hindoo zodiac, interspersed with *Lotos* flowers, and other emblems, similarly painted in water colors, for a ceiling; but the floor is plastered with the diluted ordure of the sacred cow. Whatever riches the Dewalé may possess, which, doubtless, are great, are carefully concealed from European eyes; and this ostensible appearance of poverty is probably a scheme to increase them, for it is well known, that during the Kandyan rebellion of 1817-18, this temple was made a deposit for the most valuable property belonging to those who had compromised themselves with our government.

Although the commanding Malay officer had intimated, that no European was allowed to enter the inner apartment, the chief priest, (a venerable personage in point of age and length of beard, his forehead well striped with marks of caste, habited in a crimson robe, carelessly thrown over the left shoulder, and a waist-cloth of the same color, over a dirty *Sarong,* with a long string of perfumed seeds, besides his *Zennuar,* round his neck, and a similar ornament over his right arm,) appeared to confer with the *Basnaike Ralé,* or lay comptroller of the Dewalé, (occasionally looking at "the Europeans'" boots,) and then with the three *Kappurales,* or priests* of Pattiné, of whom twelve belong to the temple, as if expecting that Captain Driberg† and myself were about to propose to enter the *sanctum,* which I really think we might have been allowed to have done *barefoot,* if we had particularly desired it.

* The priestess is called *Pattinée-Hame*

† At that time Commandant of Hambantott.

I confess that my curiosity was so much excited, that I was on the point of proposing to enter without boots, not for the moment considering that by so doing, it involved an apparent compromise of principles of a higher order, but which immediately suggested itself to my friend, (to whom all the credit of it is due;) and we retired, apparently satisfied with the *Basnaike Ralé's* assurances that the inner room contained nothing more than the *Halamba* of Pattiné, and similar paintings to those that decorated the outer apartment, which was separated from the former by a painted cotton screen. It afterwards occurred to me, that the existing objections might arise from Europeans wearing boots made of the "sacred animal's" leather; and, upon our arrival at Mahagam, I could not help expressing my regret, and much to my friend's amusement, that we had not told them our boots were made of monkey leather, which was the case, and endeavoured to see the *sanctum*.

During the rains, the water of the Parapa-Oya, which, at other times, is as translucid as crystal, and as sweet and wholesome as if it had been filtered or distilled, becomes the reverse of both, from the quantity of decaying foliage, borne down by the stream from the Ouva mountains, and the accumulations from its well-wooded banks, in its progress to the sea.

At this season, the priests send to a considerable distance for "rock water" for their own use, as well as for the sacred purposes of the temple, where certain ablutions are necessary before the priest on duty dares enter the "holy of holies;" and for this purpose, there are two vessels containing water, the smaller for the hands, and the larger for the feet, at the left of the screened entrance.

The smaller square contains the chief Brahmin's residence, a rest-house for pilgrims, and a wretched hovel, called a *Kowila,* dedicated to some demon or other, and in a small apartment, screened by a painted curtain, are a diminutive image and slippers of a god, within a small arched case, or *Karandua;* but the priests objected to our passing the threshold. In the chief Brahmin's apartment, stands a sort of easy chair, covered with the skins of chetahs, on which the state bows and arrows of the different gods and goddesses are placed, and having a fire by its side, which is never allowed to be extinguished. The chair itself is said to be formed of a sort of sacred clay, from the banks of the river Ganges, and is held in great veneration, as having been the seat of the founder of the Dewalé, who is represented to have "stepped from it, from earth to heaven, without passing through the gates of death!!"

The priests sent us some fruit, eggs, milk, and tyre as a compliment, but the surface of the cream of the latter having been tinged with turmeric, prevented us from using it. Our coolies were, however, better pleased that we did not, for it was very acceptable to them.

Both Dewalés and Vihares have lands attached to them, which are exempted from taxes; and these are, in general, the best planted and cultivated, in the native manner, throughout the country, because the priests care more about them than for the state of the temples; emolument first, and influence next, being the great objects of the Buddhist priesthood; and the Devil priests are also an easy going set of fellows, for they pay for nothing; but, on the contrary, receive allowances from government towards their infernal rites and ceremonies, and levy contributions from every pilgrim!

The native officer in command of the detachment of the invalid company of the Ceylon rifle corps, from the garrison of Hambantotté, will render every possible assistance and accommodation to the tourist; and the *Basnaike Ralé* will readily procure him every requisite supply that the place affords.

The religion of Buddha is so extremely inoffensive, the offerings presented by its followers, which consist only of odoriferous flowers, so pure, and the doctrines it inculcates are altogether so humane, when contrasted with the obscene and sanguinary rites of that of Brahma, that it is more to be lamented than otherwise, thst the existing unnatural medley and apparent connexion which these superstitions exhibit at the periodical festivals, should have contaminated the simpler worship of Sommona-Codom.

"Where, free to range the temple through,
No hallow'd shrine withheld from view;
No gloomy rites that shun the light,
Involv'd in mystery and night,
But all is open to the eye
As the surrounding woods and sky!
Oh, how unlike, in each degree,
The Hindoo's foul idolatry,
Whose pond'rous pyramidal pile,
What strange disgusting rites defile!
Where crafty Brahmins guard those shrines
On which no lively sunbeam shines,
Where never strangers' searching eyes
Can pierce their horrid mysteries,
And where in many a dark recess
Forms that no language can express
Vile beastly idols grin around,
And grisly monstrous gods abound!
May never such a horrid creed,
To Buddha's simpler faith succeed!"

CAPTAIN ANDERSON, 19*th Infantry*.

CHAP. XXXIV

Hell upon earth—Route from Kattregam to Hambantotte—Route resumed from Yalle—Ahamadewe, or Turtle Cove—Hawk's-bill turtles eggs wholesome, notwithstanding the noxious properties of the flesh—Method of taking the turtle, and divesting it of the Tortoise-shell of commerce—Dutch method of solving the hypothesis of the periodical visits of the turtle to the scene of its original despoliation—Turtling season—Choice of Tortoise-shell—Exported in a raw and manufactured state—Successful experiment of hatching turtles eggs—Paltoopané—Wild tea—Its uses—Assistant Staff Surgeon Crawford—Tea plant (Thea Bohea, L.) indigenous—Mahagamme—Kirinde Oya—Mahagammé rest-house—The son of the Malay Moodliar presents the Author with a couple of elephant's tusks, and a specimen of the supposed Gaulama, or Demon Bird—Great dread of it manifested by the palankin bearers—Insuperable impediments to its preservation—Description of the specimen of the supposed Gaulama—Major General Thomas Hardwicke, F. R. S., F. L. S.—His opinion of the Gaulama—Supposed to be a species of the Aluco owl, the Ulula of the Romans, and Nycticorax of the Greeks—A superstitious M. D.—A Buddhist priest's anecdote of the demon bird—Wallewe Aratchy—Fatal effects of eating Hawk's-bill turtle—Devil ceremonies for a remedy—Aratchy's death and funeral obsequies.

Leaving that "hell upon earth," Kattregam, the tourist, if he intend to proceed direct to Hambantotté, after having crossed the Parapa-Oya at the ford, will take the road through the villages of Mahagammé and (crossing the Kirindé-Oya) Boondellé, to Hambantotte, a distance altogether of about 30 miles;—but, as by so doing, the opportunity of visiting Ahamadewé, or Turtle Cove, would be lost, let it be supposed, that he does not diverge from the sea coast, but, after having crossed the Yallé river at the ferry, resumes his original and direct route to Ahamadewé, which is about 10 miles from Yallė.

When the turtle season approaches, the fish renter of the district assembles his people at Ahamadewé, where they construct huts, and a sort of temporary bazaar, for the sale of the usual articles of their simple diet, which are daily brought in by the villagers residing within eight or ten miles of the Cove.

As the turtles land only at night, the fishers (who are ever on the *qui vive* for the sport) begin to look out for their expected prey soon after sunset; and, as much depends on the state of the night, they distribute themselves, early or late, as those best accustomed to the habits of the animals may determine, along the edge of the low jungle bordering the Cove, where they lie ambushed until the signal be passed for them to act.

2 M

If the night be fine, and very little wind stirring, the turtles are generally observed to land just as

> "The pale moon, from out her cloudy cave,
> *Drops* her still anchor in the twilight wave,"*

and soon commence the flapping noise, most agreeable to the ears of the expectant "turtling gang;" by which they know that the "Hawk's-bills" are busily engaged in preparing holes in the sands, for the reception of their numerous *ova*, which often amount to a hundred at one time, and are very wholesome, notwithstanding the noxious properties of the flesh.

Although these reptiles are undisturbed during the process of incubation, the experienced Headman knows so well when sufficient grace has been allowed for that purpose, that he seldom omits giving the signal at the proper moment; this is done by whisper along the whole line of the ambuscade; from whence, a simultaneous onset is made by the whole gang, each carrying a stout Bamboo pole, and ligatures of the twisted bark of certain jungle trees, for the purpose of securing the turtles, as they are turned upon their backs, by tying the opposite fins, or rather *feet*; together; without which precaution, this species, (the Hawk's-bill, *Testudo imbricata*, L., *Chelonia caretta*, C., and *Lili-kas-bewa* of the Singhalese,) from its feet being longer, and back, or *shield*, more convex than those of the other varieties, would easily regain its natural position, and probably escape; for it defends itself with great fury, and bites severely, as many a Singhalese fisherman knows to his cost.

The fishers having secured as many turtles as they can, fires are lighted upon the spot; a bamboo pole is then passed longitudinally between the tied feet and breastplate of each turtle, by which it is suspended over the blazing fire, until the dorsal plates (or scales, as they are usually called) become heated and start from their horizontal position, when they are rapidly stripped off, beginning with the plate nearest the head, which is the largest, until the whole thirteen plates that cover the disk, are removed; but the marginal plates, of which there are twenty five, are seldom taken, unless unusually large; and as soon as the stripping is over, the despoiled animal is liberated, and allowed a free egress to the sea.

Although one would naturally infer, from all the circumstances of so apparently cruel a process, that instinct would prevent the same turtles from re-visiting the place of their former despoliation, the fact is otherwise; for those that survive the inter-

* Rev John Mitford, A. M.

mediate dangers which everywhere beset them, return to the Cove at the same season (viz. from the middle of April to the end of May) in the ensuing year.

This fact was fully ascertained by a Dutch gentleman, who had charge of the district in 1794; who, to satisfy his doubts upon the point, caused brass rings, marked with the dates of the capture of the turtles, in Dutch and Malay, to be attached to a fin of a certain number selected for the purpose; and, in 1826, the fish renter of the district brought me one of these rings, which he had removed from a turtle of 400lbs weight. The ring was about two-thirds of an inch in width at the largest part, and had been rivetted on, but the characters were obliterated by the action of the water; and the renter positively affirmed, that the same turtle had, to his knowledge, revisited the Cove for thirty two successive years. As soon as the ring had been engraven with my initials, in Singhalese, and dated 1826, by the second Moodliar's *Liené Aratchy*, or *Ola* writer, (who did it as deeply as he could with his iron style,) it was replaced upon the turtle, which was allowed to depart without further molestation.

The turtle season may be said to continue till the end of June; and any quantity of "tortoise shell" of the harvest may be purchased of the fish renter, upon the spot, at 100 per cent. less than the cost of the same article at Galle. The brown and black shell, which is invariably the thickest, is most valued; and the foremost plate of the disk, which is the largest in point of size, of quadrangular shape, and the anterior part convex, is considered the best.

Ceylon exports tortoise-shell, both in a raw and manufactured state, the natives being very expert at making betel and snuff boxes, cigar cases, combs of every description, tea caddies, and writing desks; for which latter purposes, they flatten the shell, by means of steam, into thin veneers. Betel boxes are always made of the best shell, (the largest and thickest plates being requisite for that purpose,) and are superbly ornamented with gold and silver filligree work.

A Portuguese lady at Point de Galle, the wife of an officer of the late 3rd Ceylon regiment, (Nicholas Austin, Esq., of the colonial staff,) by way of experiment, placed some Hawk's-bill turtles' eggs in a bason of sea-sand and small dead shells, and exposed them to the sun, until the young turtles were hatched; these were then transferred to a bason of sea water, where they continued until a larger vessel was requisite by their increased size; and ultimately they were removed to a place that had been constructed for them around the margin of the well, in the court yard, where they were supplied with salt water every day, and, in less than two years, had attained from two to three feet in length. The shields having been kept clean, were very beautiful, from the variety of transparent tints they displayed (but more particularly when salt water was thrown over them) in the sunshine.

From Ahamadewé to Paltoopané, the distance is 5 miles; the face of the country, as between Yallé and the former place, jungle and sand, sand and jungle, with an occasional glimpse of the sea.

At Paltoopané there is a small but well-built and modern fort, garrisoned by a non-commissioned officer's detachment of the invalid company of the Ceylon rifle corps, which affords an agreeable change to the traveller, as something approaching to civilization; for he will find very comfortable quarters during his stay, and every attention from the clerk (of the Hambantotté cutchery) in charge of the salt stores.

The fortification having been originally intended for a sea defence, is low, but strongly built, and capable of mounting several heavy guns; nature has, however, providently defended this part of the coast by a fortification of madrepore, more effectual against an invading enemy than all that the art of man could oppose.

This district is particularly subject to long drought, sometimes for ten or eleven months together, and the burnt state of the herbage displays a melancholy contrast to every other part of the island.

The jungles adjoining this place, and throughout the Mahagampattoo district, abound with the "wild tea tree," as it is called, but which, I am informed, is a species of *Orchis*. It bears yellow flowers; and the poorest people are accustomed to use the leaf both for food and drink; for the former, boiled and mixed with *Tyre*, and for the latter, an infusion of the green leaf. It is called *Gal-Kuroo* by the Singhalese; who also employ the leaf of another plant, which greatly resembles that of the *Thea Bohea*, L., and is called by them *Rata-Thé-Kola*, (or Red-Tea leaf,) in a similar manner.

Although the infusion of the green leaf is a very bitter drink, it is an excellent tonic, and its taste may be greatly improved by the addition of the indigenous lemon grass (*Andropogon Schœnanthus*, L.) and sugar; but that made with the dried leaf, is a tolerable substitute for Bohea tea.

The late Assistant Staff Surgeon Crawford, at the time he superintended the hospital duties at Batticaloa, in 1826, sent me, by a native *Dhoney* bound to Hambantotté, a collection* of insects and plants; and, among the latter, a very fine specimen of what he considered the real tea, in flower. It fully answered the generic description of the *Thea Bohea* of Linnæus; and, as it both flowered and seeded freely, I made a sketch

* This included the *Buprestis chrysis*, C., noticed in page 252.

of it, of which an engraving is annexed, but I was altogether unsuccessful in my own researches for the plant in the jungles of the Mahagampattoo.

Mr. Crawford did not assume any merit to himself as having made a new discovery, and it is very clear that the Dutch were well aware of the tea plant being indigenous in the eastern province; but it is to be wondered at, that the government has not, long ere this, directed its attention to so important an object of commerce; for if it be worth while to cultivate tea in so distant a country as Assam, with all its inconveniencies and dangers, surely it would be a more lucrative speculation, in a colony so much nearer home, and with increased facilities of export. But this, like the bread fruit tree, is another *chance* discovery; and a better acquaintance with Ceylon in 1787—1789, would have rendered the two expensive trips to Otaheite, for supplying the West Indies with bread fruit plants, inexpedient; for they could have been obtained in any quantity from this island, and have obviated all the disastrous consequences of the mutiny on board His Majesty's ship "Bounty."

Captain Percival, in his "Account of Ceylon," published in 1805, informs us, "that the tea plant has also been discovered native in the forests of the island. It grows spontaneously in the neighbourhood of Trincomalé, and other northern parts of Ceylon. General Champagné informed me that the soldiers of the garrison frequently use it. They cut the branches and twigs, and hang them in the sun to dry; they then take off the leaves, and boil them to extract the juice, which has all the properties of that of the China leaf. I have in my pocket a letter from an officer in the 80th regiment, in which he states that he had found the real tea plant, in the woods of Ceylon, of a quality equal to any that ever grew in China, and that it was in his power to point out to government the means of cultivating it in a proper manner."

From Paltoopané to Mahagammé, where the Kirindé-Oya is forded, the distance is $9\frac{1}{4}$ miles; the rest-house lies in the midst of low jungle, where mosquitos, ants, and sand-flies are extremely troublesome, and snakes* occasionally obtrusive.

Whilst halting at this place, in 1826, on my way to the ruins of the ancient and once splendid city of Mahagammé, or Mahagam, but which I was prevented from accomplishing, by a severe attack of jungle fever, that compelled me to retrace my steps to Hambantotté, the son of the Malay Moodliar, who had tracked a tusked elephant from the Kirindé-Oya to the jungle in which these celebrated ruins stand, brought me, in addition to a very large tusk, and the half of another which had been broken and become quite carious, a most extraordinary bird, which was neither owl nor raven, but in some respects resembled both.

* See page 111.

He called it the "Devil's Bird," and two of my bearers pretended to know it as the *Gaulama*, or Demon Bird; but the others shcok their heads doubtingly, and one of them remarked to my interpreter, that "no man can kill *him*, for that arrow cr ball would come back (rebound) as from a washerman's stone!" Such is the effect of superstition! The arguments to which this gave rise, among the coolies, each of whom had something to say about the *Gaulama*, but I could not get any one of them to touch "*him*," seemed interminable; and,

"Who shall decide, when *doctors* disagree?"

I had reason to regret, that in my very feverish state at the time, and the incipient putrefaction of the bird, which rapidly increased to a most offensive degree, I could not have taken off and preserved the skin, however anxious to have so done, even if I had had every necessary material; and, not being able to procure arrack in which to immerse it for future examination, all that remained in my power was to make a note of the circumstance; of itself, at such a time, an arduous task.

The bird, when held as nearly as possible in its natural position, by the son of the Malay Moodliar, (Noureddin,) was about eighteen inches from the point of the beak to the claws; head very round, and sunk within a cavity formed by its feathers; eyes also sunk, and surrounded with small iron-grey feathers, the iris of a brownish black; bill of a greenish hue; the upper part of the body a rufous black, intermixed with lighter and dark grey spots; wings three feet six inches between the extremities; tail about five or six inches; legs black, covered with black and white feathers, and breast a greyish white, with transverse bars.

My lamented friend the late Major General Thomas Hardwicke, of the Bengal artillery, to whom, soon after my arrival from Ceylon, I had offered my notes upon the indigenous productions of that island, and who then had it in contemplation to publish a *Fauna Indica*, having inquired very particularly respecting the *Ulama* or *Gaulama*, I referred him to the note I had made at Mahagammé respecting the supposed Demon Bird. The General subsequently informed me, that by my description of its size and plumage, and of its horrid screams, which resemble those that one might imagine to proceed from some conscience-stricken wretch, in an extremity of pain and despair, and subsequently change into a howling moan, but of a deeper and more gloomy tone than that of a dog baying the moon, that it is a species of *Aluco*,* or black owl,

* *La Hulotte* of Buffon.—*Ulula* of Brisson; so called by the Romans, from its cry resembling the howling of wolves (*Ululare*).

or the night raven (*Nycticorax*) of the Greeks, hitherto known only in Europe and the north of Asia; which, according to Salerne, howls "with so gloomy a moan as to terrify women and children."

Although I never heard the *Gaulama* but once, it is impossible ever to forget it; and that was at Wanderopé, in 1826, about midnight. The bird had taken post upon a branch of the ancient *Bogaha* tree in the temple grounds, which were merely separated from my compound by the high road. Dr. Casement, at that time the assistant surgeon in charge of the hospital duties at Hambantotté, was with me, and I never saw any one more strangely affected than he was; for, being both timid and superstitious, he insisted upon its being a prognosticator of more deaths, (of which we had just experienced several awful instances,) and he commenced firing his double-barrelled gun, in order "to frighten the devil away," as he called it; which he continued to do, at intervals, for the greater part of the night, much to my amusement, although it deprived me of sleep.—And therefore, as there are superstitious people amongst educated Europeans, one cannot much wonder at the effects of similar notions upon untutored Indians.—So much for the *Gaulama!*

> "For ravens, though as birds of omen,
> They teach both conjurors and old women
> To tell us what is to befall,
> Can't prophecy themselves at all."—COWPER.

I may mention another instance of superstition, connected with this extraordinary bird.—The *Oonansé*, or Buddhist priest of the *Pansala** at Wanderopé, who positively vouched for the fact, "that the *Gaulama* had been heard for three successive nights antecedent to the death of the Aratchy of the district," seriously expressed his belief to me, that, after such an omen, "his recovery was impossible, for that neither medicinal remedies nor Devil dancing (of which last he spoke most contemptuously) could have any effect against fate."

The Aratchy, who was one of the finest specimens of the human figure, literally of "Herculean mould," that I ever saw in any part of the world, fell a victim to his superstition, when it is very probable, that a dose of tincture of rhubarb and laudanum might have saved his life.

This Headman had been down to Paltoopané, on duty; where, from eating curry made of the hawk's-bill turtle, a violent diarrhæa ensued, which so greatly reduced his strength in the short space of forty hours, as to render it necessary to convey him in a *Dooley* to his house at Pybocké, a distance of nineteen miles, where I visited him the

* Synonymous with the *Pandal* of the Hindoos,—literally "a house made of leaves."

day after his arrival, for I felt much interested in the fate of so indefatigable and honest a Singhalese Headman, (as he really was,) and had hoped to have prevailed upon him to accept the services of the native medical assistant, Mr. Heyn, (for, at that period, there was no European medical officer nearer than Galle, a distance of seventy miles from Pybocké,) or such remedies as I could offer him from my portable medicine case.

Upon approaching within a mile or two of the village, I heard the sound of *Tam-a-tams*, as if some native marriage or rejoicing was taking place, but which, upon entering the house, I found to proceed from a "devil ceremony" going on in the inner room, where lay the poor Aratchy, stretched at full length upon a mat, with merely his *Sarong* about his loins, and another rolled up under his head by way of pillow. Immediately facing him, were three gigantic figures of Shiva, Brahma, and Vishnu, formed of sticks and clay, plastered over with chunam, and painted, in their order, yellow, white, and blue. In the middle of each figure was a small staple, to which a string, made of the fibre of the *Pandanus odoratissimus*, and neatly platted of the size of a small fishing line, was fastened, and the three lines having been brought to an apex upon the patient's exposed abdomen, (the seat of pain,) were joined to another string, which was passed round the body.

On the right of the Aratchy, sat a Kapuralé of Pattiné, with the copper bangles of the Dewalé passed over each great toe, which he kept in a revolving motion, to the horrid din of "native music;" whilst another Devil priest, masked and habited, as represented in the annexed engraving from a native drawing, kept up a clatter from the several cylindrical copper spheres about his person, as he clanked his chains and whirled about!

In this state, the poor Aratchy had passed the whole night; and I felt glad that I had visited him at so early an hour, (just before sunrise,) for he had not even the assistance of a native doctor, and trusted entirely to the "God of Kattregam" to restore him!! After remaining with him nearly two hours, during the whole of which time the devil dance continued without intermission, and having merely succeeded in obtaining a promise, that, "if the devil did not cure him in another day and night, he would take English medicine," I took leave of this most infatuated man, and gave over all hope of seeing him alive at the expiration of the time he had mentioned.

My fears were but too true; that very evening, the dying Aratchy was removed to the compound by his children, (in order to save the house, which was an excellent Singhalese farm house, with tiled roof, from being pulled down, in the event of their parent dying within it,) where, about midnight, he ceased from pain and life together; and, two days after, on passing over the plains about a mile from his house, I saw the *ola*-ornamented bamboo arch, (where the body had been burnt, just in the style described by Knox,) that marked the obsequies of the Vidahn Aratchy of the Mahagampattoo!

CHAP. XXXV.

Neglected state of Mahagammé—Fertility of the soil—Capabilities of irrigation—Ruins of ancient Mahagam—Gigantic Ipomœa—Route to Hambantotté—Face of the country—Pasturage, but no sheep—Kirindé-Oya, or Mahagam river—Tellulé—Wellegangoddé—Boondellé—Fishing village of Alut Kangallé—Exhausted Leway—Udumallé—Matellé-Aar—Fertility of the district—Exceptions—Temperature of the interior of the island favorable to the growth of wool, but that of the maritime provinces against it—Jaffna sheep thrive well upon the pasturage of the Mahagampattoo—Indigenous species of Samphire—Euphorbia Tirucalli—Hambantotté—Quaker fortifications—Population—Public buildings—View of the Koholonkalé, Maha, Karaganaré, and Sitricalé Leways—Seven hills of Kattregam—Depôt of salt, and of red sand—Termes fatale, L., its destructiveness—Sand hills—Result of digging for water—Rapid accumulation of sand—Starvation—Formation of salt at the Leways—Rapid evaporation—Crystalization—Effects of heavy rains anticipated—Suggestions as to the original deposit of salt where no basis of rock salt exists—Summary of reports to the Governor upon the state of the Mahagampattoo district—Wesleyan mission inadequately supplied with missionaries.

Mahagammé, now a straggling village, has, within the last fifty years, presented a very different appearance to its present one; a fact, attested by the remains of several extensive gardens, where many varieties of exotic fruit trees still remain, as if to challenge the present generation with neglect and indifference; and with justice, if it be considered, that the soil is extremely fertile, the means of irrigating many thousands of acres (requiring only the repairing of tanks and re-opening of water courses, which would require a very moderate expenditure of capital, when contrasted with the certain benefits and remunerating profit that would result from it) at hand, and labour cheap.

The soil, which appeared to me to bear a greater resemblance to that of the pepper and nutmeg plantations at Prince of Wales Island, in the Straits of Malacca, than to any other, is well adapted to the culture of sugar, cotton, pepper, cloves, and nutmegs; and sufficient paddee might be grown for the consumption of the whole district, within the range of irrigation by the Kirindé-Oya, exclusively of the immense area that might be sown with the same grain, and supplied with water from artificial tanks.

According to the best accounts I could obtain, the ruins of the ancient city of Mahagam, about 5 miles from Virawellé, display sufficient vestiges of its pristine magnificence to interest the antiquarian. These, are said to consist of massive granite pillars, bases, and capitals, lying in every direction amid the jungle, which has overgrown them; others, still standing, from ten to thirteen feet in height, some more,

2 N

some less, and partially covered with a variety of parasitic plants, and creepers, (including the *Cecropia peltata*, and a gigantic species of *Ipomæa*, a perennial, whose rose colored umbels are four inches in diameter,) Sacred Fig, and other trees; the remains of an extensive tank, and of a *Dagobah*, or depository of a relic of Buddha.

From the rest-house of Mahagammé, the route to Hambantotté, the next stage, distant 14½ miles, is through a neglected country, in some places cultivated with paddee, small grains, and maize, and in others waste and desolate, particularly the downs near the *Leways*, where there is excellent pasturage for sheep, but not one of these animals to be seen.

Having crossed the Kirindé-Oya, (or Mahagam* river, as it is also called,) which is fordable, except during the rains, when the stream is wide and rapid, and only to be crossed in boats, the road lies through the small villages of Tellulé and Wellegangoddé. These, are scarcely worth notice, the inhabitants being very few, and their means of cultivation limited to yams, paddee, maize, and korakan. Thence to Boondellé, upon the banks of the *Leway* of that name, about a quarter of a mile from the sea, from which it is separated by a bar of sand. Beyond Boondellé, at a village called Alut Kangallé, inhabited by fishers, very fine sur-mullet, soles, seir-fish, and prawns may be procured at a merely nominal rate. This village is situate upon the banks of an exhausted *Leway*, called Matellé Kalapoor, but the tourist had better halt at Udumallé rest-house, upon the left bank of the Matellé-Aar, which is dry, except during, and for a short period after, the rains.

From Udumallé, the usual road is between the Koholonkalé and Maha *Leways* and the sand hills; but as the sea-breeze is preferable to the monotony of the *Leway* downs, by edging to the left, the rest of the journey by the sea beach will be found the most pleasant part of it.

Always excepting the neighbourhood of the *Leways*, (in speaking of the Mahagampattoo,) the soil is so remarkably fertile, that industry and capital are the only requisites to make it one of the most productive districts in the island; and as cultivation extends, the country will be gradually abandoned by the wild beasts that infest its woods and jungles, and become as healthy as any in the maritime provinces.

Although the interior of the island presents many favorable situations for feeding large flocks of sheep for the growth of wool, and that such a speculation as the introduction of the best breeds for the purpose, would doubtless be a very profitable one,

* Mahagam and Hambantotte being the usual English pronunciation, I have used it indiscriminately with the native method, viz. Mahagammé and Hambantotté.

the climate of the maritime provinces is altogether against it; but Jaffna sheep thrive admirably well upon the stunted grass, which resembles the "*short bite*" (as it is called in some counties) of our English downs, and is so impregnated with saline particles, that these animals are very partial to it; and also to a species of Samphire (*Crithmum maritimum*, L.), which is abundant upon the borders of the exhausted *Leways*, and a most nutritious fodder. This plant may also be used for culinary purposes.

The plains surrounding the *Leways* are altogether free from jungle to a considerable extent, nevertheless, the most watchful care is required on the part of the shepherd, whilst so many leopards and jackalls abound in the adjoining jungles, or a flock of sheep would sòon yield but a "Flemish account."

The approach to Hambantotté is remarkable for the deep red color of the road, and the dark green hue of the milky hedge (*Euphorbia Tirucalli*, L.), with which the enclosures are fenced. Its roots extend in every direction, and where the stems are ligneous, the bark resembles that of the maple, or as if sun-cracked. The wood itself is white and hard, and its erect dark green branches, which are composed of straight cylindrical joints, of the size of small goose quills from two to four or five inches long, (but thickest at the joints,) produce, upon the slightest puncture, a thick cream-like juice. Goats eat the shrub with impunity, and buffalos *are said* to be partial to it; but this I doubt, because bullocks, where there is little or no herbage, would also eat it; and yet, although they are kept in enclosures formed exclusively of milky hedge, there is no instance of their doing so. The native doctors attribute extraordinary medicinal properties to the juice, which I know, from casual experience, to be of a most caustic nature.

Hambantotté (derived from the Singhalese words *Hambané*, "country boats," and *Totté*, "creek," or small bay) is situate in latitude 6° 15′ north, and longitude 81° 20 east, according to Captain Horsburgh; and, by the Master Attendant at Galle, Mr. Twynam's survey in 1837, in latitude 6° 6′ 58″ north, and longitude 81° 14′ 44″ east; and a more solitary or barren situation cannot well be conceived.

In the last edition of Captain Horsburgh's Directory, (1836,) no notice is taken either of the anchorage in Hambantotté Roads, or of the Bay; the latter, may have arisen from the circumstance of its being considered merely as a harbour for small coasting craft, as its Singhalese name implies, but it affords good anchorage for vessels from 150 to 200 tons burthen.

The town lies under a hilly promontory, (projecting seaward towards the south-east, and forming the south-west side of the small bay, which convexes to the northward and eastward, and is about 1¾ mile across to the eastern extremity,) upon which stands a sort of *half-caste* Martello tower, that half a dozen 32lb shot would annihilate, in lieu of a regular fortification, which, in the event of a war, will be indispensable; and this, with the fort of Paltoopané, (both, in these peaceable times, without cannon, and garrisoned by the invalid company of the Ceylon rifle regiment,) are the only military (*Quaker?*) defences of the coast from Batticaloa to Tangalle, a distance of 175 miles!

The town itself, which contains about 1300 inhabitants, chiefly consists of mud-built houses, thatched with *Cajans;* but there are a few tiled houses, belonging to the principal Mahomedans. The gaol, cutchery, and Assistant Government Agent's house, are situate on the hill, which commands an extensive view of the sea, the Koholonkalé, Maha, Karaganare, and Sitricalé *Leways*, and of the seven hills of Kattregam, the local *Vatican* of paganism; and the Commandant's house is on the east side of the hill, within 50 yards of the sea.

This place is the grand depôt for the salt gathered in the Mahagampattoo; and it may also be said, of red dust, which gives every thing a Cayenne-peppery appearance, whether it be the paper one writes upon, the dress one wears, the furniture, the table cloth, and what not?—and even letters, when casually sent *outside* the *Tappal*, are as well known at the Galle and Colombo post-offices by the red edges, as by the post marks.

The white ant (*Termes fatale*, L., Order *Aptera*), is quite in its element here, the red sand enabling it to burrow to a great depth, and under the very foundations of the houses; and from the brick-dust appearance of every thing upon which its minute particles are deposited by the wind, these destructive insects are enabled to carry their *covered ways* to the roof, without being perceived even by the most careful servant; but although they destroyed several boxes and portmanteaus, and a great deal of wine, by eating the corks, they showed no disposition to keep *me* in office, for they neither attacked the treasury notes or *vouchers** in my official custody.

Between the sea and the town, the enormous hills of sea-sand, (upon which a heavy carriage may be driven as easily as upon the best Mac-Adamized road,) whose eastern and western sides are covered with *Asclepiadæ*, encroach so very rapidly, that houses are being continually pulled down, and rebuilt at a greater distance, to prevent their being overwhelmed; and as the place had but one well of pure drinkable water, which is situate beyond the town, between the Karaganaré *Leway* and the sand hills, (close to the latter, and the Assistant Government Agent's garden,) I was anxious to sink another; but, upon digging to the same level, and within six feet of the former well,

* See page 236.

the result was, black mud, of a very offensive smell, mixed with fossil shells, and impregnated with salt.

The accumulation of sand must have been as rapid as the growth of the adjoining coco-nut trees; for some of sixty feet in height, are buried up to the crests, the only parts visible above the surface, and the bunches of nuts lie upon the sand, as if they were the produce of a gigantic plant, instead of being the fruit of one of the tallest of the *Palm* family, and may be cut from their stalks by a child.

So much has already been stated upon the subject of the salt* collected in the Mahagampattoo, that further allusion to it, except in regard to its formation, is unnecessary.

The *Leways* are extremely shallow; the greatest depth, except where there are holes, seldom exceeds four or five feet, after the rains in January and February; but the incrustation generally forms in the hot months of June, July, and August, when the south-west monsoon wafts a parching heat over the snow-white surface, (far more intolerable than the Sicilian *Scirocco,*) which, together with the nature of salt-gathering, causes such dreadful excoriations in the hands and feet of the coolies employed, that not even the horror of famine, or the necessity, to which indolence drives them, of subsisting upon wild roots and leaves, mixed with sour buffalo-milk, will induce them to collect the government salt, for which they are paid the full labourer's wages of four fanams (sixpence) a day, unless *pressed for that service.*

Here, then, is one proof, that the statements which have occasionally appeared, "that starvation is unknown in Ceylon, where there are always fruits and roots so abundant as to suffice nature," even if the Authors had never heard or read of its repeated visitation by famine, through failure in the rice crops, are unfounded; and similar recurrences must be expected, where such indolent habits predominate: but where, in the Mahagampattoo district, for instance, are these fruits and roots to be obtained for an idle and starving population? starving, I admit, through idleness, where no one need starve, for industry only is required to insure plenty; and, even if there were still greater abundance, agriculturists cannot be expected to part with their produce for nothing.

The excessive heat causes the most rapid evaporation, drying up some parts of the *Leways* altogether, and, in others, leaving only a few inches of water above the incrustation, which varies from half an inch, to ten or twelve inches in thickness; but the formation of the salt never extends over the whole *Leway,* nor does it exist in all the *Leways* at the same time. In the *Maha Leway,* as in the others, salt forms at one time in one quarter, perhaps over an eighth of the surface, and in another the next.

* See pages 162—166.

If a branch of a *Mimosa*, L., (which is the best for the purpose,) be laid down when the crystalization commences, and taken up upon its completion, the dazzling whiteness it displays, when exposed to the rays of the sun, is as novel and gratifying to the eye, as it is indescribable by the pen.

During the heavy rains, it has occasionally been necessary to cut through the bar of sand between the *Leways* and the sea, in order to carry off the superabundant water, which would otherwise have prevented the reaction of the brine, and consequent formation of the salt. But, in regard to the local origin of its deposit, as I have no pretensions to science, it may perhaps be deemed presumptuous in me to offer an opinion, opposed to that of my more able predecessors, upon this important subject; none of whom, in any work upon Ceylon to which I have had access, have taken the least notice of, or made any remarks upon, the presence of the innumerable fossil shells, (chiefly bivalves,) that are intermixed with the black mud and grey sand of the beds of the *Leways*; and it has long since been ascertained, that no basis of rock salt exists there.

The most general opinion is, that the presence of salt is caused by sea water percolating the sands; but if such were its origin, it would surely affect *all* the *Leways* in an equal ratio; instead of which, although their relative positions and that of the sea continue unchanged, whilst some of the nearest are exhausted, and have produced nothing but brackish water for many years, others are as prolific as ever.

The intermixture of fossil shells with the mud and sand of the *Leways*, suggests the probability, that at some remote period the whole of the land where the *Leways* are situate, had been recovered from the sea, by the gradual formation of the enormous natural embankments of sand, which now form so conspicuous a feature in the barren scenery of this part of the coast;—that for an indefinite number of years, the evaporation of the brine from the shallower parts of the enclosed space produced a certain proportion of salt, and then became exhausted; that the deeper cavities, or what are now called *Leways*, continued to yield their quota of salt, according to their depth, and the quantity of sea-water absorbed, until the brine of the shallowest had also been exhausted by evaporation; and that the deepest reservoirs will continue to yield salt so long only as any portion of brine remains, unless they are replenished from the sea by artificial means.

As the substance of my reports to His Excellency the Governor, in 1827, may give a tolerably clear representation of the state of the district, both at the period of my taking charge of it, and of leaving it, upon receiving orders to return to England, a few extracts may not be considered supererogatory.

" 1st. That I had abolished the assumed power of flogging convicts with the rattan cane, by the Fiscal's *Peons,* but had unsuccessfully suggested the expediency of improving the state of the district gaol, which was an unfit place for the imprisonment of human beings.*

" 2ndly. That, at Hambantotté, I had converted a small muddy pool, usually dry for several months in the year, into a tank 100 feet long by 45 feet wide, in order to contribute to the health and conciliate the prejudices of the inhabitants, (chiefly Mahomedans, whose religion enjoins frequent ablutions,) and provide rain water for the Cattle Establishment attached to the Salt Department; which, notwithstanding the great revenue derived from that article, had been so much neglected, that, prior to the construction of the reservoir, the poor emaciated bullocks had been occasionally driven, after a hard day's work, to assuage their thirst in the river Wallewé, many of them dying on the road from the want of sufficient food and water.

" 3rdly. That I had formed a flat road from the cutchery to the town, and planted trees on each side of it.†

" 4thly. That having ascertained by experiment that the opium poppy would attain the greatest possible perfection in Ceylon, I requested the Governor to authorize the distribution of the box of seeds from Malwah, that accompanied my report, to such Stations as might be best adapted to the culture of so valuable an article of Eastern commerce.

" 5thly. That upon my introduction ‡ of the poppy into culture in the island, the plants had appeared above ground in six days from the time of sowing the seed, and were in full bloom in less than six weeks; after which, an abundance of capsules formed, and yielded seed enough for twelve large beds, independently of a proportion given to some Malays in the neighbourhood; but, that not calculating upon the rise of the Wallewé river in October, I had been deprived of the means of collecting opium,§ and prevented from preserving a part of the native seed, by inundation.

" 6thly. That since I had been in the Mahagampattoo, I had endeavoured, by example, and the offer of rewards, to induce the inhabitants to habits of industry and cultivation, and with some prospects of success.

" 7thly. That I had erected a bungalow, on a piece of Government ground, at Wallewé, and planted the first coffee garden ever known in the Mahagampattoo; that my introduction of the *Cammanioc,* had been hailed as a blessing by the Malays, by

* See page 266, for the substance of the rest of this paragraph in the report.

† *Ficus Bengalensis,* L., and *Hibiscus populneus,* L.

‡ This was intimated to the Literary & Agricultural Society by His Excellency Sir Edward Barnes, in Dec. 1826.

§ I subsequently ascertained, that my Malay gardener had collected a very fine specimen of opium during my illness, but had kept it for his own use.

whom it was being cultivated with great assiduity; and that I sanguinely hoped that in less than eighteen months, the whole of the waste lands near the town of Hambantotté would be planted with it; for, that after the reports I had received of the numbers of natives who had died, chiefly from starvation, and the consequence of eating leaves mixed with tyre, I should have been callous to the distresses of my fellow-creatures, if I had not employed every resource of mind, and that my official position afforded, to provide against future contingencies, by encouraging the propagation of that root, as a certain supply of wholesome food, and within the reach of all who would cultivate it.

"8thly. That I had introduced the Guinea grass from Galle, but had failed to induce any of the native cattle owners to follow my example in cultivating it; and that, in the course of one year, it would ensure supplies of excellent fodder for the Government bullocks, by four or five coolies being attached to the Cattle Establishment, for the purpose of planting it.

"9thly. That my garden had produced very fine grapes, from vines that I had originally introduced from Teneriffe, in the year 1821, some of which had reached the Collector of Tangalle in the highest perfection; and that I had also introduced the Teneriffe mulberry, (preparatory to my intended importation of the silk worm,) Portugal fig, Bengal dholl, and nutmeg, all which were thriving well, together with almost every sort of vegetable for the table; thereby showing what is capable of being effected, even with limited means, but with a determined mind, in the neglected, and, comparatively, almost depopulated Mahagampattoo.

"Lastly. That, among other means for improving the temporal condition of the natives, who, because their climate had been, from time immemorial, considered the most unhealthy in the maritime provinces, had been alike neglected by the Protestant and Roman Catholic hierarchies, and were consequently the most uncivilized, with the exception only of the *Veddahs*, I had not lost sight of a still greater object; and, considering the deplorable situation of the Mahagampattoo, which was altogether destitute of a single place of Christian worship, and contiguous to the very meridian of paganism, (Kattregam,) to present an extensive field for Missionary labours, I had offered my house at Wanderopé (upon the banks of the river Wallewé, within a mile of the sea, and in the most healthy part of the district) for a Missionary residence, and to erect a temporary chapel free of expense to the Mission; and that, in answer to my proposition, I had received an assurance, by letter from the excellent Wesleyan Missionary, the Rev. Mr. Clough, dated 22nd September, 1826, "*that if the Mission could stretch its lines as far as my regions, a Missionary should be sent there;*""—but the *Veddahs* have had the preference, and the Mahagampattoo is as destitute as ever!

CHAP. XXXVI.

Paucity of Missionaries—Character of the Wesleyan mission—The Rev. Benjamin Clough—Dr. Adam Clarke—No rest-house at Hambantotté—Deficiency supplied by the hospitality of the public authorities—Deaths of Captain and Mrs. Driberg on the same day—Consequent extraordinary determination of the Commander of the Forces—Native superstition—A puzzler—Official difficulties—Europeans at Hambantotté contrasted with French pilots—Incipient panic confirmed by an official declaration—Friendly importunities and suggestions—An Englishwoman's determination—Paramount duty—Neglect of the district by the Government and by individuals—Suggestions for establishing a fish factory, grounded upon ascertained facts—Kandyan Tavelams—Kandyan produce for sale or barter—Hints to the Manchester manufacturer, as to articles adapted to the Singhalese costume; and to the Birmingham manufacturer, respecting their implements of husbandry—Wellassé famous for the Talipat palm—Sickness attributed to its fetid flowers—Important objects to be anticipated from establishing a fish factory at Hambantotté, by a British Company, and consequent results to the town and district—Cetacea—Amber—Sea Dragon—Phosphorescent appearance of the sea—Cancer fulgens—Soldier Crab—Anatomical specimens.

Referring to the preceding page, and to obviate the possible misconstruction of its concluding paragraph, I feel it my duty towards the inestimable Wesleyan mission, to add a few words.

That the Mahagampattoo district has been so long neglected, has doubtless arisen from the paucity of Missionaries in the island, and not from any latent disposition to circumscribe the range of their usefulness.

The motto of the Wesleyan mission is not, "a fair field and no favor," for there can scarcely be a fairer field, than this island presents, for Christian labour; and the Mission does want, and righteously deserves, *all* the favor that can be bestowed upon it, in furtherance of the grand object of its beneficent operations.

Since the first establishment of the Wesleyans in Ceylon, is there an individual, (I would ask,) who, however bigotted he may be to any particular creed or sect, can point out one exceptionable character that has belonged to it, whether as a Christian and a loyal and devoted subject, or as a husband, father, brother, or friend?—I might long pause for a reply, because it is irrefragable upon any axiom founded in truth.

Although it has been suggested to me by a friend to missions, that, instead of the brief extract from the Rev. Mr. Clough's letter, in the preceding page, in answer to my proposition for a resident Missionary in this district, I should have inserted that communication entire, together with extracts from my correspondence with my late revered and sincere friend, Dr. Adam Clarke, (to whom I was originally introduced by the same worthy Missionary,) who honored me with his invaluable friendship, until called from the scene of his earthly labours, it would have savoured so much of egotism on my part, and have been altogether so incompatible with the nature of this work, that I have felt it necessary to omit them.

My solicitude both for the temporal and spiritual welfare of the population of the Mahagampattoo, induces the hope, that ere long it will also form part of the Christian phalanx against its long-dominant Apollyon; and my reasons for that solicitude, which is now as fresh, after a lapse of fifteen years, as at the moment of my leaving the district, in 1827, will be found in the subsequent pages.

Hambantotté, although the principal station in the Mahagampatto, is without a rest-house, and, as for an inn or hotel, one may just as easily find such a place among the Patagonians: the deficiency is, however, supplied by the hospitality of the local authorities.

The civil departments are superintended by an Assistant Government Agent for the Southern Province, and the military by a Captain of the Ceylon Rifle Regiment, (subordinate to the Commandant of the Galle district, of which, Hambantotté is a military dependency,) a proof of the station having improved in point of salubrity since my superintendence of the district, during the mortality in 1826-1827, when it was considered such a post of danger, that, after the lamented deaths of the Commandant and his wife, on the 8th October, 1826, the Deputy Adjutant General, in conveying to me the Governor's thanks for my conduct upon the occasion, intimated His Excellency's determination, "not to send any officer to command the garrison, (at that time consisting of 130 men,) until more favorable accounts of the healthy state of the district should have been received;" and, for six months, it remained in that anomalous and neglected state.

At that period, there was scarcely a house without some one or other of its inmates dead or dying; and so destitute was the place, including the Government Stores, that there was not even a plank of wood, *or the means of sawing a tree into planks*, for coffins for my departed friends, to be got in the district; but it so happened that I possessed some slabs of satin-wood, which had been partly prepared for a set of dinner tables, by carpenters whom I had hired from Morottoo, a distance of 162 miles; but, in consequence of three out of the four dying almost immediately after their arrival, the tables had been left unfinished, and thus the last sad offices of humanity were accidentally provided for.

The superstitious inhabitants confidently attributed the death of Captain Driberg to his having shot a peacock† in the preceding August, during the period of the Kattregam

† Sacred to *Kartikeya*.

festival, and that of his excellent wife, to her having partaken of it; but how to account for my having survived a like visitation, after having repeatedly incurred a similar penalty, with a view of exposing the absurdity of their notions; or for the recovery of Captain Driberg's children (who, including an infant only six weeks old, had been removed to my house immediately after the deaths of their parents) from the same fever, and, in the natives' opinion, from the same cause, was indeed a puzzler!

It is scarcely possible for language to describe the difficulties with which I had to contend, independently of personal suffering, from a very severe attack of the jungle fever; for I had those about me, who reminded me very much of certain "French pilots" from the Channel Islands, employed in our cruizers during the war, and notorious for finding a *shoal* wherever they anticipated a *shot;* for "the fever" was ever an excuse, when the stale ones, for "attending a dying parent" at one place, or the "wedding of a sister" at another, were exhausted; anything to get to a distance from the district: and every idea seemed to be absorbed in their *sauve qui peut* selfishness, for, with very few exceptions, those had generally the fever at their elbows, whose hands were most wanted:—nevertheless, some little excuse may be made for them, when it is considered, that the official intimation that the Governor had deemed the place too unhealthy for an European officer to take the command of the garrison, had confirmed the incipient panic.

During my convalescence, for I had been the first object of attack, and when scarcely strong enough to attend the bedsides of my dying friends, I was much importuned by those, who felt for my situation, to quit the place; and one, high in the civil service, wrote me, on the 12th October, 1826, in as urgent terms as could well be penned:—"Perhaps it is also your duty, for the sake of your wife, to remove from the horrid unhealthy place you are in, for a time. If you agree with me in this opinion, *move* without delay to Galle. You can easily get Sir Edward Barnes's leave, and report to government, that only extreme ill health has compelled you to the measure. The air you breathe, is impregnated with the pestilence that is destroying all around you, and you are momentarily subject to a relapse, and too weak to support yourself through another severe attack."

But another duty was paramount, and I was not disposed to adopt a new system, after nearly twenty two years service;—a determination, in which, I was supported by *her* for whose life so great an interest had been manifested, and who replied to my intreaties, that she would retire to Galle, "So long as your duty keeps *you* here, so long will *my* duty keep *me*."—In our humane friend's anxiety for us, he had either forgotten, or was in a great degree ignorant of, the actual state of affairs at the station, (which last is the most probable,) or he would never have recommended a measure, that, if I judge him rightly, and I think I do, he would rather have sacrificed his own life, than, under similar circumstances, have himself adopted.

But, notwithstanding the numerous casualties that death had caused in the district, it was even then, as it now is, more worthy of the attention of the Government, and of individual capitalists, than it has hitherto experienced; for, as if satisfied with the revenue derived from the natural salt pans, very little has since been done for it by the former, after an interval of sixteen years; and the latter have been deterred, through want of information, or prejudice, from expending capital in its improvement.

The capabilities of this part of the district include one of the most important objects connected with the trade of the interior. It is an admirable place for establishing a factory on an extensive scale for curing fish for the Kandyan markets, where it is in general and great demand; and the reasons for my suggestions may be briefly stated, after what has been already said upon the subject, in connexion with the government monopoly in salt.*

1st. A less population than any other district of the maritime provinces, and, consequently, a proportionally limited demand for fresh fish; but even if there were an hundred times the number of mouths, there would still be a superabundance of fish to afford employment for any number of canoes; for, notwithstanding the great distance, the Colombo and Galle fishermen very often come to this part of the coast to fish.

2ndly. Land may be purchased from the Crown at five shillings per acre; but, for such a national purpose, as this may justly be called, it can hardly be doubted that the Government would grant the land gratuitously, except in as far as regards the expenses of survey and transfer.

3rdly. The scite best adapted for a fish factory, is equi-distant from the town of Hambantotté and the Maha *Leway*, and within a hundred yards of the sea beach, so that whatever smell the cleaning and curing process might diffuse, would, like that which is inseparable from the pearl fishery, affect none but the persons immediately connected with the factory, and to them, it would soon become "second nature."

4thly. It would be of such importance to the revenue to reduce the price of salt for the purpose of fish curing, that no possible objection can well be anticipated on the part of the Government upon this point; because salt might be supplied at the *Leway*, (where the cost of collecting it is about 1½*d*. per parah,†) and thereby, the expense of carting it to the storehouses, and thence to the beach for shipment, and the freight

* See pages 162—168.

† About two-thirds of a Winchester bushel.

that the quantity so disposed of at the *Leway* would otherwise cost, would be saved to the public, which would also derive considerable profit upon the salt that might be sold, at the reduced rate, to the factory.

5thly. Timber, of excellent quality for building, may be felled in the forests of Mahagammé, by license from the Assistant Government Agent of the district, upon payment of the duty of ten per cent. upon the estimated value of the quantity required. The best timber for the purpose is the *Halmilleel*, which is also preferred for cart building.

6thly. Lime will be attended with no further expense than that of collecting dead shells and madrepore, and burning them upon the spot:—and the native mode of building would answer the purpose of a factory very well, viz. with timber, sticks of various sizes, clay (which might be mixed with lime and cow-hair to give it greater durability,) and *Koir* cord. This method of building, if substantially done, will last for thirty or forty years, particularly if the roof be tiled. Pantiles, flooring bricks, and bricks can be procured in any quantity from Colombo by *Dhoneys* during the south-west monsoon; the former at about fourteen or fifteen shillings per thousand, (the price of the second sort will depend upon the size required,) and the third may be contracted for at from ten to twelve shillings per thousand. Indeed, it is best to contract for all these materials, as well as for erecting the necessary buildings, within a given time. *Cajan* thatch might answer best for a temporary roof, and may be procured in any quantity from Matura, Belligammé, or Galle.

7thly. Because the Kandyan *Tavelams** from Badulla, in the central province, the eastern part of Saffregam, and from Lower Ouva and Wellassé, in the northern part of this province, make Hambantotté their *bivouac*, to and from Point de Galle, the present nearest mart for their ivory, bees' wax, cotton, pepper, coffee, ginger, cardamoms, honey, turmeric, deer horns, skins, ghee, and various vegetable drugs used in the native condiments; and their return lading from Galle usually consists of salt fish, common cotton handkerchiefs and cloths, generally "country made," or of Indian manufacture, and other articles of native consumption, part of which, they usually barter at this place for salt.

It does not appear to have been considered by our Manchester and Birmingham

* An indefinite number of bullocks, laden with produce, and attended by the proprietors and drovers. Each bullock has an uncouth-shaped bell suspended from the neck, some few of which are of brass or copper, but the rest are of wood, of an oblong square shape, and in appearance like a small inverted box without a lid The distant sound of a *Tavelam* may be called musical, and is more agreeable than otherwise to the ear.

manufacturers, that the natives of Ceylon are so wedded to their native costume, and implements of agriculture, that centuries may elapse, ere they altogether abandon their old habits for European ones; and this is worthy of attention.

For instance, the use of the needle is simply resorted to in the jackets and waistcoats of the men, and jackets of the women; all the rest consists of a cloth about 15 *cubits,** or 7½ English yards in length, and about forty inches in width, with a selvage at each end, for the former, and called a *Sarong*, which is tightly wrapped round the waist, like a petticoat, and simply fastened by tucking in one corner next the body. The higher classes wear a peculiar chintz pattern, which might be easily imitated by our cotton printers; and the middle classes, plain white, which they prefer of unbleached cotton, and of rather a thick quality; or, white with a narrow red or deep blue stripe, about three inches from the selvage. The lower classes wear them narrower, so as to descend to a little below the knee, and of plain white, but of the same length. The cloth of the women, which is white, and called *Cambay*, is of the same length as the *Sarong*, and is put on in a similar manner, without strings of any kind, but it does not exceed one yard in width.

These, with coarse cotton handkerchiefs, of a thick quality, and cross-barred with blue or red, the intermediate squares being from an inch to an inch and a half, would obtain a ready sale in the Kandyan markets, and ensure rapid returns to the importer, by way of barter, in the produce of the interior.

If the Birmingham manufacturer were once to see a spade in the hands of a Singhalese or Malabar labourer, he would require no further argument to convince him that for the naked foot there is no implement less adapted; for if he use it at all, it is by squatting down upon his haunches, (making his heels answer the purpose of a seat,) and, holding the handle of the spade with both hands, immediately above its junction with the iron part of it, the labourer digs away in a vertical direction, as if pounding rice in a mortar, and consequently takes as much time for turning up a square foot of ground, as an English labourer would for a dozen square yards.

The favorite implement of the Singhalese, the *Mamotie*, was introduced by the Dutch, and is something of the shape of a shovel, but fastened to the handle horizontally, like that of the English hoe; they also prefer our axes to their native *Pröah*; and, if it were not for the difference in the expense, our hand-plough might soon supersede their simple *Naguelah*. Their reaping hook (*Kopanadakkat*) has not so great a curve as the sickle in common use with us, but the edge of it is similarly serrated;

* A measure reaching from the elbow to the extremity of the middle finger.

Drawn by J. W. Bennett. *Michelia Champaca L.* Engraved by W. C. Edwards.

and they would soon get accustomed to English sickles and reaping hooks, bill-hooks, and hoes. These, with heavy broad-bladed chopping knives, but round instead of pointed, might be made a profitable export to Ceylon, (where there is no import duty levied upon agricultural implements,) provided the prices were such as to place them within the reach of the husbandman.

The *Tavelam* people are chiefly natives of the districts of Lower Ouva and Wellassé, in this province, and resemble Malabars more than Kandyans, or Singhalese of the lowlands. They adopt the costume of the former, and many of them wear enormous ear-rings, which form no part of the Kandyan, or Singhalese dress. These people are all worshippers of *Pattiné*, to whom they make offerings, before undertaking any thing of moment, (of which, smuggling salt is the chief,) and attribute bad luck, as well as bad harvests and sickness, to her wrath.

Wellassé is famed for its honey, bees' wax, coffee, and ivory, and for the superabundance of the Talipat palm; to this latter, when several of these trees are in flower at the same time, they attribute whatever sickness may prevail, the fetid odour of the flowers being very diffusive.

Now it is but reasonable to anticipate, that if the *Tavelams* could also be supplied at Hambantotté* with their chief lading, next to salt,—viz. salt fish, of a better quality, and at a cheaper rate, than they now are at Galle,† and with common cloths and agricultural implements adapted to their customs, they would not extend their journey 158 miles, (the distance of going to and returning from that port,) because the very same object that is now attended with benefit, in one point only, at Galle, would then be attained with threefold advantage at Hambantotté. 1st. The saving of time and expense in the difference of the journey, which would enable them to sell their produce much cheaper at the latter place.—2ndly. The factory on the spot would supply them with salt fish at a cheaper rate by fifty per cent. at least.—Lastly. Five trips to, and from, Hambantotté would be attended with less expense and consumption of time than two journies to, and from, Galle; and the temptation, now so general, to smuggle stolen salt into the interior, would be diminished, by the means the former place will then afford of loading their bullocks with a variety of lighter and more profitable articles.

The formation of a Company for the purpose, in this country, would prove one of the most lucrative concerns that has been undertaken for the last century, in proportion to the extent of capital requisite. The first public result to Hambantotté would be a great influx of Kandyans; for the establishment of a fish factory, where

* See Map of Ceylon, for the relative distances. † Where it is chiefly imported from the Maldive Islands.

their produce might be bartered for the chief articles of consumption, would induce the settlement of merchants, or their agents, to supply the place with European merchandize, of which it is now destitute, and gradually lead to its commercial importance, in comparison with its present state;—to the sounding of the anchorage of its bay and roads, and its correct insertion in the charts of the coast;—to its having a regular customs' establishment;—and ultimately, perhaps, to its being made a port of export and import to, and from, Europe, as its value may increase in the fiscal scale.

Although whales are not common upon the Ceylon coasts, a dead one is occasionally thrown ashore; but some species of the same family (*Cetacea*) are abundant, particularly the Gladiator Dolphin (*Delphinus gladiator*, C.), whose dorsal fin is from five to six feet in length, convexing towards the head, and nearly two feet broad at the base; the Grampus (*D. orca*, C.), Common Porpoise (*D. phocæna*, C.), and Dolphin (*D. Delphis*, C.).

I once fell in with a large heap of amber lying upon the beach, within half a mile of the salt stores at Hambantotté, which was several feet in circumference at the base, and nearly three feet in height, beautifully transparent, and of the consistence and color of the calf's feet jelly of our pastry cooks. I have already noticed the *pseudo* amber,* but although there was nothing in the shape of an insect throughout this mass, I found in it a living specimen of the Sea Dragon (*Pegasus draconis*, C.), about four inches in length; which, upon being uncovered, leaped to a distance of several inches. I preserved the specimen in spirits, and subsequently presented it to my highly esteemed friend, the Rev. Rowland Morgan, Rector of Wattisfield, and Vicar of Rendham, in Suffolk.

This coast occasionally presents a phosphorescent appearance at night, as far as the eye can reach, arising from myriads of a minute species of Shrimp (*Cancer fulgens*, L.). The *Soldier Crab* is also very common; and if the collector of anatomical specimens were to search the world through for a locality favorable to preparing a collection, he could not find a place to excel this, even if it equalled it, for facilitating his object. I have had the carcases of almost every description of indigenous animal, and the heads of elephants, buried in the sand, to the eastward of the town, and within a few yards of the sea, which, in less than a month, have been made perfect skeletons, by the innumerable small crabs, that everywhere abound in the sands near the sea.

* See page 130.

CHAP. XXXVII.

Further details connected with the suggested Fish Factory inexpedient here—Qualifications for the superintendent—Schemes for the public welfare abortive—Chord struck at first hearing the notes of the skylark in Ceylon—Mournful reflections—Reluctant Native labourers—The Right Honorable the Earl of Ripon—Colombo lighthouse—Consequences of an official omission—Jungle fever—Unwelcome New-year's gift—Medical officer's pusillanimity—Its result—Timidity of Headmen infectious—Effective plan of recalling them to their duty—"Old Malay of Mahagam"—Opportune relief, the result of a gratuitous distribution of garden seeds—A Fatalist agreeably disappointed—Captain Dawson, Royal Engineers—His lamented death, a great public loss to the colony—Native Medical Assistant's consolation—A better doctor than prophet—Domestic mortality—Convicts in chains humane nurses—Their strict and commendable honesty—Regret for their fate—Convicts' gratitude and petition—An enraged elephant kills its victim, and effects its escape, in the open day—Hint to the Ornithologist—Kandyan pellet tube—A skilful shot—Hard water pearls—Parting word in favor of the native population of the Mahagampattoo.

If the formation of a "Ceylon Fish Factory Company," should be the result of my suggestions, there are several points upon which further information can be given, but the nature and limits of the present Work will not admit of their detail.

The person selected to superintend the Factory, should be of active habits and strong mind, and be liberally remunerated; for he must not anticipate personal comfort in connexion with the place or neighbourhood, for the first twelve or eighteen months at least, (and, as the Agent of a Public Company, he will not have the consolatory anticipation of making money for himself, which may have peculiar charms, and include every comfort, with some people, but I cannot speak from any experience in the matter,) and even after that period, it will entirely depend upon his own resolution; for it is only by resisting the least tendency to indolence and *ennui*, and keeping both mind and body actively employed, that he can hope to do justice to his employers, or credit to himself.

Little anticipating how soon all my schemes for the improvement of the town and district, and for the welfare of its population, would be rendered abortive, I had, during an evening's ramble upon the *Leway* downs, fixed upon a scite for a future factory, in the well-grounded hope, as I, at the time, believed it to be, that even were no one disposed to second me, I should be enabled, in the course of four or five years, if I survived that period, to test my theory by practice, through my own means.

Whilst ruminating upon these prospective plans, as the best means of resisting the obtrusion of less pleasant objects of contemplation to add to the disagreeables that I had to contend with, I all at once heard with delight, equalled only by my surprise, the well-remembered notes of the Skylark (*Alauda arvensis*, L.), for as I was ignorant of its being indigenous, or one of the migratory birds that periodically visit the island, the appearance of the ethereal warbler, as a sudden visitor from one's native land, to be, as it were, a comforter in the wilderness, excited feelings and awakened recollections not easily to be forgotten :—and however trifling the incident may be reckoned by many, it will be estimated in a very different light by others, who will readily recollect the unsophisticated pleasure derived, both by officers and men, during the invasion of Kandy, in 1815, from the discovery of one of the oldest acquaintances of their boyhood, the common blackberry bramble (*Rubus fructicosus*, L.), in an indigenous production of the interior.*

So unexpected a gratification, where all around was silence, sterility, and desolation, recalled to mind the consolatory words of Kirby :—" Of all the endowments of birds, none is more striking, and ministers more to the pleasure and delight of man, than their varied song. When *the time of the singing of birds* is come, and the *voice of the turtle is heard in our land*, who can be dead to the goodness which has provided for all ? Such an unbought orchestra tuning the soul, not only to joy, but to mutual good will ; reviving all the best and kindliest feelings of our nature ; and calming, at least for a time, those that harmonize less with the scene before us."—But even this temporary pleasure had its antithesis ; for the melancholy reflection, that the ears of those, who had, till recently, been the constant companions of my evenings' drive, or walk, to this very spot, were closed in death, superseded the transient schemes that I had been revolving in mind, and the mournful reality became uppermost !

More and severer trials were, however, in store for me ; and the sequel will show with what reluctance the native Headmen and coolies (who could not enter into the philanthropic feelings, upon which the requisition for their labour was based) undertook a public duty, even when the best offices of humanity were involved in its punctual

* "Whilst we were at dinner in this miserable hut, on the banks of the river Awatska, the guests of a people with whose existence we had before been scarce acquainted, and at the extremity of the habitable globe, a solitary half-worn pewter spoon, whose shape was familiar to us, attracted our attention ; and, on examination, we found it stamped on the back with the word *London*. I cannot pass over this circumstance in silence, out of gratitude for the many pleasant thoughts, the anxious hopes, and tender remembrances it excited in us. Those who have experienced the effects that long absence and extreme distance from their native country produce on the mind, will readily conceive the pleasure such a trifling incident can give."—*King's Voyages*.

performance, and for which the latter were well paid, notwithstanding that the Public Service system (*Rajah Karia*, subsequently abolished by the Right Honorable the Earl of Ripon) was then in force.

The Government having determined to erect a light-house in the Port of Colombo, I had received orders for 500 *Halmilleel* trees to be felled for the Commissariat Department; but in sending the dimensions of the required timber, the technical words, "*in the clear*," had been omitted; and the consequence was, that very few of the trees originally felled, would answer the purpose. Although I had never been accustomed to anything of the sort, to have allowed the public service to stand still for a matter of mere ceremony, or through indisposition to exertion, would have been criminal; and therefore, in order to explain the literal meaning to the native Headmen, I assisted in selecting and measuring, under exposure to a burning sun, such timber as appeared of the required size, as it lay upon the beach for shipment; and at the same time I explained to them the important nature and object of a light-house, and "that if, through fear of fever, they neglected this duty, many ships and more lives might be placed in jeopardy, if not altogether lost."

A second attack of jungle fever was the almost immediate consequence; and a few days after, viz. on the 1st of January, 1827, I received an order to return to England, and the very inadequate allowance of £256 for the passage;—an unwelcome new-year's gift from the Colonial Department, for my long services; and unaccompanied by any proviso as to a homeward-bound ship or no ship being in port at the time.

It so happened, that no European civilian would *volunteer* for the Station, and the Government could not consistently *order* one to relieve me of my official duties, after its declaration of the 26th October, in regard to an European Commandant. I therefore retained office for two months after that order had reached me; but there was not a ship, by which I could obtain a passage, until the 26th of the following June, for which I paid £300; and I had neither salary nor allowances, during the intermediate period!

Upon this order, it does not become me to offer a single comment in these pages. There is only One, from whom the future is not obscured; and justice may still lie in prospective. It is satisfactory to know, that as time does not run against the Crown, its equity towards the injured knows no proscription.—But, at the moment that I received the order, and when the fever was at its height, and the result uncertain, my position, (*parvum componere magno,*) recalled to mind the memorable last words of "a faithful servant of his Sovereign," with all their applicableness, solemnity, and truth; for I, too, felt conscious, that I had not served my God, as faithfully as I had served my King and country!

As it was, the Army Medical officer of the district presumed that both my case and my wife's were hopeless; and, being a very nervous individual, the moment he felt the first symptoms of ague in himself, he considered it a sufficient reason for taking French leave, and proceeding to Galle, without even once intimating his intentions; and his coolies had been pressed with so much secrecy, that I only heard of his departure several hours after he had left, and by that time he had stolen a march of twenty miles upon the express sent after him.—This, as it generally happens when people run away from danger, ended in the very disease he had been so desirous of evading: his *deserted patients* got better first; and a trip by sea to Galle, whither I had been summoned to attend the sessions of the Honorable the Supreme Court, (as the Committing Magistrate of three persons in that district, for murder,) had so far restored me, that I began to consider myself *pretty well seasoned.*

At Galle, I had the honor to meet Major General Sir Hudson Lowe, Second in Command of the Forces, who was about to proceed, on his tour of inspection, through my district; and, as soon as the Court had dispensed with my attendance, I followed the General, in the hope of overtaking him, and being at my post to receive him:—but in this, I was disappointed by a relapse, which detained me twenty four hours at Tangalle; and, on my arrival at Hambantotté, I found that Sir Hudson had proceeded on his tour;—that the district Headmen and wood cutters, whom I had left employed in executing the requisition for the Colombo light-house, had relinquished their duty in the woods of Mahagammé, upon losing a few hands from fever;—and moreover, to add to my annoyance, that my active and fearless secretary, (Mr. Lambias,) having been subpœnaed to attend the sessions of the Supreme Court at Matura, had proceeded thither.

Thus left, without any assistance but that of an aged clerk of seventy eight,—the report staring me in the face, that the Headmen had the fever,—the wood cutters had the fever,—and indeed those who had it not, pretending to have it, my only alternative was, at once to adopt a plan, which is very strongly recommended to others, who may hereafter be similarly circumstanced, in the course of service, with native Headmen.

I forthwith despatched a circular *Ola* through the villages, to the effect, "that as there were no Headmen fit for duty, I should, within forty eight hours, proceed to the jungle, to superintend the felling of the trees, and there remain until that duty had been accomplished;—report the truantship of every Headman who might be absent under any pretence whatever, except that of actual inability through illness, of which, I should require proofs, by affidavits made in the presence of a priest; and that, under every circumstance, I should hold each Headman responsible for the absence of his quota of coolies."

At the expiration of the stated time, I proceeded to the woods; but, on my arrival at Mahagammé, I found that one Headman and about thirty coolies had preceded me by a few hours, and resumed their work; soon afterwards, the Arabocké Moodliar, (who had been attacked with *intermittent* fever, ere he had left the duty he was superintending,) and about twenty wood cutters made their appearance, and the rest joined by fives and sixes at a time, until the required number was complete. It was evident, from these circumstances, that, with their usual depth of cunning, they had actually waited till my palankin bearers were pressed for the service, (a proof that I was in earnest,) ere they took their departure for the jungle.

Whether this return to the duty which they had abandoned, under a false pretence, generated by their fears, (for not a symptom of fever was perceptible in any one cooley,) was the effect of shame, at having forced me to the steps I had taken, or that the Headmen began to quake at the prospect of losing their titles and swords, by a contrary conduct, the circular had effected the desired object. The Moodliar urgently entreated me to return home, and solemnly assured me, "that he would not quit the place until the whole of the Government requisition was completed." He kept his word, and the duty was accomplished.

But, notwithstanding my weak state, I had a great desire to visit the ruins of ancient Mahagam, which I had been prevented from doing on a former occasion. At that time, a Buddhist priest presented me with a very old Pali book, written upon the talipat leaf, as a history of Mahagam, which I subsequently gave to Captain Dawson, of the Royal Engineers, during his stay at Hambantotté, whilst on a tour of inspection of the district, in 1826; this would, I doubt not, have been published, as he intended, had not the great arm of death prematurely interposed, and snatched another victim from the service of his country, of which, Captain Dawson was a most zealous officer.

Fate, however, was against me a second time; for before I left the rest-house, so much excitement and exertion had caused another relapse; but, providentially, a military pensioner,* known as the "Old Malay of Mahagam," who resided there, displayed such anxiety to render himself useful to me, that I shall never forget it, nor his nostrum for relieving the dreadful head-ache which accompanied the fever, by cutting a huge Water melon longitudinally, and suddenly applying the parts to each side of my head and face, to "put out the fire," as he called it. This was followed by a grateful and

* Of the 1st Ceylon Regiment, now the Ceylon Rifle Regiment. The Invalid Company of this splendid regiment is an excellent body of men, against whom scarcely a complaint is ever heard. Their duties at Hambantotté are comparatively light, except during the time when the salt is formed at the *Leways*, and then every vigilance is required to preserve it, as well as the salt heaps, from plunder, until removed into store.

reviving coolness; and my new doctor then sliced a Persian melon into water, and gave it to me, to assuage the insatiable thirst, the fever's inseparable companion, for which purpose, it is even preferable to iced water.

This was an unexpected result of my own introductions; for, in sending the industrious old soldier a supply of exotic seeds, which included those of several varieties of the melon and cucumber, with cuttings of the manioc, arrow root, and Guinea grass (*Panicum polygonum*, L.), some months previously, (for which he thanked me as heartily as if I had scattered gold over his garden,) I had never contemplated the probability of any part of their produce being so opportunely presented to myself.

On the same morning, a most extraordinary incident had occurred to cause great alarm to my Malay friend; who, being at work in his garden, was interrupted by the intrusion and gambols of a very young bear (*Ursus labiolus*, C.) over the arrow root and melon beds.—He soon caught the cub, and tied it to a coco-nut tree; but had scarcely so done, and was about to resume his labour, ere a leopard entered by the same gap; when believing, as a fatalist, his "hour at hand," for he had neither gun nor kriss with him, the old man, fixing his eyes upon the animal, thus addressed it:—"Good Captain Tiger, surely you are not come for me yet,—pray come when I am too old to work in my garden, and I shall then be glad to see you;" whereupon, to his great surprise, and still greater delight, the leopard, lashing its tail, retreated very leisurely by the way it had entered.

Determining to play the old soldier in future, and run no second chance of such a similar surprise, the gardener went to his hut, which was situated outside the fence, for his "cut-down" musket and kriss; and, upon re-entering the garden, the returned leopard, with the cub's neck between its teeth, was struggling to force its prey from the tree. In a moment, the animal relinquished its hold, for a well-planted ball had levelled it with its victim; and then, to make "assurance doubly sure," the Malay gave the *coup de graçe* with his kriss. He subsequently dried the skins, and sent them to me, in remembrance of the occasion, and of his gratitude for the supply of ammunition that I had left with him.

Although temporarily relieved by the old Malay's kindness, I had scarcely reached Hambantotte, ere the fever returned with full force; and, in a few hours, the worthy Native Medical Assistant, (Mr. Heyn,) considering, from its rapid increase, spite of copious bleeding, and from the appearance of the blood, that my case was hopeless, intimated his opinion, with all due solemnity, and much feeling, that "*a better world*" was close at hand!"—But he proved a much better doctor than prophet!

At this time, my *Appo*, or head servant, lay dead, and my cook's eldest daughter next shared the same fate; the other servants were suffering from fever, to such a degree, that our only active attendants were convicts in chains, (many of them for life); and yet the patience with which these poor creatures went to a great distance for spring water, several times a day, as cold suffusion was ordered, and the care and kindness they all showed, induced the wish, that they had not merited so hard a fate.

All that I could do to lighten the *weight* of their chains, I did; for, during the whole time, and when almost every thing in the house was within their reach, not an article of even the most trifling nature was pilfered, nor did they ever attempt to escape, although they might have succeeded without any very great difficulty: and, when we were about to leave the district, the Head Constable brought me a petition from these grateful convicts, "that, as a last favor, they might be allowed to be our palankin bearers to the beach!"

Under all the circumstances, and after so much affliction, I might perhaps have been justified in leaving the district, upon receipt of the official order to return to England; but I contented myself with making a respectful appeal to the proper Authorities, and continued at my post, till the Collector of the Province had made the best temporary arrangements he could, for the safety of the public stores and treasure under my official charge; because, where example was everything, it would not have been acting the part of an Englishman, for the only one in the district to have quitted it, at the very moment when his presence was most necessary to the interests of the public service.

Such was the state of the Mahagampattoo district, in 1826-1827, that wild elephants repeatedly entered the town of Hambantotté at night, and helped themselves to rice and fruit, by stripping off the *Cajan* thatch that enclosed the various small stalls in the bazaar; but a still more daring occurrence took place in 1819, when an elephant chased a native, who had wounded it, whilst grazing near the *Maha Leway*, into the town, in the middle of the day. This person was the cook of the then Commandant, Captain Roberts, and had been often upon excursions after elephants. The animal followed him through the most populous part of the place, where, in spite of the shouts of the people in the shops at each side of the street, it succeeded in seizing and trampling to death the object of its revenge; and, before a single soldier of the Malay invalids could arm himself and reach the spot, the elephant had escaped beyond the reach of spear or shot.

Having given a hint to the collector of anatomical specimens in the preceding chapter, I ought not to omit one of equal utility to the Ornithologist.

During my residence here, I employed a native to supply my table with game, and also to bring me specimens of the indigenous birds; for this, he was very well satisfied to receive eight rix dollars (twelve shillings) monthly, with a moderate allowance of powder and shot.

At first, it appeared very strange to me, how this sportsman contrived to shoot all the smaller specimens, from the size of a thrush, to that of the diminutive Tailor bird, (*Sylvia sutoria*, L.), without a single feather being injured, or a shot in their bodies. This was effected (at a great saving of the powder and shot for his own use) by means of a wooden tube of about five feet in length, through which he blew small pellets of soft clay or common mould, about the size of a swan shot, with great accuracy, a dozen or fifteen paces.

To test his skill, I placed a small wafer upon the first joint of my fore finger, and, extending my arm, sent him to a distance of a dozen yards, and told him "to hit it if he could;" and, out of twenty shots, he never once missed the mark. It was attended with no pain whatever, but was quite sufficient to stun a small bird. These tubes are drilled in Kandy, and are beautifully ornamented with red, yellow, black, and green lacker, in a similar manner to the Kandyan state bows, arrows, and walking sticks.

Hail storms are so uncommon, that I never witnessed but two, during the many years that I resided in the island; one, at Arabocké, near Hambantotté, and the other, at Kurunugallé, about 26 miles from Kandy. The then oldest resident, the venerable "Chief," or, as he was commonly called, "Salt Moodliar," a Malay of Batavia, (Matjam-Boorah-Aboocassim,) had never previously seen a fall of "*hard water pearls*," according to his definition of hail stones.

And now a parting word for the native population of the place:—I had heard so much to the prejudice of the inhabitants, before an opportunity offered of judging how far reports were, or were not, correct, that the first thing I did, upon taking charge of the district, was to erect a flogging post in the bazaar. This, naturally gave rise to the supposition, that they had *a terrible Tartar* come amongst them; but, after an experience of twelve months, as the only magistrate in the district, during which period, I had neither occasion to commit one native for trial, or to resort to summary punishment within my own jurisdiction, extending over seventy six miles in length,) either by the lash or imprisonment, except in one instance of the latter, in order to give a place of refuge to a Malabar vagrant, I had the supreme pleasure of ordering the removal of the *maiden* flogging post, as the last act of my authority there: and, when the extent of the district be considered, this tribute is nothing more than is, in justice, due to the native inhabitants of the Mahagampattoo, whom I left, *malgré* all that I had suffered there, with heartfelt regret.

CHAP. XXXVIII.

Suggestions for the introduction of the Camel into Ceylon—Soil of the Mahagampattoo favorable to its employment in the district as a beast of burthen—Habits of the camel—Possible objections to its employment groundless—Route from Hambantotté to Wallewé—Karaganaré Leway—Village of Arabocké—Euphorbia antiquorum—Apathy of the natives in regard to its gum—Presumed qualities of its timber—Sitricalé Leway—Nepenthes distillatoria—Air plant—Arabian gum tree—Escape from a tusked elephant—Cobra di Capello—Pybocké—Plains—Mushrooms—Extraordinary production of fish—Malay officer's opinion of the cause—Game—Tank—Extraordinary bird—Village of Wanderopé—Temple Title deed—The Honorable Sir Hardinge Giffard, late Chief Justice of Ceylon—Temple lands exempt from taxes—Exemption extended to Kandy, and integrity of the Buddhist religion guaranteed, by the Convention of 1815*—Wallewé river—Sailing directions—Village of Wallewé—Soil—Its bad name, and suggestions for giving it a better—Cotton fly unknown here—Tranquil locality for the growth of silk—Suggestions for employing a few Chinese settlers.*

Among other experiments for the benefit of the island, I would suggest the introduction of the Arabian Camel* (*Camelus Dromedarius*, L.), by way of throwing the thousands of draught bullocks, that might be employed for agricultural purposes, but are now monopolized by the Government Salt Department, and Tavelams, into the hands of the native farmers; and the sandy soil of the Mahagampattoo is another consideration in favor of the introduction of the camel into this district.

This might be tried upon a moderate scale at first, and at an inconsiderable expense to the Government, by importing a certain number of camels from the coast of Coromandel; and if the result prove a considerable public saving, as well as of general benefit to the district, both which may be justly anticipated from the habits of these animals, future supplies, to an indefinite extent, can be obtained from the Arabian Gulf.

The sale of the Government bullocks to the native farmers, would not be the only benefit to them; for that of its large cart establishment would naturally follow, and thereby distribute the means of transit among the agriculturists, of which, they are now nearly destitute, because they cannot afford to send 100 miles from the district to buy carts; and the only wheelwrights, within that distance, are those employed by the Government, and at double wages.

* This animal is commonly called the Dromedary, as a distinction from the double-hunched, or Bactrian, Camel, (*Camelus Bactrianus*, L.).

2 Q

A camel conveniently carries a burthen of between 700 and 800 lbs weight,* for fourteen hours out of the twenty four; which, at its usual pace of 2½ miles an hour, is a much greater distance than can be performed by bullocks, even when well fed, and with a comparatively slight load, between sunrise and sunset; and the former is so very docile an animal, that it is easily trained, and soon becomes acquainted with its driver.

Once introduced into use in the island, the value of the camel would be soon sufficiently appreciated to induce its extensive importation from Arabia, as a matter of speculation; and its general employment in the conveyance of produce, for exportation, from the interior to the sea coasts, in lieu of draught bullocks, that are now the principal means of transit, would doubtlessly follow the first successful result.

One need not refer to scripture† for the antiquity of the "Ship of the Desert," as the best adapted of all domestic animals, for the purposes of burthen, and over which the several Eastern nations had acquired early dominion; nor to its history, for perseverance, moderation, partiality for spinous plants, that other animals (the ass only excepted, which comes nearest to the camel in the coarseness of its food) will not eat; the peculiarity of its divided upper lip, which enables it to nip off the smallest shoots of grass, whether of the best or coarsest kind, and turn them into its mouth with facility; and the most Providential and extraordinary nature of its internal structure, by which, it has the power of drinking sufficient water at one time, and of storing it, for several days.

The employment of the camel in Ceylon may be objected to, by those, who have not given much consideration to the circumstance, that this animal and the elephant are conjointly employed in the Indian armies,‡ upon the grounds that the timidity of the former, and the habitual dread of the elephant attributed to it by some writers, would render it all but useless, where that animal abounds.

In this matter, I would suggest, as I have often found it necessary to do, when I have seen persons disposed to throw away valuable exotic seeds, with the wholesale condemnation of, "these are useless, they won't grow here," to "*try them;*" and rarely did t fail, where proper attention was paid to the object in view.

Leaving Hambantotté for Wallewé rest-house, the next stage, and distant 8½ miles, the road lies to the right of the eastern extremity of the Karaganaré, or Long *Leway,*

* Linnæus says, 1200 lbs weight.

† Genesis xxiv. 10, 11.

‡ The officers of the Bengal and Madras auxiliary troops, through whose timely arrival at Ceylon, and gallant assistance, in 1818, the then formidable rebellion was crushed, felt the greatest inconvenience from the want of baggage camels.

adjoining the high promontory by which the small bay of Hambantotté is formed. This *Leway* lies considerably below the level of the sea, and might be filled with salt water, by cutting through about 130 yards of sand.

The *Leway* stretches nearly along the sea shore for about three miles, and is about half a mile broad; a small quantity of very bitter salt occasionally forms upon its edges, which, the Native Medical Assistant informed me, had all the medicinal properties of the Glauber salts.

The village of Arabocké, the residence of the Second Moodliar, where paddee, maize, and Korakan, form the chief objects of culture, lies to the right of the high road, and is famed for its forests of Euphorbia trees (*Euphorbia antiquorum*, L.), which are from fifteen to twenty feet in height; the timber white and solid, and such as a superficial observer would consider very well adapted for the purposes of the musical instrument maker.

The apathy of the natives in regard to the gum of this extraordinary tree, which is generally believed to be peculiar to Ceylon, has been already noticed;* but, with the improvement of the district, it is to be hoped, that this, and its timber, will be turned to their appropriate purposes in domestic economy, instead of merely continuing to fill a certain space for a time, and then decay and rot upon its surface.

A neglected plantation of coco-nut trees, on the right of the road, points out the scite of a former agricultural village, where there is not a house or hut to be now seen;—these, must have been taken great care of for several years, or, where so many elephants abound, they would never have attained their present height; and it affords one melancholy instance, among the many, of the depopulation of this once well-peopled and cultivated district.

Between two and three miles beyond the Karaganaré *Leway*, the exhausted Sitricalé *Leway*, having the appearance of a large oval fish pond, about a mile, or a mile and a half in circumference, lies to the right of the road, which is between it and the sea, from which its distance is about 250 yards. The sea shore is bounded by a high sand bank, and the intermediate space, to the left of the road, filled with thick jungle.

About half a mile beyond the Sitricalé *Leway*, is the Lesser Sitricalé, the furthest from the sea, and called by the natives, *Koda-Leawava*. Upon the borders of this *Leway*, I once observed a huge crocodile basking in the sun, and a buffalo lying equally at its ease, and within twenty yards of each other. A rifle ball soon made the former take to the water, but had no effect in disturbing the latter.

* See page 128.

The *Nepenthes distillatoria*, L., abounds in the jungle, as well as a beautiful species of air plant, and the Arabian gum tree (*Mimosa Nilotica*, L., and *Acacia Arabica* of Wildenow), which is almost always in bloom, and has a beautiful appearance, from its globular yellow blossoms, whose fragrance is very diffusive, and similar to that of the Gilly flower (*Mathiola incana* of R. Brown).

Between this place and the small village of Pybocké, at the narrowest part of the jungle, one of the most providential escapes that ever happened to a small party, of ten persons, occurred in 1827. I had arrived at Wanderopé, upon the river Wallewé, about 4 P. M., for the purpose of superintending the planting of some exotics that I had introduced, and, as usual, immediately dismissed my palankin bearers, who belonged to the adjoining villages; but, shortly after sunset, I received an express, which rendered it imperative upon me to return to Hambantotté; and I should have gone on foot, rather than not at all, if a great part of the country between the villages of Pybocké and Arabocké had not been inundated.

Fortunately, my Malay Interpreter-Mohandiram, (Ibrahim Doole,) and the Maha Vidahn of the Fisher-caste, (Hettéwehagay Don Christian,) who had attended me from Hambantotté, had not left me; and, through their exertions, in about an hour, six coolies and a *Chule* bearer were procured; but as these had never carried a palankin, and were not enough for that purpose for such a distance, an arm chair was slung for me upon a couple of bamboo poles; and in lieu of *Cajan Chules*, some resinous sticks were formed into small fagots, one of which was lighted, and, thus prepared, we proceeded, *en route*, to Hambantotté, without even a brass *Tallea*, or *Tam-a-tam*, to scare the elephants.

About a mile beyond Pybocké, and at the narrowest part of the jungle, the Mohandiram, and Maha Vidahn, each armed with a long Dutch gun, being in a line with the extremities of the chair poles, having the *Chule* bearer between them, and all moving as silently as if about to make a night attack upon an enemy, the latter, as usual upon occasion, struck the *Chule* against the ground, (the native way of raising flame,) when, by the sudden blaze, we found ourselves within reach of the proboscis of an enormous tusked elephant, which was, at that moment, raised perpendicularly in the air.

" *Bang,—bang*," from the muskets of my escort,—my sudden ejection from the chair into the jungle, to the right of the road, where I fell upon my right side, with my rifle under me, which accidently went off,—the coolies, instead of escaping into the jungle, falling upon their knees, and, with uplifted hands, imploring the *Maha Dewyo Alia*, or " Great God Elephant," to spare them,—the trumpeting of the wounded elephant, as it rushed into the opposite jungle,—and the joyful exclamations of the shotsmen, at having hit the animal, appeared but the work of a moment, and formed a *coup d' œil,* easier to be imagined than described.

Never, I believe, was destruction nearer, without some injury following; and I give my companions credit for every proper feeling upon the occasion; for myself, I confess, that never, in my whole period of service, did I ever offer my prayers more fervently, upon going into action, that I might do my duty faithfully, than I did my heartfelt thanks, upon the occasion of this most providential, and, indeed, almost miraculous escape.

We had scarcely walked a mile beyond the place of the elephant's *bivouac,* when the Mohandiram again fired, and shot the largest *Cobra di Capello* that I ever saw in Ceylon, which had crossed our path, almost, I may say, within reach of our feet. It measured five feet in length, and was full of *ova,* in a cluster like grapes.

Two *Tappal* bearers having been killed by an elephant some time previously, about the same neighbourhood, I sent people the next day to track the animal, whose route was soon discovered by the blood sprinkled over the bushes, for a considerable distance, but they could not come up with the chase.

About a fortnight after this occurrence, a native of Jahadegammé, on the left bank of the Kirindé-Oya, complained of having been plundered of two elephant's tusks by the priests of the Kattregam temple; for that, having fallen in with a wounded elephant, he had shot it in the neck with an arrow, and followed the animal for several miles, till at length it fell within the temple lands of Kattregam, where it died, and the priests had impounded the tusks.

Inquiry, as to the right of the priests to the tusks so claimed, took place through the Agent of Government at Alipoot, Captain Fletcher, which was decided in their favor, after an official correspondence on the subject, between that excellent and distinguished officer and myself; and greatly to the loss and disappointment of the poor villager, to whom, the priests did not make the slightest acknowledgment or compensation.

Soon after the setting in of the rains, the spacious plains adjoining Pybocké present a most novel appearance to a stranger, at early dawn; patches of white, interspersed with the bright green of the herbage, meet the eye in every direction: these, upon a nearer approach, are found to be mushrooms, which, for size and flavor, are not to be surpassed in any part of the world.—But how tastes differ! The natives will not eat the mushroom with pinkish lamellæ, the most prized by Europeans, but prefer that with the white or yellowish, which we consider noxious.—During the same period, the several pools of water on the plains, notwithstanding that they had previously been for some months merely dry pits, exposing the sun-cracks at the bottom, become full of a species of perch, from five to six inches in length, in the course of six weeks.

An intelligent Malay officer thus stated his opinion of this natural phenomenon :—"Sun very much too strong, take him up little fish egg, keep him in cloud, and when water come, let him fall one fish for get too much large." The literal meaning is, that during the hot season, the sun's power is so great, that the spawn is exhaled into, and nourished by, the atmosphere, where it remains suspended until the next rains, when the pools are supplied with the living fishes. But it appears to me more reasonable to suppose, that the spawn remains imbedded in the clay, at the bottom of the pits, where it finds sufficient moisture, although imperceptible to the human eye, until its *habitat* is again supplied with water, for ensuring the means of existence to its produce.

At night, these plains appear studded with fire-flies; and, at sunrise, teem with elephants, wild hogs, in herds of some hundreds, spotted deer, and peafowl; and the adjoining larger patches of water, bordered by the jungle, with flamingos, spoonbills, wild ducks, widgeon, pelicans, herons, toucans, and kingfishers, as if inviting the attention of the sportsman and ornithologist.

Here is also a large artificial tank, but of modern construction, capable of holding sufficient water to irrigate 100 ammonams of paddee ground, of which, the average produce is 1600 parahs, or 1066⅔ Winchester bushels. This tank is the *habitat* of a very large white bird, considerably exceeding the swan in size, which has no dread of the crocodile; but I could not succeed in getting a very near view of it, there being no canoe; and the people not being disposed to venture into the tank, for fear of crocodiles, I would not allow a shot to be fired at it, as my Malay escort were very desirous of doing. It resembled, as it swam on the water, the white Albatross (*Diomedea exulans*, L.) of the Cape of Good Hope.

Wanderopé is the name of the next village, after leaving Pybocké, upon the left bank of the river Wallewé; and, with the exception of the old *Pansala*, and the cottage that I built in 1826, upon Government land, which was subsequently granted to me, by the then Governor, His Excellency Lieutenant General Sir Edward Barnes, G. C. B., consists of scattered cottages and huts, of which, a few of the former are tiled.

The only thing to interest the antiquarian, is a granite post, resembling an old English milestone, under an umbrageous *Bogaha*, in the area of the temple, which, as the priest informed me, constituted its title to the adjoining lands, "*so long as the sun and moon may endure.*"

Of this *title deed* I made a sketch, and, having copied the characters as well as I could, sent it, with a variety of drawings of the fruits of Ceylon, to the then Chief

Justice, Sir Hardinge Giffard, (through whose great kindness I had been much assisted with books, in prosecuting my Icthylogical inquiries,) at that time about to proceed to England, in consequence of ill health; but, unfortunately, Sir Hardinge had sailed before my packet reached him, and, still more unfortunately for his country, died on the voyage; leaving behind him a lasting memorial of sincere and affectionate respect for his memory in the hearts of all who thoroughly knew him; for a more humane and charitable member of society, a more loyal and devoted subject, or a more just and consistent administrator of the laws, never yet filled the justice seat at Ceylon; and if, in these eminent qualifications, one or two may have equalled, none have excelled Sir Hardinge Giffard.—The drawings were transmitted to England after Sir Hardinge had sailed, by his Private Secretary, John Frederick Giffening, Esq., but were lost in the ship Alexander.

All lands belonging to the temples are registered, and the Cutchery certificates are the only admitted proofs of their exemption from taxation; but one seldom or ever sees or hears of any part of the produce of such lands being appropriated to the repair of the temples, which everywhere appear to be fast falling into decay.

The remission of taxes (viz. a tenth of their produce) upon temple lands, extend also to those belonging to the former kingdom of Kandy, and is a considerable loss to the public revenue, for these privileged domains are of enormous extent:—but there is no help for it; for, by the Convention between the British Government and the Priests, Chiefs, and People, consequent upon the dethronement of the King, and banishment of the Royal Family, in 1815, by which, the entire dominion of the Kandyan kingdom was vested in the Imperial Crown, upon the condition, (among others,) that "*the Buddhist religion should be inviolable, and its temples, rites, privileges, and worship be maintained and protected,*" it is morally impossible, without a breach of the national faith and dignity, to alter or amend it, except by way of compromise; and it is far from improbable, that even the bare suggestion of such a measure would have the effect of fomenting a rebellion, of a far more general and formidable nature than we have hitherto had to contend against, and of which, the priests have generally been the fomenters or abettors.

"Wallewé or Walleway River bears about E. by N. ½ N. four leagues from Tangalle; the coast between them is low and barren close to the sea, but several coco-nut trees are seen near the river's mouth; the coast is high inland, and may be approached to 25 fathoms, within four or five miles of the shore. Off the entrance* of the river,

* See page 27.

at the distance of three or four miles, there is a rock, on which the sea generally breaks, said to have a channel with 7 and 8 fathoms water, sandy bottom, between it and the shore, through which small vessels may occasionally pass. A little inland from the entrance of the river, stands a small mountain, of barren aspect."

The light, but rich alluvial soil, upon the banks of this river, is admirably calculated for the cultivation of sugar, pepper, ginger, cotton, turmeric, cardamoms, arrow root, and the much neglected but most nutritious *Canna glauca.* Few even of the indispensable articles, as condiments, used in almost every sort of native food, are grown here, although immense quantities might be grown in the waste lands, without any other trouble than of planting and weeding. Here also, lands may be obtained at a merely nominal rent, or purchased for a very trifle, because this place also has a *bad name* with some people; but, in my humble opinion, it is as healthy as many other places that have better names.

The straggling village of Wallewé is on the right bank of the river. At such a place as this, the general improvement of a district should commence; and, if once it was cleared, by cutting down and burning the underwood, and thinning the trees, *not a general cutting down of the whole,* and planted with the mulberry, sugar, cotton, coffee, pepper, indigo, anatto, cardamoms, &c. &c., one would hear no more of its malaria, but as its riches increased, so would its character, till it became second to none in the island.

The fly so destructive to the cotton plantations near Galle, is never seen here; for I planted several cotton shrubs, including the perennial Bourbon cotton; of these, the former bore abundantly, and were uninjured by either fly or caterpillar; but the latter, requiring at least two years to attain maturity, I can give no account of its produce. The *Tavelam* people bring down picked cotton from Kandy, and sell it here for about 2*d.* per pound; and the cotton grower might excel it in quality, (viz. length of staple,) if I may judge from what was grown upon the spot, and sell it very profitably to himself, *clean* and *pressed,* for 4*d.* or 4½*d.* per pound, at the now nearest port of export, Galle, distant 70½ miles.

This is just the tranquil locality adapted to the silk worm; and the mulberry thrives here luxuriantly. Wells can be easily sunk, and the purest water be obtained, within twenty yards of the river.

A few Chinese settlers, by way of setting industrious examples to the indolent natives, and particularly in their native method of transplanting paddee, would soon give a very novel and fertile appearance to this now neglected neighbourhood.

CHAP. XXXIX.

River Wallewé—Horse boats—Double canoes—Seasons of sowing and reaping—Clay for the manufacture of bricks—Reported abundance of limestone rock—Pansala at Wanderopé—Buddhist priest objects to sell the bricks of the ruined temple for lay purposes—Cultivates the grape vine successfully—Wallewé tank—District but little improved for the last sixteen years—Author's desire to innoculate British capitalists with some of his own virus in favor of the Mahayampattoo—Mouth of the river Wallewé—Native objections to the sea breeze apparently insuperable—Girrawah-pattoo, or Parrot district—Wallewé rest-house—Its savage occupants in 1826—Peculiar sand of rubies, sapphires, and cats'-eyes—Roads—Government Cattle Kraal—Leways—Ranné bridge and rest-house—Crocodile Kraal—The Porcupine—Ancient tank at Ranné—Face of the country—Approach to Tangalle—What any enemy might do, upon a sudden breaking out of war—Nature the best defender of the Ceylon coast—Singhalese not to be depended upon to face an enemy—Kandyans and their characteristics—Precaution necessary—Sailing directions—Suggested Signal Station for communicating with India bound ships from England making Dondra Head, the southernmost point of Ceylon.

THE River Wallewé, which is fordable at the Ferry, except during the rains, becomes, at that season, a deep and rapid stream, and can only be crossed in boats.—The "horse-boat" in general use at the Ceylon ferries, is a very convenient one for horses and carriages, for, being flat-bottomed, it draws only a few inches of water; and as it is strongly built, about eighteen feet in length, and six or seven in breadth from head to stern, both which are square, the upper part abutting about three or four feet from the bottom, is capable of conveying a considerable burthen.

The common method of ferrying five or six passengers across the Wallewé river, is by joining two canoes, and placing a platform over them, capable of containing as many chairs conveniently. This is also the best for excursions up the river, for a temporary awning may be fitted in ten minutes; and a couple of boatmen, one being seated in the bow of the near canoe, and the other in the stern of the off one, (or vice versâ,) propel it along rapidly with their short paddles, and seldom fail to secure whatever birds may be shot, and fall into the water from the overhanging trees, without moving from their seats.

Paddee is sown in this district in October and November, and is reaped in January and February, but that called the *second sort*, is reaped in December and January; Maize (*Iringhée* of the Singhalese) is sown in August and September, and reaped in November and December; the brown and white Korakan (*Cynosurus Coracanus*, L.)

are sown in August and September, and reaped in November and December; Moong (*Phaseolus Mungo*, L.) and *Badhamu*, an excellent substitute for rice, are sown in October and November, and reaped in January and February.

I regret that my information is so limited, as it is, upon the important district of the Mahagampattoo; but even that little was obtained, as my time would admit of it, amid various official duties and difficulties, within the short period of twelve months. If my stay had been protracted, as I had anticipated upon taking charge of the district, (in which, it was my first Revenue appointment,) I should, as I was naturally anxious to have done, have made myself master of its capabilities, and, in the course of three years, either have lost my life, or known every square mile of it; for my object, from the first, was to have ascertained, from personal examination, the various scites of its antiquities, the quantum of its original means of irrigation, which were of the most extensive description, the several localities for raising clay for the purposes of brick making, and of its reported abundance of limestone rock, which are said to be numerous.

The *Pansala* at Wanderopé is a very low building, covered with pantiles, and the *Vihare* a mere heap of brick ruins; but these afford very ample proof of the excellence of the quality of the materials employed in their manufacture, which, as the priest informed me, had been procured in the neighbourhood, and made upon the spot. I endeavoured to induce him to sell me the bricks, for more useful objects than filling a nook in the jungle, but unsuccessfully, because he considered it a desecration of the sacred relics of the ancient *Vihare*, to part with them for lay purposes. These ruins, which are partly covered with jungle underwood, lie within an enclosure on the left hand, immediately adjoining the high road, and about a hundred yards from the ferry; but the Buddhists have not the means, if they had the intention, of re-employing the materials in the restoration of the *Vihare*.

I was glad to find that great attention had been paid by the resident priest to a couple of Teneriffe vines, which I had given him of those I first introduced into the district, with instructions for training them upon a trellis; for in about six months they were in full bearing, and the grapes equalled in flavor the best in my own garden.

There was a considerable difference in the size of the bunches, although none in the quality of the grapes. I used bones as a manure, and the bunches were double the size of those grown in the natural (alluvial) soil of the *Pansala* grounds. The priest attributed the difference to the shade of the magnificent Bogaha (*Ficus religiosa*, L.) that overshadowed the *Pansala*, and not to any virtue in the manure that I had employed.

Tanks, for irrigating the surrounding country, might be constructed here, and on the opposite bank of the Wallewé, to any extent; but the old Wallewé tank having been formed above the level of the river, could only be supplied from it during its periodical rise in the rainy season, when water is least wanted.

I regret to learn, by recent intelligence from Ceylon, that the state of this district is nearly the same as when I left it; and the Government, after an interval of nearly sixteen years, but little, if anything, more enlightened in regard to its capabilities, than it was at that period. This is partly attributed, by many, to dread of the climate; by others, to the circumstance of the interior being the present field of individual speculation, where coffee planting is the prevailing (*Anglo*) *mania;* and, next to it, the culture of the sugar cane; but the latter, although successful, is not likely to be carried to any extent, in comparison with that of the former object of speculation. Sugar might be brought to still greater perfection here, where the cane grows luxuriantly, but the natives are fearful of planting it except in small patches near their dwellings, for making syrups, and for their children's use in a raw state, in consequence of the numerous elephants that infest the country.

If it were possible to innoculate some of our British capitalists with a portion of my own *virus* in favor of the Mahagampattoo, there would be no local difficulties that perseverance might not overcome, in the course of a few years; when this now neglected district might rival, in its productions and trade, the most favored parts of the island; and these, gradually extending along the whole of the south-eastern and eastern coast to Trincomalé, would render that splendid harbour, where few merchant ships are now to be seen, as great a resort for stock and produce as any of the present most frequented Indian ports.

The beautiful river Wallewé, whose banks are shaded by some of the most magnificent trees that adorn the surface of the globe, debouches between two coco-nut topes, by percolating the high bank of sand at its mouth. The villagers on each side appear to have an insuperable objection to the sea breeze, for they allow the underwood to grow so densely, as altogether to preclude its cool and wholesome influence. If this were not the case, the village might become as notorious for its salubrity as any of the intermediate places from Tangalle to Colombo.

Having crossed from the left to the right bank of this river, the tourist enters the Girrawah-pattoo, or Parrot District, as it is properly called; for just before sunset, the trees, on the banks of the Wallewé, particularly those that are leafless at the time, are frequently covered with these birds, as if they sought, by their presence, to act as a temporary substitute for the absent foliage.

The rest-house is about a hundred yards from the ferry, on the left of the highway, which there begins to assume some sort of road-like appearance, and intersects the jungle, by which, that large and convenient building is surrounded; but although the compound is strongly fenced, it is subject to the nocturnal incursions of elephants. In 1826, so little had this rest-house been required, that, for several months together, it had never been once used, until the then Collector of the province ordered it to be got ready for my reception; and upon the coolies entering the house, they found a male and female chetah (*Felis venatica*, C.) already in possession, and not disposed to quit. The besiegers were consequently under the necessity of retreating, in order to get assistance from the neighbouring villagers, who, armed with guns, and bows and arrows, soon dispatched the larger animals, and secured their cubs.

A sand, composed of rubies, sapphires, and cats'-eyes, is peculiar to this district, and used in making transverse sections of the molar teeth of elephants, and for many of the purposes of diamond powder.

The road is a very dangerous one by night, owing to the numerous wild elephants that infest it. About a mile above the rest-house is the Government cattle *Kraal*, where the bullocks belonging to the Salt Department at Hambantotté, which are sent to this distant place to graze, are penned; but still the chetahs occasionally contrive to seize and devour a bullock at night, and to get off with impunity.

The *Kraal* lies in the middle of an extensive plain, which is crossed to the left, in the route by the sea side (by far the most preferable) to the village of Wellepattanvellé, about a mile and a half from the Wallewé, from whence the road rises by a gradual ascent. From the summit, where there is a delightful spot for a residence, the prospect commands a very extensive range of both sea and land, including Tangalle, the Mahagampattoo, and the Kattregam hills, in the distance.

Near the straggling village of Loonawé, situate at the eastern extremity of the Tamboora Gallé *Leway*, which lies much nearer to the sea than the Konakatté *Leway*, the country has a delightfully verdant appearance after the rains; but, being entirely dependent upon a small tank, which is filled at that season, for its irrigation, the produce is very limited, in proportion to what it might be, under more favorable circumstances; and the remains of former embankments and drains, in almost all the villages in this district, are plain evidences that its former state of cultivation was much more extensive than its present one. The native farmers aver, that whilst the paddee crops yield not more than eight or nine fold, the white and brown *Korakan*, and *Badhamu*, yield twenty five and often thirty fold.

The post-bag, or *Tappal* bearers, have here a very extraordinary but common custom of transferring their charge, upon reaching the relief stations. Although large remittances are occasionally sent by the mail, the leathern bag *has no lock*, and upon the bearer reaching the station in the night, he merely gives notice to his successor, by loudly exclaiming "*Tappal*," and then, hanging the mail bag to the stump of a tree, retires to his dwelling;—nevertheless, the letters are as safely delivered as at any town in England, and without even an occasional casualty.

After crossing the wooden bridge over the Ranné-Oya, where that river is about twenty feet wide, the rest-house, which is elevated a few feet above the road on the right hand, as one ascends the hill, offers shelter from sun and rain, but no comfort, being both hot and disagreeable, from its low roof and small size. The village of Ranné is 11 miles from Wallewé, and 9 from Tangalle.

Crocodiles infest the river, and the natives catch them in *Kraals* composed of strong and high stakes. The Aratchy presented me with a string of 25 crocodiles' eggs, nearly as large as those of the goose, but more oblong, and of a beautiful white.

The porcupine (*Histrix cristata*, L.) abounds here. It burrows to a great depth, and its retreat having but one entrance, it is easily unearthed. This animal is seldom to be seen during the day, but at night sallies forth in quest of roots or fruits, and is most destructive to young plantations. When the skin is taken off, the flesh has a honeycomb resemblance, from the indentations made by the pressure of the quills, and this extraordinary appearance of the surface, has given rise to much prejudice against its use; but this is transient, for after a trial or two, the exquisite delicacy and flavor of a roasted porcupine, generally obliterate the recollection of the original objections of the recently-arrived European, and establish its claim to rank among the choicest viands of a Ceylon dinner; of which, however, it seldom forms a part, except it be at a distance from fashionable society, or, according to local parlance, at "out-stations."

About a mile and a quarter from the bridge, on the right hand, there is a spacious but dilapidated tank, which was formerly capable of affording irrigation to 300 ammonams of land, the annual average produce of which, in the two harvests, amounted to 9600 parahs of paddee, equal to 6200 Winchester bushels.

Throughout this part of the Southern Province (the former province of Tangalle) the remains of innumerable tanks, some of very remote antiquity, afford ample proofs of the skill of its ancient population, in the collection and distribution of water. Many are excavated on level plains, which were supplied by dams across rivers, and over deep ravines; others, by water courses carried from hill to hill, over vallies, forming extensive reservoirs for irrigation, when drought precluded a supply of water from natural sources.

In my very humble view of the case, there is no plan more feasible for the restoration of these artificial reservoirs, and consequently for the regeneration of the local agriculture, than by the Government resuming possession of all lands, originally granted as *Accommodesans*, wherever their conditions have been infringed or forfeited; making the tanks, throughout the island, Crown property; putting them into perfect repair, as Public works, and levying a moderate water rate on all lands benefitted by the irrigation thereby afforded, upon the principle of the New River Company.

A few miles before one enters Tangalle, the belt of coco-nut palms, which borders the sea in myriads, begins, and continues, with but trifling exception, all the way to Colombo, but not a palmyra tree is to be seen.

There is an excellent Government house, formerly the residence of the Collector, at Tangalle; but bugs are by no means scarce there, and I gladly left the Collector's best bed for a sofa in the verandah. The house is immediately under the hill where the fort stands, and has a spacious verandah; between which and the sea, there is a magnificent row of trees (*Mimusops Elengi*, L.).

There is no other civil officer at Tangalle than the District Judge, and not even a sub-custom-house establishment; and the only military force, a Sergeant's guard of the Ceylon rifle regiment.

An enemy,* upon a sudden breaking out of war, might land at Turtle Cove, and, with a very inconsiderable force, march to Colombo, taking Paltoopané, Hambantotté, Tangalle, and Matura, and even Point de Galle, before a redoubt of any consequence could be erected at the latter place; and if redoubts were thrown up upon the several hills by which the fortified town of Galle is commanded, the capture of the former would insure the fall or destruction of the latter.

Nature is the best defender of all the Ceylon coast, except where the fortifications of Colombo and Trincomalé boldly bid an enemy "come on and try;" and at both these places, the usual gallantry of our invincible army would, doubtlessly, be displayed.

But as to any dependence upon the Singhalese, in the event of an attack by an European power, the greater part of them would do, as has been already remarked of certain pilots; for they are naturally an effeminate and cowardly race, but just such a race as may be easily and quietly governed! The Kandyans, on the contrary, are a distinct species of the genus *Felis*; over whom, prudence and past experience suggest, that a wary eye should be kept; for although they may assume the ass's skin, as a

* Upon the supposition of the possibility of an enemy having a temporary command of the Indian seas.

convenient disguise, it is best to treat them as if they still occupied that of the tiger or the leopard, for they retain all the treacherous characteristics of that genus, which they will be sure to display, whenever a safe opportunity may present itself; but, although it is to be hoped the time is far distant, caution, like civility, costs nothing, and safety is the result.

Wealthy and public-spirited individuals, who would spare neither personal exertions nor private expense, are the persons most wanted here; and if the capabilities of Ceylon were fully developed, there would not be a square mile of land throughout the island, except the portion of its surface devoted to purposes of grazing, that might not teem with produce, in the course of the next ten years; for the most valuable inter-tropical productions of one kind or other will grow everywhere throughout the maritime provinces, and wheat and other European productions in the central province; so that, from east to west, and from north to south, if mere justice be done the colony, by giving proper encouragement to agriculture, the greatest abundance would be the certain result of the outlay of capital.

"Tangalle may be seen a great way off from the offing, and is easily known by the small Fort and ruins of an old Pagoda, situate on an elevated and projecting point, on the west side of the Bay. The Bay itself is of considerable extent, being four miles from Tangalle Point to the extreme point of land opposite. The shore is sandy. From each point run extensive and dangerous reefs.

"Within the reefs is good anchorage, and shelter during the S. W. monsoon. The proper entrance to the Bay lies betwixt the western rock and a breaker bearing N. N. E. ½ E. of it. Betwixt the rock and breaker, is a channel of the depth of 8½ and 9 fathoms. The rock is always visible, being very large, and rising several feet above the surface of the water. A vessel may keep very near the rock, which is of steep descent, but must not come nearer the breaker than soundings of 7½ fathoms. Should the swell be so considerable, which it commonly is, to show the breakers, the best entrance is midway betwixt it and the rock, in 8 or 9 fathoms, over a fine sandy bottom. When here, steer N. W. ½ W. direct for a small double hill, rising considerably inland, and bearing exactly in the middle of an opening in a plantation of coco-nut trees. Continue steering this course until in 7 fathoms, fine grey sand, when either anchor or run further into the harbour, as circumstances require. Should you incline to the latter, and being in 7 fathoms, with the bottom fine black sand, when you see a small white pagoda, bearing nearly W. N. W. ¾ W., steer for it, or for a small conical-shaped hill, appearing over the end of the coco-nut grove. Steering for either of these objects, will bring the vessel directly into the harbour.

"In the middle of the harbour lies a bank, on which are 2 fathoms water, and a breaker is seen over it. Inside of this bank are $4\frac{1}{2}$ fathoms, the bottom fine sand. Should you incline to anchor inside of it, pass it to the northward, leaving it on your starboard hand, when you will find a channel of $4\frac{1}{2}$ fathoms, over a sandy bottom. Betwixt it and the reef that runs off Tangalle Point, there is also a channel, but the bottom is rocky, and the soundings irregular. This breaker almost always shows itself, and can therefore be easily avoided. Within it a vessel is completely sheltered from the west and south-west wind, and rides in tolerably smooth water, the reef of rock which runs off Tangalle Point, breaking the force of the southerly swell.

"The landing-place, which is perfectly free from surf, lies under the rising ground upon which the fort stands, having the ruins of a house a little to the south of it. About a quarter of a mile from the landing-place, passing the fort, is a well containing good water. A path-way leads directly from the fort to the well, where water may be filled, and the casks rolled down to the beach. A small jetty, built at the landing-place, would greatly facilitate the loading of the boats.

"This bay lies completely exposed to the east and south-east winds, which are most severe on this coast. These commonly prevail during the months of October, November, and in some measure in December, and blow with most violence at the full and change of the moon; but being of short duration, ships may avoid touching at Tangalle while they last. My stay here was too short to enable me to speak with certainty of the tides; but, from the observations I was able to make, the rise is inconsiderable. It is high water at full and change. The tide runs N. N. W. and S. S. E."*

The harbour of Tangalle might be made capable of affording shelter to large ships, and is deserving of greater attention from the Government than it has hitherto had. A large Indigo† Establishment might be made very profitable here. The inhabitants are principally occupied in agriculture and fishing.

The view is extensive and beautiful from the fort, which is an excellent place for a signal station, for communicating with vessels making Dondra Head, which many ships from England, bound to India, endeavour to do.

* This account of Tangalle Harbour was derived from an official document in the possession of the late William Gisborne, Esq., of the Ceylon Civil Service.

† See pages 74—79.

CHAP. XL.

Present advantages to the formation of an Indigo Factory Company over the prospective ones of the original scheme—Dam, and Canal of Kirimé, for the conveyance of produce to Tangalle—William Gisborne, Esq.—Honorary rewards conferred upon the Headmen of Tangalle, by the Governor in person, upon the completion of the Kirimé canal—Tobacco of Lower Ouva considered by the Dutch equal to that of Havannah—Tobacco farm suggested—Suggestions for a Company of moderate capitalists as settlers at Ceylon—Precautionary measures recommended—European labourers may be advantageously located in certain parts of the island—Facilities to immigrants to establish farms, contrasted with the original difficulties to settlers in new colonies—Suggestions for planting the Portugal Hop—District of Lower Ouva—Its beautiful country and delightful temperature—Soil—District of Saffregam—Produce—Route from Tangalle to Dickwellé—Face of the country—Dondra Head—Ancient Hindoo temple—Magnificent colonnade—Relics—Viharé and Dewalé—Dondra festival—Curious division of offerings—Approach to Matura—Lines—Fort—Town—Fish—Sailing directions—Government officers—Suggested Farm and Fish Factory—Variety of grasses—Matura famous for poultry—Manufactures—Petrified Tamarind wood—Zircon sold as Matura or Ceylon diamond—True diamond not native of Ceylon.

Having endeavoured, in the preceding pages,* to draw public attention to the abundance of indigenous Indigo in this district of the Southern Province, and to the originally intended formation of a "Tangalle Indigo Factory Company," under the auspices of His Excellency the then Governor, the late General Sir Edward Barnes, G. C. B., which, having been in abeyance, after the death of the intended Superintendent of the Factory, (Mr. Tranchell,) had been altogether abandoned, upon His Excellency's appointment to the Command-in-chief of the Bengal Army; it may not be considered supererogatory, in connexion with the Kirimé Canal, commenced and completed under the same energetic Governor, to refer to the additional advantages, thereby presented to British capitalists for the resumption of the original scheme, (but which, at the time it was first in contemplation, were only prospective,) for facilitating the conveyance of manufactured indigo, and other produce, to Tangalle, for shipment to the ports of export.

Of the several national and arduous undertakings of the Government of Ceylon, during Sir Edward Barnes's administration, the canal of Kirimé is justly entitled to rank with the foremost in agricultural importance, and as a splendid memorial of skill, talent, and perseverance. It was commenced in the year 1824, under the personal

* See pages 74—79.

superintendence of one of the most zealous public officers that ever did honor to the civil service of the colony,* and was completed in 1827.

This most important auxiliary to native agriculture was begun at Kirimé, about thirty miles to the northward of Tangalle, situate at the foot of the lofty mountains called Rameli-Kandi, which divide it from the Morua Korle in this province, by constructing a dam, 52 feet in height, 540 feet in length, and gradually diminishing in breadth to 12 feet, from a base of 160 feet; which latter was indispensable, in consequence of the rapid rise and fall of the mountain streams during the rains.

Into this reservoir, which is composed entirely of fine red† soil, with scarcely a pebble to be found in it, the course of a mountain rivulet was diverted; and the Kirimé canal, which, as a work of labour, excels even that of the dam, was the next object of the attention of its able and zealous superintendent. The completion of these splendid works was followed by the distribution of honorary titles and gold medals, which were conferred upon the most deserving Headmen by His Excellency the Governor in person; by way of marking, in a public manner, the unqualified approbation of their conduct and services by the Executive.

I have accidentally omitted to mention, that tobacco is one of the staple productions of the fertile soil of Lower Ouva, (now a northern district of this province, but originally part of the extensive Dessavony of Ouva, under the Malabar dynasty of the Kandyan kingdom,) which form part of the ladings of the numerous *Tavelams*, from the Interior to Point de Galle, *viâ* Hambantotté.‡ It is lighter in color than that of Jaffna; and, according to the Dutch, whose opinions in the matter are received as orthodox, equal in flavor to the best specimens of Havannah. A Tobacco Farm presents an additional object of advantageous speculation, which might be entered into, either separately, or conjointly with that of an Indigo Factory.

It has often occurred to me as somewhat extraordinary, that among the very many emigration schemes which, within the last few years, have occupied the attention of the British public, the formation of a company of moderate capitalists, for establishing

* The late William Gisborne, Esq., who died at Hastings on the 25th of December, 1839, after a public service of twenty two years; and of whom it may truly be said, "*Multis ille bonis flebilis occidit.*"

† Among the several names for Ceylon, Pliny calls it *Terra Antichthonum*, which has been generally considered analogous to *Antipodes*. May it not be more properly intended for the "Country of Red Earth, as suggested to me by that admirable writer, B. E. Pote, Esq., late Editor of the Foreign Quarterly Review, from the Greek words, *Αντις*, *red* or *copper*, (and also *giant* in Asiatic tongues,) and *Θονες*, *earth*. Pliny may have applied it in the latter sense, as the "Land of Giants."

‡ See page 293.

themselves at Ceylon, has never once been suggested, by any of the speculative individuals who have been prominent in such objects of public utility.

Although the climate is generally adverse to the employment of European labourers, there are numerous places of great extent where they may be profitably, and to themselves advantageously located; but it is to persons of moderate capital alone, who may be disposed to emigrate, that I presume to suggest the establishment of such a company; and, in order to obviate the possibility of their being misled, by hearsay or books, either for, or against, the climate or the country, to involve expenses upon uncertain grounds, or the probability of having to repent at leisure for having prematurely incurred them, no plan is more feasible, as a preliminary measure, than for a deputation of competent individuals to proceed to Ceylon, for the investigation of the state of the island, its climate and capabilities, at the expense of the company; for which purpose, it might make a temporary arrangement, with the understanding that ulterior measures were to be dependent upon the official report of such deputation or committee of investigation.

Where ardent spirits are so cheaply purchased, and the virtue of teetotalism would be put to greater tests than in this country, the selection of labourers cannot be made in too strict a manner. Those who might be employed in the temperate parts of the interior, would have none of the disadvantages of agricultural labourers proceeding to new colonies, where their habitations and daily allowances of animal food are dependent upon the log-houses and the quantity of stock carried with them; for within a short time, at Ceylon, roomy cottages can be constructed, and, in a few weeks, grounds fenced, and wheat, rice, and other seeds sown, which, in as many months, yield their harvest.

Of European fruits, grapes and strawberries thrive best; and vegetables, including the potato, onion, cabbage, cauliflower, turnip, carrot, pulse, asparagus, radish, celery, endive, cucumber, and indeed every species cultivated at home, rapidly attain perfection, when compared with their growth in this country.—Butchers' meat, poultry, and game, are generally abundant, and bread cheap; so that, whenever a farm is about to be established, contracts for bread, biscuit, flour, and seed wheat, may be entered into at the nearest seaport, until it produces sufficient for the consumption of its inhabitants; and a farm yard may be amply stocked with swine and poultry at a very cheap rate:—but as regards cattle and sheep, the reader is referred to the preceding pages.*

There can be little doubt, that as Portugal produces a very fine species of Hop (*Humulus lupulus*, L.) in abundance, the several parts of the interior of Ceylon, where

* See pages 109, 110.

the climate is, at certain seasons, very similar to that of the banks of the Tagus, the Lusitanian Hop would thrive, if the British species should not. I know of no experiment having been made, and therefore cannot anticipate why the Hop should not be equally as successful as that of other European introductions. Persons who have resided in Portugal, may recollect the great horror with which the Hop bine is regarded, and spoken of, by the Portuguese, (who consider it a deadly poison,) notwithstanding their partiality for British malt liquors, when they can afford to purchase them.

Where wheat will attain the perfection it does in the interior of Ceylon, there can be no doubt of British barley, oats, and grasses, being as easily naturalized.

The northern part of this province presents such a diversity of hill and dale, forest and plain, and consequently of climate, which in the upper parts may be styled temperate, the thermometer in the morning being as low as 50° degrees, that it is more surprising than otherwise that the tide of immigration of moderate capitalists has not yet set towards Ouva. The potato flourishes there in the greatest perfection and abundance, and is now largely cultivated by the natives; and the gentle acclivities of the country are very favorable to the growth of the vine.

The Kandyan farmers of Ouva display great ingenuity in cultivating the slopes of their mountainous country, by shelving them into narrow paddee fields. These are watered in an ample, but artificial manner, by diverting the streams which everywhere flow from the heights, so that, after irrigating the upper tier, the surplus water answers the same purpose for the inferior ones. Grain is the principal staple, and the fertility of the vallies amply rewards the labour of the agriculturist; whilst, from the higher passes, the country presents such a continuation of green hills and intermediate vallies, that one can scarcely behold the beautiful prospect beneath him, without feeling both regret and disappointment at the inadequacy of its population.

For the lover of nature, or the recluse, no part of the known world offers a more delightful retreat than the gentle acclivity of the green hills of Ouva. It is there that the tranquil mind would readily subscribe to the truism, that

> " ———————— The fall of kings,
> The rage of nations, and the crush of states,
> Move not the man who, from the world escaped,
> In still retreats, and flowery solitudes,
> To nature's voice attends, from month to month,
> And day to day, through the revolving year."

The average quality of the soil is a pure vegetable mould, resting on iron-stone clay, or coarse limestone, of a porous nature.

Image of the Kousta Rajah (කුෂ්ඨරාජා *) or Seprous King.*

Saffregam, another northern district of this province, but situate to the westward of the adjoining district of Lower Ouva, was also a province and Dessavony of itself, prior to the late division of the whole island into five provinces. It abounds with Areka nuts, coffee, pepper, cardamoms, bees' wax, excellent honey, and jaggery, and is one of the most beautiful and fertile provinces in the island, rivalling in luxuriance of soil and exuberance of vegetation the most favored country in the world, and producing sufficient rice for the consumption of its population.

Although it is generally understood, that metals and other minerals are chiefly discovered in poor and barren soils, it does not apply to Saffregam, which presents considerable inducement to the mineralogist, valuable gems being occasionally found in the beds of its rivers.

The soil of Saffregam is very similar to that of Ouva; but as the former district will be further noticed in its proper place, the direct route from Tangalle may as well be resumed.

From Tangalle to Dickwellé, the distance is 11 miles, and a great part of the road hilly; but, although tolerably good, it is much broken up during the rains. From the more elevated parts of the road the country appears to the greatest advantage at that season, when the verdure of the surrounding scenery is very grateful to the European eye. Paddee fields abound in every direction, but no symptoms of indigo and cotton being classed as staple productions of the district,—the small quantity of the latter being scarcely deserving of notice.

Passing so very near the well-known "Dondra Head," 9 miles from Dickwellé, and about 2½ or 3 miles from Matura, the tourist will find it well worth his time, to diverge to the left from the main road, and visit the ruins of the ancient Hindoo temple there.

Dondra Head, the southernmost point of Ceylon, is a steep and rugged promontory, overlooking, and about a mile to the eastward of, a low tongue of land, covered with coco-nut trees, which appear in one from the sea. Within less than half a mile of its extremity, there is a colonnade, formed by about 200 stone pillars, of Hindoo architecture, extremely well executed; of these, many had evidently been raised in the rough state, for they are unfinished: other rows of pillars branch off at right angles, and, in the middle, stand two square pillars, supporting a lintel, of the same material, (apparently the remains of a doorway,) sculptured on one side with the heads of deities, within a scroll of foliage.

Some of the scattered relics, which include the fragments of images and a well-executed head of *Ganesa*, would be an acquisition to the British Museum. The sacred well of the temple is covered with a flat stone, upon which the human right and left foot are sculptured, having between them a square orifice in the centre, for the admission of a vessel to draw water. The well adjoins an obscene specimen of Hindoo worship, surmounted by a canopy of sacred leaves.

Near this stand a Buddha Viharé, with its usual accompaniments, and a Hindoo Dewalé dedicated to the great *Vishnu*, (*Govinda* of the Singhalese,) and similarly ornamented in its interior to the Kattregam temple. Among the painted figures of the Hindoo Pantheon, that of *Kartikeya*, the peacock-riding deity, is prominently conspicuous; but the most valuable article, as a curiosity, is an ancient stone figure of the elephant-headed Hindoo deity *Ganesa*. The temples are delightfully shaded by coco-nut and areka palms, yellow Bignonia (*Bignonia Indica*, L.), Bogaha, and plantain trees, and afford a cool and pleasant lounge during the heat of the day. The priests and attendants are extremely civil and obliging to strangers, as if pleased at the temple being noticed by Europeans.

Dondra itself, although now a mere village, was the capital of Ceylon in the seventh century, during the reign of the Singhalese Rajah, Sri Singha Bo II., and is still famed for its annual festival. The present ruins are supposed to have belonged to a celebrated temple, erected about that period.

At the time of the Perahara* of Kandy, the Dondra festival takes place, under the superintendence of the Moodliar of the district, as Basnaiké Nilamé. The Kapuralé of the *Vishnu* Dewalé commences the ceremony at the first quarter after the new moon, at the appointed nekata,† by a rite called kaphitaweema, when six kowilas, or temporary Dewalés, are erected for the gods *Katragama*, *Natha*, *Saman*, and *Alut*, and the goddess *Pattiné*. All the Kapuwas bathe in pure water; but before any offerings are made, the Tam-a-tam beaters, singers, and dancers, the latter in grotesque masks, with the chief Kapuwas bearing the sacred emblems, walk in procession through the villages. The Basnaiké Nilamé makes the first offering at each of the shrines; and the Kapuwa who stands at the entrance of the Dewalé whilst the people present their offerings, anoints their foreheads with a preparation of sandal-wood, and invokes blessings upon them. This continues uninterruptedly for 36 hours.

The expenses of the ceremony are defrayed from the offerings; but the Basnaiké Nilamé, who is appointed by the Government, and appoints the Kapuralés in turn,

* The *Perahara* (literally, *procession*) commences on the day of the new moon in the month *Eysala*: which, like other Eastern festivals, from the imperfect systems of native astronomy, traverses through all the months of the year. The first observance of this festival, after the annexation of the Kandyan kingdom to our former possessions in Ceylon, took place in the month of July.

† Situation of the moon.

receives the money, and distributes it, and the offerings, in five portions,—to the Moodliar two-fifths; the remainder having been subdivided into five portions, two-fifths belong to the Kapuwas; the remainder is again divided into five portions, of which, the Aratchy takes two-fifths; and the last remainder is given to the washermen, potters, Tam-a-tam beaters, and other musicians, who have assisted in the procession.

Approaching Matura from the eastward, the country is very beautiful, presenting extensive grazing plains and paddee fields, intersected with canals and rivulets, and interspersed with coco-nut and areka palms.

The town lies low, and the Lines that remain upon the left bank of the Blue river, or Nil-Ganga, suffice to show that, under the Dutch, the fortifications were very extensive. On the right bank there is a small stone built fort of five bastions, that commands the bridges, which are connected by an islet, and the ferry. There are several excellent private houses, chiefly of *Kabook*, or iron-stone clay, a District Court-house, chapel, and barracks. The Cutchery is an extensive building, and there are also a Wesleyan Mission-house and chapel.

The country round Matura is so extremely fertile, that every article of food is abundant and cheap; and no place is better supplied with fish, including the Seir Fish (a fine species of *Scomber*), Red Sur-mullet, Pomfret, Coal Fish, Rock Cod, Soles, Eels, Skate, Crabs, a species of Cray Fish, locally called Lobster, huge Prawns, and Shrimps.

The neighbourhood of Matura affords the most delightful walks and drives, completely sheltered by a variety of umbrageous trees and dense coco-nut topes from even a mid-day sun; and it is here that the inquiring mind may picture to itself what might be done by the "magic hand of cultivation."

"The town lies in latitude 5° 58 north, and longitude 80° 37 east, and bears about E. ½ S. from Red Point, the east point of Red Bay, distant eight miles; the land between them is moderately elevated, and the coast very steep, having 60 fathoms water in some places within two miles of the shore.

"Matura is a considerable town, with a fort conspicuous from seaward when it bears between N. N. W. and N. E. Ships may anchor here in the N. E. monsoon, abreast of the town, in 20 and 22 fathoms, the bottom is generally foul. Plenty of wood and good water, poultry, fish, fruits, roots, and vegetables, may be procured here; the two former at the entrance of the river, or very near it, about half a mile to the westward of the fort.

"Matura Island stands opposite the fort, and near the shore; is small and rocky, resembling a haycock. Boats find shelter under it, the surf being generally high on shore. Canoes are used for passing to the main."

An Assistant Government Agent in charge of the revenue, and a District Judge, are the only public officers resident here during peace.

An extensive farm, and a factory for curing fish, would be good speculations; and if there were but a few moderate capitalists settled here, Matura might become one of the richest districts in the island; for no place can be better adapted to the cultivation of pepper, indigo, cardamoms, coffee, cotton, and ginger;—and why not sugar?

The district produces as great a variety of grasses as any in the island, exclusively of the esculent species that are cultivated under the name of "small grains." Of the former, the chief are called by the Singhalese, *Moththu*, *Pendah* (or bird's tail), *Urukiri* (sow's milk), *Kawula*, *Haspan*, *Hælin*, *Ranmoththa*, *Kalandura*, *Kalanduru*, *Welkiri*, *Nalaghas*, *Mangarudeli*, *Sewendara*, *Bintana*, *Hadutana*, *Meneritana*, *Itana*, *Idalhu*, *Mahakiri* (great milk), *Kokmoththa*, *Karabukiri*, and *Ilinkiri*;—but a Botanist would find employment for twelve months in describing and classifying the *Gramineæ* of Ceylon.

Matura, long famous for its poultry, may be called the "Norwich of Ceylon" for turkies, with which the Galle and Colombo markets are supplied; but *Koir*, arrack, and coço-nuts, are its principal staples. Beautiful sofa and palankin mats, and carved figures of the native castes, are manufactured here for sale to the curious; and the petrified wood of the Tamarind tree (*Tamarindus Indicus*, L.), which is much esteemed, is commonly manufactured into snuff-boxes and seals, and sold at reasonable prices.

White *Zircon* is here called "*Matura diamond*," by which name, and that of "*Ceylon diamond*," many, in ignorance of the difference, have been misled to attribute to the island the production of the true diamond, a gem never yet known to have been found there. Of other gems, there are three species of garnet, hyacinths, inferior rubies, and topazes. These are either found in the beds of rivers, or in alluvial ground, which, both here and in Saffregam, is of the same kind, and derived from the decomposition of gneiss or granitic rock.

The Singhalese aver, that the most valuable gems are found at the roots of Jack trees (*Artocarpus integrifolia*, L.) of a certain age; and this story is either founded upon occasionally successful researches in such localities, or is a *ruse* to mislead others from searching where they are more likely to be found.

CHAP. XLI.

Minerals—Extraordinary combinations in petrifactions of wood discovered by M. L'Eschenault de Latour, whilst Naturalist to his late Most Christian Majesty, Charles X., during his tour through the interior—Constituents of Beligam rock—Opinion of Dr. John Davy, F. R. S., opposed to the statements of Ptolemy, Knox, Percival, Cordiner, and Ive, in regard to the indigenous minerals of Ceylon—Possibility of the tables being turned, upon the mineral resources of the island being fully developed—Discovery of indigenous coal attributed to the Dutch, and their reasons for neglecting it—Coal an object of too great importance for its presence, or otherwise, to remain longer hypothetical—Face of the country between Matura and Beligam—Village of Beligam, or Beligammé—Birds, fish, fruits, and vegetables—Esculent Euphorbia—Agraboddigané Viharé and Dagobah—Extraordinary tradition of the Koustah Rajah, or Leprous King—Temples and Dagobahs—Captain Anderson's description of a Buddhist temple applicable to all.

THE island produces nitre in limited quantities, alum, magnesia, limestone, mica or glimmer, felspar in variety, as well as quartz, (of which, the amethyst, both of the Brazilian and oriental purple, is found in large masses); iron, equal to Swedish; cinnamon stone, opal, black, brown, yellowish and white crystal, (which last the native jewellers impose upon strangers as white sapphire); cats' eye or *pseudo*-opal, ruby, topaz, blue sapphire, electric tourmalin, chrysoberyl, moonstone, precious and common garnet, Ceylonite,* grey manganese, globules of iron-stone clay, granitic rock, sandstone, by which the island may be said to be surrounded; potters' clay (*Argilla fritilaria*), and *Kabook*, or iron-stone clay.

In 1820, M. L'Eschenault de Latour, at that time Naturalist to His Most Christian Majesty, Charles X., discovered, during his tour through the interior, petrifactions of wood, combining quartz and felspar, which he considered a novelty in mineralogy, the latter substance never having been found, or if found, never made public, in petrifactions of a similar nature;—also, moonstone embodied in porphyric rock, in large masses, and of greater beauty than moonstone hitherto dug from rocks of decomposed white clay. These discoveries were the more valuable, because the minerals are precious and beautiful in themselves, and were at that time altogether new, even to the learned in mineralogy.

* This mineral was originally supposed to be exclusively confined to the island from which its name is derived, but it has since been found in Germany and Naples.

A piece of Beligam rock, presented to a late eminent mineralogist,* was found to contain "schalstone, quartz, and cinnamon-stone; schalstone the principal constituent —the quartz regularly distributed, and without any appearance of crystalization—the cinnamon stone in grains, and distributed throughout the mass; but very few of them exhibited any traces of a crystaline form, and in those in which that appearance was at all discernible, it was extremely imperfect."

In Ptolemy's account of the island, plumbago† is included with iron and copper, as indigenous; and, in the year 1681, Knox mentioned the former as a native mineral.

In Captain Percival's History of Ceylon, it is affirmed, that, in 1797, a quicksilver mine was discovered at Kotta, about six miles from Colombo, and several pounds of that metal obtained.

In the description of Ceylon by the Rev. James Cordiner, formerly chaplain to the Garrison of Colombo, published in 1807, it is stated, that plumbago and quicksilver had been found there;—and it is further recorded, that, in 1755, a Cornish gentleman, of the name of Thomas,‡ discovered the presence of tin ore in the island, and subsequently found as fine a specimen of it as he had ever seen in his native county; and that Mr. Ive (the author) had also found there veins of black crystal intermixed with spar and iron, and black lead and copper ores.

To these statements, Dr. Davy thus opposes his opinion in rather an unqualified manner:—"Wherever I have been amongst the mountains, I have sought more particularly for tin and copper, but in vain, having never observed the least traces of either, or of lead. It has been asserted, in some publications, that gold and mercury occur native in Ceylon. The result of the inquiries I have made, satisfy me the assertion is unfounded, and that neither metal, in any state, has yet been met with in the island."

Now, as Dr. Davy was altogether not more than three years and a half at Ceylon, (during nearly one half of which period the Kandyans were in rebellion, and he himself Physician to the Forces,) one would suppose that, even with his known ardour and scientific acquirements, an area of 24,000 square miles was rather too large for so minute an investigation of its geology as would warrant the Doctor's assumption, that the statements of his predecessors (in authorship upon Ceylon) are groundless; and should further investigation, and consequent developement of its mineralogical resources, nullify Dr. Davy's opinion altogether, by the production of gold, silver, lead, tin, copper, and mercury, how deservedly will the tables have been turned!

* Mr. Phillips, of the Society of Friends, Author of a well-known Treatise on Mineralogy.

† Plumbago has of late years been largely imported into this country from Ceylon.

‡ Ive's Voyages.

The late Mr. Reckerman, Fiscal of Colombo, informed me that coal had been discovered in the island by the Dutch; but, from there being such an abundance of wood, and charcoal the only fuel used by the native cooks, no notice whatever was taken of the discovery. That mineral is now become an object of such great and general importance, as to be worthy of the most particular research, for the purpose of supplying fuel to steam vessels, touching at Ceylon, on their voyages to, and from, Madras, Bengal, and the Red Sea, and would be one of the greatest acquisitions to the colony that discovery has ever produced.

It is therefore to be anticipated, that, *malgré* prejudiced opinions to the contrary mineralogists may yet be induced to turn their attention to the developement of the geology of this magnificent country; for there can be little doubt that it will increase the present number of its known mineral productions, if it do not include both gold and silver.

The next stage from Matura is Beligam, distant rather more than 11 miles; and, according to Horsburgh, " situate upon Red Bay, in about 5° 57' north, and longitude 80° 33' 20 east; a fishing hamlet, densely wooded with coco-nut, bread-fruit, jack, areka, and other trees;" from one of which, Beli (*Cratæva Marmelos*, L.) and gammé, (village,) its name is derived. The intermediate country is fertile and well cultivated, and the road excellent.

Snipe and teal abound in the lower grounds, and a variety of doves, mango-birds, bulbuls, parrots, and finches, in the upper. The finest fish is to be purchased for a very trifle, as well as green turtle, large prawns, and crabs in abundance; and no part of the province is better supplied with indigenous fruits and vegetables, including the esculent Euphorbia (*Euphorbia esculenta*). The rest-house is a substantial stone building, approached by an avenue of splendid teak trees; and upon the hill, overlooking the bay, is a very large and commodious house, the country residence of Joseph Read, Esq., the Prince of Ceylon merchants.

Although the Agraboddigane Viharé and Dagobah, as well as the Dagobah in the midst of the dense coco-nut tope to the right of the high road to Galle, are worthy of a visit from the traveller, the most curious relic of antiquity, near Beligam, is the image of the Koustah Rajah, or Leprous King, as its Singhalese name implies, on the left of the high road, and about half a mile from the village. This gigantic image is of granite, and appears as if sculptured out of the solid rock; but the general opinion is, that it was separately executed, and then fixed in the niche where it now stands. It is very conspicuous to persons proceeding to Galle, but it may be passed unnoticed by those returning from thence, unless previously aware of its position.

At that particular spot, the road is so overshadowed by an umbrageous Jack (*Artocarpus integrifolia*, L.), Kettule (*Caryota urens*, L.), Coco-nut, and other trees, that the place has a delightfully cool appearance, even under a meridian sun.

There are many versions of the tradition respecting the Koustah Rajah; but, from the source the following is derived, it is very probably the original and most correct one. I have to acknowledge my obligations for it to the Head Priest of the Karangoddé Viharé in Saffregam, where, during a sojourn of some days, in 1825, in consequence of a severe attack of intermittent fever, I experienced the utmost possible attention and kindness from that Oonansé and his assistant priests, who related to me several of their native legends, through my Interpreter.—The tradition ascribes the original discovery of the coco-nut tree, the principal of all vegetable productions, which omnipotent wisdom and munificence has so liberally bestowed upon the sable portion of mankind, to a vision.—I have altered the style of the relator, in some points, but have adhered, as nearly as possible, to the substance of the tradition.

"A Singhalese king, or sovereign prince, (as the term "Rajah" implies,) of the most devout conduct and character, became suddenly afflicted with a cutaneous disease, which covered him with a white scaly substance from head to foot, to so great a degree as almost to deprive him of human appearance; and so rapidly had the loathsome distemper extended its malignant influence over the Rajah's person, that sacrifices were resorted to by his people, in the hope of thereby appeasing the anger of the Great Demon, (*Maha Yaka*,) the supposed author of their prince's sufferings.

The afflicted Rajah objected to assist in person at any such diabolical ceremonies; and, *malgré* the prejudices of his people, and their faith in their eventual efficacy, preferred an humble submission to the decrees of that Superior Power from whom alone the *Maha Yaka* could have derived dominion, if he really possessed any, over the destinies of mankind.

The Rajah having, with all due humility, offered odoriferous flowers,* according to the Buddhist rites, and repeated the Buddha-Sarana,† fell into a trance, which lasted for several days; and during that period, a vision represented to him a large expanse of water, which he tasted, and found both salt and nauseous, although it was of a fine green‡ color near, and blue in the distance; its margin covered with groves of trees

* Generally of Bignonia Indica, Tabernæ montana, Jasminum odoratissimum, J. Zeylanicum, J. luteum, Polyanthes tuberosa, Nyctanthes arbor tristis, Michelia Champaca, Nerium odoratissimum, Mimosa Arabica, and Lawsonia inermis, of Linnæus.

† In worship of Buddha, and acknowledgment of his being the Omniscient.

‡ A liberty is here taken with the tradition, blue and green being synonymous in Singhalese, (*Nil-pata*).

of a rare kind, such as he had never before seen;* for, instead of branches in various directions, as trees had in his country, their tops appeared crowned with a tuft of feathery leaves.

The Koustah Rajah, having awakened from his trance deeply impressed with the unusual nature of his dream, renewed his oblations and prayers for a display of omnipotent mercy towards him.

A Naya (*Cobra di Capello*, and *Coluber Naja*, L.), the sacred snake of the Buddhists, shortly afterwards approached the Rajah, and, having expanded its spectacle-marked hood, raised its head a cubit from the ground, and observed the prince steadily for some moments; then, extending its blue forked tongue, the reptile bent its head thrice, and lapped water from the leaf in which it had been reserved for the Rajah's particular use. It thrice repeated the draught, and then, with its eyes fixed on the Rajah, retrograded to the jungle. This, to the mind of the resigned and suffering prince, was conviction strong of Buddha's† favor.

Again the prince felt his eyelids grow weary, but having determined, in his then state of disease, to occupy no place of shelter save that of the shady Bogaha, he again sought repose under its umbrageous branches; but scarcely had sleep a second time exerted its magic influence, than the Rajah's former vision recurred, with the additional appearance of an aged man, whose face bore the appearance of the moon in all its splendour. It was *Maha Sudona*, the father of the God Buddha, who thus accosted the astounded prince:—

"From ignorance of the sacredness of the ground over which the God's favorite tree casts its honored shade, thou once didst omit the usual respect due to it from all his creatures. Its deeply pointed leaf distinguishes it above all other trees as sacred to Buddha; and, under another tree of the same heavenly character, thou now liest a leprous mass, which disease, at the great Deity's command, the impurity of the red water within the large and small rivers of thy body has brought upon thee. But since the sacred and kind snake, the shelterer of the God Buddha when on earth, has thrice partaken of thy drink, thou wilt derive health and long life by obeying the high commands which I now bear thee. In that direction [pointing to the southward] lies thy

* At the remote period of the tradition, the Coco-nut tree was unknown in the interior of Ceylon, and even to this day, its scarcity is remarked by every traveller who visits the late Kandyan territory.

† Supposed to be derived from a Tamul word, "*Bodhi*," which signifies *Wisdom*. The present object of Singhalese worship is the fourth Buddha, called *Goutama Buddha Arkabandoo*, or, Descendant from the Sun, and considered by many learned Indians an incarnation of Vishnu; and his religion to be founded on that of Brahma.

remedy. One hundred hours' journey will bring thee to those trees, which thou shalt see in reality, and taste their fruits to thy benefit; but as on the top only they are produced, by fire only can they be obtained. The inside, of transparent liquid, and of innocent pulp, must be thy sole diet, till thrice the Great Moon (*Maha Handah*) shall have given and refused her light :—at the expiration of that time, disease will leave thee, and thou wilt be clean again; but forget not, with the renewal of the skin of thy flesh, by the red color of the fountains of thy life being restored, to offer fragrant flowers and fruits,* with much thanksgiving, to that Great Brahma of all Brahmas,† to whom all other gods, and even demons, pay homage; through whose mercy, and the forgiveness of thy neglect and transgressions, thy bodily vigour will have been restored, and thy days of enjoyment in the splendour of the mighty and flaming Chief Ruler ‡ of the Moon prolonged."

A sound as of ten thousand Tam-a-tams simultaneously struck, seemed, to the delighted Rajah, a corroboration of the messenger's authority, and reverberated on his ear for hours together, after he had awakened from his second trance. Impressed with the belief that the Invisible Powers had thus intimated their especial protection, and that consequently it was his bounden duty to obey commands so mysteriously conveyed, the Rajah, placing the palms of his hands across his forehead, and bending to the ground, prayed for strength to act in obedience to the Ruler and Creator of all gods and demons, (*Ossah Pollah Dewyo,*) and of the *plane* world itself.

Having summoned his followers from their various resting places, (constructed with the branches and leaves of the neighbouring trees, by way of temporary shelter,) the delighted Rajah repeated to them the prophetic words of the divine messenger; and, having gone through the ceremony of making a propitiatory offering under the Bogaha tree, of fruits, Betel leaves, and flowers, he proceeded with his retinue in a direct course through rivers and forests, and over very high mountains, to the southward, as directed by the *Maha Sudona*.

The one hundred hours' journey having been miraculously performed, for it had been accomplished without fatigue either to himself or attendants, the long and anxiously anticipated view of that boundless expanse of blue water, and on its margin immense groves of trees, with crests of leaves, (which he then for the first time perceived to be large fronds,) gratified his astonished and delighted sight, as his visions

* The Head Priest informed me, that although fruits were originally offered, in addition to flowers, the former had been dispensed with for more than twelve centuries, in consequence of the poverty of the people.

† Brahmata-Brahma, a name of Buddha.

‡ Anadewara, also a name of Buddha.

had foretold. Beneath the fronds, sheltered from the vertical sun, hung large clusters of fruit, much larger than any he had ever seen in his own country of the interior, of which, the color of some was green, yellow, and orange, and of others, approaching to black.*

At that period, the coast was destitute of population; but there were wild beasts, such as elephants, leopards, bears, sloths, and monkies innumerable. To climb the coco-nut tree (the promised source of health) was then unknown, and considered beyond the power of mortal man; but fire having been pointed out as the means of obtaining its fruit, the Rajah's followers soon kindled it, after their own fashion, by the friction of wood and dried leaves; and scarcely had an hour elapsed, after the fire had encircled the foot of one of these matchless palms, ere, with a tremendous crash, it fell prostrate to the earth.

The novel fruit was, at first, with some difficulty opened; but the Rajah's superstitions were more powerful than even hunger itself. With awe he approached the beach, over which wave followed wave in quick succession; and, mute with astonishment at the vast expanse of ocean, bent to taste the liquid element. It was as his vision had prognosticated. Again his wonder was increased; but his faith had kept pace with it, that, "ere the great moon had thrice given and refused her light," he would be cleansed from his foul distemper, and his disrespect to the sacred Bogaha, which had originally drawn down upon him the anger of the All-seeing,† be forgiven.

The Rajah and his followers confined themselves to the prescribed diet; the former, in obedience to the commands conveyed by the *Maha Sudona*, and the latter from necessity, there being none of their accustomed fruits, rice, or roots, to be met with so near the ocean. They found the water‡ within the nuts sweet and delicious, and pure as crystal itself, (of which mineral their country produced a variety and abundance,) whilst the fleshy part of it was a cooling and grateful food.

Time rolled on, and day after day the delighted followers of their suffering prince acknowledged that Truth came from above, for the Rajah gradually lost the white and scaly skin which had enveloped him like the armour of the Great Ant-eater of the interior,§ whilst the glow of heat which pervaded his extremities, convinced him of the near approach of his promised recovery. Thankful to his Great Preserver, he omitted not to perform the duties dictated by his visions; and, on the first rock that

* The Singhalese language has no signification for brown, reddish, orange-colored, scarlet, or pink, which are all expressed by the word *rat*, (red); and a very dark brown, by *kalu*, (black).

† "Samanta-chacksa," covered with eyes. ‡ The green coco-nut, called in Singhalese, *Koroomba*.

§ Probably the ant-eater (*Manis tetradactyla*), *Kaballé* of the Singhalese, and called Negombo Devil by Europeans.

appeared durable and beyond the reach of the sea, the Rajah, with the assistance of his followers, carved the gigantic figure of himself, in the rock at Beligammé; remarking, "that its great height would show the wonderful recovery he had experienced, (being a very little man in stature); for he had risen, by the blessing of the God of all gods, to an undeserved degree of happiness and bodily vigour; of which, the memorial would thus be handed down to millions yet unborn.""

In regard to the temples of Buddha, and the Dagobahs, or repositories of the sacred relic, my account must be brief, for these can scarcely be said to enter into the original plan or object of the present work; and yet it is hardly possible to avoid some notice of them, in a description of Ceylon.

The several Christian Missions established in the island, have, each in their turn, transmitted such correct details of the ceremonials and mythology of the Brahmins and Buddhists, that there is no room left even for novelty. There is, too, such a great sameness in the internal decorations of their temples, that, unless where anything remarkable in the architecture presents itself to notice, it may truly be said, "see one, see all;" and Captain Anderson's description of a Viharé, taken generally, is as correct as can possibly be given.

"The vaulted roof is studded o'er
With various hieroglyphic lore;
Touch'd by the artist's glowing hand,
Flowers of all colors here expand;
There, some wild legend lives portray'd,
Here, all the zodiac stands display'd,
While every vacant space between,
Some uncouth form, or shape, is seen!
With yellow robes, and shaven head,
The priests around that altar tread,
Near Buddha's giant figure stand,
And incense shed with lavish hand;
Then bending at his sacred feet,
Their wishes, wants, and vows repeat!
Though painted robes the figure screen,
And but the countenance is seen,
One may a due proportion trace,
Throughout his giant form and face;
No lion look, no eagle eye,
But that serene philanthropy,
Which plainly indicates a breast
With every milder virtue blest!"

CHAP. XLII.

Numerous antiquities in the Southern Province—No excavated or rock temples—Agraboddigane Vihare—Image of Buddha described—Emblematical and historical paintings—Dagobah, or repository of a relic of Buddha—Charles Edward Layard, Esq., causes an ancient Dagobah to be opened—Its contents indicative of affinity to certain Egyptian antiquities, described by B. E. Pote, Esq., in his account of a mummy discovered in a tomb in the Necropolis of Memphis in 1824—The Bogaha as much venerated by the Buddhists as the oak by the Druids—Epoch of Buddha's appearance—Interesting conversion of a High Priest of Buddha to Christianity—High character of the convert not affected among the Priesthood by his apostacy—Example followed by other priests—Honors conferred upon the convert—Road from Beligam to Galle—Serpentine lake of Cogel—Bungalow Island—Indigenous Momordica—Crocodiles—Leopards—Approach to Galle—Sailing direction into the Harbour.

It is beyond my power to describe the antiquities of this province, for it would require a volume; and I have reluctantly omitted many extracts from notes in my possession, which might have interested the Antiquary, and curtailed others, rather than exceed the professed object of the present Work, or swell it beyond ordinary limits.*

In the maritime provinces, there are no excavated or rock temples, which may be considered peculiar to the interior of the island; and one of the largest Viharés is that of Agraboddigané, situate upon a gentle eminence, about three furlongs from Beligam, to the left of the high road to Galle, and approached by flights of numerous well-worn stone steps.

Here, as in all the temples of Buddha that I have visited, the recumbent image of the God is on the left hand upon entering the sanctum, and this is most probably general. This gigantic figure is about thirty feet in length, and covered with the beautiful lacker in use among the Singhalese, with a surface as smooth as polished marble.

The body of the idol is a light yellow, (the right arm and breast exposed,) the eyeballs white, mouth red, eyes and hair a deep black, the latter *Kaffer*-like, or woolly: and, upon the crown of the head, is a representation of the πυρ, or sacred flame, which completes the physiognomy of the Singhalese deity.

The robe, in wavy folds, and fitted close to the body, is of sacred yellow or saffron color, and reaches to the ankles; and over the left shoulder is a bright vermillion scarf,

* For this reason, I have omitted all mention of the method of catching elephants in *Kraals*. This was one of the feudal and unpaid services to which the natives were subject, until Lord Goderich abolished the *Rajah Karia* system.

which, instead of falling with the position of the Buddha, retains its place horizontally to the waist, as if fastened to the outer robe, or as might be supposed its proper place in an erect, instead of a recumbent figure.

Amongst other emblems, the sacred Naya, and innumerable images of the Hindoo deities, are prominently conspicuous. A long narrow table, nearly the length of the image, before which is suspended a painted cotton curtain, displays the fragrant diurnal offerings of the neighbouring villagers; among which, the *Nelumbium speciosum*, the *Rat-manel-mal* of the Singhalese, is one of the chief in point of beauty and odour.

The walls, decorated with native paintings in the primitive style of outline and color, without regard to shade or perspective, of both which the Singhalese are ignorant, display a most extraordinary historical and emblematical medley. Here are to be seen the pagan deities holding female figures in their arms; kings and queens receiving homage, the former seated on thrones, within moveable palaces, drawn by elephants; the latter in chariots of Roman shape, propelled by means of a pole, as boats are in shallow water; *Bo*-trees, palms, and *Lotos* flowers, intermixed with executioners, in the act of decapitating criminals, and blue, white, and red-eyed devils, some forcing their victims into the flames, others tormenting them in the most excruciating forms: and, by way of finish, the condemned to endless torment in eternal flame, enveloped in the latter, which is as vivid as red and yellow paint can make it.

The Dagobah,* or repository of a relic of Buddha, is a hand-bell shaped building, with a white exterior, from a thick coating of stucco, which, in Ceylon as well as upon the coast of Coromandel, is a mixture of fine sand, shell lime (*Chunam*), green coco-nut water, and coarse sugar or *Jaggery;* and, when laid on by experienced plasterers, it displays the polish and appearance of marble. In some, the bell is raised on a number of circular terraces, which gradually decrease in width from the base; in others, the centre overhangs the rest so much as almost to cover the basement; but there are many Dagobahs which have merely annular projections, like so many convex borders, by way of finish to the bell. Some Dagobahs have entrances ascended by a flight of steps, and others are entirely without.

A Dagobah in a state of great dilapidation was opened in 1820, by order of Charles Edward Layard, Esq., of the Civil Service, at that time Collector of Colombo, (the gentleman who transmitted to England the model of a Viharé, and recumbent image of Buddha, exhibited at Exeter Hall in the years 1831—1832,) in a part of his district

* Defined by an excellent Singhalese scholar, the late Rev. William Buckley Fox, to mean "a womby, or capacious place."

called the Rygam Korle.—Mr. Layard's museum contains very valuable specimens of Chinese, Japanese, Siamese, and Pali books, maps, and coins, images of Buddha, and of the Hindoo deities; but, perhaps, the contents of the Dagobah may be as rare as any, if not more so than all, as bearing some affinity to Egyptian, and also to Mexican antiquities.

The interior of the Dagobah contained a small square compartment of brick-work, mathematically correct in its bearings towards the cardinal points, and having in the centre, in a vertical line from the supposed position of the minaret that had surmounted the Dagobah, a hollow vase of granitic rock, covered with a round top of the same material. Within this cylinder was found a small piece of bone and some thin pieces of plate-gold, which probably at a very remote period had enveloped the relic, as in the case of the mummy discovered in 1824, in a tomb in the Necropolis of Memphis, described in Mr. Pote's admirable "Inquiry into the Phonetic reading of the Ashburnham Signet, in reference to the Patriarch Joseph;" a few old rings, (as in the Egyptian tomb,) three small pearls, crystal and cornelian beads, small specimens of the white zircon, ruby, blue sapphire, and also of glass; a small but solid pyramid of cement, a few clay images of the sacred Naya, (*Coluber Naja*, L.), two lamps, one of brass, the other of clay, and similar in shape to those in present use among the natives.

There appears to have been no fixed rule for the elevation or size of Dagobahs, some of which have exceeded 200 feet in height, both which are indefinite: and the chief uniformity consists in their circular bell-shape. Dagobahs are generally shaded by the tremulous and sacred Bogaha,* which is as much venerated by the Buddhists as the oak was by the Druids.

According to the best authorities extant, the Buddhist priests left in Thibet and China the precise epoch of the real or imagined appearance of the God Buddha; which information, having been preserved in writing, was compared by the Christian missionaries and scholars with our own era, and, notwithstanding their difference in point of dates, the time of Buddha, the ninth incarnation of Vishnu, may be fixed, from the meridian of the four accounts of this epoch, in the year 1014 before Christ, or 2857 years ago.†

One of the most unlooked for and extraordinary instances of conversion to Christianity, was that of a Maha Nayaka Oonansé, or High Priest of Buddha; the peculiar circumstances of which have established claims to attention as matter of history, and

* See page 56. † Asiatic Researches, vol. i. page 425, but the difference of date altered to 1843.

will be considered interesting by all who have sincerely at heart the propagation of the Gospel of Christ.

In the year 1808, Nadoris de Zilva, the Head Priest of a temple in this district, left Ceylon, with eighteen pupils under his charge, to perfect himself in the mysteries of his religion at the grand depôt of Pagan superstition and error, Amerapoora, or the Eternal City, the capital of the Burmese empire. Going by way of Madras, he resided there several months, and devoted himself to the study of the Sanscrit language; from thence he proceeded to the capital of Ava, where he perfected himself in all the dogmas of Buddhism; and at length, among other marks of Royal favor, "His Golden Footed Majesty" conferred upon him the High-Priestly title of "Maha Nayaka Oonansé."

Having returned to Ceylon, this highly dignified Priest resided some time at his former temple in this district, occasionally visiting other Viharés and Bana Maduwas, or places for reading the history of Buddha's incarnations. His fame for morality, and profound knowledge of the Buddhist mysteries and mythology, made the Maha Nayaka Oonansé the more conspicuous, when, about the time of the first translated portion of the New Testament into the Singhalese language being circulated, he displayed a most anxious and restless curiosity to become acquainted with the religious tenets of the European Christians, as contradistinguished from the Portuguese Christians of Goä, upon the coast of Malabar; or, in other words, of the Roman Catholic mission of the Oratorio of San Felippe de Neri.

Having succeeded in attaining his first object, namely, a Singhalese copy of the New Testament, he devoted himself carefully and exclusively to its study. The vast difference between the plain and simple doctrines of Christianity, and the confounding medley of the mythology of Buddha, became so apparent, that his desire was augmented, in proportion as conviction arose; and he has repeatedly assured me, that he thought "every hour a day," after he had determined to seek additional information, before he accomplished his wishes, by an interview with the Wesleyan Missionaries; from whom, as well as from the late archdeacon, the Honorable and Venerable Dr. Twisleton, who was their zealous supporter and firm friend, the anxious candidate for conversion received the most cordial assistance, and every requisite information, in regard to the essentials of Divine revelation.

The result (which, upon becoming public, spread like wild-fire from temple to temple and from hut to hut) was, that the Maha Nayaka Oonansé, with one of his pupils, after a long and deliberate comparison of the Christian with the Buddhist doctrine, abandoned at once their saffron-colored robes of Priesthood and the delusive dogmas of Paganism, and ardently embraced Christianity.

This high convert was received into our church by the baptismal ceremony, and named George, after his godfather, the Rev. George Bissett, the Governor's brother-in-law and private secretary. The other godfather was the Rev. William Harvard, Wesleyan Missionary. In this case, it was no ignorant man of humble degree who had been inveigled into apostacy from the faith of his fathers; no boy, who had been entrapped into Christian baptism before his reasoning faculties had attained their meridian; no poor native who had nominally become a Christian for the sake of a situation in a missionary establishment, but a High Priest of Buddha, upon whom the cheering ray of Almighty favor had so pre-eminently displayed itself; a man of science and education, an adept in all the dogmas of the Buddhist mythology, and reverenced almost to adoration by his brethren; with whom, notwithstanding his conversion, their former High Priest's reputation lost nothing in point of respect, and other converts amongst the priesthood soon followed the example of the Maha Nayaka Oonansé.

The then Governor, Sir Robert Brownrigg, conferred the title and sword of a Moodliar upon this eminent convert, who subsequently perfected himself in English, and showed himself indefatigable in assisting to translate the Old Testament into Singhalese.

From Beligam to Galle, distant about 17 miles, the whole line of road is excellent, and entirely shaded by dense coco-nut topes, or, where these are not, by ever-green and umbrageous Sea Pomegranate trees (*Barringtonia speciosa*, L.).

About midway, the serpentine lake of Cogel, which, during the rains, overflows the road between it and the sea, presents one of the prettiest and most tranquil scenes to be met with in the island; and, notwithstanding that it is scarcely four miles long, and about a mile and a half broad, it is well worth a day to visit the pretty islands which ornament its waters. This delightful basin is surrounded with a natural amphitheatre of verdant hills, covered to the very top with shrubs and trees of every hue that the most luxuriant foliage can present; and from its translucent bosom rise three curious rocks, which the late Major General Lord Viscount Molesworth named *Brahma*, *Vishnu*, and *Siva*.

From the island where the Agent of Government's bungalow stands, the scenery is worthy of the graphic pencil of a Daniell.* The Cajan roofed Bana Maduwas to the southward of the lake, from their extraordinary pagoda-like shape, have a very novel appearance to the European; and, embowered as they are among the deep green foliage of talipat, king coco-nut, and areka palms, shadock and bread-fruit trees,

* The late William Daniell, Esq., R. A.

indicate the calm and delightful solitude that is most congenial to the admirer of nature and the philosopher.

Pic-nic parties from Galle frequently visit this charming spot, and tiffins and dinners are occasionally given at the bungalow, the use of which is never refused by the Agent of Government to respectable parties, for such festive occasions.

When I was last at the bungalow, in 1827, the Cutchery Moodliar pointed out to me five species of *Momordica*, growing wild upon the island, which he distinguished by the names of *Tubukarawila*, *Karabila*, *Katukarawila*, *Tubakwila*, and *Domella*, all which are extremely bitter, and their leaves, upon being touched, impart a most offensive odour to the fingers.

There are many crocodiles in the lake, which afford abundant sport to the amateur: and, upon its northern and eastern borders, there is plenty of game; but it produces no other species of fish than has already been noticed, and these are so lightly esteemed, where supplies from the sea are abundant, that they are never sought after by the fisherman.

When the natives observe a crocodile in the water, they endeavour to attract attention to it by exclaiming, "*Onna! onna! Mahotmeya*," (there! there! Sir); but, for some time, the "Freshman," or "Griffin," looks about him in vain; at length he also perceives what to him appears a large cork floating upon the surface, but which proves to be the tip of a crocodile's snout.

The natives ridicule our notion of the crocodile turning with difficulty, and it is very well ascertained, that, by means of its pinnated tail, it can turn as rapidly as any other of the *Lacerta* genus. This animal has been known to seize buffalos whilst swimming across rivers, drag them to the bottom, and there suffocate them amongst the roots of trees and weeds.

In the year 1821, this part of the district was so infested by leopards, that in less than a week, a young man was carried off to the jungle from the village of Labadowé and a boy and girl from that of Etelligoddé.

The face of the country between Cogel and Galle is undulating, and extremely fertile; in many places, the road is cut through hills of ironstone clay, and, upon descending the road from the eastward, and opening the harbour of Galle, the view through the lines of the densely shading coco-nut trees, is one of the most delightful and grateful to the eye that a tropical climate can present.

From the offing, Galle has a very pretty appearance, when distinctly seen; but the first object, upon "making the land," is the Haycock, peering above the intermediate clouds; and the next, the reflection of the coco-nut trees, that line the shore, in the water, long before the trees are visible.

"Point de Galle Flag-staff is in latitude 6° 1 north, by observations taken on shore by Captain Basil Hall, Royal Navy, in 1815. Captain James Horsburgh, F. R. S., made it in longitude 80° 17′ 42″ east, by chronometers, which placed it 17° 22½′ east from Bombay castle, 2° 36′ east of Cape Comorin, and 2 miles west of Madras flag-staff, measured by chronometers, when the flag-staff of Point de Galle was bearing north.

"Captain David Ross, Marine Surveyor, made it in latitude 6° 0′ 59″ north, by observations taken close to the flag-staff in January 1824, and in longitude 80° 10′ 50 east, by chronometers from Bombay. Mr. Goldenham, the astronomer, made it 19 west of Madras Observatory, by chronometer, or in longitude 80° 17′ 2″ east." Mr. Twynam, Master Attendant of Point de Galle, made the latitude of Galle 6° 1 46 north, and longitude 80° 20′ east.

"The Town and Fort are built on the Point, which is rocky and bluff to seaward, with a rocky islet near it, called Pigeon Island, surrounded by smaller ones. The Bay or Harbour is formed between the Point and a piece of sloping high land to the eastward, which projects farther out to seaward than the true point. The entrance of the Bay is about a mile wide, the soundings in it from 7½ to 4½ fathoms; but there being many rocks covered with different depths, from 3 or 4 to 12 and 14 feet water, scattered over the entrance and also inside, a pilot is requisite to carry a ship into the Harbour, where they moor in 5 or 5½ fathoms abreast the Town.

"Captain D. Inverarity's excellent survey of this Harbour will be found useful as a guide; in which marks are given to avoid the dangerous rocks, thirteen in number within the entrance, exclusive of two outside. The following directions for sailing into Point de Galle Harbour are taken from that survey.

"In going in to the eastward of the 12 and 15 feet outermost shoals, steer along the eastern shore, giving the Bellows Rock, which always breaks, a good berth, keeping the New Belfry open to the northward of the Flag-staff until you open the White Mark or pointed rock with Watering Point, both situate on the eastern shore; then steer for Cook's House at the bottom of the Bay, keeping it its own breadth open to the westward of the rocks off the west end of Gibbet Island, until you bring the two Belfries in one; then haul over to the westward, keeping the New Belfry a little open to the northward of Pigeon Island, or the extreme of Utrecht or Eastern Bastion nearly on with the Flag-staff: you may then haul in to the northward for the anchoring ground, steering direct for Alexander's House, which is a large quarter of a mile to the westward of Cook's House, till in 4½ fathoms; this depth being a good berth for a small ship. This track between the central and north-easternmost shoals is the best for working into the Harbour without a pilot, although not used by them.

"Going in by the western track, keep the White Mark well open with Watering Point, and steer to the north-eastward until the Gull Rock, situated in the N. W. part of the Harbour, is open to the westward of a bushy tree called Pilots' Tree, and the outermost Flag-staff Rock bearing W. ½ S., then steer direct for the westernmost turret of Cook's House, (now the Cutchery,) keeping it on or a little open with the Haycock, carries you fair in between the 2 and 5 feet shoals, also between the 12 and 16 feet shoals, into a good berth for anchoring. This is the best track in the westerly monsoon, if the Haycock can be seen, as it is a leading wind into your berth; but it would not be prudent for a stranger to run into the Harbour without a pilot, except in possession of Captain D. Inverarity's survey mentioned above, (which was published in 1804, by the late Mr. Dalrymple,) *and then only in a case of necessity.*

"Galle Harbour is considered a safe place in all seasons of the year, but with strong S. W. winds, a ground swell tumbles in. A low sandy beach, with some rocky islets near it, and myriads of coco-nut trees behind, form the bottom of the Bay, and in the S. E. corner of it, on the north side of the high rocky point at the entrance, there is a wharf and an excellent spring of water at the bottom of a Cove, where a small ship may be careened: this bears from the Flag-staff about E. by. S. ½ S. a large mile.

"The outer Rock off the entrance of the Bay, bears from the Flag-staff about S. by E. ¾ E., distant near three-quarters of a mile: it is called the 15 feet Rock or Shoal, has 10 fathoms water close to, all around, and covered with 15 feet. At a small distance from it nearly north, another Rock, covered with 12 feet water, lies in 9 fathoms.

"The best anchorage in the Road is to the south-westward of these rocks, in 16 to 18 fathoms, soft bottom, with the Flag-staff on the Point bearing from N. N. E. to N. N. E. ¾ E, off the town nearly two miles; but when passengers or any articles are to be landed, or ships being in want of provisions and water, you will have a more convenient berth by anchoring in the same depth with the Flag-staff bearing N. ½ E. or N. by E. Out in 20 fathoms, the bottom is rocky, where several ships have lost their anchors. In 21 fathoms, with the Flag-staff N. E. by N., Captain Horsburgh had his cable cut through by the rocks in 24 hours, and lost the anchor, although the weather was fine, with very little swell.

"When the S. W. monsoon blows strong, it is unpleasant to anchor in the Road, as the Bellows Point or projecting land on the eastern side then becomes a lee shore, which is steep and rocky. On one of the outermost rocks, called the Bellows, near to this steep point, the sea breaks very high in bad weather."

CHAP. XLIII.

Sailing directions into the Harbour of Galle continued—Bank of soundings to the southward of Point de Galle—Coast between Galle and Colombo—General opinion respecting the Port of Galle, in regard to steam vessels—Anticipated benefits from the suggested removal of the seat of Government to Galle, and cutting a road direct to Kandy—Fortifying Galle, and other important measures suggested, with reference to our command of the seas during the last war, and the different position of France at this day—Trade of Galle—Supplies for shipping—The Elephanthiasis prevalent—Goitre—Dread of the Galle water—Cattle stealing—Cruelty to animals not provided against by Legislative enactment—Alteration in the mode of registering cattle suggested—Fort of Galle—M. Wilmot, Esq.—Garrison of Galle—Ceylon Rifle Regiment—Establishment of a large English hotel and farm suggested—Society of Galle—Dutch families—Climate of Galle—Maldivian fleet—Coco-nuts imported from the Maldive Islands—Kumblemos—Tavarkaré—Maldive ambassador—Sultan's letter and presents.

"When the Bellows Point bears N. W. 4 or 5 leagues, it may be known by a clump of trees, and if the weather be clear, the Flag-staff will be seen about two points open to the westward. To approach the anchorage, the Haycock, a little open to the westward of the Flag-staff, N. by E. ½ E., is a good leading mark, and with the same bearing, or N. N. E., is the best anchorage in 16 fathoms water, the Western Breakers W. ½ N., and the Bellows or Eastern Breakers E. S. E.

"From Point de Galle Road, the Haycock bears nearly N. by E., distant 7¼ leagues. This is a high conical mountain, in about latitude 6° 19½' north, which is very conspicuous from the offing, in sailing round the S. W. part of the island from Colombo to Dondra Head. About 3 leagues eastward from the Haycock, there is a table hill, with a nob or hummock on it, which is also visible from the Road. The land to the westward is generally low, with coco-nut trees fronting the sea, but to the north-eastward of Point de Galle it is formed of several ridges of hills of various aspects.

"The bank of soundings extends 3 or 4 leagues distance to the southward of Point de Galle, on which ships may anchor with a stream or kedge, should the wind fail and the current be unfavorable. In such case, they may anchor in from 20 to 40 fathoms on any part of it between Point de Galle and Colombo: the bottom is often sand and gravel, but in some places rocky.* In coasting along from the former place to the westward, a ship ought not to come under 26 or 28 fathoms during the night until she

* The charge for Pilotage being the same at Galle whether a Pilot may have been employed or not, no Captain, except upon a very urgent occasion, will risk the safety of his ship, by being his own Pilot into the Harbour. Author.

approach Kaltura, for these depths are sometimes found within 3 or 4 miles of the shore. Between Kaltura and Colombo the coast is more safe, and may be approached to 15 or 16 fathoms in the day, but these depths are too close to stand in during the night."

It is the general opinion at Ceylon, that whether steam vessels from the Red Sea viâ Bombay, or from England viâ the Cape, touch there, on their way to Calcutta, Galle,* being the nearest, and a very safe Port, will surely be the best, and, of course, become the grand depôt for coals.

If the removal of the seat of Government from Colombo to Galle, fortifying the hills that command the latter fortress, and cutting a road direct to Kandy, be ultimately determined by Her Majesty's Secretary of State for the Colonies, these important measures, and most expedient improvements, conjointly with the establishment of farms and factories, the culture of indigenous articles of commerce, abundant but now altogether neglected, the general extension of agriculture throughout the island, and the developement of its mineral resources, cannot fail to render it not only a place of commerce worthy of connexion with Great Britain, but, without exception, the most valuable, as it is, from its natural position as the Key of British India, the most important jewel in the Imperial Crown.

The great drawback hitherto experienced in the culture of the soil, by the persevering efforts to keep up the price of land, and the ill-favor consequent upon the alleged monopolies, which the Government are accused of encouraging, are giving way; and the recent reduction in the export duty of cinnamon, will induce many to exert their energies to increase the products of the country. A recent advance in the value of all descriptions of property, with a greater demand for domestic articles, show a good basis for the increased stability of business.

Under any circumstances, Galle must be better fortified, in the event of war, let the matter be handled which way it may; for although throughout the last, Great Britain had the command of the seas, and the combined fleets of France and Spain had either been destroyed, or transferred to English ports, or were cooped up within their own, the freedom of the seas, consequent upon the peace, and the naval exertions of France, have enabled her sailors to acquire experience in seamanship which has long since made them *all but equal to our own tars*, and worthy of fighting in the same cause, under the chief command of a British Admiral; and none are more ready than our own gallant sailors to do justice to the courage of both officers and men of the French navy, by acknowledging, that they require no instructions how to support, under whatever be the disadvantage of their position, the national honor, and glory of their country.

* Or "Gallé," according to the Singhalese, signifying *Rock*.

The trade of Galle chiefly consists in exports, but is by no means equal to what might be expected from its natural position. For nearly twenty years, it may be said to have been monopolized by one English firm, which dabbled in everything, from making *Koir* rope to selling the humblest crockery utensil; but soon after the accession of a partner of great commercial knowledge and tact, combined with all the best qualities of a British merchant, the old system was by degrees abandoned, the junior partner despatched to Colombo to superintend the retail sale of the most extraordinary medley that ever a Ceylon "store" contained, and the House assumed a footing rather more in accordance with the commercial importance of the head British firm in the island.

Galle, formerly, exported great quantities of salt fish to the continent of India; but that trade has declined considerably, although, of late years, endeavours have been made to re-establish it. There is more *Koir* rope, coco-nut oil, arrack, and Choya root exported from this province, than from all the other parts of the island together; and a considerable portion of the trade in coffee, cotton, rice, ivory, cinnamon, and tortoise shell, is carried on here. Exclusively of our own naturalized Dutch and Portuguese subjects, the trading part of the native population includes Moormen, Hindoos, Chitties, Arabs, Parsees, and Maldivians.

Ships may obtain better supplies here than elsewhere in the island; and fish, vegetables, and fruits, are cheap and abundant. Great attention is paid to onion gardens within and without the fort;—the sort cultivated is the shalot (*Allium Ascalonicum*, L.).

The very useful medicinal plant, the prickly poppy (*Argemone Mexicana*, L.), is here a mere weed, and found in abundance near the Dutch church and the old salt store.

The eastern extremity of the fort is low; the western, high, and much exposed: and, owing to the inequality of the intermediate ground, whilst, in some houses, the general complaint is, the total exclusion of the sea breeze, owing to the height of the fortifications, the Venetian'd doors and windows of others are every now and then forced open by its violence.—Ortolans (*Hortulana emberiza*, L.) are, at certain seasons, abundant upon the higher grounds and western ramparts.

One can scarcely walk through the streets of Galle without meeting objects of the greatest pity, from the dreadful effects of the Elephant leprosy (*Elephanthiasis*); but to what cause to attribute the disease, which, amongst the various maladies that afflict mankind, may be ranked as the most distressful, is at present hypothetical.

This disease is all-powerful:—the legs assume the shape and size of those of a young elephant, and the skin their roughness and wrinkles; these the patient drags along with the greatest difficulty, at a very slow pace. This dreadful disease leaves the sufferer without a hope of cure, unless the most powerful remedies be resorted to upon its very first appearance: then, indeed, the native doctors, who are extremely clever in cutaneous diseases, may succeed in eradicating it, but I could never obtain satisfactory proof of a cure having been effected in the course of three years that I resided in the district.

The most intelligent of all the native doctors at Galle,* informed me that the only cure for the complaint, which he called *Alia* and *Koraah*, was arsenic, if resorted to in the incipient state of the disease, when it is exhibited in pills, and applied, mixed with *Ghee*, as an external ointment.

The Swiss complaint "*Goitre*" is by no means uncommon here, but the cause must be very different from that to which it is attributed in Switzerland, namely, the use of snow water. I have never seen a European or native male afflicted with it, although it is not uncommon with native females, whose guttural protuberance renders their appearance very disgusting.

Nevertheless, almost all Europeans who reside in the fort of Galle, are greatly prejudiced against the use of the water from the springs within its walls, except that from the well near the Land Port Gate Barracks; and although crystal itself is not more transparent than the fort water, none will drink it; but it is seldom objected to for culinary purposes, and those who can afford it, employ a Puckalie to supply their wants from the spring between the burial ground and the Pettah. This expense may be easily obviated, by first boiling the water, and then filtering it. Shipping is well supplied with pure water from the well under the hill called Bòna Vista, which forms the east end of the harbour.

The natives of this district are notorious cattle stealers; and, notwithstanding the cruel and very disgusting manner in which they scarify the sides of their small lean cattle, by branding the owners' initials, or names, in Singhalese characters, *from twelve to eighteen inches diameter*, a Regulation exists, that every bullock, before being slaughtered, shall be exposed in the bazaar (under a shed it is true, but generally without food or even water) for twenty four hours, in order that if the animal may have been stolen, the proprietor, upon discovering his loss, may have time to claim it.

But, among other institutions of utility and charity of which the island may justly boast, it is to be lamented that there exists none for preventing cruelty to animals, notwithstanding the torture daily inflicted upon humanity, at beholding cattle driven

* Madung Appo, already repeatedly noticed in the preceding pages.

along the roads, in the heat of the day, with their *freshly scarified* sides covered with flies and other insects. I have often wished, that if only for one moment, the infliction were transferred to the owners' backs! how very soon would the cowardly and cruel wretches apply the upper surface of a cool plantain leaf to relieve their intolerable anguish! and then, perhaps, but never till some equally effective plan be tried, will they learn to appreciate the agonies of an animal, which, let its sufferings be what they may, can neither express them, nor appeal for mercy!

Legislative interference is surely desirable in order to prevent these long-standing and accumulating cruelties; and surely the substitution of a painted brand mark would be equally as effectual as scarification for the protection of the owner. But the registry of all cattle, and of the marks of proprietors, by the Headmen of villages, binding the parties selling or transferring cattle, to report the same, under a heavy penalty in case of omission, is as easy as the present plan of registering the names and marks of the animals slaughtered; and, *where cattle stealing thrives so very well as it does in Ceylon*, and the object is to protect property, Regulations can neither be too strict, nor penalties too severe.

The Fort is very extensive, being nearly 1½ mile in circumference, and has a considerable town within its walls: but is only strong as a sea defence, the promontory upon which it is built being rocky and fronted by coral islets; for it is completely commanded by the hills upon which the Roman Catholic church and Bona Vista stand, and from the hill over the burial ground, a shot might be fired through the Land Port into the main Guard-room!

The ramparts on the sea face afford delightful walks in the morning and evening, and the umbrageous *Suria* trees on the north ramparts, which, as well as some very fine bread-fruit trees, are numerous in the fort, enable one to walk there free from exposure to the sun throughout the day. In front of the Government House stands a superb row of exotic trees (*Mimusops elengi*, L.), which were originally introduced from Java.

The great improvements in the Pettah Bazaar do honor to the public spirit of M. Wilmot, Esq., of the Civil Service, a brother of the late lamented Sir Robert Wilmot Horton.

In time of peace, the garrison of Point de Galle seldom exceeds 200 men, including a proportion of the Ceylon Rifle Regiment, which is composed of Malays, and is as fine a corps as can be brought into the field, being scarcely inferior in discipline to any under the Crown. The officers of this regiment are much beloved by their Malay soldiers, and are a fine gentlemanly set of gallant fellows.

During the liberal administration of General the Honorable Thomas Maitland, the

Commandant of Galle had a good table allowance, which enabled him to display hospitality without involving himself. But now there is no such thing, and strangers arriving from England bound to India, and vice versâ, expect to receive as much hospitality from the Military Commandant, who may or may not be a field officer, as as if his table were provided at the public expense.

Very many commandants of Galle have, before now, been *seriously inconvenienced* by supporting the hospitality expected from their situation, by those who are ignorant of its trifling emoluments; and the delicacy of an officer so situated will not admit of *his* intimating that "*he has no table allowance.*"

The establishment of a large hotel upon the English plan, would be a very excellent speculation here, conjointly with a farm for the supply of shipping with stock, and prove a source of relief to the society of the place, which is limited and exclusively English, with but a solitary exception here and there; for the old and most respectable of the Dutch colonists who had survived the restoration of Java and its several dependencies, except Ceylon, to the Netherlands, removed to Batavia as soon as the treaty of 1815 had destroyed their long and anxiously entertained hopes of the island once again reverting to the Dutch flag.

Of the few remaining families, scarcely a trace remains of that independence and wealth by which the Dutch gentry of Point de Galle were distinguished antecedently, and for a long time subsequently to the cession of the island to the British arms: for these families, which, during the dominion of the East India Company of the Netherlands, lived in the best style, and in a manner suitable to their opulent circumstances, are, from their sudden privation of emoluments, and consequent changes, reduced to a condition of considerable embarassment; living by the sale of their jewels and other valuables that may remain from the wreck of better days!

To sink at once from opulence to a bare competence is quite reverse enough; but from the latter to poverty, from a condition that claimed and received respect from all ranks and classes, to that which the world too often treats with coolness bordering upon contempt, are circumstances that augment the sense of misery, and aggravate the horrors of misfortune.

The climate of Galle is salubrious, but the atmosphere is damp, and consequently inimical to books, drawing and other papers, and to steel and iron instruments:—the best preservative of the latter is a coating of thin bees' wax, which is to be preferred to mercurial ointment, notwithstanding that the latter is commonly used for preserving surgical instruments, swords, and other cutlery from rust; but keys are generally mounted with silver, and, occasionally, the smaller ones with gold.

Soon after the setting in of the south-west monsoon, the annual fleet of boats arrives from the Maldive* Islands, which extend nearly in a meridian line from latitude 7° 6 north to 0° 40′ south, and are called *Atols* by the natives.

Some of these islands are altogether uninhabited; the others produce immense quantities of coco-nuts, a species of *Scomber*, which, in its dried state, is called *Kumblemos* by the Maldivians, and *Umbella Kadda* by the natives of Ceylon, and Cowrie shells † (*Cypræa moneta*, L.).

The Sea Coco-nut, the *Tavarkaré* of the Maldivians (*Cocos Maldivica*, L.), and peculiar to the Seychelles Islands, is said to be also a native of the Maldive Islands; but, from the great value attached to its medicinal properties, and its high price, this may be doubted, in the absence of more positive information, and for the additional reason, that every specimen which I have seen imported, had the coal-black surface peculiar to the sea coco-nuts picked up in certain latitudes.[1]

The dried stuff called *Kumblemos*, has just the appearance of a ship's block divided longitudinally into several pieces, and is almost as hard; nevertheless, it is in great demand, and, after having been well soaked and beaten, is rasped into an edible consistency for *Sambols*, a sort of *olla* of chopped cucumber, onion, bilimbi, chillies, lime juice, and pepper, as an accompaniment to rice and curries, both at European and native tables.

Since the increased demand for coco-nut oil, Ceylon, notwithstanding the immense quantities of its own produce, has imported coco-nuts from the Maldives. For these, and their salt and dried fish, are bartered coco-nut oil, Koir rope, shaddocks, ananas, oranges, and limes, for the Madras and Calcutta markets, where the Maldivian boats generally arrive towards the end of the south-west monsoon, so as to exchange their cargoes for rice and cloths for their return ladings by the north-east monsoon, generally touching at Galle on the homeward-bound voyage.

The Maldive boats are remarkably well built, and have a pretty external appearance at a distance, the sides being painted or plastered with white and red streaks, with black imitations of ports; and, having a large eye painted on each bow, and the head and stern being alike, they at first sight appear like Spanish or Portuguese fishing boats.

The Head Nakodah of the Maldivian fleet is the bearer of a letter from his Sultan to the Commandant of Galle, of which, the annexed fac simile from the original, will serve to convince those who will take the trouble to compare the characters with the

* Derived from *Mal*, a thousand, and *Diva*, an island.

† These small shells pass current for money among the lower classes, in various parts of India, at the rate of 64 to a pice; and as there are 64 pice to a Sicca rupee, it takes 4096 cowries to make the value of 2*s*. 3*d*. sterling.

Singhalese, that, so far from the latter being also the language of the Maldivians, as some Authors have asserted, there really is no affinity between them.

The Nakodah is honored by the Ceylon Gazette with the title of "Maldivian Ambassador," and is escorted from the Jetty to the Government House in the Fort by a non-commissioned officer's guard of the Ceylon Rifle Corps, preceded by native music, and bearing on his head his Sovereign's letter, enclosed in a small bag of crimson silk, over which is an envelope of yellow silk, and an outer one of spangled muslin.

The Nakodah, having first respectfully touched his forehead with the Royal letter, presents it kneeling, and with repeated *salams*, after which are introduced the Royal presents, consisting of a sort of almond cake, called sweetmeats, a sea coco-nut, salt fish, bags of Cowrie shells, and some very beautifully made sofa or palankin mats; and the "Ambassador" having been informed that he should bear to his Sultan an answer and presents in return, and told that "he may go," (an easy but truly Asiatic way of getting rid of him,) respectfully takes his departure from the Government House, with the same escort and native band; and almost immediately afterwards "His Excellency" may be seen upon the beach, bargaining for Koir rope, coco-nut oil, and fruit, in his own character of Nakodah.

The stench arising from the Royal presents, made the Government house smell like a fish bazaar in the heat of the day; but, upon being ordered to be cleared away, the scramble for the salt fish, and "Royal sweetmeats," which, from having been huddled together, separated only by a covering of dried plantain leaves that enveloped the latter, must have imbibed the offensiveness of the most diffusive of the two, soon caused a clearance of the nuisance; the mats were distributed by the Commandant to his own friends, and the Cowries, and Sea coco-nut, deposited in the Government stores.

In 1825, the letter* from the Sultan of the Maldive Islands, having been translated by the only one in the district capable of doing it, was presented to me as a "memento of the occasion!!"

Upon the Maldivian fleet's return to Galle, the Ambassador is informed that the answer to the Sultan's letter, and the usual presents, consisting of scarlet cloth, (a color exclusively worn by the Sovereign, whose cap is of scarlet cloth, laced with gold, and having on the top a large gold button, set with a precious jewel,) a few pounds of cinnamon, some *China* writing paper, and other minor articles, scarcely worth enumerating, will be ready at the time fixed for his departure; when he takes leave, with similar ceremonies to those of presenting the Sultan's letter, upon his original arrival at Galle.

* See Appendix, for the translation.

CHAP. XLIV.

Maldivian process for increasing the size of coco-nut trees, similar to that of the Chinese for dwarfing, and of the Singhalese for propagating trees—The latter method described—Fishes—Author's Work upon the Ichthyology of Ceylon—Causes of its interruption—Ruinous consequences of the suppression of facts by an officious but irresponsible officer—Unauthorized and capricious rejection of the Author's appeal against the tyrannical measures pursued towards him, and upon groundless and false premises, in the name of the Right Honorable Lord Viscount Goderich—His Lordship's entire ignorance of the unjust rejection of the appeal to be presumed from subsequent facts and correspondence, and the high character of His Lordship—Anticipated justice, if ever the plain facts of the case reach the proper Authority—His Majesty George IV. specially patronizes the Author's Work on the "Fishes of Ceylon"—Face of the country—Morua Korle—Its first production of the potato—Salubrity of Galle—Dutch mode of burial a public nuisance—James Rowland Morgan, Esq. a victim to his own philanthropy—Dreadful catastrophe—Not a life boat nor a single Manby's mortar along the coast, extending 900 miles—Suggestions in behalf of humanity—Wesleyan Mission-house and Chapel—Admirable method of cooling the air during Divine service—Roman Catholic Chapel—Crucifixion represented by wooden figures—Mussulman festival of the Mohurrum—Dutch monopolies—Baddegammé, the Church Missionary Station—Extensive cultivation of arrow root—Indigenus Maranta.

THE Ambassador informed me, through the Cutchery Interpreter, that the same process adopted at Ceylon for propagating trees, viz. by the annular incision, obtained at the Maldive Islands for increasing the bulk of coco-nut trees intended for boat-building purposes. Hence, perhaps, the superiority of their coco-nut wood for building vessels, over that of Ceylon, which, unless it be above fifty years old at least, is scarcely fit for anything except fuel, fences, and aqueducts; and certainly not for the purpose it is stated to be by a certain Author, who would richly deserve, not only an exclusive patent for the manufacture of coco-nut-tree sago for life, but the highest reward in the gift of the Society of Arts, if he could but make out a satisfactory specification of his discovery, or of "the Singhalese mode of extracting some nutritious matter resembling sago from the heart of the stem."

The annular incision is also adopted in China for *dwarfing* trees; and it may therefore be presumed, that the different results arise from the rapidity of vegetation in the two former countries, and from its tardiness in the latter.

The annexed plate will afford some idea of the simplicity of the process adopted by the Singhalese.

Having selected a handsome branch of the required height, an annular incision is made, from an inch to two or three inches in length, according to the size of the branch, and the proportion of root required;* the ba k is then carefully removed, avoiding to cut the wood; and a thick compost of mould laid over the decorticated part, within an envelope of straw or koir,† which is fastened at the top and bottom as in figure 3. This part is regularly watered every morning and evening; but, in many places, a coco-nut is suspended over the covered part, with a hole in the bottom, just large enough to allow one drop of water to pass at a time; and this is more certain than the former method, because the mould is always kept moist where the incipient roots form.

In about three weeks, or a month at farthest, by attention being paid to keeping up the supply of water, the roots will appear, as in figure 4, at which period every caution is necessary; and therefore, in order not to over check the circulation, a moderate notch must first be cut at the thick end of the branch, at about two inches below the incipient roots; in two or three days, the notch may be increased, and so on gradually, until the radicated part of the branch becomes too heavy for its base, and breaks down, when it may be sawed off and planted wherever the future tree is to remain. It is, however, necessary to do all these things about a month before the setting in of the rains, and by watering the roots well morning and evening, and keeping the plants shaded during the day, scarcely ten in a thousand will fail.

Of the varieties of fish, the rock fish is superior to every other sort except the Seir fish, (*Tora-malu* of the Singhalese,) of which, the female is the most delicious, resembling salmon so much, that, were it not for the difference of color, the flesh of the former being white, one would believe it to be salmon. The finest rock fish is spotted, and known as "General Maitland's Fish" by the old fishers; but the smaller rock fish, called *Lawa Kossah,* which at first sight is thought to resemble the yellow trout, is also very firm and wholesome. Gourmands, however, prefer the sea-woodcock, or red sur-mullet (*Mullus barbatus*, L.), although, from its abundance, it is no rarity.

So extensive is the variety of useful and of peculiarly beautiful fishes upon this coast, that a long life devoted to their delineation and description would be too short to effect the object of the Ichthyologist. I had commenced the laborious undertaking in 1825, in the hope that, notwithstanding my very few hours of leisure from official duties during the day, my stay in the island would have enabled me to have carried it to some considerable extent, and that I should have been succeeded by others more competent to the task, if not more zealous in performing it, and who would ultimately have completed the Ichthyological branch of the Natural History of Ceylon.

But although I was originally encouraged by the spontaneous patronage of the

* See figure 1 of the annexed plate.

† Figure 2.

Singhalese method of Propagating Trees and Plants.

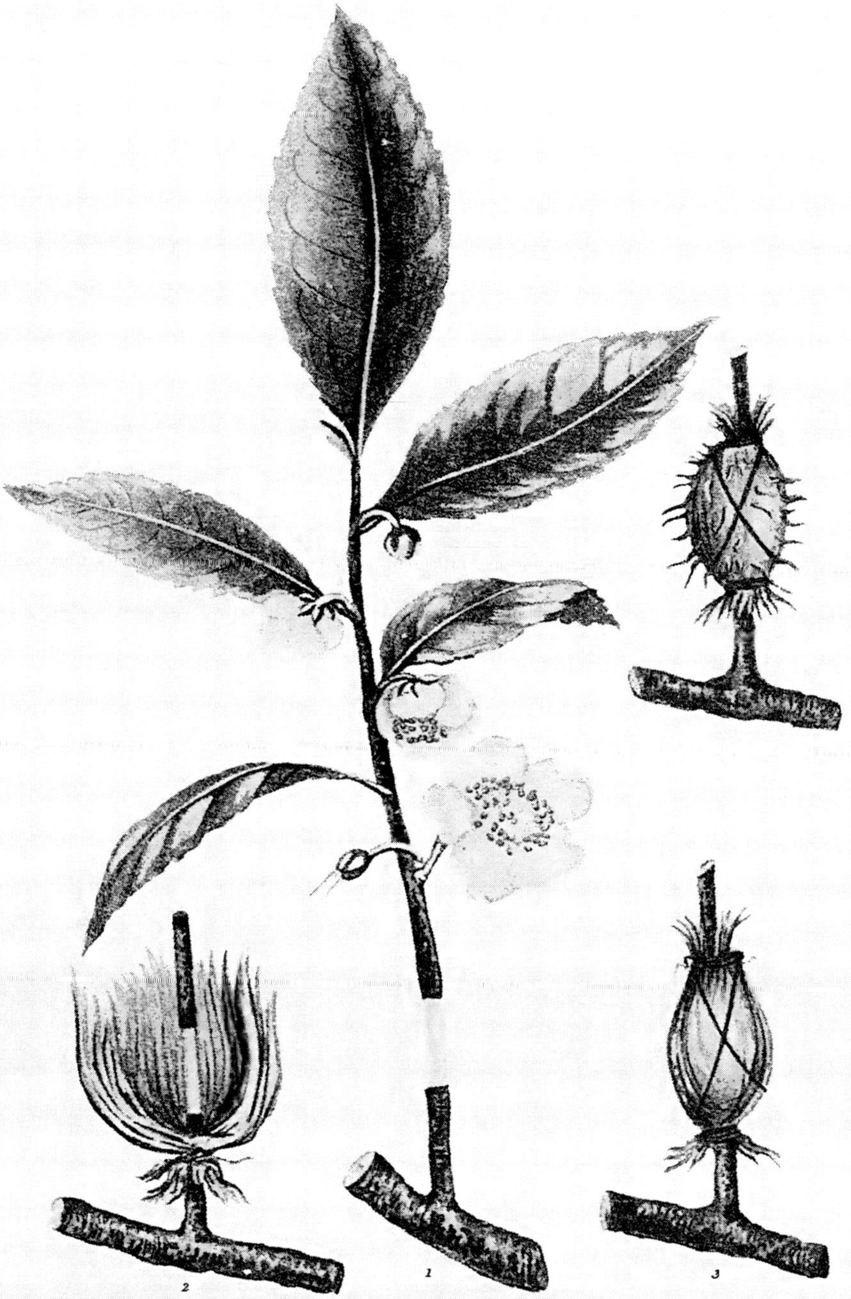

EXPLANATION.

1. *Annular Decortication.*
2. *Envelope of Coir or Straw, for the reception of Garden Mould.*
3. *The Envelope fastened, enclosing the Mould.*
4. *The Incipient Roots striking through the Envelope.*

Government of Ceylon, I had scarcely transmitted a selection of the most curious of the fishes of the southern coast for publication, than my object was nipped in its bud, by an order to return to England.* At the time, it was impossible for me to believe otherwise than that my absence would be but temporary; but I subsequently found, that the most unparalleled stretch of official power and injustice that had ever till then been exercised in the public service of this, or of any other country boasting a free Government, had been resorted to, and false and groundless pretexts employed, as a reason for rejecting my appeal against the atrocious proceeding; and this last, in the name, and as if by the authority, of the High and Noble Patron of my present Work.

It may boldly be presumed, from subsequently admitted facts and correspondence, that His Lordship was utterly unconscious of the unjust decision given in his name, and that my appeal had never been referred to His Lordship on the occasion; and thus was I, after a faithful and unimpeachable Public Service of twenty two years, through secret misrepresentations, but without the slightest cause, suddenly bereft of every prospect of Official promotion, (to which my half-pay as a First Lieutenant in the Royal Marines had been originally sacrificed, at the suggestion of Lord Viscount Goderich's noble predecessor in the Colonial Department, in 1827,) and deprived of a comparatively competent income, until it may be the pleasure of Her Majesty's Government, either to re-employ my services, or to grant me compensation; or, at least, to admit me to the Superannuation Fund, under the IXth clause of the Act passed in the 4th and 5th year of the reign of His Majesty King William IV., entitled "An Act to alter, amend, and consolidate the Pensions, Compensations, and Allowances to be made to Persons in respect of their having held Civil Offices in His Majesty's Service;" if, after all, the latter *can* be considered by Her Majesty's Government an *adequate* compensation for the unmitigated oppressions and relentless persecutions to which I have hitherto been the victim, involving deprivation of office, promotion, and emolument, for the last sixteen years; whilst the intermediate officer by whose unqualified and unauthorized use of Lord Goderich's noble name and official authority, by *himself deciding* that my appeal should be rejected, on the 20th of May, 1827, (only twenty days after Lord Goderich's assumption of the Colonial Seals; and that it was upon false and groundless premises it was so rejected, the London Gazette of the 20th of the *preceding* March affords ample proofs,) instead of submitting it, and the actual *facts* of the case, as it was his duty to have done, to His Majesty's Principal Secretary of State, all these ruinous and irreparable consequences were entailed upon me, enjoys, as he has done for many years past, a pension of £1000 a year!!

* See page 299.

The MSS. of the Ceylon Fishes having been submitted to His Majesty George IV., who honored the work with His Royal approbation, the first edition was published under His Majesty's most august Patronage, in 1828. These, contained drawings from life of the Gini-Maha (*Scorpæna volitans*), Seweya (*Acanthurus vittatus*), Koppra Girawah (*Gomphosus fuscus*), Ratoo Pahaya (*Holocentrus ruber*), Kola Handah (*Chætodon vespertilio*), Pookoorowah (*Holocentrus Argenteus*), Gal-Lellah (*Chætodon vagabundus*), Kaha Bartikyah (*Chætodon Brownriggii*), Ratoo Gini Maha (*Scorpæna miles*), Ratoopotobarah, or Mol-Kotah (*Balistes aculeatus β viridis*), Kara-Hamoowah (*Acanthurus hirudo*), Mal-Girawah (*Sparus Hardwickii*), Dewé-Boraloowah (*Bodian Cuvieri*), Hembili-Girawah (*Sparus decussatus*), Ankatilla (*Balistes biaculeatus*), Ratoo-Girawah (*Labrus formosus*), Gal-Handah (*Chætodon arancus*), Dewé-Koraleyah (*Chætodon atromaculatus*), Kaha-Laweyah (*Perca flava-purpurea*), Tic-Girawah (*Labrus aureo-maculatus*), Jul-Potobarah (*Tetrodon ocellatus*), Sepelawah (*Perca argentea*), Panoo-Girawah (*Scarus quinque-fasciatus*), Lena-Girawah (*Scarus Georgii Quarti*), Radeya (*Chætodon Tyrwhitti*), Inguru-Parawah (*Scomber Heberi*), Tik Kossah (*Gerranus Tankervillæ*), Laboo-Girawah (*Scarus Magrathii*), Pol-Kitchyah (*Anthias Clarkii*), and Nil Talapat-Girawah (*Gomphosus viridis*), as specimens of the more brilliant species of the Ichthyological genera of the Ceylon coasts and rivers.

The face of this part of the Southern Province is beautiful, and generally well cultivated with rice and a variety of other grains. Intersected by streams and canals, the vegetation is luxuriant and verdant throughout the year; and the succession of distant hills, adds to the variegated beauty which the landscape everywhere presents.

Within a few miles, the most favorable situations may be found for an extensive cultivation of sugar, coffee, cotton, cocoa, and indigo. The Government commenced planting cotton upon some of the waste lands in 1822, but as there was no regular superintendent, and it was left to the casual inspection of the Collector, who depended too much on native Headmen, through whose neglect it was ravaged by the cotton fly, it ended in nothing beneficial. Moreover, the cotton was planted within the influence of the sea breeze, which was a grand point against its success.

The Morua Korle, where the originally successful attempt to cultivate the potato was made by J. F. Lourenz, Esq., the Sitting Magistrate, in 1815, also presents a very healthy climate and delightful country, being well watered, and having a rich soil for every species of inter-tropical produce. Here numerous planters might advantageously locate themselves, every material for building being cheap, and meat, poultry, game, rice, fruit, and vegetables abundant.

Galle has hitherto escaped the ravages of Asiatic Cholera, whilst other parts of the island suffered severely from its visitation; but the proximity of the burial ground to the high road is here a very great nuisance; for, during the prevalence of the south-west monsoon, the pestiferous stench that is diffused by the abominable custom of allowing coffins to be laid one over the other in the tombs, and considerably above the surface, is indescribable. Where putrefaction is so extremely rapid, it is wonderful that the Legislature has not long since enacted an Ordinance for enforcing the interment of all bodies in the earth, unless additional tin or lead coffins be made use of.

The process of opening one of these tombs, for the reception of an additional occupant, involves the greatest danger to the people so employed; and that they escape so well, may be attributed to their precautionary use of vinegar externally to their hands and faces, and a due proportion of arrack internally, whilst their occupation continues.

Many years ago, I requested the attention of successive Collectors of Galle to this disgusting and dangerous practice; but, whether from apathy, or a desire not to interfere with matters connected with the Dutch church and burial ground, (for the English have neither,) about which the Dutch inhabitants are extremely jealous, the nuisance still continues, although fraught with peril to the living; and, if the burial ground had been within the Fort or Pettah, instead of being nearly equi-distant from both, every way calculated to effect an alarming change in the salubrity of a place equalled by few, and excelled by none, in India.

This repository of mortality contains a tomb remarkable for its architecture, and bearing the following inscription:—

SACRED TO THE MEMORY

OF

JAMES ROWLAND MORGAN, ESQ.,

ASSISTANT STAFF SURGEON TO THE FORCES,

WHO DIED AT GALLE THE 16TH SEPTEMBER, 1825,

AGED THIRTY ONE YEARS.

The inhabitants of Galle and Matura have erected this humble tribute of their grateful respect to departed worth.

By profession fitted for the noblest offices of humanity, Mr. Morgan devoted himself to their exercise in the hour of sickness and distress, to all in need of his assistance, whether rich or poor, white or black. No consideration of personal trouble or inconvenience interposed between him and that which he had marked out as his line of duty towards his fellow creatures.

His death-bed afforded the best proof of his real principles. For him, the last enemy had no terrors; and, cheered by the best hope, he bowed with resignation to the will of his Creator, and left this world of trial, under the blessed influence of faith in Christ.

GLORIA DEO.

On the 27th of June, 1823, Mr. Morgan arrived in Colombo Roads, with his wife and three little children, two of whom were girls, and the other an infant boy :—he soon afterwards landed, and having made the requisite arrangements for their reception, returned to the wharf, for the purpose of going on board for his family; but the wind blew dead upon the land, it being the south-west monsoon, and not a boat would venture out.

Soon afterwards, two boats were observed to leave the ship, of which, when about midway one was upset, and Mr. Morgan liberally offered money and used every intreaty in his power to urge the native boatmen to go to the assistance of their fellow creatures; little imagining, that at the time he was so zealous in humanity's cause, the chief sufferers were those most dear to himself, until the other boat reached the shore, when the first objects that met his view, were his two apparently lifeless children, and the corpse of the poor child's maid, with the dead infant in her arms, in the bottom of the boat; but the body of his wife had disappeared.

The two children, both girls, survived the dreadful catastrophe. For a time, the effect upon Mr. Morgan's mind was so great, that the very worst consequences were dreaded; but his naturally robust constitution, and religious temperament, enabled him to "weather the storm," and he gradually acquired the tranquility so necessary for the prosecution of his professional duties; but, in little more than two years, that constitution, which had been gratuitously and constantly exposed to all the vicissitudes of weather and a tropical sun, through his zeal for the benefit of his suffering fellow creatures, sunk under the intense exertions of philantropy; and the gratitude of the inhabitants of the districts of Galle and Matura was thus publicly acknowledged in honor of his memory.

Notwithstanding these and numerous other casualties that have happened in Colombo Roads within the last thirty years, strange to say, there is no such thing as a life boat belonging to any port of the island; and not even a single apparatus for projecting a rope from the shore to a ship in distress, from any part of this (in many places dangerous) coast, extending 900 miles!

Captain Manby's invention is so very cheap an apparatus to the Government, that it may be hoped attention will ere long be given to the general claims of humanity upon the provident foresight of our Colonial Administration, for nothing can be better adapted for Ceylon. Moreover, the Government, by establishing Manby's Mortar Stations at the most dangerous points of the coast, and placing them under the care of retired non-commissioned officers of long service and good character, with a small salary in addition to their well-earned pensions, will have the means of rewarding them in a manner more commensurate with past valuable and efficient services.

The Wesleyan Mission-house is a most convenient building, and the Chapel neat, substantial, and commodious; and, however peculiar *Punkahs* suspended from the ceiling may, at first, appear in a place of worship, it is acknowledged to be an admirable custom for rendering the air cool and delightful during Divine service, and one that is worthy of general adoption within the tropics.

The Roman Catholic chapel is a very spacious building, but destitute of internal splendour. On Good Friday, the Crucifixion is represented upon a stage in front of the high altar, by wooden figures of the size of life; one circumstance of which is particularly impressed on my memory, that upon unclasping the Virgin's arms, which embraced the cross, in order to take down the wooden representative of the body of the crucified Saviour, they fell down with a considerable noise, and, as they hung, were parallel with the ankles.

The Mussulmans of Galle celebrate the annual festival of the *Mohurrum*, as they also do in the Northern Province, during the first ten days of the first month of their year, (*Hægira*, or Flight,) in memory of the death of Hossein, the second son of Mohamed, by Fatima, who, according to the records, was killed whilst supporting his infant son Asher, who had been mortally wounded by an arrow, whilst in his (Hossein's) arms, on the 10th of the 1st month, by the army of the Caliph Yuzzed, on the banks of the Euphrates.

On the first day, the whole history of Hossein and his brother Hassan is so emphatically recited by the Muftis, that the feelings of the audience are excited to enthusiasm, and every expression of their sorrow and lamentation is shown, as if it were a recent, instead of so very remote a catastrophe. The military pageant is well got up, and horses are borrowed for the occasion, which, as well as their riders, are caparisoned as superbly as the circumstances of the Mussulmans, and gold and silver tinsel, can make them. The tenth day is the most solemn, being that of the interment of the slain; and, by way of conclusion, curses and imprecations are lavished upon the Caliph Yuzzed, and all his army and followers, whilst Hossein and Hassan are blessed and eulogized as martyrs.

This tragical story, which occupies a large quarto of MS., was formerly in the possession of an old Lebbe, or Moorman, at Galle, called Markair, who kept it enveloped in a valuable Cashmere shawl, and was as particular to prevent its being defiled by the touch of the hand as if it were the Koran itself.

Cinnamon abounds in this province, and is of excellent quality; but, notwithstanding the selfishness of the Dutch in regard to their own monopolies in cloves and nutmegs, and that they attached the penalty of death to the clandestine exportation of a single plant, and that of the torture to the crime of smuggling either the one or the other, they are not very particular in their manner of obtaining prohibited plants from the natives of British colonies; and experience ought to guard us against a repetition of conduct so every way degrading to national dignity on the one hand, and insulting to a friendly Government on the other, as that which was successfully practiced at Galle in the year 1825.*

Bread-fruit, Jack, and Angelica trees are abundant throughout this district; but the former is merely valued for its fruit, notwithstanding that the wood, when very old, is superior to that of the jack tree, and bears a nearer resemblance to mahogany (*Swietenia mahogani*, L.); and there is scarcely any part of the tree that is not useful; for excellent and strong ropes may be manufactured from its bark, and there cannot be a better substitute for pitch or dammer, for *paying* the bottoms of vessels, than may be obtained by tapping the tree, collecting the thick white juice that abundantly exudes, and, after hardening it in the sun, boiling it, when it acquires the property of pitch. Cattle are partial to bread-fruit-tree leaves, and therefore all young plants, or offsets from the roots, by which the tree is propagated, require to be fenced and protected by thorny bushes, until they may have shot up beyond the reach of the quadruped pilferers.

At Baddegammé,† the Church Missionary Station, arrow root (*Maranta arundinacea*, L.) is extensively cultivated, and the natives are greatly indebted to the example originally set them by the Rev. Messrs. Ward and Mayor, for the introduction of this invaluable root into culture in this district; and, from the low price of arrow root flour at Ceylon, and its comparitively high price in the home markets, it is doubtlessly a profitable article of commerce. It is made from the same plant as the arrow root manufactured at Barbadoes and Bermuda, and is not inferior in quality to the produce of either of these places.

There is a species of indigenous *Maranta*, called by the Singhalese *Get-Oloowa*,‡ but its root possesses very inferior qualities to that of the naturalized exotic *Maranta arundinacea*, L. In 1827, I presented a dried specimen of this plant to my highly esteemed, and now lamented friend, the late Major General Thomas Hardwicke, of the Bengal Artillery, which was nine feet in height, exceeding that of the *M. arundinacea* by nearly five feet.

* See pages 133, 134.

† Derived from *Baddé*, Jungle, and *gammé*, a village.

‡ From *Get*, a knot, and *Oloowa*, a head.

Class 1, *Monandria*, Order 1, *Monogynia*. Natural order, *Canneæ*.

CHAP. XLV.

Galle jewellers—Cabinet makers—Their objections to British tools—Suggestions to the hardware manufacturer—Veneering unknown to the Singhalese—Leaf employed for polishing wood—Revenue and Medical Departments—Post Office—The high duty upon Arrack above Bengal rum tantamount to a prohibition, and injurious to the Ceylon distiller and the British importer—Representation to the late Board of Trade—Moral state of the Galle district contrasted with that of the Mahagampattoo—Witchcraft, and the wizard—Effect of superstition upon the prosecutor—Samuel Tolfrey, Esq., author of the first English and Singhalese Grammar—Liberality of the Colonial Department—Tradition of the origin of the Singhalese Castes—Insects—Reptiles—Mygale, or musk rat—Singhalese pottery—Gindurah river—Gindurah rock—Sailing directions—Dodondewé—Rest-houses—Face of the country.

As regards the native jewellers, the remarks already made upon their brethren at Trincomalé,* are equally applicable to those of Galle and Colombo.

The master cabinet makers are generally Portuguese, but the workmen Singhalese;—these make very durable and beautiful cabinet furniture of every description, but they complain greatly of English tools, as being very badly adapted to the hardness of ebony and satin-wood timber. I would therefore suggest to the British manufacturer to study the shape and temper of the native tools, which are of the most simple construction, and thereby ensure certain and profitable returns for their exports to the Ceylon markets.

Veneering is unknown, except in the English-made furniture, which, in ignorance of the excellent workmanship of the Ceylon cabinet makers, passengers may have carried with them;—every article of furniture, from the camp stool to the splendid calamander side board, is solid, and reasonable in price. In lieu of sand or glass paper, for polishing wood, the native cabinet makers employ the under surface of a leaf, called *Welakola* or *Wellé-kola*.†

Galle is famous for calamander and tortoise-shell writing desks, work boxes, &c.; but the former soon wharp, and the import duty at home is so great, that they are scarcely worth the expense of importing them.

The Agent of Government for the Southern Province resides at the Cutchery, which is called in Horsburgh's Directory, "Cook's House;" and he is also a member

* See page 234.

† From *Wellé*, sand, and *Kola*, leaf.

of the Galle branch of the "Commission for the General Superintendence of Education." The District Court is superintended by a District Judge, at a salary of £1000 a year, with an establishment of Assessor, Secretary, Clerks, and Interpreter, at a further charge to the public of £308.

The Medical Department consists of a Staff Assistant Surgeon, who is also Superintendent of Vaccination, assisted by two Medical Sub-assistants, two Medical Pupils, and one Native Vaccinator.

The Post Office is superintended by a Cutchery Clerk; and, as it may be an object of utility to merchants and individuals going to Ceylon, I have added the Rates of Inland Postage,—the Rules established by the Governor General of India in Council for the management of the Post Office Department,—Rules for establishing a Parcel Tappal,—and the Table of Warehouse Rates, according to the Ordinance of the Governor and Council of Ceylon.*

Arrack, of an excellent quality, is extensively distilled in this district; but the import duty being 6*s.* per gallon more than that charged upon Bengal rum, it is so much against the British importer, that it is tantamount to a prohibition.†

By way of contrast to the moral state of the native community of this and the Mahagampattoo district, and making every fair allowance for the disproportion of their respective populations, I reluctantly acknowledge, that between 26th April, 1823, and 1st April, 1826, I had to decide, as Sitting Magistrate and one of His Majesty's Justices of the Peace, 3074 Civil, and 339 Criminal cases, exclusively of 5 commitments for murder (to be tried by the Supreme Court) and 5 inquests. These, do not include the Criminal decisions of the Joint Sitting Magistrate for the district, nor the Civil and Criminal cases decided by the inferior Magistrate of Ballepittyé Modera during the same period!

A few cases of witchcraft came before me at Galle, wherein the general charge was, "putting the complainant in fear of his life."

Upon one occasion, the wizard was detected in his incantations, and, with all his apparatus, brought to the Court; and if ever human being approached what is generally considered a demon in appearance, the defendant did. In some of the old Spanish prints of Asmodeus, this person is depicted to the life. The *Hembili*, or basket, contained a hen's egg, enveloped in the glume of the *Pandanus odoratissimus*, with

* See Appendix.

† See Appendix, for Letter to the late Vice President of the Board of Trade upon this subject, which, it is to be anticipated, may yet be honored with the favorable consideration of the present noble Head of that Department.

some of the flower of that plant, and an *ola*, invoking the devil "to dissolve the body of Madugammegay Appo, as fast as the waxen effigy, (about a foot in length, and not a very bad representation of the trembling prosecutor,) might melt before the fire." The egg and its accompaniments were to have been buried, "at a certain time of the moon," in the path by which the intended victim went to his cottage from the high road. The emaciated appearance of the care-worn and timid prosecutor may be in some degree imagined from Shakspeare's apothecary in "Romeo and Juliet," but even that is but a faint description of the Singhalese *anatomie vivante!*

Argument was in vain to convince the prosecutor of the futility of the supposition of any mortal's possessing the power of influencing spirits "of air, water, or the infernal regions," to do him bodily harm; for "he had already felt his body begin to dissolve!!" but he subsequently became more composed, upon handling the effigy, and *assuring himself* that it had not yet been submitted to the action of fire.

Upon subsequent conversation between the friends of the parties, and the prosecutor having agreed to pay the value of some twelfth share of a Jack and coco-nut tree, which, in the usual language of Singhalese proctors, he had been charged with having "usurped from the heirs," the emblems of witchcraft were destroyed, and the parties reconciled, without the Diary of the Court being made a record of perhaps fifty depositions in support of the prosecution, and of as many for the defence.

The defendant in this action was of the low caste called *Pidayné danno*, who make offerings to devils; and his assistant of the *Kustarogiyo* caste, who worship devils by dancing.

In regard to the observances of caste among the Singhalese, the well-known Singhalese scholar, Samuel Tolfrey, Esq., of the Ceylon Civil Service, (whose English and Singhalese Grammar was the first that appeared, and was patronized by the then liberal Secretary of State for the Colonies, who presented its Author a donation of £1000,) has given the most distinct account of their divisions and subdivisions, together with the tradition of their first establishment; a fabulous narration, fully detailing the original cause of castes, but nevertheless, believed by the most learned Oonansés.

According to this account, the present epoch is called by the Singhalese *Mahabadre Kalpaya*, of which, they have two modes of computing the duration; viz. five *Autagh Kalpas* make one *Mahabadré Kalpée.* In the course of 1000 years, the earth increases in height one finger's breadth. A span, *Viyata*, or twelve fingers' breadth, make one *Riyana*, (or cubit, 18 inches); seven *Riyanas*, one *Yaté*; twenty one *Yate*, one *Assumba*; eighty *Assumbas*, one *Kosa*; four *Kosas*, one *Gowa*; and 7½ *Gowas*, one *Anta Kalpa*. Or, there is a stone four cubits square, which a god, habited in white muslin, passes once in a hundred years; the muslin robe, waved by the wind, touches this stone as it passes; and when, by the attrition this occasions, the stone shall have been reduced to the size of a grain of mustard, one *Autagh Kalpé* will have elapsed.

But, previous to the *Mahabadré Kalpaya*, a thousand millions of *Sacvals*, or worlds, had been consumed by fire. Two only of the worlds remained; namely, that of *Brahma* in the highest region, and the *world of winds* in the lowest. All living creatures having been destroyed with the *Sacvals* that were consumed, they were regenerated in the uppermost region, and became Brahmans without any distinction of caste. Some of these Brahmans returned to the *Sacvals* they had originally inhabited, upon their being reproduced, but from avarice they degenerated so much as to begin to steal, which latter crime caused numberless disputes; and, having no Chief among them to decide between the litigants, the wisest of the Brahmans, reflecting that order could not exist without some form of Government, assembled a Council, and having selected a Brahman eminent for wisdom, they chose him their King, and invested him with a right over *one tenth* of whatever substance the people might acquire, appointing him the "JUDGE AND RULER" over them.

This King, from having been chosen by a great assembly, was called, according to the signification of those words, *Maha Sammata;* and, after his elevation, he proceeded to divide his people into the following classification of castes.

Rajah Wansaya, or King's caste; *Brahmana Wansaya*, caste of Brahmins skilled in science; *Wanija Wansaya*, caste of merchants; *Gowi Wansaya*, caste of cultivators, or agriculturists, which, in Singhalese general parlance, although not a Singhalese word, is known by the name of *Vellalé;* and which, from there now being none of the three higher castes in Ceylon, is considered the highest.

The following castes are constituted to serve the four preceding castes; namely,

Danduwaduyo, carpenters; *Wiyanno*, weavers; *Raduda*, washermen; *Aymbaythayo*, barbers; *Hannali*, tailors; *Rata Karayo*, carriage makers; *Badalu*, workers in metals; *Malakarayo*, planters of flowering shrubs and garland makers; *Kumbalu*, potters; *Sittaru*, painters; *Gahalayo*, those who build *walls* of houses only; *Hinnawo*, mat and sieve makers; *Liyana Waduwo*, turners; *Achari*, blacksmiths; *Diyaluwo*, water carriers; *Vinakarayo*, players upon the *Vinah*, a stringed instrument; *Aimaduwo*, arrow makers; *Nalakarayo*, players upon wind instruments; *Ayttalayo*, feeders of elephants; *Pupawéléndo*, cake sellers; *Raawélêndo*, toddy sellers; *Seppidiwijji Karayo*, wizards; *Sukari Kayo*, pig butchers; *Magawi Kayo*, deer killers; *Sakani Kayo*, bird killers; *Waguri Kayo*, fishermen who use nets only; *Bari Kayo*, carriers; *Baak-kayo*, purveyors of food; *Daasayo*, slaves; *Chanda layo*, inhabitants of forests who make thongs of the skins of animals for the Royal use only; *Vedda* or *Veddah*, wild people who subsist by the chase.

This account of castes was extracted from Singhalese books, lent by the Mohandiram, Don Andrias, of Colombo, a learned native; but although these castes are generally recognized by Buddhists, there is another system, which was established by the first King of Ceylon,* who arrived in the island from the kingdom of *Laaladesaye*, of whose King, *Sinhaba*, he was the son, in the 56th year of the era of the last Buddha, seven days after he had become *Nivani*, or a state of happiness, although the death of the soul; which, according to the Buddhist creed, becomes again mortal after it has attained a state of purity. The present year (1843) is the year of Buddha 2386.

According to the *Nitiyah*, a book said to have been written in the Singhalese language by Vijiah Rajah himself, he found Ceylon inhabited by devils only, which he destroyed with the army of 700 giants which accompanied him from *Laaladesayé*, and then made the country a fit residence for human beings. During his reign of 38 years, he established the following castes for the performance of personal service in his palace, and the punishment of criminals.

Duravos, or *Chandoos;* the former not a Singhalese word, and meaning, from the two words it is composed of, *come from afar;* of which caste, there are ten subdivisions; namely,

Pati Karayo, cowherds; *Porawa Karayo*, timber fellers; *Hari Duravo*, proper duravos; *Magul Duravo*, riders of the Royal elephants; *Aynadi*, servants to these four castes, for carrying their talipats, pingos, &c.; *Kuttadi*, dancers; *Balibattu*, persons who offer rice to the images of the nine planets, and who alone may eat of that rice; *Pannayo*, elephant feeders; *Nattambu*, toddy drawers; *Hiwattayo*, washermen of this caste.

Karawo. Of this caste, commonly called Fishers' Caste, there are nine subdivisions. *Karawo*, a compound word, signifies "Evil-doers," because the occupation of the caste is the destruction of animals, which the Buddhist religion forbids; namely,

Dunuwaayeli, archers; *Williya*, catchers of birds in snares; *Wadekayo*, executioners; *Ugulwaydi*, trap makers, for animals; *Kayman wadi*, catchers of crocodiles; *Paksi wadi*, bird catchers; *Muhududaye wadi*, fishers with nets in the sea only; *Kaywulo*, anglers and those who fish with hooks and lines only; *Maswikunanno*, fishmongers.

Pass mehe Karayo. Five performers of service.

Danduwaduwo, carpenters; *Wiyamao*, weavers; *Radda*, washermen; *Ambattayo*, barbers; *Sommaru*, sandal makers.

* *Vijiah*, whose capital was *Tamanha Newara*, B. C. 543, or the 1st year of Buddha.

NAWAYMIYO. The nine services,—Servants to the four highest castes; namely, *Sittaru,* painters; *Achari,* ironsmiths; *Liyana waduwo,* turners; *Gal waduwo,* lapidaries; *Ee waduwo,* arrow makers; *Ranhallo,* goldsmiths; *Yamanu,* solderers of metals; *Oli,* mask makers; *Hommaru,* persons who remove the dead bodies of animals, and dress the skins.

TOLIL KARAYO. Particular service.

Hannali, tailors; *Hakuro,* cooks; *Hurma,* chunam makers; *Berawayo,* tam-a-tam beaters; *Paduwo,* palankin bearers.

LOW CASTES.

Gauraykawallu, village watchmen; *Andi,* beggars by caste; *Wallu,* slaves; *Pidaynidanno,* offering makers to devils; *Gahalayo,* scavengers; *Horu,* thieves; *Kannu,* persons born blind!! *Koru,* persons born lame!! *Hinganno,* paupers; *Dés ayrawo,* strangers travelling for amusement!! *Yaka duru,* devil worshippers; *Pilu,* persons born deaf and dumb!! *Koostarogiyo,* lepers, and those who worship devils by dancing; *Kappuwo,* temple watchmen; *Henawalayo,* fine mat makers; *Pali,* washermen to low castes; *Hinnarayo,* mat makers; *Rodiyo,* skinners, living in woods; *Kontayo,* persons who carry the frame upon which the King's palankin is placed when he travels; *Hinawah,* washermen to the *Gahalayos* or scavengers.

This arrangement of castes is considered one of the strong features in the religion of Buddha, of resemblance to that of Brahma, and a proof of their being derived from one and the same origin.

There are a variety of names of castes given at the present day to other trades, such as *Pesa Karayan,* to *Chalias,* or cinnamon peelers; the former names signifying, "makers of cloth strainers to filter water." This caste has assumed consequence from their employment in peeling cinnamon for Europeans; which, from its importance, has given the *Chalias* such an ascendancy, that they dispute rank with the Fishers' Caste; and, during the Government monopoly in cinnamon, they received considerable advantages above other castes in regard to the jurisdiction to which they were liable.

The Entomologist may collect almost every variety of the *Arachnida* family, which "Live in each thread, and feel along the line," known to the island, within a few miles of Galle; and a great many from the godowns, &c. of the old Dutch houses, where they abound, as if enjoying peculiar privileges of exemption from the sweeper's broom. Of these, the largest are, the Long-bodied Spider (*Tetraganatha extensa*), and the Tarantula or Tarentula (*Fabricius* of Latreille).

Lizards are innumerable. These reptiles abound in every garden, and upon the walls of every house, both within and without. The smallest or white Lizard is very disgusting, for it occasionally falls from the ceiling upon the table, and, by the concussion, loses its tail, which continues for some time to exhibit motion after its separation from the body. The Garden Lizard is that called the Nimble Lizard (*Lacerta agilis*, L.), but the most beautiful in color is the large Green Lizard of the woods, with head and ridge of the back of a bright orange red.

Cockroaches (*Blatta orientalis*), Green Bugs (*Cimex viridis*), and a great variety of *Scaratides*, enter with the lighting of the lamps at night, and annoy one above board, whilst the tiny but most troublesome Mosquito (*Culex molestus*) draws all the blood it can, particularly from the Griffin, below.

Common Rats (*Mus decumanus*) of large size are numerous; and the *Mygale*, or Musk Rat, as it is vulgarly called, although neither allied to the Rat nor Beaver, but more nearly approaching to that of the Shrew (*Sorex*) than to any other family, is an occasional visitor to the godowns, or wine cellars. This animal has much the appearance of a mole, being nearly of the same color, and having a similar, but not so pointed a snout; in the shape of the head, number of teeth, want of external ears, minute eyes, and turn of the paws in a vertical direction, with the soles backward; and appears, from the slowness of its motion, compared to that of a rat or mouse, better adapted for water than land. Musked wine and ale is very often the consequence of the trail of these animals over empty bottles, or the corks of full ones.

A great deal of common earthenware, for native use, is manufactured in this district; but the Singhalese have no knowledge of the art of glazing it. Their tools are extremely simple, the principal being a wheel, made of teak (*Tectona grandis*) or ironwood (*Mesua ferrea*, L.) timber, which revolves in a stone pivot, well supplied with oil to prevent friction, and resting within the hollow of a stone in the ground, in which it is sunk to within a fourth of its length. The top of the pivot is fixed to a hole in the centre of the under surface of the wheel. This is turned by a boy; and the only other tools are, a smooth piece of stone, and a mallet, similar in shape to that used by our wine coopers. Some of these potters' wheels, although very old, are still useful, and regarded as valuable heir-looms of the family.

Many of the Singhalese earthen vessels are beautifully formed, but not equal to those of Kandyan manufacture; and those who can afford it, use the common blue and white stone China, which is preferred to, and cheaper than, British manufacture, and imported in considerable quantities by the Portuguese vessels which annually touch at Galle, on their homeward-bound voyage from Macao to Goä.

The next stage from Galle is Hiccode, or, as the Singhalese call it, *Hiccodewa*, distant 12 miles. The Gindurah river, four miles from Galle, will not fail to attract the traveller's observation, for its pretty, not magnificent, scenery; and the Botanist will find a great deal to interest him, both on the river and upon its banks.

"Off this river, there is a dangerous rock, called Gindurah Rock, about three or four miles to the southward of Ragamma Point, and two miles distant from the shore, opposite to a Reddish Hummock standing near the sea. In passing this danger, the rocky islet contiguous to Ragamma Point should not be brought so far out as to be in one with the northern extreme of the coast; but the surest guide is not to borrow under 22 fathoms, or 20 fathoms, the latter depth being within two or three ship's lengths of this dangerous rock.

"About three miles to the eastward of Gindurah Rock, and nearer the shore, there are two rocks, covered with 5 or 6 feet water, on which the sea generally breaks, having 15 and 16 fathoms about a cable's length outside of them, with irregular rocky bottom between them and the shore, from 10 to 5 fathoms. Boats or small craft passing inside of these rocks, should keep nearer to them than the shore; but it is dangerous to be among them in the night. These two rocks are three or four miles to the westward of Point de Galle."

After crossing the Gindurah river, the next village is the fishing hamlet of Dodondewé, where there is a Bana Madewa, a little out of the high road on the right hand, and a minor custom-house. A whale was driven ashore at this place in 1823, and this was such a rare occurrence, that people came from far and near to see the "great fish which suckled its young." The animal yielded a great quantity of oil, which became the Governor's property, as Vice Admiral.

The rest-houses throughout the whole line of road from Galle to Colombo are excellent, and there are Postholders at the intermediate stations to supply refreshments to travellers at 25 per cent. above the bazaar prices, which profit is allowed them for their trouble, fuel, cooking, &c.; and, where every necessary article of supply is so cheap, cannot well be objected to, even if it were not authorized by Government.

The face of the country is generally flat, but, in certain places, undulating, and the roads are excellent. One continued tope of coco-nut trees, along the sea shore, and line of road, renders travelling delightful, whether by day or night, in carriage, buggy, palankin, or on horseback. The country is intersected by beautiful rivers, whose banks are covered with verdant trees and paddee fields; and horse-boats and passage boats at every ferry render travelling any thing but irksome, the delay being very trifling at either.

CHAP. XLVI.

Hiccode rest-house—The resort of pic-nic parties from Galle—Body of a native cut out of a crocodile—Amblangoddé—Madampé river—Kosgoddé—Bentotte—Face of the country—Native farms—Singhalese culture of the pine apple—Oyster divers—Bentotte oysters—River scenery—Vihare and its neighbourhood—Govinda yields a superior indigo—Population of the Southern Province—Barberyn—Sailing directions—Barberyn village—Bazaar—Imports and exports—Minor Custom-house—Road to Kaltura—A double coco-nut tree considered ominous of good fortune—Kaltura—Sailing directions—Government House—Cutchery—Wesleyan Mission-house, chapel, and school—Fort—The Honorable John Rodney's Patterero—Experiments with the large black, and small brown scorpions—Vulgar opinion controverted by the results—View of the Kalu-Gunga from Mount Layard—Canal to Colombo—Kobra Guyon—Lacerta Nilotica—L. Gecko—Traffic between Kaltura and Saffregam—Dr. de Hoedt—Carpenter insect—Painted bat.

It was at Hiccode rest-house, which is most pleasantly situated, and a great resort of pic-nic parties from Galle, that, on one of these occasions, I saw the body of a native, who had been swallowed by a crocodile, cut out of the animal's belly;* which, although uncommon, was not a solitary instance of its anthropophagy; but it is to be anticipated, that with the increase of cultivation, through the medium of British capital, *and the settlement of some of its possessors in this incomparable colony,* the number of elephants will be reduced to a certain limit, and crocodiles be altogether extirpated.

The road, level and good, lies through an uninterrupted tope of tall and ever-verdant coco-nut palms, a prominent feature of the western coast of Ceylon, which in myriads fan the air, whilst they form an agreeable and almost impervious shade from even a meridian sun.

The next rest-house, after leaving Hiccode, is that of Amblangoddé, distant 7 miles, crossing the Madampé river by a well-constructed wooden bridge; and from thence, through the village of Kosgoddé, to Bentotte, the distance is $14\frac{3}{4}$ miles. The rest-house, a strong and extensive Dutch building, is one of the best in the island, and most delightfully situate upon a level green, at a pleasant but not too remote a distance from the sea, from whence the breeze is wafted over the river with a refreshing and unusual coolness, when contrasted with its passage over the sands.

* See pages 185, 186.

The means of irrigation are everywhere so abundant, that the face of the country is one vast scene of cultivation. Coffee grounds, fields of country hemp (*Crotalaria Juncea*) for fishing nets, paddee fields, arum (*Arum Macrorhigon*, L.), yam (*Dioscorea bulbifera*, L.), and sweet potato (*Convolvolus Batat* L.) plantations, and also of a country potato, very small, but in some respects like that of Europe (*Solanum tuberosum*), give an air of plenty and of luxuriance to the general scenery of this part of the island.

A great variety of useful and profitable grains and pulse, that are now altogether neglected or unknown in the province, might be brought into cultivation in the district at a comparatively small expense; but the natives seem too much attached to their old habits to patronize novelties, either in their agricultural implements, mode of tillage, or articles of produce.

The native farms and villages are surrounded by indigenous fruit trees, including the shadock, orange, lime, and jambo. Pine apples require neither care nor culture; for, with the Singhalese, to twist off the crown and fling it into the hedge, or carelessly stick it into the ground, or on the top of an old wall, is sufficient to insure its yielding fruit in due season. In many places, I have observed seven perfectly ripe orange Ananas upon the same stalk; of which, six encircled the centre pine as regularly as if trained with mathematical precision.

Sea and fresh-water fish are plentiful and cheap, and the Bentotte river supplies a very excellent oyster (*Ostrea edulis*, L.):—this the Singhalese divers detach from the rocks at the bottom of the river with mallets; for which purpose I have often employed them during my excursions upon the river.—Here is a strong argument against the theory of locomotion in the oyster, independently of its being destitute of feet, or substitutes for them, which the pearl oyster (*Mytilus margaritifera*) possesses.

The diver descends without any of the precautions or apparatus used at the Pearl Fishery, notwithstanding that sharks have occasionally been seen in the river, and with merely a net, attached to a line from the canoe, in one hand, and a mallet in the other. Having reached the bottom, a depth of some fathoms, he begins to knock off the oysters from the rocks, (an operation which may be plainly heard upon the surface,) and having filled his net, jerks the rope, as a signal for hauling it up; but, being more buoyant, the diver reaches the surface first, and having inhaled a fresh supply of air, repeats his labour, till the quantity of oysters required is obtained.

Upon a cursory view of the Bentotte oyster, it has the appearance of a lump of uneven rock.—Oysters should never be taken at low water, but at mid tide; because, in the former case, they are not edible until after a day or two's purging in very salt water.—The villagers are entirely ignorant of the method of feeding oysters, although their river supplies Colombo, Galle, and the intermediate places. Oysters are altogether so little esteemed by the natives, who are extremely simple in their diet, and content withal, that they never trouble themselves about luxuries, when the least extra cost attends their acquirement.

It is here, that persons of small income, disposed to retirement, and to be contented with inter-tropical productions, may live well upon a very moderate income; and, with a small additional capital of about £500 to begin with, would be considered rich among the Singhalese.

The scenery up this river is beautiful, the sides covered with the curious Mangrove (*Rhizophora Mangle*, L.), and a variety of magnificent timber trees, among which, innumerable monkies play their destructive gambols, every now and then descending to plunder the fruit trees of the adjacent farms, which they do with perfect impunity.

If the tourist leave Bentotte in a *Pardie* or covered boat overnight, he will be in the midst of a fine country, abounding in game, and intersected by small streams, where there is just room enough for the boat to pass clear of the overhanging trees and underwood, by daylight. Upon one excursion, and just as the people in my Pardie were quietly eating their dinner, a fine Samver (*Cervus Aristotelis*, L.) came to the edge of the water, without perceiving the boat, and was shot from the branch of an intervening Mangrove tree.

A few miles above Bentotte, there is an ancient and substantially-built Viharé, which is approached by a wide avenue of fruit trees, and by several flights of granitic stone steps. In the temple grounds, a variety of palms and other trees, displaying every shade of foliage, some bearing fruits, others flowers, present a delightful change from the ever-noisy variety of Ceylon towns, and an indescribable tranquillity of scene, which is interrupted only by the cooing of the turtle dove.

The priests seem to be most partial to the large yellow Bignonia (*B. Indica*), the double Pomegranate (*Punica granatum, var duplex*), Bauhinias (*Bauhinia acuminata*, L., *B. tomentosa*, L.), the sorrowful tree (*Nyctanthes arbor tristis*, L.), white and yellow Jessamins, Arabian Jessamin (*Nerium coronarium*, L.), Four o'clock flower (*Mirabilis Jalapa*), African Marigold, and the double pink and white Oleander.

At noon day, the avenue is delightfully shaded from the sun, and the rills of pure water which flow to the right of the road, where there is also an ancient and sacred well, almost as cold as if saltpetre were being dissolved in it, and which soon imparts coolness to wine, render it a charming rendezvous for the pic-nic, after a day's excursion in the neighbourhood.

Here the botanist, the entomologist, the zoologist, the ornithologist, and the sportsman, have an ample field to gratify their several tastes and pursuits, without an opportunity being afforded to either of justly charging all-bountiful nature with having been more liberal to one than to the other; and whilst the table is spread under the luxuriant foliage, and enjoyment enhanced by good appetite is the order of the day, the neatly dressed village girls, in all the innocence of early life, may be seen ascending the temple steps, and, with the awe and humility prescribed by their harmless superstition, bearing the choicest of their native odoriferous flowers, of which, the pink *Lotos* is one of the most fragrant and beautiful. as a votive offering to their deity.

Upon the left bank of this river, a shrub, called by the Singhalese *Govinda*, abounds, whose leaf yields a superior indigo; hence its name, in honor of *Vishnu*, who is also called *Govinda*, and represented of that color.

The Bentotte river separates the Western from the Southern Province, of which, the superficies is 6,032 square miles, and population 268,400, according to the Census of 1835, making the average number to the square mile, 44.48; viz.

	MALES.	FEMALES.	TOTAL.
Whites, including Military and their families	768	678	1,446
Free Blacks, ditto ditto	143,332	122,276	265,608
Slaves	431	342	773
Aliens and resident strangers	......	......	573
			268,400

Of these, 71,694 are employed in agriculture; 11,366 in manufactures, and 9040 in commerce. The marriages, in the year 1835, were 1796; births, 11,320; and deaths, 5123; leaving a surplus in favor of the population of the province, of 6197.

Having crossed the Bentotte ferry, we re-enter the Western Province, and the next village is Barberyn, distant 6¾ miles; road excellent, occasionally undulating and hilly, but well shaded with coco-nut palms, tamarind (*Tamarindus Indica*, L.), and various other beautiful trees, including the *Ficus Benjamina*, L., *F. racemosa*, L., *F. Bengalensis*, L., *Strychnos nux vomica*, L., *Cerbera Manghas*, *Bignonia Indica*, *Tabernæmontana alternifolia*, *T. Citrifolia*, *Sterculia Balanghas*, *Morinda citrifolia*, *Clerodendrum infortunatum*, L., *Bombyx pentandrum*, *B. heptaphyllum*, *Barringtonia speciosa*, L., *Hibiscus Subdariffa*, *H. tiliaceus*, *Terminalia Catappa*, and *Melia Azadirachta*.

"Barberyn Island, in latitude 6° 28′ north, bears about S. by E. ½ E. from Kaltura, distant eight miles: being small and close to the coast, it is not easily perceived, unless when passing very near. There is said to be anchoring ground to the north of it, in 6 or 7 fathoms, and a small Bay within it, with 2 or 3 fathoms, sand, where small vessels may anchor, but large ships passing between Kaltura and this island seldom come under 17 or 18 fathoms, from 2 to 3 miles off shore. Rocks project from the N. W. end of the island, with 17 fathoms water very near them, which must be avoided in passing, and the lead constantly kept going.

"Point Cocacheira bears from Barberyn Island about S. by E. $\frac{3}{4}$ E., distant $4\frac{1}{2}$ or 5 leagues. The coast between them is generally of moderate height, and should not be approached under 20 fathoms by large ships, except about 2 or 3 miles to the south of Barberyn Island, where there is said to be good anchorage in 12 or 13 fathoms, black sand, near the entrance of a small river. The depths along this part of the coast are not always regular, 20 or 22 fathoms is about 2 miles off shore, and 60 or 65 fathoms is from 3 to 4 leagues off, nearly on the edge of soundings. With the Haycock bearing about 6°, there is a rocky bank, with 30 and 32 fathoms on it, and 37 or 38 fathoms inside, between it and the land; this bank seems to about 5 leagues off shore, extending a considerable distance to the southward."

Barberyn is a large fishing village, with a spacious native bazaar. Fish is salted here in considerable quantities, but in the usual careless manner of the Singhalese, for the Kandyan markets; where, spite of its inferior preparation, it is ever in demand. The trade coastwise is considerable, and a great deal of koir cord and rope is manufactured, and exported coastwise, as well as coco-nuts and areka nuts.

The principal imports consist of cloth, and common handkerchiefs, sarongs, and cambays from the Coromandel coast, Jaffna, and Chilaw; all of which are manufactured of cotton. The principal traders are Hindoos, Chitties, and Moormen, who also carry on a considerable trade with Saffregam by the Kalu-Ganga, or Kaltura river.

There being no rest-house at Barberyn, the tourist will be certain of every attention from the Officer in charge of the minor custom-house there. Near the village, upon a projecting promontory, there is a small mosque, which is more remarkable for its delightful scite, than for any peculiar merit it possesses as a specimen of a place of Mussulman worship.

From Barberyn to Kaltura, distant $5\frac{1}{2}$ miles, the road is excellent, in some places cut through hills of Kabook clay, and the country undulating and well cultivated. Nearly equi-distant between the two villages, there is an extraordinary *lusus naturæ*, on the right hand, in a double coco-nut tree, the heads of which branch off at about sixty feet from the ground, like the letter Y, and its average produce is equal to that of two good trees. I have heard of other instances of it, but this is the only one I ever saw, and it is considered by the superstitious natives an omen of great good fortune to the family to whom it may belong.

"Kaltura, or Caliture, on the left bank of the Kalu-Ganga, in the western province, is in latitude 6° 36′ north, and bears S. by E. from Pantura, distant about three leagues. The coast between them, fronting the sea, is mostly low and woody, and should not be approached under 15 or 16 fathoms, in large ships. This place may be easily known in passing along, by a small Fort close to the sea, where the land is a little elevated. Ships should not come under 10 or 12 fathoms, on account of foul ground both to the north and south of the Fort, except they intend to anchor in the Road. The mark to steer in with, is to keep the Fort between two hummocks, which are near each other, and not far from the shore, the northernmost being the lowest. With this mark, a ship may run in and anchor in 5½ or 6 fathoms, tolerable ground, but it is rocky out in 15 or 16 fathoms. About S. W. ½ S. from the Fort, is a rock, having on it 12 or 13 feet water: small vessels can pass between it and the shore, in 4 fathoms, but large ships ought not to come nearer it than 10 or 11 fathoms, for it is said to lie about two miles off shore."

The Government House is a large and substantial building, having a spacious verandah in front and rear; the former shaded by several beautifully grown Jambo trees, and the latter open to the ever welcome cool sea breeze, passing over the Kalu-Ganga, as it winds between the grounds and the sandy ridge that intervenes between the river and the sea, to its embouchere to the westward of the village. The adjoining Cutchery is also a very substantial building, and shaded in front by some fine specimens of the India-rubber tree (*Ignatia elastica*, L.).

The Wesleyan Mission has a large and commodious house, and a neat and well-constructed chapel and school, both which are constantly and well attended.

The Fort is large for the place, and was, at one period, important as a defence against the Kandyans, and as commanding the ferry over the Kalu-Ganga. It has been dismantled since tranquility was restored in the Kandyan province, in 1818, and has been for very many years a stranger to the sound of any other ordnance than that of the morning and evening *Patterero* of the Honorable John Rodney, who resided here at intervals, during the latter years of his Chief Secretaryship in the island.

Coffee, of a very superior kind, is grown in this district; and I know of no place in the island better calculated, from its shade and moisture, for growing Caoutchouc (*Ignatia Elastica*). Land may be purchased at moderate prices where there are no coco-nut trees, its value being usually estimated by the number of these palms growing upon it.

For cotton, the soil is admirably well adapted, as well as for the cultivation of the chocolate nut (*Theobroma Cacao*, L.), which requires much shade. I would plant all the rising grounds to a certain extent with the former, and the latter is well adapted to the vallies.

Pepper too (*Piper nigrum*) is fond of shade, and might be grown in sufficient quantities, in this province only, to render the island altogether independent of the Malabar coast for that spice to fill up the interstices in the stowage of the cinnamon for exportation to Europe.

The large black scorpion is common here. It attains the length of from seven to eight inches, and runs remarkably fast, with its tail forming an arch over its back. Its *habitat* is the coco-nut palm. This species of the genus *Scorpio*, L. (*Scorpionidæ* family of Leach) is never met with in houses or places frequented by the brown scorpion (*Scorpio australis*, L.).

From experiments that I made at Kaltura, in presence of the Collector, Wesleyan Missionary, and several officers, to ascertain how far the vulgar opinion, that the scorpion, when closely surrounded by fire, would destroy itself, was well founded or otherwise, I can vouch from the results that it is groundless, as far as six distinct experiments with the black and brown scorpion may be considered a fair trial. The insects ran about in a state of the greatest irritation, and one was much singed by attempting to cross the burning charcoal; but with this the mischief ended, and the rest were unanimously acquitted of all disposition towards suicidal monomania.

The view from Mount Layard, the country residence of Charles Edward Layard, Esq., on the left bank of the river, is beautiful; but one scarcely knows which of the two reaches of the river to admire most:—the old fort, an island, and the open sea over the sandy ridge, make the view down the river the finest, but for the Indian impression given by the areka trees and coco-nut topes;—but the mellow richness of the scenery up the river towards Gal-Pata, would, to a Cockney, appear a Richmond Hill style of beauty, and of course be in his eyes the most interesting.

There is a canal from this river to Colombo, of which the naturalist may advantageously avail himself. The extraordinary Lizard called *Kobra guyon* (whose habits are similar to that of the *Lacerta Nilotica*, or Monitor of the Nile, but its appearance in regard to color nearer to that of the Monitor of the Congo) is common upon the banks of the canal, wherever there is underwood. It makes a noise similar to that of a goose when protecting its young from an imaginary enemy, but is equally harmless. It subsists upon frogs and insects. The *L. Gecko* is also found in similar places.

The process of ploughing gives one a good idea of the simple state of Singhalese agriculture. A team of mud-covered buffalos dragging the *Naguelah* through the dark and slimy soil, which the all but naked husbandman, his head alone sheltered by a huge basket hat from the vertical sun, assays to guide free from the frequent sprawling matches to which, from the nature of the soil, he is continually liable, and often extended at full length, to the amusement of the passing traveller.

On either side the Kalu-Ganga are extensive paddee, korakan, mustard, and millet (*Panicum Italicum*, L., and *Tanna-hal* of the Singhalese) fields.

The trade is carried on by Pardie boats between Kaltura and Ratnapoora in Saffregam, freighted from hence, chiefly by the Moormen from Barberyn, with salt fish, white and colored cotton cloths, kerchiefs, country soap, &c., for the Kandyan markets, which they barter for areka nuts, bees' wax, and Jaggery. The priests at the Pansalas near the river afford very great accommodation to the traders, by allowing depôts to be made there for the collection of the areka nuts, which are purchased by the *ammonam* of 25,000.

The intelligent and most obliging little gentleman who has for many years been stationed here as Medical Sub-assistant, Mr. Frederick William de Hoedt, is perhaps better acquainted with the natural productions of this district than any other in the island; and he will readily assist the collector of natural specimens to procure them. The Kaltura, or left bank of the Kalu-Ganga abounds with monkies and peafowl; and at Balgoddé there is wild duck, widgeon, and snipe shooting, equal to any place in the island, or perhaps in India. The roads are beautifully shaded; and, during an evening's walk in the village, the insect called the "*Carpenter*" may be heard by its whirling and shrill noise, whilst at work in drilling a hole into the heart of a coconut tree, at a considerable distance off. Dr. de Hoedt, as he is generally called, procured for me several specimens of the painted bat (*Vespertilio picta*) with orange-colored and blackish wings; of the black and white, and black and brown widow birds, vulgarly called Ceylon Birds of Paradise, and by the Singhalese, *Sudu-kalu Pili-hora*, and *Rattoo Pili-hora*;* and a large *Pimbera's* (*Python*) skin, seventeen feet in length.

Terrestrial Molluscs of large size are commonly found upon the Papaw tree (*Carica Papya*, L.), of which, some specimens are beautifully marked with white and crimson.

* Anglicé, White and black, and red cotton stealers.

CHAP. XLVII.

Rapidity of the Kalu-Ganga—Ellas—Mount Karangoddé—Extraordinary Pine-apple leaves—Residence of the priests—Rock temple of Buddha—Gigantic Groundsel—View from the summit of Mount Karangoddé—A priest's caution neglected, and the consequences—Bromelia flax—Lieutenant Malcolm, of the First Ceylon Regiment, the first European known to have ascended Adam's Peak—Description of his tour—Buddhist priest's prediction—Lieutenant Malcolm disregards it, and proceeds—View from the Peak—Scarlet Rhododendron—Jewels very like glass—Volley of small arms fired from the Peak—A second priestly warning treated with more deference than the first—Kandyan army passes over the mountain into Saffregam, under the Second Adikar, Molligoddé, in pursuit of the revolted First Adikar, Eheylepola, who escapes into the British territories—Route from Kaltura to Colombo resumed—Pantura—River fishes—Fish Kraals—Bird's tail grass employed as a bait for the Dewé-Koraleyah—Morotte—Cinnamon plantations—A village of carpenters.

The stream of the Kalu-Ganga is so extremely rapid, that I was five days in going about forty miles in a Pardie, that I accomplished in twelve hours in returning, namely, from Kaltura to Ratnapoora, and vice versâ. In the former case, I had occasionally from forty to fifty of the neighbouring villagers to drag the boat, by rattan ropes, against the stream, at the falls between the rocks, or, as the Singhalese call them, *Ellas.*

About twenty miles above Kaltura, the scenery is beautiful; but it beggars description from Mount Karangoddé, a few miles beyond, and to the north-east of, Ratnapoora. Indeed, the prospect from Table Mountain at the Cape of Good Hope, or from the summit of Gibraltar, is no more to be compared to it, than the view from the terrace of Somerset House to that from the cross of St. Paul's.

The ascent to the first landing is by some hundreds of broad steps, hewn in the solid rock, which is covered with jungle, and pine apple plants, (produced from the offsets, and crests of the fruit that had been casually thrown there and taken root,) whose leaves are from five to six feet in length, a proof of the effect of shade upon that plant. Upon the first landing is the residence of the priests, an extensive and substantial stone building, having a large interior square, with wide and covered verandahs, into which the dormitories open.

A similar but less inclined flight of rock steps leads to the second landing place, where a rock Viharé displays Buddha's recumbent image, daubed over with the usual quantum of red and yellow lacker, behind an old Palampore by way of curtain, surrounded as usual with Hindoo deities, and having an oblong table before it, profusely covered with flowers. But the chief attraction to the European, is a well of the purest water, of so very cold a temperature, that in five minutes a bottle of claret was cooled as well as if an experienced *Hopdar* * had iced it.

From hence, the approach to the summit is extremely rugged, and covered with the Gigantic Groundsel (*Senecio giganteus*, L), exceeding twenty feet in height, jungle, and grass; both well tenanted with snakes and land leeches (*Hirudo Zeylanicus*); but one is amply rewarded for toil, trouble, and even danger, by the magnificent panorama which, on gaining the crown of the mountain, bursts upon the view. Here, castellated Ratnapoora, and surrounding country, interspersed with every variety of champaign, undulating, and hilly lands, intersected by the meandering and (for boats) navigable Kalu-Ganga;—there, the Peak,† towering high above the clouds to the north-eastward, and the various villages dispersed upon the banks of the river and its tributary streams, bordered by extensive areka, kettule, and coco-nut topes, with occasional patches of intervening jungle, scattered among verdant tracts of pasture land, as if by way of contrast to the golden glare of paddee and mustard fields in their approaching maturity; and everywhere, teeming with abundance; the nearest plains covered with innumerable herds of bullocks and buffalos, and the distant ones with deer and elephants.

Although I had felt it extremely cold in ascending from the Viharé before daybreak, I felt the sun oppressively hot by 9 o'clock, and gladly descended from the "Mountain's top" to the cool temple of the rock, where I found an excellent breakfast of all the good things the country produced that had never "breathed the breath of life;" for I had previously given strict injunctions to my servants not to prepare any animal food for my use within the temple's precincts, the destruction of life being altogether opposed to the merciful tenets of the Buddhist religion, (whose priests live entirely on roots, vegetables, fruits, milk, tyre, and water,) it being but just to respect the prejudices of others.

After rising in the morning, I had incautiously drunk a bowl of milk fresh from the cow; a worse thing I could not have done, for I had scarcely descended the mountain, ere I had every symptom of fever. If I had considered for a moment where I was, I should have followed the kind priest's advice, and either have had the milk boiled, or have added brandy to it. As it was, a severe attack of intermittent fever ensued, which confined me for several days to the Viharé, where I received every possible care and attention, and was accommodated with an excellent bed, having mosquito curtains,

* A Hindoo, whose sole business is the refrigeration of liquids for the table. † Adam's Peak.

altogether an unexpected comfort, but of which I had very little need, from the usual cool composition* of my bedroom floor.

Upon my arrival at Ratnapoora, a carpenter's wife, near whose hut my Pardie was moored, and who was employed in weaving *Hembilis*† and boxes with prepared fibre, prepared some for me with the pine apple leaves, which my cook had given her, in the following simple manner :—having removed the spines from each side, she beat the leaf throughout its length very gently with a wooden mallet; and then, laying the largest end upon her lap, over which a thickly-folded cloth was laid, and pressing a blunt knife upon the leaf with her left hand, just allowing room enough for her right hand to retain the end of it firmly, she withdrew the whole of the leaf quickly from between the knife and the cloth into most delicate fibres; these she soaked for some time in water, again passed them under the blunt knife, and dried them in the sun; after which, having immersed them for a few minutes in spring water, she dried them in the shade.

This woman wove some of the most beautiful Hembilis I ever saw; and she described to my cook, who was also my interpreter, that she "had never seen the *Anasi kola* (or pine apple leaf) used for that purpose by any one except herself, and had first been shown it by the Portuguese Padre who had made her a Christian; that the *Wetta kola* (leaf of the *Pandanus odoratissimus*) produced a very superior fibre to that she had just made for me, but that as there was none to be procured "*in that country*,"‡ she employed the pine apple leaf for her basket work."

Nambapané rest-house, situate on the scite of an old Kandyan fort, on the right bank of the river, and about midway between Kaltura and Ratnapoora, presents just such a spot as a Madeira wine grower would select for a vineyard, the alluvial soil being both rich and stony, and water abundant.

The direct distance from Ratnapoora to Adam's Peak is 20 miles, through Gillemallé, (7 miles,) Pallabadoolla, (5 miles,) and Diabetmé, (4 miles,) to the Peak, (4 miles.) The country as magnificent as the most romantic mind can imagine, and the vallies extremely fertile, and cultivated in the Kandyan manner.

Ratnapoora, the residence of an Assistant Agent of Government, is 61 miles south-east of Colombo, and has a very pretty fort, with good barracks, and quite strong enough to resist a considerable Kandyan army. It is commanded by a Captain of the Ceylon Rifle Regiment, and a Staff Assistant Surgeon superintends the medical duties

* See page 213. Among other uses for the sacred animal's ordure, it is mixed with turmeric and coco-nut water, and plastered over a bruised or sprained limb, and considered an infallible remedy.

† Baskets made of the dried strips of various palm leaves and fibrous plants.

‡ A common expression of the Singhalese;—anywhere distant from their immediate home is "another country."

of the garrison. Beautifully situate upon the right bank of the river, it is very healthy, and has an extensive bazaar, where every necessary article of life can be procured at a cheap rate. The country abounds with game, and the rivers and tanks with fish.

The first stage in the direct route from hence to Colombo, is to Kuruwitté rest-house, distant 8 miles; the second to Nahakandella rest-house, 11 miles; the third to Handipangoddé rest-house, 15 miles; the fourth to Pittipané rest-house, 9 miles; the fifth to Godagammua rest-house, 10 miles; and thence to Colombo, 8 miles:—total 61 miles. The face of the country is alternately woody and hilly, undulating and champaign, but well irrigated, being intersected by the Kalané-Ganga, which river takes its rise in the mountainous region of Adam's Peak; and, from the confluence of the two streams of the Maskellé and Kehelmua Gangas, flows to the sea, a distance of 43 miles, under the name of the Kalané-Ganga, and debouches at Modera, about 4 miles from Colombo, where its local name is the Mutwal rive.—Gems are found in this river by what is called "streaming."

The continuance of the fever prevented me from ascending the mountain called by the Portuguese "Pico d' Adam," by the Singhalese *Samenella*, and by us Adam's Peak, and it was with very great reluctance that I limited my wanderings to Batugedera.

Lieutenant Malcolm, of the First Ceylon Regiment, first set the example to Europeans of ascending the Peak in 1815; and as he had given me a transcript of his notes during the journey, which I had preserved for my guidance, in the event of having a future opportunity of ascending it, I took it with me into Saffregam; but as wishing to ascend a mountain, and ascending it, are widely different things, I have substituted Mr. Malcolm's statement, in the correctness of which the fullest confidence may be placed, and in, as nearly as possible, his own words.

"On the morning of 26th April, 1815, I left Batugedera with a small escort of a sergeant and four Malays, (of the First Ceylon Regiment,) for the purpose of ascending Adam's Peak; for I had been so repeatedly disappointed in expectation of guides, which the Headman of Batugedera, Dolip Nillamé, had promised, that I determined to take my chance of obtaining them at Gillemallé on my way. I merely took with me a few blankets, a quadrant, and measuring chain, and three days' provisions for my party. The route winded with the Kalu-Ganga, or Kaltura river, which, about two miles from Batugedera, receives the Mugellé-Oya, about two chains in breadth at the confluence. On the left bank, there are ruins of a Kandyan fort, erected during the late war to command the ford.

"From the Mugellé river to the rest-house of Gillemallé, the distance is about three miles and a half. At this place I procured two guides, after some delay, and leaving the

Gillemallé rest-house, we immediately crossed the Malmelloe river, and about half a mile further on, the Maskellé river.

"From the banks of the latter, we entered a forest of magnificent trees, straight as pines, and from fifty to seventy feet in height; and about four P. M. we arrived at Palabadoolla, ten miles and eighteen chains from Batugedera. Here there is a considerable temple of Buddha, and a large rest-house for pilgrims on their way to the Peak.

"About two hundred pilgrims, of both sexes and of all castes and conditions, were here assembled, some on their way to, and others on their return from, the Peak. The dance was continued without intermission, to the sound of Tam-a-tams and other instruments of Singhalese music, until the pilgrims, who were about to ascend the mountain, began to prepare their lights; and at about eight P. M. they proceeded onwards in distinct parties.

"The Head Priest, from whom I received every possible attention, tried all the persuasive rhetoric he could muster, to prevent me from proceeding further towards the Peak; assuring me, that "no white man ever did and never could ascend the mountain." I soon convinced the benevolent Oonansé that I was not a white man to be dissuaded from the attempt through any dread of ulterior danger; and therefore, having been well refreshed, and our Chules ready, we took leave of the priest, and left Palabadoolla about eleven at night.

"After passing three small forts that had been thrown up during the war, we began to ascend the first mountain, and reached the summit in four hours. From the next, the Kalu-Ganga descends rapidly; and, about five A. M., we breakfasted upon the rocks bordering its stream, and then continued our route up the mountain, Adam's Peak still towering far above our heads;

"Nil mortalium arduum est—Cœlum ipsum petimus,"

and, after surmounting two other distinct ascents, equally steep, but of less height, we came to the foot of the Peak itself. The face of the hill here appeared quite perpendicular, and the pilgrims, in advance of my party, were seen climbing up the precipice by the assistance of the iron chains which are fixed in the rock for that purpose. We halted a few minutes to take breath, and after great exertions, we reached the top between eight and nine A. M. of the 27th April.

"The view from this great elevation far surpassed my most sanguine expectation, it was so magnificently extensive. On one side displaying a vast extent of mountain, champaign, and forest scenery, the latter so variegated in foliage and so irregular in form that I could only compare it to an ocean of woods, whose waves had suddenly become fixed in an unalterable position; on the others, the tops of the hills rising above dense fogs, and resembling innumerable islands covered with wood and scattered over the sea that apparently filled the space below. Batugedera was seen on one side, as if almost under our feet, and on the other, in the distance, the Kandyan mountains, interspersed with clouds.—But, alas! whilst in the full enjoyment of this splendid scene, a thick fog arose from the bottom of the mountain, and drew a curtain over its sublimity.

"The area of the summit of the Peak is 72 feet long and 54 broad, and is enclosed by a parapet wall five feet high; this has partly fallen down on the east side, which is covered with scarlet Rhododendrons (*Rhododendron arboreum*), and the remainder is sadly out of repair. In the middle of this area is a large rock of Kabooc or iron-stone, upon which is a mark of Adam's left foot, called *Sri Pada* by the Singhalese;* but it requires a great deal of help from imagination to trace it out. This sacred footstep is covered over with a small building formed of the most durable wood, 12 feet long, 9 broad, and 4½ to the tiles, with which it is surmounted. Upon the inside it is enclosed by a frame of copper fitted to its shape, and ornamented with numerous jewels set in four rows, but not of the best or *most precious gems* the island has been known to produce, for to me they looked very like glass.

"We were not, I regret to say, provided with an "Union Jack," but we fired three vollies, to the great astonishment of the Buddhists, as a memorial to them that a British armed party had reached the summit, spite of the prediction of the priest of Palabadoolla. The priest having warned us of approaching rain, we *had* some faith in that warning, as the result of his experience, and made the best of our way down the mountain, which we found far more laborious to descend than it had been to climb.

"The rain, which fell in torrents, increased the difficulties of the abominable roads, over rocks and fragments of iron-stone, to Palabadoolla, which we reached about 4 P. M. and returned to my quarters at Batugedera the next morning.

"Sound lungs and hard feet are indispensable to the performance of such a trip, for in many places we had to climb barefoot over the iron-stone. As to palankins, they

* *Sri Pada*, or fancied impression of Buddha's foot, of which, many wise in their own conceit pretend to trace the toes, and aver that they point to the westward, and moreover that it is the impress of the *left* foot. This alone is an extraordinary coincidence with the Balic account of Sommona Codom's in Siam, which the Siamese call *Prabát*, or the venerated foot. This M. de la Loubère, in his admirable account of Siam, states to be derived from the Balic words *Pra*, venerable, and *Bat*, foot, as *Pad* in Sanscrit; and the same excellent Author further states, that the Siamese call their deity "SOMMONA CODOM, the son of a King of the famous Ceylon, who placed his *right* foot upon their *Prabát*, and his *left* upon *Lanka*." AUTHOR.

are quite out of the question. There may be some risk in ascending Adam's Peak in heavy rains, but surely not in fine weather.*

"The summit of the mountain was only clear about a quarter of an hour, which did not even allow me time to satisfy my curiosity, or to take any bearings, which latter circumstance I particularly regret."

The elevation of the Peak is 7420 feet above the level of the sea; and it was across this mountain that the Second Adikar, Molligoddé, upon the defection of the First Adikar being reported to the then King of Kandy, Sree Wickremé Rajah Singha, in 1814, entered Saffregam at the head of a Kandyan army, but Eheylepola, who had formerly been the Dessave of the province, and had many supporters there, preferred the safer asylum of the British territories.

This gave rise to the massacre of all his family in a manner so revolting to human nature, that, were the facts hypothetical, or not founded upon official reports of the highest authority, and subsequently proclaimed as such by the British Government of Ceylon, would be altogether incredible. To this, I shall hereafter advert.

Resuming our route by land from Kaltura, the next stage is Pantura, situate upon the left bank of the river of the same name, and distant 10 miles; roads level, good, and well shaded.

"Pantura, bearing from Colombo about S. $\frac{3}{4}$ E., distant $4\frac{1}{2}$ leagues, is a small river, with two rocks on the north side of the entrance, near half a mile from the shore. There is anchorage to the south of these in 10 or 12 fathoms, off shore about 2 miles. About half-way between this place and Colombo, there is, in a small Bay called Galkisse, a few houses, to the north of which the coast may be approached to 12 fathoms occasionally, about 2 and 3 miles off; but further to the southward the shore becomes more steep and rocky, making it prudent not to come under 16 or 17 fathoms towards it, these depths being from 2 to 3 miles off shore. About 2 leagues off, there is from 23 to 26 fathoms, and from 30 to 35 fathoms 4 or 5 leagues off, from whence the depth increases suddenly, on the edge of the bank, to no ground, in standing to the westward."

There is a very substantial rest-house at Pantura, which faces the ferry, and the verandah is generally so cool, as to afford a pleasant reading place during the heat of the day. The best fish obtained here is a species of *Gadus*, (a *Merlingus*, or whiting, having peculiarly hard bone-plates over the eyes, which some people esteem as curiosities,) called *Kalandah*, and the *Dewé-Koraleyah*† (*Chætodon atro-maculatus*); the latter of

* Since this was written, several Ladies have overcome the difficulties of ascending the Peak.

† This curious fish is also caught with hook and line; the former, baited with a grass, called *Pendah*, or bird's tail grass.

which is figured in my selection of Ceylon Fishes, originally published in 1828. The *Kalandah* is superior, both in flavor and firmness, to the whiting of the British seas.

The native method of catching these fish is worth looking at; the *Kraals* (a Dutch name for them) are extremely curious and intricate, and the fish once in, find their retreat cut off. these *Kraals* extend directly across the river, just leaving space enough for the Pardie boats to pass and repass.

A few mats for palankins and sofas may be purchased here, but it has neither scenery nor manufactures to recommend it. Like the whole of this coast, it abounds with coconut trees; and the principal objects of agriculture are paddee and sweet potatos.

A District Judge resides here, and the place has a minor Custom-house establishment, in charge of a Supervisor, who, after thirty years' service, has a salary of about £40 a year!

After crossing the river, the road leads through the village of Morotto, or *Morottowa*, near which the Government cinnamon gardens or plantations occupy an extent of from 300 to 400 square acres. These have recently been selling for about £3 10*s*. to £5 an acre. The village is inhabited by carpenters only, who may be seen felling Jack trees, sawing them into planks, and working them into every article of household furniture upon the spot, and generally after the most recent English patterns, which they contrive to borrow by way of "muster."*

Every Monday morning, and whenever ships arrive at Colombo, a troop of coolies may be seen in their usual jog-trot, wending their way towards the Fort, with tables of every kind, bedsteads, tripods, wardrobes or almiras, sofas, Cleopatra couches, easy and library chairs, elbow chairs, book cases, drawers, and even clothes-horses and stands for water goglets. If this furniture were not made of unseasoned wood, it would be much better; but being at first a bright yellow color, and the grain not very compact, the use of *Dornatil*, or wood oil, in order to give it a mahogany color when dry, leaves a whitish substance in the interstices, which although at first indistinct, is exposed by age.

A large house may be completely furnished (including rattan cane mats throughout) with Morotto furniture for less than £50; but those whose means are not limited, will do well to wait and purchase the best satin, ebony, calamander, and superior *old* jack wood furniture at sales, or from long resident Civilians about to retire from the Colonial Service; and that is also the best way to get *good* wine.

The Malays of Ceylon are excellent workers in rattan cane: they bottom sofas and chairs so finely as to resemble network, and their door tatties and floor mats are extremely neat and durable.

* Local name for *pattern*.

A Masked Devil dancer of the Koostarogiyo Caste
from a drawing by a Native.

CHAP. XLVIII.

Route from Morotto to Colombo—Galkisse—Road—Seir fishery—English chapel—Buddha temple—A priestly courtier—Mount Lavinia—Anecdote of Governor (the late General the Right Honorable Sir Thomas) Maitland, G. C. B., *and Samuel Daniell, Esq., known by the soubriquets of King Tom and Sam—How to get a Civil Appointment—A halt at the Tamarind Tree suggested—Completion of the tour round the island—Origin of the war in Kandy, which resulted in the annexation of that kingdom to the British dominions, but partially known or understood—Local improvements in Ceylon date from Sir George Murray's accession to the Colonial Seals in* 1828—*Lord Viscount Goderich follows them up by additional advantages and improvements—Mutilation of ten British subjects by order of the Kandyan Despot, Sree Wickremé Rajah Singha—Explanation demanded and refused—Revolting cruelties upon the family of Eheylepola, and native Chiefs—The Governor leads the army in person—Kandy taken—Geographical position of the former Kandyan kingdom—Scite of Kandy and its origin.*

Morotto is 15¼ miles from Colombo, and the intermediate road lies through the large but straggling villages of Galkisse* and Colpetty; and, throughout the distance, as level as a bowling-green, thickly shaded by a variety of beautiful and useful trees, and the sea side bordered by coco-nut palms.

The former village may be said to be one continuous bazaar, and is very well supplied with fish; of which, the Seir is chiefly esteemed for the market, and consequently the most valuable to the fisherman. This delicious fish is caught with hook and line, whilst the canoes appear to skim the surface of the water at a rail-road pace, and in such quantities, that, after supplying the bazaar at Galkisse, the Renter of the fish farm sends the surplus, morning and evening, to the Colombo bazaar, by coolies, who actually bend under the weight of their Pingo loads.

Galkisse has a very pretty English chapel, and there is another at Morotto, of both which, the duties are performed by a Singhalese Colonial Chaplain, who is better off than many an English curate, with a salary of £130 per annum, exclusively of "pickings."

Strangers visiting the Buddha temple near this, will meet with every civility from the priest, Vanantenakedana Oonansé, who is superlatively *au fait* at flattering Governors. Nature most certainly intended him for a courtier, for he makes nothing of comparing the Governor to the sun, and the Governor's wife to the moon, in their full splendour!! Alas, poor humanity!

* For sailing directions, see page 383.

Galkisse is of more importance than it would otherwise be, from its proximity to the Governor's country seat, Mount Lavinia;—a name which gives rise to a very pleasing and extraordinary reminiscence; for it was at this place, (not at the modern Palace, but at the former capacious and delightful Bungalow of one floor, when Ceylon Governors were wont to be content with the cool and delightful native way of building,) that the then eccentric Samuel Daniell, Esq., Ranger of the Woods and Forests, availed himself of the hospitality of his excellent friend, Governor the Honorable Thomas Maitland, and of his own peculiar rights and royalties, as a generally acknowledged *privileged character*, and the wag and idol of the British community, to do whatever he pleased, without involving the least risk of serious consequences to himself.

Mr. Daniell, celebrated for his beautiful drawings of the animals of Ceylon, was known throughout the island by the soubriquet of "Sam," and Governor Maitland (the late Right Honorable Sir Thomas, G. C. B.) by that of "King Tom," to whom he had been originally recommended for a civil appointment in the colony; but having the general *entrée* of the King's House, as the Governor's residence was, at that time, called, and good dinners, beds, horses, and carriages, always at hand, "Sam" did not press His Excellency for an appointment, until it was bruited about that "King Tom" was about to resign the Government. "Sam" then became more than ever anxious to be appointed to the Civil Establishment, and hit upon the following scheme "to get rid of the complaint in his *chest*," as he facetiously called an empty purse.

One morning, soon after Gun-fire, the Governor, whilst walking in the compound, *en robe de chambre*, with Captain Prager, at that time one of his Aids-de-camp, in a similar dishabille, observed an unusual train of coolies approaching the lodge gates, with "Sam" at their head, on horseback, and his right arm extended, as if directing them towards the eastern verandah of the bungalow.

These carried so many trunks, chairs, saddles, guns, spears, parrot cages, tiger traps, fryingpans, gridirons, and camp equipage, that it quite startled the good Governor, who immediately despatched Prager to "command a halt, and to tell *Mister* Sam, that although his company was not wanted at the Mount, he might stay breakfast, and then depart for other quarters."

The A. D. C. delivered the message verbatim, and "Sam" laughed heartily at it. "King Tom (said he) thinks he has taken a very cheap way of getting rid of me; but its *no go*, Prager, and so I shall tell the General, for I am very hard up, and moreover as hungry as a Trojan." By this time, "Sam" and the A. D. C. had approached the toddy tree, under which the Governor was seated in a high back'd Dutch elbow chair, and as stately as Royalty could possibly be. "Well, *Mister* Sam (said His Excellency) here ye are again, and upon the *old score*, I suppose; but what mean ye *maan* by bringing an army of black rascals to the Mount? Ye had better mind your Ps and Qs, *Mister* Sam, or ye'll tire General Maitland out."—Then addressing the Aid-de-camp, "Order breakfast, Prager; Sam appears hungry, and it must not be said he was starved at the Mount!" to all which "Sam" bowed assent, and pledged himself to do honor to the Governor's hospitality. "I do not doubt ye, Sam, I do not doubt ye; so go and make yourself decent for the breakfast table, as ye'll find some *weemen* there."

As soon as breakfast was served, the Governor, forgetful of his assumed anger at "Sam's" mode of coming to the Mount, recommended him to "do his best;" and *certes*, if Harlequin had been at his elbow, the curry and rice, kabobed prawns, fish balls and cutlets, pigeon pie, snipe cutlets, soused seir fish, cold ham, eggs, muffins, and all the usual entremêts of a Ceylon breakfast, could not have vanished sooner than under the powerful masticators of the delighted Sam, and much to His Excellency's amusement.

"You may have the run of your teeth here, till ye get tired of the Mount, *Mister* Sam, (said the Governor,) so long as your infernal tiger traps and parrot cages and the black fellows are kept away. We may perhaps get rid of you in a month or two, but at all events we must make the best of a bad bargain, for I dare say you are a little afraid of the Supreme Court:" to all which, the self-invited guest bowed assent.

The dejeuner finished, and the second chillum supplied to the Governor's Hookah, His Excellency, pretending to be very serious, "begged to ask *Mister* Sam a question or two."

"Ten thousand, if Your Excellency pleases, now that I may exclaim, "*Ohe jam satis!*" of all the good things before us, or, which is nearly the same, that were recently before us."

"Sam, your impudence will hang ye yet! but what claims,—what claims I say, have you upon General Maitland, that you always quarter upon Mount Lavinia when you want money, *as I know you do now*, and at *no other* time?"

"The best claims in the world, Your Excellency!—Have I not a thousand times heard you call me "Your own Sam;" vow to others that "Sam kept your life and soul together;" express your regret that you could not make me Vice-Treasurer, or find some place that would keep my head above water for life?" Here King Tom smilingly dissented, puffed away more rapidly than usual at his Hookah, and then said, "not quite so fast, Sam, as all that."—"Secondly, (continued Sam,) how *many* would feel the obligation to be on *their* side, if "Your Excellency's own Sam" would condescend to allow them to supply cash for his wants? but no, no, Your Excellency, I always prefer the Head of the Well, and no one shall ever *boast* of being Sam's banker *except* Your Excellency!—Thirdly, can Your Excellency wonder at the constant remarks, that I, "Your own Sam," should have been so long upon the shelf?"—Here His Excellency the Governor motioned a pause, with his well-known sceptre of Royalty, *his fore finger*, and referring to the Aids-de-camp "if they had ever heard him so express himself," they fearlessly and unhesitatingly (for King Tom detested *China Carriers* and hypocrites) answered, "repeatedly!" and if all Her Majesty's Governors and Colonial Secretaries of State resembled him in this respect, "toad eating," lying, and fawning would soon be at a discount in the colonies!

"Sam" resumed his interrupted statement of *claims*. "Whilst any Italian fiddler, or French vagabond with a *pretty* wife, or ———

"Stop, Sam! (said His Excellency,) no more! you've hit me in a *tender part!* but never mind, you didn't mean it, I suppose; and therefore, let me know what in the world you are at all fit for, except to roam the jungles like a wild beast. You are not likely to get a place in the Revenue, for you would spend all the rix dollars, and do as others have done, swear that the white ants had eaten them, and leave the public to pay the piper. But if you can point out, within five minutes by the watch, (suiting the action to the word,) any place that will relieve me from being your Chancellor of Exchequer, without your interfering with any body but the wild beasts, with whom, the Moodliars tell me, you appear on such good terms, that they stand still to let you draw their pictures,* you shall have it, upon your solemn promise never to come to the Mount again, *until I send for you*."

"Done! done! done! Your Excellency, (exclaimed Sam,) "*Dictum factum reddidi*,"

"RANGER OF THE WOODS AND FORESTS!!"†

"Well, Sam, you are the devil himself! but General Maitland is a man of his word;" and, extending his right hand, said, "you have it, Sam, and 800 rupees a month to begin with;" and then directing the Deputy Secretary (who had just come in) to Gazette the appointment, and order the Paymaster General to advance "*Mister* Sam" six months' pay, the Ranger of the Woods and Forests, with, as he subsequently declared, "his heart up to his throat," attempted to express his thanks. The good General, observing "Sam" overcome by his feelings, and the salt spray in his eyes, again took him by the hand, and shook it heartily. "Well, Sam, (said His Excellency,)

* This arose from Mr. Daniell's accurate delineations of the quadrupeds of Ceylon.

† This appointment was made expressly for the occasion, and has been vacant ever since Mr. Daniell's death.

God bless you! no piping;—mind the elephants;—come to the Mount when you please;—always welcome; but do not again come in character, or, *may the de'il tak ye*, you'll be the death of General Maitland if you do!"

Throughout the whole line of road between Galkisse and Colombo, one may walk under coco-nut trees by the sea side, without the least exposure to the sun. On the right of the high road, where cinnamon plantations do not intervene, plantations of plantain and anatto trees would be a profitable speculation.

If the tourist sleep at Pantura, and leave before Gun-fire, with the view of breakfasting at Colombo, a halt at the "Tamarind tree," about three miles from the Fort, for a glass of the delicious toddy always to be had there from sun-rise till eight o'clock, fresh from the flower, (sending on his palankin to wait for him at the entrance of the Esplanade, or, as it is locally called, the "Galle Face,") and the walk through the beautiful avenue of trees which the whole line of road presents, will well reward him for the exertion.

Having now completed the tour round the island, the traveller may discharge his palankin coolies, and, for a time, lay up his palankin and canteens "in ordinary," and at his leisure book himself by the mail coach for the Central Province. If, however, he be desirous of continuing his palankin travelling, he will have the advantage of leisurely seeing and exploring that interesting and romantic country; and the French pocket edition of "Knox's Ceylon" will (presuming that, as almost everybody knows that language now, or is supposed to do so, he is able to understand it) give him a clearer view of the still unchanged customs, agriculture, &c., of the Kandyans, than any other hitherto published.

Notwithstanding that much has been written respecting the origin of the last Kandyan war in 1814, and its termination by the annexation of the kingdom of the deposed monarch, Sree Wickremé Rajah Singha, to the former British territories by which it was belted, in 1815, it appears to be known but to few, in comparison with the public importance of the acquisition; and to these few, either in an incorrect or partial degree.

Nothing great, except in point of neglect, had been done for Ceylon by the Home Authorities, from the time of the conquest of the interior, in 1815, to the Right Honorable Sir George Murray's accession to the Colonial Seals in 1828; from which period whatever good has since been extended to Ceylon, whether in respect of local improvements, increase of revenue, or rise in the estimation of the mercantile world, may justly be said to date.

To these national benefits, the Right Honorable and gallant officer's noble successor, the then Lord Viscount Goderich, added other public advantages and improvements; which, whilst the recollection of them serves to immortalize His Lordship's administration with the Singhalese, have raised that nation in the scale of humanity, and rendered the island of Ceylon the choicest colonial jewel in the Imperial diadem.

As my official position in the island, soon after the termination of the war, and during the whole of the subsequent rebellion, may be supposed to have enabled me to collect the best information, the following may be relied on for its accuracy.

Early in November, 1814, it was reported to His Excellency, Lieutenant General Brownrigg, the then Governor and Commander-in-chief of the British Settlements at Ceylon, that ten Singhalese inhabitants of the village Mahara, in the Sinna Korle, who had entered the Kandyan province of the Seven Korles (now part of the Western Province) for the purposes of trade, had been dreadfully mutilated in the Kandyan capital; that seven had died of their sufferings on the spot, and that the three survivors had arrived in a most deplorable state at Colombo, each with his nose, ears, and one arm hanging by a cord round his neck!

An explanation was immediately demanded from the Court of Kandy; and, without awaiting the result, the inhabitants of the British territories were cautioned not to enter the dominions of the Kandyan despot, Sree Wickremé Rajah Singha. At the same time, notice was given by proclamation to all Kandyan subjects within the British possessions to pursue their commercial occupations, so long as they conducted themselves conformably to the laws; and the Government further guaranteed to such Kandyan subjects full security and protection for their persons and property.

The Kandyan despot having refused either explanation or satisfaction, war was determined upon by the Governor in Council, the time being most favorable for such an undertaking, discontent being almost general throughout the Kandyan kingdom; and the defection of the First Adikar, Eheylepola,* who was also Dessave of Saffregam, gave an impulse to rebellion against the tyrant, and ensured the assistance of the disaffected in supplying the British army during its march upon the capital.

To relate the revolting cruelties exercised upon the Chiefs† suspected of correspondence with the First Adikar, as well as upon those actually connected with him, would fill a volume; but of all the great tragedies of human life, none ever exceeded in horror the fate of the wife and family of Eheylepola, through whom the ferocious miscreant determined to be fully revenged, and immediately sentenced the Adikar's

* See page 383.

† Of these, forty seven were impaled at Kandy.

wife and children, and then Eheylepola's brother and his wife, to the most ignominious deaths.

The children were ordered to be decapitated before their mother's face, and their heads to be pounded in a rice-mortar by their mother's hands! which, to save herself from the *most diabolical* torture and ignominious exposure, she submitted to attempt. The eldest boy shrunk from the dread ordeal, and clung to his agonized parent for safety, but his younger brother stepped forward and encouraged him to submit to his fate, placing himself at the same time before the executioner, by way of setting his elder brother an example how to die!* The last of the children to be beheaded was an infant at the breast, from which it was brutally torn away, the mother's milk flowing from its mouth, to be sacrificed to the tyrant's rage.

The Adikar's brother having been also beheaded, the sisters-in-law were bound together, and large stones having been tied to their legs, and ropes placed round their necks, were drowned in a neighbouring tank.—All Kandy, except near the palace, was for many days a scene of mourning and fasting; but the people were ripe for that revolt, which, upon the approach of General Brownrigg's army, effectually broke out.

The brave and veteran Governor, instead of availing himself of his Civil privileges to delegate his Military command, took the field, determined to share every privation and danger with his gallant little band of British heroes, and to "seek the tiger in his lair." The whole march was a bloodless one, on the part of the British army; and the city of Kandy was taken possession of on the 14th of February, 1815. In about four days after, the King was captured by a party of his own subjects, at a lonely place, called *Meda-Maha-Neuwara;* but, instead of being hanged upon the nearest tree, this monster of depravity was treated as a Sovereign Prince, and not separated from his wife and family, in defiance of all laws, both Divine and human, as the Emperor Napoleon, the hero and regenerator of his adopted country, and the munificent patron of the Arts and Sciences was, and sent into solitary exile, "to eat his heart in comfortless despair;" but, with his numerous wives, conducted to Colombo, (his dagger still incrusted with the blood of one wife whom he had murdered!) and, after having there received every distinguished attention that false humanity, not policy, dictated, the remorseless tyrant was conveyed to the jetty in the Governor's carriage, (followed by his wives and suite in palankins,) and embarked on board His Majesty's ship Cornwallis, Captain O'Brien, for Vellore, on the 24th of January, 1816; as if Royalty justified not only murder, but every other brutal atrocity, and placed the

* This was related to me as a fact by Lieutenant Lyttelton, 73rd regiment.

possessors of it above the laws of God and man! This sanguinary miscreant died at Vellore some years ago, and left a son, who was born in that fortress.

The Kandyan kingdom extended from latitude 6° 15′ to 8° 50′ north; and from 80° 10 to 81° 50′ east longitude; of which, the mountainous region varies in elevation from 1731 to 8280 feet above the level of the sea.

Kandy, (the *Muragrammum* of Ptolemy, and the *Maha Neuwara*, or Great City, of the Singhalese,) the chief town of this province, and late the capital of the dominions of the deposed Malabar despot, Sree Wickremé Rajah Singha, is situate in latitude 7° 18′ north, and in longitude 80° 49′ east of Greenwich, in a spacious and fertile valley, surrounded by hills and mountains, beautifully wooded, and diversified with foliage of every hue, from the very darkest to the lightest green and yellow tints of the young, and the deep red brown of the falling leaf; a scite, originally selected in consequence of an omen, to which, the soothsayers ascribed great importance.

The tradition is, that the original Malabar conqueror, after a lucky day for hunting had been determined by the soothsayers of the Court, (the *soi-disant* descendants from the ancient Magi, who maintain the doctrine of only two principles, the *cause* of all good, and the *cause* of all evil,) took the field, and, after surrounding the game for several miles, and gradually contracting the *cordon* of persons employed with firebrands, tam-a-tams, perforated conch shells, cymbals, and pipes, to drive the animals into the smallest possible space, when a pell-mell slaughter took place, the King left his attendants, accompanied only by a few Polygar dogs, and came to a spot where a considerable cover was afforded to smaller game by a single rattan bush, extending over a large tract of ground, and presenting three branches pointing in different directions; one towards the ferry of Kattogastotté, a second towards Gonaruäh, and a third towards Heywellé.

The Polygars pursued a hare into the cover which the rattan bush afforded; this she made her fortress, and kept the dogs *at bay*, to the wonder and astonishment of the observant Rajah; who, having been rejoined by the soothsayers, and his attendants, and the former declaring "that it was an omen of too great importance to be neglected," the intrepid hare was taken and cherished by the Royal hand; and the spot having been selected as the scite for the future capital, in memory of so extraordinary a defence by the most timid of all animals, Kandy was subsequently built, and the palace of the King succeeded the fortress of the hare.

CHAP. XLIX.

Choice of routes to the Central Province—Road to Kornegalle, in the Seven Korles—Kornegalle—Stupendous rocks—A Kandyan Tarpeius Mons—Civil and Military officers—Cutchery occupies the scite of an ancient royal palace—Henry Pennell, Esq.—Granite slabs sculptured with the lion, unicorn, and elephant—Time of sowing and reaping—Route to Trincomalé—Face of the country—Route to Kandy—Kalané-Ganga navigable by boats to Ruanwellé—Route to the Central Province by land viâ Koddoowellé, Hangwellé, and Avisahawellé—Sittawaka river—A rattan hawser—Rajah Singha the apostate—Ruins of a Portuguese fort—Ruanwellé—Route to Kandy over the Balané mountain—Route to the Central Province over the Idalgashina mountain more circuitous, but best for the intending settler—Major Kelly's division of the Army of Kandy crosses the Idalgashina mountain—Anticipated difficulties to the traveller—Warm clothing and fires necessary in crossing the Balané and Idalgashina passes—Balangoddé—Alut Neuwara—Upper Ouva—Successful introduction of the potato into culture—Wheat, of superior quality, grown at Kandy and Badulla—Face of the country—Limestone—Potters' clay—Brick clay—Hemp—European vegetables naturalized in the interior in the time of Captain Robert Knox, 1657—1678.

From Colombo, the tourist may proceed through the yet unnoticed parts of the Western Province, to the Central Province, either by mail coach* to Kandy, or through Kornegalle, (or Kurunegallé,) or by land or water to Ruanwellé; but, for the intending settler, either is preferable to the first as a means of seeing the country.

Having already sketched one route to Kornegalle,† the second is by the direct road from Colombo to Mahara rest-house, (crossing the Mutwal river by the bridge of boats,) distant 8¾ miles; from thence to Kosrupé mail coach station, 6½ miles; Heneratgoddé rest-house and barracks, 2 miles; Kellegeddéhainé mail coach station, 5 miles; Vaingoddé rest-house, 3 miles; Walwedenia mail coach station, 4¾ miles; Ambapassé rest-house, 6½ miles; Alawé Bridge over the Maha-Oya, 4½ miles; Polgahawellé, 6½ miles; and to Korneg. 10¼ miles; the intermediate country presenting a variety of well-irrigated champaign, undulating, and hilly lands, covered with the verdure of an eternal spring, and inferior to none other upon the surface of the globe.

The latter very romantic station, in the Seven Korles of the Western Province, derives its name from the *Kuru-naika Gallé,*‡ one of the chain of lofty and stupendous rocks, ranging in height from 300 to 600 feet, at whose base it is situate.

* See page 160.

† See page 181.

‡ *Elephant-driver rock.* This rock is said to have answered the same purposes as the *Tarpeius Mons,* in the neck-breaking system of the ancients, (but its elevation exceeds by 220 feet the height of the latter,) in order to get rid of princes who had incurred the hatred, and consequently the revenge, of the Pagan priesthood.

An Assistant Government Agent has charge of the Revenue Department, and a District Judge of the Judicial. The Garrison is commanded by a Captain in the army, and a Staff Assistant Surgeon superintends the Medical and Vaccine Departments.

The Cutchery is situate on a gentle acclivity, at the foot of "Tusked Elephant Rock,"* (upon which there is a temple, where the relic was originally kept; and there are also a Viharé and Dagobah on the way up the rock, in a very romantic situation,) which is a most appropriate name for it, from the resemblance it bears to the head and back of that animal; and, notwithstanding that the style of the building is more Muscovite than English, it has a very pretty appearance from the Trincomale road, which skirts the grounds. The Wesleyan Mission-house and chapel, also at the base of "Tusked Elephant Rock," have a peculiarly neat appearance; and the cantonment and grounds are everywhere well laid out. Here is a spacious tank of very solid construction, and capable of supplying water for the irrigation of numerous paddee fields, which are chiefly Crown property.

Kornegalle owes much to the indefatigable zeal of one of the first Superintendents of the district, as Agent of Government, (Henry Pennell, Esq.,) and one of the most enlightened of its Civil Servants, whose retirement from the service of the colony may very justly be considered a public loss.—Whilst on a visit to this excellent officer, in 1821, I had the satisfaction of seeing some very fine strawberries at Colonel Campbell's, (the Commandant of the province,) from plants produced from seeds which I had originally introduced from the Cape of Good Hope, and shared with the late Captain George Stace, at that time commanding the Ceylon Cavalry, by whom they were distributed in the interior. From the original supply, I had successfully cultivated the strawberry, both at Colombo and Galle; where, also, I found no difficulty in growing the green pea (*Pisum sativum*, L.); both which might, with care, be made as common in the maritime provinces as they now are in the interior.

This place (said to have been an ancient capital) is well ascertained to have been the scite of a royal palace, of which, many huge slabs of granite, having various animals, both known and fabulous, sculptured upon them, lie scattered about; of these, the British lion, the Caledonian unicorn, (extraordinary though it be,) and the Ceylon elephant, appear to have formed part of the Zoological medley of the ancient ornaments of a Singhalese Malagawa.

Mr. Pennell offered me my choice of these ponderous masses; but, as it may well be supposed, there were *weighty* reasons for my declining to remove them.

* *Ahéta Gallé.*

In the Kornegalle district, paddee is sown for the *Maha* harvest, in the low grounds, from July to November, and reaped in the following January and February. Fine grains are sown in the high grounds from September to November, and reaped from December to March. For the *Yalla* harvest, paddee is sown in the low grounds in April and May, and reaped in August and September; and fine grains, sown in the low grounds from April to June, are reaped from July to the end of September.

The route from hence to Trincomalé, by the new road, is to the Dedroo-Oya, 5½ miles, over which, there is a curious (native) suspension bridge for pedestrians, of Zalacca rattan (*Calamus Zalacca,* and *Mahawé-wela* of the Singhalese); Ibbagammé-Oya, 3 miles; Polegala, 3 miles; Ambanpola, 3 miles; Himbalwana-Oya, 2½ miles; Omaragolla Ella, 3¾ miles; Galawalla, 4¾ miles; Tolumbajalla, 2 miles; Damboola-Oya, 5½ miles; to the Junction Kandy Road, (about three-quarters of a mile from Damboola rest-house,) 2 miles; from whence, the route has been already described, in the line of road *from* Trincomalé;* to which port, the total distance from Kornegalle is 102 miles; the face of the country presenting every variety of the wildest and most romantic scenery, of hill and dale, mountain and valley, forest and plain, rivers, streamlets, and tanks, that can possibly be found in any part of the habitable globe.—Elephants, and game of every description known to the island, abound throughout.

From Kornegalle to Kandy, the distance is about 26½ miles, viz. to Kospotté-Oya. 8½ miles; Madawallatenné, 6¼ miles; Mavali-Ganga, 8¾ miles; entrance of the Tunnel, (which is 500 feet in length,) 1½ mile; and from thence to Kandy, 1½ mile. Road excellent, and country very healthy. Here the most magnificent scenery meets the eye in every direction: forests abounding with game, plains covered with verdure, or the golden hue of ripening paddee crops, and the Mavali-Ganga meandering through the immense area which it intersects in its course, and fertilizes as it flows.

By the Kalané-Ganga,† in a well-thatched Pardie boat, containing his palankin, canteens, coolies, and servants, the tourist has every comfort at hand; and the beautiful country which this fine river intersects, is worthy of his deliberate investigation on both banks of it, as it is also of the Oriental antiquarian and the naturalist.

The route by land, by way of Ruanwellé, is to Koddoowellé, a village 10 miles north-east from Colombo, and from thence to Hangwellé, 8 miles, (both on the left bank of the Kalané-Ganga,) where there is a rest-house. The face of the country alternately flat and undulating, but well cultivated and populated, and the road delightfully shaded by fruit trees and toddy topes.

* See page 244.

† See page 26.

Hangwellé is famous for the defeat of the King of Kandy, (in September, 1803); who, upon the successful result of the treacherous butchery of Major Davie's force, considering himself invincible, advanced into the British territories, imagining that they would prove an easy prey to his invading army. But although the village was only protected by a field work, garrisoned by a mere handful of men, not exceeding 110 rank and file, commanded by the gallant Captain Pollock, of His Majesty's 51st regiment, the Kandyan army, having been outflanked by a detachment from the garrison, whilst engaged in attacking the British redoubt in front, was defeated with immense slaughter, the King running away first, and his army following pell-mell. The loss of the Kandyans in killed exceeded thrice the number of the British garrison, of which, but two or three men were wounded. This defeat afforded an opportunity to a number of Malays and gun Lascars, who had survived the fate of Major Davie's detachment, and had been compelled to serve in the Kandyan army, to rejoin the British force.

From Hangwellé to Avisahawellé, the distance is 11 miles; this place is also on the left bank of the Kalané-Ganga, and, since the re-establishment of tranquillity in 1818, has assumed a very different appearance to that which it antecedently bore. Here extensive forests and verdant plains contrast with the most rugged and romantic scenery: the then almost entirely neglected vallies are now covered with verdant pasture and paddee fields, and cottages are no longer, like angels' visits, few and far between.

The village of Avisahawellé is situate at the base of dark and almost perpendicular rocks, of from 900 to 1000 feet elevation, but the former military post, as well as rest-house, have been abandoned since the termination of the rebellion in 1818.

In the immediate neighbourhood, at about three furlongs distance, the ferry over the Sittawaka river, which flows into the Kalané-Ganga, is crossed by means of a horse boat; and occasionally, when the stream is rapid, transport is facilitated by a stout Rattan rope (*Calamus Rotang*, L.), from 40 to 50 fathoms in length; which, being suspended over the river, and strongly fastened at each extremity, the boatmen, by hauling hand over hand upon this flexible hawser, soon effect the passage across, which is about 250 yards from bank to bank.

This place, famed in Singhalese history as the place where numerous Oonansés were put to death in the year 1600, by the then King of Ceylon, (Rajah Singha, surnamed of Sittawaka,) who had abandoned the worship of Buddha for that of the Lingam, is scarcely to be distinguished, its ruins, such as they are, being almost covered with jungle; and it is more than probable, that the Portuguese destroyed the Dewalé, or whatever may have been the original buildings, (of which, some square kabook enclosures, and a large well of excellent water, show the scite,) and with the materials constructed the *Kotua*,* whose foundation, and a part of the walls, still remain.

Sittawaka is now recovering itself, and when I last visited it, I found a very good rest-house upon the scite of the former temporary military post, and experienced every attention from the Headmen. In this neighbourhood there is excellent snipe and wigeon shooting.

If the tourist prefer the route across the Balané mountain, he should proceed from hence to Ruanwellé, a fortified post on the left bank of the Kalané-Ganga, at its confluence with the Gooroogoddé-Oya, in the district of the Four Korles of the Western Province, where there is a spacious fort, (to which a wide street leads from the landing place,) with officers' quarters and barracks, and a large bazaar, distant 9 miles. Several hundred families are now settled at Ruanwellé, where, until the period of Kandyan domination ceased by our taking possession of that kingdom, nothing but jungle was to be seen.

From Ruanwellé, the road lies through Idamalpané, 11 miles; Arranderré, 2½ miles; Hellemoellé, 5½ miles; Fort King, commanding the ferry over the Maha-Oya, 7¼ miles; and from thence, across the Balané mountain† to Amanapoora, through Gannitenné, at the base of the Balané, where there is a substantial fort, and below it excellent barracks, and a large village and bazaar, 8 miles; from thence to Dodonwellé, 5 miles; and to Kandy, 8 miles. I would, however, suggest to an intending settler to take the more circuitous route through the Three Korles into Saffregam, and, skirting the base of Adam's Peak, through Batugedera (Bamboo-house) and across the Idalgashina mountain into the lofty table land of Upper Ouva, as affording the greater scope for observing the country, in order to fix upon a locality suitable to the object he may have in view; and if for the purpose of agricultural pursuits, better adapted to a temperate than a tropical climate, the high lands of the Central Province present many advantages over every other part of the island.

In the beginning of the Kandyan war of 1815, Major Kelly's division took this route to Kandy, through the Saffregam Dessavony, over the tremendous mountain of Idalgashina, and across the fine province of Ouva, where they found the climate very different from that of the sea coast, or even of Kandy; and they were enabled to march during the middle of the day, never finding the heat in that elevated province at all oppressive.—It was upon this march, that, to the great delight of both officers and men, they found the common bramble (*Rubus fruticosus*, L.), until then

* Singhalese for Fort.

† 3000 feet above the level of the sea.

unknown to be a native of Ceylon, in abundance; a circumstance which justified the inference, that other British productions might be naturalized there.

But, in proceeding by this route, although the facilities for travelling are now much greater, the tourist must make up his mind to occasional difficulties, in traversing so extensive a country, in a state of agricultural infancy.—To occupy a shed at night, and to cross the mountain streams by fording, or upon rafts of bamboo canes, where there are neither canoes nor suspension bridges, are mere matters of course; but even these troubles to the many, will be enjoyed by the few, who are really lovers of nature, in preference to the best roads and bridges.

Both on the Balané and Idalgashina mountains, warm clothing is necessary, the thermometer seldom ranging above 77°, and in the colder months of January, February, and March, it varies from 63° to 70°. At night, a good fire is requisite, for the thermometer is occasionally below 50°; and the mean temperature throughout the year, according to data with which I was favored by William Herries Ker, Esq., at the time he was Deputy Secretary to the Ceylon Government, may be stated at 72° in the day, and 63° at night.

But very few real difficulties may be anticipated, until the tourist reaches Balangoddé, 1750 feet above the level of the sea. There is here a fort on the top of the hill, and below it a bazaar, and a large house belonging to the principal native Headman. Climate delightfully cool and healthy, but the country very hilly and but partially cultivated. The Guava (*Psidium pyriferum*, L.) is here as wild as any jungle tree; and to the northward of the fort, the scenery presents an amphitheatre of lofty mountains, in successive degrees of elevation, and varying in their form and color from the most verdant hue in the foreground to the lightest indigo blue in the distance.

After leaving Balangoddé, and crossing the Wallewé river about 1¼ mile beyond it, which at some seasons may be forded, and at others crossed on bamboo rafts, or upon a platform raised upon a couple of small canoes, the route lies through the abandoned military post of Alut Neuwara to the ancient Dewalé of that name, (distant about eight miles from Balangoddé,) where there is also a small Viharé and Dagobah, the former of which affords a comfortable halting place; but the country, though beautiful and romantic in appearance, is so badly cultivated as to induce the reflection of how little has hitherto been done by man, where so much has been done by his Creator.

Crossing the Idalgashina mountain at the pass, Upper Ouva is entered. This pass is about 4400 feet above the level of the sea, and the summit of the mountain about 4750, or probably 4800 feet. Here is sufficient grass for an indefinite number of cattle, but very few are to be seen in any direction, except wild buffaloes, and the country is but thinly populated; and yet how easily a few European agriculturists, with moderate capital, might change the present wild but luxuriant face of nature into a paradise of cultivation and plenty!

The potato, although first introduced into culture in the interior at Fort Mac Donald in Upper Ouva, had been cultivated in the Morua Korle of the Southern Province with great success by J. F. Lourenz, Esq., at that time the Resident Sitting Magistrate, to whom, prior to the conquest of the Kandyan kingdom, Public thanks were about to be given; and as it was, the greatest compliments were paid him through the Government press, for the production of a few hundreds of potatos.

Mr. Lourenz planted the sets on the 1st of July, and on the following 21st of September, his crop was ripe; each set producing an average quantity of fifty two good-sized potatos, of a dryer and more farinaceous quality than those periodically imported from Bombay and Madras.

Then it was that the general cultivation of the *Solanum tuberosum* was recommended by the Government as a succedaneum for rice, although the *Jatropha Manihot*, L. would have been a much surer one, and better calculated for the maritime provinces, in cases of failure in the crops through excessive drought; but it was altogether unheeded, and Ceylon continued dependent upon Bombay and Madras for its periodical supplies, until the potato was so successfully cultivated at Fort Mac Donald as to exceed the anticipations of the most sanguine of our military horticulturalists.

This invaluable root is more extensively grown in this province than elsewhere in the island, and of very good size and quality. In 1826-7, I received regular supplies by the Kandyan Tavelams, at the average price of about 2*d.* a pound, or 80 lbs. (the quantity brought at each time) for 13*s.* sterling;—but it is now cheaper, in proportion as its propagation has increased.

The potato was soon planted with equal success in other high lands of the interior, and the maritime provinces consequently became independent of extraneous produce, and possessed of a surplus for ships touching at the island; and Madras itself is not better, if so well supplied from the Mysore country, than the maritime provinces of Ceylon are from the interior; nor is the Mysore potato equal in its farinaceous properties to the Kandyan. This root is cultivated extensively by the natives, and is become a great favorite with the entire population, being eaten by every caste and class.

The first attempt to grow wheat in this province was made in 1815, and although on a small scale, it completely succeeded, both at Kandy and Badulla; for the return was great, and when compared with some seed wheat that had been sent from Colombo, was found superior in weight and fineness of grain. But where bread is already cheap, and the demand for it limited to the Europeans, (for rice is the principal staff of life to all classes of the native population,) the growth of wheat may scarcely be an object of extensive cultivation, or of profit worthy the attention of the European agriculturist, until a more general influx of European settlers might make it otherwise.

In this beautiful and magnificent country, diversified with hills, undulating and champaign lands, and watered by numerous perennial mountain streams, which gradually increase in size and depth from tributary waters, in their meanderings towards the sea, the settler may choose his own soil and climate, according as either or both may suit his agricultural or horticultural pursuits; and surely, to those moderate capitalists who are bent upon emigrating to new and unknown lands, it is worthy of attention and serious consideration, that a country is open to them, where the productions of temperate and inter-tropical climes thrive luxuriantly: and where, by an introduction of European grasses and domestic animals, the native breed may in a very few years be so much improved, that the Highlands of the interior of Ceylon would scarcely be known as part of an Indian colony, except by name.

Limestone has been found in abundance, and potters' clay (*Argilla figuli*) in several localities, of excellent quality. Clay for brick making is obtained in Ceylon of such consistency as to require none of the artificial auxiliaries employed at home; and of timber, the builder may pick and choose, from the durable *Tectona* to the light *Dillenia*.

The cultivation of the Hemp (*Cannabis Sativa*, L.) would be a most profitable speculation in the event of war, notwithstanding the quantity of koir rope made in the maritime provinces, and the abandonment by the Government of the culture of the former (after having been proved of excellent quality) at Delft Island in the Northern Province.

So far back as Captain Knox's captivity in Kandy, between the years 1657 and 1678, the European colewort, carrot, radish, fennel, and balsam, as well as mustard and spearmint, the two last indigenous, were common enough there; and his opinion, that the climate was favorable to almost every European vegetable, experience has proved to have been a very just one, by the successful cultivation of such European fruits and vegetables as have hitherto been tried in the various places in the interior adapted to their growth.

For my own part, after having visited almost all but the northern regions of the globe, I have seen nothing to equal this incomparable country, to which I am so ardently attached, that, notwithstanding the *unparalleled injustice* with which my long services have hitherto been rewarded, it is ever present to my recollection, and its welfare inseparable from the best wishes of my heart.

CHAP. L.

Country between Alut Neuwara and Kalapahane at the base of the Idalgashina mountain—Native agriculture—Cataracts—Kalapahané—Cattle—Welanghena—Extensive panorama—Rhododendron arboreum—Laurus serrata—Andropogon schœnanthus—Hilloya—Passera—Alipoot—Wallassé—Bintenné and Veddah Ratté—Efforts to civilize the wild Veddahs attended with encouraging success—Anticipations of the result—Mountain of Namini Kooli—Badulla—Route to Kandy—Intermediate country intersected by eight rivers—Route from Passera to Neuwara Eliya—Hembliatewellé—Scenery—Limestone—Extraordinary contrasts—Fires and blankets indispensable, and ice not uncommon, in the very same province where sugar and coffee grow luxuriantly—Sanitory station established by Governor Sir Edward Barnes at Neuwara Eliya—Descent through the forests to Ramboddé—Chetahs—Cascades—Pusselawa rest-house—Mavali-Ganga navigable by boats between Gampola and Paradenia—Royal Botanic garden—Race course—Satin-wood bridge—Proclamation for the preservation of roads from inundation—Dodonwelle a favorite retreat of Rajah Singha—Splendid avenue of iron-wood trees, and magnificent Bogaha—City of Kandy as it was at the time of its capitulation—Delada Malagawa—British improvements—Hall of Audience—Hindoo Pagodas—Asgiri Vihare—Royal cemetery—Malwatté Viharé—Lakes—Massive pillars—Buddhist priesthood.

THE country between the villages of Alut Neuwara and Kalapahané, at the base of the Idalgashina mountain, a distance of 14½ miles, affords proof of the ample means of irrigation this part of the island possesses; and although it is but inadequately populated, paddee is extensively cultivated near the former place. The water necessary to supply the growing crops, is conveyed with an almost Chinese skill and economy over the terraced sides of hills, and through vallies beneath, chiefly from the Bellahool and Halgaran Oyas; the latter, descending in cataracts amidst the grandest and truly Alpine scenery.

Kalapahané was formerly a military post, which was abandoned soon after the termination of the rebellion of 1818; but many of the inhabitants who had at that time deserted it, have since returned, and to these belong the occasional patches of paddee that intervene between the well-wooded and grass-covered hills, with which, the neighbourhood of the village (about 2350 feet below the top of the Idalgashina pass) is studded; and the mountain itself is covered from its base to about midway, where the woody region commences, with verdure throughout the year. The district affords an infinite variety of grasses for cattle, which, exclusively of draught buffalos, are a species of black Zebu, chiefly employed in Tavelams, (there being no consumption of beef, except when European troops may be stationed in the neighbourhood,) and presents a delightful climate for speculative European agriculturists.

3 E

About $2\frac{1}{4}$ miles beyond the summit of the pass, by a gradual descent of several hundred feet, stands the village of Welanghena, formerly a military station, which overlooks a very deep valley, or rather ravine, for it has more the appearance of one, from the steepness of its grass-covered sides; and from this place the panorama is as magnificent as it is extensive.—Park-like grounds, interspersed with hills and vallies, covered with verdure, and surrounded by the immense mountains of Pedrotalagalla, 8280 feet above the level of the sea, on the N. W., the Idalgashina pass on the S. W., Apotella pass on the south, the Bamberagam pass on the east, and the high lands above Hembliatewellé and Passera on the N. E.;—the whole range occupying a delightfully cool and healthy climate, and presenting a natural amphitheatre, in the distance of from 15 to 30 miles, in all the varied colors of the most beautiful Italian landscape; and in the immediate foreground, clumps of flowering jungle, among which, the bright scarlet corols of the tree *Rhododendron*, a common production of many of the high lands of the interior, afford a striking contrast to the white ones of the wild orange, shaddock, and Mendya (*Laurus serrata*, L.); and at one's feet, the Lemon grass (*Andropogon schœnanthus*, L.) in wild abundance. The view altogether induces a most favorable opinion of the agricultural capabilities of Upper Ouva.*

The route from hence to Alipoot lies through Hilloya and Passera, the former distant about 12 miles from Welanghena, and the latter 15 from Hilloya. From Passera to Alipoot, the road is due east, and very rugged and hilly throughout the descent of nearly 800 feet in the distance of about 9 miles; the country everywhere beautiful, and although scarcely a coco-nut tree is to be seen, its absence is in a great degree compensated for by numerous jack, shaddock, jaggery, and wild talipat trees.

Alipoot is the residence of an Assistant Government Agent for the Southern Province, who has charge of the Revenue of the district, and is also a District Judge of the Eastern Circuit of the Supreme Court. It is not now, as formerly, a Military Command, but a dependency of Badulla.

This station is by no means so cool in point of temperature as one might expect from its position, but it is nevertheless remarkably healthy; and, as such, affords a strong contrast to the lower country of Wallassé, which, from the end of June to the beginning of October, is unhealthy.

The district of Wallassé is chiefly inhabited by Moormen, who are very industrious: and as the land affords abundant pasturage, these people, who have considerable herds of cattle and flocks of goats, are in easy circumstances. Paddee is cultivated in places

* See pages 322—324.

where the supply of water, by natural or artificial means, admits of it, and they have the coco-nut, talipat, and sugar palms in profusion.

Wallassé adjoins Bintenné and Veddah Ratté, the country of the *wild* Veddahs; but it may now be anticipated, that through the zealous exertions of the Wesleyan Mission, (which have already been attended with the most encouraging success,) under the auspices of Her Majesty's Colonial Government, and the cordial co-operation of the Assistant Government Agent at Batticaloa, to civilize this savage portion of our fellow creatures, the day is not far distant, when a road direct from Kandy to Batticaloa, through the now dense forests of the Veddah country, may connect the commercial relations of the central province with those of the eastern parts of the island; and cultivated lands, and populous villages, supersede the present hunting grounds and scantily inhabited forests of the wild descendants of the *Antichthones* of ancient Taprobane.

But, for the intending colonist, if the green plains and hills of Upper Ouva should fail to please him, or fall short of his original anticipations, (and if so, he must be hard to please,) he cannot do better than retrace his steps from Alipoot to the valley of Passera, and from thence proceed to Badulla, in the Central Province, 8½ miles further; between which places, the Namini Kooli mountain, nearly 7000 feet above the level of the sea, and covered with forest trees to the summit, and the basaltic-capp'd Lunagallé, destitute of trees, but covered with verdant grass, appear in conspicuous contrast with each other.

The scite of Badulla is one of the most beautiful that imagination can paint. The fort and village are seated in the midst of an amphitheatre of hills and mountains, the highest being from 3500 to 4000 feet above the level of the valley, which is fertile by nature and well irrigated by art; for advantage has been taken of the several mountain streams to form canals sufficient for supplying the numerous paddee fields, everywhere interspersed with rising grounds, covered with coco-nut and sugar palms.

The fort of Badulla is said to have been the scite of the residence of a famous Rajah or King of Ouva, an independent sovereign, who held his court there about 200 years ago, and is now the station of the Commandant of the district, a Captain of the Ceylon Rifle Regiment, (who is also Assistant Government Agent and District Judge,) and of the Native Medical Assistant in charge of the Hospital duties of the Garrison. A Hindoo temple, and a Buddha Viharé, with its usual accompaniment, a Dagobah, or tomb of a relic, are the principal native buildings.

The country between Badulla and Kandy, a distance of 52½ miles, is intersected by eight rivers, besides minor streams; and the direct route lies through Taldenné, 9¾ miles; Vella-Oya, 9 miles; Ooma-Oya, 6½ miles; Kurundu-Oya, 5¾ miles; Bellahool-

Oya, 4¾ miles; Gannegammé, 3¼ miles; Maha-Oya, 3½ miles; Harrackgammé-Oya, 2 miles; Talatoo-Oya, 5 miles; Kondesalé Ferry, ¼ mile; and Kandy, 3¾ miles; the whole road good, but gradually descending from the mountainous to the hilly, and, from about the centre of the country, between the high mountains of Neuwara Eliya to the southward and those beyond Kandy to the northward, the view is as unrivalled for beauty and extent as the scenery is for richness and magnificence.

If, however, the higher lands of Ceylon be the tourist's object, instead of proceeding from Alipoot to Badulla, he might take the road to Neuwara Eliya, from Passera, viâ Hembliatewellé, distant 10½ miles, a military station on the top of a mountain, about 3900 feet above the level of the sea, and forming a strong contrast in point of verdure with the green and hilly patches of the district of Upper Ouva, of which, the prospect is very extensive from the fort. From Hembliatewellé to Neuwara Eliya the distance is 27¼ miles, through Attangpittyé, 3 miles, (where there is now an excellent rest-house, built in 1839); Mahatettilla-Oya, 2¼ miles; Wilson's Bungalow, upon the verge of Wilson's plain, (so called after Major General Sir John Wilson, K. C. B., late Lieutenant Governor of Ceylon,) where there is a rest-house, 9 miles; and from thence to the rest-house of Neuwara Eliya, the *ne plus ultra* of climate for an Englishman, 13 miles.

Throughout the whole of this route, such a variety of mountain scenery presents itself, that, (in the words of my correspondent, to whom I am principally indebted for the information, this sanitory station having been established since I left the island,) "Pen can but inadequately describe,—imagination but faintly pourtray it; the province everywhere presenting a fine and extensive field for the speculative capitalist and the intending immigrant; and if the English settler prefer the agricultural system of his own country, he may purchase any quantity of excellent land adapted to his purposes, at a cheap rate. Limestone has been discovered in abundance, at less than 2000 feet below Neuwara Eliya; where, as in other places in the same province, fires and blankets are indispensable at night, and ice not uncommon;—and yet, the sugar, cotton, indigo, and coffee planter need be at no loss for appropriate localities for their culture; and all between the parallels of 6° 40′ and 8° 10′ of north latitude, and of 80° 30′ and 81° 20′ of east longitude!"

His Excellency the late Lieutenant General Sir Edward Barnes established this sanitory station in 1828, and built a substantial mansion, military quarters, and storehouses; than which, nothing could possibly be more beneficial to the forces employed in the island, as the result has proved; and if a reference be made to the returns of expenses incurred for sending invalid soldiers to Europe, for ten years prior to the establishment of a convalescent station at Neuwara Eliya, and for a similar subsequent period, according to the relative proportion of European troops, during both periods, in the island, the result will be the best panegyric in favor of Neuwara Eliya, and of His Excellency s provident foresight and regard for the health of the troops under his command.

From Neuwara* Eliya to Kandy the distance is 52 miles, and the direct carriage road is, to Ramboddé rest-house, 15 miles, through a dense forest, abounding with chetahs, and a gradual descent of nearly 3000 feet. The village is romantically situate on a rather steep acclivity, between two of the numerous cascades which flow from the neighbouring mountains. From Ramboddé to Pusselawa rest-house, 14 miles; and from thence to Gampola, a large village in a delightfully level and fertile country, and salubrious climate, 8 miles. From Gampola to Kandy, the distance is 15 miles; but the traveller may proceed by water to Paradenia bridge, a distance of 9 miles, which reduces the distance to Kandy from 15 to 12 miles.

Paradenia (3 miles S. W. of Kandy on the Colombo road) may justly boast of its Botanic Garden, race course, and bridge of satin-wood of a single arch, having a span of 205 feet over the Mavali-Ganga. The former was commenced under Governor, the late General Sir Robert Brownrigg's auspices, in 1819; and the two last, are among the many memorials of the energy and devotion to the improvement of the colony, which distinguished the administration of His Excellency's immediate successor, the late Lieutenant General Sir Edward Barnes.

That the former almost impenetrable fastnesses of this fine country were superseded by such excellent roads, and that they still continue so, may justly be attributed to Sir Edward Barnes, under whose constant and zealous supervision they were formed; for having in view the inundations to which such works were liable, if the natives were allowed their own way, His Excellency issued a Proclamation, on the 7th September, 1820, to the effect "that all persons having paddee land on either side of a road, should, in cultivating the same, leave a space of not less than four feet between the road and the cultivated land; and that it should not be lawful for any person to lay across the road pipes or other machinery for conveying water; or to fence across or over any part of the road, or otherwise encroach thereon, on pain of fine and imprisonment at hard labour, at the discretion of any Agent of Government before whom he might be convicted, in addition to being obliged, at his own cost and labour, to repair

* The repeated recurrence of the word *Neuwara,* literally city, requires explanation. Neuwara means also a royal residence, whether under a temporary bungalow of Cajan thatch, or one more appropriate to the dignity of Royalty. Wherever a King sojourned, whether when a fugitive from his excited subjects, or other occasion, that place from thenceforth was dignified with the name of Neuwara.

all damage. And it was further declared, that as it was the intention of Government by all means in its power to encourage agriculture, orders had been given, wherever the conveyance of water was required from one side of the road to the other, to leave sufficient drains or channels for the same, the situations of which to be pointed out by the different Headmen* to the Agents of Government or other Officers superintending the working parties; and that where such were found to be wanting, the Headman, or the Proprietor of the land adjacent, was at full liberty, and was invited to make the same known to the Agent of Government in the district, who would take measures for affording the accommodation required, if he considered the application reasonable; but that no person, of his own authority, was to presume to cut across or otherwise damage the road, on pain of punishment as above directed."

After viewing the Botanic Garden at Paradenia, the tourist may as well visit Dodonwellé, about 8 miles from Kandy; from whence it is a most delightful ride, although the approach to it is by a steep and rugged ascent. The temples are of ancient construction, but very small and paltry, and present nothing worthy of notice, except by way of contrast to the magnificent avenue of iron-wood trees (*Mesua ferrea*, L., and *Naghas* of the Singhalese). From the entrance, the avenue is upwards of a quarter of a mile in length, and from fifty to sixty feet in width, and at the extremity is a circular area containing the temples, shaded by an umbrageous Bogaha in all its majesty and luxuriance, and venerated as much from its great size and age as the most famed of its species, the *Pra si Maha Pout* of the Siamese.†

* The Majoraals or Majoraales of the Districts are the Superintendents of agriculture, tanks, and embankments for the irrigation of lands.—AUTHOR.

† The supposed parent of the tree originally planted at Anarajahpoora, to which place it is believed by the Buddhists to have been miraculously conveyed from Siam.—See note to page 56 for the reason of its additional name of *Sassalada*, or tremulous leaf.

According to M. de la Loubère's account of Siam, the Bogaha (*Ficus religiosa*, L.) is the *Pra si Maha Pout*, or tree of the Great Pout, (the *Ton-Po* of the vulgar Siamese,) which he erroneously supposed to mean the God Mercury, by his remarks that "*Pout* or *Poot* is the name of that planet in the Bali term for Wednesday, and that Pout is one of the names of Sommona-Codom (or Buddha)."

Wednesday is called the day of Bod or Buddha in the Hindoo, as well as in the Singhalese languages, (*Buddha-da* in the latter,) and M. de la Loubère considered that "as the Tamulic has no *b* the *p* brings it very near the Bali mode of writing it, *Pout*, which, among the Siamese, is another name for Sommona-Codom, and is itself a corruption of the word Buddha, the Mercury of the Greeks and Latins."

In this, M. de la Loubère has fallen into the same mistake that the late Sir William Jones did; but, with his usual candour, Sir William subsequently acknowledged his original error.*

* Asiatic Researches, vol. ii. Chronology of the Hindoos.

The analogy of the sacred fig tree with the oak of the Druids is further strengthened by a huge spherical mass of granitic rock lying near, in which there are two steps, but for what purpose these were originally hewn, the priests are themselves ignorant.

It was here that the late King, when temporarily tired of the ferocious pleasure of impaling his subjects, was wont to retire to a decorated summer-house, which formerly stood at the extremity of the avenue, where the foliage is so dense as to be impervious even to the meridian sun; and when that sanguinary despot fled to Meda-Maha-Neuwara in 1815, the priests of Dodonwellé abandoned their temples and accompanied him in his flight.

Kandy originally contained but few tiled houses, in proportion to the rest; these belonged to the Chiefs, were elevated from the ground, and approached by steps. The other habitations were built of *Waretchie* sticks and mud, and thatched with paddee straw, the whole forming five streets; and, from their inclination from the eastward and westward towards the north, appear as if the original intention had been to form the city in the shape of a triangle, with its apex to the northward, and its base bounded by the two artificial lakes, of which, that called the new lake was formed during the reign of the late Malabar despot, Sree Wickremé Rajah Singha.

The relatives and connexions of the Royal Family, whom the jealousy of the reigning Sovereign had separated from the rest of the Kandyan community, were restricted to a part of the city called Malabar Street, which takes a south-easterly direction from the Delada Malagawa, having the hospital on its right, and between it and the lake. But (by the recent information I have received) so great have been the improvements in Kandy, since the erection of the Pavilion by Sir Edward Barnes, and the subsequent improvements in laying out the grounds by Sir Wilmot Horton, and the pretty villas which have sprung up, as if by magic, under the skilful management of British architects, that if the late tyrannous and sanguinary Rajah were to revisit the scene of his former despotism upon earth, he would scarcely recognize the scite of his own palace, for all that remains of it are the Hall of Audience and the Pateripoa; the former, now much better employed as the Court House on week days, and as a chapel on Sundays, and the latter as a military "Black Hole."

Between the Kandyan part of the town and Malabar Street, there is a large intervening space, which contains the principal temple of Delada Malagawa, (literally, palace of the tooth,) and the Hindoo Pagodas or Dewalés of *Pattiné* and *Nata;* the former stands to the southward and westward, and the latter to the westward, of the palace, and between it and the Pagoda of *Pattiné*, in separate and extensive areas. The *Maha Vishnu* Dewalé is situate nearly north of the *Nata* Dewalé, and the

Kattregam Dewalé about west of the *Pattiné* Dewale, and all are shaded by umbrageous palms and other trees.

The Asgiri Viharé adjoins the original burial place of the Kandyan Kings, and is situate to the north-westward of the principal street from which one enters the enclosure of the Awadánamadewa, or Royal cemetery; and the Malwatté Vihare (which, with the former, may be considered the Oxford and Cambridge of Buddhism) is situate on the south side of the new lake, and nearly facing the small artificial island, where originally stood the late despot's favorite pavilion or summer-house; but which, subsequently to our occupation of Kandy, was converted into a magazine.

The lakes are about a mile in length but vary from a hundred to five hundred yards in width, and are well stocked with fish, which the despot would never allow to be caught; so that, whatever may have been the extent of the misery he inflicted upon his oppressed subjects, he displayed one trait of humanity, and the only one he was ever known to have possessed, towards the finny tribe. These lakes are a great improvement to the town, and are 1800 feet above the level of the sea.

In addition to the splendid natural amphitheatre which Kandy presents,* and the magnificence of the surrounding scenery, there is a solemnity about the Malwatté Viharé that is altogether opposed to our notions of pagan worship, or its temples; and, in contemplating the massive pillars of stone, sixteen cubits in height, and of proportionate circumference, each formed of one block only, which support the roof of the College Hall, and contrasting these, and innumerable other vestiges of the remotest antiquity, with the best architecture of the Singhalese of the present day, one is puzzled to believe that they are descended from the wonderful architects whose gigantic works astound all who behold them, and which have so long set time and the destructive efforts of worse than Barbarian conquerors (the *Christian* Portuguese) at defiance.

The principal offices of priesthood in the colleges of Malwatté and Asgiri are in the gift of the Government. The former has one Arch Priest, called Maha Nayaka Oonansé; a First and Second Deputy, called Anoo Nayaka Oonansé; and ten Nayakas of districts. The latter, one Maha Nayaka Oonansé, one Deputy, or Anoo Nayaka Oonansé, and five Nayakas of districts. The Lay Chiefs, or Basnaiké Nilamés of the principal Dewalés, are appointed by the Government. The former are appointed by the Governor's warrant, the latter by the Agent of Government for the province.

* See page 392.

CHAP. LI.

Sequel to the possession of Kandy—Person of the deposed King—Bad policy of the Portuguese—Additional reasons for the war with Kandy—Regalia of Kandy—Honors conferred upon the conquerors, the Head Civil Servant, and the Kandyan Adikar Eheylepola, by His Royal Highness the Prince Regent—Political humbug—Political importance of the relic, or tooth of Gautama Buddha, contrasted with that of the Trojan Palladium—Imposing ceremonial of the restoration of the relic to the temple of Delada Malagawa, or palace of the tooth, under a salute from the Royal Artillery of the garrison—The Head Civil Officer presents an offering to the temple in the name and on behalf of the Governor, Lieutenant General Sir Robert Brownrigg, G. C. B.—Hypothesis respecting the relic—Mandelsloh's account of certain sacred relics made from the tusks of an elephant of the King of Pegu—The idol of less importance in its sacred than in its political character—Custody of the idol—Military sentinel at the entrance of the Delada Malagawa—Zealotry—Stipendiary priests of Buddha—Kandy the meridian of Buddhist and Demon worship in Ceylon—Expenses of idolatrous festivals borne by the Government.

THE possession of Kandy* was followed by the formal annexation of it to the British Empire, by the unanimous consent of Priests, Chiefs, and People. The Governor's reception in the capital was of the most gratifying description; and every honor that native pomp and ingenuity could display, in the welcome of the deliverer of the nation from the most cruel and galling yoke that ever oppressed a people, was paid to His Excellency and his gallant followers; and, in that same "Hall of Audience" where the dethroned despot was wont to issue his mandates of death, privation of sight, and mutilation of limbs, the Governor conferred honors and rewards upon the most active in affording assistance to the troops during their advance upon the capital.

This triumph over a barbarous power, which had long set every moral obligation at defiance, and made wanton sport of human misery, regarding the infliction of the most excruciating bodily torture upon his subjects as mere pastime, and seeking only for new pleasures in the invention and exercise of new brutalities, was the dawn of better days for the Kandyan nation; and the occupation of Kandy having been followed by the capture of the King's mother and thirty seven other ladies of the Royal *Zenanah*, with a considerable treasure, by Major Kelly, at Mungallé Doboddagammé, on the 16th of that month, and soon afterwards by that of the tyrant himself, the Convention † took place, and the entire island of Ceylon formed, for the first time, an integral part of the British Empire.

* See pages 391, 392.

† See Appendix, for the Convention.

The judgment and determination of His Excellency the Governor, (Lieut. General Brownrigg,) in seizing the proper moment to commence war upon just grounds, were not based upon a solitary principle. So long as there was the smallest chance of the island being restored to the Dutch, it might have been bad policy to have interfered with the Kandyans; but when, through the wisdom which directed His Majesty's Councils,—the energy of the then illustrious and gallant Prince who conducted the army at home,—and the steady valour and transcendant skill of the immortal Chief, who, to the eternal admiration of his country and of the world, had led that army through so long and glorious a career of victory, this island was confirmed to the Imperial Crown, it would have been disgraceful to Sir Robert Brownrigg as a politician, if he had left Kandy as he had found it in 1812, in possession of the Malabar despot; for our maritime possessions could never have been secure, when the whole of the interior was possessed by a people who had at all times shown themselves unfriendly towards us; and when our retention of the coast was the mere possession of a fortress, whilst the enemy occupied the citadel.

In vain had the conquest of the interior been attempted for two or three centuries by our Portuguese and Dutch predecessors in the maritime provinces, although they had been repeatedly masters of the capital; at one period, indeed, the former had conquered all except the impregnable position called *Kandi Udda,* in the centre of the mountainous region, surrounded by impervious jungles, and with secret approaches for only one man at a time, to that last refuge of Kandyan independence:—but the Portuguese Governors could not have adopted a worse policy than they did by giving commands in their army to Kandyans. One of their very first considerations, after conquest, ought surely to have been the study of the national characteristics of the conquered; and it would have required but little to have satisfied them, that the principal features of the Kandyans were merely human imitations of their own indigenous leopard,—treachery and ferocity, as circumstances might give them an opportunity of profiting by the one, or of gratifying their vengeance by the other.

The deposed King, Sree Wickremé Rajah Singha, was a stout good-looking Malabar, with a peculiarly keen and rolling eye, and a restlessness of manner, which, according to some opinions, "stamped him at first sight as a person of irascible temper," and to others, of "unbridled passions." Of these qualifications, he was so well known to be in the fullest possession, that the colonial physiognomists did not display any very great spirit of prophecy in their judgment.

The ancient Royal crown of gold, and sword of state mounted with the same metal, together with the sceptre and throne of Kandy were sent to His Royal Highness the

Prince Regent, and arrived in England on the 12th of October, 1815, the very day that one of the highest compliments was publicly paid to the army in Ceylon, by the transmission of the Royal standard of Kandy to be deposited in Whitehall Chapel, in company with the Imperial eagles and colors taken at Waterloo. The gallant Governor and Commander of the Forces was honored with the Grand Cross of the Most Honorable Military Order of the Bath, and a Baronetcy; his son and Aid-de-camp, who was the bearer of his despatches, with the Brevet rank of Lieutenant Colonel; the Chief Singhalese Translator, Mr. D'Oyley, of the Civil Service, with a Baronetcy; a few field officers with a step by Brevet; and Eheylepola, the former Chief Kandyan Adikar, although disappointed in his hopes of succeeding to the throne, was honored with the Prince Regent's portrait set with brilliants, to be worn round his neck, suspended from a magnificent gold chain.

The Governor's first object, after the Convention had been formally executed, was to ensure the fidelity of the Kandyans to the new order of things and the conquest that had been so bloodlessly achieved, by the adoption of a little political humbug; but which, being perfectly in accordance with the superstitious notions of the conquered, was one of the most likely means to effect the ulterior object that His Excellency had in view, although at the risk of future censure for having exceeded the ordinary limits of Christian propriety in a British Governor.

The Kandyans attach as much importance to the possession of a sacred relic, called *Delada*, or tooth of Gautama Buddha, (who must have been a most extraordinary specimen of the *Homo Sapiens*, to have had a tooth two inches in length and one in diameter, the reputed* size of the *Delada;* and miraculous also has been its preservation, if it be true that its original and natural possessor died 543 years before the advent of Christ,) as the Trojans of old did to their statue of Pallas;† and, entertaining the same belief, that once in an enemy's power, it involved the dominion of the

* This is not in accordance with Dr. Davy's account of the Delada, which he saw at Kandy in 1817; for the Doctor has given a drawing of its shape and size, the latter being about 1½ inch in length, and nearly an inch in circumference at the largest part.

† Its fabled fall from heaven before the tent of Ilus, whilst building the citadel of Ilium, B. C. 1174, gives it precedence, in point of antiquity, by 631 years, to the Kandyan Palladium, and of fiction also, notwithstanding the various relations of the original rescue of the latter from the funeral pile, (according to the converted High Priest, Moodliar George Nadoris de Zilvas's information, which he derived from Pali works of great antiquity, whilst at Ava, and to whom I am obliged for the account of it,) by one of Gautama Buddha's disciples, a priest of the Upasampada order, near Kossidera, in Hindoostan, B. C. 543, and its numerous escapes, subsequently to to its expulsion by the Brahmins from Dantapoora, or city of the tooth, in the fourth century.

country, much greater importance was attached to our possession of it, than even to the capture of the King and Royal Family. It was, therefore, considered sound policy to show that we were equally as conscious of the political value of the relic as the Kandyans themselves; and an imposing ceremonial was ordered for restoring the Palladium (which, spite of tradition, is thought by many to be an Ourang Outang's tooth, and, by others who have seen it, artificial) to the Delada Malagawa, or Palace of the Tooth, from which it had been removed during the army's advance upon the capital.

I was favored with the details of the procession, by Lieutenant William Henry Lyttelton, of the 73rd regiment, who was present at the ceremonial, in April, 1815; than which, no public *spectacle* could have been more gratifying to the idolatrous worshippers of Gautama Buddha, or, in some respects, more disgusting to Christians;—but, nevertheless, they may prove interesting to the reader.

"1. Eight large elephants with enormous tusks, richly covered, and attended by several splendidly-dressed individuals.

2. The Maha Nayaka Oonansé, or Arch Priest, supported by two young priests in their saffron-colored robes.

3. One hundred and fifty priests in saffron-colored robes.

4. A sacred image, covered with gold brocade and carried in a *Muncheel,** with a canopy over it.

5. Sixty banners, &c. of various colors.

6. Trumpets and tam-a-tams.

7. Devadasi, or dancing girls.

8. Adikar's whips, of great length, without handles, but gradually tapering from the thickness of several inches in circumference to that of whip-cord, made of the *Sensiviera Zeylanica*, or bow-string hemp.—With these emblems of authority, the Adikar's attendants precede him, and make a tremendous cracking, as a warning to offenders against the law.

9. First Adikar, (Molligoddé,) but more properly *Adikaaram*, attended by numerous Chiefs, in full state dress.

10. Two hundred principal Headmen, in full state dress.

11. Ginjals, or grasshopper guns belonging to the temples.

12. *Drums of the Ceylon regiments.*

13. Five full-grown elephants, their tusks magnificently ornamented;—the centre elephant's tusks cased in pure gold, and carrying the *Karandua*, composed of several

* A cot, suspended from a bamboo pole, as in the annexed plate, (from a colored drawing by a Kandyan artist, as a specimen of the state of the art in Ceylon,) but more splendidly ornamented.

splendidly ornamented and jewelled cases, in the innermost of which the relic is contained. The elephants covered with cloth of gold, and the two first and two last elephants carrying the attendants upon the centre elephant, bearing gold-mounted fans and umbrellas.

14. The Second Adikar, (Kappuwatté,) with some hundreds of followers in full state dress.

15. Six large elephants, magnificently covered and ornamented, each carrying a sacred image.

16. Eheylepola on horseback, with a numerous and splendid suite.

The procession extended upwards of a mile in length, and reached the palace in which the temple of Delada Malagawa is situate, about four P. M., but as, according to the soothsayers, "the propitious moment had not arrived," the procession, by way of passing the intermediate time, moved round the grand square of the palace.

Upon a second time reaching the temple, a salute was fired from the temple ginjals, *and returned by the Royal Artillery of the garrison;* after which, the relic was removed from the elephant's back by two servants of the temple, whose mouths were covered, to prevent their breath from contaminating the object of so much profound veneration. The priests then retired within the temple, which, *after having put off our shoes!!* we were invited to enter.

Mr. D'Oyley, the Chief Commissioner for the Kandyan Provinces, having intimated to the Maha Nayaka Oonansé that "*he was commissioned by His Excellency the Governor to make an offering to the temple,*" retired for a minute or two, and then returned, bringing a most beautiful musical clock, which he formally presented as the offering in the Governor's name!!—The burst of applause, which continued for some minutes, proved their high estimation of *the Governor's offering to the temple;* but when, as if by magic, the machinery was put in motion, the general expression of delight, of Priests, Chiefs, and People, exceeded all belief, and beggars description.

The streets through which the procession passed, were strewed with white composition and flowers, emblematic of purity; and the houses were ornamented with young plantain trees. The decorations of the temple were most beautifully arranged, and all concluded without the slightest accident.

The square in front of the palace was illuminated at night, and groups of boys, dressed as dancing girls, were exhibiting in all quarters."

Be the relic what it may, traditions and opinions are as abundant as they are conflicting, and in a great degree incredible; and if it were not for its reputed antiquity, (which is extraordinary, when contrasted with the fact, that the priests admit that it was carried in procession for the first time in 1775,) one might, upon a cursory perusal of Mandelsloh's Travels, venture an hypothesis which, under other circumstances, would not have been more remote from the truth than the tales in circulation respecting it, (reasoning upon the grounds of the great existing analogy between the rites and ceremonies of Buddha's worship in Ava and Ceylon,) that the supposed tooth of the God Buddha had been one of the many articles manufactured from the tusks of the celebrated elephant, upon which the King of Pegu, about the middle of the sixteenth century, advanced at the head of his army against his uncle, the King of Ava, his vassal, who had refused to do him homage.

The battle was for the possession of a *White Elephant*, and was decided in favor of the former, who killed his uncle in single combat, in view of their respective armies; and the elephant of the King of Pegu, after having rendered his Royal rider the greatest service during the combat, soon afterwards fell dead at his feet, when the King, as an acknowledgment of the noble animal's merits, caused a variety of idols to be manufactured of its tusks, and placed in various Pagodas or temples.

The shape of the idols is not stated by my authority,* but it would not have been unreasonable to conclude, that some of them were made in imitation of a sacred relic, called the "tooth of Buddha," of which, the original was of great interest and importance in the view of the Buddhist priesthood, and that one of these imitations had been transmitted to Ceylon, with some rigmarole story respecting it, to accredit it as sacred and inestimable to the superstitious devotee.

This idol is of less importance in its sacred than in its political character and effect upon the superstitious population; and a mistaken notion appears to prevail, as to the object of the British Government in placing the entrance of the Malagawa, where this Kandyan Palladium is deposited, under the charge of a sentinel, from sunset till sunrise; but as that object is founded on the sound policy of preventing its clandestine removal by ambitious Chiefs, or discontented Priests, for the purpose of exciting rebellion against British dominion, there cannot be a safer plan than that now adopted of keeping it under military *surveillance*, although this caution is erroneously attributed to other motives, such as doing honor to the Delada, or tooth of Buddha, and supporting the reign of idolatry.

The Government Agent has the custody of the keys of the room, and of the cases, or *Karanduwa*, in which the Delada is deposited; but the most sceptical may be satisfied, that as Christianity extends, (and that it is on the increase in Ceylon, no one

* Mandelsloh's Travels into the Indies.

who will retrograde to the year 1815, and contrast the state of the churches there at that period with the present, will doubt,) the native superstition will diminish; the dread of the power of malignant demons gradually cease to overawe the minds of the now idolatrous Kandyans; and that in the course of time it will be no more expedient to keep the relic under military safeguard, than the Druidical remains of Stonehenge, because it will cease to be regarded with the reverence originally implanted, reared, and supported, by superstition and ignorance.

Nevertheless, we have some zealots who would adopt the Portuguese system to extirpate Buddhism and the Hindoo worship in Ceylon, by absolutely prohibiting the exercise of the rites of either within the British dominions! Others, for the Dutch system of toleration, but limiting the employment of natives in the Public Service to those only who may openly become apostates to their own religion, and very probably hypocrites, under the profession of Christianity! but if the British Government were capable of assuming the office of "persecutor for religion's sake," and of adopting either the Dutch or Portuguese model, it would merit the charge of having obtained the possession of the Kandyan kingdom, by the full and free consent of Priests, Chiefs, and People, under the falsest and basest pretences;* and, as far as the old Dutch system had obtained, if general opinion may be credited, there was no lack of apostates, in the one sense, or of hypocrites, in the other, for the sake of office under Government.

The Government allows a monthly stipend to forty two Buddhist priests; namely, to two Maha Nayaka Oonansés and to two officiating priests at the Delada Malagawa, in money and paddee; and to the remainder in paddee, with a proportion of salt and oil, or a commutation in money for these articles. The total expense may be estimated at from £150 to £200 per annum, and the remission of the tenth part of the produce of temple lands† to about 25,000 parahs of paddee, or from £1250 to £1500 more, according as the price of the latter may be in the market.

Kandy is the meridian of the medley of Buddhist and Demon worship that obtains at Ceylon; but as I have no pretensions to an acquaintance with the dogmas of Buddhism, or the incarnations of Vishnu, except that which the "Asiatic Researches" copiously afford, I would beg leave to refer the curious upon such points to that elaborate work; and, for the most correct accounts of the original possessions of the Portuguese and Dutch in Ceylon, to their national authors; or to those of our own country who have availed themselves of such original information, and have long since

* See the 4th and 5th Clauses of the Kandyan Convention, in the Appendix. † See page 272.

exhausted that subject so far as to leave nothing for others to relate, except by extracting from their voluminous works: of these, I have occasionally availed myself, as I have also done of official and private accounts of the observances of the Kandyan festivals.*

The chief festival is that of the *Perraherra*, or "Cutting of the Water ceremonial;" and as this is announced to take place when the Royal Astrologers have ascertained the favorable time for commencing it, all persons desirous of contracting for supplying the various articles required for the celebration, are invited by beat of tam-a-tam "to send in their tenders to the Government Agent;"† viz. "For oil and cloth for lights to the procession,—For articles for the Delada Malagawa and four Dewalés,—For canopy bearers over the relic,—For *Walliyakun*, or devil dancing,—and for the *Perraherras* at thirteen outstations!!!" But none of these processions can possibly excel in splondour the restoration of the relic to the Delada Malagawa in 1815.

Everything emanating from the Government, in the slightest degree complimentary to idolatry, militates against the Gospel of Christ, whilst it gives importance to the former, with the Pagan part of the population, which it ought not to derive from such a source, and could not otherwise command; and therefore, all contributions to the heathen festivals, on the part of a Christian Government, as well as the insertion of the names and titles of Buddhist and Devil Priests, and Lay Chiefs of temples, in succession to the Ecclesiastical, Civil, and Judicial Establishments of the island, in the Calendar, annually published by Authority, ought to be abandoned at once and for ever.

* See Appendix.

† The expenses of this and of the other festivals may surely be dispensed with on the part of a Christian Government, without incurring a breach of faith under the Convention of 1816; and it is to be deplored, that when the rebellion of 1817 was put down by force of arms in the following year, the then most favorable moment had not been taken advantage of by the British Government either to annul the objectionable clauses in that Convention, upon the grounds that a breach of it had originated with the Kandyan Conventionalists, or to abrogate it altogether.

But the Colonial Government did not show any particular fastidiousness about the Convention in another matter, in 1819; for, not satisfied with issuing a Proclamation for a registry of the Temple lands, which it had an undoubted right to do, upon the grounds of preventing imposition upon the Public Revenue, it assumed the despotic power of preventing proprietors of land from assigning their property to the temples, without the express *sanction* of the Government. Now, if a power were to be assumed in Great Britain or Ireland, to prevent donations, or assignments of lands to religious purposes, without a license from the Government, it is not very difficult to conceive the excitement so arbitrary a measure would create, although it may be beyond one's power to predict the result of it.

CHAP. LII.

Extraordinary facts elicited after taking possession of Kandy in 1815, respecting the King's military resources at the time Major Davie capitulated in 1803—Secret service money—Deplorable consequences of want of information as to the true state of Kandyan resources—Pilamé Talawé, apparently a traitor to his sovereign, makes the British Government his dupe—Prince Mootto Sawmé—Pilamé Talawé enters into an armistice with Major Davie, and breaks it—British troops, with few exceptions, massacred in detail—Captain Arthur Johnston, in 1804, with a much less force, marched from Batticaloa, took Kandy, and reached Trincomalé with little loss—Governor's first object after the conquest of Kandy in 1816—Roads—Eheylepola—William Tolfrey, Esq., receives private intimation of Eheylepola's intended treachery—His information treated with contempt—Consequences—Murder of S. D. Wilson, Esq., by Veddahs—Rebellion of 1817—The Pretender—Critical position of the army—Honorable East India Company's auxiliary troops—Recovery of the relic—Military casualties—Fate of the rebel Chiefs—Governor's triumphant return to Colombo—Incipient rebellions in 1834 and 1842—Faithless Princes—Supposed origin of the rebellion of 1817—War cry of the 19th regiment—The Kandyans—Kandyan arts and sciences, domestic habits and manners—Agriculture—Climate of Kandy—Government Clerks and Headmen—Governor's Minute—Garrison of Kandy—Public Departments—Citadel—Algallé—Neuwera Eliya potatos—Caste no disqualification for tenure of lands—Suggestions to capitalists—Rest-houses—Indigenous iron, alum, and saltpetre—Suggestions for a farm for supplying cured and salted provisions to shipping—Area and population of the Central Province—Conclusion.

The British troops had been but a very short time in possession of the capital of the late kingdom of Kandy, ere attention was drawn to the extraordinary facts, which had been elicited after particular inquiry, and were fully corroborated by the First Adikar, (Molligoddé,) that at the time Major Davie capitulated, on the 24th of June, 1803, the Royal store of gunpowder did not exceed 750 lbs avoirdupois, and that the best Kandyan arms were inferior, in point of efficiency, to those of any temporarily excited European rabble.

It appears almost a mystery, how the British Government of the maritime provinces, considering that it displayed no niggardly economy in the expenditure of "secret service money," could have been so deplorably ignorant, at the time, of the state of the Kandyan population, military force, and resources, as subsequent events have proved it to have been.

To what purpose then, was the very natural question, had the secret service money, from 1796 to 1803, been appropriated? Are we to believe, or doubt, in 1843, the reports in the colony, that for the intervening seven years from the cession of the island to the melancholy and disgraceful calamity that befel Major Davie's detachment at Wattépolowa, after having ceded Kandy by capitulation, the secret service money was not employed as the public had been led to believe, but for secret services of a very different nature and complexion to the political purposes for which the Home Government had so liberally allowed it in the Colonial expenditure ?—But for this ever to be regretted want of information, either the capitulation might never have taken place, or the treacherous breach of it, and subsequent dreadful massacre of Major Davie's detachment, would not have been so long unrevenged ; nor the twelve years, between that eventful period and the conquest of Kandy, have been thrown away in endeavours to bring the then reigning despot to a treaty of amity and commerce.

It may scarcely be necessary to state here, what the reader is perhaps already well acquainted with, that after the cession of the Dutch possessions in Ceylon, during the war with the French Republic and Empire, the arrangements for governing the new acquisitions furnished a pretty specimen of jobbing ; the result of which was a disastrous war with the King of Kandy, a mere puppet in the hands of a powerful minister, (Pilamé Talawé,) who had previously set aside Prince Mootto Sawmé, the alleged lawful heir to the throne, but whose claim to it was far from being clearly established.

That Prince having fled to the British settlements, was hospitably received ; but there was not, for a time, the slightest intention of supporting his pretensions to the crown, nor until the war had commenced with the King of Kandy ;—then, indeed, it was determined to place Mootto Sawmé upon the throne from which he had been excluded. Kandy was taken, and the Prince became a nominal King ; but had scarcely been invested with the title and in possession of the palace, ere Major General Macdowall and the Second Adikar entered into negociations for reducing the new sovereign to the position of a pensioner, delivering up Rajah Singha to the care of the British Government, and investing Pilamé Talawé with sovereign power, under the title of "The Great Prince.

An armistice having been concluded, Major General Macdowall returned to Colombo with the greater part of the British force ; but Pilamé Talawé, thinking it, after all, to be his best policy to adhere to the fugitive Rajah, and to further ingratiate himself in the royal favor, broke the armistice, by attacking Kandy, where Major Davie, after a gallant defence, hoisted a flag of truce, and then capitulated, upon the condition of retaining his small arms and baggage, and retiring unmolested to Colombo. At Wattépolowa, a demand was made for the surrender of Mootto Sawmé, who accompanied the garrison. This was at first resisted, but ultimately complied with ; the national faith was broken in a dastardly manner, and Mootto Sawmé given up and murdered ! The British troops were then required to march back to Kandy ; but all, with few exceptions, were massacred by twos and threes, *en route* to the city, where also 120 of their sick comrades, for whose good treatment the Kandyan minister had pledged himself, were murdered in their beds in the hospital!!!

In 1804, the gallant Captain Arthur Johnston, of the 19th regiment, who is second to none in the annals of Ceylon for the bravery and cool determination of a British officer, marched from Batticaloa to Trincomalé, taking Kandy *en passant*, with a small detachment, not exceeding, officers included, 150 men; and, spite of all the impediments which the King of Kandy and the nature of the country opposed to his indomitable band, reached his destination with a very inconsiderable loss. Captain Johnston had thus, by his skill and intrepidity, overcome every obstacle; and by his noble example, inspired the brave troops under his command with a persevering endurance of sufferings, hardships, and privations, as severe as ever tried the fortitude of a soldier in any part of the world.

These are irrefragable facts, and whilst they speak volumes against the inexplicable conduct of the former Commandant of Kandy, it is greatly to be deplored, that the strong arm of death prevented that officer (Major Davie*) from having an opportunity of clearing it to the satisfaction of his country, before a Court of his military peers, instead of leaving his fame and honor as a soldier to the mercy of every historian.

To revert to the year 1816:—One of the most important objects, after the formal execution of the convention, by His Excellency the Governor, had been to secure the advantages which that treaty had confirmed; and working parties, under Assistant Engineers, who were selected from the officers of the several regiments, were established for the formation of substantial military roads and bridges through every part of the country; the improved state of which, as regards matters connected with the fulfilment of the pledges given by the Convention with the Chiefs, Priests, and People, may be more correctly estimated from His Excellency's Address of the 20th of May, 1816,† than from any other account of it.

But whilst so much was being done for the Kandyan people, by fiscal and judicial arrangements, and for facilitating commerce, a desire was manifested on their part to relinquish the merciful government of a Christian power, in order to revert to the sanguinary rule of the Malabar dynasty; and, for a time, rebellion impeded the chief operations upon the line of road from Colombo on the west, to Trincomalé on the east side of the island, the connexion of these two ports being of paramount importance, for establishing the means of transport between them, when interrupted by sea, as the north-east or south-west monsoons might respectively prevail.

* Of His Majesty's Malay Regiment, now Her Majesty's Ceylon Rifle Regiment.

† See Appendix.

The treacherous Eheylepola, upon whom, the Governor, after giving him and the two Adikars private audiences, on the 18th March, 1816, had publicly conferred the high and honorable appointment of *Maduwé Gankam Lekam,* (Chief of regular soldiers or Lascoreens who possess lands for their service,) with *Pali wahala Gabadu Gam,* (King's villages,) and who had doubtlessly expected the vacant throne, but had received no sort of encouragement in any such anticipations, brooding over his blighted ambition, but ever *professing it his greatest pride to be considered the friend of the British Government,* secretly fomented an extensive rebellion, whilst he masked his proceedings by the most specious appearances of loyalty, and of devotion to the changes that had taken place.

So great, indeed, was the Governor's confidence in this man, and in his gratitude to the British nation, that when His Excellency, with Lady Brownrigg, visited Trincomalé, Eheylepola and his armed retinue formed their principal escort of honor; and, at this very time, when the Governor was completely in that Chieftain's power, (and if his plans had been a little nearer maturity, there can scarcely exist a doubt but that he would have availed himself of that power,) Mr. William Tolfrey of the Civil Service, who had succeeded Mr. D'Oyley as Chief Singhalese Translator to Government, was daily receiving anonymous but friendly *Olas* from loyal natives of the interior, of the projected rebellion, and the Governor's danger, through the intended treachery of Eheylepola. But although Mr. Tolfrey forthwith communicated his fears to the Deputy Secretary, and laid before him the anonymous grounds for entertaining them, the intimations were treated with the contempt they would have deserved in private life, but not equally so in political matters, as fabrications, by way of a hoax; and Mr. Tolfrey himself was thought scarcely less than a lunatic for viewing them in a more serious light; but his original impression was daily strengthened by reiterated cautions from the interior; and, fortunately, in the interim, the Governor had himself received timely warnings of the danger that awaited him.

The absolute disregard of Mr. Tolfrey's communications by the official Head of the Secret and Political Department, had a fatal effect, and involved a serious loss to the Public Service, of which, he was an old, zealous, and efficient officer. Mr. Tolfrey had been for a long time occupied in translating the Scriptures into Singhalese, was constitutionally of a melancholy turn of mind, and the excitement, which had at first driven him to madness, ended in death.

The rebellion soon afterwards broke out extensively. It commenced by a partial display of insurrection by armed Veddahs, who murdered my esteemed friend Sylvester Douglas Wilson, Esq., with their arrows, whilst stooping to wash his face in a rivulet, to which he had advanced unarmed; and from that moment, every day brought intelligence of the revolt of province after province, till the whole kingdom was arrayed against us, except the Three Korles, Four Korles, Yattineura, Oudineura, and a part of Saffregam, adjoining the Kaltura, Galle, Matura, and Hambantotté districts.

A Pretender, a Malabar, and formerly a priest, was acknowledged as king; and the brother-in-law of Eheylepola, named Kappitipola, the Dessave of Ouva, made himself the conspicuous head of the rebellion. This man was joined by almost every Chief of note, except the First Adikar and a few others; but Eheylepola, and the Second Adikar, (Kappuwatté,) were the secret abettors of Kappitipola and his colleagues.

At one time, the position of our brave and veteran Governor, and his gallant little army, exhausted with fatigue, privation, and sickness, was extremely precarious; and if His Excellency's official reports of it were now before public review, they would show how much suffering and privation British officers and soldiers can cheerfully undergo for their country's honor.

Fortunately, dissentions among the rebels, and the opportune arrival of auxiliary troops from the Honorable East India Company's Presidencies of Bengal and Madras, soon altered the complexion of affairs; and Kappitipola and other Chiefs having been taken, and the relic restored to the Delada Malagawa, tranquillity was re-established in October, 1818.

It is invariably the first object of the Kandyans, in their attempts at rebellion, to possess themselves of the Delada. In 1817, notwithstanding the great care taken for its security, it was clandestinely removed by the priests connected with the incipient rebellion; and its subsequent recovery by our gallant troops was considered of far greater importance towards the restoration and maintenance of tranquillity than the capture of the rebel Chiefs; and in the last fruitless attempt at rebellion, in 1834, the first object of the disaffected was to possess themselves of the relic; but, fortunately for the peace of the interior, they were defeated, through the active and watchful energy of the Agent of Government, and fidelity of certain priests, whose appointments he had either himself conferred, or been instrumental in obtaining.

Medical officers in the field estimated the loss of the army, from casualties, (chiefly from disease,) at one fifth of the whole; and that of the rebels from ten to fifteen thousand. Kappitipola and another Chief were beheaded, and the arch rebel Pilamé Talawé* banished to the Mauritius. The Kandyans never came to open action, but resorted to every possible mode of harassing our troops, and showed considerable tact in Guerilla warfare.

* This Chief was the son of the old traitor Pilamé Talawé, the chief actor in the massacre of our troops in 1803, who was subsequently hanged for treason in 1812.

The Governor, who had never relinquished the command during the rebellion, having re-established (as the result of 25 years' experience, with very trifling exceptions, has proved) permanent tranquillity in the interior, returned to Colombo, where he was received with the highest honors that every class and caste could show to the Pacificator of Kandy.

Although it is not generally known in this country, scarcely eight years have elapsed since an attempt was in contemplation to murder the Governor, the Agent of Government, and indeed every European, and to fire the bridge of Paradenia during the flooding of the Mavali-Ganga, with a view to cut off a retreat from Kandy! That such an attempt would have failed in the *grand* point, there is scarcely a doubt, but much injury and bloodshed must have ensued, had the warning of friendly priests been disregarded; and, so far, the system of paying a certain number may have been good policy, and the same system may have an equally potent effect, if tried upon the Roman Catholic priesthood elsewhere.

History has recorded so many instances of the worse than Punic faith of the native Princes of India, that it is almost incredible how any British officer can expect the observance of it, on their part, for a moment longer than it may suit the convenience of such a faithless race; and the Kandyan Chiefs of the present day are not at all worthier of confidence than they were in 1803, for they can no more change their cat-like nature than the leopard its spots; and the Kandyan of that date will prove himself to be the Kandyan still, if ever a favorable opportunity present itself.*

Various were the grounds assigned for the rebellion of 1817; amongst others, that it had originated in a misunderstanding, or ignorance, of the ranks and customs of the people of the two countries; and that our soldiers, being strangers to the language, and to the courtesies due to, and expected by, the Kandyan Chiefs, and Buddhist priesthood, (whose saffron-colored robes and shaven heads they regarded with contempt and ridicule,) had passed both these high ranks without *deigning* to pay the slightest respect to either.

This feeling of offended dignity was increased by the general *hauteur* of the conquerors towards the conquered; and the Chiefs failed not to urge this on the people

* "The Kandyans again begin to make a disturbance. They intend, I hear, to begin from Badulla and Veddah Ratté: in the latter place, more than 4000 Veddahs are collected with bows and arrows; within a week, the Kandyans have purchased 300 guns from the bazaar here; a native proctor in Kandy left his house some days ago, saying that his brother is sick at Madawaletenné, but instead of going to his country, he went to another direction, supposed to join them; most part of the low country people have left the place."—*Kandy, 15th March, 1842. Ceylon Herald.*

until the feeling burst out into absolute rebellion. Infringement upon the honors of the former, led to disgust on the part of the latter, who are naturally fond of official pomp and splendour, which, from time immemorial, they have been accustomed to associate with, and regard as inseparable from, the possession of authority and power.

It was but natural that our gallant soldiers, particularly of the 19th,* whose brave companions in arms, with others of the 23rd and 51st regiments, had been basely massacred at Wattépolowa, in 1803, whilst in full confidence that the terms of capitulation entered into by their commanding officer would have been strictly observed; and, moreover, recollecting that 120 of their comrades had been *basely murdered in their beds in the hospital,* should feel dissatisfied at Kandyan treachery having been so *slightly revenged.* The wonder is, that humanity so far prevailed with the 19th regiment as to allow the life of a single Kandyan to be spared; not that they could not *degrade* themselves by paying respect to Chiefs, known to have been *actors* in that dreadful tragedy.

The basis of the former Government of the Kandyans was the distribution of the lands and classification of the population, and consequently the Chiefs possessed all the power in regard to judicial and fiscal matters; and these were exempted from taxes for their own lands, in return for their services in superintending the public duties of the people in their respective provinces and districts, over whom, their influence was unbounded.

The Kandyans, or Ceylon Highlanders, a superior race of men to those of the lowlands, or maritime districts, are naturally hardy, capable of long abstinence and great fatigue, and very independent in their notions, since their chains fell off by the abolition of personal service in 1832; prior to which period, it must be confessed, that although the Chiefs themselves were for the most part exempted from the public burthens, the people had had grounds for discontent, from the incessant calls for their services and labour, (occasionally exceeding the duties which they had formerly been liable to under the Malabar dynasty,) and which had been enforced, regardless of the ancient customs of the country, or the claims and condition of individuals.—The Kandyan women, too, surpass in beauty and figure, their sisters of the maritime provinces.

As regards the arts and sciences among them, and their domestic habits and manners, they continue unchanged since the period that Captain Robert Knox wrote his plain-sailing and accurate account of them, in the year 1681. In some points, their agriculture is improving, by the force of English example, and the introduction of

* "WATTEPOLOWA" subsequently became their war cry in the execution of ample vengeance. The loss of the Kandyans, of from 10,000 to 15,000, between the commencement of the rebellion in 1817, and its termination in the following year, was some atonement to the *manes* of the officers and soldiers of the 19th, 23rd, and 51st regiments, massacred in Kandy in 1803.

useful exotics, particularly the potato, into general cultivation, and by the regular system of sugar planting originally introduced at Kondesalé,* about four miles from Kandy, on the opposite bank of the river, the scite of an ancient royal palace. It was here that the first arrack still, for supplying the troops, was established in 1816.

The mean daily variation of the temperature at Kandy is 6°, and the annual range of Fahrenheit's thermometer from 66° to 86°; the climate is quite delightful, and as healthy as any part of Europe; nevertheless, so great was the dread entertained by the Government Clerks and native Headmen of being employed in Kandy, and which had continued unabated from 1815 to 1820, that it became expedient for the Governor to issue the Minute of which a copy is subjoined,† as the best cure for *that* species of *Hambantotté fever*,‡ which generated skulking, when their services were most in request.

The Garrison of Kandy consists of the Head Quarters, and a few companies of a Regiment of the Line and of the Ceylon Rifle Corps, with a proportion of Artillery and Engineers.

The Ecclesiastical duties are discharged by a Colonial Chaplain, and the Judicial ones by a District Judge. Inferior District Judges are stationed at each of the other principal places in the province; namely, at Madawallatenné, Matellé, Badulla, and Neuwara Eliya, in the Eastern Circuit of the Supreme Court of Judicature.

The Revenue Department of this Province is superintended by an Agent of Government, who has an Assistant at each of the following places,—Kandy, Badulla, Malették, Madawallatenné, and Neuwara Eliya.

The citadel of Kandy, situate on One-tree Hill, communicates with Atgallé (a strong military post, about 8 miles from Kandy on the Trincomalé road, and beautifully situate on a commanding eminence) by signals; and, during the rebellion, it was of great importance. From Atgallé, the mountains of Hellemoetté are distinctly seen over

* See page 34.

† "Experience having shown, that although during the period of active operations in 1818, the troops employed in the interior became, from fatigues and privations, naturally subject to disease, yet that the climate of the Kandyan Provinces is in general as salubrious as that of the maritime districts, the Lieutenant Governor will no longer admit of any excuses from persons in the employ of Government, either as Clerks or native Headmen, whom he may promote to situations in the Kandyan Provinces, of which the pay has been fixed at higher rates than in the offices in the maritime districts, against proceeding forthwith on their appointment to the destination ordered, but such persons will be, in the event of refusing the office proposed, absolutely dismissed from any situation or rank they may have held, and be considered disqualified for further service under Government.—Heads of departments in the maritime provinces will explain this Minute distinctly to the Clerks and native Headmen employed under them, and its rules are to be considered equally applicable to the removal of the servants of Government from any one part of the island to another for the public advantage. *May 10th*, 1820."

‡ See page 291.

the Balané mountain, and the prospect, like the generality of Kandyan views, from the bold and romantic highlands over a beautiful and fertile country, where there is one perpetual spring and harvest, is worthy of the pencil, both of a Salvator Rosa, and of a Gaspar Poussin.

Atgalle was the third place where the culture of the potato, cabbage, cauliflower, and turnip, which had been introduced into Kandy and Badulla in 1815, was successful; but although the produce exceeded that of the latter places in size and quality, the potatos grown at Neuwara Eliya have proved superior in size and farinaceous properties to all others grown in the island. Excellent wheat was also grown at Atgallé so far back as 1816; and, when compared with a second supply of seed wheat from Bengal, was found to excel it both in weight and fineness.

As caste is no disqualification for the acquisition of landed property in Ceylon, where it is only liable to an assessment of one tenth of the produce, while those on the Indian Peninsula are commonly assessed at one third or one half, surely there is ample inducement for the agricultural classes of the Malabar and Coromandel coasts to become settlers in the island; and capitalists might employ their money advantageously in the repair of tanks, by which immense tracts of excellent but now waste lands would be reclaimed and rendered productive. At present, the high rates of Indian assessment are rigorously imposed; but the landholders are at full liberty to make the most of their labour, in the best market that offers.

In regard to Rest-Houses, the only accounts published of the roads being the few pages devoted to that purpose in the Ceylon Calendar, are calculated to mislead the traveller; and I have myself been much annoyed at finding mere sheds, scarcely fit to lodge one's horse, which are therein styled "Rest-Houses;" and once in particular, at Kornegalle, where the Agent of Government had actually transformed the Rest-House for travellers into a stable for his own horses. Until the Government shall have taken this matter into its favorable consideration, the temporary Rest-Houses in several places of the Interior, and Northern and Eastern Provinces, will be constantly exposed to destruction by white ants, and the places mentioned in the Calendar be known only by the site they previously occupied.

The plan I adopted in the Mahagampattoo district, might be made general with advantage to the public; and that was, for the Headmen of the villages adjoining rest-houses, to report their condition every week, and thus, by timely care, dilapidation was prevented, at a very trifling cost to the public.

Iron, alum, and saltpetre are found in this province; and Dr. Davy enumerates twenty two places in the island which are famous for nitric caves.

The beneficial effects arising from the Kandyan territories, have already proved their importance, and justified the sacrifices which were necessarily made to retain possession of them; and it may be anticipated, that a vigilant and enlightened Government will rapidly develope their resources, and amply prove, that without the command of the interior, Ceylon could never have been a colony either valuable or safe.

Having already suggested* the formation of a central agricultural and grazing farm, by way of a model to Kandyan farmers, I strongly recommend the establishment of another at Neuwara Eliya, for salting and curing provisions for the maritime provinces, and for supplying the Royal Navy in the Indian seas, and merchant ships touching at Ceylon.

The superficies of the Central Province is 3016 square miles, and the population, agreeably to the Census taken in 1835, was 164,411, making the average number to the square mile, 54.51; viz.

	MALES.	FEMALES.	TOTAL.
Whites, including Military and their families	900	304	1,204
Free Blacks, ditto ditto	85,822	72,170	157,992
Slaves	687	694	1381
Aliens and resident strangers	......	......	3834
			164,411

Of these, there were employed in agriculture, 84,727; in manufactures, 3931; and in commerce, 8531. The marriages, in the year 1835, were 1841; births, 2508; and deaths, 1598; leaving a surplus in favor of the population of the province, of 910.

We have now the whole of this magnificent country in our possession, and secure, as far as human foresight can anticipate, by splendid military roads, and, let us hope, an adequate defensive force. But whilst we continue ever watchful against Kandvan duplicity, treachery, and stratagem, our chief reliance should be upon that *moral* power which is the strongest and firmest support of empire; and our soundest policy, that which is founded upon humanity and justice towards all, whom the accident of conquest, country, or color, may have made our dependants. These, co-existing and co-operating with education and religious toleration, the encouragement of the arts and sciences, the improvement of agriculture, and the gradual developement of the natural and great resources of this incomparable colony, will insure both the stability and perpetuity of the British Government.

* See pages 111, 177.

The rising generation of Kandyans, profiting by the benefits of education, may, in time, lose the treacherous characteristics of their forefathers, as the wild orange tree loses its spines by cultivation; and, upon contrasting their own happy lot, under a benign, just, and merciful sovereign, with that of their ancestors under a race of sanguinary Malabar despots, with whom, unproved suspicion usurped the place of fair trial, the fiat of the sovereign condemned to death instead of the decision of justice, and a bold contempt of every just and moral principle set at naught every public duty, dispensed with the necessity of accusation, and chose helpless and innocent women, uncharged with the least offence, and infants incapable of crime, for their victims, rejoice in the blessings they enjoy and can bequeath to their posterity, confident that they are as imperishable as the power which confers them, and are wholly exempt from their former precarious condition, when even a temporary change could only be hoped for at the risk of rebellion, and all the dreadful consequences of civil war.

CORRIGENDA.

Page 34, line 4, *for* only could, *read* could only

45, 10, *for* is, *read* include

58, 23, *for* Gri, *read* Gre

60, 14, *for* 1815, *read* 1814

62, 19, *for* to belong to, *read* or belong to

64, 79, *for* and deputy inspector at £84 10*s*. &c., *read* in addition to other emoluments of £84 10*s*

78, 21, *for* precipitate, *read* precipitant

117, 17, *for* lactera, *read* Cachew

228, 25, *for* which river separates this part of the Northern from the Eastern Province, *read* which river intersects the northernmost part of the Eastern Province

258, 32, *for* during my residence in the island, *read* ; but, although, during my residence in the island, no European officers were killed, several had very narrow escapes, &c. &c.

274 10, *for* incubation, *read* laying

APPENDIX.

THE CHARTER OF JUSTICE,

Referred to in pages 52, 53.

WILLIAM the FOURTH, by the grace of God, of the United Kingdom of Great Britain and Ireland King, Defender of the Faith, to all to whom these presents shall come, Greeting.

Recital of Letters Patent.

1. WHEREAS his late majesty King George the Third, by three several Charters and Letters Patent under the Great Seal of the United Kingdom of Great Britain and Ireland, bearing date respectively at Westminster the eighteenth day of April in the year of our Lord one thousand eight hundred and one, the sixth day of August in the year of our Lord one thousand eight hundred and ten, and the thirtieth day of October in the year of our Lord one thousand eight hundred and eleven, did establish within his said late Majesty's Settlements of the island of Ceylon and the Territories and Dependencies thereof a certain Court called the Supreme Court of Judicature in the island of Ceylon, and a certain other Court called the High Court of Appeal in the island of Ceylon, and did make certain other provisions for the due administration of justice in the said Settlements, Territories, and Dependencies.

And annexation of the Kandyan Provinces.

And whereas since the day on which the last of the said several Charters and Letters Patent bears date, a certain Territory in the interior of the said island of Ceylon, called the Kingdom of Kandy, or the Kandyan Provinces of the island of Ceylon, hath become and now is subject to His Majesty, whereby the whole island of Ceylon with its Dependencies has become and now is part of His Majesty's dominions.

And of Power reserved in the former Charters for repealing them.

And whereas it is provided by each and every of the said several Charters and Letters Patent that nothing therein respectively contained, or any Act which should be done under the authority thereof respectively, should extend or be deemed or construed to extend to prevent his said late Majesty his Heirs and Successors from making such further or other provision for the administration of justice throughout the said Settlements and Territories in the said island of Ceylon with their Dependencies, at his and their will and pleasure and as circumstances might require, his said late Majesty meaning and intending fully and absolutely and to all intents and purposes whatsoever to reserve to Himself his Heirs and Successors such and the same rights and powers in and over the said Settlements, Territories, and Dependencies, and every part thereof, and especially touching the administration of justice therein, and all other matters and things in and by the said several Charters and Letters Patent provided for, as if the said several Charters and Letters Patent had not been made, any thing therein contained or any Law Custom Usage matter or thing whatsoever to the contrary in anywise notwithstanding. And whereas it is expedient to make more general and more effectual provision for the administration of justice in the said Island and its Dependencies. Now know ye that We, upon full consideration of the premises and of our certain knowledge and mere motion, have thought fit to revoke and annul, And We hereby revoke and annul each and every of the said Charters and Letters Patent, such revocation to take effect at and from after the time when (as hereinafter mentioned) this our Charter will come into operation in our said Island.

Necessity for a new Charter.

Old Charters repealed.

Recital of subordinate Courts.

2. And whereas in the several Districts and Provinces of the said Island there now are several Courts appointed to administer justice by the exercise of Original Jurisdiction to the inhabitants of the said Districts and Provinces. known respectively by the names and titles of the Provincial Courts, the Courts of the Sitting Magistrates, the Court of the Judicial Commissioner, the Court of the Judicial Agent, the Courts of the Agents of Government, the Revenue Courts, and the Court of the Sitting Magistrate of the Mahabadde, And whereas such Courts differ among themselves in respect of their constitution, of their rules of procedure, and of the kinds and degrees of the jurisdictions which they exercise within the limits of their respective Districts or Provinces, Now know ye that We, upon full consideration of the premises, have thought fit to direct ordain and appoint that the said Provincial Courts, the said Courts of the Sitting Magistrates, the said Court of the Judicial Commissioner, the said Court of the Judicial Agent, the said Courts of the Agents of Government, the said Revenue Courts, and the said Court of the Sitting Magistrate of the Mahabadde, shall be and the same are hereby respectively abolished, such abolition to take effect at and from after the time when (as hereinafter mentioned) this our Charter will come into operation in our said Island.

Such Courts abolished.

Reciting Courts of Appellate Jurisdiction.

3. And whereas the Governor of our said Island for the time being and the said Court of the Judicial Commissioner have hitherto exercised an Appellate Jurisdiction for the administration of justice in certain cases arising in the Kandyan Provinces of our said Island, And whereas certain Courts called the Minor Courts of Appeal, and certain Courts called the Minor Courts of Appeal from Revenue Cases, have hitherto exercised an Appellate Jurisdiction for the administration of justice in certain cases arising in the Maritime Provinces of the said Island, And whereas the existence of several independent Appellate Judicatures in the said Island tends to introduce uncertainty into the administration of justice

Uncertainty thence arising.

Abolition of such Appellate Courts.

there, Now know ye that We, upon full consideration of the premises, have thought fit to direct and ordain and do hereby direct and ordain that the said Appellate Jurisdictions of the Governor of the said Island, and of the said Court of the Judicial Commissioner respectively, shall be and the same are hereby respectively abolished, and that the said Minor Courts of Appeal and the said Minor Courts of Appeal for Revenue Cases, and such their Appellate Jurisdiction, shall be and the same are hereby abolished.

The Courts hereby erected, to have an exclusive jurisdiction.

Saving the Rights of the Court of Vice Admiralty and the Piracy Commission Court.

The Governor may not establish Courts.

Exception.

4. And to provide for the administration of justice hereafter in our said Island, our will and pleasure is, and We do hereby direct, that the entire Administration of Justice Civil and Criminal therein shall be vested exclusively in the Courts erected and constituted by this our Charter. And in such other Courts as may be holden within the said Island under any Commission issued or to be issued in pursuance of the Statutes in that case made and provided for the trial of offences committed on the seas, or within the jurisdiction of our Lord High Admiral, or the Commissioners for executing his office, or under any Commission issued or to be issued by our Lord High Admiral, or by the Commissioners for executing his office for the time being, And it is our pleasure and We hereby declare that it is not and shall not be competent to the Governor of our said Island, by any Law or Ordinance to be by him made with the advice of the Legislative Council thereof or otherwise howsoever, to constitute or establish any Court for the administration of justice in any case civil or criminal, save as hereinafter is expressly saved and provided, Provided nevertheless and We do hereby declare that nothing herein contained shall extend or be construed to extend to prevent any person from submitting their differences to the Arbitration of certain Assemblies of the inhabitants of villages known in our said Island by the name of Gangsabes.

Supreme Court established.

5. And We do hereby grant direct and appoint that there shall be within the said island of Ceylon one Supreme Court, which shall be called "The Supreme Court of the island of Ceylon."

To consist of a Chief Justice and two Puisne Judges.

Title of Chief Justice.

Judges how to be appointed.

6. And We do direct and appoint that the said Supreme Court of the island of Ceylon shall consist of and be holden by and before one Chief Justice and two Puisne Justices, And that the Chief Justice shall be called and known by the name and style of "The Chief Justice of the island of Ceylon," And that the said Chief Justice and Puisne Justices shall from time to time be nominated and appointed to such their offices by Letters Patent to be issued under the Public Seal of the said Island in pursuance of Warrants to be from time to time issued by Us, our Heirs and Successors, under our or their Sign Manual, and shall hold such their offices during the pleasure of Us, our Heirs and Successors.

7. And We do further direct and appoint that upon the death, resignation, sickness, or incapacity of the said Chief Justice or any of the said Puisne Justices, or in case of the absence of any of them from the said Island, or in case of any such suspension from office as hereinafter mentioned of any such Chief Justice or Puisne Justice, It shall and may be lawful to and for the Governor of our said Island for the time being by Letters Patent to be by him for that purpose made and issued under the Public Seal of the said Island, to nominate and appoint some fit and proper person or persons to act as and in the place and stead of any such Chief Justice or Puisne Justice so dying or resigning, or labouring under such sickness or incapacity as aforesaid, or being so absent as aforesaid from the said Colony, or being so suspended, until the vacancy or vacancies so created by any such death or resignation or sickness or incapacity or absence or suspension shall be supplied by a new appointment to be made in manner aforesaid, or until the Chief Justice or Puisne Justice so becoming sick or incapable, or being absent or suspended as aforesaid, shall resume such his office and enter into the discharge of the duties thereof.

The Governor may provisionally appoint Judges in cases of death, resignation, incapacity, absence, or suspension.

8. And whereas cases may arise in which it may seem necessary to our Governor for the time being of our said Island that a Judge of the said Court should be suspended from the exercise of his functions therein provisionally until Our pleasure can be known, And it is expedient that no such act of suspension should take place except upon the most evident necessity and after the most mature deliberation, And that in any such event the Judge who may be so suspended should receive the most early, complete, and authentic information of the grounds of such proceedings against him, We do therefore declare direct and appoint that it shall and may be lawful for the Governor of our said Island for the time being, by any Order or Orders to be by him for that purpose made and issued under the Public Seal of the said Island, with the advice and consent of the Executive Council of the said Island or the major part of them, upon proof of the misconduct or incapacity of any such Chief Justice or Puisne Justice as aforesaid, but not otherwise, to suspend him from such his office and from the discharge of the duties thereof, Provided that in every such case the said Governor shall immediately report for Our information through one of our Principal Secretaries of State the grounds and causes of such suspension, And provided also that a full statement be entered on the Minutes of the said Executive Council of the grounds of such proceeding and of the evidence upon which the same may be founded, a full copy of which minutes and evidence shall by such Governor be transmitted to such Judge, together with the Order suspending him from such his office, And We do hereby reserve to Us, our Heirs and Successors, with the advice of our or their Privy Council, full power and authority to confirm or to disallow any such suspension from office as aforesaid of any such Chief Justice or Puisne Justice.

The Governor when authorised to suspend a Judge.

Rules to be observed in such case.

Rank of the Chief Justice.

9. And We do hereby give and grant to our said Chief Justice for the time being rank and precedence above and before all our subjects whomsoever within the said Island and its Dependencies, excepting the Governor or Lieutenant-Governor for the time being thereof, and excepting such persons as by law or usage in England take place before our Chief Justice of our Court of King's Bench.

Rank of the Puisne Justices.

10. And We do hereby give and grant to the said Puisne Justices for the time being rank and precedence above and before all our subjects whomsoever within the said Island and its Dependencies, excepting the Governor or Lieutenant-Governor for the time being thereof, the said Chief Justice, and the Officer for the time being Commanding our Forces in the said Island and its Dependencies, and excepting such persons as by law or usage in England take place before our Puisne Justices of our Court of King's Bench, And We do hereby declare that the said Puisne Justices shall take rank and precedence between themselves according to the priority of their appointments respectively.

Supreme Court to have a Seal.

11. And We do further grant direct ordain and appoint that the said Supreme Court of the island of Ceylon shall have and use as occasion may require a Seal bearing a device and impression of our Royal Arms with an Exergue or Label surrounding the same with this inscription, "The Seal of the Supreme Court of the island of Ceylon," And that the said Seal shall be delivered to and shall be kept in the custody of the said Chief Justice, with full liberty to deliver the same to any Puisne Justice of the said Court for any temporary purpose, and in case of the vacancy of or suspension from the office of the Chief Justice, the same shall be delivered over to and kept in the custody of such person as shall be appointed by the said Governor of the said Island to act as and in the place and stead of the Chief Justice.

The custody of the Seal.

Judges incapable of holding other offices of profit.

12. And We do further direct and appoint that no such Chief Justice or Puisne Justice as aforesaid shall be capable of accepting taking or performing any other office, place of profit, or emolument within the said Island, on pain that the acceptance of such other office as aforesaid shall be ipso facto an avoidance of such his office of Chief Justice or Puisne Justice as the case may be, and the Salary thereof shall cease accordingly from the time of such acceptance of any other office or place, Provided nevertheless that no such Chief Justice or Puisne Justice shall be rendered incapable of holding his office or shall forfeit his Salary by accepting the office of Judge of the Court of Vice Admiralty in the said Island, or of Commissioner for the trial and adjudication of Prize Causes and other maritime questions arising in India.

Exception.

Appointment of the Judges by name.

13. And We do hereby constitute and appoint our trusty and wellbeloved Sir Charles Marshall, Knight, to be the first Chief Justice of the said Supreme

Court, and our trusty and wellbeloved William Rough, Esquire, Serjeant at Law, to be the senior Puisne Justice of the said Supreme Court, and our trusty and wellbeloved William Norris, Esquire, to be the second Puisne Justice of the said Supreme Court.

Ministerial Officers of the Court: their number how to be determined.

14. And We do hereby direct ordain appoint and declare that there shall be attached and belong to the said Court an Officer to be styled the Register and Keeper of Records of the said Court, and such and so many other Officers as to our Chief Justice of the said Court for the time being from time to time appear to be necessary for the administration of justice and the due execution of the powers and authorities which are granted and committed to the said Court by these our Letters Patent, Provided nevertheless that no office shall be created in the said Court unless the Governor of the said Island for the time being shall first signify his approbation thereof to the said Chief Justice for the time being in writing under the hand of such Governor.

Ministerial Officers how to be appointed.

The Judges to appoint their own Private Secretaries.

15. And We do further direct and declare our will to be that all the subordinate Officers of the said Court shall be appointed to such their offices by Us, or by the Governor of the said Island on our behalf by Commissions to be for that purpose used under the Public Seal of the said Island, Provided nevertheless that all persons who shall be attached to or hold any office in the said Court as Clerk or Private Secretary to any of the Judges thereof shall be appointed to such office by the Judge for the time being whom such person may so serve in any such capacity.

Subordinate Officers to hold during pleasure of the King, but liable to suspension by the Court.

16. And We do further direct and appoint that the several Officers of the said Supreme Court shall hold their respective offices during the pleasure of Us, our Heirs and Successors, and shall be subject to be suspended from their offices therein by the said Court for misconduct or other sufficient cause.

Admission of Advocates and Proctors.

17. And We do hereby authorise and empower the said Supreme Court to admit and enrol as Advocates or Proctors in the said Supreme Court all such persons, being of good repute, as shall upon examination by one or more of the said Justices of the said Supreme Court appear to be of competent knowledge and ability, Provided always that whenever the said Supreme Court shall refuse to admit and enrol any person applying to be admitted and enrolled as an Advocate or Proctor in the said Supreme Court, the Judges of the said Court shall in open Court assign and declare the reasons of refusal. And We do direct and declare that no person whatsoever not so admitted and enrolled as aforesaid shall be allowed to appear, plead, or act in the said Supreme Court for or on behalf of any other person being a Suitor in the said Court.

No person not so admitted capable of acting as such.

The Island to be divided into three Circuits.

Their limits described.

18. And We do further declare our pleasure to be, and do hereby ordain and appoint, that for the purpose of the administration of justice under this our Charter, the said island of Ceylon shall be divided into the District of Colombo, and three Circuits to be called respectively the Northern Circuit, the Southern Circuit, and the Eastern Circuit, and that the said Northern Circuit shall comprize the District of Jaffna together with the several Districts which are parcel of the Maritime Provinces of the said Island and which lie to the westward of the Kandyan Provinces of the said Island between the said District of Jaffna and the District of Colombo, and that the said Southern Circuit shall cor prize the District of the Mahagampattoo and all the Districts parcel of the Maritime Provinces of the said Island lying to the westward and southward of the Kandyan Provinces of the said Island between the District of the Mahagampattoo and the District of Colombo, and that the said Eastern Circuit shall comprize all the Kandyan Provinces of the said Island and all the Districts parcel of the Maritime Provinces of the said Island lying to the eastward of the Kandyan Provinces of the said Island between the District of Jaffna and the District of Mahagampattoo, Provided nevertheless that it shall be lawful for the Governor for the time being of our said Island, on any application to him for that purpose made in writing under the hands of the Judges for the time being of the said Supreme Court or the major part of them, but not otherwise, by any Proclamation or Proclamations to be from time to time for that purpose issued, to alter as occasion may require the beforementioned division of the said Island as aforesaid and to establish any other division or divisions thereof for that purpose which may appear to the said Governor and the whole or the major part of such Judges more conducive to the public convenience and the effective administration of justice in the said Island.

The Governor on application from the Judges may by Proclamation alter such limits.

The Governor may subdivide the Circuits into Districts.

19. And We hereby authorise and require the Governor for the time being of our said Island with the concurrence of the Judges of the said Supreme Court or the major part of them, but not otherwise, by any Proclamation or Proclamations to be by him for that purpose from time to time issued, to subdivide into Districts each of the Circuits into which the said Island, exclusive of the District of Colombo, is or shall be in manner aforesaid divided, and from time to time with the like concurrence but not otherwise to revoke alter and amend any such Proclamation or Proclamations as occasion may require, and which appointment of the said Circuits and Districts shall be made in such a manner as may best consist with and promote the prompt and effectual administration of justice therein as hereinafter mentioned. Provided always that until the said Circuits shall in manner aforesaid be divided into Districts in pursuance of this our Charter, the existing divisions of our said Island comprized within the respective limits of the said Circuits respectively shall for the purposes hereof be deemed and taken to be such Districts as aforesaid.

Existing Divisions to remain for the present.

District Courts established.

20. And We do further grant direct and appoint that within each and every District of the said Island there shall be one Court to be called the District Court of such District, and that every such District Court shall be holden by and before one Judge to be called the District Judge and three Assessors, And that every such District Judge shall be appointed to such his office by Letters Patent to be for that purpose issued under the Public Seal of the said Island by the Governor thereof for the time being in pursuance of Warrants to be for that purpose addressed to him by Us, our Heirs and Successors, Provided that such Governor may and he is hereby authorized and required to issue such Letters Patent as aforesaid provisionally and subject to the future signification of the pleasure of Us, our Heirs and Successors, and without any such Warrant or Warrants as aforesaid on any occasions on which it may be necessary to make any such appointment or appointments before the pleasure of Us, our Heirs and Successors can be known. And We do hereby declare that the said District Judges respectively shall hold such their offices during the pleasure of Us, our Heirs and Successors.

District Judges how to be appointed.

District Judges to hold during pleasure.

Assessors how to be chosen.

21. And We do further direct and appoint that the before mentioned Assessors shall be selected from amongst our subjects inhabiting the said Island, whether natives thereof or otherwise, and being respectively men of the full age of twenty-one years and upwards, and possessing such qualifications as shall from time to time be determined by any Rules and Orders of Court to be made in the manner hereinafter mentioned, and not having been convicted of any infamous crime, nor labouring under any such bodily or mental incapacity as would render them unfit for the discharge of that office. And We do hereby reserve to Ourselves, our Heirs and Successors, the right of appointing in each of the said District Courts one person to act as a Permanent Assessor, but in respect of all Assessors until any such appointment shall be made and after any such appointment shall be made in respect of all Assessors not so appointed, it is our pleasure and We do hereby direct and declare that they shall be selected, summoned, and required to serve in the said office in such manner as shall be provided by such Rules and Orders of Court as are hereinbefore particularly mentioned.

Right of appointing a permanent Assessor in each District reserved.

Assessors to be chosen and summoned as before mentioned.

Appointment of subordinate Officers of District Courts.

22. And We do hereby further direct that the Ministerial and other Subordinate Officers of the said District Courts respectively shall respectively be appointed to and shall hold such their offices therein in such and the like manner in every respect as is hereinbefore provided with regard to the Ministerial and other Officers of the said Supreme Court, And that the admission and enrolment of persons to appear, plead, or act in any of the said District Courts as Advocates or Proctors shall be regulated and provided for by such general Rules and Orders of Court as are hereinafter mentioned.

Admission of Advocates and Proctors in District Courts.

Supreme Court to be held at Colombo. Except for Circuits. District Courts to be holden at places to be appointed by the Governor.

23. And We do further direct and appoint that the said Supreme Court shall be holden at Colombo in the said Island, Excepting for the purpose of such Circuits as are hereinafter mentioned, And that every such District Court as aforesaid shall be holden at such convenient place within every such District as the Governor for the time being of our said Island shall from time to time for that purpose appoint by any Proclamation or Proclamations to be by him in manner aforesaid issued for such division as aforesaid of the said Island into Districts.

Civil Jurisdiction of District Courts.

24. And We do further grant direct and appoint that each of the said District Courts shall be a Court of Civil Jurisdiction and shall have cognizance of and full power to hear and determine all pleas suits and actions in which the party or parties Defendant shall be resident within the District in which any such suit or action shall be brought or in which the act matter or thing in respect of which any such suit or action shall be brought shall have been done or performed within such District, Provided nevertheless that no such District Court as aforesaid shall be competent to hold Jurisdiction of or to hear or to determine any cause suit or action wherein the Judge of such Court shall himself be a party Plaintiff or Defendant, but that every cause suit or action which according to the provisions aforesaid would have been cognizable in any District Court if the Judge of such Court had not been a party thereto shall in that case be cognizable in the Court of any District immediately adjoining.

If the District Judge be a Party, the Court of the next adjoining District shall have cognizance of the cause.

Criminal Jurisdiction of Distrit Courts.

25. And We do further grant direct and appoint that each of the said District Courts shall be a Court of Criminal Jurisdiction and shall have full power and authority to enquire of all crimes and offences committed wholly or in part within the District to which such Court may belong and to hear try and determine all prosecutions which shall be commenced against any person or persons for or in respect of any such crimes or offences or alleged crimes or offences, Provided always that such Criminal Jurisdiction as aforesaid shall not extend to any case in which the person or persons accused shall be charged with any crime which according to any Law now or hereafter to be enforced within our said Island shall be punishable with death or transportation or banishment or imprisonment for more than twelve calendar months or by whipping exceeding one hundred lashes or by fine exceeding ten pounds.

District Courts to have the custody of Persons and Estates of Lunatics within the District.

26. And We do further grant direct and appoint that each of the said District Courts shall have the care and custody of the Persons and Estates of all Idiots and Lunatics and others of insane or nonsane mind resident within such Districts respectively with full power to appoint Guardians and Curators of all such Persons and their Estates and to make order for the

maintenance of such Persons and the proper management of their Estates and to take proper Securities for such management from such Guardians and Curators and to call them to account and to charge them with any Balance which may be due to any such Persons as aforesaid or to their Estates and to enforce the payment thereof and to take order for the secure Investment of any such Balances, and such Guardians and Curators from time to time to remove and replace as occasion may require.

District Courts to appoint Administrators to the Estates of Intestates.

And to adjudicate on the validity of Wills.

And to grant Probate.

And to appoint Administrators.

27. And We do further give and grant to the said District Courts respectively in their said respective Districts full power and authority to appoint Administrators of the Estates and Effects of any persons dying within such respective Districts Intestate or who may not have by any Last Will or Testament appointed any Executors or Trustees for the administration or execution thereof, And like power and authority to enquire into and determine upon the validity of any document or documents adduced before them as and for the Last Will and Testament of any person who may have died within such Districts respectively and to record the same and to grant Probate thereof with like power and authority to appoint Administrators for the administration or execution of the trusts of any such Last Will or Testament as aforesaid in cases where the Executors or Trustees thereby appointed shall not appear and take out Probate thereof or having appeared and taken out such Probate shall by death or otherwise become incapable to carry any such trusts fully into execution. And We do further authorise and empower the said District Courts in their said respective Districts to take proper Securities from all Executors and Administrators of the Last Wills and Testaments of any deceased persons or of the Estates and Effects of any persons who may have died Intestate for the faithful performance of such trusts and for the proper accounting to such Courts respectively for what may come to their hands or be by them expended in the execution thereof with like power and authority to call all such Executors and Administrators to account and to charge them with any Balances which may be due to the Estates of any such deceased persons and to enforce the payment thereof and to take order for the secure Investment of any such Balances, and such Executors and Administrators from time to time to remove and replace as occasion may require.

And to take Securities from Executors and Administrators.

And to call them to account, and enforce the payment of or take security for Balances.

And to remove and replace Executors & Administrators.

28. And whereas doubts might arise whether by virtue of the provisions aforesaid and without an express authority in that behalf the said District Courts would be competent to entertain Suits therein brought for the protection of our Revenue and for the punishment of offences committed against the Revenue Laws of our said Island, Now therefore for the removal of any such doubts We do hereby expressly declare that all causes affecting our Revenue arising within our said Island and all

District Courts to take cognizance of all Revenue Cases.

prosecutions for the punishment of offences committed against the Revenue Laws thereof shall be cognizable within the said District Courts respectively in such and the same manner as any other suits or prosecutions, Saving nevertheless and reserving to all Courts of Vice Admiralty established or to be established within our said Island all such rights powers jurisdictions and authority as are by Law vested in them as fully as if this our Charter had not been made. Provided nevertheless that no such prosecution for any offence committed against the Revenue Laws shall be cognizable within any such District Court in cases where the punishment may be of greater degree or amount than such District Court can under the provisions aforesaid award upon prosecutions for any other offences.

Saving the rights of the Courts of Vice Admiralty.

Limitation of Jurisdiction in such cases.

Jurisdiction of District Courts to be exclusive.

29. And We do further grant and declare that the several Jurisdictions so vested as aforesaid in the said District Courts is and shall be an exclusive Jurisdiction and shall not on any plea or pretext whatsoever be assumed or exercised by any other Court Tribunal or Judge within our said Island, Save and except in so far as cognizance of the same suits causes actions prosecutions matters and things is hereinafter expressly given by way of Appeal to the Supreme Court aforesaid or to the respective Judges thereof, And also save and except in so far as an Original Jurisdiction in certain suits causes actions prosecutions matters and things is hereinafter vested in the said Supreme Court or in the Judges thereof, And also save and except in as far as respects the Jurisdiction of the Court of Vice Admiralty in the said Island.

Exceptions.

Judgments of District Courts how to be pronounced.

30. And We do further direct and appoint that every final Sentence or Judgment of the said District Courts respectively and that every interlocutory Order of the said Courts having the effect of a final Sentence or Judgment and that every Order of any such Court having the effect of postponing the final decision of any cause or prosecution there pending and any other Order which to the Judge of any such Court may appear of adequate importance shall by such Judge be pronounced in open Court, And that such Judge shall in all such cases state in the presence and hearing of the Assessors before mentioned what are the Questions of Law and of Fact which have arisen for Adjudication and which are to be decided upon any such occasion together with his Opinion upon every such Question with the grounds and reasons of every such Opinion. And that every such Assessor shall also in open Court and in the presence and hearing of the Judge and the other Assessors declare his Opinion and deliver his Vote upon each and every Question which the Judge shall have previously declared to have arisen for Adjudication whether such Questions shall relate to any matter of Law or any matter of Fact, Provided nevertheless that in case of any difference of Opinion between any such Judge and the majority or the whole of such Assessors upon any Question of Law or of Fact depending before any such District Court the Opinion of such Judge

Assessors to give their opinions and votes.

In case of a difference of opinion, that of the Judge to prevail.

b 2

shall prevail and shall be taken as the Sentence Judgment or Order of the whole Court, But in every such case a Record shall be made and preserved among the Records of the said Court of the Questions declared by the Judge to have arisen for Adjudication and of the Vote of such Judge and of every such Assessor upon each such Question.

But Record to be made of Questions and Votes.

Appellate Jurisdiction of Supreme Court.

31. And We do hereby grant declare direct and appoint that the Supreme Court of the island of Ceylon shall be a Court of Appellate Jurisdiction for the correction of all Errors in Fact or in Law which shall be committed by the said respective District Courts and shall have sole and exclusive cognizance by way of Appeal of all causes suits actions prosecutions matters and things of which such District Courts may in pursuance of the provisions of this our Charter or any of them take cognizance by way of Original Jurisdiction. And We do further grant to the said Supreme Court power jurisdiction and authority to hold an Original Jurisdiction for enquiring of all crimes and offences committed throughout the said Island and for the hearing trying and determining all prosecutions which shall be commenced against any person or persons for or in respect of any such crimes or offences or alleged crimes or offences. And to provide for the due execution of the powers and authorities and jurisdictions so vested as aforesaid in the said Supreme Court it is Our further pleasure and We do direct ordain and appoint that Civil and Criminal Sessions of the said Supreme Court shall be holden by some one of the Judges thereof in each of the Circuits into which our said Island is or shall be so divided as aforesaid.

Original Jurisdiction of Supreme Court.

Civil and Criminal Sessions of the Supreme Court how to be holden.

Such Sessions to be holden twice a year in each Circuit.

32. And We do further direct and appoint that such Sessions as aforesaid of the said Supreme Court shall be holden twice in each year within the Northern Southern and Eastern Circuits of the said Island respectively hereinbefore described or referred to at such places within such respective Circuits and at such particular times in each year as the Governor for the time being of our said Island shall after previous consultation with the Judges of the said Supreme Court by Proclamations to be by him from time to time for that purpose issued direct and appoint, Provided always that the times and places for holding such Civil and Criminal Sessions of the said Supreme Court on such Circuits shall be so arranged as that all the Judges of the said Supreme Court shall never at the same time be absent from Colombo, and that all such Judges shall be resident at the same time at Colombo not less than one month twice in each year. And We do direct and appoint that the Chief Justice of the said Court shall first choose the Circuit on which he will proceed for the purposes aforesaid and that the second choice shall be made by the Senior Puisne Judge for the time being.

At times and places to be appointed by the Governor, in consultation with the Judges.

Choice of Circuits by the Judges.

At Civil Sessions of Supreme Court, Assessors to be associated with the Judge.

At the Criminal Sessions thirteen Jurors.

33. And We do further direct ordain and appoint that at every Civil Sessions of the Supreme Court to be holden on any such Circuit as aforesaid three Assessors shall be associated with the Judge, And that every Criminal Sessions of the Supreme Court to be holden on any such Circuit shall be holden before such Judge and a Jury of thirteen Men, which Assessors and Jurors shall be selected summoned and required to appear and serve in such manner and form as shall be provided by such general Rules and Orders of Court as hereinafter mentioned.

Appellate & Original Jurisdiction of the Supreme Court how to be exercised on Circuit.

34. And We do will ordain and appoint that within each and every of the said Circuits respectively all and every the Appellate Powers Jurisdictions and Authorities hereby vested in the said Supreme Court shall be exercised by the Judge for the time being of such Circuit and the Assessors so to be associated with him as aforesaid, And that within each and every of the said Circuits respectively all and every the Original Powers Jurisdictions and Authorities hereby vested in the said Supreme Court shall be exercised by the Judge for the time being of such Circuit who upon the trial of any crimes made cognizable by the said Supreme Court by way of such Original Jurisdiction as aforesaid shall be associated with such Jurors as aforesaid.

At Civil Sessions the Court to hear all Appeals from District Courts of the Circuit.

With power to remand Causes for further hearing or new Evidence.

New Evidence may be admitted or rejected by the Court at such Sessions.

35. And We do further direct and appoint that at every Civil Sessions of the said Supreme Court so to be holden as aforesaid on every such Circuit the said Court shall proceed to hear and determine all Appeals which may be then depending from any sentence judgment decree or order of any District Court within the limits of any such Circuit and to affirm reverse correct alter and vary every such sentence judgment decree or order according to Law, and if necessary to remand to the District Court for a further hearing or for the admission of any further Evidence any cause suit or action in which any such Appeal as aforesaid shall have been brought, And upon hearing every such Appeal it shall also be competent to the said Supreme Court to receive and admit or to exclude and reject new Evidence touching the matters at issue in any such original cause suit or action as Justice may require.

With power to grant Prohibitions, &c. to the District Courts of the Circuit, and to transfer causes from one District Court to another.

36. And We do further direct and appoint that the Supreme Court aforesaid at any Civil Sessions to be holden on any such Circuit as aforesaid shall have full power and authority to grant and issue Mandates in the nature of Writs of Mandamus Procedendo and Prohibition against any District Court within the limits of such Circuit and to make order for the transfer of any cause suit or action depending in any one District Court in such Circuit to any other District Court within the same Circuit if it shall be made to appear

to the satisfaction of the said Supreme Court at any such Civil Sessions as aforesaid that there is any sufficient cause or reason to conclude that in such particular cause suit or action Justice would not probably be done in the District Court in which the same had so been commenced, And in every such case the District Court to which any such cause suit or action shall be so traneferred shall take cognizance thereof and have Power and Jurisdiction for the hearing trial and decision of the same as fully and effectually to all intents and purposes as the District Court in which the same was originally brought could or might have had.

Form of proceeding at Civil Sessions of Supreme Court.

37. And We do further direct declare and appoint that the Judge of the Supreme Court holding any such Civil Sessions thereof as aforesaid on any such Circuit shall in open Court state and declare in the presence and hearing of the Assessors beforementioned what are the Questions of Law and of Fact arising for Adjudication upon every Appeal brought before the said Supreme Court at such Sessions and which are then to be decided and shall then pronounce his Opinion upon every such Question with the grounds and reasons of every such Opinion, and that every such Assessor shall thereupon also in open Court and in the presence and hearing of such Judge and the other Assessors declare his Opinion and deliver his Vote upon such and every Question which the Judge shall have previously declared to have arisen for Adjudication whether such Question shall relate to any matter of Law or to any matter of Fact, And in case of any difference of Opinion between any such Judge and the majority or the whole of such Assessors upon any Question of Law or of Fact depending upon such Appeal the Opinion of such Judge shall prevail and shall be taken as the Sentence Judgment or Order of the whole Court, But in every such case a Record shall be made and preserved among the Records of the said Supreme Court of the Questions declared by the Judge to have arisen for Adjudication and of the Vote of such Judge and of every such Assessor upon every such Question.

At Criminal Sessions the Supreme Court to hear Appeals from Judgments of the District Courts in Criminal Cases.

And to receive or reject new Evidence.

38. And We do further direct ordain and appoint that at every Criminal Sessions of the said Supreme Court to be holden on any such Circuit as aforesaid such Court shall proceed to hear and determine all Appeals which may be then depending from any Sentence or Judgment pronounced by any District Court within the limits of any such Circuit in any criminal prosecution and to affirm reverse correct alter and vary every such Sentence and Judgment according to Law, And upon hearing every such Appeal it shall also be competent to the said Supreme Court to receive and admit or to exclude and reject new Evidence touching the matters at issue in any such original prosecution as Justice may require, And it shall also be lawful for the said Supreme Court at any such Criminal Sessions as aforesaid to make Order for the Transfer of any prosecution depending in any one District Court in such Circuit to any other District Court within the same Circuit if it shall be made to appear to the satisfaction of the said Supreme Court at any such Criminal Sessions as aforesaid that there is any sufficient cause or reason to

conclude that in such particular prosecutions Justice would not probably be done in the District Court in which the same had been so commenced, And in every such case the District Court to which any such prosecution shall be so transferred shall take cognizance thereof and shall have Power and Jurisdiction for the hearing trial and decision of the same as fully and effectually to all intents and purposes as the District Court in which the same was originally brought could or might have had.

Appeals in Criminal Cases.

39. And We do further declare and ordain that notwithstanding the right of Appeal hereby given from the Judgments and Sentences of the said District Courts upon such Criminal Prosecutions as aforesaid no such Appeal shall have the effect of staying the execution of any Sentence or Judgment pronounced by any such District Court upon any prosecution unless the Judge of such District Court shall in the exercise of his discretion see fit to make Order for the stay of any such execution pending such Appeal.

At Criminal Sessions Supreme Court to exercise its Original Jurisdiction.

40. And We do further direct ordain and appoint that at every Criminal Sessions of the said Supreme Court so to be holden as aforesaid on every such Circuit the said Supreme Court shall inquire of all crimes and offences committed within the Limits of any such Circuit for the trial of which such Original Jurisdiction as aforesaid is by this our Charter vested in the said Supreme Court and which the King's Advocate or Deputy King's Advocate shall elect to prosecute before such Supreme Court and shall hear try and determine all prosecutions which shall be commenced by the said King's Advocate or Deputy King's Advocate against any person or persons for or in respect of any such crimes or offences or alleged crimes or offences.

Offences to be prosecuted by Information in the name of the Advocate Fiscal.

Without a Grand Jury.

41. And We do further direct and ordain that all crimes and offences cognizable before any of the Courts constituted by these Presents or deriving authority from the same shall be prosecuted and that all fines penalties and forfeitures recoverable therein to Our use shall be sued for and recovered in the name of our Advocate Fiscal of our said Island and by him or by some Deputy Advocate Fiscal by an Information to be exhibited without the previous finding of any inquest by any Grand Jury or otherwise, Provided nevertheless that it shall be competent to the said Supreme Court by such Rules and Orders of Court as after mentioned to make any other and more convenient provision for the prosecuting before the said District Courts breaches of the peace petty assaults and other minor offences of the like nature.

Questions of Fact on Criminal Prosecutions at such Sessions how to be decided.

42. And We do further direct and ordain that all Questions of Fact upon which issue shall be joined at any such Criminal Sessions as aforesaid of the said Supreme Court on any such Circuit as aforesaid shall be decided by such Jury of thirteen Men as aforesaid, And that the Verdict of such Jury

shall be pronounced in open Court by the mouth of the Foreman, and that if such Jury shall not agree upon their Verdict then the Verdict of the major part of such Jury shall be received and taken as the Verdict of the Jury collectively.

All Questions of Law to be decided by the Judge.

43. And We do further direct and ordain that all Questions of Law which shall arise for Adjudication at any such Criminal Sessions as aforesaid of the said Supreme Court on any such Circuit as aforesaid shall be decided by the Judge presiding at such Sessions, who shall pronounce his Judgment thereupon in open Court and assign the grounds and reasons of such Judgment, Saving nevertheless to every such Judge the right of reserving such Questions for the decision of the Judges of the said Supreme Court collectively at their General Sessions in manner hereinafter mentioned.

Who may reserve them for the decision of the whole Court.

Sentence of death is to be respited till the Case has been reported to the Governor.

44. And We do further appoint declare and direct that in every case where any person shall be adjudged to die by any Sentence of the Supreme Court of our said Island at any such Criminal Sessions as aforesaid the execution of such Sentence shall be respited until the Case of such person shall have been reported by the Chief Justice or Puisne Justice who shall have presided at such trial to the Governor of the said Island for the time being which report shall be made as soon after the passing of such Sentence as conveniently may be.

The Judge at the Criminal Sessions is to issue a Mandate to all Jailors within the Circuits to return a Calendar of Prisoners.

45. And We do further appoint declare and direct that the Judge on any such Circuit as aforesaid holding the said Criminal Sessions of the said Supreme Court shall and may issue his Mandate under his Hand and directed to all and every of the Fiscals and other Keepers of Prisons within the Limits of his Circuit to certify to the said Judge the several persons then and there in any of their custody committed for and Charged with any crimes or offences whatsoever, And the said Fiscals or other Keepers of Prisons shall and are hereby required to make certify and transmit due Returns to such Mandate by specifying in a Calendar or List to be annexed to such Mandate respectively the time and times when all and every of the said persons so in their custody was or were committed and by whose authority particularly and on what charge or charges crime or crimes respectively in writing, And to the said List or Calendar shall also be annexed such Information or Informations upon oath as may have been taken against them or any of them and be then remaining in the hands of the said Fiscals or Keepers of Prisons or true copies thereof attached by the said Fiscals or Keepers of Prisons respectively, And if need be according to the tenor and exigency of such Mandate such Fiscals or Keepers of Prisons shall bring the said persons so

The contents of the Calendar.

The Informations on oath against any Prisoner to be attached to it.

The Jailors to bring Prisoners before the

Judge holding such Criminal Sessions. With the Witnesses whose Names may be endorsed on the Commitments.

in their custody or any of them before the said Judge wheresoever the said Judge shall then be holding the Criminal Sessions of the said Supreme Court Together with such Witness or Witnesses whose name or names shall appear to be written or endorsed on the respective Commitments by virtue of which such prisoners or prisoner were or was delivered into their custody respectively in order that such prisoners or prisoner may be dealt with according to Law, Provided always that wherever any party or parties shall after the making out of any such Calendar or List and while such Judge shall be holding the Criminal Sessions of the said Supreme Court in the town or place wherein such Calendar or List was delivered be apprehended or committed on any criminal charge it shall and may be lawful for the Officer of such Supreme Court to insert the name or names of such person or persons in such Calendar or List.

Proviso for the insertion in the Calendar of the Names of Persons committed during the Sessions.

The Judge at Colombo to hold the Civil and Criminal Sessions of the Supreme Court for that District.

46. And We do further direct declare and appoint that any Judge of the Supreme Court remaining at Colombo shall within the Limits of the District of Colombo exercise the same Jurisdiction and hold such and the same Civil and Criminal Sessions as the said Judges of the Supreme Court are by these Presents directed appointed and ordained to exercise and to hold on their respective Circuits within the Limits of their respective Circuits

Judge on Circuit or at Colombo may reserve Questions of Law, &c., for the whole Court in General Sessions.

47. And We do further ordain and appoint that whenever any Question of Law Pleading Evidence or Practice shall arise for Adjudication at any Civil or Criminal Sessions of the said Supreme Court at any such Circuit as aforesaid or within the said District of Colombo which shall appear to the Judge presiding at such Sessions to be a Question of doubt and difficulty it shall be lawful for such Judge to reserve such Question of Law Pleading Evidence or Practice for the decision of the Judges of the said Supreme Court collectively and to report any Question so reserved to the said Judges at some General Sessions of the said Supreme Court to be held for that purpose as hereinafter mentioned. And We do further direct and appoint that the Judges of the said Supreme Court shall from time to time as occasion may require collectively hold a General Sessions at Colombo to hear and inquire of any Questions of Law Pleading Evidence or Practice so reserved as aforesaid and to decide the same according to Law.

Judges to compare the Records of District Courts. If the practice vary, to prepare draft of

48. And We further authorize and require the respective Judges of the said Supreme Court on such Circuits as aforesaid and at the Sessions so to be holden for the District of Colombo to inspect and examine the Records of the different District Courts, And if it shall appear to them that contradictory or inconsistent decisions have been given by different District Courts

Laws on Questions of Law or Evidence, & Rules of Court on Pleading or practice.

or by the same District Court upon different occasions upon any matters of Law Evidence Pleading or Practice then and in every such case the said Judges of the Supreme Court shall report to the Judges of the Supreme Court at Colombo at such General Sessions as aforesaid any such contradictions or inconsistencies, And the said Judges of the Supreme Court shall after due consideration of the matters so brought before them prepare the draft of such a declaratory Law upon any matter of Law or Evidence in respect to which such contradictory or inconsistent decisions shall have been given as the occasion shall appear to them to require and shall transmit such draft under the Seal of the said Court to the Governor for the time being of our said Island who shall thereupon lay the draft of such declaratory Law before the Legislative Council of the said Island for their consideration. And We further direct and ordain that the said Judges of the Supreme Court shall in pursuance of the Powers hereinafter vested in them after due consideration of any Reports so to be made as aforesaid by any such Judge of any such contradiction or inconsistency as aforesaid in any matter of Pleading or Practice make or establish such General Rules or Orders of Court for the removal of any doubts respecting any such matters as the occasion shall appear to them to require.

Supreme Court, &c. may issue writs of Habeas Corpus;

49. And We do further ordain and appoint that the said Supreme Court or any Judge thereof at any Sessions so to bo holden as aforesaid on any such Circuit as aforesaid or in the District of Colombo or at any General Sessions of the Judges of the said Court collectively shall be and are hereby authorized to grant and issue Mandates in the nature of Writs of Habeas Corpus and to grant or refuse such Mandates to bring up the body of any person who shall be imprisoned within any part of the said Island or its Dependencies and to discharge or remand any person so brought up or otherwise deal with such person according to Law. And We do further direct and appoint that the said Supreme Court or any Judge thereof at any Sessions so to be holden on any such Circuit as aforesaid or in the District of Colombo or at any General Sessions of the said Court collectively shall be and they and he are and is hereby authorized to grant and issue Injunctions to prevent any irremediable mischief which might ensue before the party making application for such Injunction could prevent the same by bringing an Action in any District Court, Provided always that it shall not be lawful for the said Supreme Court nor for any Judge thereof in any case to grant an Injunction to prevent any person from suing or prosecuting a suit in any District Court or to prevent any party to any suit in any District Court from appealing or prosecuting an appeal to any Court of Appeal or to prevent any party to any suit in any Court of Original Jurisdiction or in any Court of Appeal from insisting upon any Ground of Action Defence or Appeal.

and Injunctions;

but not to prevent parties from sueing, defending or appealing.

And may order the Records of cases on

50. And whereas it may be expedient that the Judges of the said Supreme Court of Colombo previous to the commencement of any such Circuits as

appeal to be transmitted to Colombo; and to decide the same, by consent, at General Sessions.

aforesaid should be enabled to inspect and examine the Records of the said District Courts in cases upon which Appeals may have been entered, And it may also be convenient that with the consent of the litigant parties the hearing of such Appeals should take place before the Judges of the said Court collectively at their General Sessions at Colombo and not at such Circuits as aforesaid, And it may also be convenient that in certain cases the Judges of the said Supreme Court collectively at such General Sessions should be authorized to decide in a summary way and without further argument Questions arising upon any such Appeals, We do therefore further will direct ordain and appoint that it shall be lawful for the Judges of the said Supreme Court by such General Rules and Orders as hereinafter mentioned to require the said District Courts to transmit to them at Colombo the Records of such District Courts in any cases upon which Appeals may be entered, And We do authorize and empower the Judges of the said Supreme Court collectively at any such General Sessions as aforesaid with the consent of all the litigant parties but not otherwise (save as hereinafter provided in cases Appealed to Us in our Privy Council) to hear any such Appeals or to decide the same or any particular Question or Questions arising thereupon in a summary way and without further argument and to remit any such Records with such their final decision thereupon to such District Courts to be by them carried into execution.

And may make Rules of Court,

51. And whereas for carrying into effect the various Provisions of this present Charter and for the more prompt and effectual administration of Justice in our said Island it is necessary that Regulations should be made respecting the course and manner of proceeding to be observed and followed in all suits actions and criminal prosecutions and other proceedings whatsoever to be brought commenced had or taken within the said District Courts and the said Supreme Court respectively which Regulations cannot be properly made except by the Judges of the said Supreme Court, We do therefore hereby further declare Our pleasure to be and do will ordain direct and appoint that it shall be lawful for the Judges of the said Supreme Court collectively at any General Sessions to be by them holden at Colombo as aforesaid from time to time to frame constitute and establish such General Rules and Orders of Court as to them shall seem meet touching and concerning the time and place of holding any General Sessions of the Judges of the said Supreme Court collectively and any Civil or Criminal Sessions of the said Supreme Court on any such Circuits as aforesaid or in the District of Colombo and the said several District Courts as shall not be inconsistent with the authority hereinbefore granted to the Governor of our said Island respecting the appointing of the times at which and the places to which the Judges of the said Supreme Court shall perform their Circuits together with such General Rules and Orders as to them shall seem meet touching and concerning the form and manner of proceeding to be observed in the said Supreme Court at any General Sessions and at such Civil and Criminal Sessions as aforesaid on such Circuit as aforesaid or in the

as to the time and place of Sessions,

and as to the Procedure, Civil & Criminal, of the Supreme and District Courts, and of Fiscals.

District of Colombo and in such District Courts respectively and touching and concerning the Practice and Pleadings upon all actions suits and other matters both Civil and Criminal to be therein brought the Proceedings of the Fiscals and other Ministerial Officers of the said Courts respectively the Process of the said Courts and the mode of executing the same the qualifications summoning impannelling and challenging of Assessors and the summoning impannelling and challenging of Jurors Arrest on Mesne Process or in Execution the taking of Bail the duties of Jailors and others charged with the custody of Prisoners in so far as respects the making due Returns to the respective Judges of the said Supreme Court of all Prisoners in their custody and respecting the mode of Prosecuting such Appeals as aforesaid from the said District Courts the admission of Advocates and Proctors in the said Courts respectively together with all such General Rules and Orders as may be necessary for giving full and complete effect to the Provisions of this present Charter, in whatsoever respects the form and manner of administering Justice in the several Courts hereby constituted and all such Rules Orders and Regulations from time to time to revoke alter amend or renew as occasion may require, Provided always that no such Rules Orders or Regulations shall be repugnant to this our Charter and that the same shall be so framed as to promote as far as may be the discovery of Truth and Economy and Expedition in the despatch of the business of the said several Courts respectively and that the same be drawn up in plain succinct and compendious terms avoiding all unnecessary repetitions and obscurity and promulgated in the most public and authentic manner in the said Island as long before the same shall operate and take effect as to such Judges may appear practicable and convenient, And provided always that all such Rules Orders and Regulations shall forthwith be transmitted to Us our Heirs and Successors under the Seal of the said Court for our or their approbation or disallowance.

and as to Process, Assessors, Jurors, Arrest, Bail, & Jailors, and as to Appeals, and admission of Advocates and Proctors. Not to be repugnant to this Charter, and to be transmitted for H. M.'s approval or disallowance.

Appeal to His Majesty in Council.

52. And We do further grant ordain direct and appoint that it shall be lawful for any Person or Persons being a party or parties to any civil suit or action depending in the said Supreme Court to Appeal to Us our Heirs and Successors in our or their Privy Council against any final Judgment Decree or Sentence or against any Rule or Order made in any such civil suit or action and having the effect of a final or definite Sentence and which Appeals shall be made subject to the Rules and Limitations following—First, That before any such Appeal shall be so brought such Judgment Decree Sentence Rule or Order shall be brought by way of Review before the Judges of the said Supreme Court collectively holding a General Sessions at Colombo at which all the said Judges of the said Supreme Court shall be present and assisting which Judges shall by such Rules and Orders as aforesaid regulate the form and manner of Proceeding to be observed in bringing every such Judgment Decree Sentence Rule or Order by way of Review before them and shall thereupon pronounce Judgment

Cause to be first heard at General Sessions of Supreme Court.

according to Law the Judgment of the majority of which Judges shall be taken and recorded as the Judgment of the said Court collectively—Secondly, Every

Amount appealable.

such Judgment Decree Order or Sentence from which such an Appeal shall be admitted to Us our Heirs and Successors as aforesaid shall be given or pronounced for or in respect of a sum or matter at issue above the amount or value of Five Hundred Pounds sterling or shall involve directly or indirectly the Title to Property or to some Civil Right exceeding the value of Five Hundred Pounds sterling—Thirdly, The

Application for leave to appeal to be made within 14 days.

Person or Persons feeling aggrieved by such Judgment Decree Order or Sentence shall within fourteen days next after the same shall have been pronounced made or given apply to the said Supreme Court at such General Sessions as aforesaid by Petition for leave to Appeal therefrom to Us our Heirs and Successors in our or their Privy Council—Fourthly, If such leave

Judgment to be executed on securities being given for restitution.

to Appeal shall be prayed by the party or parties who is or are adjudged to pay any sum of money or to perform any duty the said Supreme Court shall direct that the Judgment Decree or Sentence Appealed from shall be carried into execution if the party or parties Respondent shall give Security for the immediate performance of any Judgment Decree or Sentence which may be pronounced or made by Us our Heirs and Successors in our or their Privy Council upon any such Appeal and until such Security be given the execution of the Judgment Decree Order or Sentence Appealed from shall be stayed—Fifthly, Provided nevertheless that if

Court may stay execution when Justice requires it, Appellant giving Security.

the party or parties Appellant shall establish to the satisfaction of the said Supreme Court that real and substantial Justice requires that pending such Appeals execution should be stayed it shall be lawful for such Supreme Court to order the execution of such Judgment Decree Order or Sentence to be stayed pending such Appeal if the party or parties Appellant shall give Security for the immediate performance of any Judgment Decree or Sentence which may be pronounced or made by Us our Heirs and Successors in our or their Privy Council upon any such Appeal—

Appellant to give Security for prosecution of Appeal and payment of Costs.

Sixthly, In all cases Security shall also be given by the party or parties Appellant for the prosecution of the Appeal and for the payment of all such Costs as may be awarded by Us our Heirs and Successors to the party or parties Respondent—Seventhly, The Court from which any such Appeal as

Court to determine Security.

aforesaid shall be brought shall subject to the Conditions hereinafter mentioned determine the nature amount and sufficiency of the several Securities so to be taken as aforesaid—Eighthly, Provided nevertheless that in any case

If title to immoveable property be subject of Appeal, Security not required, if occupation, how to be determined.

where the subject of litigation shall consist of Immoveable Property and the Judgment Decree Order or Sentence Appealed from shall not change affect or relate to the actual occupation thereof no Security shall be demanded either from the party or parties Respondent or from the party or parties Appellant for the performance of the Judgment or Sentence to be pronounced or made upon such Appeal but if such Judgment Decree Order or Sentence shall change affect or relate to the occupation of any such Property then such Security shall not be of greater amount than may be necessary to secure the restitution free from all damage or loss of such Property or of the intermediate Profit which pending any such Appeal may probably accrue from the intermediate occupation thereof—Ninthly, In any case where the subject of litigation shall consist of Money or other Chattels or of any personal Debt or Demand the Security to be demanded either from the party or parties Respondent or from the party or parties Appellant for the performance of the Judgment or Sentence to be pronounced or made upon such Appeal shall be either a Bond to be entered into in the amount or value of such subject of litigation by one or more sufficient Surety or Sureties or such Security shall be given by way of mortgage or voluntary condemnation of or upon some Immoveable Property situate and being within such Island and being of the full value of such subject of litigation over and above the amount of all mortgages and charges of whatever nature upon or affecting the same—Tenthly, The Security to be given by the party or parties Appellant for the prosecution of the Appeal and for the payment of Costs shall in no case exceed the sum of Three Hundred Pounds sterling and shall be given either by such Surety or Sureties or by such mortgage or voluntary condemnation as aforesaid—Eleventhly, If the Security to be given by the party or parties Appellant for the prosecution of the Appeal and for the payment of such Costs as may be awarded shall in manner aforesaid be completed within three months from the date of the Petition for leave to Appeal then and not otherwise the said Supreme Court shall make an Order allowing such Appeal and the party or parties Appellant shall be at liberty to prefer and prosecute his her or their Appeal to Us our Heirs and Successors in our or their Privy Council in such manner and under such Rules as are observed in Appeals made to Us in our Privy Council from our Plantations or Colonies—Twelfthly, Provided nevertheless that any Person or Persons feeling aggrieved by any Order which may be made by or by any proceedings of the said Supreme Court respecting the Security to be taken upon any such Appeal as aforesaid shall be and is hereby authorized by his her or their Petition to Us in our Privy Council to apply for redress in the Premises.

If moveable property be the subject of Appeal, Bond to be given.

Security for prosecution of Appeal never to exceed £300.

Appellant to be allowed three months to enter into Securities.

Application may be made to His Majesty in Council against orders on the subject of Securities.

Reservation to His Majesty of the right of admitting Appeals without regard to these Rules.

53. Provided always and We do further ordain direct and declare that nothing herein contained doth or shall extend to take away or abridge the undoubted Right or Authority of Us our Heirs and Successors to admit and receive any Appeal from any Judgment Decree Sentence or Order of the said Supreme Court on the humble Petition of any Person or Persons aggrieved thereby in any case in which and subject to any Conditions or Restrictions upon and under which it may seem meet to Us our Heirs and Successors so to admit and receive any such Appeal.

Transcripts of Records to be transmitted to His Majesty in Council.

54. And We do further direct and ordain that in all cases of Appeal allowed by the said Supreme Court or by Us our Heirs and Successors such Court shall on the application and at the costs of the party or parties Appellant certify and transmit to Us our Heirs and Successors in our or their Privy Council a true and exact Copy of all Proceedings Evidence Judgments Decrees and Orders had or made in such Causes so Appealed so far as the same have relation to the matter of Appeal such Copies to be certified under the Seal of the said Court.

Supreme Court to execute Judgments pronounced by His Majesty in Council on Appeals.

55. And We do further ordain and direct that the said Supreme Court shall in all cases of Appeal to Us our Heirs and Successors conform to execute and carry into immediate effect such Judgments and Orders as We our Heirs and Successors in our or their Privy Council shall make thereupon in such manner as any Original Judgment or Decree of the said Supreme Court can or may be executed.

Revocation of all Laws repugnant to this Charter.

56. And We do further ordain and direct that all Laws Customs and Usages now or at any time heretofore established or in force in the said Island so far as such Laws or Usages are in any wise repugnant to or at variance with this present Charter shall be and the same are hereby revoked abrogated rescinded and annulled.

Definition of the title "Governor."

57. And We do further declare that for the purpose and within the meaning of the present Charter any Person lawfully administering for the time being the Government of the said Island shall be deemed and taken to be the Governor thereof.

Governor to fix the time at which the Charter is to come into operation, when all Suits pending are to be transferred to the new limits.

58. And We do further ordain and direct that at the expiration of two Calendar months next after the arrival within the said Island of these Presents or at such earlier period as the Governor for the time being of the said Island shall by a Proclamation to be for that purpose issued appoint this our Charter shall come into operation within the said Island and from that time forward every suit action complaint matter or thing which shall be then depending before any Court administering Justice by Original or Appellate Jurisdiction in the said Island and its Dependencies shall and may be proceeded upon in the Court in which it ought to have been instituted or to which it ought to have been carried up in Appeal if it had been instituted or carried up in Appeal after the time when the Provisions herein contained shall have come into operation and all Proceedings which shall hereafter be had in such suit action complaint matter or thing respectively shall be conducted in like manner as if such suit action complaint matter or thing had been instituted or carried up in Appeal in or to such last mentioned Court and all the Records Muniments and Proceedings

whatsoever belonging or pertaining to any such suit action complaint matter or thing shall when the Provisions herein contained shall have come into operation be delivered over by the Court in which such suit action complaint matter or thing shall be then depending to the Court in or to which such suit action complaint matter or thing ought to have been instituted or carried up in Appeal if it had been instituted or carried up in Appeal after the time when the Provisions herein contained shall have come into operation.

All persons to aid in the execution of the Charter.

59. And We do hereby strictly charge and command all Governors Commanders Magistrates Ministers Civil and Military and all our Liege Subjects within and belonging to the said Island and its Dependencies that in the execution of the several Powers Jurisdictions and Authorities hereby granted made given or created they be aiding and assisting and obedient in all things as they will answer the contrary at their Peril.

Reservation of right to revoke and amend the Charter.

60. Provided always that nothing in these Presents contained or any Act which shall be done under the Authority thereof shall extend or be deemed or construed to extend to prevent Us our Heirs and Successors by any other Letters Patent to be by Us or Them from time to time for that purpose issued under the Great Seal of the United Kingdom from revoking this our Charter or any part thereof or from making such further or other Provision for the administration of Justice throughout the said Island and its dependencies at our and their Will and Pleasure as circumstances may require We meaning and intending fully and absolutely to all intents and purposes whatsoever to reserve to Ourselves our Heirs and Successors such and the same rights and powers in and over the said Island and its Dependencies and especially touching the administration of Justice therein and all other matters and things in and by these Presents provided for as if these Presents had not been made any thing in these Presents contained or any Law Custom Usage matter or thing whatsoever to the contrary in any wise notwithstanding.

In Witness whereof We have caused these our Letters to be made Patent Witness Ourself at Westminster the Eighteenth day of February in the Third year of our Reign.

By Writ of Privy Seal.

BATHURST.

INFORMATION FOR THE USE OF MILITARY AND NAVAL OFFICERS PROPOSING TO SETTLE IN THE BRITISH COLONIES.

Referred to in page 80.

GENERAL ORDER.

Horse Guards, 16th April, 1840.

The General Commanding-in-Chief announces to the Army, that the advantages provided for Military and Naval Officers becoming Settlers in the Australian Colonies, under the Memorandum dated Colonial Office, 15th August, 1834, which was annexed to the General Order of the 25th of that month, are now extended by Her Majesty's Government to Officers of the Army and Navy who may be desirous of settling in the Island of CEYLON, under the Regulations and Conditions specified in the said Memorandum, copy of which is likewise hereunto annexed.

By Command of the Right Honorable

GENERAL LORD HILL,

Commanding-in-Chief.

JOHN MACDONALD,

Adjutant General.

Colonial Office, 15th August, 1834.

1. Annexed is a Statement of the Regulations according to which, with such modifications as local circumstances may render necessary, Lands belonging to the Crown are disposed of in the several British Colonies in North America, as well as a Statement of the Regulations in force in the Australian Colonies.

2. Under these Regulations Military and Naval Officers cannot receive free grants of land; but, in buying land, they are allowed a remission of the purchase money, according to the undermentioned scale:—

Field Officers of twenty-five years' service and upwards, in the whole £300.

Field Officers of twenty years' service and upwards, in the whole £250.

Field Officers of fifteen or less years' service, in the whole £200.

Captains of twenty years' service and upwards, in the whole £200.

Captains of fifteen years' service or less, in the whole £150.

Subalterns of twenty years' service and upwards, in the whole £150.

Subalterns of seven years' service or less, in the whole £100.

Regimental Staff Officers and Medical Officers of the Army and Navy will be deemed to come within the benefit of this Rule.

3. Officers of the Army or Navy, who propose to proceed to the Colonies in order to take advantage of this indulgence, should provide themselves with Certificates from the office of the General Commanding in Chief, or of the Lords Commissioners of the Admiralty, showing that their emigration has been sanctioned, and stating exactly their rank and length of service. No document from the office of the Secretary of State is necessary.

4. Officers on half-pay, residing in the Colony where they propose to settle, may be admitted to the privileges of Military and Naval Settlers, without referring to this country for testimonials, provided they can satisfy the Governor that there is no objection to their being allowed the indulgence, and that their return of their rank and length of service is accurate, and provided, if they belong to the Navy, that they produce their letter of leave of absence from the Admiralty.

5. Military Chaplains, Commissariat Officers, and Officers of any of the Civil Departments connected with the Army, cannot be allowed any privileges on the subject of land.—Pursers, Chaplains, Midshipmen, Warrant Officers of every description, and Officers of any of the Civil Departments connected with the Navy, must also be considered as not qualified for those privileges. Although members of these classes may have been admitted formerly, and under a different state of circumstances, they must now be excluded.

6. Gentlemen who have ceased to belong to His Majesty's Service cannot be allowed the advantages to which they were entitled while in the Army or Navy. It is not, however, proposed to affect by this rule Officers who desire to quit the service for the express purpose of settling in the Colonies: it is only required, that when they resign their Commissions, they should apply for a certificate from the General Commanding in Chief, or from the Lords Commissioners of the Admiralty, that they do so with the view of emigrating; and such certificate, if produced to the Governor of any Colony, within one year from its date, *but not otherwise,* will be a sufficient warrant for allowing the bearer the same advantages as Officers still in His Majesty's Service.—Officers who have sold out within the last twelve months preceding the date of this Memerandum will be allowed the usual privileges, notwithstanding their want of the certificate required by these regulations, if they present themselves to the Governor of the Colony within a year from the present date. And all Officers who have already been recommended by the General Commanding in Chief will be entitled to their privileges, without regard to any obstruction which might otherwise be offered by the Regulations now established.

7. Officers cannot be allowed the advantages in the acquisition of land in any Colony, unless it be their intention to fix their residence in that Colony. In order to insure the observance of rule, it has been determined that the Titles to lands obtained by Officers who take advantage of the peculiar Regulations existing in their favour, shall be withholden for a period sufficient to prove that they have not repaired to the Colony for the mere purpose of gaining possession of a portion of land, and then departing. Two years is the period for which it has been decided that the Titles shall be kept back. This delay will be sufficient for the salutary object in view, and will not constitute any serious inconvenience to the *bonâ fide* Settler.

8. By the annexed Regulations for the disposal of Crown lands, it will be observed that the general sales will take place periodically. But in order to prevent inconvenience to Officers who

may arrive in the intervals between those sales, and be desirous at once to obtain an allotment, the Governors of the Colonies are authorized to allow Officers to acquire, at any time, on payment of the upset price, lands which have previously been offered for sale at some general sale, and not been bought.—Officers will thus be relieved from delay at the time of establishing themselves in the Colony. They will also be enabled by this arrangement, which will permit them to obtain their land at a fixed price, to choose such a quantity as shall be exactly equivalent to the amount of the remission to which they are entitled, instead of being liable to be called upon to pay a balance, which must be the case if they bid for lands at a sale by auction.

9. There being little or no Crown land available in Prince Edward's Island, Officers cannot be offered any privileges in the acquision of land in that Colony. In Cape Breton, an Island in which the natural inducements for the settlement of Officers are not very considerable, it is necessary, from local circumstances, that there should not be a remission of purchase money as in other Colonies: to such Officers as may wish to settle in this Island, allotments of land will be granted on the same scale and conditions as before the general introduction of the system of selling the Crown Lands, viz. to a Lieutenant-Colonel, 1200 acres; to a Major, 1000; to a Captain, 800; to a Subaltern, 500.—The same Rule will be observed in Nova Scotia.

Regulations for the disposal of Lands belonging to the Crown in the British North American Provinces.

The lands are no longer to be given away by free grants, but are to be sold.

The Commissioner of the Crown lands will, at least once in every year, submit to the Governor a Report of the land which it may be expedient to offer for sale within the then ensuing year, and the upset price per acre at which he would recommend it to be offered; the land so offered having been previously surveyed and valued in one or more contiguous tracts of those which are most adapted for settlement, according to the local peculiarities of the Province, and in proportion to the number of deputy-surveyors who can be employed.

The lands to be laid out in lots of 100 acres each, and plans of such parts as are surveyed to be prepared for public inspection, which plans may be inspected in the office of the Surveyor-General, or in that of his deputies in each district, on payment of the fee of 2*s.* 6*d.*

The Commissioner of Crown lands will proceed to the sale in the following manner:—He will give public notice in the Gazette, and in such other newspapers as may be circulated in the Province, as well as in any other manner that circumstances will admit of, of the time and place appointed for the sale of the lands in each district, and of the upset price at which the lands are proposed to be offered; he will give notice that the lots will be sold to the highest bidder; and if no offer be made at the upset price, that the lands will be reserved for future sale in a similar manner by auction.

The purchase money will be required to be paid down at the time of sale, or by four instalments with interest; the first instalment at the time of the sale, and the second, third, and fourth instalments at intervals of half a year.

If the instalments are not regularly paid, the deposit-money will be forfeited, and the land again referred to sale.

Public notice will be given in each district, in every year, stating the names of the persons in each district who may be in arrears for the instalments of their purchases, and announcing that if the arrears are not paid up before the commencement of the sales in that district for the following years, the lands in respect of which the instalments may be due will be the first lots to be exposed to auction at the ensuing sales; and if any surplus of the produce of the sale of each lot should remain, after satisfying the Crown of the sum due, the same will be paid to the original purchasers of the land who made default in payment.

The patent for the land will not be issued, nor any transfer of the property allowed, until the whole of the instalments are paid. The lands sold under this regulation are not to be chargeable with quit-rents, or any farther payment beyond the purchase money and the expense of the patent.

Persons desirous of buying land in situations not included in the tracts already surveyed, must previously pay for the expense of survey, and the price must of course depend upon the quality of the land and its local situation.

The Crown will reserve to itself the right of making and constructing such roads and bridges as may be necessary for public purposes in all lands purchased as above; and also to such indigenous timber, stone, and other materials, the produce of the land, as may be required for making and keeping the said roads and bridges in repair, and for any other public works. The Crown further reserves to itself all mines of precious metals.

The regulations for granting licences to cut timber will be learned by application to the Surveyor-General's office in the respective Colonies.

Colonial Office, 7th March, 1831.

Terms upon which the Crown Lands will be disposed of in New South Wales and Van Diemen's Land.

It has been determined by his Majesty's Government, that no land shall, in future, be disposed of in New South Wales or Van Diemen's Land, otherwise than by public sale, and it has therefore been deemed expedient to prepare, for the information of settlers, the following summary of the Rules which it has been thought fit to lay down for regulating the sales of land in those Colonies.

1. A division of the whole territory into counties, hundreds, and parishes, is in progress. When that division shall be completed, each parish will comprise an area of about twenty-five square miles.

2. All the lands in the Colony not hitherto granted, and not appropriated for public purposes, will be put up to sale. The price will of course depend upon the quality of the land and its local situation, but no land will be sold below the rate of 5*s.* per acre.

3. All persons proposing to purchase lands not advertised for sale, must transmit a written application to the Governor, in a certain prescribed form, which will be delivered at the Surveyor-General's office to all persons applying, on paying the requisite fee of 2*s.* 6*d.*

4. Those persons who are desirous of purchasing will be allowed to select, within certain defined limits, such portions of land as they may wish to acquire in that manner. These portions of land will be advertised for sale for three calendar months, and will then be sold to the highest bidder, provided that such bidding shall at least amount to the price fixed by Article 2.

5. A deposit of £10 per cent. upon the whole value of the purchase must be paid down at the time of sale, and the remainder must be paid within one calendar month from the day of sale, previous to which the purchaser will not be put in possession of the land; and in case of payment not being made within the prescribed period, the sale will be considered void and the deposit forfeited.

6. On payment of the money, a grant will be made in fee-simple. to the purchaser, at the nominal quit-rent of a pepper-corn. Previous to the delivery of such grant, a fee of forty shillings will be payable to the Colonial Secretary for preparing the grant, and another fee of five shillings to the Registrar of the Supreme Court for enrolling it.

7. The land will generally be put up to sale in lots of one square mile, or 640 acres; but smaller lots than 640 acres may, under particular circumstances, be purchased, on making application to the Governor, in writing, with full explanations of the reasons for which the parties wish to purchase a smaller quantity.

8. The Crown reserves to itself the right of making anu constructing such roads and bridges as may be necessary for public purposes in all lands purchased as above; and also to such indigenous timber, stone, and other materials, the produce of the land, as may be required for making and keeping the said roads and bridges in repair, and for any other public works. The Crown further reserves to itself all mines of precious metals.

Colonial Office, 20th January, 1831.

Terms upon which the Crown Lands will be disposed of in the New Settlement in Western Australia.

It has been determined by His Majesty's Government, that land shall in future be disposed of in Western Australia, upon the same principles as in New South Wales and Van Diemen's Land; but the encouragement hitherto given to persons who might incur the expense of taking out labouring persons to the Colony, will not be entirely withdrawn at present.

The following is a summary of the Rules which it has been thought fit to substitute for those dated the 20th of July, 1830.

1. A division of the whole territory into counties, hundreds, and parishes, is in progress. When that division shall be completed, each parish will comprise an area of about twenty-five square miles.

2. All the lands in the Colony not hitherto granted, and not appropriated for public purposes, will be put up to sale. The price will of course depend upon the quality of the land and its local situation, but no land will be sold below the rate of 5*s.* per acre.

3. All persons proposing to purchase lands not advertised for sale, must transmit a written application to the Governor, in a certain prescribed form, which will be delivered at the Surveyor-General's office to all persons applying, on payment of the requisite fee of 2*s.* 6*d.*

4. Those persons who are desirous of purchasing will be allowed to select, within certain defined limits, such portions of land as they may wish to acquire in that manner. These portions of land will be advertised for sale for three calendar months, and will then be sold to the highest bidder, provided that such bidding shall at least amount to the price fixed in Article 2.

5. A deposit of £10 per cent. upon the whole value of the purchase must be paid down at the time of sale, and the remainder must be paid within one calendar month from the day of sale, previous to which the purchaser will not be put in possession of the land; and in case of payment not being made within the prescribed period, the sale will be considered void, and the deposit forfeited.

6. On payment of the money, a grant will be made, in fee-simple, to the purchaser, at the nominal quit-rent of a pepper-corn. Previous to the delivery of such grant, a fee of forty shillings will be payable to the Colonial Secretary for preparing the grant, and another fee of five shillings for enrolling it.

7. The land will generally be put up to sale in lots of one square mile, or 640 acres; but smaller lots than 640 acres may, under particular circumstances, be purchased, on making application to the Governor, in writing, with full explanations of the reasons for which the parties wish to purchase a smaller quantity.

8. The Crown reserves to itself the right of making and constructing such roads and bridges as may be necessary for public purposes in all lands purchased as above, and also to such indigenous timber, stone, and other materials, the produce of the land, as may be required for making and keeping the said roads and bridges in repair, and for any other public works. The Crown further reserves to itself all mines of precious metals.

9. Those Settlers who may incur the expense of taking out labouring persons to the settlement, will be entitled to an abatement of the price at which the land may have been purchased, at the rate of £20 for the passage of every married labourer and his family.

10. Persons claiming such an abatement from the price paid for land, will be held responsible for any expense the Colonial Authorities may be compelled to incur for the maintenance (during the first year after their arrival) of the labourers in respect of whom it has been allowed.

Colonial Office, 1st March, 1831.

REGULATION OF GOVERNMENT,

(Referred to in page 135,)

For promoting the Growth of certain Articles of Agricultural produce in the Island of Ceylon, and for the encouragement of Agricultural speculation.

Whereas it is proper and expedient to afford every practicable encouragement to Agricultural speculations and pursuits in this Island and more particularly to the growth of certain articles of produce hereafter specified, And whereas it has been represented to His Excellency the Governor that some persons have been deterred from engaging in such speculations and pursuits by an apprehension that they might be liable to pay a proportion of the produce thereby raised as a tax due and payable to Government,

1. For removing therefore all such apprehensions, it is hereby enacted by His Excellency in Council, that no part of any Coffee, Cotton, Sugar, Indigo, Opium, or Silk, of the growth or produce of the Island, or of any part of its Dependencies, has hitherto been, or will be demanded or claimed by Government for the period of twelve years from this date.

2. And whereas by Regulation of Government, No. 9, of 1825, therein referred to, Coffee and Cotton are permitted to be exported from any port of this Island, free of duty, but no mention is made of the other articles of produce herein enumerated, it is therefore hereby further declared that all Sugar, Opium, Indigo, or Silk, the growth or produce as before named, may be exported from any port of this Island or its Dependencies free of all duties whatever.

3. And it is further enacted, that all Implements, Tools, and Machinery used for the purposes of Agriculture, or of any kind of Manufacture, may from henceforth be imported into this Island free of all duty whatever.

4. And with a view to the further encouragement of Agricultural speculations, it is also enacted that all Labourers, of whatever nation or description, who shall be *bonâ fide* employed in any plantation of Coffee, Cotton, Sugar, Indigo, Opium, or Silk, or in the manufacture or produce thereof, shall be exempt from being called out in the public service during the period of such *bonâ fide* employ, except during actual war, and for the purpose of repelling invasion, or during internal commotion. Provided, that in order to exempt from such public service those otherwise liable, a certificate from the Proprietor of such plantation, or manufacture, or from his Agent, be produced to the Collector of the District. And any Proprietor or Agent issuing to any Labourer a certificate which shall be wilfully false in any particular, shall, on conviction, be liable to a fine not exceeding Twenty Pounds; and in default of payment, to imprisonment for any term not less than Two calendar months, nor more than Six calendar months.

Given at Colombo 21st September, 1829.

By order of the Council, T. EDEN,
Secretary to Council

REGULATION OF GOVERNMENT,

(Referred to in page 162,)

PRESENT, THE HONORABLE THE LIEUTENANT GOVERNOR IN COUNCIL.

A. D. 1821. REGULATION NO. 6.

For the encouragement of the preparation of Salt Fish within this Island.

Preamble. Expedient to encourage the preparation of Salt Fish.

1. WHEREAS it is expedient to encourage the preparation of Salt Fish within this Island,

From 1st April, 1821, the Duty on Salt Fish imported is raised to 15 per cent. on Invoice price or prime cost.

2. It is therefore enacted, by the Lieutenant Governor in Council, that from and after the first day of April next, a duty on Salt Fish of every description imported into this Island shall be levied at the rate of Fifteen per Cent. on the Invoiced value or prime cost thereof; such value or cost to be ascertained in the manner in and by the 4th and 5th Sections of the 6th Regulation of the year 1820 laid down.

No Export Duty on Salt Fish used in Ceylon exported Coast ways.

3. And it is further enacted, that from the date aforesaid, no Export duty shall be levied on any Salt Fish exported from any port within this Island to another; and that the rates of export and import duty assessed by the said 6th Regulation of 1820, on Salt Fish, shall be and the same are hereby repealed.

Given at Colombo this 17th day of March, 1821.

By order of the Council,

GEORGE LUSIGNAN,

Secretary to Council.

By the Lieut. Governor's command,

JOHN RODNEY,

Chief Secretary to Government.

ORDINANCE ENACTED BY THE GOVERNOR OF CEYLON, WITH THE ADVICE AND CONSENT OF THE LEGISLATIVE COUNCIL THEREOF.

(Referred to in page 240.)

No. 5. *An Ordinance to amend the Laws Relating to the Ports and Customs.*

Preamble. WHEREAS it is expedient to repeal the several Regulations now in force relating to the general Regulation and Management of the Ports and Customs, and to make other Provisions in lieu thereof,

Former Regulations repealed. 1. It is therefore hereby enacted, by the Governor of Ceylon, with the advice and consent of the Legislative Council thereof, that from and after the eleventh day of October, one thousand eight hundred and thirty seven, the Regulation No. 9 of 1825, entitled "For repealing all former Laws relating to the collection of Customs, and enacting new Laws, Rules, and Tables for collecting the same, and for the Export or Import of Goods, and Landing and Shipping the same, and for granting certain Drawbacks, and also allowing the Warehousing of certain Goods for re-exportation, and also for preventing the introduction of any pestilential or contagious disease into this Island," the Regulation No. 2 of 1826, entitled "For defining the application of the provisions of the Regulation No. 9 of 1825, relating to the registering of Vessels and the granting of Certificates of Registry, and for amending and altering certain other provisions of the said Regulation with reference to the Act of Parliament intituled an Act for the Registering of British Vessels," the Regulation No. 1 of 1828, entitled "For the protection and encouragement of the growth of Tobacco in this Island," the Regulation No. 4 of 1830, entitled "For diminishing the duties on certain articles of Export, for permitting the import of Military Clothing duty free, and for empowering the Governor to assign to Informers a share of penalties levied under the Regulation No. 9 of 1825," and the Ordinance No. 7 of 1836, entitled "For establishing a new Tariff of Duties on Goods exported and imported," shall be and the same are hereby repealed, except in so far as respects any Offences already committed, or any Fines, Penalties, Dues, Forfeitures, or Liabilities incurred thereunder, or the Repeal of any previous Regulations thereby.

Duties payable on Goods. *And Drawbacks allowed* 2. And it is further enacted, that from and after the said eleventh day of October, one thousand eight hundred and thirty seven, there shall be collected on all Goods imported into or exported from this Island, the several Duties of Customs, and there shall be allowed the several Drawbacks, as the same are respectively inserted, described, and set forth in Figures in the Tables marked A. and B. to this Ordinance annexed.

Deposit may be made for Duties.

3. And it is further enacted, that in all cases where the Amount of Duties payable under the preceding Clause upon any Goods imported into or exported from this Island, shall exceed Thirty Pounds, it shall be lawful for the Importer or Exporter of such Goods to lodge Security by Deposit for the full amount of such Duties, such Deposit to be valued and approved of by the Collector of Customs: Provided always, that Interest shall be levied on the said Amount of Duties for any period exceeding Three Months that the same may be left unpaid, at the rate of Seven per cent. per annum: And provided further, that no Grain, Provisions, or other articles of a perishable nature, shall be received as Deposit: and if any such Deposit shall not be redeemed within Six Months from the time of its being lodged in the Custom House, it shall be sold for the satisfaction of the Claims of the Crown, the Duties, Interest, and other Charges deducted from the Proceeds, and the Balance, if any, paid to the Owner.

Conditions.

Port Dues.

4. And it is further enacted, that upon all Ships and Vessels anchoring in any Port of this Island, save and except Chartered Transports and Vessels belonging to this Government, Port Dues shall be levied at the rate of Four Pence per Ton of the registered Tonnage of such Vessel: Provided always, that such Dues shall not be payable, unless such Ship or Vessel shall have remained at anchor for Eight Days, or unless such Ship or Vessel shall have discharged any Goods, or taken any Goods on board, when the Quantity of Goods landed or shipped shall exceed One Ton for every Hundred Tons registered of such Vessel, the Baggage of Passengers excepted.

Composition for Dues.

5. And it is further enacted, that any Vessel employed for the Conveyance of Goods or Passengers between one Port and another of this Island only, shall be allowed to compound for Port Dues for Twelve Months, at the rate of One Shilling per Ton of the registered Tonnage, and on payment thereof the Collector and Controller of Customs shall grant a Certificate which shall exempt such Vessel, while so employed, from any further demand for Port Dues during the period above stated; and no Vessel making a Coasting Voyage shall be liable to pay Port Dues within Thirty Days from the date of the last payment thereof.

Coasting vessel not again liable within 30 days.

Pilotage.

6. And it is further enacted, that the rates of Pilotage into the several Ports of Colombo, Trincomalé, and Galle, payable to the Master Attendant for the use of the Pilots employed in the Pilotage of such Vessels, shall be those specified in the Table C. to this Ordinance annexed.

Ballast not to be thrown overboard in Port.

7. And it is further enacted, that if any Master of a Vessel, or in the absence of such Master, the Mate, or other person in principal charge of a Vessel, shall throw or cause or permit to be thrown overboard from such

Vessel, being in any Port of this Island, any Ballast or Rubbish whatever, such Master, Mate, or other person in charge shall be liable to a Fine not exceeding Ten Pounds.

INWARDS.

No Goods to be landed nor Bulk broken before report and Entry.

8. And whereas it is expedient that the Officers of Customs should have full Cognizance of all Ships coming into any Port in this Island, or approaching the Coasts thereof, and of all Goods on board, or which may have been on board such Ships, and also of all Goods unladen from any Ship in any Port or Place in this Island; It is therefore enacted, that no Goods shall be unladen from any Ship arriving from parts beyond the seas at any Port or Place in this Island, nor shall Bulk be broken after the arrival of such Ship within One League of the Coasts thereof respectively, before due Report of such Ship and due Entry of such Goods shall have been made, and Warrant granted, in manner hereinafter directed; and that no Goods shall be so unladen except at such Times and Places, and in such Manner, and by such Persons, and under the care of such Officers, as is and are hereinafter directed; and that all Goods not duly reported, or which shall be unladen contrary hereto, shall be forfeited; and if Bulk be broken contrary hereto, the Master of such Ship shall forfeit the sum of One Hundred Pounds; and if, after the arrival of any Ship within One League of the Coasts of this Island, any alteration be made in the stowage of the Cargo of such Ship, so as to facilitate the unlading of any part of such Cargo, or if any part be staved, destroyed, or thrown overboard, or any Package be opened, such Ship shall be deemed to have broken Bulk: Provided always, that Coin or Bullion may be landed without Report, and previous to Entry or Warrant.

Penalty.

Except Coin and Bullion.

Report to be made within 24 hours of arrival of Ship.

Particulars of Report.

9. And it is further enacted, that the Master of every Ship arriving from parts beyond the Seas at any Port in this Island, whether laden or in ballast, shall within Twenty-four Hours after such arrival, and before Bulk be broken, make due Report of such Ship, and shall make and subscribe a Declaration to the truth of the same, before the Collector or Controller of such Port; and such Report shall contain an account of the particular Marks, Numbers, and Contents of all the different Packages or Parcels of the Goods on board such Ship, and the particulars of such Goods as are stowed loose, to the best of his knowledge, and of the Place or Places where such Goods were respectively taken on board, and of the Burthen of such Ship, and of the Country where such Ship was built, or if British, of the Port of Registry, and of the Country of the People to whom such Ship belongs, and of the Name and Country of the Person who was Master during the Voyage, and of the Number of the People by whom such Ship was navigated, stating how many are subjects of the Country to which such Ship belongs, and how many are of some other Country and in such Report it shall be further declared, whether and in what cases such ship has broken Bulk in the course of her Voyage; and if any Goods be unladen from any Ship before such Report be made, or if the Master fail to make such Report,

Penalty. or make an untrue Report, he shall forfeit the sum of One Hundred Pounds; and if any Goods be not reported, such Goods shall be forfeited.

Master to deliver Manifest. And Bill of Lading or Copy. And answer questions. 10. And it is further enacted, that the Master of every Ship shall, at the time of making such Report, deliver to the Collector or Controller the Manifest of the Cargo of such Ship, where a Manifest is required, and, if required by the Collector or Controller, shall produce to him any Bill or Bills of Lading, or a true Copy thereof, for any and every part of the Cargo laden on board; and shall answer all such Questions relating to the Ship and Cargo, and Crew and Voyage, as shall be put to him by such Collector or Controller; and in case of failure or refusal to produce such Manifest, or to answer such Questions, or to answer them truly, or to produce such Bill of Lading or Copy, or if such Manifest, or Bill of Lading or Copy, shall be false, or if any Bill of Lading be altered by any Master, and the Goods expressed therein shall not have been *bonâ fide* shipped on board such Ship, or if any Bill of Lading uttered or produced by any Master shall not have been signed by him, or any such Copy shall not have been received or made by him previously to his leaving the place where the Goods expressed in such Bill of Lading or Copy were shipped, then and *Or forfeit £100.* in every such case such Master shall forfeit the sum of One Hundred Pounds.

Officers to board Ships. And secure Goods. 11. And it is further enacted, that it shall be lawful for the proper Officers of the Customs to board any Ship arriving at any Port in this Island, and freely to stay on board until all the Goods laden therein shall have been duly delivered from the same; and such Officers shall have free access to every part of the Ship, with power to fasten down Hatchways, and to mark any Goods before landing, and to lock up, seal, mark, or otherwise secure any Goods on board such Ship; and if any Place, or any Box or Chest, be locked, and the Keys be withheld, such Officers, if they be of a degree superior to Tidesmen, may open any such Place, Box, or Chest in the best manner in their power; and if they be Tidesmen, or only of that degree, they shall send for their superior Officer, who may open or cause to be opened any such *Goods concealed forfeited.* Place, Box, or Chest in the best manner in his power; and if any Goods be found concealed on board any such Ship, they shall be forfeited; and if the Officer shall place any lock, mark, or seal upon any Goods on board, and *Penalty on secret removal of any such Goods, etc.* such lock, mark, or seal be wilfully opened, altered, or broken before due delivery of such Goods, or if any such Goods be secretly conveyed away, or if the Hatchways, after having been fastened down by the Officer, be opened, the Master of such Ship shall forfeit the sum of One Hundred Pounds.

Importer to deliver Bill of Entry of Goods. 12. And it is further enacted, that the Person entering any Goods Inwards, (whether for payment of Duty, or to be warehoused for Exportation, or whether such Goods be free of Duty) shall deliver to the Collector or

Controller a Bill of the Entry of such Goods, fairly written in Words at length, expressing the Name of the Ship, and of the Master of the Ship in which the Goods were imported, and of the Place from whence they were brought, and the description and situation of the Warehouse if they are to be warehoused, and the Name of the Person in whose name the Goods are to be entered, and the Quantity and Description of the Goods, and the Number and Denomination or Description of the respective Packages containing the Goods, and in the Margin of such Bill shall delineate the respective Marks and Numbers of such Packages, and shall pay down any Duties which may be payable upon the Goods mentioned in such Entry: and such Person shall also deliver at the same time Two or more Duplicates, as the case may require, of such Bill, in which all Sums and Numbers may be expressed in Figures; and the Particulars to be contained in such Bill shall be written and arranged in such Form and Manner, and the Number of such Duplicates shall be such, as the Collector and Controller shall require; and such Bill being duly signed by the Collector and Controller, and transmitted to the Landing Waiter, shall be the Warrant to him for the Landing or Delivery of such Goods.

Duplicates.

Entry to agree with Manifest, etc.

13. And it is further enacted, that no Entry, nor any Warrant for the landing of any Goods, or for the taking of any Goods out of any Warehouse, shall be deemed valid, unless the Particulars of the Goods and Packages in such Entry shall correspond with the Particulars of the Goods and Packages purporting to be the same, in the Report of the Ship, and in the Manifest, where a Manifest is required, and in the Certificate or other Document, where any is required, by which the Importation or Entry of such Goods is authorized, nor unless the Goods shall have been properly described in such Entry by the Denominations and with the Characters and Circumstances according to which such Goods are charged with Duty or may be Imported, either to be used in the Island, or to be warehoused for Exportation only; and any Goods taken or delivered out of any Ship, or out of any Warehouse, or for the Delivery of which, or for any Order for the Delivery of which from any Warehouse, Demand shall have been made, not having been duly Entered, shall be forfeited.

Goods not duly entered, forfeited.

Importer to declare the Value of Goods ad valorem.

14. And it is further enacted, that in all cases where the Duties imposed by this Act upon the Importation of Articles are charged not according to the Weight, Tale, Gauge, or Measure, but according to the Value thereof, such Value shall be ascertained by the Declaration of the Importer of such Articles, or his known Agent, in Manner and Form following; (that is to say,)

I, A. B., of (*place of abode,*) do hereby declare that I am (the Importer, or authorized by the Importer) of the Goods contained in this Entry, and that I enter the same (*stating which, if part only*) at the sum of Witness my hand the day of

A. B.

Goods under valued to be detained.

15. And it is further enacted, that if upon Examination it shall appear to the Officers of the customs that such Goods are not valued according to the true Value thereof, it shall be lawful for such Officers to detain and secure such Goods, and (within Four Days from the date of such Declaration being made) take such Goods for the use of the Crown; and the Collector and Controller shall thereupon cause the Amount of such Valuation, together with an addition of Ten Pounds *per centum* thereon, and also the Duties paid upon such Entry, to be paid to the Importer or Proprietor of such Goods, in full Satisfaction for the same, and shall dispose of such Goods for the benefit of the Crown; and if the Produce of such Sale shall exceed the Sums so paid, and all Charges incurred by the Crown, one Moiety of the Overplus shall be given to the Officer or Officers who had detained and taken the Goods; and the Money retained for the benefit of the Crown shall be paid into the hands of the Collector of the Customs, with the knowledge of the Controller, and carried to Account as Duties of Customs.

And sold for the benefit of the Crown.

Bill of Sight, if Goods not known.

16. And it is further enacted, that if the Importer of any Goods, or his Agent, after full Conference with him, shall declare before the Collector or Controller that he cannot for want of full Information make a full or perfect Entry of such Goods, and shall make and subscribe a Declaration to the truth thereof, it shall be lawful for the Collector and Controller to receive an Entry by Bill of Sight for the Packages or Parcels of such Goods by the best Description which can be given, and to grant a Warrant thereupon, in order that the same may be provisionally landed, and may be seen and examined by such Importer, in Presence of the proper Officers; and within Three Days after any Goods shall have been so landed, the Importer shall make a full or perfect Entry thereof, and shall either pay down all Duties which shall be due and payable upon such Goods, or shall duly warehouse the same; and in default of such Entry, such Goods shall be taken to the King's Warehouse; and if the Importer shall not, within One Month after such landing, make perfect Entry of such Goods, and pay the Duties due thereon, together with the Charges of Removal and Warehouse Rent, such Goods shall be sold for the payment thereof, and the Overplus, if any, shall be paid to the Proprietor of the Goods.

Perfect Entry to be made within 3 days.

Cotton Cloths, not British, to be Stamped.

17. And it is further enacted, that all Cotton Cloths, not being of the Manufacture of Great Britain, shall, previous to their being passed through the Custom House, be there marked and stamped at one end of every Piece with such Mark or Stamp as the Governor may from time to time order or appoint to be made and used for that purpose, and any Cotton Cloths as aforesaid, which may be found in any House or Place within this Island, except by the written Permission of the proper Officer of Customs, without being marked or stamped at one end of every entire Piece, shall be liable to be seized and forfeited, and after Condemnation shall be publicly

Or forfeited.

Other Goods may be Stamped by order of the Governor. sold to the highest bidder: And it shall be lawful for the Governor, by any Proclamation to be by him issued and published in the Gazette, to make and appoint such other Regulations for the properly stamping or marking of any other Goods, as may be deemed expedient for more effectually securing the Duties thereon; and any Goods which may be required to be stamped or marked under any such Proclamation as aforesaid, which may be found in any House or Place within this Island, not being stamped or marked as aforesaid, except by the written Permission of the proper Officer of Customs, shall be liable to be forfeited and sold, and the Proceeds thereof shall be disposed of in like manner as is hereby directed in respect to Cotton Cloths.

Abatement of Duties on Goods damaged during voyage. 18. And it is further enacted, that if any Goods which are rated to pay Duty according to the Number, Measure, or Weight thereof, shall receive Damage during the Voyage, an Abatement of such Duties shall be allowed in proportion to the Damage so received; provided Proof be made to the satisfaction of the Collector and Controller of Customs, or of any Officer of Customs acting therein under their Directions, that such Damage was received after the Goods were shipped: and provided Claim to such Abatement of Duties be made at the time of the first Examination of such Goods.

Proportion of damage how to be ascertained. 19. And it is further enacted, that the Officers of the Customs shall thereupon examine such Goods with reference to such Damage, and may state the Proportion of Damage which, in their Opinion, such Goods have so received, and may make a proportionate Abatement of Duties; but if the Officers be incompetent to estimate such Damage, or if the Importer be not satisfied with the Abatement made by them, the Collector or Controller shall choose Two indifferent Merchants experienced in the Nature and Value of such Goods, who shall examine the same, and shall make and subscribe a Declaration, stating in what Proportion, according to their Judgment, such Goods are lessened in their Value by reason of such Damage; and thereupon the Officers of Customs may make an Abatement of the Duties according to the Proportion of Damage so declared by such Merchants.

Surplus stores subject as Goods. 20. And it is further enacted, that the surplus Stores of every Ship arriving from parts beyond the Seas in this Island, shall be subject to the same Duties, and the same Prohibitions, Restrictions, and Regulations, as the like Sorts of Goods shall be subject to when imported by way of Merchandize; but if it shall appear to the Collector and Controller that the Quantity or Description of such Stores is not excessive or unsuitable, under all the Circumstances of the Voyage, it shall be lawful for them to permit such surplus Stores to be entered for the private use of the Master, Purser, or Owner of such Ship, or of any Passenger of such Ship to whom any such

May be entered for use of Master, etc. or warehoused.

surplus Stores may belong, on payment of the proper Duties, or to be warehoused for the future use of such Ship, although the same could not be legally imported by way of Merchandize.

Certificate of Goods of British Possession. 21. And it is further enacted, that no Goods shall be entered as being of or from any British Possession (if any Benefit attach to such Distinction) unless the Master of the Ship importing the same shall have delivered to the Collector or Controller a Certificate, under the Hand of the proper Officer of the Place where such Goods were taken on board, of the due Clearance of such Ship from thence, containing an Account of such Goods.

Searcher to examine Goods. 22. And it is further enacted, that it shall be lawful for the Searcher to open all Packages, and fully to examine all Goods unshipped or landed at any Place in this Island, and if any Goods so examined shall be found to correspond in all respects with the Bill of Entry for the same, such Goods shall be re-packed at the Charge of such Searcher, who may be allowed such Charge by the Governor, if he shall see fit so to do: Provided always, that it shall be lawful for the Officer of Customs to count, weigh, measure, or gauge all Goods imported, when the same shall be necessary to ascertain the Amount of Duty payable thereon; and the unshipping, carrying, and landing of all such Goods, and the bringing of the same to the proper Place after landing for Examination or for weighing, and the putting of the same into the Scales, and the taking of the same out of and from the Scales after weighing, shall be performed by or at the Expense of the Importer.

Goods to be unshipped, etc. at expense of Importer.

Baggage accompanying Owner, free. 23. And it is further enacted, that all wearing Apparel and personal Baggage of whatever description, accompanying the Owner, shall be admitted to importation Duty free, except such portion thereof as shall on Examination appear to the Collector or Controller of Custōms to be imported for the purpose of Sale.

Public Property Free. 24. And it is further enacted, that all Articles consigned to any Officer of a Public Department in Ceylon, and being the Property of the Crown, are to be passed Duty free, on the Public Officer to whom they are consigned delivering to the Collector of Customs a List of the Articles, and certifying at the foot thereof that they are *boná fide* Public Property.

Prohibitions and Restrictions. 25. And it is further enacted, that the several Sorts of Goods enumerated or described in the Table following, denominated "A Table of Prohibitions and Restrictions Inwards," shall either be absolutely prohibited to be imported into this Island, or shall be imported only under the Restrictions mentioned in such Table, according as the several Sorts of such Goods are respectively set forth therein; (that is to say,)

A Table of Prohibitions and Restrictions Inwards.

A List of Goods absolutely Prohibited to be Imported.

Arms, Amunition, and Utensils of War, by way of Merchandize, except by License from His Majesty for furnishing His Majesty's public Stores only, or under special Authority of the Governor.

Cinnamon, Cinnamon Oil, Cassia, or Cassia Buds.

Coin; viz.—False Money, or Counterfeit Sterling.—Silver of the Realm, or any Money purporting to be such, not being of the established Standard in Weight or Fineness.

Gunpowder, except by License from His Majesty, such License to be granted for the furnishing His Majesty's Stores, or under special Authority of the Governor.

Forfeiture. And if any Goods shall be imported into this Island contrary to any of the Prohibitions or Restrictions mentioned in such Table in respect of such Goods, the same shall be forfeited.

OUTWARDS.

Ship to be entered and Goods cleared before shipment. 26. And whereas it is expedient that the Officers of Customs should have full Cognizance of all Ships departing from any Port or Place in this Island for parts beyond the Seas, and of all Goods taken out of this Island; and it is therefore necessary to make Regulations for the entering and clearing outwards of all such Ships, and for the entering, clearing, and shipping of all such Goods; It is therefore enacted, that no Goods shall be shipped, or waterborne to be shipped on board any Ship in any Port or Place in this Island, to be carried to parts beyond the Seas, before due entry outwards of such Ship and due entry of such Goods shall have been made, and Warrant granted, nor before such Goods shall have been duly cleared for shipment in manner hereinafter directed.

Victualling Bill for Stores. 27. And it is further enacted, that the Master of every Ship which is to depart from any Port in this Island for parts beyond the Seas, shall, upon due Application made by him, receive a Victualling Bill for the shipment of such Stores as he shall require, and as shall be allowed by the Collector or Controller, for the use of such Ship, according to the Voyage upon which she is about to depart; and that no Articles taken on board any Ship shall be deemed to be Stores except such as shall be borne upon the Victualling Bill for the same.

Bill of Entry. 28. And it is further enacted, that the Person entering Outwards any Goods to be exported to parts beyond the Seas, from any Port in this Island, shall deliver to the Collector or Controller a Bill of the Entry thereof, fairly written in Words at length, expressing the Name of the Ship, and of the Master, and of the Place to which the Goods are to be exported, and of the Person in whose name the Goods are to be entered, and the Quantities and proper Denominations or Descriptions of the several Sorts of Goods, and shall pay down

Duplicates. any Duties which may be due upon the Exportation of any such Goods; and such Person shall also deliver at the same time One or more Duplicates of such Bill, in which all Sums and Numbers may be expressed in Figures; and the Particulars to be contained in such Bill shall be written and arranged in such Form and Manner, and the Number of Duplicates shall be such, as the Collector and Controller shall require; and thereupon the Collector and Controller shall grant a Warrant *Warrant.* for the shipment of such Goods.

Goods for Drawback. Duty Goods. Goods under Restriction. 29. And it is further enacted, that if any Drawback be allowable upon the Exportation of any such Goods, or any Duty be payable thereon, or any Exemption from Duty claimed, or if any such Goods be exportable only according to some particular Rule or Regulation, or under some Restriction or Condition, or for some particular Purpose or Destination, such Goods shall be entered and cleared for shipment by such Denominations or Descriptions as are used, mentioned, or referred to in the granting of such Drawback, or in the levying of such Duty, or granting such Exemption, or in the directing of such Rules, Regulations, Restrictions, Conditions, Purpose, or Destination; and if the Goods in such *Ad valorem Goods. Declaration of value.* Entry are charged to pay Duty according to the Value thereof, such Value shall be stated in the Entry, and shall be affirmed by the Declaration of the Exporter or his known Agent, to be made upon the Entry, and attested by his Signature; and if any Person shall make such Declaration, not being the Exporter of such Goods, nor his Agent duly authorized by him, such Person shall forfeit the Sum of One Hundred Pounds; and such Declaration shall be in Manner and Form following, and shall be binding upon the Person making the same; (that is to say,)

I, A. B., of (*place of abode,*) do hereby declare, that I am the Exporter of the Goods mentioned in this Entry, (or, that I am duly authorized by him,) and I do enter the same at the value of Witness my hand the day of A. B.

Goods under valued to be detained and sold for the benefit of the Crown. 30. And it is further enacted, that if upon Examination it shall appear to the Officers of the Customs that such Goods are not valued according to the true Value thereof, the same may be detained and (within Four Days) taken and disposed of for the benefit of the Crown, in like manner as is herein before provided in respect of Goods imported, except that no Sum in addition to the Amount of the Valuation and the Duties paid shall be paid to the Exporter or Proprietor of the Goods.

Entry of Foreign Goods for Drawback. 31. And it is further enacted, that the Person intending to enter Outwards any Foreign Goods for Drawback, at any other Port than that at which the Duties Inwards on such Goods had been paid, shall first deliver to the

Collector or Controller of the Port where the Duties on such Goods were paid, Two or more Bills, as the case may require, of the Particulars of the Importation of such Goods, and of the Entry Outwards intended to be made; and thereupon such Collector or Controller, finding such Bills to agree with the Entry Inwards, shall write off such Goods from the same, and shall issue Certificate of such Entry, with such Particulars thereof as shall be necessary for the Computation of the Drawback allowable on such Goods, and setting forth in such Certificate the Destination of the Goods, and the Person in whose name they are to be entered for Exportation, and also the Name of such other Port; and such Certificate, together with Two or more Bills of the same, as the case may require, in which all Sums and Numbers may be expressed in Figures, being delivered to the Collector or Controller of the Port from which the Goods are to be exported, shall be the Entry Outwards of such Goods; and such Collector and Controller shall thereupon cause a Warrant to be delivered for the shipment of such Goods.

Certificate.

Goods not agreeing with Bill of Entry forfeited.

32. And it is further enacted, that if any Goods which are subject to any Duty or Restriction in respect of Exportation, or if any Goods which are to be shipped for any Drawback, shall be brought to any Quay, Wharf, or other Place, to be shipped for Exportation, and such Goods shall not agree with the Bill of Entry, the same shall be forfeited; and if any Goods prohibited to be exported be found in any Package brought as aforesaid, such Package and every thing contained therein shall be forfeited.

Prohibited Goods.

Searcher to examine Goods.

33. And it is further enacted, that it shall be lawful for the Searcher to open all Packages, and fully to examine all Goods shipped or brought for shipment at any Place in this Island; and if any Goods so examined shall be found to correspond in all respects with the Bill of Entry for the same, such Goods shall be re-packed at the Charge of such Searcher, who may be allowed such Charge by the Governor, if he shall see fit so to do.

Master to deliver Content.

34. And it is further enacted, that before any Ship shall be cleared Outwards at any Port in this Island for parts beyond the Seas, with any Goods shipped on board the same in such Port, the Master shall deliver a Content of such Ship, setting forth the Name and Tonnage of such Ship, and the Place or Places of her Destination, and the Name of the Master, and also an Account of the Goods shipped on board, and of the Packages containing such Goods, and of the Marks and Numbers upon such Packages, and a like Account of the Goods on board, if any, which had been reported Inwards for Exportation in such Ship, so far as any of such Particulars can be known by him; and the Master of the Ship shall make and sign a Declaration before the Collector or Controller to the Truth of such Content, and shall also answer to the Collector or Controller such Questions concerning the Ship, the Cargo, and the intended

And answer Questions.

Certificate of Clearance. Voyage, as shall be demanded of him; and thereupon the Collector or Controller, or other proper Officer, if such Ship be laden, shall make out and give to the Master a Certificate of the Clearance of such Ship for her intended Voyage, containing an Account of the total Quantities of the several Sorts of Goods laden therein, or a Certificate of her Clearance in Ballast, as the Case may be; and if the Ship shall depart without such Clearance, or if the Master shall deliver a false Content, he shall forfeit the Sum of One Hundred Pounds.

Officers may board Vessels after Clearance. 35. And it is further enacted, that it shall be lawful for the Officers of the Customs to go on Board any Ship after Clearance Outwards, within the Limits of any Port in this Island, or within Two Leagues of the Coast thereof, and to demand the Certificate of Clearance and the Victualling Bill, and if there be any Goods or Stores on Board not contained in the Certificate of Clearance nor in the Victualling Bill, such Goods or Stores shall be forfeited.

DRAWBACKS.

Entry by real Owner or Commission Merchant. 36. And it is further enacted, that no Drawback shall be allowed upon the Exportation from this Island of any Goods unless such Goods shall have been entered in the Name of the Person who was the real Owner thereof at the time of Entry and Shipping, or of the Person who had actually purchased and shipped the same, in his own Name and at his own Liability and Risk, on Commission, according to the Practice of Merchants, and who was and shall have continued to be entitled in his own Right to such Drawback, except in the cases hereinafter provided for.

Declaration to Exportation and Right. 37. And it is further enacted, that such Owner or Commission Merchant shall make and subscribe a Declaration upon the Debenture that the Goods mentioned therein have been actually exported, and have not been relanded and are not intended to be relanded in any Port of this Island, and that he was the real Owner thereof at the time of Entry and Shipping, or that he had purchased and shipped the said Goods in his own Name and at his own Liability and Risk, on Commission, as the case may be, and that he was and continued to be entitled to Drawback thereon in his own Right: Provided always, that if such Owner or Merchant shall not have purchased the Right to such Drawback, he shall declare under his Hand upon the Entry and upon the Debenture the Person who is entitled thereto, and the Name of such Person shall be stated in the Entry and in the Debenture; and the Receipt of such Person on the Debenture shall be the Discharge for such Drawback.

Limitation of the Drawback. 38. And it is further enacted, that no Drawback shall be allowed upon the Exportation of any Parcel, Package, or other Assortment of Goods which may not be entire and the same as imported, except with the special Permission of the Collector and Controller, nor unless such Goods be shipped within Two Years after the payment of the Duties Inward thereon, nor unless such Goods shall exceed Forty Pounds in Value; and that no Drawback shall be allowed upon any Goods which by reason of Damage or Decay shall have become of less Value for the use of the Island than the Amount of such Drawback, and all Goods so damaged which shall be cleared for any Drawback, shall be forfeited, and the Person who caused such Goods to be so cleared shall forfeit the Sum of Two Hundred Pounds, or Treble the Amount of the Drawback in such case, on the decision of the Governor.

Issuing & passing Debenture.

39. And it is further enacted, that for the purpose of computing and paying any Drawback payable upon any Goods duly entered, shipped, and exported, a Debenture shall, in due time after such Entry, be prepared by the Collector and Controller, certifying in the first instance the Entry Outwards of such Goods; and so soon as the same shall have been duly exported, and a Notice containing the Particulars of the Goods shall have been delivered by the Exporter to the Searcher, the Shipment and Exportation thereof shall be certified to the Collector and Controller, upon such Debenture, by the Searcher, and the Debenture shall thereupon be computed and passed with all convenient dispatch, and be delivered to the Person entitled to receive the same.

Duty on Drawback Goods relanded.

40. And it is further enacted, that if any Goods which have been taken from the Warehouse to be exported from the same, or any Goods which have been cleared to be exported for any Drawback, be relanded at any Port in this Island, such Goods shall be subject to pay the same Duties as Goods first entered.

GOODS WAREHOUSED FOR EXPORTATION.

Goods may be entered to be Warehoused, if of the value of £150.

41. And it is further enacted, that it shall and may be lawful to the Proprietor of any Goods, (except Cinnamon, Cinnamon Oil, Cassia, or Cassia Buds,) who may import the same into the Ports of Colombo, Trincomalé, Point de Galle, and Jaffna, to enter the same, or any part thereof, not being in the Aggregate of less Value than One Hundred and Fifty Pounds, for Exportation; and on such Entry, it shall and may be lawful for such Proprietor to store and warehouse the Goods, Wares, and Merchandize so entered, in any Store or Warehouse to be approved by the Collector of the Customs of any of the abovementioned Ports, under the joint Keys of the said Collector and the said Proprietor, without payment at the time of any Custom Duty; and that the said Goods may remain in the Store or Warehouse aforesaid, at the sole Risk of the Proprietor, until the same shall be taken therefrom for Exportation; and the same may be exported (due Notice being given to the Officers of the Customs) from the said Ports, either by the original Proprietor importing, or by any other Person to whom he may sell the same for the purpose of Exportation, without payment of any Duty thereon: Provided always, that if the said Goods, or any part thereof, shall be taken out for sale or Consumption within this Island, the full Import Duties shall be paid thereon, and in addition thereto a Duty of One per cent. on the Value thereof in this market: And provided further,

Conditions.

that the Warehouse or Store in which such Goods are deposited, shall be subject to the Visitation of the Collector of Customs or other Officer of the Customs deputed by such Collector by Writing under his Hand, at any time of the day, on Notice to the Proprietor or other Person acting on his behalf in Charge and Custody of the Goods; and such Goods shall be so arranged in such Store, as to admit of easy and prompt Access thereto.

Goods may be sorted and repacked.

42. And it is further enacted, that it shall be lawful for the Collector and Controller, under such Regulations as they shall see fit, to permit the Proprietor or other Person having Control over any Goods so warehoused, to sort, separate, pack, and repack any such Goods, and to make such lawful Alterations therein, or Arrangements and Assortments thereof, as may be necessary for the Preservation of such Goods, or in order to the Sale, Shipment, or legal Disposal of the same. and no single Delivery of Goods shall take place for Exportation of less Value than Forty Pounds, according to the invoiced Value of such Goods.

No Delivery under the value of £40.

On removal of Goods, Duty to be paid on deficiency.

43. And it is further enacted, that when any Goods, Wares, or Merchandize are intended to be taken out of any Warehouse or Place in which the same shall have been lodged or secured, according to the directions of this Regulation, for Exportation, the proper Officer of the Customs shall re-examine such Goods, Wares, or Merchandize; and in case it shall appear on such re-examination that the Quantity or Contents of any such Goods, Wares, or Merchandize is or are less than the Quantity or Contents entered at the first Examination of such Goods, after a reasonable allowance for Wastage or Leakage on such Goods as are subject thereto, then and in such case, the Importer or Importers, Proprietor or Proprietors, Consignee or Consignees, of such Goods, Wares, and Merchandize, shall, before the same are delivered out of the Warehouse for the purpose aforesaid, pay the full Duty of Customs on such deficient Quantity.

Goods fraudulently removed or concealed forfeited.

44. And it is further enacted, that if any Goods, Wares, or Merchandize warehoused under the authority of this Regulation, shall be fraudulently and clandestinely hid or concealed in, or removed out of, any Warehouse or Place where the same shall be lodged, with intent to evade the Duty payable on the Importation or Exportation thereof, all such Goods or Merchandize so fraudulently or clandestinely hid, or concealed, or removed, shall be forfeited, and shall and may be seized by any Officer of the Customs; and the Person or Persons so hiding, concealing, or removing the same, or aiding or assisting therein, or to whose hands the same shall knowingly come, shall be subject to the like Penalties, as if such Goods, Wares, and Merchandize had been fraudulently landed, or removed without payment of Duty.

Goods not exported within eighteen

45. And it is further enacted, that all Goods, Wares, and Merchandize which may be warehoused for Exportation under the Provisions of this

months liable to Duty.

Or to be sold or destroyed.

Ordinance, which shall not be Exported within Eighteen Months from the date of the first Entry thereof, shall be liable to the full rate of Import Duties imposed on Goods of a similar Description; and in default of such Duties being paid, it shall and may be lawful for the Collector and Controller of Customs to cause all such Goods, Wares, and Merchandize to be publicly sold, or exposed to Sale; and after such Sale, the Produce shall be applied to the payment of the Duties thereon, and the Surplus, if any, paid to the Proprietor or other Person authorized to receive the same: Provided always, that if at the Expiration of Eighteen Months as aforesaid, it shall appear to the Collector and Controller that such Goods, Wares, or Merchandize are so much damaged as to be no longer in a marketable state, it shall be lawful for the said Collector and Controller to destroy the same; and the Proprietor or Owner of such Goods shall have no Claim, either in Law or Equity, to the Value of the same, or any part thereof destroyed as aforesaid.

No Goods to be imported or exported in Vessels of less than 15 tons.

Unless by Proclamation by Governor.

46. And it is further enacted, that no Goods shall be imported into or exported from this Island, from or to parts beyond the Seas, in any Vessel or Boat of less Burthen than Fifteen Tons, on pain of Forfeiture of all such Goods: Provided always, that it shall and may be lawful for the Governor by any Proclamation to be by him issued and published in the Gazette for that purpose, to allow any Vessels or Boats under Fifteen Tons Burthen to import or export any Goods from or to parts beyond the Seas, at such Ports or Places, and during such Periods or Times, and in such Manner as may be deemed expedient, upon any Pearl Fishery or other occasion appearing to require the same.

REGULATIONS COASTWISE.

Officers of Customs to have Cognizance of Ships and Goods Coastwise.

47. And it is further enacted, that Ships conveying Goods Coastwise, and all Goods imported or exported Coastwise, shall be liable to the like Cognizance of the Customs, and be subject to the same Prohibitions, Restrictions, and Regulations as Goods imported from or exported to parts beyond the Seas: Provided always, that it shall be lawful for the Governor to make and appoint such other Regulations, by any Proclamation to be by him issued and published in the Gazette, for the carrying Coastwise of any Goods, as to him shall appear expedient.

License for Boat under Fifteen Tons Burthen.

48. And it is further enacted, that all Vessels or Boats under Fifteen Tons Burthen, wholly owned by British subjects, shall be allowed to carry Goods Coastwise from one Part of the Island to another: Provided nevertheless, that such Vessel or Boat shall be licensed by the Collector of the District to which the said Vessel or Boat belongs; and every such License shall specify the Burthen of the said Boat, the Name of the Owner and the Tindal thereof, and shall be in force for the Year in which the same may be granted; and any such Vessel or Boat carrying Goods

Coastwise as aforesaid, without being duly licensed as required by this Clause, shall be liable to Forfeiture, together with all the Goods so carried.

Collector to grant Permit for conveyance of Goods within his Province.

49. And whereas it is expedient to grant Facilities to the Navigation round the Coasts of this Island, for the purpose of collecting a Cargo for the Export of Vessels belonging to the same; It is therefore enacted, that all Boats, Dhonies, or other Vessels belonging to any of the Ports of this Island and duly registered as British Vessels, or licensed in manner required in the preceding Clause, may by Permission in writing from any Collector of Customs, and having such written Permission on board, in the room of a Port Clearance, proceed to any part of the Coast situate within the Province in which such Collector is stationed, and there take in Goods of the Description in the said Permission to be mentioned, which Goods are to be brought to the Port of regular Entry and Clearance defined in this Ordinance from which the said Permit is granted, there to be inspected and regularly cleared for Exportation; and also, by such written Permission, and having the same on board, such Boats, Dhonies, or other Vessels may convey from a Port of regular Entry, Goods duly imported and entered, the Description and Quantity being stated in such Permit, to such Part of the Coast, situate within the Province in which such Collector is stationed, as in the said Permit shall be mentioned.

Duty on Goods exported Coastwise to be repaid on Certificate.

50. And it is further enacted, that whenever Goods shall have been exported Coastwise from any one Port to any other Port of this Island, the full Amount of Customs Duty paid on the Export thereof shall be repaid to the Shipper or his Agent, on production of a Certificate, signed by the Collector or Controller of Customs at the Place of relanding, (and which such Collector or Controller is hereby required to give without delay,) that such Goods have been relanded in the same Packages unopened; provided such Shipper or Agent shall on so exporting the same, have entered such Goods to be carried Coastwise, and shall have specified the Place or Places of relanding; and provided such Certificate shall be produced within the period of Three Months from the date of Exportation.

GENERAL REGULATIONS.

Ships to use their own Boats.

Or licensed Boats.

License.

51. And it is further enacted, that Ships and Vessels of all kinds may, in landing or taking on board any Cargo or Goods, either make use of their own Boats, or (excepting at the Ports of Colombo, Galle, and Trincomalé) of any other Boats; and at the said excepted Ports, of such Boats as shall be Licensed for that purpose, by Licenses under the Hand of the Collector and Controller of Customs at such Port respectively, to be issued and recalled or taken away in case of any Misconduct by the Owner, Tindal, or any of the Boatmen thereof, at the discretion of the Collector and Controller; and such Licenses shall be in force for such Period as may be expressed therein, unless

previous to the expiration thereof, the same shall be recalled or taken away as aforesaid, and shall specify the Burthen of the said Boat, the Name of the Owner and the Tindal thereof, and the Number of Seamen to be employed in the same, and shall be registered in the Offices of the Master Attendant at each Port respectively; and all Ships requiring Boats shall apply for the same at the said Offices.

Restriction not to extend to Dhonies.

52. Provided always, that the Restriction of employing licensed Boats, or the Boats belonging to the Vessel itself, at the Ports aforesaid of Colombo, Trincomalé, and Galle, shall not extend, or be construed to extend, to any Dhoney, but only to square-rigged Vessels, Sloops, and Schooners.

Governor to fix rate of Boat Hire.

Tindal demanding more.

53. And it is further enacted, that the Charges for Boat Hire which may be demanded by Boats licensed to ship and land Goods in the Ports of Colombo, Galle, and Trincomalé, shall be such as shall be fixed from time to time by the Governor of this Island, and publicly notified by Advertisement; and the Tindal or the principal Person of any licensed Boat, who shall demand any higher Rate, shall, on Conviction before the District Court, be liable to a Fine of Two Pounds, and, in default of payment, to imprisonment at hard labour for One Calendar Month, unless the Fine be sooner paid.

If Boat absent.

Or Tindal disobey orders.

If Boatmen absent.

Penalty.

54. And it is further enacted, that all Tindals and Boatmen of licensed Boats shall obey the lawful orders of the Collector and Controller of Customs and of the Master Attendant of the Port and the Officers of his Department, and no licensed Boat shall be absent from the Port without leave of the said Officers; and if the Tindal or principal Person of any licensed Boat, on any verbal or written Notice being given to him by the Master Attendant of the Port, or any Officer of his Department, ordering such Boat to proceed on board any Ship or square-rigged Vessel, or to convey to the same any Cargo or Passenger, or to bring on shore any Cargo or Passenger, shall refuse to comply with such Order, not being manifestly prevented therefrom by Stress of Weather; or if he shall when so required to proceed have fewer Seamen on board his Boat than the Number specified in his License, unless by Permission of the Collector or Controller of Customs, who may in such case at their discretion order a proportionate reduction of the charges payable for the Hire of such Boat, such Tindal or principal Person shall, upon proof of such refusal or deficiency before the District Court, be liable to a Fine not exceeding Ten Pounds, which Fine may be levied by seizure and sale of such Boat, and of such Tindal's Property, and in default of his having sufficient Property, he may be committed to Hard Labour for the term of Three Months; and the License of such Boat may be revoked.

Goods removed in unlicensed Boat forfeited, with Boat.

55. And it is further enacted, that if any Goods be landed from, or shipped to any Ship or Vessel anchoring or being at anchor in the Port of Colombo, Galle, and Trincomalé, except in Boats licensed as abovementioned, or in Boats belonging to such Vessel, the said Goods, and the unlicensed Boat in which they may have been landed or shipped, shall, upon proof thereof before any Court having Jurisdiction under this Ordinance, be confiscated.

Note of contents of Boat.

56. And it is further enacted, that in landing the Cargoes of Vessels, (the Masters or Supercargoes of which are Europeans,) each separate Boatload shall be accompanied by a Note, addressed to the Collector of Customs, specifying the Quantity, Nature, and Quality (when necessary) of the Goods so sent, and the Marks and Numbers affixed to them: And in Default of Compliance with the said Provision, the said Master or Supercargo shall be liable to a Fine not exceeding Ten Pounds, and to be imprisoned till the same is paid.

Power for Governor to appoint Ports and legal Quays.

57. And it is further enacted, that it shall be lawful for the Governor, by any Proclamation to be issued by him for that Purpose from time to time, to appoint any Port, Haven, or Creek in the Island of Ceylon, and to set out the Limits thereof, and to appoint the proper Places within the same, to be legal Quays for the lading and unlading of Goods, and to declare that any Place that had been set out as a legal Quay by such Authority, shall be no longer a legal Quay for the lading and unlading of Goods: Provided always, that all Ports, Havens, and Creeks, and the respective Limits thereof, and all legal Quays, appointed and set out and existing as such at the Commencement of this Ordinance, under any Law till then in force, shall continue to be such Ports, Havens, Creeks, Limits, and legal Quays respectively, as if the same had been appointed and set out under the Authority of this Ordinance.

Collector and Controller to appoint Sufferance Wharfs.

58. And it is further enacted, that it shall be lawful for the Collector and Controller of His Majesty's Customs, from time to time, by any Order under their Hands, to appoint Places to be Sufferance Wharfs, for the lading and unlading of Goods by Sufferance, to be duly issued by them, or by the Proper Officers under their Directions, in such Manner and in such Cases as they shall see fit.

Times for landing and shipping.

59. And it is further enacted, that no Goods shall be unshipped or landed, or shall be put off from any Wharf, Quay, or other Place, or shall be waterborne in order to be exported, but only on Days not being Sunday, Christmas Day, or Good Friday, or before Six o'clock in the Morning, or later than Five o'clock in the Afternoon, and in the Presence and with the Authority of the proper Officer of the Customs: Provided always, that Coin, Bullion, and personal Baggage to the extent of Two Trunks and

Two Parcels, and no more, shall be permitted to pass at all convenient Hours, on being searched by any Officer of the Customs.

Transhipment of Goods.

60. And it is further enacted, that all Goods which shall be transhipped in Port without the previous Permission of the Collector or Controller of Customs, or which shall be shipped on board of any other Vessel than that for which they have been passed at the Custom House, shall be liable, as well as the Vessel on which they are shipped, to Confiscation, which Penalty may be reduced to Treble the Amount of Duties, at the Discretion of Government.

No Vessel to be hauled on shore without permission.

Boat to be removed from Wharf when directed.

Penalty.

61. And it is further enacted, that no Vessel or Boat shall be hauled on Shore at any Wharf, Quay, or Landing Place in this Island, for the Purpose of Repairs or otherwise, without Permission from the Collector or Controller of Customs and the Master Attendant; and no Boat shall remain alongside of any Wharf or Landing Place, after the Owner or Person in Charge shall be directed to remove the same by the proper Officer of the Customs: And any Person hauling any Vessel or Boat on Shore without such Permission as aforesaid, and the Owner or Person in Charge of any Boat refusing or neglecting to remove the same when ordered as aforesaid, shall be liable to a Penalty of Five Pounds, and in default of payment, to imprisonment until such Fine be paid.

No Timber, etc. to be left on Wharf for more than two days.

62. And it is further enacted, that if any Timber or other bulky Articles be left on any public Wharf or Landing Place in this Island for more than Two Days, so as to interrupt or hinder the free use thereof, it shall be lawful for the Collector and Controller of Customs, after Twenty Four Hours Notice in writing given to the Owner thereof, to remove the same; and such Owner shall be liable to a Penalty of Five Pounds: And such Goods shall not be delivered up to the Owner thereof until after payment of the said Penalty, together with the charges attending the Removal of the same: And if such Goods shall not be claimed and removed within Six Days after Notice given as aforesaid, it shall be lawful for the Collector and Controller to sell the same by public Auction, and to deduct from the Proceeds the Amount of such Penalty, and all Charges which may have been incurred on account of such Goods, and the Surplus, if any, shall be paid to the Owner.

Ballast, etc. to be removed to proper place within 24 hours.

Penalty.

63. And it is further enacted, that if any Ballast or Rubbish landed from any Vessel on any Wharf, Quay, or other Landing Place, or in any Place prohibited by public Notice, be not removed within Twenty Four Hours after the same shall be landed, to the Depositories appointed by the Collector and Controller and the Master Attendant, the Master or other Person landing the same shall be liable to a Penalty not exceeding Ten Pounds.

Power to charge Rent in King's Warehouse.

64. And it is further enacted, that in all cases where Goods Imported (save and except such as are in Deposit) or Goods intended for Exportation are not removed from the Custom House within the term of Seven Days, it shall and may be lawful for the Collector or Controller of Customs to charge and demand and receive Warehouse Rent for such Goods for all such Time as the same shall remain in such Warehouse, at such Rate as may from time to time be fixed by Government as Warehouse Rent payable for Goods lodged in any King's Warehouse; and no Goods upon which Warehouse Rent may be due shall be removed until the same be paid.

Power to sell Goods not cleared.

65. And it is further enacted, that if any Goods shall be left in any Custom House or King's Warehouse of this Island without payment of Duty for a longer Period than Six Months, unless permitted to remain by this or any other Ordinance, or by the special Permission of Government, such Goods shall be, after public Advertisement, sold by Auction to answer the Duties and Warehouse Rent due thereon, and any Surplus shall be repaid or reserved to be paid to the Owner, who shall have no further Claim touching the same: Provided, that if any such Goods shall happen to be of a perishable nature, such Advertisement and Sale may take place at such earlier Period as may appear to Government, on a Representation and Consideration of the Case, necessary.

Goods warehoused to be at risk of the Owner.

Penalty on Officers embezzling, etc.

66. And it is further enacted, that if any Goods lodged in any Custom House or King's Warehouse of this Island, shall be destroyed by fire, or stolen therefrom, the Owner thereof shall not have any Claim on the Crown to Compensation thereof, but shall in that case be exempted from payment of any Duties thereon: Provided always, that any officers employed in and about the Customs, who shall embezzle any Property lodged therein, belonging to an Individual, or by whose Negligence such Property may be stolen therefrom, shall be liable to make good to the Party injured Double the Value thereof, upon the Fact being proved before a competent Court, in an Action to be brought within One Year from the Date at which such Embezzlement, or Theft, and Negligence, is alleged to have taken place.

Weights and Measures.

67. And it is further enacted, that all Duties and Drawbacks of Customs shall be paid and received in the several Descriptions of Money herein enumerated, and at the Rates of Exchange specified, viz. in British Gold or Silver Money, or in such other Description of Money and at such Rate of Exchange as may from time to time be established by Government, and according to the Standard Weights and Measures of this Island; and that in all cases where such Duties and Drawbacks are imposed and allowed according to any specific Quantity or any specific Value, the same shall be deemed to apply in the same Proportion to any greater or less Quantity or Value.

Bonds to be taken by Collector & Controller.
When void.

68. And it is further enacted, that all Bonds relating to the Customs required to be given in respect of Goods or Ships, shall be taken by the Collector and Controller for the use of His Majesty; and after the Expiration of Three Years from the Date thereof, or from the Time, if any, limited therein for the Performance of the Condition thereof, every such Bond upon which no Prosecution or Suit shall have been commenced, shall be void, and may be cancelled and destroyed.

No act invalidated by absence of Controller.

69. And it is further enacted, that every Act, Matter, or Thing required by any Law at any time in force to be done or performed by, to, or with the Collector and Controller of Customs, shall and may be done or performed at such Ports or Places where there is no Controller of Customs, by, to, or with the Collector or other principal Officer of Customs, and shall be as valid and effectual in Law as if the same had been done and performed by, to, or with any Collector and Controller of Customs under any Law now in force or hereafter to be made.

Officer may be stationed in Ship within Limits of a Port.

70. And it is further enacted, that it shall be lawful for the Collector and Controller of any Port in this Island, to station Officers on board any Ship while within the Limits of such Port; and the Master of every Ship on board of which any Officer is so stationed, shall provide every such Officer sufficient Room under the Deck, in some part of the Forecastle or Steerage, for his Bed or Hammock; and in case of Neglect or Refusal so to do, shall forfeit the Sum of One Hundred Pounds.

Officers may board Ships hovering on the Coasts.
And bring them into Port.

71. And it is further enacted, that it shall be lawful for the Officers of Customs to go on board any Ship or Vessel hovering within One League of the Coast of this Island, and to rummage and search all parts of such Ship for prohibited and uncustomed Goods, and freely to stay on board such Ship or Vessel, so long as she shall remain within such Distance; and if any such ship shall be bound elsewhere, and shall continue so hovering for the space of twenty-four Hours after the Master shall have been required to depart, it shall be lawful for the Officer of the Customs to bring such Ship into Port, and to search and examine her Cargo, and to examine the Master touching the Cargo and Voyage; and if there be any Goods on board prohibited to be imported into this Island, such Ship or Vessel and her Cargo shall be forfeited; and if the Master shall not truly answer the Questions which shall be demanded of him on such Examination, he shall forfeit the Sum of One Hundred Pounds.

Writ of Assistance to search for and seize Goods.

72. And it is further enacted, that under Authority of a Writ of Assistance, granted by the Supreme Court or Court of Vice-Admiralty, (who are hereby authorized and required to grant such Writ of Assistance, upon Application made to them for that Purpose by the Principal Officers of His

Majesty's Customs,) it shall be lawful for any Officer of the Customs, taking with him a Peace Officer, to enter any Building or other Place in the Daytime, and to search for and seize and secure any Goods liable to Forfeiture under this Act, and, in case of Necessity, to break open any Doors and any Chests or other Packages for that Purpose; and such Writ of Assistance, when issued, shall be deemed to be in force during the whole of the Reign in which the same shall have been granted, and for Twelve Months from the Conclusion of such Reign.

Obstruction or bribery of Officer.

73. And it is further enacted, that any Person shipping or landing any Goods, or receiving the same on board, or on shore, contrary to the Provisions of this Ordinance, or, in either situation, obstructing or molesting any Custom House Officer in the Execution of his Duty, or bribing or offering to bribe any such Officer, or knowingly assisting in any such Acts, shall, on Conviction before the District Court, be liable to a Fine not exceeding One Hundred Pounds, and to be imprisoned for any Term not exceeding Six Months, according to the nature of the Misdemeanour; and the Goods so attempted to be shipped or landed, shall be liable to Confiscation. And it is further enacted, that any Person who shall be convicted of giving or offering to any Person employed in the Collection of the Customs, directly or indirectly, any Present, Fee, or Gratuity, shall be liable to a Fine not exceeding One Hundred Pounds, and to be imprisoned till such Fine be paid; and that any such Person so employed in the Collection of the Customs, convicted of receiving any Bribe, Present, Fee, or Gratuity, shall be punishable by Fine and Imprisonment, with or without Hard Labour, at the Discretion of the District Court, such Fine not exceeding One Hundred Pounds, and such Imprisonment not exceeding Six Months.

Penalty on Officer receiving Bribe.

Falsification of Stamp or Document.

74. And it is further enacted, that if any Person shall counterfeit or falsify, or wilfully use when counterfeited or falsified, any Stamp or Mark used in the Customs to denote that Goods have duly passed through the same and the Duty been charged thereon, or any Entry, Warrant, Cocket, or Transire, or other Document for the unlading, lading, entering, exporting, or clearing of any Ship or Vessel, or for the landing or shipping of any Goods, Stores, Baggage, or Article whatever, or shall by any false Statement procure any Writing or Document to be made for any of such Purposes, every Person so offending shall for every such Offence forfeit the Sum of Two Hundred Pounds: Provided always, that this Penalty shall not attach to any particular Offence for which any other Penalty shall be expressly imposed by any Law in force for the time being.

Penalty on false Declaration & Answer.

75. And it is further enacted, that if any Declaration required to be made by this Ordinance or by any other Ordinance relating to the Customs, (except Declarations to the Value of Goods,) be untrue in any Particular, or if any Person required by this Ordinance or by any other Ordinance relating to the Customs to answer Questions put to him by the Officers of the Customs, touching certain Matters, shall not truly

answer such Questions, the Person making such Declaration, or answering such Questions, shall, over and above any other Penalty to which he may become subject, forfeit the Sum of One Hundred Pounds.

Seizures.

Ship to include Guns, Tackle, etc.

76. And it is further enacted, that all Goods, and all Ships, and Vessels, and Boats, which by this Ordinance or any other Ordinance at any time in force relating to the Customs, shall be declared to be forfeited, shall and may be seized by any Officer of the Customs; and such Forfeiture of any Ship, Vessel, or Boat, shall be deemed to include the Guns, Tackle, Apparel, and Furniture of the same; and such Forfeiture of any Goods shall be deemed to include the proper Packages in which the same are contained.

Forfeiture of Goods to include means of removal.

77. And it is further enacted, that all Vessels, Boats, Carriages, and Cattle made use of in the Removal of any Goods liable to Forfeiture under this Act, shall be forfeited.

Return of Duty overpaid.

78. And it is further enacted, that although any Duty of Customs shall have been overpaid, or although after any Duty of Customs shall have been charged and paid, it shall appear or be judicially established that the same had been charged under an erroneous Construction of the Law, it shall not be lawful to return any such Overcharge, after the expiration of Three Years from the Date of such Payment.

Recovery of Penalties and Forfeitures.

79. And it is further enacted, that all Penalties and Forfeitures which shall be incurred under this or any other Ordinance, or under any Act of Parliament relating to the Customs, shall and may be sued for and recovered in the respective Courts of this Island, in like manner as other Revenue Cases therein.

Averment of Offence.

80. And it is further enacted, that in any Information or other Proceeding for any Offence against any Ordinance made or to be made relating to the Customs, the Averment that such Offence was committed within the Limits of any Port, shall be sufficient, without Proof of such Limits, unless the contrary be proved.

Proof of payment of Duties to be on Owner.

81. And it is further enacted, that if any Goods shall be seized for Non-payment of Duties, or any other Cause of Forfeiture, and any Dispute shall arise whether the Duties have been paid for the same, or the same have been lawfully imported, or lawfully laden or exported, the Proof thereof shall lie on the Owner or Claimer of such Goods, and not on the Officers who shall seize and stop the same.

Disposal of forfeited property. 82. And it is further enacted, that no Claim to any Thing seized under this Act, and returned into any of His Majesty's Courts, for Adjudication, shall be admitted, unless such Claim be entered in the Name of the Owner, with his Residence and Occupation, nor unless a Declaration to the Property in such Thing be made by the Owner, or by his Attorney or Agent, by whom such Claim shall be entered, to the best of his Knowledge and Belief; and every Person making a false Declaration thereto, shall be deemed guilty of a Misdemeanour, and shall be liable to the Pains and Penalties to which Persons are liable for a Misdemeanour.

Claim to Thing seized to be entered in name of Owner. 83. And it is further enacted, that all Ships, Boats, Goods, and other Things which shall be seized as forfeited under this Ordinance or any Law relating to the Customs, shall be deemed and taken to be condemned, and may be dealt with in the manner directed by Law in respect to Vessels, Boats, Goods, and other Things seized and condemned for Breach of any such Laws, unless the Person from whom such Ships, Boats, Goods, and other Things shall have been seized, or the Owner of them, or some Person authorized by him, shall, within One Calendar Month from the day of seizing the same, give Notice in writing to the Person or Persons seizing the same, or to the Collector, Controller, or other chief Officer of Customs, at the nearest Port, that he claims the Ship, Boat, Goods, or other Things, or intends to claim them.

Claimant to give Security. 84. And it is further enacted, that no Person shall be admitted to enter a Claim to any Thing seized in pursuance of this Ordinance, until sufficient Security shall have been given in the Court where such Seizure is prosecuted, to answer and prosecute without delay such Claim; and in default of giving such Security, such Things shall be adjudged to be forfeited, and shall be condemned.

Restoration of property seized. 85. And it is further enacted, that in case any Goods, Ships, Vessels, or Boats shall be seized as forfeited, or detained as undervalued, under this or any other Ordinance relating to the Customs, it shall be lawful for the Collector and Controller of the Customs, with the Sanction of the Governor, to order the same to be restored in such Manner and on such Terms and Conditions as they shall think fit to direct; and if the Proprietor of the same shall accept the Terms and Conditions prescribed by the said Collector and Controller, he shall not have or maintain any Action for Recompence or Damage on account of such Seizure or Detention; and the Person making such Seizure shall not proceed in any Manner for Condemnation.

Remission of Forfeitures & Penalties. 86. And it is further enacted, that if any Ship shall have become liable to Forfeiture on account of any Goods laden therein or unladen therefrom, or if the Master of any Ship shall have become liable to any Penalty on account of any Goods laden in such Ship or unladen therefrom, and such Goods shall be small in Quantity or of trifling Value, and it shall be made appear to the Satisfaction of the Collector and Controller of His Majesty's Customs that such Goods had been laden or unladen contrary to the Intention of the Owners of such Ship, or without the Privity of the Master thereof, as the case may be, it shall be lawful for the said Collector and Controller, having received the previous Sanction of Government, to remit such Forfeiture, and also to remit or mitigate such Penalty, as they shall see Reason to acquit such Master of all Blame in respect of such Offence, or more or less to attribute the Commission of such Offence to Neglect of Duty on his part as Master of such Ship: and every Forfeiture and every Penalty, or part thereof, so remitted, shall be null and void, and no Suit or Action shall be brought or maintained by any Person whatever on account thereof.

Informers' share of Penalties.

87. And it is further enacted, that of the Value of any Property confiscated under this Ordinance, one-half shall be paid to any among any Person or Persons who shall give such Information as shall lead to the Discovery and Conviction of the Offence for which the said Property is confiscated; and that when there may be more than one Person entitled to share in this or any other Reward assigned under this Ordinance, the Court which shall declare the Property confiscated, or assess the Penalty or Fine, shall also apportion the Shares in the Reward: Provided always, that neither the Collector of Customs nor any Assistant Custom Master at the Port where the Offence may be committed, shall be entitled to share in any part of such Confiscation: And provided further, that it shall be fully competent to the Governor to remit the whole of such Confiscation, or any part thereof, or the whole or any part of any Penalty or Forfeiture which may be incurred under the Enactments of this Ordinance, as he may consider expedient on Representation of particular Circumstances in any Case.

Definition of time of an Importation.

88. And it is further enacted, that if upon the first levying or repealing of any Duty, or upon the first granting or repealing of any Drawback, or upon the first permitting or prohibiting of any Importation or Exportation, whether Inwards, Outwards, or Coastwise in the Island of Ceylon, it shall become necessary to determine the precise Time at which an Importation or Exportation of any Goods made and completed shall be deemed to have had effect, such Time, in respect of Importation, shall be deemed to be the Time at which the Ship importing such Goods had actually come within the Limits of the Port at which such Ship shall in due course be reported, and such Goods be discharged; and that such Time, in respect of Exportation, shall be deemed to be the Time at which the Goods had been shipped on board the Ship in which they had been exported; and that if such Question shall arise upon the Arrival or Departure of any Ship, in respect of any Charge or Allowance upon such Ship, exclusive of any Cargo, the Time of such Arrival shall be deemed to be the Time at which the Report of such Ship shall have been or ought to have been made; and the Time of such Departure shall be deemed to be the Time of the last Clearance of such Ship with the Collector and Controller for the Voyage upon which she had departed.

And of an Exportation.

And of an Arrival.

And of a Departure.

Ships arriving not to communicate with Shore, until visited by Health Officer, & Certificate of Health granted.

89. And it is further enacted, that it shall not be lawful for the Master of any Ship or Vessel, except Dhonies, arriving at any Port or Place of this Island, or any Person on board thereof, to communicate with the Shores, or with any other Ship, or with any Boat from any other Ship or from the Shore, or for such Master to allow any Person on board so to do, until such Ship arriving as aforesaid shall have been visited, and a Certificate of Health granted, by the Health Officer, and the Health Flag shall have been hoisted at the head of the main or loftiest Mast of the Ship, in manner hereinafter mentioned, umder a Penalty not exceeding Twenty Pounds for every such Offence: And if it shall be proved that any malignant Disease, of a Contagious or Infectious nature, did within the knowledge of the Master or other Person so offending, actually prevail on board the said Ship, or if such Ship shall have been placed under Quarantine at the time when such Communication or Attempt at Communication took place, every such Master or other Person so offending, or aiding, assisting, and abetting in such Communication or Attempt, shall be subject to perform Quarantine, and shall be liable, on conviction thereof, to be punished for a Misdemeanour.

Nor Dhonies or Boats, until after Report made and Certificate of Health obtained.

90. And it is further enacted, that the Masters or Tindals of all Dhonies or Boats arriving in any Port or Place in this Island, shall with the least possible delay attend at the Custom House of such Port, and sign a Declaration of Health, and obtain a Certificate from the Health Officer, as required by this Ordinance; and if any Master or Tindal aforesaid shall without reasonable Cause neglect or delay to obtain such Certificate of Health as aforesaid, or if any other Person on board of such Dhoney or Boat shall land or communicate or attempt to land or communicate with any Ship or Dhoney, or with any Boat from any Ship or Dhoney or from the Shore, until such Certificate of Health shall have been granted, every Master, Tindal, or other Person so offending, or aiding, assisting, or abetting in such Communication, or Attempt, shall be liable to a Penalty not exceeding Twenty Pounds, or Imprisonment with or without Hard Labour; and if it shall be proved, that at the time of such Communication or Attempt, any malignant Disease of a Contagious or Infectious nature did within the knowledge of the Master or Tindal, or other Person so offending, actually prevail on board the said Dhoney or Boat, the said Master, Tindal, or other Person so offending, and every Person aiding, assisting, or abetting in such Communication or Attempt, shall be subject to perform Quarantine, and be liable moreover to be punished, upon conviction thereof, for a Misdemeanour.

Health Officer to visit Ships arriving, and Master to sign Certificate of Health.

91. And it is further enacted, that on the Arrival of any Ship or Vessel, except Dhonies, at any Port or Place in this Island, the Health Officer shall with the least possible Delay go alongside such Vessel, and keeping to the windward thereof shall hand up a printed Declaration of Health, according to the Form D. hereunto annexed; and if the Master of such Vessel shall feel himself authorized, from the perfect state of Health of every Person on board, to sign the

said Declaration, then and in that case it shall be lawful for the said Health Officer on receiving such Declaration duly signed by the said Master, to grant a Certificate of Health according to the Form E. hereunto annexed, when the Captain or Master shall hoist the Union Jack, or Flag of the Nation to which the Vessel may belong, at the head of the main or loftiest Mast in such Vessel, as the Health Flag.

Additional Punishment on Master for false Declaration or Answer.

92. And it is further enacted, that if any Master or Tindal of any Ship, Dhoney, or Boat arriving at any Port or Place in this Island, shall sign the Declaration of Health as required by the preceding Clauses of this Ordinance, and it shall subsequently appear that any malignant Disease of a Contagious or Infectious nature had shown itself on board of such Ship, Dhoney, or Boat during her Voyage to this Island, or did actually prevail on board the said Ship, Dhoney, or Boat at the time such Declaration was signed, with the knowledge of the said Master or Tindal, or if it shall appear that any Statement made in such Declaration, or in the Answers to the Questions therein inserted, whether made verbally or in writing, in any way wilfully misrepresented the true Facts of the Case, such Master or Tindal signing such Declaration as aforesaid, shall on conviction thereof, besides being subject to the Penalty imposed by this Ordinance on all Persons making any false Declarations or Answers, be moreover liable to be punished for a Misdemeanour.

Where Contagious Disease on board, Health Officer to refuse Certificate and Yellow Flag to be hoisted.

93. And it is further enacted, that whenever it shall happen that the Master or Tindal of any Ship, Dhoney, or Boat arriving at any Port or Place in this Island, shall, from the ill state of Health of any of the Persons on board his Ship, Dhoney, or Boat, not deem himself authorized to sign the above mentioned Declaration of Health; or whensoever it shall appear to the Health Officer that one or more Persons on board of any Ship, Dhoney, or Boat are labouring under any malignant Disease of a Contagious or Infectious nature, or where from any reasonable cause of Doubt or Suspicion existing thereon, the said Health Officer shall deem it necessary to place the said Ship, Dhoney, or Boat in Quarantine, he shall notify the same to the Master or Tindal thereof, by a refusal in writing to grant a Certificate of Health to the said Ship, Dhoney, or Boat, and shall order the said Master or Tindal to hoist a Yellow Flag at the head of the main or loftiest Mast of the said Ship, Dhoney, or Boat, and should the Master or Tindal of any Ship, Dhoney, or Boat so placed in Quarantine, not have a Yellow Flag on board, the Health Officer shall order one to be furnished forthwith at the expense of the said Master or Tindal, who shall hoist the same, or cause it to be hoisted as directed, and to be kept up during the Day, so long as the Ship, Dhoney, or Boat may be detained in Quarantine, under a Penalty of not exceeding Twenty Pounds for neglecting so to do; and during the Night, the Master or Tindal of any Ship, Dhoney, or Boat so placed in Quarantine, shall in lieu of such Yellow Flag, hoist, or cause to be hoisted, at the head of the main or loftiest Mast of the said Ship, Dhoney, or Boat, two lighted Lanterns, one over the other, under a similar Penalty of not exceeding Twenty Pounds in case of contravention.

Duty of Health Officer and Collector in regard to Ships placed in Quarentine.

94. And it is further enacted, that upon any Ship, Dhoney, or Boat being placed under Quarantine by the Health Officer as directed by the preceding Clause, the said Health Officer shall without any delay report the same if at Colombo, to the Colonial Secretary, and if at Out-stations to the Collector of the Customs of the District in which the Port is situated, and such last mentioned Officer, in concert with the Principal Medical Officer of the Province, is hereby authorized and required, upon any such Report being made to him by the Health Officer as aforesaid, to adopt such necessary Measures as the case may require to prevent all Communication with the said Ship, Dhoney, or Boat for such time as may be needful, except by the Health Officer, or other Persons duly appointed for furnishing under proper Precautions the said Ship, Dhoney, or Boat with any supplies she may be in want of, and for the relief of the sick, and he shall report the same forthwith to Government for its Orders.

Governor to declare time of operation of Quarentine Regulations.

And alter or repeal the same.

And give special directions in particular cases.

95. And it is further enacted, that the 89th, 90th, 91st, 92nd, 93rd, and 94th Clauses of this Ordinance shall not take effect within these Settlements until after Proclamation by the Governor to that effect, to be by him published in the Gazette: And provided further, that it shall be lawful for the Governor in like manner to repeal and alter any of the general Provisions of Quarantine provided for by this Ordinance, or to make any other general Regulations in lieu thereof, or in addition thereto, as it shall appear to be necessary and expedient; and it shall be lawful for the Governor (without any Proclamation being published as aforesaid) upon any particular Case or Cases with respect to any Ship, Dhoney, or Boat arriving in any Port or Place in this Island, and having any malignant Disease of an infectious or contagious nature on board, or on board of which any such Disease may have appeared in the course of the Voyage, or arriving under any other alarming or suspicious circumstances as to Public Health, to give Special Directions through the Health Officer or other Competent Officer acting for him, for cutting off all Communication between any Persons infected with any such Disease, and the rest of His Majesty's Subjects or Inhabitants of this Island, by placing the said Ship, Dhoney, or Boat, together with their Crews, Passengers, Letters, Goods, Wares, and other Merchandize, in Quarantine according to the circumstances of each particular Case; and likewise to give Orders for shortening the Period of Quarantine, or for mitigating it, or for wholly releasing the said Persons, Goods, Ships, or Vessels from Quarantine, according to circumstances, and as to him shall seem proper.

Terms used in Ordinance.

96. And in order to avoid the frequent Use of numerous Terms and Expressions in this Ordinance, and any other Ordinances relating to the Customs, and to prevent any Misconstruction of the Terms and Expressions used therein, it is further enacted, that whenever the several Terms or Expressions following shall occur in this Ordinance or in any other Ordinance relating to the Customs, the same shall be construed

respectively in the Manner hereinafter directed; (that is to say,) that the Term "Ship" shall be construed to mean Ship or Vessel generally, unless such Term shall be used to distinguish a Ship from Sloops, Brigantines, and other Classes of Vessels; that the Term "Master" of any Ship shall be construed to mean the Person having or taking the Charge or Command of such Ship; that the Term "Owners" and the Term "Owner" of any Ship shall be construed alike to mean one Owner, if there be only one, and any or all the Owners, if there be more than one; that the Term "Mate" of any Ship shall be construed to mean the Person next in Command of such Ship to the Master thereof; that the Term "Seaman" shall be construed to mean alike Seaman, Mariner, Sailor, or Landsman, being one of the Crew of any Ship; that the Term "*British* Possession" shall be construed to mean Colony, Plantation, Island, Territory, or Settlement belonging to His Majesty; that the Term "His Majesty" shall be construed to mean His Majesty, his Heirs and Successors; that the Term "Governor" shall be construed to mean the Governor, Lieutenant Governor, or the Officer administering the Government of these Settlements for the time being; that the Term "East India Company" shall be construed to mean the United Company of Merchants of *England* trading to the East Indies; that the Term "Limits of the East India Company's Charter" shall be construed to mean all Places and Seas Eastward of the *Cape of Good Hope* to the Straits of Magellan; that the Terms "Collector and Controller" shall be construed to mean the Collector or Assistant Collector and Controller of the Customs of the Port intended in the sentence; that the Term "Health Officer" shall be construed to mean the Officer appointed by Government for inspecting Vessels, and reporting on the Health of the Persons on board; that whenever mention is made of any public Officer the Officer mentioned shall be deemed to be such Officer for the time being; that the Term "Warehouse" shall be construed to mean any place, whether House, Shed, Yard, Timber Pound, or other Place in which Goods entered to be Warehoused upon Importation may be lodged, kept, and secured without payment of Duty or although prohibited to be used in the Island of Ceylon; that the Term "King's Warehouse" shall be construed to mean any Place provided by the Crown for lodging Goods therein for the security of the Customs.

Ship. *Master.* *Owner or Owners.* *Mate.* *Seaman.* *British Possession.* *His Majesty.* *Governor.* *East India Company.* *Charter.* *Collector and Controller.* *Health Officer.* *Officer.* *Warehouse.* *King's Warehonse.*

A.

Table of Duties payable on Goods Imported into Ceylon, and of the Drawbacks to be allowed on the Exportation of such Goods.

	£	s.	d.
Ale, Porter, and all other Malt Liquors in Casks, per gallon	0	0	2½
Ditto, per dozen quarts in bottles	0	0	6
Opium, per lb.	0	1	0
Paddee, per bushel	0	0	3
Rice, per bushel	0	0	7
Spirits and Liqueurs, per gallon	0	4	6
Goods, Wares, and Merchandize, not otherwise charged with Duty, and not herein declared to be Free of Duty, being of the Growth, Produce, or Manufacture of the United Kingdom, or of any of His Majesty's Possessions abroad, other than the Possessions of the East India Company, for every One Hundred Pounds of the Value thereof in this Market	4	0	0
Goods, Wares, and Merchandize, not otherwise charged with Duty, and not herein declared to be Free of Duty, being of the Growth, Produce, or Manufacture of any Foreign State, or of the Possessions of the East India Company, for every One Hundred Pounds of the Value thereof in this Market	10	0	0
Books, printed—Bullion, Coin, Pearls, and Precious Stones—Garden Seeds and Plants—Horses, Mules, Asses, Neat Cattle, and all other Live Stock—Instruments, scientific—Machinery, Implements, and Tools for Agriculture and for any kind of Manufacture—Maps—Regimental Clothing and Accoutrements—Timber	FREE.		

B.

Table of Duties payable on Goods Exported from Ceylon.

	£	s.	d.
Cinnamon, per lb.*	0	2	6
Ditto, if assorted as the third sort by the Government assorters, per lb.	0	2	0
Cinnamon Oil, per oz.	0	1	0
Goods, Wares, and Merchandize, of the Growth, Produce, or Manufacture of the Island of Ceylon, not being subject to other Export Duty, nor particularly exempted from Export Duty, for every One Hundred Pounds of the Value thereof	2	10	0
Books, printed—Bullion, Coin, Pearls, and Precious Stones—Horses, Asses, Mules, Neat Cattle, and all other Live Stock—Plants and Seeds—Wearing Apparel and Personal Baggage	FREE.		

* This has been recently reduced by Her Majesty's present Administration to 1*s.* per lb.—AUTHOR.

C.

Schedule of the rates of Pilotage payable by all Square-rigged Vessels, Sloops, or Schooners, at the Ports of Colombo, Trincomalé, and Galle.

Port	Vessels		£	s.	d.		£	s.	d.
COLOMBO,							0	15	0
TRINCOMALE,	Vessels of 600 Tons and upwards	Back Bay	2	0	0	Inner Harbour	4	0	0
	400 and under 600	—	1	10	0	—	3	0	0
	200 and under 100	—	1	1	0	—	2	2	0
	100 and under 200	—	0	10	6	—	1	1	0
	Under 100	—	0	6	0	—	0	15	0
GALLE,	Vessels of 600 Tons and upwards		3	0	0				
	400 and under 600		2	5	0				
	200 and under 400		1	10	0				
	100 and under 200		1	2	6				
	Under 100		0	15	0				

The above Rates of Pilotage will be charged to all Vessels going into the Inner Harbour of Trincomale and the Harbour of Galle, whether they may make a signal for a Pilot or not. In Colombo, and the Back Bay at Trincomalé, the charge will only be made, if the Vessel make the signal, and a Pilot actually repair on board.

D.

Form of Declaration of Health.

1. Name of Vessel and Commander.
2. From what Port, and whither bound.
3. When sailed.
4. At what intermediate Port or Place touched on the Voyage, and the date of sailing thence.
5. With what Vessels communicated during the Voyage.
6. Date or dates of such communication.
7. Has any Person on board suffered any illness of any kind during the Voyage; if so, what are the symptoms of the complaint.

I do hereby declare to the best of my knowledge and belief, that the (*Insert here the Description and Name of Ship or Boat*) under my command is in a perfectly healthy state; and that during the Voyage, neither Measles, Small Pox, Cholera Morbus, or any other malignant disease, of a contagious or infectious nature, have made their appearance on board; and that I have not touched at any Port, excepting as above-mentioned, or been boarded by, or communicated with, any Vessel having, to my knowledge and belief, any of the above diseases on board.

Signed Master.

E.

Form of Certificate of Health.

I do hereby certify that the (*Insert here the Description and Name of Ship or Boat*) appears to have neither Measles, Small Pox, Cholera Morbus, nor any other malignant disease of a contagious or infectious nature on board thereof, but to be in a Healthy state,—and the said Vessel is accordingly allowed to communicate with the Shore, and Ships in this Port.

Signed Health Officer.

Given at Colombo, this Twenty-second day of September One Thousand Eight Hundred and Thirty Seven.

By His Excellency's command,

P. ANSTRUTHER, *Colonial Secretary.*

LITERAL TRANSLATION OF THE LETTER FROM THE SULTAN, OR KING OF THE MALDIVE ISLANDS,

(L. S.)

Referred to in page 352.

" Hass, Sultan, Mohammed, Mohayedian, Iskander, Koollesoontoré, Katteribowené Maha Radoon presenting thousand millions of salams and compliments.

" I beg leave to inform the Chief Officer at Galle of my hope of continuing to enjoy the friendship which has always existed between your predecessors in office and the King or Kings of the Maldive Islands, and I solicit the protection of your Government for my Country from all enemies. In case any boats or vessels belonging to my Country should meet with any accident, I request you will be pleased to afford every assistance in your power.

" I have herewith despatched to you a trivial present, in charge of Mohammedoo Kaiwy, and beg you to excuse him for any error on his part, and to assist him so as to return in time."

Interpreted by me,

D. P. F. OBEYESEKERE,

Second Attepattoo Moodliar, and
Second Interpreter of the Cutchery of Galle.

GALLE, 9 November, 1825.

POSTAGE RATES, POST OFFICE REGULATIONS, WAREHOUSE RATES, &c.,

Referred to in page 362.

Rates of Inland Postage, according to the Ordinance No. 8 of 1836.

			D.				D.
For any distance not exceeding	10 miles	..	1	For any distance not exceeding	95 miles	..	7
— —	20 —	..	2	— —	120 —	..	8
— —	35 —	..	3	— —	150 —	..	9
— —	50 —	..	4	— —	180 —	..	10
— —	65 —	..	5	— —	210 —	..	11
— —	80 —	..	6	— exceeding ..	210 —	..	12

Extract from the Rules for the Management of the Post Office Department, passed by the Governor General of India in Council, on the 30th of August, 1837.

" Receipt of Letters &c. for dispatch by Land or Sea.

Letters, Papers, and Parcels shall be received wherever a Post Master or Post Office Writer is stationed, for dispatch by *Land* to every part of India or to Ceylon, and by *Sea* to every part of the World with which there is a Post Office communication: the letter, unless superscribed for some particular Ship, will be sent by the first Vessel that sails direct to the country to which the letter is addressed, and if there be no Vessels so proceeding direct to the place addressed, the letter shall be forwarded by such circuitous route as shall appear to the Post Master General or Post Master to afford the means of most speedy and secure transmission.

Letters to Ceylon to be paid in advance.

Excepting letters received from Sea.

On Letters, Papers, or Parcels, intended for delivery in Ceylon, Postage must be paid in advance to Point Calimere, except in case of letters received for Ceylon from Ship, which may be forwarded Bearing Postage. If letters for Ceylon are received from Ship under cover to residents in India, such letters, superscribed " Ship Letters," and Bearing Postage as such, will be received for transmission to their destination in like manner as if received direct from the Ship.

Letters from Ceylon to be charged Postage.

Letters from Ceylon will be charged Inland Postage from Point Calimere, or the place where the same are landed in India."

The Right Honorable the Governor is pleased to direct that the following Rules for establishing a Parcel Tappal be published for general information.

By His Excellency's Command,

P. ANSTRUTHER,
Colonial Secretary.

Colonial Secretary's Office,
Colombo, 24th November, 1837.

It having been found expedient to establish for the public convenience a Parcel Tappal between Colombo and the principal Outstations, Notice is hereby given, that from the 1st of January next, such a Tappal shall be established under the following Rules and Conditions, with a proviso, however, that the conveyance of parcels through the Post Office will be given up as soon as any establishment of the same nature shall be set up by private persons, and with the exception of the road between Kandy and Colombo, on which a conveyance of that nature already exists.

The following Rules will be strictly abided by:

1. The Tappal will be despatched twice a week, namely, each Tuesday and Friday, from Colombo, and arrangements will be made with the Post Offices at Outstations for parcels being brought to Colombo also twice a week, on days to be fixed by the several Government Agents.

2. All private parcels, not exceeding six pounds in weight, and being made up in a form which can be conveniently carried, which may be brought to the Post Office before five on the days above-mentioned, will be duly forwarded.

3. In order that the Parcel Tappal may not interfere with the regular post, the Post Master General, or Government Agent or Assistant Government Agent at Outstations, will be authorized to call on any person sending or receiving a parcel in which he may suspect letters to be enclosed, to open it at the Post Office in his presence.

4. No parcel can be franked; all below one pound shall be charged as if they were of that weight, and the following Rates will be levied:—Double letter postage for every parcel of a pound weight, or less than a pound, and two pence for every extra pound for each distance of 72 miles, and an additional charge of ten shillings for every single letter found in any parcel.

5. The Post Office will be answerable for no parcels containing money or jewels, but for additional security, any person sending such parcels should give notice at the time to the Post Office Clerk, and take a receipt in writing, specifying the weight of the parcel.

By virtue of the Powers in him vested by the 64th clause of the Ordinance No. 5 of 1837, the Right Honorable the Governor has been pleased to establish the following to be the Rates of Warehouse Rent to be charged upon all Goods imported and remaining in any Queen's Warehouse for a longer term than Seven days, and to publish the same for general information.

TABLE OF WAREHOUSE RATES.

For every	PER WEEK.
Ton butt	1s. 0d.
Leaguer Cask	0 9
Half Leaguer	0 4
Pipe or Puncheon	0 6
Hogshead	0 4
Barrel	0 2
Cask or Keg of smaller size	0 1
Case containing one dozen of Liquors	0 1
Crate, Cask, or Case of Hardware, Earthenware, or Ironmongery	0 6

For every	PER WEEK.
Bale of Cloth, Indian	0s. 6d.
Half Bale ditto	0 3
Quarter Bale ditto	0 2
Bale, Case, or Box, not exceeding half a Ton measurement	0 6
Ditto, exceeding half a Ton	1 0
Bag of Rice, Sugar, or Coffee	0 1
Small Package not otherwise enumerated	0 1
Ton of Heavy Goods not otherwise enumerated	1 3

By His Excellency's Command,

P. ANSTRUTHER,
Colonial Secretary.

Colonial Secretary's Office,
Colombo, 11th November, 1837.

EXTRACT FROM A LETTER TO THE RIGHT HONORABLE HENRY LABOUCHERE,

PRESIDENT OF THE BOARD OF TRADE, &c. &c. &c.

Referred to in page 362.

"With reference to your Bill for the "*Equalization of the Rum Duties,*" I hope I may be pardoned for suggesting the insertion of a clause for the admission of Arrack, produced from the toddy of the coco-nut palm, in the island of Ceylon, into this country, upon the payment of such Duty as may be determined for East and West India Rums.—An erroneous notion prevails, that Ceylon Arrack is produced from rice, and that it would be greatly injurious to the island to encourage the appropriation of the "Natives' staff of life" to such a purpose.—Arrack is held to be a great luxury in this country, but the Duties have been tantamount to prohibition; and it is well known, that, at places of public amusement, Vauxhall for instance, enormous prices were obtained for *supposed* Arrack Punch, which was merely an addition of Benzoic acid to the *commonest* Rum, and the other usual materials.—The Arrack of Batavia is manufactured exclusively of rice."

THE KANDYAN CONVENTION OF 1815,

Referred to in page 409.

At a Convention held on the second day of March, in the year of Christ 1815, and the Singhalese year 1736, at the Palace in the city of Kandy, between His Excellency Lieutenant General Robert Brownrigg, Governor and Commander-in-Chief in and over the British Settlements and Territories in the island of Ceylon, acting in the name and on behalf of His Majesty George the Third, King, and His Royal Highness George Prince of Wales, Regent of the United Kingdom of Great Britain and Ireland on the one part, and the Adikars, Dessaves, and other principal Chiefs of the Kandyan Provinces, on behalf of the Inhabitants, and in presence of the Mohottales, Coraals, Vidaans, and other subordinate Headmen from the several provinces, and of the people then and there assembled on the other part, it is agreed and established as follows:

1st. That the cruelties and oppressions of the Malabar Ruler, in the arbitrary and unjust infliction of bodily tortures and the pains of death without Trial, and sometimes without an accusation or the possibility of a crime, and in the general contempt and contravention of all Civil Rights have become flagrant, enormous, and intolerable, the acts and maxims of His Government being equally and entirely devoid of that Justice which should secure the safety of his subjects, and of that good faith which might obtain a beneficial intercourse with the neighbouring settlements.

2nd. That the Rajah, Sree Wickreme Rajah Singha, by the habitual violation of the chief and most sacred duties of a Sovereign, has forfeited all claims to that title, or the powers annexed to the same, and is declared fallen and deposed from the office of King; his family and relatives, whether in the ascending, descending, or collateral line, and whether by affinity or blood, are also for ever excluded from the Throne; and all claim and title of the Malabar race to the dominion of the Kandyan Provinces is abolished and extinguished.

3rd. That all male persons being or pretending to be relations of the late Rajah, Sree Wickreme Rajah Singha either by affinity or blood, and whether in the ascending, descending, or collateral line, are hereby declared enemies to the Government of the Kandyan Provinces, and excluded and prohibited from entering those Provinces on any pretence whatever, without a written permission for that purpose by the authority of the British Government, under the pains and penalties of Martial Law, which is hereby declared to be in force for that purpose; and all male persons of the Malabar caste now expelled from the said Provinces, are under the same penalties prohibited from returning except with the permission before mentioned.

4th. The Dominion of the Kandyan Provinces is vested in the Sovereign of the British Empire, and to be exercised through the Governors or Lieutenant Governors of Ceylon for the time being and their accredited Agents, saving to the Adikars, Dessaves, Mohottales, Coraals, Vidahns, and all other chief and subordinate native Headmen, lawfully appointed by authority of the British Government, the Rights, Privileges, and Powers of their respective offices, and to all classes of the people the safety of their persons and property, with their Civil rights and immunities, according to the laws, institutions, and customs established and in force amongst them.

5th. The Religion of Buddha, professed by the Chiefs and Inhabitants of these Provinces, is declared inviolable, and its Rites, Ministers, and Places of Worship are to be maintained and protected.

6th. Every species of bodily torture, and all mutilation of limb, member, or organ, are prohibited and abolished.

7th. No Sentence of Death can be carried into execution against any inhabitant, except by the written Warrant of the British Governor or Lieutenant Governor for the time being, founded on a Report of the case made to him through the accredited Agent or Agents of the Government resident in the Interior, in whose presence all trials for Capital offences are to take place.

8th. Subject to these Conditions, the administration of Civil and Criminal Justice and Police over the Kandyan Inhabitants of the said Provinces is to be exercised according to established Forms and by the ordinary Authorities, Saving always the Inherent Right of Government to redress grievances and reform abuses in all instances whatever, particular or general, where such interposition shall become necessary.

9th. Over all other persons, Civil or Military, residing in or resorting to these Provinces, not being Kandyans, Civil and Criminal Justice, together with Police, shall, until the pleasure of His Majesty's Government in England may be otherwise declared, be administered in manner following,

First. All persons, not being Commissioned or Non Commissioned Military Officers, Soldiers, or Followers of the Army usually held liable to Military Discipline, shall be subject to the Magistracy of the accredited Agent or Agents of the British Government in all cases except charges of Murder, which shall be tried by special Commissions to be issued from time to time by the Governor for that Purpose: Provided always as to such charges of Murder wherein any British Subject may be defendant, who might be tried for the same by the Laws of the United Kingdom of Great Britain and Ireland in force for the Trial of offences committed by British Subjects in Foreign Parts, no such British Subject shall be tried on any charge of Murder alleged to have been perpetrated in the Kandyan Provinces, otherwise than by virtue of such Laws of the United Kingdom.

Second. Commissioned or Non Commissioned Military Officers, Soldiers, or Followers of the Army usually held amenable to Military Discipline, shall in all Civil and Criminal Cases wherein they may be defendants, be liable to the Laws, Regulations, and Customs of War, reserving to the Governor and Commander in Chief in all cases falling under this Ninth Article, an unlimited right of review over every proceeding, Civil or Military, had by virtue thereof, and reserving also full power to make such particular provisions conformably to the general spirit of the said Article as may be found necessary to carry its principle into full effect.

10th. Provided always, that the operation of the several preceding clauses shall not be contravened by the provisions of any temporary or partial proclamation published during the advance of the army, which provisions, in so far as incompatible with the said preceding articles, are hereby repealed.

11th. The Royal Dues and Revenues of the Kandyan Provinces are to be managed and collected for His Majesty's use and the support of the Provincial Establishment, according to lawful

Custom, and under the direction and superintendence of the accredited Agent or Agents of the British Government.

12th. His Excellency the Governor will adopt provisionally and recommend to the confirmation of His Royal Highness the Prince Regent, in the name and on behalf of His Majesty, such Dispositions in favor of the Trade of these Provinces as may facilitate the Export of their products, and improve the Returns, whether in Money, or in Salt, Cloths, or other Commodities, useful and desirable to the Inhabitants of the Kandyan Country.

GOD SAVE THE KING.

By His Excellency's Command,

JAMES SUTHERLAND, *Deputy Secretary.*

THE KANDYAN FESTIVALS,*

Referred to in page 416.

THE PERRAHERRA.

The word Perraherra means literally a procession, and though the epithet may be applied to any procession, it is used emphatically of a festival held annually in the city of Kandy, which commenced this year (1841) on the day of the new moon in August.

We have tried in vain to obtain an account of its origin from the natives; they say that its history is lost in the darkness of antiquity. A Kaparulé of Udanuwara refers it to the time of Gajabahu, who reigned A. D. 113, and says that this king was a native of some foreign country, where these processions were in common use. This account cannot be correct, as Gajabahu was the son of a native prince; but on referring to the history of this monarch, there are circumstances related which may assist us in our researches.

Gajabahu resided at Anarajahpoora. One night, when walking through the city in disguise, he saw a widow weeping, whose sons had been taken captive by the Solli king, in an invasion of Ceylon from the continent, during the previous reign. The king made a mark upon the door of the house, and returned to his palace. Next morning he called his nobles, and asked what injustice had been committed in the city. They replied, that the whole city was as free from injustice as a house wherein a festival is celebrated; when the king, in anger, sent for the woman whose dwelling he had marked, and asked her why she was crying upon the previous evening. She said that in the reign of the king's father, the people of Solli had taken 12,000 captives from Ceylon, among whom were two of her sons, and that it was on this account she wept. Upon hearing this, they collected an army, and proceeding to Yapapatuna, (Jaffna,) he informed his

* For the details of these Pagan Festivals, I have to express my obligations to an anonymous contributor, under the signature of Philo-veritas, as having been compiled from "Extracts from the columns of a Colombo Periodical, called the Friend, and the Ceylon Calendar." Author.

people, that as the Solli king had taken captive his subjects, he must go and bring them back to their own homes. With Neela, a giant, he arrived at the sea shore, where he dismissed his army, and taking an iron rod he struck the sea, which divided, and he and the giant went over to the continent. The Solli king was in great fear; and, to increase his terror, Neela took one of the royal elepnants, and dashed it against another with such force, that both the animals died. In the same manner, the giant devastated the country. The Solli king, when he heard of these things from his nobles, asked Gajabahu why he had come with an army to destroy his realm; to which he replied, that he had brought no army besides his giant, and proceeded,—"In the days of your father, when my father reigned, he went over to Ceylon and seized 12,000 persons, and brought them hither captive, and I have come to demand them." The Solli king answered forthwith, "Though you go to Dewyalokaya, and receive the assistance of the Asoors, you will not be able to overcome me. Gajabahu was greatly enraged at this refusal to deliver up the captives, and declared that he would not only take his own subjects, but 12,000 other captives as well; and he threatened to burn the royal city to ashes in case of refusal. To show his great strength, that the threats were not idle words, he squeezed water out of a handful of dry sand, and afterwards out of the iron rod, which frightened the Solli king to such a degree, that he delivered up the 24,000 persons demanded, the golden Halamba of Pattiné, the sacred utensils of four Dewalés, and "the refection dish" of Buddha; and with these Gajabahu returned to Ceylon. The 12,000 Singhalese were sent to their respective homes, and the 12,000 captives were allowed to reside in Alootkoorakorle, a district to the northward of Colombo, the inhabitants of which to this day retain many marks of their continental origin.

The sacred vessels here referred to had been taken away in the reign of Walagambahu, B. C. 90, and there can be little doubt that it was to commemorate their return the Perraherra was originally established, as the carrying of the Halamba and other relics seems to be the most essential part of the procession; and to the dividing of the waters also a reference will afterwards be made. It is not clear from the narrative whether the Halamba had been previously in Ceylon, though, from other traditions we have heard, we should suppose they had; but this will make little difference in the intention of the festival, as it may still be held to celebrate their arrival. It is upon these relics that the heathen natives swear in the courts of justice. The origin of the Perraherra is therefore to be dated as far back as the second century of the Christian æra.

In the Ceylon Almanac for 1834, is a "Description of the four principal Kandyan festivals, compiled from materials furnished by a native chief." From this document, we learn that until the reign of king Kirtisree (A. D. 1747—1780) the Perraherra was celebrated exclusively in honor of the four deities, Nata, Vishnu, Kattregam, and Pattine, and altogether unconnected with Buddhism. The sacred delada relic of Buddha was first carried in procession together with the insignia of the four gods, in 1775. The circumstances which gave rise to this innovation were as follows:—The Siamese priests who were invited here by king Kirtisree, for the purpose of restoring the Upasampadawa, the highest order of Buddhist ordination, one day hearing the noise of ginjals,* &c., enquired the cause, and were informed that preparations were being made for cele-

* Small guns upon grasshopper carriages.—AUTHOR.

brating a festival in honor of the gods. They took umbrage at this, and observed that they had been made to believe that Buddhism was the established religion of the kingdom, and they had never expected to see Hindooism triumphant in Kandy. To appease them, the king sent to assure them that this festival of the Perraherra was chiefly intended to glorify the memory of Buddha; and, to convince them of it, the king gave directions that the great relic should be carried foremost in the procession, dedicating his own howdah for its reception.

There can be little doubt that the Perraherra received the countenance of the native princes, rather from a political than a religious motive, though these circumstances would vary with the disposition of the reigning king. It was one of the few occasions upon which the monarch presented himself to the public gaze. The most imposing edifice connected with the palace was the Pateripoa, an octagan of two stories, the upper story having a balcony that overlooked the principal square of the royal city, on one side of which was a lake, and on the other various religious and consecrated places. The procession was collected in the square, that the king might see it from the balcony; and when the curtain which shrouded his majesty at his entrance was withdrawn, and the assembly did lowly reverence, amidst the clamor of the drums and pipes,—the sight of the prostrate thousands, the elephants richly caparisoned, the royal guard in proud array, the countless banners floating in the breeze, and the Adikars and other chiefs at the head of their respective clans, all arranged in due order and degree, must have produced an effect that is not often equaled even in the festive scenes of far mightier kingdoms. On some occasions the king joined in the procession, but in this there was no uniformity of observance, his majesty being at one time on foot, and at another, we are told, in a golden chariot drawn by eight horses.

The Perraherra afforded an excellent opportunity to the king to examine into the state of the provinces, the conduct of the governors, and the obedience of the people. The refractory were punished, the loyal rewarded, and new regulations were now promulgated, that they might be carried to the more distant districts of the island. To the inhabitants generally it must have been a time of grateful festivity, especially during the reigns of the more popular kings, as it was a spectacle of splendour, and the various chiefs were able to exhibit their consequence in the presence of the assembled kingdom.

The Perraherra begins on the day of the new moon in the month of æsala, which this year answers to our August. The commencement is regulated by the nekata, or situation of the moon; and at the appointed moment, which must be either in the evening or morning, never at mid-day, the kapuralé of the Vishnu dewalé cuts down a young jack tree which has been previously chosen, and is consecrated for the purpose by mysterious rites. The day before, the kapuralé must bathe in pure water, anoint his head with the juice of the lime, and clothe himself in clean garments. In ancient times flowers were used, as mentioned by Knox, and these were the flowers of the æhæla (*Cathantocarpus fistulata*), but either because this tree does not now bear flowers in the proper season, or because another tree is more conveniently found, the jack has been substituted in its place, which, however for the time, receives the name of æhæla. When Knox wrote, the procession was in June; when Davy wrote, in July; it is now in August:

and, like all other eastern festivals, from the imperfection of the native astronomy, it traverses through all the months of the year. The painted stick of Knox, adorned with flowers, appears to be commemorative of the wonder-working rod of Gajabahu, and the *Jack* is undoubtedly an innovation. When the tree has been cut down, it is divided into four sections, one of which is conveyed to each of the dewalés, under a white canopy, and accompanied by music. The section is cleaned at the dewalé, and put into a hole, after which offerings of cakes are presented, called Ganabodana. The Gana are an order of inferior deities attendant upon the gods, and bodana is the Eloo form of bhojana, food.

The consecrated wood is adorned with leaves, flowers, and fruit; and during the first five days the procession simply passes round it, the Kapuralés bearing the sacred vessels and implements. After this time they are brought beyond the precincts of the dewalé, and paraded through the principal streets of Kandy. On the night of the full moon, the procession is joined by the delada magnificently accompanied, which is afterwards carried to the Adahana Maluwa, a consecrated place, near which are the tombs of the ancient kings and other individuals of the royal race. The Maluwa is encircled by stones, within which, it is said, the kings had no jurisdiction; it was a kind of sanctuary. The relic receives the adoration of the crowd until the morning, when it is returned to the temple.

Towards the end of the festival, the procession approaches the river, at the ancient ferry not far from the Paradenia bridge, and whilst the multitude remains upon the bank, the Kapuralés enter a boat that has been splendidly decorated for the occasion. The boat is rowed to some distance, when the Kapuralé takes a golden sword and strikes the water. At the same instant a brazen vessel is dipped into the river, and whilst the water is yet disparted, a portion is taken up, which is kept until the vessel can be filled in the same manner at the next festival. The water which had been taken the previous year is at the same time poured back into the river.

There is a close analogy between this striking of the river and the striking of the sea by Gajabahu, though what is meant by the dividing of the waters we cannot tell. It is probable that there was something extraordinary connected with the passage of the king, which tradition afterwards magnified into this miracle. Were we disposed to be fanciful, we might notice the resemblance which the striking of the sea by a rod, the squeezing of water from the dry sand, the errand of the king to demand captives, and some other circumstances, bear to certain facts in the Israelitish Exodus, but we have seen so many similar constructions levelled to the ground at a single blow, that we forbear to pursue the parallel.

The general arrangement of the Perraherra is the same now as in former times, but in the grandeur of the spectacle there can be no comparison. There are still elephants richly adorned; flags, pennons, and banners; several bands of drums, tam-a-tams, and pipes; the palankins of the gods, the sacred utensils; and the chiefs of the dewalés, &c. with their separate retinues. The streets are lighted by vessels of oil, placed upon poles, and carried by men, after the manner of the meshals of the Arab tribes. There are several who have a light at each end of the pole, which they whirl round at intervals with some velocity. The din of the tam-a-tams cannot be better described than in the words of Knox, " they make such a great and loud noise, that nothing else besides them can be heard." The chiefs walk alone, the crowd being kept off by their attendants; the stiffness of their gait, as they are wrapped round with manifold layers of cloth, being in perfect contrast to their usual ease, indeed we may say gracefulness of manner. The long whips were cracked before the adikar until the present year, but no one has been appointed to this office since the death of the old man whose presence we now miss, and no other individual is entitled to the honor. The whole procession may extend about a quarter of a mile, but this is only towards its conclusion, as it gradually increases in the number of its attendant elephants, &c. from the commencement. The natives who attend as spectators are now few, even in comparison with recent years, and it would seem that in a little while its interest will vanish away, with many a better remembrance of the olden time. The procession was one day prevented from taking its accustomed round, as a man had hung himself in one of the streets through which it must have passed. The natives are very unwilling to enter into conversation respecting the detail of this ceremony, and say that there are many mysteries connected with it which they cannot reveal.

The history of the Perraherra is another evidence how tenaciously the people adhere to the Brahminical superstitions, and would tend to prove, that even when Buddhism was predominant upon the continent of India, it must have had very little hold upon the mass of the population, and this may account for its almost total destruction, after it had once the ability to erect the splendid temples that yet remain, monuments at once of its majesty and its weakness. Buddhism is too philosophical, too cold and cheerless, to be a popular creed, and it is only its present alliance with its deadly antagonist of former times, that now preserves it in the place it occupies as the national religion of Ceylon.

THE AWURUDHA FESTIVAL.

This New-year's day festival is held when the sun enters Aries, which in the present year (1841) was on the 21st of March. It is both a state pageant and a religious festival, but connected with the greatest astrological absurdities. Under the Kandyan Government, the inferior chiefs were at this period reinstated in office, on the payment of a fine.

THE NANAMURA (*Bathing*) FESTIVAL.

The ceremonies take place when, according to the calculation of the Malabar soothsayer or astrologer, it will be fortunate to bathe for the first time after their new-year's day *(Awurudha)*.

THE FIVE WAHALA PINKAMAS.*

The Buddhists believe that all events are consequences of merit or demerit, *kusala* or *akusala*. *Kusala*, or *pin*, is good; *akusala*, evil.

Wahala signifies "the royal gate," and these festivals were so called, because their principal ceremonies were performed in the palace, and for the benefit of the king's household.

* *Pin* means religious merit, or moral virtue acquired by a course of moral action. It is usually applied by the natives to charity, or almsgiving. *Kama* means a manufacture.

THE KATINA PINKAMA,

Relates to an ordinance of Buddha as to the itinerant life a priest ought to lead, and not to reside under any other roof than that of leaves, or *Pansala*, except during the rains, when they read the life of Buddha in *Bana Madewas* to the people, and receive in return cloth and dye for their robes; these are often made from the raw cotton, and dyed within a certain number of hours. On some occasions, the Government provides the cloth for the robes.

THE KARTIYA FESTIVAL.

This festival is celebrated in the month Kartteka, answering to December, (1841,) on the night of the full moon. The people formerly presented offerings of oil to the king, for illuminating the triangular niches in the walls of the palace, in which lamps were placed, and lighted at a particular moment *(nekata)* determined by the astrologer. The great square, dewalés, and principal streets, were also illuminated, and the relic was carried in grand procession. This festival was instituted in honor of the Great Bali, the hero of Indian romance.

THE ALUT SAL (*New Rice*) FESTIVAL.

This festival is also determined by the astrologer, when new rice shall be first brought into the city from the royal farms. These ceremonies are splendidly got up, but having described the principal, there is such a sameness throughout, as to render repetition unnecessary; but the best ceremony to the poor is that of eating the rice, and for which an astrologer's nekata is also indispensable.

The paddee was put into new earthen pots, and the rice into clean white bags. Those for the Malagawa were conveyed on an elephant; those for the dewalés, by men shaded by canopies of white cloth; those for the palace, by the people of the king's villages, in their best apparel, and with their mouths covered with white cloth. These were attended by tam-a-tams, flags, and other honors, under a salute of ginjals, and were met on the way from the farms by the adikars and chiefs, who accompanied them to the great square.

At the nekata, a salute was fired from ginjals, and also when the rice and paddee were carried to the respective places for which they were destined. At the same nekata, or fortunate hour, both chiefs and people brought new rice and paddee from their own fields and houses; and at the nekata for eating the new rice, the portion for the gods was eaten by the priests selected for their known morality and religious lives.

THE WALIYAKUN.

Yakun signifies demi-gods, or (*more Romano*) deified heroes, but regarded by the people as devils. The Waliyakun signifies three heroes, one the offspring of Vishnu, the second sprung from the *Nymphæa Nelundo*, and the third from grass. The Waliyakun is thus described by Knox: "At this time they have a *superstition*, which lasteth six or seven days, too foolish to write; it consists in dancing, singing, and juggling. The reason of which is, lest the eyes of the people or the power of the *Jaccos*, or infernal spirits, might any ways prove prejudicial or noisome to the aforesaid gods in their progress abroad.

During the celebration of this great festival, there are no drums allowed to be beaten to any particular gods, at any private sacrifices.

In the month of November, the night when the moon is at the full, there is another great solemn feast, called in their language *Cawtha Poujah*, which is celebrated only by lighting of lamps round about the Pagoda; at which time, they stick up the longest poles they can get in the woods, at the doors of the Pagodas, and of the king's palace; upon which, they make contrivances to set lamps in rows, one above the other, even unto the very tops of the poles, which they call *Tor-nes*. To maintain the charge thereof, all the country, in general, do contribute, and bring in oil.—In this *Poujah*, or sacrifice, the King seems to take delight; the reason of which may be, because he participates far more of the honor than the gods do, in whose names it is celebrated; his palace being far more decked and adorned with high poles and lights than the temples are."

ADDRESS OF HIS EXCELLENCY THE GOVERNOR OF CEYLON,

TO THE

KANDYAN ADIKARS AND CHIEFS, ON THE 20th MAY, 1816,

Referred to in page 419.

Adikars and Chiefs,—Having now gone through a long series of Public Audiences, assisted by the Principal Native Officers of His Majesty's Government in the Kandyan Country, I have to express my satisfaction in the opportunity that has been afforded me of a close and confidential personal intercourse with you, on a variety of subjects intimately connected with the welfare and prosperity of these Provinces.

After listening to every complaint preferred during so considerable a period of free and open Audience, justice demands from me the avowal, that nothing material has arisen out of these complaints to be reprehended on the part of the Chiefs, and that I have found much which deserves my commendation.

A general call for all Civil and Criminal Prisoners to be brought before me was the first step of my proceedings here, a measure dictated not less by duty than by feeling, and one which, as it was wholly unexpected, was a fair test of the exercise of coercive authority in all Departments entrusted with it. The whole number of Prisoners was six, of whom, one was released, after a long enquiry into the merits of an intricate transaction; one case was accommodated, and four Prisoners were committed. It would be quite superfluous to add any comment to this simple statement.

In the further progress of the business, it was found, partly from the casual manner in which applications came forward, and partly owing to the different branches of Judicature not being digested into separate Departments, or regulated by settled forms of proceeding, that it would not be possible, without much delay, to adapt the Sittings to any rule of classification, and the Causes were in consequence entered upon as they arose.

Amongst them, there were many of considerable importance, and some which, besides the value of large Estates, involved feelings and interests of the greatest delicacy.

It may not be improper to recapitulate a few of the principal.

1st. The Estate of a deceased Chief, Rattwatté, Dessave of Dewimeddé, who was executed by the deposed King, on suspicion of treason. This property was claimed by Rattwatté, the male Heir of the family, and now Dessave of Matellé ; by Kappittipola, Dessave of Ouva, the Cousin of the deceased by the mother's side ; and by Mollegoddé, Dessave of the Three Korles, under a testamentary disposition in favor of the deceased's widow, whom he has since married.

2ndly. The Lands of Matamagoda, enjoyed under a King's Grant by Matamagoda, late Dessave, for twenty five years antecedent to the recent troubles, but who was dispossessed by Kanatotté Mohottalé during the march of the troops.

3rdly. Certain confiscated Lands granted to the temple of Nata Dewalé, in compensation of others overflowed with water in the formation of the great tank of Kandy, but in part recovered by the construction of a new dam.

4thly. A portion of the Lands of Asgiri Viharé, supposed to have been originally private property, and erroneously included in a Grant to the temple by the King, engraved on a Rock in the wall of the building, and dated 160 years back.

5thly. The Temple of Deguldora and its Lands, confiscated on the execution of a suspected Priest, and afterwards granted by the King to the High Priest of Kandy, but now reclaimed by the Pupils of the deceased, on the ground of local custom and the rules of the Buddha religion.

6thly. A variety of cases between individuals respecting Lands ; on questions of Title, chiefly originating in confiscations by the King, and subsequent grants.

7thly. Numerous applications to Government for the restitution of Lands confiscated at various periods.

In all these cases, and throughout the Sittings, I have to acknowledge the aid of candid and independent opinions, in which natural known motives of attachment and good-will were obviously sacrificed to justice and public duty.

By such assistance, a number of cases, and all which were ready for hearing, have been disposed of, and those which remain in the progress of enquiry have been classed and referred as follows, with the exception of a small number not reducible to any class, and left with Mr. D'Oyley to be put in the proper course.

1st. Such disputes between individuals as concern also the rights of Government, to be investigated by the Resident in presence of the Chiefs.

2ndly. Those which lie entirely between private parties, referred to the Chiefs according to their jurisdiction, namely, to Chiefs of Provinces and Districts for matters merely local ; to the Adikars in their respective Divisions for those which arise in King's Villages and other regal jurisdictions ; and to the assembled Chiefs for matters of general import, or controversies of great Families.

3rdly. Claims for restitution of forfeited Lands have been postponed until the completion of a general Register of such Claims, embracing all necessary particulars.

To these Claimants of Lands formerly confiscated, it is proper to offer some explanation of the principles which will govern my opinion on that important subject.

In cases of ancient forfeiture, the former Proprietors can hardly be encouraged to expect the recovery of property so long alienated;—any plan of that kind would form a dangerous opening to indefinite changes of property, and the domains of Government would be reduced below that standard which is absolutely necessary for its independence and respectability, and to its possessing the means of rewarding faithful Service.

Grants made by the late Government subsequent to confiscation, and perfected by possession on the part of the new Proprietors, ought to be considered as being in almost every instance a species of impediment fatal to the revival of antecedent Titles.

Chiefs, Headmen, and others who have distinguished themselves by adherence to the British Government during the late troubles, cannot be refused the restitution of Family Property to which they may be Heirs, if lost within any reasonable period back, and if still remaining at the disposal of Government, free from the Claims of intermediate Grantees. As it has been understood, that the people of Oudinura and Yattinura early discovered a friendly disposition towards the British cause, I am happy to have had an opportunity of acknowledging their attachment, by a favorable consideration of the losses sustained by the inhabitants of those Districts, at the period when the Adikar Pilamé Talawé lost his life; which being (comparatively with other confiscations) a recent period, it may be expected by all parties whose Estates were then confiscated, that unless opposed by adverse Claims of individuals, their Lands will be restored to them by the relinquishment of the Right of Government.

Many curious and valuable facts concerning the institutions, customs, and if not the laws, at least the principles of Justice acknowledged in the Kandyan Country, have in the course of these proceedings been disclosed and recorded on respectable evidence.

It is to me a most pleasing discovery, that principles of that nature, and of a leading and comprehensive character, are thus demonstrated to subsist in force, as they will happily afford the grounds of uniform decision as to Civil rights, and secure the stability of private property.

The existence of a body of acknowledged usages, regulating the succession of Estates, and other principal branches of Civil Judicature, serves also to prove, that the misfortunes under which these Provinces have laboured for many years past, are not, as has been supposed, imputable to the absence of Legal rule, but to the total disregard of common Justice, to the wanton abuse of absolute power, the merciless and precipitate infliction of capital punishment, the rapacious assumption of private property, and the ruin of entire and numerous Families for the real or supposed transgression of a single individual.

A very poor tribute indeed would be paid to the dominion of our just and merciful Sovereign, by my informing you, that such enormities are no longer to be feared. I believe no one of those who surround me, is so unacquainted with the principles of British Government, as to require any assurance on that head.

But it is undoubtedly somewhat remarkable, that in the multiplicity and variety of Cases in which I have benefitted by your presence as my Assessors, there has not been a single opinion offered by you to which I have not been able to yield my hearty concurrence, nor any proposition suggested on my part, but has received your acquiescence, as consonant to those immemorial Institutions and Customs on which the rights of the Kandyan People depend.

A flattering and happy presage of future cordiality may be drawn from so extraordinary a concurrence of opinion, and a solid ground is thus laid for the hope, that the Chiefs and Inhabitants of this beautiful and fertile country will place that confidence in the just and honorable intentions of Government, which will most facilitate and best tend to support the public measures; assuring themselves that those measures will be invariably directed to the benefit and improvement of the country, and the happiness of the Chiefs and People, and guided by a strict observance of their native institutions.

The business of the Sittings in Criminal matters has, I am happy to say, been extremely light. No Cases of that kind deserving of particular notice have appeared, excepting two; one a charge of murder against Kerulageddere, Mohottalé of the village of Vialna, in the province of Walapané, who having at first disobeyed the summons of Mr. Wright, the Agent of Government at Badulla, has since absconded, and cannot at present be discovered. The other is the complaint of a man of Ouva, who being suspected of theft by a relation of his own, was cruelly scorched on various parts of the body, and lamed of one hand. The Complainant was ordered to accompany me from Badulla to this place, for the purpose of having the Case tried during my stay here, but it has not been possible to assemble all the witnesses.

In the Civil and Political Branch, I am also indebted to your assistance for a number of important particulars, in answer to enquiries which I took this occasion to address to the Dessaves, on the subject of their Provinces, and to all Heads of Departments respecting the constitution, duties, and management of their several Charges. From the short notice at which this request was made, it would be unfair to expect methodical or complete statements; but a variety of information is contained in them, which was much wanted and wished for; and I assure myself that any future queries which may be found necessary on perusal and consideration of what has thus been furnished, will be answered with equal promptitude, and with the same zealous desire to aid my views for the benefit of this country, by the lights of your local knowledge and experience.

I will now take occasion to notice some measures of Government having reference to the Kandyan Country, and shall also offer a few practical remarks as to the course of the public business best adapted for the present state of affairs, and finally advert in a summary manner to certain objects material to be held in view by the Chiefs in general, but more especially those entrusted with the Charge of Provinces and Districts, as calculated to secure the happiness and improve the condition of the People.

In the public act of Settlement by which the Kandyan Country became joined with the Maritime Provinces, under the dominion of His Britannic Majesty, I thought it consonant to the spirit of His Majesty's Government to engage, (by an article of the Convention,) that an early consideration would be given " to make such dispositions in favor of the Trade of the Interior Country as might facilitate the Export of its Products, and improve the returns, whether in money or in commodities, such as Salt, Cloths, or other things useful and desirable to the inhabitants." This object I have been unceasingly anxious to effect, and trust I may now state that it has been accomplished, and that the pledge of Government has been fairly fulfilled.

The restrictions and Custom Duties heretofore in force in passing from one district to another in the Low Country, have been withdrawn as an impediment to Trade, and a Proclamation is now ready to be published here for abolishing the Gravett Duties between the Maritime Settlements and the Interior. By these means, the mutual exchange of Commodities between the two Countries is facilitated and promoted in the way of Trade, (that rich source of wealth and prosperity,) a branch hitherto little understood in these Provinces; but it will daily extend itself, and in a short time be felt in the ready and cheap supply of all articles desirable here, also in the increasing wealth of the Trading Classes, who, when duly sensible of these advantages, will occupy the Trade and secure the profits at present enjoyed by other Merchants: the benefit resulting from the measures just noticed, will then fully appear and be properly appreciated.

In the Three Korles a vigorous Trade offers itself both by land and water conveyance; but at the accession of the present Government, was found cramped and nearly suppressed by a restrictive monopoly of Areka Nuts; this emolument was early relinquished on the part of Government, and the restriction withdrawn, in consequence of which, the People of that and the adjoining Province of the Four Korles are rapidly enriching themselves.

A similar restriction, and on the same grounds, has hitherto existed in the Province of Saffregam and Lower Bulatgammé, but will be immediately removed by a Proclamation already prepared for the purpose. The happy consequences of this change will immediately appear in that fine and fertile Province, closely connected as it is with the sea coast, in the means of commercial intercourse by the Kaltura river; it will quickly be discovered by every Owner of Land, that the value of his Estate is materially increased, and the Cultivator who shares the Produce, will feel his means of subsisting himself and family improved in a considerable degree. Another class, hitherto few and inexperienced, the Traders, will also find (in daily increasing numbers) a comfortable and independent subsistence, in the business of exporting the Commodities of their own Province to the sea coast, and bringing back such Articles as are wanted in the Interior from that quarter. whether of Produce or Import.

The adjoining but more remote Province of Ouva will not fail to experience the benefits of these privileges, both in a more advantageous market for its Grain, and in a cheaper, more various, and more abundant supply from the Low Country.

During my visit at Badulla, I had an opportunity of informing myself, (amongst other particulars of the state of that Country,) that the Inhabitants experienced some disadvantage in the supply of Salt, their stock of Grain, for which Salt was exchanged, being nearly exhausted, and having in consequence risen in value in the Bazaar, so that the exchange in kind was rather unfavoruble to them. This complaint, I trust, will have been relieved, by an order which I issued yesterday, directing a sale of Salt from the Government Stores for money, at the rate of five

Doodoes and one Challie, or sixteen Challies, for the measure. That rate is strictly calculated on the price at which Salt is issued by Government to the inhabitants of the sea coast, namely, fifteen Fanams the Parah, adding only the exact amount of the charge of carriage. A free permission has also been intimated to the People of Ouva to supply themselves with Salt at the Stores of Hambantotté and Paltoopané, on the same terms above-mentioned, viz. fifteen Fanams the Parah.

The Province of the Seven Korles, and other parts of the Interior adjoining the District of Chilaw and Putlam, will benefit by a similar permission in that direction; and the Northern Provinces will enjoy the same liberty of supply from Batticaloa and Trincomalé. By these arrangements, His Majesty's Kandyan subjects and those of the sea coast are placed, with regard to the necessary article of Salt, on a footing of exact equality.

Amongst the means of facilitating trade, the adjustment of the standard of Dutch Challie money ought not to be forgot, but as it has been already fully explained at a former Audience, it is only necessary at present to notice it in a summary manner.

By the effect of that measure, every proprietor of a sum of money in Challies increased the value of his capital at the date of the Proclamation by one fourth part.

The subsequent issues of the same money, passing in circulation at the appointed rate, and being freely received by Government either as Revenue or in exchange for Bills, could occasion no prejudice anywhere; but if the old rate had been allowed to prevail, while money of a lower intrinsic value passed current for the same amount, the People of this Country would have been stripped of all their Coin by the more experienced Traders from the Coast; and as it would never again have appeared in the shape of currency, the Kandyan Provinces must have experienced all those inconveniences and disadvantages which necessarily arise from a want of specie.

The measures here enumerated have had the good of this Country for their direct and single object.

In others, when the Dues of Government have been concerned, I trust it will have been observed, that moderate exaction and a tender consideration for the People have never been lost sight of.

The article of Revenue has been very sparingly pressed in any quarter, so that the Country and all classes of the Inhabitants have had a full opportunity of recovering from the effects of the late troubles.—If the establishment and provisioning of new military stations has led to extensive calls for labour, it has not been exacted on the bare ground of public service, but the inducement of money allowances has been added in almost all cases, without any strict inquiry how much of the Duty might have been demanded by Government as a right, free of any charge.

Connected with this subject, I have to mention a change which is about to take place in the branch of Revenue and Public Service. In order to relieve the Honorable the Resident of some part of the multifarious occupations which engross his valuable time, it is proposed to transfer the charge of the Revenue and Public Services tc Simon Sawers, Esq., by the title of Revenue Agent.

Under the guidance of Mr. D'Oyley's experience, and by virtue of special and peremptory Instructions which will be communicated from Government, the system of Mr. Sawer's Department will be strictly governed by established Rules and Usages, and as I undertake to promise for that Gentleman, that his intercourse with the Chiefs will be conducted with all that respect, politeness, and circumspection so necessary to the maintenance of mutual cordiality, I must express my hope, that the Chiefs with whom he may from time to time have occasion to communicate, will regard him as a Gentleman, who at the same time that he holds a respectable Rank in His Majesty's Civil Service, and a high station in the Government of the Interior, occupies also an eminent place in my good opinion and favor.

I firmly persuade myself that he will receive the ready aid and support of the Heads of Provinces and Departments, and of the Chiefs of Villages, in reducing the Public Revenue and the Government Services to a regular system. It is particularly desirable that all communications made by the Revenue Agent should be promptly replied to, and every explanation afforded from which Mr. Sawers, in the responsible charge thus committed to his management, may be enabled to judge, and to report for my information, what assistance he can from time to time depend on, from the respective Provinces and other Establishments.

I shall not trouble the assembly with the further notice of any public measures in particular. but must repeat my assurance that none will be adopted as applicable to this Country without the direct and immediate motive of public good.

Proceeding to offer some practical remarks on the course of Public Business, I shall principally (though perhaps not entirely) deduce them from the subjects which have occupied our deliberations for the last month. Amongst these, the resort of Complainants to Colombo, and the reference of their cases back for decision here, is one which has drawn my particular attention.

To prevent the necessity and occasion of such reference, is a most desirable object, and will be best obviated by establishing, both on the part of the Chiefs and of the Resident, some Rules by which every Complainant, whenever he presents himself, shall have his name and cause entered, and be appointed for a certain fixed time to appear again; that whenever he does appear, he may receive a distinct answer, and instruction for his further proceeding; and in all stages of the Case be fairly and patiently heard, and fully informed of the state and progress of his cause, and of the next appointed time for proceeding in it.

With regard to the references to Colombo or to the Resident, when once made, I have already explained at a former Audience that it is an indispensable part of my Public Duty, and of that of the British Agent, to return an answer to the party; first taking proper means to be accurately informed of all proceedings in the Case, with the Decision and the reasons on which it is grounded.

Mr. D'Oyley will make arrangements for conducting all such Cases in a regular progress, until the final Report for my information.

Sudden and informal changes of possession in Landed Property, and the unauthorized seizure of Produce, have appeared in the course of my business here to be a fertile source of litigation and complaint, and one great cause of the difficulty and embarassment which attends the disposal of disputed Titles; as the original relative state of the parties in the suit is in most instances reversed, by the Claimant forcing himself into actual possession, and obliging the other party to prove his Title, instead of defending it.

The practice on the part of Dessaves, in granting Chittoos or interlocutory orders on a summary hearing, originated no doubt in the laudable design of supporting peaceable and lawful possession; but it appears that those Documents have deviated into the nature of Decrees, which being founded on slight enquiries, lay the foundation of many disputes, and introduce much confusion. I therefore strongly recommend to all Chiefs of Provinces and Districts to confine their Interlocutory Orders called Chittoos, to the single purpose of maintaining the first Possession, and to grant no Document which can by any perversion be considered a Decision, until after a full hearing of Parties and Witnesses.

Trespasses by Parties themselves, whether by intrusion into possession of Land, or by seizure of the Produce without the interposition of Lawful Authority, cannot be justified by any pretence of Title, and must on all Cases be treated and punished as offences against the Public Peace.

In almost all Cases of change of Possession, there is an allegation of personal violence and spoliation of moveable Property; these Complaints are no doubt exaggerated, and perhaps in many instances entirely false; their existence however suggests the necessity of much precaution and regularity in carrying even judicial Process into execution, and that all persons entrusted with such duties, should be seriously admonished and held strictly responsible to conduct the business in a peaceable, orderly, and deliberate manner, avoiding all violence, and carefully observing to have any moveable Property which they may be authorized to seize, entered in the first instance in a written List, in presence of Witnesses.

Observations of this nature might be extended to a considerable length, but perhaps they may be more proper as a subject of memorandums for the Resident, than to be further pursued at the present time.

I shall therefore conclude this long address with a few remarks of a more general nature, as to those duties which attach to Chiefs of Provinces, and other Chiefs having appointments of authority over any Classes of the Inhabitants.

1st. To make themselves thoroughly acquainted with the condition and circumstances of those under their Jurisdiction, as the necessary ground-work of an administration just and humane towards the People, and advantageous to the State.

2ndly. To show every countenance and encouragement to moral conduct and orderly behaviour, and mark all contrary instances with their displeasure.

3rdly. To promote industrious pursuits, encourage manufactures, and give every facility and protection to commercial dealings and trading intercourse.

In these attentions the most effectual means will be found of suppressing vice and preventing crimes, but where such precautions fail, the coercion and penalties of Criminal justice must be enforced; and the Peace of the Country will be essentially promoted by the prompt apprehension of Offenders, and a strict watch over persons known to be of dangerous character: observing however as to Culprits of every description, the necessity of public and regular proceedings, fair and patient enquiry, and a strict adherence to established rules.

Of Revenue and Public Services I have already delivered all that I intend to observe; but as the Chiefs may have remarked a great anxiety on my part to have the Country opened by clearing the principal Roads, it is proper to explain, that this operation (which I avow to have much at heart) is one of those which will most of all conduce to secure the general benefits derivable from the intercourse of different Provinces with each other, but more particularly to make way for the free progress of Trade from the Sea Coast, by which the Interior Country has every thing to gain.

I cannot entirely quit the subject of public improvements, and that of facilitating the intercourse between the British Government and the Kandyan Chiefs and People, without mentioning my intention of establishing at this place a Seminary for teaching the English Language, the cultivation of which by the younger branches of families here, and the attention of English Gentlemen to acquire a knowledge of the Singhalese, will furnish those means of acquaintance which must necessarily tend to promote mutual esteem and cordiality.

It is with much pleasure I have learnt, that the Heads of Families, both in and out of Office, look forward with satisfaction to the intended plan of education for their young men, and express an anxiety to have them thus qualified for Public Employ. In return for such a proof of zeal and confidence towards the present Government, it is my duty to declare, that all fair and reasonable Claims for service and promotion, according to the just pretensions of families, and the Custom of the Country, will meet with due and impartial consideration, from time to time, as Vacancies and opportunities occur.

I have now to express my thanks for the respectful attentions I have received in various parts of the Country, during my present Tour.

To the Oedagampaha Adikar, Dessave of the Saffregam Province, where I entered the Kandyan Country, I have already expressed my obligations; but I must further beg leave to make public mention of the zealous and efficient services of Ekneligoddé Nilamé, the second in authority in the Province of Saffregam, being Dessavony Mohottalé there, and also Madigey Dessave for the Four Korles. The attentions and useful services of Mahavellytenné Gonbaddé, Dessave of Ouva, during my progress through the Meddépattoo, and across the Idalgashina Pass, also demand my approbation and thanks.

It remains only to add, that I shall enjoy the truest feelings of satisfaction, in transmitting the very favorable Report I have to make of my observations here, to His Majesty's Government in England, for the information of his Royal Highness the Prince Regent, whose parental regard for the Chiefs and People of this Country, will excite in His Royal mind an anxious desire to receive accounts of their well-being, their attachment to the British Government, and their unanimity and good understanding amongst themselves.

I shall now conclude with my cordial good wishes for the health and happiness of yourselves and families, trusting that at my next visit to Kandy, which I propose to make in a short period, I shall meet you in the same feeling of mutual regard, which I am confident prevails among us at the present moment of our parting.

THE END.